19世纪西方传教士编汉语方言词典

丛书主编　姚小平　姚喜明　　副主编　杨文波

西 蜀 方 言

Western Mandarin, or the Spoken Language of Western China

［英］钟秀芝（Adam Grainger） 编著

杨文波　黄自然　杨昱华　彭玉康　吴卸耀　校注

薛才德　审订

上海大学出版社
·上海·

图书在版编目（CIP）数据

　　西蜀方言/（英）钟秀芝编著；杨文波等校注. —2版. —上海：上海大学出版社, 2022.3
　　（19世纪西方传教士编汉语方言词典）
　　ISBN 978-7-5671-4450-7

　　Ⅰ. ①西… Ⅱ. ①钟… ②杨… Ⅲ. ①西南官话—词汇—汇编—四川 Ⅳ. ① H172.3

　　中国版本图书馆CIP数据核字(2022)第031063号

本书由上海文化发展基金会图书出版专项基金资助出版

书　　　名	西 蜀 方 言
编　　　著	钟秀芝（英）
校　　　注	杨文波　黄自然　杨昱华　彭玉康　吴卸耀
审　　　订	薛才德
责任编辑	陈　强
装帧设计	柯国富
技术编辑	金　鑫　钱宇坤
出版发行	上海大学出版社
社　　　址	上海市上大路99号
邮政编码	200444
网　　　址	http://www.shupress.cn
发行热线	021-66135112
出　版　人	戴骏豪
印　　　刷	上海华业装潢印刷厂有限公司
经　　　销	各地新华书店
开　　　本	787mm×1092mm　1/16
印　　　张	52
字　　　数	1040千
版　　　次	2022年3月第2版
印　　　次	2022年3月第1次
定　　　价	180.00元
书　　　号	ISBN 978-7-5671-4450-7/H·401

版权所有　侵权必究
如发现本书有印装质量问题请与印刷厂质量科联系
联系电话：021-56495919

《19世纪西方传教士编汉语方言词典》编委会

主　编　姚小平　姚喜明

副主编　杨文波

编　委　姚小平　游汝杰　薛才德
　　　　陶飞亚　姚喜明　杨文波

总　序

　　中西语言学传统各有所长：西方长于语法，中国长于辞书。公元前1世纪，希腊语文学者色雷克氏便撰成《语法术》，对本族语的语法体系做了分析，整理出名、动、代、介等八大词类。约在同一时期，中国人有了第一部语文词典《尔雅》，分19个义组及语类，收列词汇并做解释。《尔雅》被奉为十三经之一，足见古人对词典的看重。两汉有《方言》《急就篇》《说文》《释名》，或搜辑方言词语，或意在教人识字，或系统梳理文字，或以阐释词源为旨，——这种以辞书服务于语文教学、进而带动语言文字研究的繁荣景象，在同时期的罗马帝国是绝对看不到的。这些辞书当中，尤其值得一提的是《说文解字》，它是第一部严格意义上的字典，所发明的部首析字和检索法一直沿用至今。这之后的发展不烦细述，总之辞书越出越多，到了明末传教士来华，一方面发现中国人没有语法书，觉得不可思议，以为是中国学术的一大缺憾；另一方面，看到中国辞书种类奇多，代代传承而编纂有方，则不能不大为叹服。

　　外国人学习和教授汉语，尤其需要了解它的语法体系，把握它的运作规则。由于没有现成的中国语法书可用，传教士必须自力更生，花大力气编写汉语语法书。此时，欧洲传统的语法学范畴、概念、分析方法等便开始发挥作用，颇能供传教士编撰汉语语法书借力。当然坏处也在这里，即常为今人诟病的套用。然而词典不同。词典中国人有的是，所以传教士虽然不能拿来就用而得自编，但因为有中国本土词典当作样本，从整体框架、编纂路数到字词条目的设立和释义，都可以参考利用，于是就能省力许多；甚至直接就拿本土词典（如明末清初畅行的《字汇》）当母本，把其上的字条悉数或者挑选一部分译成西文，便算是编成了一部西洋汉语词典，也就是汉欧双语词典。这样的汉欧词典，常见的编排方式有两种：一种采用中国传统的部首笔画法，一种采用音序法。后者又分中式的和西式的：中式的，即按中国韵书如《广韵》上所见的韵类编排西式的，即根据拉丁注音，按字母的顺序排列。用作检索的方法，部首法和音序法各有便利与不便，所以，有些考虑周全的编纂者会为部首词典配上一个音序检索表；反过来也一样，音序词典的后面经常附有部首检字表。这说的是汉欧词典，以汉语字词立条，用欧语诠释意义。如果是欧汉词典，用欧语的词目立条，以带出汉语对应词，则一般就采用西式的音序法。

早期传教士来中国，都是走海路，从华南口岸入境。入华之初，逗留于广东、福建等地，有些人就在那里播教而终其一生；有些人得以继续北上，抵达江浙、华北以及中国西部。而正是在粤、闽两省，方言问题较之其他省份更加突出：官话主要通行于公务人员、学者书生中间，日常生活中传教士们仍不得不面对难以听懂的方言土语。所以，在早期的西洋汉语词典上，官话与方言混杂的现象十分普遍；即便是万济国所编的西班牙语—汉语词典，明确题作《官话词汇》（*Francisco Varo. Vocabulario de la Lengua Mandarina.* 1679），也夹杂着许多闽方言的语词，其中有些可能是无意间混入的，有些则可能明知属于方言，而仍予以收录，只是没有说明而已。后来的词典家更倾向于区分，虽然也常把明显不属于官话的词语收进词典，但会刻意说明来源。这种把方言与官话分开处理的意识逐渐增强，至19世纪中期应中西交往大增之需，便终于促成了各种方言词典的产生。收于本系列的《上海方言词汇集》（1869）、《英粤字典》（1891）、《宁波方言字语汇解》（1876）、《西蜀方言》（1900）、《客英词典》（1905），就是其中较重要的五种；细分之，前三种为欧汉型，后两种则属于汉欧型。

中国古代不是没有记录方言的著述。两千年前，西汉扬雄便辑有《方言》，可以划归辞书之属。可惜之后的十多个世纪里，再也没有出现堪与扬雄之著比肩的同类作品。直到明清，似乎才有了起色：与一批搜辑俚言俗语的著作一道，出现了一些考索某一特定地区方言词语的专书，如明末李实的《蜀语》，康熙时毛奇龄的《越语肯綮录》，乾隆年间茹敦和的《越言释》以及胡文英的《吴下方言考》。这些方言书上所见的词条，从百余到近千不等，均为编著者出于个人偏好而选收，或多或少显露出猎奇之趣，其诠释则经常带有溯源或考据的目的。

对比之后，我们会发现西士所编的方言词典很不一样：

一是使用拉丁字母注音，较准确地记录了当时汉语方言的实际音值；

二是为日常交际服务，着眼于听和说，更全面地收集了一种方言的普通词汇，包括大量常用的词组和短句；

三是载录了19世纪我国各口岸及商埠洞开以后进入汉语的大批西洋物名、西学概念、西语表达及其汉译。

对于今人考察中国近代方言发展史以及中西语言文化交通史，这批西洋汉语方言词典独具价值，非中国本土的任何方言著作所能取代。唯其种类颇多，本次组织重印并予注释的仅为其中的一小部分，期盼未来能有更多同类的著作，以这种具有研究性质的重刊本形式面世。

姚小平

2016年2月22日

出版说明

《西蜀方言》(*Western Mandarin, or the Spoken Language of Western China*)是清朝末期由中国内地会(China Inland Mission)传教士钟秀芝(Adam Grainger)编著,上海美华书馆(Shanghai: American Presbyterian Mission Press)于1900年出版的一部蜀地方言词典。钟秀芝,英国人,生平不详,1889年到中国,长期居住在成都金马街37号,1904年创办"圣经学堂",1921年在成都去世。

《西蜀方言》既是一部词典,也是一部用于传教士学习当地语言的口语教材。该书内容丰富,较完整地反映了19世纪末川西方言的状况,涉及语音、词汇、语法、民俗等诸多方面。据杜晓莉(2011):"该书专收当地人口语中的常用语,共收字头3786个、异体字112个、无字词191个、方言用例13484条(含401条成语)","《西蜀方言》全书共分七个部分:1.前言;2.部首索引;3.有字词;4.无字词;5.亲属称谓表;6.音节索引;7.英语索引。书末还附有勘误表。其中第3、4是该书的正文部分,5、6、7是附录。"

部首索引共引214部,按笔画多少排列。正文包含有字词和无字词两部分。有字词是指有音又有记录它的文字的词,是本书的主要部分。词头按部首分部排列,同部首的字按笔画多少排列。无字词是指有音却不能确定记录它的文字的词,共191个,编者用自造字来记录,并用罗马字及代表声调的数字来为其注音,或者直接用罗马字及代表声调的数字注音来记录。音节索引,是以音节为单位在正文中出现过的词编的索引,每一个词下面分别列出其英文意思和在书中出现的页码。英文索引不是词头的英文索引,而是为英文解释中出现过的英文词编的索引,利用该索引寻找方言用例,可以使读者了解一个意思的多种汉语表达方式。甄尚灵(1988)、郭莉莎(2003)、黄灵燕(2010)、李晓东(2011)、杜晓莉(2011)、马正玲(2012)等学者都曾对此书进行过专门的研究和论述。

本次再版,为保存原书全貌,除列出全部字头(括号外为原字形,保留繁体字与异体字,括号内为该字的简体字或规范字)及音标外,只对具有四川方言特点的部分词目予以注释,并按顺序列于页面侧边,予以注释的词目全部改用简体字,例如:

側(侧)[tsʰe⁵] [tse⁵] [tsʰa⁵]

【侧黑】将近天黑,傍晚。

在无字词部分,所列字头为编者钟秀芝的自造字,注释中"丨"代替字头。例如:

𠂇[tʂʰoŋ⁴]

【丨鼻子】刺鼻。

另有一部分无字词编者并未为其造字,而是直接用罗马字及代表声调的数字注音来记录。例如:

[tʂʰoŋ⁴]

【筋筋丨丨】(食物)多筋的。

词典注音参照了甄尚灵(1988)的注音体例,但略有不同。现将修改后的音系转写对照表列下:

(1)声调表

调类	例字
1阴平	包征期弯
2阳平	盆聊柔云
3上声	摆女偶晚
4去声	冒坠共望
5入声	木立族骨

(2)声母表

p[p] 补摆兵	pʻ[pʰ] 皮飘偏	m[m] 木猫门	f[f] 呼番纷		
t[t] 低堆灯	tʻ[tʰ] 途挑吞				l[l] 立雷南

续表

ts[ts] 栽簪遭	ts'[tsʰ] 醋猜操	s[s] 苏腮三	
ch[tʂ] 斋沾招	ch'[tʂʰ] 处钗超	sh[ʂ] 书筛山	r[z] 弱锐然
ch[tɕ] 佳决鸠	ch'[tɕʰ] 缺求轻	sh[ɕ] 学靴熏	n[n̠] 泥女牛
k[k] 瓜该宫	k'[kʰ] 夸开宽	h[x] 花鞋欢	ng[ŋ] 恶哀恩
Ø[Ø]衣弯渊			

（3）韵母表

i[ɿ]资思次			
i[ʅ]知施日	i[i]彼低衣	u[u]木苏枯	ü[y]驴虽居
a[a]爬他沙	ia[ia]佳恰鸭	ua[ua]抓刷花	
o[o]波若哥	io[io]略脚学		
e[e]德色遮	ie[ie]灭姐茄	ue[ue]国阔或	üe[ye]靴确药
e[ei]杯媒非		ue[uei]堆吹规	
ao[ao]包刀高	iao[iao]描挑妖		
eo[əu]偷走柔	iu[iəu]丢秋休		
ai[ai]拜来腮	iai[iai]皆孩芥	uai[uai]衰乖块	
an[an]班丹三	ien[ien]偏天先	uan[uan]端川官	üen[yen]全捐渊
en[ən]门类人	in[in]平林英	uen[uən]准绳温	üin[yn]巡群君
ang[ɑŋ]邦当昌	iang[iɑŋ]良香江	uang[uɑŋ]庄双光	
ong[oŋ]蒙冬松	iong[ioŋ]穷凶容		

注：（1）声调只标调类，不标注具体调值。

（2）中括号前为《西蜀方言》中的注音，中括号内为笔者转写注音。

（3）ch、ch'、sh组声母在开口呼与合口呼前音值分别为[tʂ]、[tʂʰ]和[ʂ]，在齐齿呼与撮口呼前音值分别为[tɕ]、[tɕʰ]、[ɕ]。

（4）笔者对《西蜀方言》止开三日母字的记音转写与甄尚灵先生不同，另文详述。

（5）e[ei]、ue[uei]与非入声调相配，e[e]、ue[ue]与入声调相配。

在本书的校注过程中，上海大学国际交流学院给予了大力支持和帮助。参与校勘整理工作的人员有姚喜明、杨文波、黄自然、杨昱华、彭玉康、吴卸耀、周城芮等。其中，姚喜明负责全书统稿及英译校对，杨文波负责全书音标核对及书中部分词条的校对和注释，黄自然、杨昱华、彭玉康、吴卸耀等负责书中部分词条的校对和注释工作。全书由薛才德先生审订。西南官话发音人吴雪颖女士对本书校注帮助颇多,谨此致谢。

词典校注参考了《西蜀方言与成都语音》、《四川方言词典》、《成都方言词典》、《成都通览》、《〈西蜀方言〉研究》、《〈西蜀方言〉词汇研究》、《〈西蜀方言〉句法研究》等文献。

此次《西蜀方言》修订与再版,由于笔者时间和精力有限,疏漏之处在所难免,书中谬误及不足之处敬请诸位专家学者指正。

参考文献

[1] 北京大学中国语言文学系语言学教研室.汉语方音字汇(第二版)[M].北京:文字改革出版社,1989。

[2] 杜晓莉.浅谈一部传教士编著的四川方言辞书——《西蜀方言》[J].四川民族学院学报,2011(6):51—55.

[3] 傅崇矩.成都通览[M].成都:成都时代出版社,2006.

[4] 郭莉莎.《西蜀方言》词汇研究[D].四川师范大学硕士学位论文,2003.

[5] 黄灵燕.再论钟秀芝《西蜀方言》入声和基础音系问题[J].语言科学,2010(4):402—415.

[6] 李思敬.汉语"儿"[ɚ]音史研究[M].北京:商务印书馆,1986.

[7] 李晓东.《西蜀方言》研究[D].四川师范大学硕士学位论文,2011.

[8] 梁德曼.《成都方言词典》引论[J].方言,1993(1):2—13.

[9] 梁德曼,黄尚军.成都方言词典[M].南京:江苏教育出版社,1998.

[10] 马正玲.《西蜀方言》句法研究[D].南京大学硕士学位论文,2012.

[11] 彭金祥.四川方音在宋代以后的发展[J].乐山师范学院学报,2006(3):50—54.

[12] 四川大学方言调查工作组.四川方言音系[J].四川大学学报(社会科学版),1960(3):3—68.

[13] 王文虎,张一舟,周家筠.四川方言词典[M].成都:四川人民出版社,1987.

[14] 杨时逢.云南方言调查报告(汉语部分)[M].台湾"中央研究院"历史语言研究所,1969.

[15] 甄尚灵.成都语音的初步研究[J].四川大学学报(社会科学版),1958(1):1—30.

[16] 甄尚灵.《西蜀方言》与成都语音[J].方言,1988(3):209—218.

[17] Edkins, Joseph. *A Grammar of the Chinese Colloquial Language, Commonly Called the Mandarin Dialect*[M]. Shanghai: Shanghai American Presbyterian Mission Press, 1864.

[18] Grainger, Adam. *Western Mandarin, or the Spoken Language of Western China*[M]. Shanghai: Shanghai American Presbyterian Mission Press, 1900.

西蜀方言

WESTERN MANDARIN,

OR THE

SPOKEN LANGUAGE OF WESTERN CHINA;

WITH

SYLLABIC AND ENGLISH INDEXES.

COMPILED BY

ADAM GRAINGER,

China Inland Mission.

SHANGHAI:
AMERICAN PRESBYTERIAN MISSION PRESS.
1900.

CONTENTS.

		Page.
1.	Introduction	i
2.	Radical Index	iv
3.	Words with Characters, arranged according to the radicals	1
4.	Words without Characters, arranged alphabetically	567
5.	Table of Relationships	617
6.	Syllabic Index	629
7.	English Index	709

目 录

简介 /1

部首索引 /1

有字词 /1-596

无字词 /597-616

亲属称谓表 /617-628

音节索引 /629-708

英语索引 /709-802

勘误表 /803

译文

简 介

论及著书初衷，原因有二：一则赖于密切的工作往来，作者亟需掌握当地用语；二则源于缺乏帮助，作者无从学习该语言。悉闻此书将对同在巴蜀务工的同伴大有益处，作者至此着手出版。

范围：本书名为《西蜀方言》，明确了该书适用范围。单以口语与书面语为界，试图对方言加以区分，实属不易。学者所用之词因过于"文绉绉"而多被舍弃，但另一方面，没有词因过于普通就不被收录。本词典共收字头3786个，含112个异体字、191个无字词，用例13484条，含成语401条。所收例句均为本地口语，外来词如宗教用语等均不收录，因为这些词可从其他途径很方便地查到。

结构：第一部分，即最主要部分，按部首进行排列。第二部分，包括无字词在内，按字母顺序排列。音节索引确保学生能由发音找到与之对应的文字。同时，英语索引则有助于其成为一本完备的英汉词典。末尾的称谓表，旨在帮助人们梳理脉络，理清复杂的人际关系。

罗马拼音：其使用旨在修正中国内地会的拼写系统。其规则变化如下：当k置于i或ü之前，则变为ch，例：江—chiang, 去—ch'ü；当hs出现在i或ü之前，则变为sh，如：下—shia, 玄—shüen; ae, i, ei及eh统一写为e，如：这—che, 雷—lue, 背—pe, 白—pe。

释义：一个词与不同词语搭配，意义会发生变化，而罗列释义很难真实表达这些意义。

通常，针对某个词的不同用法，本书均逐一示例；在翻译过程中，文字因种种联系而产生的不同字面意义均用斜体表示。当

INTRODUCTION.

The need of a thorough knowledge of the every-day language of the people among whom the writer's work lay, and the lack of adequate helps to the attainment of that knowledge, led to the preparation of this vocabulary. Being assured that it would prove of use to his fellow-labourers in Western China, he has arranged it for publication.

Scope:—The name of the book, "The Spoken Language of Western China," indicates pretty clearly the scope of the work. It is difficult to draw a line between what is spoken and what is written only. Many phrases used by scholars have been rejected as too "bookish," but, on the other hand, nothing has been regarded as too common for insertion. The work contains 3,786 characters, 112 duplicate characters, 191 words without characters, and 13,484 examples, including 401 proverbs. The examples have been taken in every case from the lips of the natives. No phrases of foreign origin—religious or otherwise—have been collected, as students can easily obtain such from other sources.

Arrangement:—The first and chief part of the work is arranged according to the radicals. The second part, which consists of words without characters, is arranged alphabetically. A syllabic index enables the student to find any word from the sound, and an English index gives the advantages of a very full English-Chinese dictionary. An appendix on relationships, is an attempt to clear up what many have found to be a somewhat perplexing subject.

Romanization:—The Romanization used is a modification of the China Inland Mission system. The principal alterations are as follows:—*k*, before *i* or *ü*, is changed to *ch*, as in 江 *chiang*, or 去 *ch'ü*; *hs*, before *i* or *ü*, is changed to *sh*, as in 下 *shia*, or 玄 *shüen*; *ae*, *i*, *ei*, and *eh*, are uniformly written *e*, as in 这 *che*, 雷 *lue*, 背 *pe*, or 白 *pe*.

Definitions:—As the meanings of a word are often modified by association with other words, no list of definitions can give a true

[ii]

idea of these meanings. As a general rule, one example of each use of a word has been given, and, in the translation, the different shades of meaning in its various connections have been indicated by italics. When an English word covers more ground than the Chinese word, only a part of the English word is italicized. A word may have other meanings in the classical language, but only such as are used in the spoken language are given.

Translation:—The rendering into English of the word to be illustrated sometimes entails a cumbrous or roundabout sentence. The aim has been to translate the word in each sentence correctly. The remaining words are often freely translated. In some instances the meaning is obvious but not translatable into idiomatic English, and, in a few cases, the derivation, or reference, is quite obscure.

No doubt, in many instances, the characters did not originally bear all the meanings given, but, owing to the scarcity of characters of a certain sound or tone, one character has, in time, come to do duty for many and varied meanings; e. g., 巴 *pa*, page 195.

Emphasis sometimes alters the meaning; e. g., page 117, line 26, "*hao ta ti sï*," with the emphasis on "*ta*," means "How big is the affair?"; but, with the emphasis on "*hao*," the same phrase means "What a big affair!", either really or sarcastically.

The student should be careful to discriminate between phrases that are similar in sound but quite different in meaning; e. g., 乘轎子 and 陞轎子, or 你們與不與 and 你們信不信, etc.

Tones:—The tones are marked in the usual order from 1 to 5. In Western Mandarin the tones differ from Northern Mandarin on the one hand, and from Southern Mandarin on the other. The names of the tones are the same, but the sounds are different. The 1st tone in Western Mandarin is similar to the 3rd in Southern Mandarin, the 2nd like the 1st, the 3rd like the 4th, and the 4th like the 2nd. The 5th tone is sometimes difficult to distinguish from the 2nd, being less abrupt than the 5th tone in Southern Mandarin. Still, it is a distinct tone and is not confounded with the other four tones as in Northern Mandarin. In double words, such as 娃娃, etc., the second word usually rises in tone.

Duplicates:—Where one character may be written in two or more forms, that form which is commonly used has been adopted. Where two forms are commonly written, both have been inserted;

译文

种或多种形式，则取其常用形式收录。如两种形式均使用广泛，则都收入。然而，由于本字典旨在罗列口语表达，所以尽可能少地收录这类异体字。

数量修饰词：N.A.代表"数量修饰词"，即"量词"。该类词通常置于用例末尾。诸如不可译之词，则被归为"数量修饰词"类。而可译之词则被划为常规词类，如："（一）捆"、"（一）把"等。

谚语：稍加阅览可发现常用谚语遍布全书。此类主题则以"谚语"为索引，编入其下。

无字词：大部分无字词常见且实用。其中一部分或许能依据部首，但出于对其类别某种程度上的不确定，编者并未将它们进行划分。

省略：省略十分重要，通常须格外注意。如："上⁴"在诗歌中有两种声调，而在会话则只有一种；同样，"去⁴"及其他一些汉字亦然。

勘误表：由于不时离开中国，作者在出版过程中无法兼顾各个细节。如若不是上海友人协助，出版或许会延误更长时间。

同时，已出版书中依然存在一些错处，无不令人遗憾。因此，使用者应留意本书末尾的勘误表，及时更正相关内容。

在此，特别感谢中国内地会成都分会斐有文先生慨然校订了大部分手稿，同时也感谢其他友人给予的帮助和鼓励。

纵观编辑过程，作者获益良多，也因此倍感愉悦。若读者能获得与作者同样的感受，即便一星半点，之于作者也是莫大的鼓舞。

真诚祈祷本词典成为各位同工的得力助手，以利于福音在中国人中传播。

钟秀芝
1900年11月于上海

[iii]

but, as the aim has been to illustrate the spoken language, as few as possible of such duplicates have been given.

Numerary Adjuncts:—N. A. stands for "Numerary Adjunct," or "Classifier." These, where they occur, are usually placed at the end of the list of examples. Such as cannot be translated are indexed under "Numerary Adjunct." Those that are translated are indexed as ordinary words; e. g., "bundle," "handful," etc.

Proverbs:—Many common proverbs will be found scattered throughout the book. The subjects of these have been indexed under the head "Proverbs."

Words without Characters:—Most of the words without characters are very common and useful words. Some of these might have been classed under certain characters, but, as there is a measure of uncertainty about their identity, the compiler has not presumed to allocate them.

Omissions:—Omissions are often significant and should be noted; e. g., 上⁴ has two tones for purposes of poetry, but only one in speaking; also 去⁴ and others.

Errata:—Unavoidable absence from China has made it impossible for the writer to do full justice to the work while passing through the press, and, but for the assistance of friends in Shanghai, its appearance would have been considerably delayed.

For the same reason it is to be regretted that some errors have passed into print. Students should carefully note the corrections given under "Errata" at the end of the book.

The writer is indebted to Mr. Vale, C. I. Mission, Ch'en-tu, who kindly revised the greater part of the manuscript, and to many other friends for help and encouragement.

If all who use the book derive from it a tithe of the profit and pleasure which the writer has obtained from the compilation of it, he will be doubly rewarded.

His earnest prayer is, that it may, above all, prove a help to his fellow-workers in their efforts to reach the Chinese with the "good news of God concerning His Son."

ADAM GRAINGER.

SHANGHAI, *November, 1900.*

RADICAL INDEX.

1-66.

No. of Rad.	Page of Dict.								
One Stroke.		16	几	42	33	士	114	52	幺	165
		17	凵	43	34	夂	115	53	广	165
		18	刀	43	35	夊	115	54	廴	169
1	一	1	„	刂	„	36	夕	116	55	廾	169
2	丨	5	19	力	53	37	大	117	56	弋	170
3	丶	6	20	勹	58	38	女	123	57	弓	170
4	丿	6	21	匕	60	39	子	132	58	彐	174
5	乙	7	22	匚	60	40	宀	135	59	彡	174
6	亅	9	23	匸	61	41	寸	145	60	彳	175
Two Strokes.					42	小	148	**Four Strokes.**		
7	二	9	24	十	61	43	尢	150			
8	亠	10	25	卜	64	44	尸	151	61	心	179
9	人	11	26	卩	64	45	屮	154	„	忄	„
„	亻	„	„	㔾	„	46	山	155	„	㣺	„
10	儿	31	27	厂	66	47	巛	156	62	戈	198
11	入	34	28	厶	67	„	川	„	63	戶	200
12	八	35	29	又	68	48	工	157	64	手	201
13	冂	37	**Three Strokes.**			49	己	158	„	扌	„
14	冖	39	30	口	71	50	巾	159	65	支	241
15	冫	39	31	囗	97	51	干	163	66	攴	241
			32	土	100				„	攵	„

67	文	247	86	灬	318	105	癶 354
68	斗	247	87	爪	329	106	白 355
69	斤	248	"	爫	"	107	皮 356
70	方	249	88	父	330	108	皿 357
71	无	251	89	爻	330	109	目 361
72	日	251	90	爿	331	"	罒 "
73	曰	258	91	片	331	110	矛 367
74	月	260	92	牙	331	111	矢 367
75	木	262	93	牛	332	112	石 368
76	欠	285	94	犬	334	113	礻 374
77	止	287	"	犭	"	"	示 "
78	歹	289	**Five Strokes**			"	ネ "
"	歺	"	95	玄	337	114	禸 377
79	殳	290	96	玉	337	115	禾 377
80	毋	291	"	王	"	116	穴 382
81	比	292	97	瓜	341	117	立 385
82	毛	293	98	瓦	342	**Six Strokes**		
83	氏	294	99	甘	342	118	竹 387
84	气	294	100	生	343	119	米 397
85	水	295	101	用	344	120	糸 400
"	氵	"	102	田	344	"	糹 "
"	氺	"	103	疋	348	121	缶 414
86	火	318	104	疒	348	122	网 415

122	皿	415
"	冖	"
123	羊	417
124	羽	419
125	老	420
126	而	421
127	耒	422
128	耳	423
129	聿	425
130	肉	425
"	月	"
131	臣	437
132	自	437
133	至	438
134	臼	438
135	舌	440
136	舛	440
137	舟	441
138	艮	441
139	色	442
140	艸	442
"	艹	"
141	虍	457

142-214.

142	虫 459	162	辵 512	179	韭 562	200	麻 590
143	血 465	,,	辶 ,,	180	音 563	Twelve Strokes.	
144	行 466	163	邑 524	181	頁 564	201	黃 590
145	衣 467	,,	阝 ,,	182	風 569	202	黍 591
,,	衤 ,,	164	酉 526	183	飛 570	203	黑 591
146	襾 473	165	釆 529	184	食 570	204	黹 593
,,	西 ,,	166	里 529	185	首 574	Thirteen Strokes.	
Seven Strokes.		Eight Strokes.		186	香 574	205	黽 593
147	見 474	167	金 530	Ten Strokes.		206	鼎 593
148	角 476	168	長 541	187	馬 575	207	鼓 593
149	言 477	,,	镸 ,,	188	骨 579	208	鼠 593
150	谷 489	169	門 542	189	高 580	Fourteen Strokes.	
151	豆 489	170	阜 547	190	髟 581	209	鼻 594
152	豕 489	,,	阝 ,,	191	鬥 582	210	齊 594
153	豸 490	171	隶 553	192	鬯 582	Fifteen Strokes.	
154	貝 490	172	隹 553	193	鬲 583		
155	赤 497	173	雨 556	194	鬼 583	211	齒 595
156	走 498	174	青 558	Eleven Strokes.		Sixteen Strokes.	
157	足 500	175	非 559	195	魚 584	212	龍 596
158	身 505	Nine Strokes.		196	鳥 586	213	龜 596
159	車 507	176	面 559	197	鹵 588	Seventeen Strokes.	
160	辛 510	177	革 560	198	鹿 588		
161	辰 511	178	韋 562	199	麥 589	214	龠 596

注释

一 [i⁵]
【鞋子做归一了】一：完结，好。
【我人今天不居一】一：舒服。

THE SPOKEN LANGUAGE OF WESTERN CHINA.

WORDS WITH CHARACTERS ARRANGED ACCORDING TO THE RADICALS.

The 1st radical. (一)

一 1⁵.

一個人	*one* person; alone.
一心一意	with *one* heart and mind.
一年一回	*once* a year.
一步一步	step *by* step.
要喫一點藥	you must take *a* little medicine.
下了一天的雨	it rained a *whole* day.
他們是一路來的	they came *together*.
一切的事情	*all* affairs.
一樣的東西	the *same* kind of thing.
天一亮的時候	*as soon as* it is daylight.
一早要起身	we will start in the *early* morning.
鞋子做歸一了	the shoes are *finished*.
都坐歸一了沒有	are they all seated *ready*?
我人今天不居一	I am *unwell* to-day.
第一章	the *first* chapter.
第一要緊的	the *most* important.
不一定	not *certain*.

一 1⁵. 1-2

1 丁 TIN¹.

丁香	cloves; lit. *nail* spice, (from the old meaning of the character).
好多人丁	how many *persons*?
成丁	to come *of age*.
丁憂	a *son* mourning for his father (official).
家丁 and 門丁	*servants* and door *keepers*.
兵丁	*soldiers*.
他兩個的力量丁對	they are about *matched* in strength.
丁㮒兩句	they *squabbled* a bit.
丁年	"tin" year, i.e., the year in the cycle in which "tin" occurs.

七 TS'I⁵, TS'IE⁵.

七百	*seven* hundred.
第七本	the *seventh* volume.
燒七	to burn cash paper after a death every *seventh* day till the 49th day.
他在那裏說七說八的	he just talked a lot of nonsense there.

2 丈 CHANG⁴.

一丈長	*ten feet* long; a Chinese *yard*.
好多丈尺	what is the *measurement*?
丈田	to *measure* fields.
丈夫	a *husband*.
大丈夫	an able *man*.
老丈人	wife's *father*.

下 SHIA⁴.

樟子底下	*under* the table.
在下面	on the *lower* side.
下等的貨	an *inferior* class of goods.
下民	the *vulgar* classes.
下半天	*after*-noon.
下月	*next* month.
快快下來	come *down* quickly.
把瓦下下來	*take down* the tiles off the house.
下馬	to *dismount* from a horse.

(2)

注　释

丁 [tin¹]
【他两个的力量丁对】丁对：相当，差不多。
【丁㮒两句】丁㮒：拌嘴，争吵。
【丁年】英文释义应为：①the age of maturity. 男子成丁之年。历代之制不一。汉以男子二十岁为丁，明清以十六岁为丁。亦泛指壮年。②the year that ding occurs in traditional way to number the years with the Heavenly Stems and Earthly Branches. 天干地支纪年中出现"丁"的年份，如丁丑年、丁亥年等。

七 [tɕʰi⁵] [tɕʰie⁵]
【烧七】做七，也称"斋七"、"理七"、"作七"、"做一日"、"七七"等。旧时汉族丧葬风俗，即人死后（或出殡后），于"头七"起即设立灵座，供木主，每日哭拜，早晚供祭，每隔七日做一次佛事，设斋祭奠，依次至"七七"四十九日除灵止。

丈 [tṣaŋ⁴]
【好多丈尺】尺寸多少？

下 [ɕia⁴]
【把瓦下下来】第一个"下"：动词，卸除，取下。

注释

【下脚钱】(行程结束时自付的)劳务费、苦力费。

三 [san¹]

【三脚】即三脚架。

上 [ṣaŋ⁴]

【利见上人】很荣幸见到尊贵的长官。

— 1⁵. 2

下手做工	to *commence* work.
下鄉	to *go into* the country.
那天下了雨	rain *fell* on that day.
生下來	to *give birth to*.
下蛋	to *lay* eggs.
下棋	to *play* chess.
下脚錢	coolie hire paid at the *end* of a journey.
下江板子	the blocks of this book have been cut *down* river.
我名下分好多	how much is there *to* my name?
天下	the empire.
下身	the *privates*.
一百錢的上下	a hundred cash or thereabout.

SAN¹.

三本書	*three* books.
我不管他三七二十一	I don't care what he says or does; lit. 3 times 7 are 21.
三脚	a *tri*-pod.
三隻手	a pick pocket.
不要三心二意	don't be irresolute.
第三天	the *third* day.
再三	*several* times; *repeatedly*.

SHANG⁴.

擱在上頭	place it on the *top*.
上好的東西	the *best* quality of goods; a *first-rate* article.
上半天	*fore*-noon.
上古以來	from the *most* ancient times.
利見上人	I am happy to be in the presence of my *superior* officer.
上諭	an *Imperial* edict.
上帝	the *Supreme* Ruler.
上省	to *go up* to the capital.
上街	to *go upon* the street.
把舖門上起	*shut up* the shop front; to *put up* the shutters.

— 1⁵. 3-5

上燈	to *light* a lamp.
拿燈來上油	bring the lamp and *pour* some oil into it.
上顏色	to *lay on* colouring.
那天上路	when will you *start* on your journey?
上學	to *begin* or *enter upon* study.
那個不上算	that does not *enter* into the reckoning; of no importance.
買上了當	I was *taken in* in buying it.
幫我達個拜上	*salute* so-and-so for me.
在街上	*on* the street.
班上的	lictors; policemen.
你看得上嗎	does it take your fancy?
不上一吊錢	not *more than* 1,000 cash.

3 不 PU⁵.
不是	it is *not*; no.
我不去	I *won't* go.

READ PO⁵.
你要不	do you want it or *not*?

4 世 SHÏ⁴.
世界	the *world*.
今世	the present *age*; this *life*.
世代	*generations*.

且 TS'IE³.
苟且了事	the business was *carelessly* done.

5 兩 LIANG³.
same as 兩.

丟 TIU¹.
丟開	to *cast* aside.
丟石頭	to *throw* a stone.
丟棄	to *reject*.
丟手	*let go* your hold!
他那一付煙癮丟不脫	he cannot *abandon* the opium habit.
丟個信在屋頭	*leave* word in the house.
丟不得手	I cannot *leave* my work.
他死丟了兩個娃娃	he died and *left* two children.

(4)

注 释

【那个不上算】不上算：不合算，吃亏。
【班上的】警察，刑吏。
【不上一吊钱】不上：不超过，没达到。
不 [puˉ⁵]
世 [sꞏ⁴]
且 [tsʰie³]
两 [liaŋ³]
丟 [tiəu¹]
【丟手】撒手，放手。
【丟不得手】"丟手"的否定用法，即"丟不开手"、"撒不了手"、"放不下手"。
【他死丟了两个娃娃】丟：同"掉"。

注 释

並(并)[pin⁴]

丫[ia¹]
【丫口】又作"垭口"。两山之间可通行的狭窄地方。

中[tʂoŋ¹][tʂoŋ⁴]
【中人】中间人，为双方介绍买卖、调解纠纷等并做见证的人。
【一个中锭】一锭约五盎司的银锭。
【看中了意】满意。

串[tʂʰuan⁴]

一 1⁵. 7 ｜. 2-6

7 並 那個地方丟荒了 — that land is *left* waste.
PIN⁴. sometimes pronounced p'in³ in the first sentence.
並排走 — to walk *side by side*, to walk *abreast*.
一並在內 — *all* included.
並不是 — it *certainly* is not.

The 2nd radical. ｜

2 丫 IA¹.
丫頭 — a slave girl; lit. *forked* head, referring to the hair.
3 丫口 — a mountain *pass*.

中 CHONG¹.
在棹子中間 — in the *centre* of the table.
中人 — a *middle*-man.
在你我中間當 } he will act as middle-man *between* you
個保人 } and me.
在衆人當中 — *among* the people.
在心中 — *in* the heart.
中等貨物 — *medium* quality of goods.
一個中錠 — a small ingot of silver, about 5 oz.
中飯 — the noonday meal; dinner.
不中用 — not *fit* for use.

READ CHONG⁴.
射中了 — he *hit* the mark.
中舉 — to *obtain* "kü-ren" degree.
6 看中了意 — it *struck* my fancy.

串 CH'UAN⁴.
錢串子 — a cash *string*.
一串錢 — a *string* of cash.
拴了一串串 — prisoners tied together in a *line* or *file*.
話是串通了的 — they are all in the secret.

(5)

ヽ 2-4 ㇒ 2

The 3rd radical. (ヽ)

丸 UAN². ÜEN².
丸藥　　　　　pills.
硬心丸　　　　a firm resolve—to abandon the opium habit.

READ ÜEN².
脎丸子　　　　meat-balls.

丹 TAN¹.
一片丹心　　　loyal-hearted; lit. a *red* heart.
探藥煉丹　　　to distil *medicines* from raw materials.
好丹方　　　　a good prescription.

主 CHU³.
房主人　　　　the *owner* or *landlord* of a house.
主人家坐下邊　the *host* takes the lowest seat.
打個主意　　　come to a decision; make up your mind; lit. a *lord's* mind.
主保的人　　　a *surety*; one who gives a guarantee.
我作不得主　　I cannot act upon my own responsibility.
可以自主　　　you may *rule* yourself; *manage* your own affairs.
長子主祭　　　the eldest son *presides* at the sacrifice.
點主　　　　　to dot the character "*chu;*" a ceremony at the erection of the tablet.

The 4th radical. (㇒)

久 CHIU³.
天長地久　　　heaven is lasting, earth is *enduring*.
喫了好久　　　how *long ago* is it since he ate it?
好久沒有來　　he has not been here for a *long time* [or a good *while*].

(6)

注　释

丸 [uan²] [yen²]
【硬心丸】（戒毒时）下定的决心。
【脎丸子】肉丸子。
丹 [tan¹]
主 [tʂu³]
【主保的人】担保人。
【点主】旧俗丧礼之一。填写神主上"主"字上端之点。
久 [tɕiəu³]

注释

之 [tʂɿ¹]
乏 [fa⁵]
【我乏力】客套语，表示希望报答对方的恩情。
乍 [tsa⁴]
乖 [kuai¹]
乘 [ʂən²]
【轿竿子乘不起】乘：承受，承担。
【我靠实乘不住了】靠实：实在是，确实是。
乘 [tʂʰən²]
【两乘轿子】乘：量词，辆。
九 [tɕiu³]
【九八银子】纯度为98%的银子。

丿 3-9 乙 1

之 3

CHĪ¹.

| 得之易失之易 | lightly come lightly go [a particle used like 的 a. v.] |
| 之字拐的路 | a *crooked* road (from the shape of the character). |

乏 4

FA⁵

脚走乏了	my feet are *tired* with walking.
穷乏得很	very *poor*.
我乏力	I am *wanting* in means to repay your kindness.

乍 7

CHA⁴.

| 乍冷乍熱 | changeable weather; lit. *suddenly* cold and *suddenly* hot. |

乖

KUAI¹.

脾氣乖張	his temper is *perverse*.
你倒乖巧	you are very *cunning*!
乖不乖	are you *good* [said to a child].

乘 9

SHEN².

乘轎子	to *ride* in a sedan chair.
乘機會	to *take advantage of* an opportunity.
找個陰地方乘涼	let us sit in a shady place *to get cool*.
轎竿子乘不起	the chair poles will not *bear* the weight.
我靠實乘不住了	I really can't *bear*, or *endure* it.

READ CH'EN².

| 兩乘轎子 | two sedan chairs [*N. A.*]. |

The 5th radical. (乙)

九 1

CHIU³.

九間房子	*nine* rooms.
一九二九懷中插手	the first *nine* and second *nine* days after midwinter, keep your hands in your bosom.
九八銀子	silver with 2 per cent alloy, $\frac{98}{100}$ silver.
第九篇	the *ninth* page.
打小九九的	a mean man; lit. one who reckons on a small *abacus*.

(7)

乙 2-12

乞 CH'IE⁵.

九子爛瘁	scrofulous ulcers on the neck (so called because several in a row.)
乞兒	a *beg*gar.

也 IE³.

你也來了	you *also* have come.
也下雨也吹風	*both* rain *and* wind.
也不喫也不說	he would *neither* eat *nor* speak.
也罷	that's an end of it!

扎 CHI¹.

| 降扎仙 | to bring down the *divining* genius. |

乳 RU³.

小兒吃乳	an infant feeds on *milk*.
乳名	the *infant* name.
拿乳鉢乳細	take the mortar and *triturate* the medicine.

乾 KAN¹.

曬乾了	*dry* through exposure to the sun.
乾得好	well *dried*.
天乾	a drought; lit. the heavens are *dry*.
乾瘡子	itch; lit. *dry* sores.
木頭乾過性了	the wood is well *seasoned*.
乾貨舖	a grocery store.
乾兒子	a kind of adopted son.
洗乾淨	wash it *clean*.
罪脫乾淨了	sin *completely* put away.
說不乾淨的話	to speak *obscene* words.
錢使得乾乾淨淨	my money is *all* gone.
我這個錢乾淨	this cash is *good*; *free from* bad cash.
他手脚不乾淨	he is not *honest*; he is a thief.
錢來得不乾淨	ill-gotten gains, dis*honest* money.
這個地方的魚乾貴	fish is *very* dear here.

READ CH'IEN².

| 乾坤顚倒 | a disorderly house; lit. *heaven* and earth are turned upside down. |

亂 LUAN.

| 亂頭髮 | *dishevelled* hair. |

(8)

注 释

【九子爛瘁】瘰疬，病名，即淋巴腺结核。俗称疬子颈，多发生在颈部，有时也发生在腋窝部。

乞 [tɕʰie⁵]

也 [ie³]

扎 [tɕi¹]

乳 [zu³]

乾（干）[kan¹]

【干疮子】疥疮，传染性皮肤病，病原体是疥虫，多发生在手腕、手指、臀部、腹部等部位。

【木头干过性了】过性：彻底，完全。

【这个地方的鱼干贵】干：非常，很。

乾 [tɕʰien²]

亂（乱）[luan⁴]

注释

了 [liao³]
【才来了】才来，埋怨人来得晚。
【了性酒】一种医治跌打劳损、腰腿酸痛的药酒。该药由明末清初著名医药师冯了性创制，故名"了性酒"。

事 [sๅ⁴]
【同事的人】同事。

二 [zๅ⁴]

丿. 1-7

亂石頭	ruby; unknown stone; cable-stones.
莫亂規矩	don't *break* or *transgress* the customs.
你亂拿東西	you take up things in a *disorderly* manner.
打胡亂說	you talk *wildly*! nonsense!

The 6th radical. (丿)

了   LIAO³.   often pronounced la³ in sentences like the last.

不得了	in a fix; lit. it cannot be *ended* or *settled*.
又了咯一件事	that's another row *settled*.
了不得	extraordinary; extreme; infinite; inexhaustible.
一看就了然	you will *understand* it as soon as you look at it.
纔來了	just come [indicates *past* time].
了性酒	a kind of medicinal wine.

事   SÏ⁴.

我的事不好	my *affairs* are in a bad state.
那是個不懂事的	he is an ignorant fellow.
好事不出門 惡事傳千里	good *deeds* never travel, but bad deeds spread a thousand miles.
辦事的	the manager of a *business*.
做事不對	you do not do your *work* properly.
沒事業	having no *occupation*.
同事的人	partners in an undertaking.
有甚麼心事	what are you grieving about; lit. what is your heart *trouble*?
惹出多少的事來	it will stir up a lot of *trouble*.
服事	to *serve*.

The 7th radical. (二)

二   RÏ⁴.

| 二百個人 | two hundred men. |

(9)

二 RÏ⁴. 2-5　⊥. 1-4

	我沒得二心	there is no *duplicity* or *indecision* about me.
	第二條街	the *second* street.
2	二天來	come *another* day.
井	TSIN³.	
	一口井	one *well*.
	天井	a square *opening* in the roof.
	說話井井有條	to speak in an *orderly* manner.
互	FU⁴.	
	互相打罵	*mutually* striking and cursing.
五	U³.	
	五行	the *five* elements.
5	五月初五	the *fifth* of *fifth* moon.
些	SIE¹.	
	一些兒	a *little*.
	有些不是	*some* are not.
	有好些人	a good *few* men.
	快些跑	run more quickly [indicates the *comparative*].
	這些小東西	these small things [indicates the *plural*].
	昨晚些	last night [a final particle].

The 8th radical. (⊥)

1	UANG².	
亡	疾病死亡	sickness and *death*.
	他逃亡了	he has *absconded*.
4	CHIAO¹.	
交	交朋友	to *contract* a friendship.
	心性相交	to have intimate *communion* with another.
	絕了交	the *intercourse* is broken off.
	我不曉得怎樣開交	I don't know how to extricate myself from this *difficulty*.
	我望個解交人	I hope someone will take me out of this *fix*.
	交戰	to *engage* in battle.
	兩交界	the *boundary* between two places.
	彼此交易	to *barter*.

(10)

注 释

【我没得二心】没得：没有。

【二天来】二天：改天，以后。

井 [tsin³]

互 [fu⁴]

五 [u³]

些 [sie¹]

【昨晚些】昨晚。

亡 [uaŋ²]

交 [tɕiao¹]

【心性相交】"心有灵犀"之意。

【我不晓得怎样开交】开交：从困境中脱身。

【我望个解交人】望：盼望。解交：汉代百官交拜之礼。官员调任对拜而去，称"解交"。此句意为希望有人将自己从困境中解救出来。

注释

【拿点交头】交头:保证金,定金,预付金。

亨 [xən¹]

享 [ɕiaŋ³]

京 [tɕin¹]

亮 [liaŋ⁴]

【亮火虫】萤火虫。

【亮皮子】造纸的嫩竹皮子,可以引火或照明。

亭 [tʰin²]

人 [zən²]

5-7

好大個交易	what a big *trade!* (sarcastic).
信沒有交到	the letter was not *delivered*.
把銀子交給他	*hand over* the silver to him.
有交接沒得	is any *gratuity* to be given?
拿點交頭	give a little *earnest money*.
坐頭一把交椅	the chief man in any matter.
不許交頭接耳	*whispering* is not allowed.

5 亨 HEN¹.

事情亨通	the affair is *successful*.

6 享 SHIANG³.

享福	to *enjoy* happiness.
享大壽	to live to a good old age.

7 京 CHIN¹.

北京	the northern *capital*; Pekin.

亮 LIANG⁴.

照個亮來	bring a *light*.
莫遮倒亮	don't intercept the *light*.
燈不亮	the lamp is not *bright*.
天氣清亮	the weather is clear and *bright*.
天亮開了	the sky has *cleared* up a little.
天亮起身	we will start at day*break*.
聲音響亮	the sound is loud and *clear*.
亮火虫	a *firefly*.
亮皮子	an *allumette*; spills of wood dipped in brimstone.

亭 T'IN².

凉亭子	a cool *arbour*.

The 9th radical. (人)

人 REN².

一個人的錢	one *person's* money.
多少人	many *people*.
天地人	heaven, earth, and *man*.
成人	to come of age; to become a *man*.
我人病了	*I* am unwell.
我們人生面不熟	we are unacquainted.

人 REN². 2-3

人人都在說	every*body* is talking about it.
盡人道	to fulfil the duties of the *human* relationships.
沒人烟的地方	where there are no *human* habitations.
做紙人人	to make paper *effigies* or *manikins*.
人參	the plant *ginseng* (extravagantly regarded as a medicine).

仇 CH'EO².

兩家成仇	the two families have become *enemies*.
有恩須當報 無仇莫結冤	if you have received a favour repay it, but where there is no *enmity* do not stir up a quarrel.

仆 P'U⁵.

仆倒在地	to *fall face downward* on the ground.
仆倒睡	to sleep *face downward*.
仆起的	hollow side *downward*; inverted.
把那個盆仆倒	turn that basin *mouth downward*.

仁 REN².

他心裏仁慈	he is *compassionate*.
手脚不仁	hands and feet paralysed; lit. not *fulfilling their duties*.
冲桃仁澄水	crush peach *kernels* and put them in the water to clear it.

仍 REN².

仍然不改	*as before* he will not change; still unrepentant.

今 CHIN¹.

今夜脫了鞋和韈 不知明日穿不穿	we cast off shoes and hose *this day*, and know not if we'll don them next.
我們如今走不得了	we can't walk *now-a-days*!
當今皇上	the *present* emperor.

仄 TSE⁵.

平聲仄聲	the even and *inclined* tones.
仄起身子過	to *sidle* past, or through.

仗 CHANG⁴.

打勝仗	to fight a winning *battle*; to gain a victory.

注 释

【做纸人人】扎纸人。
仇 [tʂʰəu²]
仆 [pʰu⁵]
【仆倒睡】胸脯和肚子朝下背朝天地睡觉。
【仆起的】器物口朝下放置。
仁 [zən²]
【手脚不仁】手脚麻痹或瘫痪，不听使唤。
仍 [zən²]
今 [tɕin¹]
【今夜脱了鞋和袜，不知明日穿不穿】比喻生死无常，世事难料。
仄 [tse⁵]
【仄起身子过】侧身通过。
仗 [tʂaŋ⁴]

注 释

付 [fu⁴]

以 [i³]
【可以而以】这样就行，未尝不可。
【有事所以不得来】不得：不会，不能。

令 [lin⁴]

仙 [sien¹]

他 [tʰa¹]
【他不管我的事】不管：不关，与……无关。

代 [tai⁴]
【好多年代】年代：年。

人 REN². 3

FU⁴.

倚仗	to *rely* on.
仰仗	to *look* to for aid.
交付清楚	to *hand* over all; to pay up.
先付一半	to *pay* one-half at the beginning.
付出去錢	*expenditure*; money *paid* out.
託付你帶個信	I *intrust* you with a letter; I *commission* you to take this letter.

I³.

可以而以	it will *do*; it may be *done*.
以德報德	*render* good for good.
你以爲人不曉得麽	did you *reckon* that people would not know?
有事所以不得來	he was busy, and *therefore* could not come.
說個所以然	give a reason *why*.
除此以外	*besides* this.
他未來以前	before he came.
他死了以後	after he died.

LIN⁴.

傳個號令出去	send out an *order*.
令人生氣	to *cause* people to get angry.
令尊康健	is your *honourable* father well?
時令很熱	the *season* is very hot.

SIEN¹.

神仙	gods and *genii*.
八仙	the eight *deified mortals*.
水仙花	the tuberose; lit. the water-*sprite* flower.
仙人掌	the cactus; lit. the hand of an *immortal*.
老神仙	an old man.

TʰA¹.

他不管我的事	*he* has nothing to do with me.
他的意思不同	*his* opinions are different.
他們不肯	*they* are unwilling.
那是他們說的	that is what *other people* say.

TAI⁴.

| 好多年代 | how many *years*? |

(13)

人 REN². 3-4

	來川有幾代人了	how many *generations* of your family have been in Sī-ch'uan?
	請個代書做呈子	engage a copyist to write an indictment; lit. one who writes *for* another.
	代館	to look after a school or office *for* another.
仔₄	TSĬ³.	
	做事要仔細	be *careful* about your work.
伐	FA⁵.	
	砍伐樹木	to *cut down* trees.
	請你作伐	will you act as *go-between*, please?
仿	FANG³.	same as 彷.
	他的話到還相仿	what he says is *like* my mind on the subject.
伏	FU⁵.	
	俯伏在地	to *fall down flat* on the ground.
	他使的有埋伏	he is up to tricks; lit. has laid an *ambush*.
	要把他降²伏得住	I will *humble* him.
	三伏天	the "*dog days*."
休	SHIU¹.	
	我兩個不得罷休	our quarrel cannot be *settled*.
	無常一到萬事皆休	when the "Messenger of Death" comes, all affairs *cease*.
	吾命休矣	my life is *ended*!
	休想活命	I'll take your life! lit. *don't* think to live!
	休來見我	*stop* coming to see me.
	休妻子	to *divorce* a wife.
伙	HO³.	
	屋裏的傢伙	the *furniture* in the house.
	木匠的傢伙	the joiner's *tools*.
	好傢伙	a fine *fellow*.
	生傢伙	half-cooked *food*.
	搭伙食	to *board* with one.
任	REN⁴.	
	重大的責任	a great *responsibility*, or *trust*.
	革職留任	to degrade in rank and yet retain in *office*.

(14)

注 释

【请个代书做呈子】代书：代写状子的人。呈子：民间向官方或下级向上级上呈的公文。

【代馆】同"代管"，替他人管理学校或办公室。

仔 [tsɿ³]

伐 [fa⁵]

【请你作伐】请你说媒，请你作媒人。

仿 [faŋ³]

【他的话到还相仿】相仿：差不多，中意。

伏 [fu⁵]

【他使的有埋伏】他在耍花招。

休 [ɕiəu¹]

伙 [xo³]

【生家伙】半生不熟的食物。

任 [zən⁴]

注释

件 [tɕien⁴]
　【还有些件件】还有些钱财。
仵 [u³]
伍 [u³]
　【在营伍里】营伍：军队。
伉 [kʰaŋ⁴]
仰 [ȵiaŋ³] [iaŋ³]
佔（占）[tʂan⁴]
　【他只占得这一门】占得：擅长。
　【占强】占上风，占优势。英文释义不准确，应为 to get the upper hand; to have the advantage over...
作 [tso⁵]
　【作房】作坊。

人 REN². 4-5

件 CHIEN⁴.

任隨他	as he pleases.
一件衣裳	an *article* of dress (*N.A.*)
好個物件兒	that's a fine *article*!
還有些件件	there are still a few *small pieces of silver*.
件件都依從他	comply with him in *each*, or *every* case.

仵 U³.

| 仵作 | the man who examines the body at an inquest: a *coroner*. |

伍 U³.

大擺隊伍	a great parade of *troops*.
行伍出身	risen from the *ranks* to office.
在營伍裏	in the *army*.

伉 K'ANG⁴.

| 伉儷和偕 | fidelity to the *marriage relationship*. |

仰 NIANG³, IANG³.

仰天嘆息	to *look up* to heaven and sigh.
久仰	I have long *thought* of you, i.e., desiring to see you.
仰起的	hollow side *upward*; face *upward*.

佔 CHAN⁴.

覇佔財產	to *usurp*; to *forcibly seize* the property of another.
侵佔邊界	to *encroach* upon the boundary of another.
佔便宜	to *take advantage* of others.
他只佔得這一門	he only *has the advantage* in this respect; he is only *good at* this one thing.
佔强	to *rely on* one's power.
我們佔上房	we *occupy* the upper part of the house.
這個東西佔地方	this thing *takes up* a lot of room.

作 TSO⁵.

| 作房 | a factory; a shop where certain articles are *made*. |
| 下作 | grasping, mean *acts*. |

(15)

人 REN². 5

	作難	to *put*, or to *be* in *distressing* circumstances.
	做作	*pretences*.
	事情發作了	the affair has *leaked out*.
	他的脾氣又發作了	his temper has *broken out* again.
住 CHU⁴.		
	在那裏住	where do you *dwell*?
	雨住了我們走	the rain has *ceased*, let us go.
	住手不消打了	*hold* your hand, don't strike.
	不住的哭	to cry without *stopping*; to weep incessantly.
	拴不住心	unable to *firmly* fix one's mind on a thing.
	靠不住	unable to rely *securely* upon anything; unreliable.
	忍不住笑	unable *steadfastly* to endure being laughed at.
	塞住	stop it up *tightly*.
佛 FU⁵.		
	拜佛	to worship *Buddha*.
	佛教	the *Buddhist* religion.
	佛手柑	the *Buddha's* hand citron.
何 HO².		
	如何得了	*how* will you do now?
	何必然	*why* will you do it? what's the good?
	沒奈何	no resource; lit. no means *whereby*; no help for it!
估 KU³.		
	不同你估堆堆	I will not *estimate* with you by the heap.
	估個價錢	*guess* the price of this article.
	估住幹	to *force* one to do a thing.
	估騙人	to obtain by *intimidation*; to get by fraud and *violence*.
	他兩個攪估了	those two men are bitterly *opposed* to each other.

(16)

注 释

住 [tṣu⁴]
【住手不消打了】不消打了: 不要打了。
佛 [fu⁵]
何 [xo²]
估 [ku³]
【不同你估堆堆】估堆堆: 乡下集市上的方式。把物品堆在一起, 根据堆的大小而不是重量出价, 价钱是否公道, 全凭买卖双方的眼力。
【估住干】现为"估到干", 强迫某人做事。
【估骗人】以恐吓、欺诈或暴力方法取得财物。
【他两个搅估了】搅估: 抬杠, 互相找茬。

注释

你 [n̠i³]
伴 [pan⁴]
伯 [pe⁵]
伸 [ʂən¹] [tʂʰən¹]
【事情闹不伸腰】事情多得没空休息。
似 [sɿ⁴]
伺 [sɿ⁴]
但 [tan⁴]
低 [ti¹]

人 5

NI³.

| 你要小心 | *you* must be careful. |
| 這不關你的事 | this is none of *your* business. |

PAN⁴.

我兩個做同伴	we two are *companions*.
少是夫妻老是伴 一時不見親吁喚	when young man and wife, when old *comrades* dear, if parted an hour, each for other call.
我陪伴你去	I will *accompany* you.

PE⁵.

| 伯伯 | *father's elder brothers*. |
| 老伯父 | my respected *senior*. |

SHEN¹.

| 大老爺伸冤 | Great Sir! *redress* my grievance! |

READ CH'EN¹.

伸出來	*thrust* it out from you.
伸手接倒	*put out* your hand and take it.
伸個懶腰	to *stretch* one's lazy body.
把腰桿伸起	*straighten up* your back.
一年到頭不得伸腰	I never get a *rest* all the year round.
事情鬧不伸腰	my affairs are never ended.

SĪ⁴.

| 似是而非的 | *like* right and yet wrong. |
| 相逢好似初相識 到老終無怨恨心 | if you always treat your friends *as* when first acquainted, friendship to old age will last, anger ne'er will taint it. |

SĪ⁴.

| 伺候倒 | *attend at your posts*! (said to official underlings). |

TAN⁴.

| 不但這樣 | not *only* thus. |
| 但不知開不開花 | *but* I don't know that it will flower. |

TI¹.

| 說話低聲些 | speak in a *lower* tone. |
| 這個銀子程分低 | this is *inferior* silver. |

人 5-6

	光棍不怕出身低 只要長大有氣力	the villain cares not if he be *base* born, his only wish is to be great and strong.
	低頭便是理	to *bow* the head is to apologise.
	我不低三下四	I will not *stoop* to do everything.
	銀價低了	the price of silver has *fallen*.

TIEN⁴.

佃田戶 — a tenant farmer; lit. one who *tills* the fields.
佃房子 — to *rent* a house.
壓佃 — the *deposit* on a rented house.

TSO⁴.

佐貳雜職 — *secondary* or *assistant* officials.

UE⁴.

請得位 — please take your *seats*.
牌位 — the *station* of the spirit tablet.
他佔的是甚麼地位 — what *position* does he hold?
他到了那個地位 — when he comes to that *position* or *condition*.
爭點位分 — deficient in *quality*, *ability*, etc.
這幾位朋友 — these few friends [*N. A.*] (respectful).

IU⁴.

保佑 — to *protect*, as God does.

CH'Ï⁴·³.

奢侈 — *extravagant*.

I¹.

依靠 — to *trust* in.
可以依從 — you may *conform to* it.
不依你的 — I won't have it! I will oppose such doings!
依舊星子照舊月 — *after* the old way; *according to* the old fashion.
依我想那個法子不對 — *to my mind*, that plan will not answer.

LIAO².

乾佬佬 — a poor *fellow*; a *person* of no means.

CHIA¹.

美貌佳人 — a *pretty* woman.

(18)

注　释

佃 [tien⁴]
【佃田户】佃户，旧时租地主土地的农民。
【佃房子】租房子。
【压佃】(租房的)押金。

佐 [tso⁴]
【佐贰杂职】即助理官员，清代州县官署内助理官吏佐贰、首领、杂职三者的统称。

位 [uei⁴]
【请得位】请坐。
【争点位分】质量有缺陷或能力不足。争点：差一点。位分：地位，职位。英文释义应为：not high enough in one's position or power to do something.

佑 [iəu⁴]
侈 [tṣʰɿ⁴], [tṣʰɿ³]
依 [i¹]
佬 [liao²]
【干佬佬】穷人；没有任何资产的人。
佳 [tɕia¹]

注 释

【不见佳】不见好。
供 [koŋ¹] [koŋ⁴]
　【吃零供】零供：子女不定期的赡养费。
伶 [lin²]
　【那么精伶的一个人】精伶：聪明伶俐。
　【你伶便些】伶便：聪明，敏捷。
来 [lai²]
　【来字】在官府里做事的底层办事员，由于官员对他们招之即来，挥之即去，所以百姓戏称他们为"来字"。
　【给我写个来账】记我账上。
侑 [iəu⁴]
　【经侑客】款待客人。
　【经侑棹子】在宴席旁助兴，劝人吃喝。英语释义疑有误。
　【经侑病人】照料病人。
　【经侑牲口】喂养牲口。

人 6

供	端候你的佳音	I will wait for *good news* from you.
	不見佳	it is not *nice*.
	KONG¹.	
	喫零供	to get irregular *support from sons*.
	審口供	give a verbal *testimony*.
	READ KONG¹·⁴.	
	供養父母	to *support* one's parents.
	READ KONG⁴.	
	供奉菩薩	to *offer* to idols.
伶	LIN².	
	那麼精伶的一個人	such an *intelligent* man as that!
	那個娃娃精伶	that child is *clever*.
	聰明伶俐	wise and *shrewd*.
	你伶便些	be a little *smarter* (at your lessons).
來	LAI².	
	還沒有來	not yet *come*.
	來字	official's servants (because they are called to *come*).
	來往	intercourse; *comings and goings*.
	拿書來	*bring* the book.
	來錢八百	*received* 800 cash.
	給我寫個來賬	put it down to my *credit*.
	來得起兩吊錢	I can *contribute* two thousand cash.
	做得來	I can *do* it.
	來世	the *future* world.
	這是甚麼來頭	what is the *cause* of this?
	沒來頭	of no *consequence*.
	一來他罵我二來他打我	in the first place he cursed me, and in the second place he beat me.
侑	IU⁴.	
	經侑客	to *entertain* guests.
	經侑棹子	to *wait* table at a feast.
	經侑病人	to *nurse* a sick person.
	經侑牲𤘅	to *look after* an animal.

(19)

人 6-7

例		LI⁴.
	官清例熟	a magistrate virtuous and well-versed in the *laws*.
	下不爲例	don't look upon this as a *custom* or *precedent*.
佩		PE⁴.
	佩服不忘	I will *remember* and follow your advice.
使		SHÏ³.
	使得使不得	can it be *used* or not?
	使用的人	servants.
	莫使氣	don't be angry.
	他在使牛	he is out ploughing.
	沒得錢使	I have no money to *spend*.
	使費大	the *expenses* are great.
佯		IANG².
	佯粧不知	to *pretend* not to know.
佾		I⁵.
	佾生	a half "siu-ts'ai;" lit. a *mummer*.
侯		HEO².
	掛印封侯	to raise to the rank of *marquis*.
係		SHI⁴.
	關係重大	great *responsibility*, great *consequences*.
	實係不好	it is *really* bad.
俠		SHIA⁵.
	豪俠之客	a man who is *zealous* for the right.
俐		LI⁴.
	伶俐乖巧	*clever*.
保		PAO³.
	有我保你	I will *protect* you.
	遞保狀	to give a *bailbond*.
	保養身體	to *take care* of one's health.
	保正	a street warden; lit. *guardian* of the upright.
	中保人	middleman; advocate.
便		PIEN⁴.
	順便	*convenient*.

(20)

注　釋

例 [li⁴]
佩 [pei⁴]
使 [sï³]
【莫使气】别生气。
【他在使牛】他去耕田了。
【使费大】使费: 花费。
佯 [iaŋ²]
佾 [i⁵]
侯 [xəu²]
係 (系) [ɕi⁴]
俠 (侠) [ɕia⁵]
俐 [li⁴]
保 [pao³]
【保正】保长; 保护法律公正的官员。
【中保人】居中作保之人。
便 [pien⁴] [pʰien²]

注释

信 [sin⁴]
【我肯信他还走得那么远】
我肯信: 不信, 怀疑。
【没信实】没诚信, 不诚实。

俗 [sio⁵] [su⁵]
【在俗人】俗人, 尘世之人。

侵 [tsʰin⁴]

促 [tsʰo⁵]
【当时把我促倒了】促: 惊, 吓。

入 7

	便壺	a chamber utensil.
	大便 and 小便	to *ease* nature.
	你隨便來	come at your *pleasure*.
	行方便	to do *beneficial* acts.
	買便買不買便罷	if you want to buy, *then* buy, if not, *then* don't.
	READ P'IEN².	
	買便易	to purchase a *cheap* article, to buy *cheaply*.
	佔人的便宜	to usurp an *advantage*.
信	SIN⁴.	
	信不信	do you *believe* it; would you *believe* it!
	我肯信他還走得那麼遠	I doubt if he could walk that distance.
	我信服他	I *trust* or *put confidence in* him.
	大信心	great faith; lit. *believing* heart.
	沒信實	no *sincerity*.
	忠信的人	a *faithful* servant.
	信口亂說	you let your mouth talk nonsense.
	帶口信	to carry *news* by word of mouth.
	一封信	a *letter*.
俗	SIO⁵ SU⁵.	
	還俗	to leave the priesthood; lit. to return to the *world*.
	在俗人	a layman; lit. a man in the *world*.
	孬風俗	a bad *custom*.
	俗話	*common* language; *proverbs*.
	鄙俗不堪	unbearably *vulgar*.
侵	TS'IN⁴.	
	侵吞家財	to *appropriate* goods.
	侵佔田地	to *usurp* lands.
促	TS'O⁵.	
	催促起程	*urge* him to start on his journey.
	當時把我促倒了	it took me by *surprise* at the time.
	光陰甚促	time is very *pressing*; "time flies."
	時候短促	the time is *short*.

(21)

人 7-8

	CHÜIN⁴.	
	人材俊俏	he is a *handsome* man.
	TS'IAO⁴.	
	收拾得俏扮	she is *handsomely* dressed.
	U³.	
8	侮慢人	to *insult* a person.
	CH'ANG⁴.	
	夫倡婦隨	the husband *leads* and the wife follows.
	CHÏ⁵.	
	適值下雨	it *happened* to rain.
	值年的保正	the street official for the *present* year.
	輪值班期	in *rotation*.
	價值多少	what is the *price*?
	不值價	not *worth* much.
	你值得我縱值不得	you *deserve* it, but I do not.
	FU³.	
	俯伏	to *fall* prostrate.
	HEO⁴.	
	莫說不報時候未到	say not there is no doom, the *time* has not yet come.
	氣候不一	the *weather* is uncertain.
	節候不同	the *periods* are not alike.
	等候同路	*wait* and we will go together.
	伺候	to *wait* upon; to *serve*, to *attend* on.
	候補州縣	to *await* appointment as a district magistrate.
	問候他的安	*ask* after his welfare.
	SHIN⁴.	
	儌倖苟免	he was *fortunate* enough to escape.
	KO⁴.	
	八個人	eight men (*N. A.*).
	個個都有	*each* person has it (*N. A.*).
	一個一個的去	go one by one (*N. A.*).
	CHÜ¹.	
	俱皆一樣	*all* alike.

(22)

注　释

俊 [tɕyn⁴]
俏 [tsʰiao⁴]
侮 [u³]
倡 [tʂʰaŋ⁴]
值 [tʂʅ⁵]
【值年的保正】当值之年的保长。
俯 [fu³]
【俯伏】趴在地上，表示低头屈服。
候 [xəu⁴]
倖（幸）[ɕin⁴]
個（个）[ko⁴]
俱 [tɕy¹]

注 释

倦 [tɕyen⁴]
們（们）[mən²] [mən¹]
倫（伦）[lən²]
倍 [pei⁴]
修 [siəu¹]
　【修个阴功】阴功：不为
　　人所知的善行。
倘 [tʰaŋ³]
倒 [tao³] [tao⁴]
　【他倒了灶】倒灶：垮台，
　　败落。
　【倒他的炉子】到主人（或
　　上司）面前诋毁中伤他
　　的仆人（或随从）。

人 8

倦們倫倍修

CHÜEN⁴.	
疲倦得很	very *tired* or *weary*.
MEN²¹.	
我們	we (indicates the *plural*).
弟兄們	brethren (indicates the *plural*).
LEN².	
人倫	human *relationships*.
PE⁴.	
加一倍	add one *fold*; to double.
SIU¹.	
修房子	to *build* a house.
修橋補路	to *repair* bridges and mend roads.
修飾華麗	to *adorn*; to beautify.
修鬍鬚	to *shave* the beard.
修脚	to *pare* the toe-nails and corns.
修脚的	a chiropodist.
修書信	to *indite* a letter.
出家修行	to become a priest; lit. to leave home to *regulate* the conduct.
修個陰功	*lay up* secret merit.

倘倒

T'ANG³.	
心裏倘若不願	*if* you are not really willing.
TAO³.	
房子倒了	the house has *fallen*.
跌倒了	he stumbled and *fell*.
把牆推倒	to *overturn* a wall.
字號倒了	the bank has *failed*; the firm is *bankrupt*.
他倒了竈	he is *ruined*.
倒他的爐子	to slander a servant to his master.
把這個拿倒	take hold of this (a particle added to many verbs).
我沒有聽倒³說	I have not heard of it (a particle).
READ TAO³,⁴.	
顛倒過來	to *invert*; to *reverse*.
READ TAO⁴.	
倒轉來	to *return*; to *turn*; to *reverse*.

(23)

人 8-9

倒一口鐘	to *cast* a large bell.
倒銅錢	to *mint* copper cash.
倒在河頭	*empty* it into the river.
倒茶來	*pour out* the tea and bring it.
倒飯	to *dismiss* from service.

倭 o¹.

倭絨	*Japanese* velvet.

倉 TS'ANG¹.

陳倉滿庫	his granary and storehouse are full (metaphorically, a rich man).
開倉吐血	to spit blood (supposed to come from *a cavity in the abdomen*).
倉倉皇皇	*flurried*.

俸 FONG⁴.

身俸	*salary; wages; pay*.

借 TSIE⁴.

借給他	*lend* it him.
借去要還	if you *borrow* you must repay.
在你這裏借個歇	may I lodge at your house to-night?
借路過	may I pass through your premises?

假 CHIA³.

分別眞假	distinguish between true and *false*.
你莫做假嗎	don't make a *pretence*.
假把意思的	*pretending; feigning*.
貓兒不喫死老鼠假慈悲	the cat won't eat a dead rat,—*hypocritical* compassion!
假若你明天不來	*supposing* you do not come to-morrow?

READ CHIA⁴.

給先生告假	ask the teacher for *leave of absence*.

偕 HAI² SHIAI².

同偕到老	may you *live happily together* till you grow old.

健 CHIEN⁴.

健壯	*strong* and *healthy*.
老先生很康健阿	you are very *hale* and *hearty* old sir!
健火	to *temper* iron tools.

(24)

注 释

【倒一口钟】倒：铸造。
【倒饭】丢掉饭碗，失去工作。
倭 [o¹]
【倭绒】日本丝绒。
仓（仓）[tsʰaŋ¹]
俸 [foŋ⁴]
【身俸】薪水。
借 [tsie⁴]
【在你这里借个歇】借个歇：借宿过夜。
假 [tɕia³] [tɕia⁴]
【假把意思的】假模假式的，装模作样的。
偕 [xai²] [ɕiai²]
健 [tɕien⁴]
【健火】烧得很旺的火（来锻造铁器）。

注释

傢（家）[tɕia¹]
 【好家伙三】好伙伴，好兄弟。
偶 [ŋəu³]
 【土木偶人】木偶。
偏 [pʰien¹]
 【偏起的】歪斜的。
 【偏性子人】性格偏执的人。
 【一偏之见】偏见。
偈 [tɕie⁵]
偷 [tʰəu¹]
偢 [tsʰiəu¹]
停 [tʰin²]

人 9

傢 CHIA¹.
傢伙 — furniture; utensils; tools; men.
好傢伙三 — a good fellow.

偶 NGEO³.
拜偶像 — to worship idols.
土木偶人 — a doll.
偶然 — casually; by chance.

偏 P'IEN¹.
偏起的 — oblique; inclined to one side.
醉得打偏偏 — staggering because of drink.
房子有點偏 — the house is leaning to one side a little.
偏頸子 — a wry-neck.
偏性子人 — a cross or crooked tempered person.
一偏之見 — a prejudiced opinion.
道理斷偏了 — the matter has been unjustly decided.
偏愛 — to love excessively; to dote on; undue partiality.
地方偏僻 — it is an out-of-the-way place.
偏耍這樣 — I certainly must have it this way.
偏偏不依你 — I am decidedly displeased with you.
有偏 — thanks, I have eaten!

偈 CHIE⁵.
念佛偈 — to repeat Buddhist rhymes.

偷 T'EO¹.
偷竊 — to steal.
偷稅 — to smuggle.
小偷 — a petty thief.
偷油婆 — a cockroach; lit. a creature that steals the oil.
偷婆娘 — to commit adultery.
偷看甚麼 — what are you spying?
偷走-了 — he has absconded.
忙裏偷閒 — to shirk work at a busy time.
偷生在世 — to live when one has no right to live.

偢 TS'IU¹.
不偢不睬 — to take no notice of a guest.

停 T'IN².
商量停當 — to discuss and adjust.

(25)

入 9-10

	停柩	to *lay out* a corpse in a coffin.
	停了工	they have *ceased* work.
	鐘停了	the clock has *stopped*.
	停食	*indigestion*.
	十停折了七停	I lost seven *parts* out of ten.

TS'E⁵ TSE⁵.

側	側邊站立	stand on one *side*.
	放平不要放側	lay it flat, not *sideways*.
	側起耳朵聽	*incline* your ear and hear.
	側近有根大樹子	there is a large tree *near by*.

TS'A⁵ TS'E⁵.

	側黑	*nearly* dark.

TSU⁴.

做	做工夫	to *do* work.
	這是怎樣做的	how is this *made*?
	燕子正在做窩	the swallows are *building* a nest.
	做官	to *act* as an official.
	做好人	to *be* a good man.
10	這個叫做甚麼名字	what is this called? (denotes the *passive*).

FU⁴.

傅	大師傅	a master *workman*.

CHIE⁵.

傑	大豪傑	a very *eminent man*; a *leader*.

LEO².

僂	僂儸	*banditti*; the followers of a rebel chief.

KUE³.

傀	傀儡戲	a *puppet* show; Punch and Judy.

PANG⁴.

傍	傍晚的時候	*near* evening.
	沒得個挨傍	I have no *supporter* or *no one to depend on*.

PI⁴.

備	作個准備	make a *provision* for it.
	萬事俱備缺少東風	everything is *ready*; we only need the east wind, i.e., money.
	防備小人賊盜	*guard against* thieves.

(26)

注 释

【停食】不消化，消化不良。

【十停折了七停】东西损失了70%。

側(侧) [tsʰe⁵] [tse⁵] [tsʰa⁵]

【侧黑】将近天黑，傍晚。

做 [tsu⁴]

【做工夫】动词，工作。

傅 [fu⁴]

傑(杰) [tɕie⁵]

僂(偻) [ləu²]

傀 [kuei³]

傍 [paŋ⁴]

【没得个挨傍】没人可以依靠。

備(备) [pi⁴]

注 释

伞(傘)[san³]
【日照伞】太阳伞,遮阳伞。
【桶伞】华盖。
【万名伞】旧时百姓送给清官的一件大礼,上面签有众多百姓的名字,用以表达对清官的崇敬。

债(債)[tṣai⁴]
【债账拉重了】负债累累。

传(傳)[tṣʰuan²][tṣuan⁴]
【他到处传闻】他到处散布小道消息。

倾(傾)[tɕʰyn¹]
【拿出去倾了】拿出去倒了。
【拿这个碎银倾个大定】拿这些碎银子铸一大锭银子。

人 10-11

	守備	a captain.
	受責備	to receive a *reprimand*.
傘	SAN³.	
	雨傘	an *umbrella*.
	日照傘	a *sun-shade* carried before officials; an *eye-shade*.
	桶傘	a large round *canopy*.
	萬名傘	a large *umbrella* covered with the names of the people, and presented to a good official.
11 債	CHAI⁴.	
	債賬拉重了	he has incurred a heavy *debt*.
傳	CH'UAN².	
	這規矩是我們祖傳	this custom has been *handed down* from our ancestors.
	傳教	to *propagate* a religion.
	他到處傳聞	he *told* the news everywhere.
	給老師傳名	I will *spread* your name for good doctoring.
	施藥不如傳方	to freely dispense medicine is not equal to *circulating* a prescription.
	傳遞呈子	to *hand in* an indictment to an official.
	傳話	to *carry* verbal messages out and in.
	傳號令	to *issue* or *send out* an order.
	傳某人來	*tell* or *order* a certain person to come.
	傳個鑼	*send round* a crier with a gong.
	傳子	the short *carrying pole* of a three or four-bearer chair.
	READ CHUAN⁴.	
	看傳書	to read *annals* or *chronicles*.
傾	CH'ÜIN¹.	
	拿出去傾了	take it out and *empty* it away.
	傾家破產	to *impoverish* the family estate.
	拿這個碎銀傾個大定	get this small silver *smelted* into an ingot.

(27)

人 11-12

	拿這程分銀子傾個漂色	get this bad silver *refined*.

傲 NGAO⁴.
驕傲	*proud*.
那個人有些傲性	he is rather *obstinate*.
這把剪刀傲性	these scissors are *stiff* to work.

傷 SHANG¹.
遭了煤傷	to meet with an accident; lit. an unintentional *hurt*.
打傷了	to *injure* by beating; to *wound*.
致命傷	a mortal *wound*.
年輕的時候傷了力	I *overstrained* my strength when I was young.
那個話有些傷人	such talk is calculated to *offend* people.
我怕傷你的臉	I am afraid of *affronting* you.
這個菜喫傷了	I have taken a dislike to this through eating too much of it.
這個話聽傷了	I am *tired* of hearing this.
傷了心	*grieved* at heart.
傷了風	to *catch* cold.
傷風壞俗	to *demoralize* the customs of the community.

催 TS'UE¹.
催起馬走	*quicken* your horse's pace.
催客坐席	*urge* the guests to come to the feast.
催討債賬	to *dun* for a debt.
差人來催糧了	the runners have come to *press* the payment of taxes.
把火催起點	make a bigger fire; make it burn brighter.
把桶箍催緊	*drive* the pail hoops on tightly.
今年莊稼不催	the harvest is late this year.

傭 IONG².
傭工做活	to *hire* oneself out as a labourer for a living.

僱 KU⁴.
當僱工	I am a *hired* labourer.
僱幾乘轎子	*hire* a few sedan chairs.

(28)

注 释

【拿这程分银子倾个漂色】将这种银子精炼提纯一下。

傲 [ŋao⁴]

【那个人有些傲性】傲性：傲气，顽固，倔强。

【这把剪刀傲性】傲性：钝。

傷（伤）[ʂaŋ¹]

【年轻的时候伤了力】年轻时过度劳累，体力不支了。

【我怕伤你的脸】我怕冒犯了你。

【这个菜吃伤了】这个菜吃得太多，不喜欢吃了。

【这个话听伤了】这种话听得太多，觉得乏味无聊了。

催 [tsʰuei¹]

【今年庄稼不催】今年庄稼成熟得晚。

傭（佣）[ioŋ²]

僱（雇）[ku⁴]

注 释

僞（伪）[uei⁴]
僚[liao²]
僕（仆）[pʰu⁵]
僬[tsiao²]
　【嫖赌僬摇】僬摇：放荡，淫乱。
　【僬矜客】荡妇，水性杨花的女人。
僧[sən¹]
　【二僧】尼姑。
像[siaŋ⁴][tsʰiaŋ⁴]
　【活像他的老汉儿】老汉儿：父亲。
儀（仪）[ŋi²]
　【送个程仪】亦称"程敬"，旧时赠送旅行者的财礼。
　【仪注】官方礼节。
價（价）[tɕia⁴]
僵[tɕiaŋ¹]

人 12-13

僞 UE⁴.
真僞難辨　　it is hard to distinguish between true and *false*.

僚 LIAO².
同僚爲官　　official *associates*.

僕 P'U⁵.
忠信的僕人　　a faithful *retainer*.
奴僕　　*slaves*.

僬 TSIAO².
嫖賭僬摇　　whoredom, gambling, and *wantonness*.
僬矜客　　a *wanton*.

僧 SEN¹.
受戒僧　　a *priest* who has taken full orders.
小僧人　　the small *Buddhist* (said by a priest of himself).
二僧　　a Buddhist *nun*.

像 SIANG⁴.
人的形像　　the *appearance* of a man.
照像　　to take a *photograph*.
塑的偶像　　a moulded *image*; a mud *idol*.

READ TS'IANG⁴.
不像個樣子　　not *like* anything; not well done.
活像他的老漢兒　　he *resembles* his father.
我像記得　　I have a slight recollection of it.

儀 NGI².
送個程儀　　to give a *present* to one starting on a journey.
好個容儀　　what a fine *deportment*!
儀注　　official *etiquette*.

價 CHIA⁴.
不講價　　we do not bargain about the *price*.
不直價　　*worth*less; of no *value*.
那個人的身價高　　he has a high *estimate* of himself.

僵 CHIANG¹.
手脚都冷僵了　　my hands and feet are *benumbed* with the cold.

(29)

人 13-15

僥	**SHIAO¹**	
	行險僥倖	to break the laws, yet *lucky* enough to escape.
儉	**CHIEN⁴**	
	穿喫節儉	he is *economical* in clothes and food.
	READ CHIEN³	
	用錢儉省些	be more *careful* in your expenditure.
僻	**P'IE⁵**	
	邪僻的人	a *depraved* person.
儒	**RU²**	
	儒教	the *Confucian* school; the *literary* class.
	儒書	the *classics*.
儘	**TSIN³**	
	儘他做	*let* him do it.
	儘够用	there is *quite* enough for use.
	儘下得去	you can *easily* manage.
	你就儘說	you speak *far too much*; you talk *incessantly*.
	我儘等你	I waited a *long time* for you (*indefinitely*).
	你儘在這裏耍	you are *always* playing here.
償	**SHANG³**	
	償還	to *restore*; to *pay back*.
	殺人償命欠賬還錢	if you kill a man you must *atone*; if you contract a debt you must repay.
儡	**LUE³**	
	傀儡	*puppets*.
	自儡其身	to *injure* oneself.
優	**IU¹**	
	品學皆優	his disposition and his learning are both *excellent*.
	優禮相待	to treat each other with *excessive* politeness.
	優游自得	to *tranquilly* stroll about and enjoy oneself.

(30)

注　釋

僥（侥）[ɕiao¹]
儉（俭）[tɕien⁴][tɕien³]
僻 [pʰie⁵]
【邪僻的人】贪腐分子。
儒 [zu²]
儘（尽）[tsin³]
【尽他做】随便他做。
【尽够用】完全够用。
【你就尽说】你就一直说。
償（偿）[ʂaŋ³]
儡 [luei³]
【自儡其身】儡：伤害。
優（优）[iəu¹]

注释

僄 [piao¹]
  【他僄ta⁵ta⁵的跑起来了】
    僄ta⁵ta⁵：飞快跑动的样子。
储（儲）[tṣʰu²]
僭 [tsien⁴]
  【我就僭分了】僭分：越分、越权，做了职责以外的事情。
  【说话僭妄】僭妄：越分而狂妄。
儳 [tsʰan⁴]
  【那是个儳头】儳头：坏人，恶棍。
儷（俪）[li⁴]
儸（罗）[lo²]
儧（攒）[tsan³]
儼（严）[n̠ien³]
儽（累）[luei⁴]
  【付累你】让你受累了。
  【这个活路累人】活路：名词，工作。
元 [yen²]

人 15-21　儿 2

僄 16	PIAO¹.	
	他 僄 ta⁵ ta⁵ 的 跑起來了	he came running *quickly*.
儲	CHʻU².	
	儲 積 貨 物	to *accumulate* goods.
	TSIEN⁴.	
僭	我 就 僭 分 了	I am *overstepping* my position.
	他 做 事 僭 分	he acts *presumptuously*; he *oversteps* his duty.
17	說 話 僭 妄	to speak *presumptuously* or *arrogantly*.
儳	TSʻAN⁴.	
19	那 是 個 儳 頭	that fellow is a *villain*.
儷	LI⁴.	For example of use see 伉.
儸	LO².	For example of use see 僂.
儧 20	TSAN³.	
	積 儧	to *economize*; to *accumulate*.
	NIEN³.	
儼	儼 然 一 個 顏 色	*exactly* the same colour.
21 儽	LUE⁴.	
	走 儽 了	*tired* with walking.
	付 儽 你	I have *wearied* you (a polite expression).
	這 個 活 路 儽 人	this work is *fatiguing*.
	心 儽	heart *weariness*, caused by general debility or consumption.

The 10th radical. **(儿)**

元 2	ÜEN².	
	元 旦	the *first* day of the year.
	光 緒 元 年	the *first* year of the reign of the Emperor Kuang-sü.
	中 元	the *great* middle festival (in the 7th moon).
	元 帥	a *general* in the army.
	中 了 狀 元	to obtain the *chief* place in Han-lin examinations.
	元 寶 滾 進 來	may the *big* ingots of silver come rolling in?

(31)

儿 2-4

	元氣不足	his *constitution* is poor; deficient in *stamina*.
	本命元神	the *spirit* of a person which is able to leave the body and return again.
	元朝	the *Yuen* or Mongol Dynasty.
允³	ÜIN³.	
	允准	to *grant*.
	你們二家依不依允	do you both submit to my *decision*?
充	CH'ONG¹.	
	充滿	to *fill* full.
	充公	to *put into* the public funds.
	沒得充饑的	to have nothing to *appease* one's hunger.
	把他的貨物拿來充公	*confiscate* his goods.
	充當首人	to *act as* headman.
	假充官長	pretending to *be* an official.
	充軍	to banish beyond the frontier (originally meant to *recruit* the army).
兄	SHIONG¹.	
	家兄舍弟	the *elder* and younger *brothers* of our family.
	兄弟	a younger brother.
	弟兄	*brethren*.
	表弟兄	*cousins*.
	老兄貴姓	what is your honourable name, *sir*?
兆⁴	CHAO⁴.	
	吉兆	a good *omen*.
	得了個豫兆	I have had a *prognostication*.
兇	SHIONG¹.	
	兇惡	*wicked; cruel*.
	兇暴	*fierce*.
	逞兇	to *murder*.
	遭兇	to be *murdered*.
	兇手	a *murderer*.

(32)

注 释

允 [yn³]

充 [tṣʰoŋ¹]

兄 [ɕioŋ¹]

【家兄舍弟】自己的哥哥弟弟。

兆 [tṣao⁴]

兇（凶）[ɕioŋ¹]

【逞凶】行凶，谋杀。

注释

光 [kuaŋ¹]
【把头发梳光生】光生：整齐。
【大头光棍】恶棍、流氓、混混等的头目；表面光滑的棍子。
【这副眼镜子是长字光】长字光：近视镜，与老花镜相对。
【他肯来光是怕父母不喜欢】他愿意来不过是怕父母不高兴罢了。

先 [sien¹]

克 [kʰe⁵]
【克苦人家】克苦：虐待，对人苛刻。

免 [mien³]
【一边出麻子一边出痘子两免】表面是说出麻子、出痘子获得免疫性，实际上是说双方的礼节都免了。

光 KUANG¹.

月過十五光明少 人到中年萬事休	after the 15th, the moon's *light* grows less; after middle life a man's affairs cease.
把銅盆擦光亮	scour the brass basin till it is *bright*.
把頭髮梳光生	comb your hair *smooth*.
他穿得光生	he is *well and cleanly* clad.
光腳板兒	*naked* feet; barefoot.
大頭光棍	the chief blackguard; lit. *barestick*.
光陰似箭日月如梭	*time* flies like an arrow, days and months like a shuttle.
光景不好	*prospects* are bad.
沾你的光	I (or may I) receive *benefits* from you.
這副眼鏡子是長字光	these spectacles have magnifying *lenses*.
光你一個人	*only* you.
他肯來光是怕父母不喜歡	he is willing to come, *but* fears his parents would not be pleased.
光是會喫	he is *merely* able to eat.

先 SIEN¹.

祖先人	*forefathers*.
先到爲君後到爲臣	the one who came *first* should have the precedence.
他先來三天	he came three days *before* that.
先前的話	*former* words.
先生	a teacher; sir; lit. one who was born *before* I was.
這是我先父遺留下的	this was left me by my *deceased* father.
先見之明	able to see *beforehand*.
爭先恐後	to push *ahead* lest one should be behind.

克 K'E⁵.

| 克勤克儉 | he *can* be both diligent and economical. |
| 克苦人家 | to *ill-treat* people. |

免 MIEN³.

| 一邊出痲子一邊出痘子兩免 | in your house you have had measles, and in ours we have had small-pox, but both have *escaped*; metaphorically: If two marriages take place on one day, both parties *escape* giving presents. |

儿 6-12 入

兔 T'U⁴.

免不得親自去	I cannot *avoid* going myself.
免得鬧嘴	in order to *avoid* a row; *lest* they should quarrel.
閒人免進	loafers *need not* come in; *don't* come in.
求官免糧	to ask the magistrate to *remit* the taxes for this year.
赦免我的罪	*forgive* my sins.
兔子	a rabbit.
守株待兔 緣木求魚 }	he'd watch a post to catch a *hare*, or climb a tree to seek for fish.
打兔子	to vomit; Uen Uang is said to have vomited a *rabbit*.

兌 TUE⁴.

兌換銀錢	to *exchange* silver and cash.
滙兌銀子	to *transmit* silver through a bank.
打兌	to *exchange*; to sleep in the same bed.
轎子在路上打兌	chair-bearers *changing* their fare on the road.

兒 RÏ².

兒子	a *son*.
兒孫滿堂	may your *children* and grandchildren fill the hall.
狗兒	a *pup*.
牛兒	a *calf*.
洋畫兒	a foreign picture (a particle attached to nouns).

兜 TEO¹.

| 在衣兜裏頭 | in the *lap*. |

兢 CHIN¹.

| 戰戰兢兢的 | *tremblingly*. |

The 11th radical. (入)

入 RU⁵.

| 出入 | going out and *coming in*. |
| 入教會 | to *enter* a religion; to *become a member of* a church. |

(34)

注 释

兔（兔）[tʰu⁴]
【打兔子】意为呕吐，传说周文王误食其长子之肉而呕出了一只白兔。

兑 [tuei⁴]
【打兑】换零钱。

兒（儿）[zʅ²]

兜 [təu¹]

兢 [tɕin¹]

入 [zu⁵]

注 释

内 [luei⁴]
【内伤外感】内科和外科疾病。

全 [tsʰyen²]
【完全了】（工作）完成了。
【路上务要保全】保全：保护（人身、财物等）使不受损害。

两（两）[liaŋ³]
【两个钱】几个钱，一些钱。
【这是好多分两】好多：多少。这个东西有多少斤两？/这个东西有多重？

八 [pa⁵]
【八德】中华传统文化表彰的八种德行，即孝、悌、忠、信、礼、义、廉、耻。
【那钱要拿来八刀】八刀：即"分"，那钱要拿来分。

入 2-6 八.

	還沒有入門	you have not yet *commenced* or *entered upon* the business.
	入學	to *begin* to study; to *graduate*.
2 入	入不敷出	*income* not equal to expenditure.
LUE⁴.		
	內外	*within* and without.
	北門內	*inside* the North Gate.
	飯在內	rice is *included*.
	是我分內的事	this is *part* of my duty.
	內人	my wife, i.e., the one who lives in the *inner* apartments.
	內兄	*own* brothers.
	內傷外感	*internal* and *external* diseases.
4 內	內科	*medical* practice.
TSʻÜEN².		
	完全了	*completed*, as a work.
	樣樣齊全	all the things are *entire*.
	路上務要保全	on the road, be careful to preserve the things *whole*.
	全家福	may your *whole* family be prosperous.
	才貌雙全的人	his abilities and his outward appearance are both *perfect*.
	心裏全然不動	my mind is *altogether* unmovable.
6 兩		
LIANG³.		
	兩個錢	*two* cash; a *few* cash.
	兩頭	*both* ends.
	二兩水烟	two *ounces* of cut tobacco.
	十兩銀子	ten *taels* of silver.
	這是好多分兩	what is the *weight* of this? (silver, etc.).

The 12th radical. (八)

		PA⁵.
	八德	the *eight* virtues.
八	中第八	to attain to the *eighth* place.
	那錢要拿來八刀	we must divide that money (a play on the character 分).

(35)

八 2-6

KONG¹.

老公公	old man; grandfather (direct address).
老人公	husband's *father*.
諸公請坐	*gentlemen*, please sit down.
小相公	young *gentlemen*.
相公行	catamites.
船上太公那去了	where has the boat *captain* gone to?
雞公	a *cock*.
公羊	a *ram*.
辦公事	to manage *public* business.
公所地方	a *public* place.
公項的錢不得私用	money that is *common* property may not be used privately.
說公道話	ask a *just* or *fair* price.
公平交易	to trade *justly*.

LU⁵.

| 六六三十六 | *six* times *six* are thirty-*six*. |
| 六月六曬衣服 | on the *sixth* of *sixth* moon air your clothes. |

KONG⁴.

共總是好多	what is the sum *total*?
不共戴天的仇	our enmity is such that we cannot live *together* in this world.
沒有共過事	we have had no dealings *together*.
我們是同鄉共井的人	we are natives of the *same* place.
公共的錢	*public* funds.

PIN¹.

喫糧當兵的人	soldiers.
操兵	to drill *troops*.
馬兵 and 步兵	cavalry and infantry.
兵器	arms.
兵船	a gun boat; a war vessel.

CHÜ⁴.

| 刑具 | *implements* of punishment. |
| 家具 | household *utensils*. |

(36)

注　釋

公 [koŋ¹]

【老公公】老人家；祖父（面称）。

【老人公】丈夫的父亲。

【相公行】成年男子。

【船上太公那去了】船上撑篙的老人家哪里去了？

【鸡公】公鸡。

【公所地方】公共场所。

六 [lu⁵]

共 [koŋ⁴]

兵 [pin¹]

具 [tɕy⁴]

注释

【我要具控你】具控:控告,起诉。

【莫看为具文】不要当作一纸空文。

其 [tɕʰi²]

典 [tien³]

【房里老典】对官府中各署之官吏的总称。

兼 [tɕien¹]

【兼扯有好多】总共有多少?

【兼高扯低卖四个钱一个】兼高扯低:总的来说。

【萝卜兼饭】萝卜炒饭。

囬(回) [xuei²]

【囬食】即呕吐。

【囬水】漩涡。

八 6-8 冂 3

其典兼	我要具控你	I will *accuse* you to the magistrate.
	莫看爲具文	do not regard it as *common*.
	CH'I².	
	受其拖累	I am involved by *him*.
	其中必有別故	there certainly is another reason in *it*.
	TIEN³.	
	字典	a dictionary; lit. a *record* of characters.
	房裏老典	*recorder* or *chief clerk* of a bureau.
8	典當舖	a *pawn*-shop.
	恩典	*grace*; *favour*.
	CHIEN¹.	
	文武兼全	he is versed in *both* civil and military affairs.
	兼扯有好多	how much is there *altogether*?
	兼高扯低賣四個錢一個	to sell at 4 cash a piece *over all*.
	蘿蔔兼飯	turnips *and* rice cooked together.
	兼之我不能	*moreover* I am unable.

The 13th radical. (冂)

3	HUE².	
囬	出遠門囬來	to *return* from a long journey.
	囬門	a bride *returning* to her parents' house after her marriage.
	苦海無邊囬頭是岸	the sea of bitterness is boundless, yet *turn* your head and you may reach the shore.
	囬鍋	to boil meat and then fry it.
	囬食	to *vomit*.
	寫封囬信	write an *answer*.
	給老師囬	to give you an *answer*, sir.
	囬心轉意	to *repent* and reform.
	牛在囬嚼	the cow is *ruminating*.
	難免輪囬	it is difficult to escape *transmigration*.
	囬水	a *whirl* pool.
	一囬生二囬熟	the first *time* we are unacquainted the second *time* we are.
	囬囬敎	*Islam*; the *Mohammedan* religion.

(37)

冊 3-9

冊 TS'E⁵.
門牌冊	the *register* of inmates hung up at the door of a house.
填冊	to enter one's name, etc., on the examination *list*.
生死冊	the *book* of fate.

再 TSAI⁴
明天再說	we will speak of it *again* to-morrow.
再三不肯	he was *repeatedly* unwilling.
再喫點	eat a little *more*.
再耍一陣	stay a while *longer*.
再少我還是要	*however* little there may be I still want it.
再猜不倒	you could *never* guess it.
再不是的	*certainly* it is not.

胄 CHEO⁴
甲胄在身不便還禮	I have donned my cuirass and *helmet*; 'tis inconvenient to return your courtesy.

冒 MAO⁴
冒名頂替	to *assume* the name of another and act in his stead.
你總冒失	you *recklessly* falsify.
冒險	to *brave* danger
假冒為善	*feigning* to be good; hypocritical.
打冒詐	to practise *deception*.
冒出幾股頭	it has *broken out* at several places.
打冒烟兒	to strike to the *effusion* of blood.
冒火	to *become* angry.
我感冒風寒	I have caught a cold; lit. *affected by* the weather.
冒二頭	a *heaped* basin of rice.
喫冒二頭	to pay for rice and lodging separately.

冕 MIEN³
皇上的冠冕	the emperor's *crown*.
辦得冠冕	*grandly* (or *superbly*) got up!
外面做得冠冕	he is *finely* decked on the outside; a whited sepulchre.

(38)

注 释

册 [tsʰe⁵]
再 [tsai⁴]
【再耍一阵】耍：玩。
【再猜不倒】永远猜不到，就是猜不到。
【再不是的】当然不是。
胄 [tʂəu⁴]
冒 [mao⁴]
【打冒诈】其义近欺诈，但属中性词。一般是并不清楚对方情况，揣测其意，以恐吓、引诱、要挟等手段让对方说出真相。
【冒出几股头】事情多出很多头绪。英文释义应为：something becomes complicated.
【打冒烟儿】打架打得很厉害。
【冒二头】四川饭店卖的一种冒尖的白米饭，北方称帽儿饭，是用一个小些的碗装满饭盖在另一装有半碗饭的碗中，让饭垒一高尖而成。也是对范姓的戏称，因"范"、"饭"同音。
【吃冒二头】吃饭和住宿分开结算。
冕 [mien³]

注 释

冠[kuan¹] [kuan⁴]
【请升冠】升冠：脱帽。
【麻冠】在我国实行火葬以前，许多地方的老人去世后，安葬的时候总要最亲的人（如儿子）拜路，三步一跪，五步一拜。送葬的人穿一身黑衣，再用一只麻袋弄成披风样式，从头顶披戴到腰间，即为麻冠。
【你这阵是冠者了】冠者：成婚的人。

冥[min²]

冬[toŋ¹]

冲[tsʰoŋ¹]
【筏子冲在鱼嘴上搁起了】鱼嘴：迎流建造的分水工程，形似鱼嘴，故名。多用块石砌筑，或用卵石堆砌。

⼌. 7-8 · 冫. 3-4

The 14th radical. (⼌)

7 冠   KUAN¹

戴冠冕	to wear a *crown*.
請升冠	please take off your *hats* (a polite expréssion).
麻冠	a coarse linen *cap* worn by the eldest son at his parent's funeral.
冠冕些	a little *grander*.
鷄冠子	a cock's *comb*.

READ KUAN⁴

你這陣是冠者了   you are a *married* man now! lit. a *crowned* one.

8 冥   MIN²

幽冥地府	*dark* hades.
我在冥王殿等你	I will await you in the hall of the King of Hades—for revenge.
那事渺渺冥冥的	that matter is very *obscure*.

The 15th radical. (冫)

3 冬   TONG¹

春夏秋冬	spring, summer, autumn, *winter*.
天門冬	*asparagus lucidus*.
麥門冬	*Ophiopogon spicatus*, grown in Sï-ch'uan for a medicine.

4 冲   CH'ONG¹

筏子冲在魚嘴上擱起了	the raft *struck* on the embankment and stuck fast.
犯冲	not having respect to the *colliding* days in the "甲子."
不要冲煞	do not *go counter* to the evil influences.
我不會說話冲撞了你	I am a dolt! I have presumed *to disagree with* you (a polite expression).
你說話不對把我冲撞了	you talk nonsense and *contradict* me.

(39)

4-5

怒氣冲天	his wrath *rose to* heaven.
冲天砲	a sky-rocket; one who is quick to stir up mischief.
出氣把燈冲息了	he *blew* out the lamp by accident.
打爛船冲些人走了	the boat was smashed and a few men *washed away*.
冲兩碗茶來	*pour out* two cups of tea.

CHÜE⁵

决

處决	to *execute* a criminal.
說話做事要有决斷	you must have *decision* in speech and action.
决意不往	I am *determined* not to go.
决不食言	I will *certainly* not retract my words.

FU⁴

冴

嘴上的油都冴起了	the fat has *congealed* about the child's mouth.

PIN¹

冰

凍起了冰	frozen into *ice*.
玉潔冰清的婦女	a pure-minded woman; i.e., a widow or virgin who does not marry.
冰冷	*icy* cold.
冰糖	*crystallized* sugar-candy.
冷得冰人	it is cold enough to *freeze* one.
放在水頭冰起	put in the water to *cool*.
冰泮大人	the middle man who arranges a betrothal.

LEN³

冷

冷茶冷飯都喫得 冷言冷語受不得	*cold* food I can take, but *cold* words I cannot bear.
今年冷凍大	the *cold* is severe this year.
冷天	winter.
親戚朋友冷淡	my relatives and friends have all grown *distant*.
那個房子冷清	that house is *lonesome*.
地方冷清	the place is *dull*.
冷箭射人	to shoot *privily* at one.
打冷定子	to *secretly* smite another.

(40)

注 释

【冲天炮】旧时一种具有很大杀伤力的大炮；比喻遇事好抢先发表激烈言论的人。

决 [tɕye⁵]

冴 [fu⁴]

【嘴上的油都冴起了】冴: 冻结, 凝固。

冰 [pin¹]

【冰泮大人】媒人。

冷 [lən³]

【今年冷冻大】今年非常冷。

【冷天】冬天。

【打冷定子】放冷箭, 偷袭。

注　释

【下冷子】下冰雹。
况 [kʰuaŋ⁴]
清 [tsʰin⁴] [tsin⁴]
【一双手冰清】清: 冷, 凉。
准 [tʂuən³]
凉 [liaŋ²]
【我凉了】我感冒受凉了。
凌 [lin²]
凋 [tiao¹]
凄 [tsʰi¹]
冻（冻）[toŋ⁴]

5-8

况	下冷子	a fall of *hail*.
	K'UANG⁴.	
	他的景况好不好	are his *circumstances* good or not?
	何况你	how *much more* you?
	况且这事他都晓得	*moreover* he knows all about this affair.
清	TS'IN⁴ TSIN⁴.	
	一双手冰清	your hands are *cold*.
	冷得清手	it *cools* the hand when you touch it.
	凉得清人	it *cools* one, as a drink of cold water on a hot day.
准	CHUEN³.	
	暗暗的做准备	to make secret *preparation*.
	案没有批准	the case is not *permitted*; the plea is not *allowed*.
	我们不准这座做	we do not *permit* these things.
	允准我们的祷告	*grant* our prayer.
凉	LIANG².	
	天气凉快	the weather is *cool* and refreshing.
	我凉了	I have *caught a chill*.
	坐倒歇凉	let us sit down and *cool* ourselves.
	菜凉了	the food is *cold*.
	他受了凉	he received a *reprimand*.
	凉糕	blanc-mange.
凌	LIN².	
	受人凌辱	to receive *insults*, to be *insulted*.
	凌剐碎剐	*ignominious* slow dismemberment.
凋	TIAO¹.	
	树叶都凋落了	the leaves are all *fallen* from the trees.
	家业凋零	our estate is *impoverished*.
凄	TS'I¹.	
	风吹得冷凄凄的	the wind blows *bitterly* cold.
	莫在那里唱凄凉腔	don't whine there in that *mournful* voice.
冻	TONG⁴.	
	今年冷冻大冻死了好些人	the *cold* is great this year, several persons have been *frozen* to death.

(41)

冫 9-15 几 1-10

9 減 CHIEN³.
脚上起了凍包	*chil*blains on the feet.
凍肉	brawn; lit. *congealed* meat.
減價	to *reduce* the price.
減筆寫	to *abbreviate* in writing.
減刑	to *abate* the punishment.
飲食減少	food is *scarce*.

湊 TS'EO⁴.
這事湊巧得很	this affair is very *opportune*.
湊少成多	*accumulate* littles and they will become much.
我湊成你	I will *make up* what you are lacking.

13 濈 CHIN⁴.
打個冷濈	to have a cold *shiver*.

凝 LIN⁴.
下凝	to *freeze*; frost.
凝冰	*ice*.
猪油凝起了	the lard has *congealed*.

15 瀆 TU⁵.
冒瀆	to be *disrespectful*.

The 16th radical. (几)

几 CHI¹.
茶几	small tea *tables* used in guest rooms.

凡 FAN².
從天下凡	to descend from heaven to this *world*.
脫凡體	to put off this *mortal* body.
凡人	*common* men; mankind.
非凡的事	an *uncommon* affair.
大凡	in *general*.
凡事	*all* affairs.

9 凰 HUANG².
	for example of use see fong 鳳.

10 凱 K'AI³.
已經凱旋了	they have already returned *triumphantly* from the war.

(42)

注 释

減 [tɕien³]

【減笔写】写汉字的简略形式,如:餐—歺。

湊 [tsʰəu⁴]

【我湊成你】我弥补你的不足或所缺。

濈 [tɕin⁴]

凝 [lin⁴]

瀆(渎) [tu⁵]

【冒渎】冒犯。

几 [tɕi¹]

凡 [fan²]

凰 [xuaŋ²]

凱(凯) [kʰai³]

注 释

凳 [tən⁴]

凶 [ɕioŋ¹]
【接一封凶信】凶信：噩耗，坏消息。
【毛钱凶】小钱（或零钱）很多。

出 [tsʰu⁵]
【把官出脱了】丢了官职，没了工作。
【出不倒气】呼吸不畅。
【他出我的气】他生我的气。
【今年肯出病】今年发病率高。

刀 [tao¹]

几 12 凵 2-4 刀

12 凳	TEN⁴.	
	板 凳	a long *form* without a back.
	踢 脚 凳	a *footstool*.

The 17th radical. (凵)

2 凶	SHIONG¹.	
	接 一 封 凶 信	I have received *bad* news.
	凶 荒 年 歲	a *calamitous* year.
	凶 日	an *unlucky* day.
	凶 星	an *inauspicious* star.
	今 年 病 症 凶	sickness is very *prevalent* this year.
	毛 錢 凶	bad cash are *plentiful*.
4 出	CH'U⁵.	
	出 去	to go *out*.
	出 門 去 了	gone *off* on a journey.
	沒 得 出 路	there is no *exit* or *outlet*.
	說 不 出 來	I cannot speak it *forth*.
	出 告 示	to *issue* a proclamation.
	出 本 錢	to *furnish* capital.
	那 個 出 錢	who is going to *pay* the money?
	大 家 出 幾 個 錢	let all *contribute* a few cash.
	他 是 甚 麽 出 身	how did he make his *début* as an official?
	出 嫁	to marry a husband; lit. to wed *out*.
	出 家	to become a priest; lit. to *leave* home.
	沒 出 息 的 人	a man of no *abilities*.
	把 官 出 脫 了	he has *lost* his office.
	出 不 倒 氣	I cannot *breathe* freely.
	他 出 我 的 氣	he got angry at me.
	出 世	to *enter* the world; to be born.
	那 個 地 方 出 甚 麽	what does that place *produce?*
	今 年 肯 出 病	sickness is prevalent this year.

The 18th radical. (刀)

刀	TAO¹.	
	菜 刀	a vegetable *knife*.

(43)

刀 1-2

一把刀	one *sword*.
剃頭刀	a *razor*.
買一把剪刀	buy a pair of *scissors*.
彎刀	a *bill-hook*.
柴刀	a wood *chopper*.
箭刀兒	an *arrow-head*.
舞弄刀筆	to handle the *pen*.
把他砍一刀	he gave him one cut with the sword. *N. A.*
一刀紙	100 sheets of paper; *N. A.* A Chinese *ream* of paper.

¹刁 TIAO¹.

刁唆	to *stir up* strife.
頂刁惡的一個人	an *unscrupulous* villain.

²分 FEN¹.

三分銀子	three tael *cents*.
三寸七分	three inches and seven *tenths*.
十分有八分我不懂	I do not understand eight *parts* in ten.
十分好	*perfect*.
在兩路口分路	the roads *diverge* at Liang-lu K'eo.
分家	to *divide* the estate.
分開	to *separate*.
分散	to *scatter*; to *disperse*.
分別善惡	to *distinguish* between good and evil.

READ FEN⁴.

分出分子來	*divide*¹ it into *parts*⁴.
安分守己	quietly mind your own *business*.
各做各的本分	each one do his *duty*.
本分人	a *simple* man.
他有甚座職分	what *office* does he hold?
一個縣分	a district (*division*); A Hsien *division*.
天分好	great *intelligence*.

切 TS'IE⁵.

反切	to spell in Chinese fashion; lit. to turn over the *parts* of a word.

(44)

注 释

刁 [tiao¹]

【刁唆】挑唆。

【顶刁恶的一个人】顶：很，非常。

分 [fən¹] [fən⁴]

【他有甚么职分】职分：职务，官职。

【一个县分】亦作"县份"，即"县"，但不与专名连用。

切 [tsʰie⁵]

注 释

【他讲的短切】短切：简短扼要。

刊[kʰan¹]

刑[ɕin²]

【头刑】杖刑。

【生庚八字有刑克】占卜术语，指生辰八字中带有坎坷。

划[xua²]

【小划子船】平底船；小划艇。

剆[pʰin¹]

列[lie⁵]

【蜂列子】蜂巢。

刎[uən³]

初[tsʰu¹]

刀 2-5

一切的言語	*all* words.
切碎	to *cut* a thing fine.
他切我的水	he has *intercepted* my water supply.
他講的短切	he speaks tersely and *concisely*.
切齒痛恨	to hate and *gnash* upon with the teeth.
切脈	to *feel* the pulse.
切切的勸戒他	*urgently* warn him.
那事切不可做	you *certainly* must not do that.

3 刊 K'AN¹.

刊刻書板子	to *engrave* blocks for printing books.

4 刑 SHIN².

刑罰	*punishment*.
頭刑	the big *baton* or rod.
生庚八字有刑尅	there are *injurious* obstructions in the horoscope.

划 HUA².

划船	to *row* a boat.
小划子船	a punt; lit. a small *row* boat.

剆 P'IN¹.

剆點給我	*share* it with me; let me have a part (at a price).

列 LIE⁵.

行行排列得勻勻淨淨	the rows of rice plants are all *arranged* evenly.
一個排列	one *partition* wall.
蜂列子	honey-*comb*.
列位請坐	please sit down gentlemen; lit. *ranked* sirs.

刎 UEN³.

刎頸之交	they are friendly enough to *cut* their throats for each other.

5 初 TS'U¹.

起初的時侯	in the *beginning*.
初一十五	the *first* and fifteenth of the moon.
我纔初到	I have *just* arrived.

西蜀方言

刀 5

LI⁴.

將本求利	to obtain *profit* from capital.
利不過三分	not more than three per cent *interest*.
有利就有害	if there is *advantage*, then there is injury.
封個利市	wrap up a present of money; lit. a *compensation* for services.
利迷心	a heart deceived by *gain*.
刀子快利	the knife is *sharp*.

MIN³.

| 刟子 | a small *hairbrush* used by women and barbers. |
| 泥水匠的刟子 | a mason's small *trowel*. |

P'AN⁴.

審判	to *judge*.
判斷曲直	to *decide* right and wrong.
判官執筆勾簿子	the *deciding* officer (in Hades) checks the register of life and death.

PAO⁴.

木匠的刨子	a joiner's *plane*.
板子刨光生	*plane* this board smooth.
刨花兒	shavings; lit. *plane* flowers.

PIE⁵.

有大分別	there is a great *distinction*.
沒得個分別	there is no *difference*.
男女有別	between men and women there are the *separations* of propriety.
分別清楚	clearly *distinguish*.
同路兩天就分別了	we will go two days together and then *separate*.
辭別父母	to *take leave* of one's parents.
辨別道理	to *discuss* doctrine.
不說別的	don't mention *other* things.
別有天地	this is like *another* world.
這把扇子別緻	this is a *rare* kind of fan.

(46)

注 釋

利 [li⁴]
【封個利市】包个红包。
刟 [min³]
【刟子】篦子，一种发梳。
【泥水匠的刟子】刟子：这里指泥刀，抹子。
判 [pʰan⁴]
刨 [pao⁴]
別 [pie⁵]

注释

刹 [tṣʰa⁴]

刎 [tiao¹]
【把箱子刎开】刎开：打开。

刐 [syen⁴]
【刐鸡】阉（公）鸡。

制 [tṣɿ⁴]
【我们用的是制钱】制钱：合法的钱。

刻 [kʰe⁵]
【刻下欠安】刻下：当下，现在。
【一个时候有八刻】时候：即时辰，一个时辰相当于现在的两个小时。

刮 [kua⁵]
【刮得四疋梁子现】弄个水落石出。

刀 6

刹	CH'A⁴.	
	寶刹有多少住持	how many priests are there in your monastery?
刎	TIAO¹.	
	把箱子刎開	to break open a box.
刐	SÜEN⁴.	
	刐雞	a castrated fowl; a capon.
制	CHȲ⁴.	
	皇上的制度	rules which the Emperor has laid down.
	有節制	there are restrictions.
	我在守制	I am in mourning; lit. observing the mourning usages.
	我們用的是制錢	we use good or legal cash.
	制作	to make.
	把他制住	control him.
	難得制伏	he is hard to tame.
	劉制臺	Viceroy Liu, Governor General of Sī-ch'uan (of riot fame).
刻	K'E⁵.	
	刻字	to cut characters in wood for printing.
	雕刻山水人物	to engrave pictures.
	一刻的工夫	a little while; a short space of time; an instant.
	刻下欠安	I am not very well at present.
	卽刻要起身	we will set out immediately.
	時時刻刻	constantly.
	一個時候有八刻	there are eight k'eh (fifteen minutes) in a Chinese hour.
	待人刻薄	to treat people meanly.
刮	KUA⁵.	
	刮子	a scraper; a curry-comb; a strike for levelling grain.
	殺豬刮毛	to kill a pig and scrape the hair off.
	刮得四疋梁子現	you strike the rice till the rim of the measure is visible.

刀 6

刺 TSʻĪ⁴.

把我脚上的刺挑出來	pick this *thorn* out of my foot.
芒刺飛在眼睛裏頭了	a *mote* has flown into my eye.
刺客	an assassin; lit. one who *stabs*.
行刺	to *stab*.
他的話能够刺透人心	his words can *pierce* the heart.
領上刺字	to *tattoo* characters on the forehead.
刺繡花草	to *embroider* flowers.

刷 SHUA⁵.

洗衣裳的刷子	a *brush* used for washing clothes.
把鞋上的泥巴刷乾淨	*brush* the dirt off the boots.
刷石灰	to *whitewash* with lime.
刷勸世文	to *print* tracts.

到 TAO⁴.

還沒有來到	they have not yet *arrived*.
成都省到過沒有	have you *visited* Chʻen-tu?
你到那裏去	where are you going *to*?
事到頭來不自由	when matters come *to* a head, you will be disconcerted.
到那個時候又來說	*when* that time comes, you may come again and say.
時候還沒有到	the time has not yet *come*.
到今年有二十年了	it is twenty years *up till* the present year.
到處都有	there are some everywhere; lit in every place *that may be reached*.
想得到做不到	I can think of it, but I can not do it.
到底你肯不肯	*after all*, are you willing.
要說到底嗎	you must speak *decisively*.
你到會說	you are able to talk (a contraction of 到底 *to* the bottom).

(48)

注　释

刺 [tsʰɿ⁴]
【芒刺飞在眼睛里头了】
　芒刺：灰尘。
刷 [ṣua⁵]
【刷劝世文】印刷《福音》
　册子。
到 [tao⁴]

注释

剁 [to⁴]
削 [sio⁵]
【那有那么削得尖蹬得齐】哪有那么恰到好处,哪有那么合适的。英文释义应为: how can one find so perfect a thing?

剃 [tʰi⁴]
则(則)[tse⁵]
【水则子】立于水中测量水位高低的标尺。
【没得凭则】凭则: 凭据。
【比个则子】比量一下。
【使平则一ha(下)】测量一下。
【人是则出来的】人是从他们所做的工作中分出高下的。

前 [tsʰien²]

刀 6-7

剁 削 剃 則 前

TO⁴.

剁牛肉	to *mince* beef.

SIO⁵.

削個尖尖	*pare* a point on it.
削皮	to *peel*, or *pare* off the skin.
削指甲子	to *cut*, or *pare* the finger nails.
那有那麼削得尖蹬得齊	wherever was there anything so *sharpened* and *levelled*? (Like Eng. "cut and dried.").
掙錢猶如針上削鐵	he strives to get money like one *scraping* iron off a needle.
削髮爲僧	to *shave* the hair off and become a Buddhist priest.
削個篾片子	*split* off a slip of bamboo.
請先生斧削	please, teacher, *revise* this.

Tʻl⁴.

剃頭	to *shave* the head.
他的鬍髭難剃	he is hard to manage; lit. his whiskers are hard to *shave*.

TSE⁵.

說話做事都有法則	speech and action must all be according to *rule*.
水則子	a *scale* for measuring the height of the water in a river; a *mark* in the river bed.
沒得憑則	there is no *evidence*.
比個則子	take a *pattern*, or the *measure*, of it.
一則來我不空二則來我不好	for one *reason* I have no time, and for another *reason* I am not well.
使平則一ha(下)	*try* it on the scales.
人是則出來的	men are *tested* by their work.

TSʻIEN².

在前頭	in *front* of.
在門前	*before* the door.
前天	the day *before* yesterday.
前頭來過沒有	have you been here *before*?
從前我在成都的時候	*formerly*, when I was in Chʻen-tu.

(49)

刀 7-9

	前任的官	former officials.
	前幾年	several years *ago*.
	在這兒跟前	here.
	我在跟前	I was *present*.
	眼前的榮華是不久的	*present* glory is not lasting.
	馬前子	the nux vomica bean.
8 剛	**KANG¹**.	
	這個木頭剛硬	this wood is *hard*.
	氣血剛強的人	a *strong* man.
	太陽加剛	the sun is growing *strong*.
	秉性剛直	of an *energetic* or *firm* disposition.
	他的性子太剛	his disposition is too *stiff*, or *unbending*.
	剛纔出街去了	he has *just* gone on the street.
剖	**P'O⁴ P'EO⁴**.	
	把魚拿來剖開	*split* open the fish.
	READ **P'O³ P'EO³**.	
	把一切的事剖訴出來	*tell* everything out *clearly*.
剝	**PO⁵**.	
	殺牛剝皮	to kill an ox and *skin* it.
	一根樹剝得倒幾層皮	how many layers of bark can you *peel* off one tree?
	把蛋壳剝下來	*remove* the shell from the egg.
剔	**T'I⁵¹ T'IE⁵¹**.	
	把這個名字剔了	*reject* this name.
	骨頭上巴的腬剔下來	*pick* the meat off the bones.
	剔燈棍兒	a small stick used for *trimming* a native lamp.
剜	**UAN¹ UA¹**.	
	牛剜人	the ox *gores* people.
	剜他兩眼	to *frown* at one.
9 副	**FU⁴**.	
	一正一副	a principal and a *second*; a chief and a *vice* or *deputy*.

(50)

注 释

剛（刚）[kaŋ¹]
【太阳加刚】阳光更耀眼了。
剖 [pʰo⁴] [pʰəu⁴] [pʰo³] [pʰəu³]
剝（剥）[po⁵]
剔 [tʰi⁵] [tʰi¹] [tʰie⁵] [tʰie¹]
【把这个名字剔了】剔：去掉。
【剔灯棍儿】用于修剪旧时油灯灯芯的小棍。
剜 [uan¹] [ua¹]
【牛剜人】牛顶人。
【剜他两眼】瞪他两眼。
副 [fu⁴]

注释

【一副枋子】枋子：棺材。
【一副对字】对字：对联。
【全副的执事】全副装备的官员，现指把所有装备都带上。

刷 [pʰien³]
【刷斧】短柄斧。
【捉倒过刷】刷：砍头。

剐（剐）[kua³]
【剐罪】凌迟。

剩 [ʂən⁴]

剪 [tsien³]
【做剪径的买卖】剪径：拦路抢劫。

創（创）[tʂʰuaŋ⁴]
【惩创恶人】惩创：惩罚。

刀 9-10

	那副臉色很好	his face is very fine. (*N.A.*)
副	一副枋子	a coffin. (*N.A.*)
	一副盌	a *set* of basins, i.e., ten. (*N.A.*)
	一副對字	a *set* of scrolls. (*N.A.*)
	全副的執事	the full *paraphernalia* of office.

P'IEN³.

刷	幾斧子就刷出來了	that can be *cut out* with a few strokes of the axe.
	刷斧	an *axe*; a *hatchet*.

READ P'IEN⁴.

	刷一盤白肉	*slice off* a plateful of cold boiled pork.
	捉倒過刷	to seize and *behead* a robber.

KUA³.

剮	剮罪	the punishment of death by *cutting in pieces*.
	色是剮骨的刀	lust is a knife that *scrapes* the bones.
	剮棕樹	to *strip* the palm trees of their fibre.
	剮皮	to *skin*; to *flay*.

SHEN⁴.

剩	家中有剩飯路上有饑人	if there is *left* rice in the house, there are hungry people on the road.
	還剩得有好多錢	how much cash is there *over*?
	把剩的布留起	leave the *surplus* cloth.

TSIEN³.

剪	一把剪刀	a pair of scissors.
	莫把料子剪壞了	don't *cut* the material to waste.
	剪羊毛	to *shear* sheep.
	剪腳指甲	to *clip* the toe nails.
10	做剪徑的買賣	to *intercept* and rob people on bye-ways.

CH'UANG⁴.

創	創造萬物	to *create* all things.
	創業容易守成難	to *found* an estate is easy, to keep one is difficult.
	新創的器具	a newly *invented* thing.
	懲創惡人	to *punish* evil men.

(51)

西蜀方言

刀 9-13

剴 割 11 勦 剚 12 劃 剮 劕 13 劍

	身上大大的受剴	I sustained a great *injury*.
K'AI³.		
	說得剴切	he spoke *decisively*; he explained it *clearly*.
KO⁵.		
	割斷	to *cut* asunder.
	屠夫割肉提刀看人	the butcher *cuts* his meat according to his customer.
	割穀子	to *reap* grain.
	割脵	to *buy* meat.
	夫婦恩愛難割捨	if husband and wife love each other, it is hard to *separate* them.
TSIAO³.		
	帶兵征勦	to take soldiers and *suppress* a rebellion.
	勦滅反寇	to *extirpate* rebels.
	把盜賊勦捕乾淨	utterly *root out* the robbers.
CH'Ï².		
	凌剚	the punishment of death by *dismemberment*.
HUA¹.		
	劃柴	to *split* firewood.
READ HUA⁴.		
	劃傷了手	I have *cut* my hand.
	把玻璃劃做兩塊	*cut* the glass into two panes.
	劃地爲牢獄	to distrain; to seize and dun for a debt.
SHAN⁴.		
		same as 騸.
TSEN³.		
	柱頭都劕了	the posts are all *rotten*.
CHIEN⁴.		
	一把寶劍	a *sword*.
	口蜜腹劍	his mouth is honey, but his belly *swords*.
	舌如龍泉劍殺人不見血	his tongue is like the Long-ts'üen *sword*, it kills without drawing blood.
	猶如刀劍挿胸膛	my grief is like a *knife* piercing my breast.

(52)

注　釋

剴（剴）[kʰai³]

【说得剴切】说话说得切中事理。

割 [ko⁵]

勦（剿）[tsiao³]

剚 [tʂʰɿ²]

【凌剚】凌迟。

劃（划）[xua¹] [xua⁴]

【划柴】割柴火。

剮 [ʂan⁴]

劕 [tsən³]

【柱头都劕了】劕：腐烂，腐朽。

劍（剑）[tɕien⁴]

注释

刽（刽）[tɕy⁴]
劈 [pʰie⁵]
【劈头一碰】撞见（某人）。
剂（剂）[tsi⁴]
鎅 [tsʰien¹]
【手上鎅个签子】尖细的木屑等刺入手上皮肤。
力 [li⁵] [lie⁵]
【估个眼力】目测一下。
加 [tɕia¹]
【加不得病】不可使病情加重。

刀 11-14　力 3

刽 CHÜ⁴.
刽子手　　　　　an *executioner*.

劈 P'IE⁵.
劈破　　　　　　to *break* open.
劈头一撞　　　　to meet one *suddenly*.

剂 TSI⁴.
一剂药　　　　　a *course* of medicine. (*N.A.*)

鎅 TS'IEN¹.
手上鎅个签子·　a splinter has *run into* my hand.

The 19th radical. (力)

力 LI⁵ LIE⁵.
气力　　　　　　*strength*.
肯为人出力　　　he is willing to work for one; lit. to put forth *strength*.
因风吹火用力不多　when the wind blows up the fire, little *labour* 'twill require.
凡事要量力而行　in all things, you ought first to estimate your *ability*.
估个眼力　　　　give an eye *estimate*.
是个得力的人　　he is a man of great *resources*; a handy man; *capable*.
不过仗他有财力　he only depends upon the *influence* of his wealth.
十六个力的硬弓　a bow of 16 *powers* used at military examinations.

加 CHIA¹.
加添两百钱　　　*add* 200 cash.
加不上去了　　　nothing can be *added* to it.
加点盐　　　　　*add* a little salt to it.
加倍奉承　　　　*doubled* flattery.
恩典有加无已　　there is no limit to the *increase* of grace.
加不得病　　　　the disease must not be *aggravated*.
加官　　　　　　to *promote* in office.

(53)

力 3-5

	加三分行利	to *charge* three per cent interest.
	加罪	to *inflict* punishment.
	加不的	I cannot *say* certainly; I could not *guess* exactly.
	沒加敢	there is no *certainty* about it.
功	KONG¹.	
	功勞	*merit*.
	自以爲功就不體面	to regard yourself as *virtuous* is unbecoming.
	這藥大有功效	this medicine has great *efficacy*.
	正值少年好用功	youth is the best season for *work*.
	成功者不可損壞	a finished *work* should not be spoilt.
	他是甚麼功名	what is his *rank*? What *honours* has he obtained?
4 劣	LI⁵ LIE⁵.	
	比較優劣	compare good and *bad*.
劤	CHIN⁴.	
	趲劤	to exert great *strength*.
5	趲嘴劤	to gossip; lit. to put forth lip *strength*.
助	TSU⁴.	
	幫助	to *help*.
	人都喜歡捐助	the people are all willing to *aid* with subscriptions.
劫	CHIE⁵.	
	劫奪	to *plunder*.
	大劫運	a great *calamity*.
	除非轉個劫來	doubtless it will be in your next life on earth (*kalpa*).
勌	CH'Ü².	
	父母勌勞之恩殺身難報	though I kill myself, I can never repay my parents' *anxious* toil.
努	LU³.	
	努力上前	*exert* your strength and press onward.

(54)

注　釋

【加不的】说不准，不确定。

【没加敢】不敢。

功[koŋ¹]

劣[li⁵] [lie⁵]

劤[tɕin⁴]

【趲劤】使劲，用力。

【趲嘴劤】耍嘴皮子。

助[tsu⁴]

劫[tɕie⁵]

勌[tɕʰy²]

努[lu³]

注释

効（效）[ɕiao⁴]
劾 [xe⁵]
勁（劲）[tɕin⁴]
【对劲的朋友】意气相投的朋友。
勉 [mien³]
勃 [pʰo⁵]
勇 [ioŋ³]
務（务）[u⁴]
勘 [kʰan¹]
勒 [le⁵]

力 6-9

6 効

SHIAO⁴.
願効犬馬之勞　　willing to *toil* like a dog or a horse.

劾
HE⁵.
劾奏一本　　　　to *impeach* another.

7 勁
CHIN⁴.
對勁的朋友　　　a *congenial* friend.

勉
MIEN³.
應當勉力爲善　　you ought to *exert* yourself in doing good.
不可勉強應承　　don't *force* yourself to answer.
強勉要得　　　　we will *make* it do; it will do at a pinch.
勉勵　　　　　　to *constrain*.
互相勸勉　　　　to mutually *exhort*.

勃
P'O⁵.
勃然生氣　　　　he *suddenly* got angry.

勇
IONG³.
勇士　　　　　　a *brave* fellow.
有勇無謀　　　　*courageous* but without stratagem.
奮勇向前　　　　press *fearlessly* to the front.
好勇　　　　　　fond of *daring*.
團勇　　　　　　*soldiers* maintained by a parish.

8 務
U⁴.
公務　　　　　　public *business*.
君子務本　　　　the princely man *gives attention to* his duty.
專務讀書　　　　*devoted* to study.
務要齊心　　　　we *must* be all of one mind.

9 勘
K'AN¹.
請官勘驗　　　　ask the magistrate to *investigate* the matter.

勒
LE⁵.
勒住馬韁繩　　　*rein* in the horse.
勒死的牲畜　　　an animal *strangled* by its halter.

(55)

力 9-10

勒揞	to *retain unjustly*.
勒索	to *extort*.
勒碑	to *carve* a stone tablet.

動 TONG⁴.

不要動	don't *move*; don't *stir*.
行動能生財	if you *bestir* yourself, you can make money.
心莫妄動	don't *excite* your mind to evil.
感動人心	to *influence* men's minds.
搖動	to *shake*.
地動	an *earthquake*.
好動的人	fond of *motion* or *stir*.
看他的動靜	observe his *conduct*, or his *movements*.
起來走動一ha(下)	get up and *walk* a bit.
動腳動手的	he *struck* with both hands and feet.
請不動	I cannot get him to *respond* to my invitation.
牢不動	incorrigibly lazy.
莫驚動他	don't *disturb* him.
動不得刀	you must not *use* a knife or a dagger.
他就動怒了	he thereupon got angry.
逯沒有動工	not yet *commenced* work.
動不得手	you must not *begin* to fight.
幾時纔動身	when will you *start* your journey?
兩國動起兵來了	the two countries have gone to war.

10 勞 LAO².

不辭勞苦	he does not shirk *toil*.
讀書勞心耕田勞力	study *tasks* the mind, farming *exercises* the strength.
勞神得很	very *toilsome*.
勞勞碌碌的	*laborious*; *wearisome*.
極大的功勞	very great *merit*.
給他道勞	thank him for his help.
不必勞心	you need not *trouble* yourself.
憂勞成病	to become sick through *distress* or *grief*.
不要勞動人	don't *annoy* people.

(56)

注 釋

【勒揞】克扣；勒索。
【勒碑】往石碑上刻字。
動（动）[toŋ⁴]
【地动】地震。
劳（劳）[lao²]
【给他道芳】向他道谢。
【不要劳动人】不要麻烦别人。

注释

勝（胜）[ṣən¹][ṣən⁴]
　【他的事不必胜言】不必胜言：不必多言。
勤 [tɕʰin²]
募 [mo⁴]
　【募化十方】十方：指东、南、西、北、东南、西南、西北、东北、上、下。到各地为寺院化缘募捐。
勢（势）[ṣɿ⁴]
　【站的势子高】势子：势力。指一个人的势力强。
　【他的门势好】他的出身好。

力 10-11

勝

SHEN¹.
不勝職任　　not *adequate* to his post.
他的事不必勝言　we need not enlarge *to the full* about his affairs.

READ SHEN⁴.
勝不過他　　I cannot *overcome* him.
打勝仗　　to *conquer* in battle.
得勝　　to be *victorious*.
好勝的人　　one who loves to have the *pre-eminence*.
結交須勝己似 }　a friend must be *better than* one's self; if
我不如無 }　he is just like one's self, one would be better without him.

11 **勤**

CH'IN².
殷勤　　*diligent*.
大富由命小富由勤 }　a great fortune depends on luck, a small one on *diligence*.
放勤快些　　be a little *smarter*.
酒斟勤點　　take your wine a little *quicker*.
他來得勤　　he comes *frequently*.

募

MO⁴.
招募兵勇　　to *enlist* soldiers.
募化十方　　to go everywhere *soliciting* subscriptions for a temple.

勢

SHÏ⁴.
站的勢子高　　his *power* is great.
仗自己的勢利　　to depend on one's *influence*.
他的門勢好　　his *influence* is great; he has a good standing.
成不起勢　　they did not gain the *ascendency* (as rebels, &c.).
大勢去了　　the *strength* has left him; the *glory* is departed.
那是勢所必然的　that is necessary because of the *conditions*; inevitable.
陽宅的形勢　　the *site* of a house.

(57)

力 11-15 ㄅ 2

陰宅的形勢	the *position* of a grave.
山的形勢	the *aspect* of a mountain.

劄 CHA⁵.

房子的柱料劄實	the timbers of the house are *strong*.
這個東西劄板	this is a *strong, durable,* or *good* article.
活路劄實	the work is *hard*.
生意劄勁	*pushing* in business.

14 勳 SHÜIN¹.

開國元勳	*loyal* officers who helped to found the kingdom; originators of any movement.

15 勵 LI⁴.

彼此勉勵	*animate* one another.
激勵	to *encourage*.
鼓勵將士	to *incite* the soldiers.
我人不勵朗	I am *unwell*.
走人戶不勵朗	I am not *free* to go visiting (as a woman with a lot of children).
做事要勵朗點	be a little *smarter* at your work.

勸 CH'ÜEN⁴.

勸化人	to *exhort* men to reform.
泥夫勸土夫	Mr. Mud *exhorting* Mr. Dirt.
人不勸不善鼓不打不鳴	men will not be good unless you *admonish* them, just as a drum will not sound unless you beat it.
不聽勸	he will not listen to *exhortations,* or *admonitions*.
勸喫酒	to *press* a person to drink wine.

The 20th radical. (ㄅ)

2 勾 KEO¹.

把債賬一筆勾銷	to *cancel* an account.
把兩邊的話勾通	to *reconcile* two parties.
勾引良民子弟	to *entice* good people to evil.
勾點醬油	*add* a little soy.

(58)

注 释

劄 [tṣa⁵]

【这个东西劄板】劄板：（料子）好，耐用。

【活路劄实】工作难做、费力。

【生意劄劲】劄劲：势头不错。生意做得很好。

勳（勋）[ɕyn¹]

勵（励）[li⁴]

【我人不励朗】我身体不舒服。

【走人户不励朗】串门不方便。

【做事要励朗点】做事要活络点。

勸（劝）[tɕʰyen⁴]

勾 [kəu¹]

【勾点酱油】添加点酱油，兑点酱油。

注　释

匀 [yn²]
【匀倒起】平分，均匀。
包 [pao¹]
【包谷】玉米。
【篾包子】竹篾串成的竹垫。
【除包皮】去皮；净重。
【脸包子】脸颊，脸蛋。
【山包包】小山头，小山包。
【包包白菜】卷心菜。
【包两棹席】订两桌酒席。
【沙钱包换】沙钱：劣质铜钱。

ㄅ 2-3

匀　ÜIN².

匀不出來	it cannot be *divided*.
匀倒起	to *divide equally*; to *equalize*.
匀匀净净的	*evenly*.
匀匀净净的走	walk *steadily* or *regularly*; keep step.
天乾容易過喫食要均匀	if it were a famine we could manage without trouble, but while we have food let us all share *alike*.
好生攪匀	stir it till it is *thoroughly mixed*.

3 包　PAO¹.

包在裏頭	*wrap* it up inside.
包穀	maize (the corn is *wrapped* up in the spathe).
包子	steamed bread (a pinch of sugar or meat is *inclosed* in it).
篾包子	bamboo mat *wrapper*.
除包皮	without the *wrappers*, or *baskets*; net weight.
小包包	a small *parcel*.
包祆	a *bundle*; a *wrapper*.
腰荷包	a *pocket*; a *fob*.
臉包子	the *cheeks*.
山包包	a *hill-top*.
包包白菜	*round* cabbages.
腦壳上長個包	I have a *tumour*, or *carbuncle* on my head.
打起一個包	the knock has raised a *bruise* or *swelling*.
都包在內	everything *included*.
怪我一身包	he blamed me for the *whole* affair.
用石頭包墳	to *encircle*, or *encase*, a grave with stone.
用白銅包口	*plate* the rim with brass.
包脚	to *bind* the feet.
包工活路	work done by *contract*.
包兩棹席	to *contract* to supply a small feast.
包席館子	a shop where feasts are *undertaken*.
沙錢包換	to *undertake* to change bad cash.

(59)

西蜀方言

ㄅ 3　ㄥ 2-3　匚 4.

包船	to *hire* a boat.
耍包無毛病唔疾	you must *guarantee* the animal free from flaw or fault.
沒得一點包涵	he has not the least *patience*.

The 21st radical. (ㄥ)

HUA⁴.

感化	to *influence*.
化錢	to *beg* or *solicit* money.
叫化子	a beggar.
化功果	to *collect* subscriptions for a temple.
教化	to *instruct*.
勸化不轉	he cannot be turned by *exhortation*; incorrigible.
造化萬物	to *create* all things.
人情風化	manners and customs.
化惡爲善化僞爲誠	to *transform* the evil into good and the false into sincere.
燒錢化紙	to *convert* paper money into invisible money by burning it.
不怕雪山高萬丈太陽一照化長江	in height, the snowy hills ten myriad feet may seem; let but the sunshine fall on them, they *melt* into a stream.
飮食不消化	my food will not *digest*.

PE⁵.

| 北極 | the *North* Pole. |
| 拜北闕 | to make obeisance toward the *Northern* Court. |

SHĬ³,¹.

| 鑰匙 | a *key*. |

The 22nd radical. (匚)

CH'IANG¹. K'UANG¹.

| 匡扶 | to *assist*. |

K'ANG⁴.

| 匠床 | a large wooden bed, or *divan*. |

(60)

注　釋

【沒得一点包涵】包涵：名词，耐心。

化 [xua¹]

【化功果】为寺院募捐。

【劝化不转】油盐不进的，不听劝告的；无可救药的。

北 [pe⁵]

匙 [ʂʅ³] [ʂʅ¹]

匡 [tɕʰiaŋ¹] [kʰuaŋ¹]

匠 [kʰaŋ⁴]

【匠床】即炕床。

注 释

匠 [tsiaŋ⁴]

匣 [ɕia⁵]
【火匣子】粗陋的小棺材，通常为红色。

匪 [fei³]
【追捕会匪】会匪：在古代和近代史上，中外官方文书和某些私人记述中，往往把民间秘密结社及其成员称为"会匪"。

匹 [pʰi³] [pʰi⁵]

匾 [pien³]

匿 [nie⁵]

区(区) [tɕʰy¹]
【别作区处】另寻方法，另外作计划。

十 [sɿ⁵]
【去了十打十个钱】花了整整十块钱。

匚 4-8　匚 2-9　十．

匚

請匠上坐　　please sit on the *divan*.
TSIANG⁴.
匠人　　　　a *mechanic*.
石匠　　　　a *worker* in stone; a stone mason.
敎書匠　　　a *schoolmaster*.

SHIA⁵.
點心匣子　　a confection *box*.
拜帖匣　　　a card *case*.
火匣子　　　a beggar's *coffin*.

FE³.
捉拿匪徒　　to arrest *vagabonds*.
土匪鬧事　　local *robbers* causing a disturbance.
追捕會匪　　to put down the *seditious*.

The 23rd radical. (匚)

P'I³⁵.
匹配得均　　well *mated*.
一匹馬　　　one horse. (*N. A.*)
小匹夫　　　a *mean* fellow.

PIEN³.
送匾　　　　to present a *laudatory inscription*.

NIE⁵.
匿喪不報　　to *conceal* the death of parents from one's superior officers.
逃匿遠方　　to *abscond*.

CH'Ü¹.
別作區處　　find another *plan*.

The 24th radical. (十)

SHĪ⁵.
幾十個人　　a few *tens* of people.
去了十打十個錢　I paid *ten* cash.
中第十名　　to attain to the *tenth* place.

(61)

十 1-2

十分之一	one part in *ten* ; a *tenth*.
十分好	*perfectly* good.
十足文銀	*pure* silver.
十方叢林	a monastery open to priests from *all* quarters.
十字路口	*cross* roads.
合十	a priest's bow (made by putting the *digits* together).

1 千 TSIEN¹.

千字文	the *thousand* character classic.
千總	a *chili*arch.
千脚虫	a centipede.
千脚泥	the mud on the front door step.
千子行	members of a *secret society* ; the *Ko-lao Hue.*
添了一個千金	you have got another daughter ; lit. a *thousand* of gold.
大千世界	the *whole* world.
千萬要做	it *must* be done.
千繁得很	*very* troublesome or mischievous.
打千	to bow on one knee to a superior.

2 升 SHEN¹.

升子	the Chinese *peck* ; the 10th of a bushel.
升天	to *ascend* to heaven.
請升堂	please *come up to* the hall.
升白糖	to *refine* sugar.
升丹	to *sublime* medicines.

午 U³.

午時	noon.
人怕老來窮穀怕午時風	man fears poverty in his old age, and grain fears a wind at *noonday* (i.e., when in flower).
過午沒有	have you had your *lunch* ?
端午節	the festival of the 5th of 5th moon.

(62)

注　释

【十方丛林】十方：见第57页注释。丛林：通常指禅宗寺院。一种寺庙管理制度，指寺庙向各方僧侣开放。

千 [tsien¹]

【千脚虫】蜈蚣。

【千脚泥】大门台阶上的泥土。

【千子行】秘密社团的成员。

【千繁得很】麻烦得很，繁琐得很。

【打千】男子下对上通行的一种礼节。流行于清代满族。其姿势为屈左膝，垂右手，上体稍向前俯。

升 [ʂən¹]

【升子】量粮食的器具，容量为一升。

【升白糖】提炼白糖。

午 [u³]

【过午没有】吃过午饭没有。

注释

卉 [xuei³]
半 [pan⁴]
【到手大半天了】时间过去大半天了。
【半边疯】偏瘫。
【话说在半边去子】说的话毫不相干；风马牛不相及。
【你半心是做甚么的】你长着一颗心是干嘛用的？意为责怪别人不小心。
【半头船】一种头宽尾窄的小型货船。
【郎当半子】女婿。
卍 [uan⁴]
協(协) [ɕie⁵]
【四镇八协】镇、协：清末新军的编制单位。
卑 [pei¹]
卒 [tɕio⁵] [tsu⁵] [tsʰo⁵] [tsʰu⁵]

+ 3-6

3 卉半

HUE³.
畫的花卉 — sketched flowers and *plants*.

PAN⁴.
耽擱半天 — to delay *half* a day.
半夜晚 — *midnight*.
年將半百 — about *half* a hundred years old; in *middle* life.
到手大半天了 — the greater *part* of the day is gone now.
莫說半面的話 — don't give only *one side* of the story.
半篇 — one *side* of the leaf of a book; a page.
半邊瘋 — *partial* paralysis.
話說在半邊去子 — that is *another* subject; your words are irrelevant.
你半心是做甚麼的 — why are you so *careless*?
多半不來 — he *probably* will not come.
半頭船 — small cargo boats, broad at the bow and narrow at the stern.
郎當半子 — a son-in-law.

4 卍

UAN⁴.
卍字格的窻子 — a window made in the pattern of the character *uan*; a la Grecque.

6 協

SHIE⁵.
同心協力 — of one mind and with *united* strength.
四鎮八協 — four brigadier-generals and eight *colonels* in Sï-ch'uan.

卑

PE¹.
分個尊卑大小 — distinguish between high and *low*, great and small.
他是個謙卑的人 — he is *humble*.
是個卑微的人 — he is a *vulgar* fellow; an *insignificant* person.
行爲太卑污了 — his conduct is *contemptible*.

卒

CHIO⁵ TSU⁵.
兵卒 — *soldiers*.

(63)

西蜀方言

十 6-10　卜 3-6　卩 4

	無名小卒	a *person* of no account.
	READ T'SO⁵ TS'U⁵.	
7	來得倉卒	to come *very hurriedly*.
南	LAN².	
	在南邊	in the *south*.
	南海普陀	P'u-t'o of the *southern* seas.
10	指南針	a compass; lit. the needle that points to the *south*.
博	PO⁵.	
	賭博	to *gamble*.

The 25th radical. (卜)

	P'U⁵.	
3	卜課	to *divine* by casting lots.
卜	CHAN¹.	
	占個吉凶	*divine* to see whether it will be lucky or unlucky.
占	CH'IA³.	
	卡房	the small *jail* in a court-house.
	卡子房	a *guard-house*.
卡	卡子路口	cross-roads.
	卡子	a kind of cross-hilted *dagger*.
	刺卡在喉嚨上	a bone has *stuck* in my throat.
6	一卡	a *span*.
卦	KUA⁴.	
	八卦	the eight *diagrams*.
	抽籤問卦	to shake out a lot and inquire by the *divining-cones*.
	打卦婆	a female fortune-teller.

The 26th radical. (卩)

4	IN⁴.	
印	用印印錢票子	*stamp* the cash tickets with your *seal*.

(64)

注　释

南 [lan²]
博 [po⁵]
卜 [pʰu⁵]
占 [tṣan¹]
卡 [tɕʰia³]
【卡房】旧时临时拘留犯人的处所。
【卡子房】收容所。
【卡子路口】十字路口。
卦 [kua⁴]
印 [in⁴]

注 释

【扤倒印把子】推翻执掌官印的人，即推翻掌权者。
【杵火印】以金属图识烙物留下的印记。
【跟倒车子印印走】跟着车辙走。
危 [uei²]
却 [tɕʰio⁵]
卷 [tɕyen⁴]
卵 [luan³]
【卵子】睾丸。
即 [tsi⁵] [tsie⁵]
卸 [sie⁴]

p 4-6

新官接印	the new magistrate receives the *official seal*.
扤倒印把子	to take over the management, or the authority.
印花兒	the impression of a *seal*.
印書	to *print* books.
杵火印	to *brand* with a hot iron.
印花布	*print* calico.
這是那個的脚印	whose foot *prints* are these?
打脚模手印	to stamp the *impression* of the foot and the hand on a deed.
跟倒車子印印走	follow the wheel-barrow *track*.
心心相印	of the *same* mind.

UE².

馬到臨巖收韁晚 事到臨危後悔遲	when o'er the cliff the steed has dropped, too late then to draw rein; when your plans down to *ruin* sink, repentance will be vain.
危險得很	very *dangerous*.
危亡	*peril* of death.

CH'IO⁶.

推却	to *refuse*.
忘却了	I *forgot* it.
却有憑據	*nevertheless* there is evidence.
却是爲何	*but*, why so?

CHÜEN⁴.

書卷	books.
上卷	the first *volume*.
卷子	essay paper, ruled and stamped.

LUAN³.

卵子	the *testicles*.

TSI⁵ TSIE⁵.

卽刻起身	we will set off *immediately* or *instantly*.

SIE⁴.

卸甲	to *doff* the armour; to *give up* a job.

(65)

卩 6-9　厂 7-8

	卸擔	to *set down* a load.
	兩官交卸	*handing over* the official papers to the new magistrate.
	卸責	to *relinquish* a post.
	車上的東西卸下來	*unload* the wheel-barrow.
	花卸了	the flowers have *faded*.
9 卿	CH'IN¹.	
	卿相	a *noble*.

The 27th radical. (厂)

7 厚	HEO⁴.	
	厚薄	*thick* and thin.
	厚的厚薄的薄	some are *thick*, and some are *thin*; some were *kindly* treated, others not.
	雪墊得厚	the snow is *deep*.
	交情甚厚	very *intimate*.
	待人厚道	to treat people *liberally*.
	那個地方的人皮厚	the people of that place are *hospitable*.
	忠厚傳家	to train the family in *honesty* from generation to generation.
	富厚	*wealthy*.
	他家底子厚	his family is *well-to-do*.
	這個官的底子厚	the present official is a *literary* man.
	田土肥厚	the soil is *rich*.
	臉皮厚	*shameless*.
	心厚	*greedy*; *grasping*.
厘	LI².	
	十厘爲一分	ten *li* make one *fen*. ($\frac{1}{1000}$th of an ounce).
	不少分厘	not the *least* discount; not a *fraction* short.
8 抽厘金		to levy a *tax on goods*.
原	ÜEN².	interchanged with 源.
	平原地方	*level* country; a *plain*.

注　釋

【花卸了】花谢了。
卿[tɕʰin¹]
厚[xəu⁴]
【那个地方的人皮厚】皮厚: 热情好客。
【心厚】贪婪。
厘[li²]
【抽厘金】抽税。
原[yen²]

注释

【原中】最初的中间人。
厦 [ʂua³]
【搭个偏厦】偏厦：侧房。
廠(厂) [tʂʰaŋ³]
【厂房】小棚。
【稀饭厂】施粥场，发放救济的场所。
【厂子铺】理发店。
厨 [tʂʰu²]
厮 [sʅ¹]
【茅厮】茅房，厕所。
厭(厌) [ien⁴]
【厌儿毛】现为"蔫儿毛"，指不靠谱的或令人生厌的朋友。
厲(厉) [li⁴]
幺 [iao¹]
【幺儿子】最小的儿子。
【幺师傅】即小师傅，服务员、店小二。

厂 8-12　厶 1

原來是這樣	it was *originally* thus.
原中	the *original* middlemen.
當原告	the accuser.
原不該做	*properly* I ought not to do it.
原本不錯	*really* it is right.
原諒	to *excuse* another.

10 厦　SHUA³.
搭個偏厦　　build a *side-room*.

12 廠　CH'ANG³.
廠房　　a *shed*.
稀飯廠　　the *enclosure* where food is distributed to the poor.
金廠　　a gold *mine* or *working*.
廠子鋪　　a barber's shop.

厨　CH'U².
厨房　　a *kitchen*.
厨子　　a *cook*.
做厨　　to *cook*.

厮　SÏ¹.
茅厮　　a *privy*.

厭　IEN⁴.
厭惡　　to *dislike*.
厭棄　　to reject with *disgust*.
討人厭　　to incur one's *displeasure*.
聽厭煩了　　I am *tired* of hearing it.
厭兒毛　　a *detestable*, or *despicable*, fellow.

厲　LI⁴.
厲鬼　　an *evil* spirit.
厲聲　　a *dreadful* sound.

The 28th radical. (厶)

1 幺　IAO¹.
幺兒子　　the *youngest* son.
幺師傅　　a waiter, one who attends to *small* matters.

(67)

ㄙ 3-9 叉 1

3 去 CH'Ü⁴.

去不去	will you *go*?
拿去	take it *away*.
去惡從善	to *put away* evil and follow after good.
去年	the *past* year.
去世了	*dead*; lit. *left* this world.
去了好多錢	how much money has been *spent*?
失去好幾樣東西	I have *lost* several things.

9 参 TS'AN¹.

過府參拜	I will come and *visit* you.
打坐參禪	to sit and *meditate*, as the Buddhists do.
他的官參革了	he is *degraded* from office.
參將	a major.

READ SEN¹.

弟兄參商	the brothers are at variance, like Orion and Lucifer (opposite constellations).
人參	the *ginseng* plant, used as a tonic.

The 29th radical. (叉)

叉 IU⁴.

今天叉有客來	guests have come to-day *also*.
叉在多嘴	talking scandal *again*!
叉不聽話	disobedient *yet*!
叉添一點	add a little *more*.
叉是一天雨	*another* whole day's rain.
打了叉罵罵了叉打	he beats *and* curses me, and curses *and* beats me.
叉冷叉餓實在難過	*both* hunger *and* cold together are hard to bear.
叉要馬兒跑得好 叉要馬兒不喫草	*on the one hand*, he wants his horse to run well, but *on the other hand*, he does not want it to eat grass; met. work and no pay.

叉 CH'A¹.

叉子	a *fork*.

(68)

注 释

去 [tɕʰy⁴]
【去了好多钱】花掉了多少钱?

参(參) [tsʰan¹] [sən¹]
【他的官参革了】他被革职了。
【弟兄参商】参、商: 星宿名, 二星此出则彼没, 永不相见。比喻兄弟之间不和睦。

叉 [iəu⁴]
叉 [tʂʰa¹]

注释

反 [fan³]
【反教】改变宗教信仰；变节。
【你那么反口吗】反口：推翻原来的话，反悔。
【他两个反起的】敌对的，对立的。

及 [tɕie⁵]

收 [ʂəu¹]

叉 1-2

魚叉	a *trident*; a fish *spear*.
羊角叉	a military *trident*.
他惡叉叉的答應我	he answered me *truculently*.

叉 2

FAN³.

知恩報恩天下少 / 反眼無情世上多	few people in this wide world know or care a kindness to repay, but many want of feeling show, and rudely from you *turn* away.
反教	to *turn* coat; to *change* one's religion; to apostatize.
你那麼反口嗎	do you *retract* thus? Do you *disavow* your agreement?
反口供	to *deny* a former confession of guilt.
易漲易退山溪水 / 一反一覆小人心	easily rises and easily falls the little mountain stream; *backwards* and forwards goes shifting about, the small man's mind so mean.
他反轉不依	*on the contrary*, he would not comply with it.
他兩個反起的	they are *opposed* or *at variance*.
造反	to *rebel*.

CHIE⁵.

來不及	unable to *reach* a place by a certain time.
累及別人	to *implicate* others.
我不及他	I do not *come up to* him. I am not equal to him.
後悔不及	to repent too late will be un*availing*.

SHEO¹.

收倒幾封信	I have *received* a few letters.
收賬	to *collect* accounts.
寫個收票	give a *receipt*.
收割時候	*reaping* time.
今年收成好	the *harvest* is good this year.
收拾東西	*pack up* your things.
收拾好	*mend* it well.

(69)

又 2-6

收心得早	repent in time; lit. *withdraw* the heart (from the world).
拿來收監	*commit* him to prison.
他生意收了	he has *given up* the business.
我收了活路來	when I have *stopped* work, I will come.
收親	to *marry* a wife.
收漿	to *steal* clothes that have been hung out to dry.
收脚跡	to die.

友 IU³.

酒肉朋友柴米夫妻	wine-and-flesh *friends*, wood-and-rice partners.
多年的老朋友	an old *associate*.
他兩個是窗友	they are old school-*mates*.
敎友	a *member* of a church.
弟兄要友愛	brothers ought to show *brotherly* affection.

6 受 SHEO⁴.

受敎	to *receive* teaching.
受緊	to *be* hard up.
受人之託	to be *intrusted* with a charge.
承受祖業	to *inherit* the ancestral estate.
受罪	to *suffer* punishment.
受談	to *be* evil spoken of.
你說這個話我不受	I won't *stand* these accusations.
熱得難受	un*endurably* hot.
受高帽子搊	*affected by* praise.
叫化子掉了棍受狗的欺	when the beggar has lost his stick, he is set on *by* the dogs.

叔 SHU⁵.

叔父	an *uncle*.
叔公	a grand-*uncle*.
小叔子	husband's younger brother.
請問老叔這是大路嗎	please, *sir*, is this the great road?

(70)

注 釋

【他生意收了】他生意停了。
【我收了活路来】工作做完我就过来。
【收亲】娶妻。
【收浆】偷窃晾在外面的衣服。
【收脚迹】死亡。
友 [iəu³]
受 [ʂəu⁴]
【受紧】缺钱，短缺。
【受谈】被人传谣。
【受高帽子搊】受人夸奖。
叔 [ʂu⁵]

注释

取 [tsʰy³]

【取耳】挖除耳垢,即掏耳屎。

【我取总没有听倒说】我从来没有听说过。

叛 [pʰan⁴]

叙 [sy⁴]

叟 [səu³]

曡(叠)[tie⁵]

叢(从)[tsʰoŋ²]

口 [kʰəu³]

叉 6-16 口

取　TSʻÜ³.

取出來	to *take* out.
取當	to *take* out of pawn.
取牙齒	to *extract* teeth.
取絲	to *unwind* the silk from the cocoon.
取耳	to *clean out* the ears, as a barber does.
主人要取房子	the landlórd wants to *take back* his house.
取一雙鞋	*buy* a pair of shoes.
拿錢票子在錢舖取錢	take this ticket and *draw* the cash at the cash shop.
給娃娃取名字	*select* a name for the child.
我取總沒有聽倒說	I *never* heard of it before.

叛　PʻאN⁴.

| 謀反叛逆 | to plot and *rebel*. |

叙　SÜ⁴.

| 叙話 | to *chat*. |

叟　SEO³.

| 老叟 | venerable *sir*. |

曡　TIE⁵.

| 灣灣曲曲路山處　曡曡到名牽　重重飛為　重重雁人不利 | by many a crooked road, o'er *serried* mountain peaks, where wild goose ne'er could fly, man fame and fortune seeks. |

叢　TSʻONG².

| 大叢林 | a *monastery*; a large temple in a *grove*. |

The 30th radical. (口)

口　KʻEO³.

開口	open your *mouth*.
人口浩繁	a lot of *mouths* (to feed); many *people*.
招口供	to plead guilty (to become evidence against *one's self*).
兩口子	husband and wife.

口.

口巴巴的	fulsomely familiar.
口信	a *verbal* message.
有口氣沒口氣	is there any *response* to the offer?
口嚌是非	*quarrelling* and scandal.
爲點口角	because of a little *tiff*, or a slight *altercation*.
使口不如自走	to tell another to do a thing is not to be compared to going one's self.
口音不同	the *accent* is different.
口前話	a common saying; common language.
城門口	in the *gateway* of the city.
口子上	at the *entrance* of the street.
海口	a sea-*port*.
渡口	a ferry.
大口岸	a busy *market*.
這幾天的市口快	*business* is brisk these days.
口外貨	goods from beyond the *frontiers* (i.e., North and West).
那是個總口子	that is an important *centre*.
看盜口	to view the *breach* made by a house breaker.
缸口	the *rim* of a jar.
刀口子	the *edge* of a knife.
刀口藥	medicine for *wounds*.
在腦壳上割了一個口口	he received a *gash* on the head from a sword.
扯了一條口	I have torn a *hole* in it.
心口痛	pain in the region of the *chest* or the *stomach*.
他會打口棻	he is good at getting *lodging and provisions* when travelling.
口棻算那個的	who pays for the *food*?
你愛喫甚麼口味	what *flavour* or *seasoning* do you like in your food?
胃口不好	my *appetite* is bad.

(72)

注　釋

【口巴巴的】啰哩啰唆的，让人生厌的说话方式。

【有口气没口气】有气无力的样子。

【使口不如自走】求人不如求己。

【口前话】俗话。

【口子上】街口。

【这几天的市口快】这几天市场生意活跃。

【口外货】进口商品，进口货物。

【那是个总口子】总口子：重要的地方，关键部位。

【看盗口】查看被窃贼进入房屋的豁口。

【刀口药】治疗刀伤的药。

【他会打口棻】（旅途中）他善于化缘和借宿。

【口棻算那个的】这顿饭谁来付钱？

注释

【他那口臭】他说话难听，不入耳。

【紧开口慢开言】少说话，多做事。

【牛的口轻】牛太小，只吃嫩草。

【好个口条】牙口真好！

只 [tʂɿ³]

【只今只说只今话】在什么时候说什么时候的话。

召 [tʂao⁴]

【待召】理发师。

叩 [kʰəu⁴]

叫（叫）[tɕiao⁴]

（"叫"当作"叫"，见803页勘误表。）

【鸡公叫，鹅公叫，各人寻倒各人要】各取所需。

口 2

這個菜可口	this food is *appetizing*.
我聞倒你的口臭	your *breath* smells offensively.
他那口臭	his *speech* is abusive.
忌口	to *abstain* from certain things.
緊開口慢開言	*speak* little and guardedly.
那狗下口咬人	that dog *bites* people.
牛不開口喫草	the cow will not *eat* grass.
牛的口輕	the cow is *young*.
好個口條	what a fine *beard*!
口袋	a *bag*; a *sack*.
一口鍋	one skillet, or Chinese pot. (*N. A.*)
一口箱子	one box. (*N. A.*)
喝一口水	drink a *mouthful* of water. (*N. A.*)
一口氣不來	dead. (*N. A.*)
把我咬一口	it bit me. (*N. A.*)

²只 CHÏ³.

我只有幾百錢	I have *only* a few hundred cash.
我們只得這一個法子	we have *but* this one plan.
只是有個毛病	*but* he has a fault.
只今只說只今話	at present, *just* speak of the *present*.

召 CHAO⁴.

| 待召 | a barber; lit. one who waits the *summons* of the Emperor. |

叩 K'EO⁴.

叩其來意	*ask* what he has come for.
叩門	*rap* at the door.
叩頭	to *knock* the head on the ground.

叫 CHIAO⁴.

這個叫作甚麼	what is this *called*?
大聲叫喚	to *cry* with a loud voice.
叫魂	to *invoke* the spirits of a rich person to return.
鷄公叫鵝公叫各人尋倒各人要	the cock *crows* and the gander *cackles*, and he who finds keeps.

口 2

喜鵲簷前叫必有貴客到	the magpie *chatters* from the eaves: distinguished guests are sure to come.
白燕子叫得好聽	the canary *sings* sweetly.
叫驢子	a *braying* donkey.
叫他快快做	*make* him do it quickly.

可 K'O³

可以回去	you *can* go home.
可不可	*may* I do it or not? *Will* it do?
可憐	piti*able*.
可惜	lament*able*!; alas!
可惡到萬倍	*hate*ful to all generations.
可是你們要曉得阿	*nevertheless* you ought to know.

古 KU³

人生七十古來稀	from *ancient* times downwards, few live to be seventy.
稀奇古怪	marvellous—like an *old* legend.
事不依古就不好	if things do not conform to *former* patterns, they are bad.
那個東西過得古	that thing will last for a *long time*.
雜而古董	*antique* articles.
老古板人	an *old-fashioned* person; a man like the ancients.
人心不古	now-a-days, men's hearts are not *good* or *sincere*.
作古證今的	true; lit. that which can be proved by that which has been.
作古了	dead.

句 CHÜ⁴

一句話	a *phrase*; a *sentence*. (*N. A.*)
彎刀鬭木橘句句都是老實話	as sure as a cleaver takes a wooden handle, every *word* is true.
話到口邊留半句理從是處讓三分	though in your mouth the words be formed, still half a *phrase* restrain; even should the right be on your side, let him three-tenths retain.

(74)

注 释

可 [kʰo³]
古 [ku³]
【事不依古就不好】事不依古：做事不遵循古法。
【那个东西过得古】过得古：经久耐用。
【杂而古董】古董。
句 [tɕy⁴]
【弯刀斗木把，句句都是老实话】指一个人说的全是实话。

注释

另 [lin⁴]
叭 [pa⁵]
史 [sɿ³]
司 [sɿ¹]
【人间司命主，天上耳目神】司命主：即掌管人生命的神。耳目神：即灶王爷。
台 [tʰai²]
叨 [tʰao¹]
(TI'AO¹当为T'AO¹，见803页勘误表。)
【叨光】受到对方好处表示谢意时用的客套话。
叼 [tiao¹]
【甚么叼嘴法】对食物非常挑剔，嘴叼。
叮 [tin¹]
【虼蚤叮我一口】虼蚤：跳蚤。

口 2

另	**LIN⁴.**	
	另起炉灶	to board *separately*.
	另自打主意	you can find a plan for yourself.
	另外还有好多	how much is there *besides*?
叭	**PA⁵.**	
	吹喇叭	to blow a *brass trumpet*.
史	**SHI³.**	
	史书	a book of *history*.
	御史	a *reporter of events* to the Emperor; Imperial *historiographer*.
司	**SI¹.**	
	各司其事	each *manage* his own affairs.
	人间司命主 天上耳目神	on earth, the lord who *presides* over life; in heaven, the god who acts as ears and eyes, i. e., the kitchen god.
	布政司	*Commissioner* of Revenue.
	有司衙门	the *magistrate's* office.
	都司	a major.
	土司	a tribal *chief*.
	活像候上司样	waiting for you is like waiting on a superior *officer*.
	打官司	to go to law.
台	**T'AI².**	same as 臺.
	兄台	*Sir*.
叨	**TI'AO¹.**	the second is sometimes read tao⁴.
	叨光	*favoured* with your custom.
	咵叨	*loquacious*.
叼	**TIAO¹.**	
	老鹰叼鸡儿	the hawk *seized* the chicken.
	甚麽叼嘴法	dainty over food; *picking* the good bits.
	叼出来	to *pick* out; to *select*.
叮	**TIN¹.**	
	再三叮嘱	to repeatedly *enjoin*.
	叮㗠叮㗠	the sound of lutes or drums.
	虼蚤叮我一口	the flea *bit* me.

(75)

西蜀方言

口 2-3

右 IU⁴.
右手 — the *right* hand.
男左女右 — the men on the left and the women *on the right*.

后³ HEO⁴.
皇后 — the *Empress*.
皇太后 — the *Empress-Dowager*.

向 SHIANG⁴.
向倒天看 — look *toward* heaven.
這個地方向陽 — this place is *exposed* to the sun.
向火 — to *face* the fire; to warm one's self at the fire.
向烘籠子 — to warm one's self with a hand stove.
向嘴 — to *look at* people eating.
向他借錢 — borrow money *from* him.
他向我說的 — he said it *to* me.
向來在做甚麼 — what has your work been *hitherto*?
立個志向 — have a *purpose*; make up your mind.
這一向不得空 — I have no leisure at this time.
指個方向 — indicate a *place*.
房子是甚麼字向 — what is the *aspect* of the house?

合 HO⁵.
他的心偏向 — his heart is *depraved*.
合縫 — to *join* at the edges.
合攏一起 — to *bring together* into one.
夜合樹 — acacia tree (so called because it *folds together* its leaves at night).
配合 — to *pair*.
照市合價 — make your price *correspond* with market prices.
合我的意 — it *suits* my mind.
合式 — *suitable*; lit. *agreeing* with the pattern.
大不合理 — very unreasonable.
合家人等 — the *whole* household.
同心合意 — of *one* heart and mind.

(76)

注 释

右 [iəu⁴]
后 [xəu⁴]
向 [ɕiaŋ⁴]
【向倒天看】向天上看。
【向火】烤火。
【向烘笼子】烘笼子：取暖用具，口大底小，底部有脚，盆口有固定的三足陶制提把。倘无提把，就用一只编织精致的半圆形竹篾倒扣住瓦盆，谓之烘笼子。
【向嘴】因嘴馋跑去看人吃饭。英文释义应为：to eye others eating covetously.
【向来在做甚么】向来：最近。
【房子是甚么字向】字向：朝向。
合 [xo⁵]
【夜合树】即合欢树。
【照市合价】根据市值定价。

注 释

【八合子】用八块部件组装成的棺材。
【扣个合同】在合同文本边缘盖个章。
【三合土】水泥。
吉 [tɕie⁵]
吃 [tʂʰʅ⁵]
【嘴上吃钝心里明白】嘴上口吃,舌头打结,可心里明白得很。
各 [ko⁵]
【你各自做就是】各自:自己。
【打各食】交易双方请中间人吃饭。
吏 [li⁴]
名 [min²]

口 3

吉 吃 各 吏 名

八合子		a coffin made of *pieces*.
扣個合同		to write a *tally* on the edge of a document.
三合土		cement (sand, mud and lime).

CHIE⁵.

擇吉入學		choose a *lucky* day to go to school.
大吉大利年月		an *auspicious* season.
吉人自有天相		heaven helps the *prosperous* man.

CHʻĪ⁵.

嘴上吃鈍心裏明白	}	although he *stammers* with his lips, he is clear in his mind.
吃力		laborious.

KO⁵.

各有各的事		*each* has his own affairs.
各處地方		*every*where.
你各自做就是		just do it *yourself*.
打各食		two parties in a transaction give a meal to the middlemen.
熱起來大家熱 冷起來各冷各	}	when the weather gets hot, all are hot alike; but when the weather grows cold, *each* man is cold for *himself*.
各樣東西		*all* kinds of things.

LI⁴.

貪官污吏		a covetous *official*.
吏房		the *civil* office in a small yamên.

MIN².

小名		the baby *name*.
混名		a *nick*name.
我名下的		to my *name*; mine.
這是甚麼地名		what is the *name* of this place?
有名無實		having the name without the reality; hypocritical.
無名帖子		an anonymous *placard*.
大有聲名		great *fame*.
全不顧自己聲名		he is not at all mindful of his *reputation*.

口 3

婦女以名節爲重	a woman regards her *reputation* as important.
出名的人	a *celebrated* person.
名教中的罪人	an offender against *established* teachings.
添一名夫	add one more coolie. (*N. A.* for persons)

吊 TIAO⁴.

吊喪	to *condole* with mourners the evening before the funeral.
吊頸死了	he has *hanged* himself dead.
拿來吊起	take it and *hang* it up.
吊刀子	a case, containing knife, chop-sticks and tooth pick, *suspended* from the belt.
事情是吊起的	the affair is *suspended*.
拿來吊秤	*weigh* it on the steelyard.
吊墨線	*plumb* line.
吊子耳環	ear-*pendants*.
鞋帶子吊起了	your shoe string is *trailing* down.
吊命	to *prolong* life for a short time.
他在後頭吊起	he *loiters* behind.
吊樓子	a house resting partly or wholly on piles; a veranda.
一吊錢	a *string* of cash; a thousand cash.

吐 T'U³.

吐口水	to *spit*.
又吐又屙	*vomiting* and purging, as in cholera.
半吞半吐	to *tell* part and keep back part.

同 T'ONG².

我們都同路	we will all go *together*.
你同倒我去	go *with* me.
同姓不同宗	of the *same* name, but not of the *same* family.
二人同了心黃土變成金	when two men are of *one* mind, even brown earth turns to gold.
大不相同	very *unlike*.
寫個合同文約	write an agreement.

(78)

注　释

【名教中的罪人】触犯宗教教条的人。
【添一名夫】添一名苦力。

吊 [tiao⁴]

【吊刀子】系悬在腰间的小器件，里面常有刀、筷子、牙签等等。
【事情是吊起的】事情拖着，没得到解决。
【鞋带子吊起了】鞋带子散开来了。
【吊命】指只剩最后一口气，也提着这口气让它一直存在；命悬一线。
【他在后头吊起】他在后面闲荡。
【吊楼子】山区的一种木板房或竹房子，下面用木桩做支柱，用梯子上下。

吐 [tʰu³]

同 [tʰoŋ²]

【你同倒我去】你跟我去。

注 释

吆[iao¹]
【吆道】用大声吆喝来让路上的人闪开。
【吆猪吆羊糯米心肠】驱使猪羊,心肠须如糯米般耐心和细心。
吵[tʂʰao³]
呈[tʂʰən²]
【哀怜呈子】诉状。
咿[i¹]
吹[tʂʰuei¹]
吨[tʰən⁴]
【说话打吨打吨的】说话犹犹豫豫的,很迟疑。
吩[fən¹]
含[xan²]
【没得含忍】没有一点耐心。
【望其海含】海含:即海涵。

口 3-4

吆	IAO¹.	
	吆道	to clear the road by *bawling*, as outrunners do.
	吆猪吆羊糯米心肠	*patience* and *kindness* are needed in *driving* pigs or sheep.
吵	CH'AO³.	
	吵鬧	to *brawl*; to make a row.
	有理說得出來的不在吵上	if you have right on your side, you may state it, only don't *wrangle*.
	他們又在吵	are you *disputing* again?
呈	CH'EN².	
	呈上去	to *hand in* to a superior.
	哀憐呈子	a *petition* for forgiveness or help.
	遞呈子	to hand in an *indictment*.
咿	I¹.	
	咿咿唔唔要說話了	the baby *chatters*: he will soon be able to speak.
吹	CH'UE¹	
	吹大風	to *blow* a gale.
	吹燈	*blow out* the lamp.
	吹笛	to *play* the flute.
	吹哨子	to *whistle*.
	請你幫我吹嘘	please *speak* a good word for me.
吨	T'EN⁴.	
	說話打吨打吨的	to speak in a *hesitating* manner.
吩	FEN¹.	
	官吩咐派差	the magistrate *ordered* runners to be sent.
	聽我吩咐	listen to my *orders*.
含	HAN².	
	沒得含忍	he has no *patience*.
	望其海含	I trust in your great *forbearance*; bear with me.
	滿面含羞	I am very much *ashamed*.
	含笑不答	he *smiled* and did not answer.

西蜀方言

口 4

	含含糊糊的答應	to answer *carelessly*.
	HEO³.	
	莫在那裏吼	don't *shout* there.
	吼班兒	*outrunners*.
	水吼	the *roaring* of water.
	吼聲如雷	a *noise* like thunder.
	P'I³.	
	我的命否	my luck is *bad*.
	CHIE⁵ SHIE⁵.	
	一呼一吸爲一息	one expiration and one *inspiration* make one breath.
	吸鴉片煙	to *smoke* opium.
	吸鐵石	*loadstone*.
	KAO⁴.	
	我要告你	I will *inform* on you.
	告狀	to *inform against* by indictment; to *accuse*.
	告假	to ask for *leave of absence*.
	告病	to *report* sickness.
	告示	an official *proclamation*.
	告白	a public *notice*.
	U².	
	道吾好者是吾賊 道吾惡者是吾師	he who speaks well of *me*, is *my* thief; he who speaks ill of *me*, is *my* teacher.
	CHIAO⁴.	same as 叫.
	CHÜIN¹.	
	君王	a *king*; a *sovereign*.
	君子愛財取之有道	the *princely man* is fond of wealth, but he seeks it in a proper way.
	幾位少君	how many *sons* have you?
	老君	Lao-tsĭ, the founder of Taoism.
	NIN⁴ LIN⁴.	
	吝嗇	*niggardly*.
	不要吝步	don't *begrudge* your steps to come and visit me.
	PA¹.	
	啞吧	a *dumb* person.

(80)

注 释

吼 [xəu³]
【吼班儿】在马车前面跑的侍从。
【水吼】波涛声, 风浪声。
否 [pʰi³]
【我的命否】否：现音 pʰie³。我的运气不好, 我的命不好。
吸 [tɕie⁵] [ɕie⁵]
告 [kao⁴]
吾 [u²]
呌（叫）[tɕiao⁴]
君 [tɕyn¹]
【几位少君】少君: 儿子。
【老君】老子, 道教创始人。
吝 [ɲin⁴] [lin⁴]
吧 [pa¹]

注释

吞 [tʰən¹]
【这个话我吞不下】我咽不下这口气，意为我忍受不了这样的侮辱。
【吞进去一步】向后退一步。
呀 [ia¹]
吟 [in²]
周 [tʂəu¹]
【还没有周堂】周堂：娶妻，成亲。
咎 [tɕiəu⁴]
咒 [tʂəu⁴]
咐 [fu⁴]
呵 [xo¹]
【要得呵嗨】玩得开心。英文释义应为：have a good time.
呼 [fu¹]

口 4-5

吞　T'EN¹.

吞鴉片煙	to *swallow* opium.
吞人家財	to *appropriate* the property of another.
這個話我吞不下	I cannot *swallow* this affront.
吞進去一步	*take back* (the wall, or partition) a few feet.

呀　IA¹.

| 哎呀 | *alas!* (an exclamation of surprise, grief, or pain). |

吟　IN².

| 背地沉吟 | to turn the back and *ponder*. |

周　CHEO¹.

周圍團轉	*all round; surrounding*.
樣樣都周全	all *complete*.
還沒有周堂	I have not yet taken a wife.
做得周到	done *properly*.
請你幫我周旋	please *speak a good word for* me.
事情做得周密	the affair was done *secretly*.

咎　CHIU⁴.

| 你不要見咎我 | overlook my *fault*; pardon me. |

咒　CHEO⁴.

咒罵人	to *curse* people.
你給我賭個咒	take an *oath* before me.
念咒語	to chant *incantations*.

咐　FU⁴.

| 我吩咐你的話　要好生記倒 | you must carefully remember what I *command* you. |

呵　HO¹.

| 打呵嗨 | to *yawn*. |
| 要得呵嗨 | *genial* in his manner. |

呼　FU¹.

| 呼吸之氣 | the air we *breathe*. |
| 氣喘呼呼 | to *pant*. |

(81)

口 5

和 HO².

稱呼人	to *address* a person.
給他招呼沒有	have you *called* him? Have you *told* him?
家和萬事興	if the family is *harmonious*, all things will prosper.
和睦鄰居	live at *peace with* your neighbours.
給他二家取和	*reconcile* the two parties.
和燒埋錢	to *conciliate* with money for the funeral (in a case of man-slaughter).
求和	to sue for *peace*.
立和約	to draw up a treaty of *peace*.
你心放平和點	be at *peace* about it; set your mind at *rest*.
和而流	to *associate* with and follow evil companions.
藥性平和	the medicine is *mild*.
心平氣和	of a *mild* disposition.
和氣能招財	a *pleasant* manner will attract wealth, i.e., draws customers.
天氣溫和	*genial* weather.
床舖和軟	the bed is *soft*.
我和你同路	I will go *with* you.
有筆和墨和紙	there are pens, ink *and* paper.
調和要勻	you must *mix* it thoroughly.
和倚	a Buddhist priest (probably a transliteration from Sanscrit).

READ HO⁴.

莫和在裏頭	don't *mix* it with the other.
口唱心和	let your heart *accord* with your voice in singing.
跟倒人家打和聲	to *agree* with everything said; to repeat idle tales.

命 MIN⁴.

不敢違命	I dare not disobey *orders*.
生命	*life*.
性命難保	difficult to preserve one's *life*.

(82)

注 釋

和 [xo²]

【給他二家取和】取和：调停，使和好。让他们双方和解。

【和烧埋钱】烧埋钱：办理丧事、安葬死者的钱。

【和而流】和坏人同流合污。

【跟倒人家打和声】人云亦云。

命 [min⁴]

注 释

【算命生先】算命先生。
呢 [n̠i²]
呸 [pʰei³]
呻 [tʂʰən¹]
咂 [tsa⁵]
【把墨线咂断】比喻制止双方争吵。
【打咂筒】拔火罐。
咀 [tsy¹]
【咀片铺】卖口含片的药铺。
呱 [ua¹] [tʂua¹]
味 [uei⁴]

口 5

死生有命富貴在天	death and life are by *decree*, prosperity and honour depend on Heaven.
心有天高命如紙薄	my desires and intention are heaven high, but my *luck* is thin as paper.
命中只有八角米走盡天下不滿升	if it is my *lot* to have but eight "koh" of rice, I may go all over the world and never make up the "shen."
算命生先	one who reckons the *horoscope*; a *fortune teller*.

呢 NI².

| 這是甚麼緣故呢 | what is the cause of this? |
| 大呢 | broad cloth. |

呸 P'E³.

| 呸你兩口 | (an insulting expression, usually preceded by *spitting* in one's face). |

呻 CH'EN¹.

| 呻喚 | to *groan*. |

咂 TSA⁵.

把菸咂燃	*suck* the pipe alight; light the pipe.
把墨線咂斷	to stop a quarrel; lit. to *bite* through the marking line.
耗子咂櫃子	the rats are *gnawing* the cupboard.
打咂筒	wet cupping.

咀 TSÜ¹.

| 咀片舖 | a medicine shop where the medicines are sold in slices for *sucking*. |

呱 UA¹ CHUA¹.

| 奶娃子呱呱的哭 | the infant *cries piteously* (imitation o the sound). |

味 UE⁴.

好味道	a good *flavour*.
山珍海味	*delicacies* from mountain and sea.
口沒味	I have no *appetite*.
淡而無味的話	insipid talk; a speech devoid of *interest*.

(83)

口 6

	要嘗倒那裏頭的滋味	you must appreciate the internal excellences of it.
	二人氣味相投	their *dispositions* are congenial.
	一味的懶惰	*invariably* lazy.

AI⁴.

	哎哟你不消說	you need not say anything!

HA¹.

	打哈哈	to *laugh* loudly (imitation of the sound).

HONG¹.

	鬧哄哄的	very *noisy*.
	他先哄進來	he *bounced* in first and began the quarrel.
	把他哄出去	*hustle* him out!

READ HONG³.

	哄騙人	to *cheat* people.
	喝喝哄哄	to *cozen*; to *deceive*.

K'E⁵.

	乾咳	a dry *cough*.
	咳得不住聲	to *cough* without ceasing.

LO⁵.

	就是咯	that will do! Just so! Of course!

MI¹.

	咩咩羊	a *lamb*.

NGAI¹.

	他是不哀憐人的	he does not *feel for* (or *commiserate*) people.
	告哀憐	to tell one's *distress*.
	哀懇	to *sorrowfully* beseech.
	哀哭	to weep *bitterly*.
	孤哀子	an orphan; fatherless and *motherless*.

P'IN³.

	一品官	an official of the highest *rank*.
	上品的藥料	the best *quality* of medicine.

(84)

注 釋

哎 [ai⁴]

【哎哟你不消說】哎呀你啥也用不着说啦!

哈 [xa¹]

哄 [xoŋ¹]

【喝喝哄哄】哄骗欺瞒。

咳 [kʰe⁵]

咯 [lo⁵]

咩 [mi¹]

哀 [ŋai¹]

【告哀怜】向别人诉说自己的不幸,以乞求对方的怜悯和施舍。

【哀恳】悲伤地恳求。

【孤哀子】孤儿。

品 [pʰin³]

注释

哉 [tsai¹]
咬 [ŋao³] [ɲiao³]
咽 [ien¹] [ien⁴]
哼 [xən¹]
哤(唠) [lao²]
咙 [maŋ³]
【咙声咙气的】指人说话声音粗，低沉。
【吹咙】乐队里吹的一种重低音乐器。
唎 [pa⁵]
【唎哥儿】即八哥。
哽 [kən³]
【咽喉哽哽吞之不下】由于悲伤，喉咙哽住无法吞咽。
【看哽倒】小心噎到。
哥 [ko¹]

口 6-7

他的品行好	his *conduct* is good.
品貌不凡	an extraordinarily fine *countenance*.
品盆	a *large* basin.
品藍	a *good* blue colour.
TSAI¹.	for example of use see 嗚.
NGAO³ NIAO³.	
那個狗咬人	that dog *bites* people.
天天夜晚狗咬	the dogs *bark* every night.
狗咬倒的	*bitten* by a dog.
蛇咬人有藥醫 人咬人沒藥醫	if a snake *bites* a man, medicines will heal him; if a man *implicates* a man there is no escape.
咬不爛	I cannot *chew* it.
IEN¹.	
咽喉	the *throat*.
READ IEN⁴.	
慢慢的咽下去	*swallow* it down slowly.
HEN¹.	
哼你在做甚麼	*ha!* what are you doing?
LAO².	
太說得哤叨	to talk *loquaciously*.
MANG³.	
咙聲咙氣的	*loud-voiced*, or *bass-voiced*.
吹咙	to play a *bass* instrument in a band.
PA⁵.	
唎哥兒	a kind of black bird or jay.
KEN³.	
咽喉哽哽吞之不下	my throat is *obstructed* and I cannot swallow (because of grief); a lump in the throat.
看哽倒	beware of *choking*.
KO¹.	
哥哥	an *elder brother*.

(85)

口 7

表哥	an *elder cousin* (male).
拔哥	a thief who snatches things and runs.
耍哥	an *idler*; a *loafer*.
袍哥痞子	a vagabond belonging to the Ko-lao Hue.

哭 K'U⁵.

| 他哭起來了 | he began to *weep*. |
| 娃娃在哭 | the baby is *crying*. |

唎 LI¹.

| 這個娃娃唎喇 | this child is very *fretful*. |

喇 READ LI⁴.

| 一張唎嘴 | very *talkative*. |

哺 FU³.

| 三年乳哺 | to *suckle* an infant for three years. |
| 羔羊跪乳烏鴉反哺 | the lamb kneels to suck, and the young crow *feeds* its aged parents; met. filial piety. |

哨 SHAO⁴.

一營分爲四哨	one garrison of soldiers is divided into four *companies*.
哨官	captain of a *company*.
哨樓	a *lookout* loft.
望哨	to *spy* out; to *scout*.
吹風打哨	to *whistle*.
鴿子帶哨筒	the dove carries a *whistle* on its tail.

唇 SHEN².

| 嘴唇 | the *lips*. |
| 這事很費唇舌 | this affair has cost a lot of *talking*. |

唔 U².

for example of use see 阡.

唆 SO¹.

挑唆是非	to *instigate* discord by gossiping.
唆訟	to *incite* to litigation.
莫囉唆人	don't *trouble*, or *annoy*, him with it.

員 ÜEN².

| 文武官員 | civil and military *officials*. |

(86)

注　釋

【拔哥】抢了东西就跑的贼。

【耍哥】游手好闲的人。

【袍哥痞子】袍哥：即哥老会，源于四川和重庆，是近代中国活跃于长江流域，声势和影响都很大的一个秘密结社组织，在四川和重庆的哥老会被称为袍哥。袍哥痞子，是对哥老会成员的民间称呼。

哭 [kʰu⁵]

唎 [li¹] [li⁴]

【这个娃娃唎喇】唎喇：焦躁不安。

哺 [fu³]

哨 [ʂao⁴]

唇 [ʂən²]

唔 [u²]

唆 [so¹]

【唆讼】煽动别人提起诉讼。

【莫啰唆人】不要麻烦别人。

員(员) [yen²]

注释

【拢了一个委员】来了一个委员。

唱 [tʂʰaŋ⁴]

【唱莲花闹】莲花闹：即莲花落，一种民间曲艺形式。早期莲花落艺人的活动一般多以"沿门"（即沿门乞讨）为主，其次也参与"赶酒"（婚丧嫁娶）和"赶会"等活动。

啄 [tʂua⁵]

【啄木关儿】啄木鸟。

【这句话被他啄上了】这句话他说得一针见血，十分中肯。

【啄瞌睡】头一点一点啄米似地打瞌睡。

【后啄啄上长个疮】后啄啄：后脑勺。

嗙 [poŋ³]

【哈哈打得脆嗙嗙的】笑得咯咯地，有不雅意。

【叮嗙了一阵】叮嗙：争吵。

啃 [kʰən³]

【他的脑壳啃不动】形容人思想顽固，很难被人说动。

商 [ʂaŋ¹]

口 7-8

	攏了一個委員	a deputy *official* has arrived.
	老員外	old gentleman ; squire (from a dignity conferred by the Emperor).
8 唱	一員官	an official. (*N. A.*)
	CH'ANG⁴.	
	唱歌	to *sing* songs.
	唱戲	to *act* plays.
	唱佛偈	to *chant* Buddhist exhortations.
	唱道情	to *chant* Taoist exhortations.
	唱蓮花鬧	to *recite* beggar's rhymes to an accompaniment of bamboo clapper.
啄	**CHUA⁵.**	
	雞啄米	the hen *pecks* rice.
	啄木關兒	the wood-*pecker*.
	這句話被他啄上了	he has *hit* the nail on the head.
	啄瞌睡	to *nod* with sleep.
	後啄啄上長個瘡	I have got a sore on the back of my head (*posterior edge of skull*).
嗙	**PONG³.**	
	花生炒得脆嗙嗙的	the peanuts are baked *crisp*.
	哈哈打得脆嗙嗙的	to laugh loudly with a *cackling* noise.
	叮嗙了一陣	to *squabble* for awhile.
啃	**K'EN³.**	
	耗子啃櫃子	the rats are *gnawing* the cupboard.
	這個草鞋啃腳	this sandal *rubs* my foot.
	他的腦殼啃不動	his head can't be *bitten*, i. e., hard-headed in business.
商	**SHANG¹.**	
	我們大家商量	let us all *consult* about it.
	士農工商	scholars, farmers, artizans and *merchants*.
	通商馬頭	a mart opened for *trade* with foreigners ; an open port.

(87)

西蜀方言

口 8-9

問 UEN⁴.

你去問明白	go and *inquire* clearly.
一問一答	*question* and answer.
問安	to *ask after* one's welfare.
問價錢	*ask* the price.
你問他要錢	*demand* the money from him.
問罪	to *investigate* crime; to *try* a case.

啞 IA³.

我再不說話啞吧都要開腔了	if I did not speak, the very *dumb* would cry out.
十啞九聾	of ten *dumb* persons, nine are deaf.
聲氣啞了	I have lost my voice; *aphonia*.
你啞了嗎	are you *dumb*?

喘 CHʻUAI³ CHʻUAN³.

喘氣	to *pant*.
喘息未定又要跑	before we have had time to *draw* breath, on we go again.
他齁喘的病又發了	his *asthma* has broken out again.

喊 HAN³.

喊兩乘轎子	*call* two chairs.
他大聲喊叫	he *cried* out with a loud voice.
喊街	to *publish* an unjust judgment on the street.
喊冤	to *demand* justice.

喉 HEO².

喉嚨痛	a sore *throat*.
氣喉食喉	the *windpipe* and the *gullet*.
一副好喉嚨	a fine *voice* for singing.
咽喉地方	an important pass; a strategic position.

喜 SHI³.

喜樂	*joy*.
歡歡喜喜的	*joyfully*.
過喜事	to get married.

注 释

問（问）[uən⁴]

啞（哑）[ia³]
【声气哑了】嗓子哑了。

喘 [tʂʰuai³] [tʂʰuan³]
【他齁喘的病又发了】齁喘：哮喘病。

喊 [xan³]
【喊街】在大街上大声谩骂人，即骂街。

喉 [xəu²]

喜 [ɕi³]
【过喜事】结婚。

注释

【找得倒个财喜不】（这生意）有利可图吗？

【脸都喜欢青了】反语，指气得脸都绿了。

【娃娃出喜事】指儿童出天花。

唧（衔）[xaŋ²] [xan²]

【锯个衔口】锯个缺口，锯个凹槽。

喝 [xo¹] [xo⁵]

【喝人】骗人。

喧 [ɕyen¹]

唤（唤）[xuan⁴]

口 9

	喜雀	the magpie (from a legend).
	你喜不喜悦	are you *pleased* or not ? Are you *agreeable* ?
	找得倒個財喜不	can we find any *money* in the business ?
	臉都喜歡青了	very di*spleased*.
	給先生道喜	I congratulate you, sir.
	恭喜發財	I *wish* you fortune.
	娃娃出喜事	the child has *small-pox*.
	有喜	enceinte.
	HANG² HAN²	
唧	口裏唧的甚麼 快吐出來	what are you *holding* in your mouth ?— spit it out at once !
	狗把肉唧起走了	the dog has run off with the meat.
	鋸個唧口	saw a *notch* in it.
	HO¹ ⁵.	
喝	喝茶	to *drink* tea ; come and *drink* tea !
	READ HO¹.	
	喝人	to *cheat* people.
	READ HO⁵.	
	沒得好喫喝	I have no good food and *drink* to set before you.
	SHŬEN¹.	
喧	喧嚷	to *wrangle*.
	HUAN⁴.	
唤	喚雞	to *call* in the chickens.
	喊你莫叫喚	don't *cry* !
	馬叫喚	the horse *neighs*.
	牛叫喚	the cow *lows*.
	羊子叫喚	the sheep *bleat*.
	狗叫喚	the dog *barks*.
	老鴉叫喚	the rooks *caw*.
	喜雀叫喚	the magpie *chatters*.
	麻雀叫喚	the sparrows *chirp*.
	燕子叫喚	the swallows *twitter*.
	鴿子叫喚	the doves *coo*.

(89)

口 9

	白燕子叫喚	the canary *sings*.
	一夜都在伸喚	he *groaned* the whole night long.
喫	CH'Ï⁵.	
	喫飯	to *eat* a meal.
	包工活路要喫自己	if you contract to do the work you must *feed* yourself.
	喫酒	to *drink* wine; to attend a feast.
	喫鴉片煙	to *smoke* opium.
	在屋頭沒得喫的	there are no *eatables* in the house.
	喫錢	to *appropriate* money.
	喫雷	to *rob* one's master by taking commission on things bought for him.
	喫死人	to *extort* money, etc., when a child or relative dies on another's hands.
	喫不起力	I cannot get room to *exert* my strength.
	喫不緊	it does not *hold* tight.
	官喫住他	the magistrate *reprimanded* and repressed him; ("sat upon him").
	喫苦	to *suffer*.
	要喫得虧纔到得堆	you must be able to *bear* a little loss and then you will get on.
	喫雷的膽子	very great courage.
喇	LA³.	
	喇叭	a brass *trumpet*.
	喇麻和尙	a Tibetan *lama* or priest.
	唎喇得很	very *peevish*.
喪	SANG¹.	
	開喪設吊	to begin the *mourning* on the day before the funeral.
	辦喪事	to manage the *funeral* affairs.
	活像鬧喪一樣	as noisy as a *funeral* or a *wake*.
	血喪	a *corpse* that is not yet decayed or dried.
	停喪	to leave a *coffin and corpse* in the house unburied.

(90)

注 释

喫（吃）[tʂʰʅ⁵]
【吃钱】拨款。
【吃雷】敲诈。
【吃死人】当有孩子或亲属死于别人手上时，家人以此来勒索谋利。
【吃不起力】使不上劲。
【吃不紧】抓不牢、钉不牢、系不紧，也指事情没搞定。
【官吃住他】吃住：训斥，惩戒，约束。
【要喫得亏才到得堆】吃小亏享大福。
喇[la³]
【唎喇得很】非常焦躁。
喪（丧）[saŋ¹]
【血丧】尸体未腐时发丧。
【停丧】即停止发丧，将棺材和尸体留在房屋内不下葬。

注 释

善 [ṣan⁴]
【善便不开腔】不随意发表意见，不乱说话。
【善便不使钱】不乱花钱。
單（单）[tan¹]
【单袜子】单层袜，薄袜。
【单条】单幅的条幅。
【生的单吊】形容人精瘦。
【单净弄】只用它（炒菜或做饭）。
【逢单日子赶场】集市在单数的日子开放。
【检一单药】按药方抓一副药。

口 9

READ SANG⁴.

中年喪妻老亦喪子大不幸也	in middle life to be *bereaved* of one's wife, or in old age to *lose* one's son, is very unfortunate.
喪膽	to *lose* courage.
喪盡天良	to *destroy* one's conscience.
喪你的德	you are *ruining* your virtue!

SHAN⁴.

善

善有善報惡有惡報	*virtue* has a good reward and wickedness has an evil one.
善良的人	a *benevolent* person; a *righteous* man.
行善	to do *good*.
善會畫花	*expert* at painting flowers.
善會做傢火	*skilful* at making furniture.
善便不開腔	he does not *thoughtlessly*, or *carelessly*, express his opinion.
善便不使錢	he does not spend money *lightly*, or *heedlessly*.

單

TAN¹.

單襪子	socks made of a *single* thickness of cloth.
開的單花	it has *single* flowers.
身上穿得單薄	very *thinly* clad.
福不雙降禍不單行	pleasures never come in pairs, and troubles never come *singly*.
單身漢	a bachelor.
單條	a long *single* scroll.
生的單吊	he has grown up *slender*.
單淨弄	cook it *by itself*.
逢單日子趕場	the market is held on the *odd* days (i. e. 1st, 3rd, 5th, etc.).
開個單子	make a *list* of the things; write out the account.
書單子	a *catalogue* of books.
藥單子	a *prescription*.
檢一單藥	to buy the medicines in a prescription. (*N.A.*)

(91)

口 9-10

	單把那一樣不見	it is *only* that one thing that I cannot find.
啼	T'I².	
	哭哭啼啼	to *weep* much.
唧	TSI¹.	
	唧唧噴噴	*chatter! chatter!*
啾	TSIU¹.	
	啾啾唧唧	continual *whining* or *moaning*.
喂	UE⁴.	
	喂娃娃	to *feed* an infant.
	喂牲口	to *fodder* a horse.
	喂的有一條牛	we *keep* a cow.
喻	ü⁴.	
10	比喻的話	an *illustration*.
嗎	MA¹.	
	是這樣嗎	is it thus?
	READ MA³.	
	對嗎	it will do!
	HO⁵.	
嗑	嗑嗑	a *hubbub*; the voice of a multitude (from the sound).
	SANG³.	
嗓	喉嗓	the *throat*.
	嗓子好	his *voice* is good.
嗇	SE⁵.	
	太客嗇	too *niggardly!*
	鄙嗇	*stingy*.
	嗇家子	a *miser*.
嘎	HA¹.	
	嘎喉嚨	a *hoarse* throat.
	嘎聲嘎氣	a *gruff* voice.
	嘎一口氣	*breathe* upon it.
	臘䏑有點嘎口	the bacon is rather *rancid*.

注 释

【单把那一样不见】单单就寻不见那样东西。

啼 [tʰi²]

唧 [tsi¹]

啾 [tsiəu¹]

喂 [uei⁴]

喻（喻）[y⁴]

嗎（吗）[ma¹] [ma³]

嗑 [xo⁵]

【嗑嗑】清嗓子的声音。

嗓 [saŋ³]

【喉嗓】喉咙，嗓子。

嗇（啬）[se⁵]

【啬家子】小气鬼，吝啬的人。

嘎 [xa¹]

【嘎喉咙】喉咙沙哑。

【嘎声嘎气】粗声粗气。

【嘎一口气】（朝某物）呼一口气，哈一口气。

【腊肉有点嘎口】嘎口：（含有油脂的食物）因变质而有陈腐味道。

注释

嗉 [su⁴]
　【狐嗉】狐狸下巴、脖子下面、部分前腹部位的毛皮。
嗣 [tsʰɿ²]
嗒 [ta⁵]
　【嗒嘴】掌嘴。
嗆（呛）[tsʰiaŋ⁴]
嗐 [xai⁴]
　【嗐呀】哎呀。
嗚（呜）[u¹]
嘗（尝）[ʂaŋ²]
鳴（鸣）[min²]
噓（嘘）[ɕy¹]
　【噓起多少高】（喷泉、水柱等）喷得非常高。
　【噓花筒】类似于烟花筒，由整节楠竹或棕树挖空内心制成筒，然后在楠竹节或棕树空心内填满配制好的火药以及铜砂、钢砂、打火石和玻璃碎沫。用干黄泥巴封口压实而成花筒，燃放时能喷出三五米高的开花火焰。
　【菜子噓了】油菜子发芽了。

口 10-11

嗉	SU⁴.	
	鷄嗉子	a chicken's *crop*.
	狐嗉	the *white fur* on a fox's *throat*.
嗣	TS'Ï².	
	抱子承嗣	to adopt a son to *succeed* to the family name and estate.
	無後嗣	having no *heirs*, i.e., *male descendants*.
嗒	TA⁵.	
	嗒嚠	to *smack* the lips.
嗆	TSI'ANG⁴.	
	硫磺烟子嗆人	the smoke of brimstone *suffocates* one.
	嗆倒了	choking and *coughing up food into the nostrils*.
嗐	HAI⁴.	
	嗐呀	an exclamation of sudden sorrow or pain, as *ah! alas!* or surprise as *O! ha! heigh!*
嗚	U¹.	
	嗚乎哀哉	*alas! alas!*—he is dead.
嘗	SHANG².	
	嘗味道	*taste* the flavour.
	嘗新	a kind of "feast of the first-fruits."
	嘗熟地方	temple lands, whose revenues are devoted to idol *worship*.
鳴	MIN².	
	去鳴個鑼	go and *sound* the gong; send round the crier.
噓	SHÜ¹.	
	噓氣一口	*blow* a breath.
	吹噓	to speak a good word for one.
	噓起多少高	to *squirt* up very high, as water from a syringe.
	噓花筒	to *fire* a species of firework.
	菜子噓了	the rape is *throwing up* weak shoots before the time.

西蜀方言

口 11-12

嘉	CHIA¹.	
	喜歡人的嘉獎	fond of *praise*.
嘔	NGEO³.	
	嘔吐	to *vomit*.
	打乾嘔	to *retch*.
啯	KU¹.	
	啯匪	*robbers*; lawless *vagabonds*.
嗛	K'ANG¹.	
	咳咳嗛嗛的	*coughing*.
	戰嗛嗛的	*tottering* with age.
嗽	SEO⁴.	
	咳嗽.	to cough and *expectorate*.
嗾	SHO³.	
	嗾狗咬人	to *hound* on a dog to bite people.
嘆	T'AN⁴.	
	嘆氣	to *sigh*.
	問嘆	to ask after *anxiously*.
	嘆家常	to *chat* about home affairs.
嘍	LEO².	
	嘍卒	*guerilla* troops.
嘈	TS'AO².	
	地方嘈嘈	the place is *noisy* and *tumultuous*.
	娃娃甚麼嘈法	the child is very *gluttonous*.
	心裏嘈得很	*weak* in the stomach for want of animal food.
嘖	TSA¹ ⁵.	
	長行唧唧嘖嘖	constantly *chattering*.
	都唧嘖我	every body *speaks* ill of me.
嘲	CH'AO².	
	怕人嘲笑	to fear *ridicule*.
嘻	SHI¹.	
	嘻嘻哈哈	*laughing*; *tittering* (imitation of the sound).

(94)

注　釋

嘉 [tɕia¹]

嘔（呕）[ŋəu³]

啯（啯）[ku¹]
【啯匪】强盗，土匪。

嗛 [kʰaŋ¹]
【咳咳嗛嗛】形容咳嗽的样子。
【战嗛嗛的】步履蹒跚的样子。

嗽 [səu¹]

嗾 [ʂo³]
【嗾狗咬人】嗾：唆使。

嘆（叹）[tʰan⁴]
【问叹】关切地问候。

嘍（喽）[ləu²]

嘈 [tsʰao²]
【娃娃甚么嘈法】这个孩子非常贪嘴。
【心里嘈得很】因饥饿而想吃荤了。

嘖（啧）[tsa¹] [tsa⁵]
【长行唧唧嘖嘖】不停地唧唧喳喳，一直唧唧喳喳。
【都唧嘖我】唧嘖：诋毁。

嘲 [tʂʰao²]

嘻 [ɕi¹]

注释

哗(哗)[xua²]
嚙[tɕʰin²]
嘹[liao²]
嘴[tsuei³]
【捏嘴巴子】被人用皮带扇了一嘴巴。
【好嘴箍子】形容人能说会道，嘴皮子利索。
【一张白嘴】形容人嘴里没一句实话，全是谎言。
【嘴筒子】动物的鼻口。
【山嘴】指山区曲折的V形谷地向河流凸出并同山岭相连的坡带。
【种子爆嘴嘴了】种子破壳发芽了。
噫[i⁴]
器[tɕʰi⁴]

口 12-13

哗 HUA².

人聲喧哗	the *clamour* of many people.

嚙 CH'IN².

拿在口頭嚙住	*retain* (the medicine) in your mouth.

嘹 LIAO².

聲音嘹喨	the sound is *clear*.

嘴 TSUE³.

嘴巴子	the *lips*.
捏嘴巴子	to be beaten on the cheek or mouth, with a piece of leather.
偷嘴	to eat on the sly ; to steal food, like a dog.
莫多嘴	don't *talk* or *gossip* so much.
嘴尖舌快	sharp-tongued.
好嘴箍子	a clever talker.
又在鬧嘴	squabbling again !
一張白嘴	a parcel of lies.
嘴筒子	the *nose, snout*, or *muzzle* of an animal.
鷄嘴壳子	a hen's *beak*.
魚嘴	a fish's *snout*.
茶壺嘴	the *spout* of a tea-pot.
河嘴上	at the *bend* of the river.
山嘴	the *corner* of the hill.
菸袋嘴	a pipe *mouth-piece*.
老鴉嘴	an iron *staple*.
種子爆嘴嘴了	the seed has brairded or germinated ; the *blade* has sprung up.

13 噫 I⁴.

噫那個放炮	Oh ! who's that shooting ?

器 CH'I⁴.

器皿	a *vessel* ; a *dish* ; a *utensil*.
好個器皿兒	that's a good *article* !
磁器	earthen-*ware*.
一套煙器	a set of opium smoking *instruments*.
以凶器爲憑據	the *weapon* is a proof of his guilt.
軍器	arms ; *weapons* of war.

(95)

口 13-17

	機器局	an arsenal.
	那個子弟邊成器	that lad will become a *capable man*.
噤	喂不成器	unable to feed it to a *full grown* animal.
	CHIN⁴.	
	噤口痢疾	dysentery and *loss of appetite*.
噥	LONG².	
	唧唧噥噥	indistinct *muttering* (imitation of the sound).
噴	FEN⁴.	
	噴水	to *spurt* water.
	打噴嚏	to *sneeze*.
	心裏噴噴不平	*disturbed* in mind.
噪	TS'AO².	
	麻雀噪林要黑了	the sparrows are *chirping* in the wood, it will soon be dark.
14 嚇	HE⁵.	
	嚇了一跳	*startled*.
	READ SHIA⁴.	
	把人嚇倒了	it *frightens*, or *scares* one.
	把我嚇一跳	it *startled* me; made me jump.
嚀	LIN².	
15 嚏	叮嚀囑咐	to *enjoin*.
	T'I⁴.	
	噴嚏打得不住聲 是那個在說我	I am continually *sneezing*; who is talking about me I wonder.
嘰	TSI⁵.	
16 嚨	嘰的一聲就跑了	it gave a *squeak* and ran away.
	LONG².	
17 嚷	喉嚨	the *throat*.
	RANG³.	
	鬧鬧嚷嚷的	scolding and *wrangling*.

(96)

注 释

【机器局】兵工厂，军械库。
噤 [tɕin⁴]
【噤口痢疾】痢疾患者不思饮食的症状。
噥（哝）[loŋ²]
噴（喷）[fən⁴]
【心里噴噴不平】噴噴不平：愤愤不平。
噪 [tsʰao²]
嚇（吓）[xe⁵] [ɕia⁴]
嚀（咛）[lin²]
嚏 [tʰi⁴]
嘰 [tsi⁵]
【嘰的一声就跑了】吱地一声就跑了。
嚨（咙）[loŋ²]
嚷 [zaŋ³]

注释

嚓 [tsa⁵]
嚴（严）[ȵien²]
嚼 [tsiao⁴] [tsio⁵]
【嚼牙巴】犹嚼舌。搬弄是非；胡扯。
囉（啰）[lo²]
囊 [laŋ²]
【一封锦囊】一条妙计。
嘱（嘱）[tṣu⁵] [tṣo⁵] [ṣo⁵] [ṣu⁵]
囚 [siəu²]
四 [sɿ⁴]
【周围四方】四面八方。

口 17-21　口 2

嚓　TSA⁵.　for example of use see 嘈.

嚴　NIEN².
嚴師出好弟子　a *strict* teacher puts forth good scholars.
十分威嚴　very *dignified*.
家嚴　my father.

18 **嚼**　TSIAO⁴.
好生嚼爛　be careful to *chew* it well.
回嚼　to *ruminate*.
嚼牙巴　to back-*bite*.
　　READ TSIO⁵.
19 馬嚼口　a horse's *bit*.

囉　LO².
嘍囉　*banditti*.

囊　LANG².
囊中空乏　the *bag* is empty; met. poverty.
收拾行囊　pack up the *baggage*.
21 一封錦囊　a *letter* of recommendation.

嘱　CHU⁵, CHO⁵.
嘱附　to *enjoin*.
嘱託　to *commission*.
　　READ SHO⁵, SHU⁵.
遺嘱　a *will*.

The 31st radical. (口)

囚　SIU².
囚籠　a *prison* cage.
囚犯　a *prisoner*.

四　SÏ⁴.
四書　the *Four* Books.
第四名　the *fourth* name on the list.
四四方方的　*square*.
周圍四方　*everywhere*.

	跑四路流差	couriers who travel in *all* directions.
	四下無人	there is no one *about*; private.
	四不像	unlike *everything*.
	很四海	very agreeable with *everybody*.
	長得四應	*fully* developed, as a man, animal or plant.
3 因	IN¹.	
	因爲	*because*.
4 困	K'UEN⁴.	
	家屋窮困	my family is *poor*.
	境遇困苦	my circumstances are *distressing*.
	筋力困乏	my strength is *exhausted*.
	精神困倦	my spirit is *depressed*; *wearied*.
	CH'ONG¹.	
	烟囪	a *flue*; a chimney.
	TEN⁴.	
5 囤	米囤子	a rice *bin*.
	KU⁴.	
	堅固	to *stablish*; stable; strong; constant.
	固執	*obstinate*.
8 固	固意那麼做	I am *determined* to do it in that way.
圈	CH'ÜEN¹.	
	打個圈圈	make a *circle*.
	圈聲音	*mark* the tones of the characters *with a circle*.
	竹圈椅	a *round*-backed bamboo chair.
	玉圈子	jade *bracelets*.
	瓜子圈	a triangular mark made with a Chinese pen.
	房圈	a *room*.
	扯多大個圈子	to gather a big *crowd* round one.
	READ CHÜEN⁴.	
	馬圈	a *stable*.
	羊圈	a sheep-*fold*.

(98)

注 释

【跑四路流差】信使。
【很四海】很善于与人打交道。
【长得四应】（人或动植物）充分发育。
因 [in¹]
困 [kʰuən⁴]
囪 [tʂʰoŋ¹]
囤 [tən⁴]
固 [ku⁴]
【固意那么做】固意：执意，决意。
圈 [tɕʰyen¹] [tɕyen⁴]
【圈声音】标示出汉字的声调。
【玉圈子】玉手镯。
【瓜子圈】用毛笔画的三角形记号。
【房圈】房屋。
【扯多大个圈子】聚拢了一大群人。

注释

國（国）[kue⁵]
【大国手】医生。

圍（围）[uei²]
【好大的围圆】周长多少？

圓（圆）[yen²]
【滴溜圆】非常圆，圆得像水滴一样。
【长圆】椭圆。
【朝圆鞋】一种鞋尖为圆弧形的鞋子。
【请你帮我方圆】请你帮我跟他说和说和（或求求情）。
【那个地方方方圆圆】方方圆圆：方正宽敞，让人觉得很舒服。
【圆成生意】（以中间人的身份）帮助某人达成交易。
【今天圆不倒工】今天的工作做不完。

園（园）[yen²]

□ 8-10

	猪圈	a pig-*pen*.
	鸡圈	a hen-*roost* or *coop*.
	柴圈	a *row of piles* in the river bed to catch drift wood.
國	**KUE⁵.**	
	中國	China; lit. the *middle* kingdom.
	外國	foreign *lands*.
	出國	to leave one's *country*.
	三國志	the annals of the Three *states*.
	大國手	a doctor.
圍	**UE².**	
	四面圍繞	to *surround* on all sides.
	圍得水洩不通	to *besiege* closely.
	周圍都是一樣	it is the same *all round*.
	築個圍墻	build an *inclosing* wall.
10	好大的圍圓	how large is the *circumference*.
圓	**ÜEN².**	
	圓棹子	a *round* table.
	十五月圓圓	on the 15th the moon is *full*.
	滴溜圓	*globular* as a drop.
	長圓	*oval*.
	朝圓鞋	*round-toed* shoes.
	一家老小圓圓	the family remains *unbroken* and *unscattered*.
	請你帮我方圓	please intercede and *set* me *right* with him.
	那個地方方方圓圓	that farm (or house) is *complete in every way*.
	圓成生意	to help one to *complete* a transaction; to be middleman.
	今天圓不倒工	I cannot *finish* the work to-day.
	圓夢	to *interpret* a dream.
	放圓通些	be more *accommodating* or *obliging*.
園	**ÜEN².**	
	菜園子	a vegetable *garden*.

(99)

口 11-19 土

11 圖	醬圜	a condiment *shop*.
	墳圜	a *grave*yard.
	T'U².	
	地理圖	a *map*.
	圖形	a *sketch*.
	圖章	a *stamp*; a *seal*.
	貪圖名利	to covet and *plan* to be famous and rich.
團	T'UAN².	
	一團發麵	a *lump* of dongh.
	團魚	turtle.
	團轉	*all round*.
	月亮團圓	the moon is *full*.
	團年	to have a family *gathering* at the New Year.
	團個學堂	to *collect* a number of boys to form a school.
	團人做錢會	to *call together* persons to form a mutual benefit society.
	團拜	officials *assembling* for new year congratulations
19 圞	團首	the head man of a *country ward*.
	LUAN².	
	團圞月	a *full* moon.

The 32nd radical. (土)

土	T'U³.	
	土肥	the *soil* is rich.
	打個土墻	build an *earth*, or a *mud* wall.
	臉上戴土色	his face is *brown*.
	買幾個土碗	buy a few *coarse earthenware* basins.
	這個地土好	this is a fine *place*.
	土地廟	the shrine of the god of the *Precinct*.
	土話	the *local* dialect.

(100)

注 释

【坟园】坟场。
圖(图)[tʰu²]
團(团)[tʰuan²]
【团鱼】乌龟。
【团转】周围。
【团个学堂】召集孩子们以兴办学堂。
【团人做钱会】召集众人做慈善。
【团拜】古代拜礼,指团聚行礼,相互庆贺。
圞[luan²]
【团圞月】满月。
土[tʰu³]
【脸上戴土色】面色发黄。

注释

地 [ti⁴] [ti¹]
【地皮钱】地租。
【地皮风】流言蜚语。
【一地地儿】一点点，一丁点，少量。
在 [tsai⁴]
【在屋头】在屋里。
【不由在我】由不得我。
【没定在】不确定。

土 3

	土人	*aboriginal* tribes.
	不服水土	not agreeing with the *climate*.

地 ³ TI⁴.

拜天地	to worship Heaven and *Earth*.
地理	Geography.
地做的宽	much of the land is laid out in *dry fields*.
地瓜儿	a sweet root with a creeping stem, grown as a field crop.
地皮錢	*ground* rent.
地皮風	a rumour.
墳地	a burial *ground*.
發地雷	to spring a *mine* under a city wall.
地壩子	an open *space*.
佔地頭	to take up *room*.
各處地方	every *place*.
地方官	the *local* magistrate.
落到這個地位	you have fallen into this *condition*.

READ TI¹.

一地地兒	a *little*; a *small* quantity.

在 TSAI⁴.

在屋頭	*in* the house.
在山上	*on* the hill.
在那邊	*at* that side; *in* that direction.
我們在喫飯	we are having our food (*present* time).
現在	*now*; *at present*.
工夫沒有在心	your work is not *on* your mind; you do not pay attention.
牛好不在角上 人好不在脚上	an ox's goodness does not *consist in* its horns being good; a woman's goodness does not *consist in* her feet being well bound.
不由在我	it does not *depend upon* me.
實在	*real; genuine; really*.
沒定在	no *certainty*.
父母在不在	are your parents *alive*?

(101)

土 3-4

	那個書還在嗎	is that book still *here* (or *in existence*).
	不在了	lost; dead; non est.
	我今天不自在	I am not *well* to day.
	心裏很不自在	very dis*pleased*.
4 址	CHǏ³.	
	房屋的基址	the *foundation* of a house.
坊	FANG¹.	
	牌坊	a monumental *archway*.
	街坊鄰居	neighbours (on a street).
	READ FANG².	
	油坊	an oil *shop*.
坎	K'AN³.	
	歷盡坎坷	*difficulty* after *difficulty*; *trouble* upon *trouble*.
	翻不翻得過那坎坎	will he be able to pass the *crisis*.
坑	K'EN¹.	
	挖個坑坑	dig a *hole* in the ground.
	餓坑難填	the hunger *pit* (i.e. the stomach) is hard to fill permanently.
	茅坑	a cess*pool*.
	坑倒人家	to *wrong* people.
均	CHÜIN¹.	
	一子一分二子均分	one son the whole, two sons *equal* shares, of the estate.
	均平	just; impartial.
坐	TSO⁴.	
	請坐	please *sit down*.
	坐轎子	to *ride* in a chair.
	有坐頭沒得	is there any *luggage* to go in the chair.
	坐船	to *travel* by boat.
	坐監牢	to *be in* prison.
	坐月	*confinement* (by child birth).

(102)

注 释

址 [tʂʅ³]
坊 [faŋ¹] [faŋ²]
坎 [kʰan³]
坑 [kʰən¹]
均 [tɕyn¹]
坐 [tso⁴]

【有坐头没得】有没有地方坐?
【坐月】即坐月子。

注释

【在那里坐】在哪里住？
【坐家人户】普通住宅，普通人家。
【没得坐当】没地方坐。
【把水坐开】把水烧开。
【缝子使漆坐紧】用漆把裂缝刷一下。
【秧子坐笕】禾苗长得矮小，发育不良。
【米价坐了】米价降了。
【房子那边坐下去了】坐下：塌陷，凹陷。

垂 [tṣʰuei²]
坷 [kʰo¹]
坤 [kʰuən¹]
（K'UEN² 当为 K'UEN¹，见803页勘误表。）

【坤道人家】妇道人家。
【挣下乾坤】出人头地，发了大财。

城 [tṣʰən²]
【万里城】即万里长城。

垇 [ŋao⁴]
坯 [pʰei¹]
坭（泥）[n.i²]
【耍泥巴饼饼】种地，做农活；玩泥巴。

土 4-5

官坐堂	the magistrate is *sitting* to try cases.
在那裏坐	where do you *live*?
坐家人戶	a *dwelling* house.
坐位	a *seat*; a *station*.
沒得坐當	no *seat*; no *place*.
把坐騎牽來	lead the *steed* out.
燈坐子	a lamp *stand*.
把水坐開	*place* the kettle on the fire to boil.
縫子使漆坐緊	*fix* the joint firmly with varnish.
秧子坐笕	the rice is *stunted*.
米價坐了	rice has *fallen* in price.
房子那邊坐下去了	that side of the house has *subsided*.

5 垂 CH'UE².

把門簾子垂下來　lower the door screen.

坷 K'O¹.

一路的坎坷　the whole road is *rugged*.
受不盡的坎坷　endless *trouble*.

坤 K'UEN².

坤道人家　*women*.
挣下乾坤　he has made his fortune; lit. he has acquired heaven and *earth*.

城 CH'EN².

萬里城　the Great *Wall*.
進城　enter the *city*.

垇 NGAO⁴.

垇口　a mountain *pass*.

坯 P'E¹.

毛坯子　an article in the rough; an unfinished article.

坭 NI².

坭巴　*mud*; *soil*.
耍坭巴餅餅　farming; lit. playing with *mud* cakes.
紅沙坭　red sandy *loam*.

(103)

土 5-7

	泥脚肝	a farm labourer; lit. *muddy* legs.
	泥塑木雕	idols; lit. the *clay*-moulded and wood-carved ones.
	一身的泥巴	you are covered with *dirt*.
	稀泥爛水	*mire*.
	泥金壺	a *terra-cotta* teapot.
	泥籬壁	to *plaster* a wall *with mud*.
	泥水匠來了沒有	has the mason come?
	桂花泥	*opium* from Kue-hua market.
坡	P'O¹.	
	下坡容易上坡難	it is easy to go down the *slope*, but difficult to go up.
	懒斜的坡	a gentle *declivity*.
	壁陡的坡	a steep *brae*.
	人在下坡勢不要搠他	don't push a man when he is going down *hill*.
	他正是上坡勢子	he is a rising man.
	太陽落坡就要黑了	the sun has set behind the *hills*, it will soon be dark.
	拿個坡坡給他爬	give him a *test* and see how he will get on.
坦	T'AN³.	
	坦平的壩子	a *level* plain.
	坦坦碗	a *shallow* basin.
	心裏坦白	a *quiet* conscience.
6 垢	KEO⁴.	
	一身的垢甲	begrimed with *filth* from top to toe.
垛	TO³.	
	箭垛子	a *target*.
	城垛眼	embrasures on the *parapet* of a city wall.
垣	ÜEN².	
	墙垣	a *wall*.
	省垣地方	a *provincial capital*.
7 埳	KAN⁴.	
	墙埳	a low mud *wall*.
	做埳埳	to act as *middleman*.

注 释

【泥金壶】陶壶。
【泥篱壁】用泥土糊起来的墙壁。
坡[pʰo¹]
坦[tʰan³]
【坦平的坝子】坝子：西南地区称平地、平原。
【坦坦碗】一种平口浅底的碗。
垢[kəu⁴]
【一身的垢甲】满身尘垢。
垛[to³]
【箭垛子】箭靶子。
【城垛眼】城墙上的射击孔。
垣[yen²]
【省垣地方】省会。
埳[kan⁴]
【墙埳】一种低矮的泥土做的墙。
【做埳埳】当中间人。

注释

【莫当埋鬼】别管闲事。
埋 [mai²]
埃 [ŋai²]
【这鱼是埃的】这鱼是死的。
【买埃了】买亏了。
执（执）[tʂʅ⁵]
【打执事】在婚丧等仪式上做跟班，参与仪仗事务。英文释义应为：to carry flags, weapons as guard of honours or cortege.
基 [tɕi¹]
【修个生基】为自己建个坟墓。
【讲个根基】问计于祖先。
坚（坚）[tɕien¹]
塔 [ta⁵]
【滑塔的一声】咔嚓一声，形容物体碎裂的声音。

土 7-8

埋	莫當埋鬼	don't be a *meddler*.
	MAI².	
	埋葬	to *bury*.
	埋怨	to *harbour* ill-feeling.
	隱姓埋名	to *hide* one's true name; to adopt an alias.
埃	埋倒腦殼	to *bow* the head; to *stoop*.
	埋伏	an *ambush*; a scheme to entrap one.
	NGAI².	
	這個魚是埃的	this fish is *dead*.
	買埃了	I have bought it *dear*; a bad bargain.
執	CHĬ⁵.	
	各執其事	each one *manage* his own affairs.
	錢交給父母執掌	give the money to your parents to *look after*.
	我執意要做	I am *determined* to do it.
	固執不通	to doggedly *maintain* one's own opinion; obstinate.
	打執事	to bear an official's *paraphernalia* before him.
基	CHI¹.	
	屋基地	a site for the *foundation* of a house.
	地基	the *site* of a house.
	修個生基	to build a new *tomb* for one's self.
	基業	an *estate*.
	講個根基	inquire into his *antecedents*.
	新主登基	the new Emperor ascends the *throne*.
堅	CHIEN¹.	
	堅固不移	*firm*; immovable.
	堅硬的心腸	a *determined* will; an *unwavering* purpose.
	堅辭不受	I *firmly* refuse to take it (polite).
	堅硬的木頭	hard, *durable* wood.
塔	TA⁵.	
	滑塔的一聲	a *crash*; a *thud*.

土 8

培 P'E².

培植菜園	to *cultivate* a garden.
栽培幾根樹子	to *raise* a few trees.
培植子弟	to *instruct* the young.
栽培心地	to *improve* the heart; to *cultivate* virtue.
修塔子培文峯	build a pagoda to *improve* the literary talent of the district.
培補身體	to *strengthen* the body.
帮我栽培幾句好話	assist me by *speaking* a few good words *for* me.

堅 TS'Ü⁴.

| 堅土 | to *pile* up earth. |

READ SÜ⁴.

| 再堅點 | *add* a little more. |

堂 T'ANG².

清官肯坐大堂	an upright magistrate is pleased to sit in the *public court-room*.
堂屋	the *reception-hall* of a house.
令堂	your respected *mother*.
母親下了堂	my mother has married again.
申家祠堂	the ancestral *hall* of the of Shen family.
客堂	a guest *hall*.
禮拜堂	a *chapel*.
在那個堂	in what *place*? In that *place*.
喊堂官來	call the waiter.
轉堂子	to go to a *brothel*.
好個明堂	what a fine *situation*!
他一輩子做事沒得個明堂	all his life long, he has never made a good *job* of any thing.
說不出個明堂	he cannot make his *meaning* plain.
看不出個明堂	I cannot make any *sense* of it.

掩 IEN³.

| 掩土 | to *cover* with soil. |

(106)

注 释

培 [pʰei²]
【修塔子培文峰】建宝塔以修文韬。

堅 [tsʰy⁴] [sy⁴]
【堅土】即堆土，将土堆起来。

堂 [tʰaŋ²]
【母亲下了堂】母亲再婚。
【喊堂官来】堂官：服务员，店小二。
【转堂子】逛妓院。
【好个明堂】明堂：即名堂。
【他一辈子做事没得个明堂】他这一生做事都糊里糊涂的。

掩 [ien³]
【掩土】用土掩上。

注释

堆 [tuei¹] [tuei³]
【堆子房】警卫室,岗哨。
【卖堆的】批发的,非零售。
场(場) [tṣʰaŋ²]
【较场坝】练兵场。
【杀场】处决犯人的场所。
【你的山场好】山场:指山中平坦的地方。
【摆场火】摆场:街上的赌博摊位。
【没说场】没说头,说了没有用。
【你尽过场】你就假装吧。
【一场事】一件事。
堪 [kʰan¹]
堦(阶) [kai¹]
【阶檐】台阶和屋檐。指进门处。

土 8-9

堆　TUE¹.

一大堆	a great *pile*.
一堆石頭	a *heap* of stones.
墳堆	a *mound* over a grave.
一堆人	a *crowd* of people.
我們在一堆坐	we live near each other ; we live in the same place.
堆子房	a *guard-house*.
堆金積玉	to *heap* up wealth.
堆起的雪	*piled* up snow.

READ TUE³.

賣堆的	to sell *wholesale*.

9　場　CH'ANG².

院場	a level *plat* ; a threshing-*floor*.
較場壩	a parade *ground*.
殺場	the execution *ground*.
趕鄉場	to go to a country *market*.
你的山場好	your hillside is very good.
進場	to enter the *examination halls*.
戲場	a *theatre*.
擺場火	to spread a gambling *stall* on the street.
做道場	to invite the Taoists in to invoke the gods.
沒說場	it has no *use* as a spoken word ; it is not spoken.
你儘過場	you are constantly feigning.
一場事	an affair. (*N. A.*)
害了一場病	he has fallen sick. (*N. A.*)
哭了一場	he cried for a *while*. (*N. A.*)

堪　K'AN¹.

貧窮不堪	un*bearably* poor.
請個堪與先生	invite a geomancer ; i. e., one who understands about *heaven* and earth.

堦　KAI¹.

堦簷	the *pavement* under the eaves.

(107)

土 9-10

報	PAO⁴.	
	報答四恩	to *recompense* the grace of heaven, prince, parents and teacher.
	有寃報寃有仇報仇	let all wrongs be *avenged*—in the examination halls.
	不是不報日子未到	it is not that there is no *retribution*, but that the day has not come.
	善惡到頭終有報只爭來早與來遲	in the end good and evil have their *reward*, the only question is will it come soon or late?
	報期	to *state* the day for a wedding.
	報喜	to *report* the birth of a child to the wife's parents.
	報單	an *announcement*; an *advertisement*.
	跑報子	to carry home the *news* that a scholar has graduated.
	信報	a *newspaper*.
	京報	the Pekin *Gazette*.
堤	T'I².	
	堤壩	a *dike* by a river; a long *mound*.
堵	TU³.	
	堵塞	to *stop up*; to *obstruct*.
	辦防堵	prepare to *guard* the highway.
	堵堵堵住	*charge! charge! charge!*
	一堵牆	a *wall*. (*N. A.*)
堰	IEN⁴.	
	河堰	a *dam* on a river.
	堰塘	an artificial *reservoir*.
塚	CHONG³.	
	義塚	a public *burying ground* for the poor.
塊	K'UAI³.	
	幾塊錢	a few cash. (*N. A.*)
	一塊田	a *field*. (*N. A.*)
	我站了半塊	I have half of the *piece* (of land.) [*N. A.*]

(108)

注 释

報（报）[pao⁴]
【报答四恩】报答天、王、父母和老师。
【报期】报期,旧时流行的婚俗习惯,即由男方提出结婚时间,经女方同意后,择定佳日送往女家,名曰"报期"。
【报单】旧时向升官、得官、考试中榜的人送去的喜报。
【跑报子】①科举放榜后报喜信的人,英文释义应为:messenger who brings the good news after the result of imperial examinations published;②一种民间舞蹈形式,通常在祈雨时在乡村中表演。
堤 [tʰi²]
【堤壩】堤防、堤坝。
堵 [tu³]
堰 [ien⁴]
【河堰】河坝。
塚（冢）[tsoŋ³]
【义冢】旧时收埋无主尸骸的墓地。
塊（块）[kʰuai³]

108 西蜀方言

注 释

【小块的】小孩子。
【块子布】格子布。
塞 [se⁵]
塕 [oŋ⁴]
　【塕城子】塕，应为"翁"。古时城市的防御设施之一，在城门外修建的护门小城。
塑 [su⁴]
塌 [tʰa⁵]
　【蒸塌了气】（米饭等）蒸得扁了或坍塌了。
塔 [tʰa⁵]
　【塔子】宝塔。
塘 [tʰaŋ²]
　【塘房】驿舍。
　【塘口上】苦力们聚集在一起趴活的地方。
　【打塘抬轿】将轿子抬着走二三十里。
填（塡）[tʰien²]

土 10

	多大一塊	a large *lump*.
	坭巴塊	a *clod* of earth.
	切塊塊	cut it into *slices*.
	小塊的	children.
	塊子布	*checked* cloth.
塞	SE⁵.	
	陰溝塞倒了	the drain is *obstructed*.
	閉塞不通	*stopped up*.
	塞住他的口	*shut* his mouth (with a bribe).
	抓人家來搪塞	to implicate others in order to *screen* oneself.
	頓開他的茅塞	clear away his *dulness*.
塕	ONG⁴.	
	塕城子	the *enclosure* between the outer and inner gates of a city; a *bastion*.
塑	SU⁴.	
	塑菩薩	to *model* an idol *in clay*.
塌	T'A⁵.	
	房子倒塌了	the house has *fallen*.
	塌鼻子	a flat, *sunken* nose.
	好生莫遭塌了	take care and not to *waste* (or *destroy*) it.
	蒸塌了氣	the rice is *unevenly* steamed.
塔	T'A⁵.	
	塔子	a *pagoda*.
塘	T'ANG².	
	池塘	a large water *tank*.
	塘房	*post-houses* 10 li apart on the main roads.
	塘口上	the *entrance to a village* or town where coolies may be hired.
	打塘抬轎	to carry a chair on a *short stage* of twenty or thirty li.
塡	T'IEN².	
	塡平	*fill it up* level.

(109)

土 10-11

填空		to *fill* a vacant post.
填房		a widower marryiug a second wife.
填還		to *repay* a debt.

T'U².

泥塗	*mud*; *mire*.
病糊塗了	*delirious* with fever.
把賬拿來塗了	*cancel* the account; *blot out* his score.
小聰明大糊塗	in small matters clever, in great matters *stupid*.

TSANG⁴.

葬喪	to *bury* the dead.
亂葬墳	a public *burying* ground.

ÜIN².

先塋	the *tombs* of one's ancestors.
墳塋的邊界	the boundaries of a *grave-yard*.

CH'EN.

灰塵	*dust*.
陽塵	*cobwebs*.
一塵不染	not defiled by one *atom* of worldliness.
紅塵世界	this *vain* world.

MAN⁴.

面海墁	to *pave* with stones.

CHIN³.

各守境界	each look ofter his own *boundaries*.
四境清平	peace on all *sides*.
貴境地方在那裏	where is your honourable *abode*?
境遇好	his *circumstances* are good.

MO⁴.

墳墓	a *grave*.
古墓	an ancient *tomb*.

SHU⁵.

義塾	a charity *school*.

(110)

注　释

塗（涂）[tʰu²]
【泥涂】湿泥；泥潭。
【把账拿来涂了】把账销掉。

葬（葬）[tsaŋ⁴]
【葬丧】埋葬死者。

塋（茔）[yn²]
【先茔】祖先的坟墓。

塵（尘）[tʂʰən²]
（CH'EN当为CH'EN²，见803页勘误表。）
【阳尘】蜘蛛网。

墁[man⁴]
【面海墁】铺石砖。

境[tɕin³]
【贵境地方在那里】您住在哪里？

墓[mo⁴]

塾[ʂu⁵]
【义塾】旧时免收学费的私塾。

注释

塴 [pʰoŋ¹]
【人都塴进屋来了】人多得都挤进屋来了。

墈 [kʰan³]
【田墈】田边的高坡。
【崖墈】悬崖,绝壁。

墊(垫)[tien⁴]
【垫的泥巴】淤泥。
【给人家垫铺】谈好价钱,货物却被别人抢先买了。
【脚有些垫】脚有些跛。
【我垫起脚要】(这个东西)我现在急需。

墜(坠)[tʂuei⁴]

墳(坟)[fən²]
【新坟不过社老坟不过清明】社:即春分,早于清明十五天。民俗上对上坟有讲究,上新坟须在春分前上,上老坟须在清明前上,上新坟需早于老坟半个月左右。新坟在春分以后上,都算"过了社"。新坟只有在"社"前上了,捎去的哀思和焚烧的纸币新亡的人才能收到,否则 就是白上了。

土 11-12

11 塴 墈 墊

Pʰong¹.

| 灰塵塴進來了 | the dust *flies* into the room. |
| 人都塴進屋來了 | the men *rushed* into my house. |

Kʻan³.

田墈	the *dike* of a rice field.
下河思命上墈 思財	when in the river his life is his care, when on the *bank* his cash he would spare.
嚴墈	a *cliff*; a *precipice*.

Tien⁴.

墊的泥巴	*deposited* mud.
雪墊的有一兩尺厚	the snow *lies* one or two feet deep.
墊話的人都有 墊錢的人沒得	there are plenty who will give advice, but none who will *advance* money.
墊賠	to be *surety* for losses another may incur.
給人家墊鋪	to make a bargain and then let another buy the goods before you.
墊子	a *cushion*.
墊坐	to *cushion* a seat.
腳有些墊	he has a slight *limp*.
墊起腳	to *tiptoe*.
我墊起腳要	I am needing it immediately.

12 墜 墳

Chue⁴.

墜落	to *fall down*.
墜底	to *tumble* or *sink* to the bottom.
帶金銀是墜人的	to carry gold or silver *weighs* one *down*.
耳墜子	ear-rings; *pendants*.
鐘墜子	the *weights* of a clock.
扇墜子	a *tassel* on a fan.

Fen².

| 新墳不過社老墳不過清明 | new graves must be attended to before "she" (i. e., about Mar. 16th) and old one's before "tsʻin-min" (about April 5th). |

西蜀方言

土 12-13

墨 ME⁵

埋在墳墓裏	to lay in the *tomb*.
墳山地	a *burial-ground*.
買一定墨	buy a stick of *ink*.
青布墨	*black* calico.
他的筆墨好	his *composition* is good.
沒有喫過墨水	he has not studied books.
墨斗線	a joiner's *marking line*.
掌墨師	the head carpenter on a job.
墨魚	the *cuttle-fish*.

墮 TO⁴

墮落在地獄裏	to *sink into* hell.
你要墮落你的兒孫	you will *ruin* your posterity by your evil ways.
墮淚	to *shed* tears.
墮胎	to cause a miscarriage.

墩 TEN¹

一墩石頭	a *block* of stone.
石墩子	oblong *blocks* of stone; stone *stairs*.
跳墩子	*squared* stepping *stones* in a stream.
墩子料	*squared* timber.
矮墩墩的	short and *stout*.

增 TSEN¹

天增歲月人增壽	heaven *adds* a year of time, and man adds a year of age—at the New Year.
功夫增長	the work has *increased*.
我飲食加增	I am able to eat *more* now-a-days.
亮增增的	*bright*; *light*; *clean*; *tidy*.

墾 K'EN³

開墾荒地	to *break up* waste land.

壁 PI⁵

壁頭	a lath and plaster *wall*.
板壁	a *wall* of thin boards.
隔壁鄰居	neighbours.

(112)

注 释

【坟山地】坟地。

墨 [me⁵]

【买一定墨】定：即"锭"，量词。

【掌墨师】掌控墨线的师傅，即传统修房造屋时全程主持建设的"总工程师"。

堕（墮）[to⁴]

【你要堕落你的儿孙】你会宠坏你的儿孙们。

墩 [tən¹]

【一墩石头】墩：量词，用于块状物。

【跳墩子】（过溪流、草地等）用于走路的石墩。

【墩子料】方木材。

增 [tsən¹]

【功夫增长】工作增加了。

垦（墾）[kʰən³]

壁 [pi⁵]

【壁头】墙壁。

【板壁】薄木板搭的墙。

注释

壇（坛）[tʰan²]
墙（墙）[tsʰiaŋ²]
【石水缸的墙子】石水缸的缸壁。
【一合墙子】棺材的两个侧边。
壅 [ioŋ³][oŋ¹]
【壅笕子】给植物培土。
【壅倒脑壳睡】蒙住头睡觉。
【壅一大堆人】围起了一大堆人。
壕 [xao²][xao⁴]
壓（压）[ia⁴]
【压马】驯马。
壙（圹）[kʰuaŋ⁴]
【那一天入圹】入圹：下葬。
壘（垒）[luei³]
壞（坏）[xuai⁴]

土 13-16

	T'AN².	
壇	社稷壇	an *altar* to the gods of the land.
	TS'IANG².	
墙	城墙	a city *wall*.
	石水缸的牆子	the *sides* of a stone water trough.
	一合牆子	the two *sides* of a coffin.
	IONG³.	
壅	壅壁	the *screen* wall in front of a court-house.
	READ ONG¹.	
	壅笕子	to *earth up* the stems of plants.
	壅倒腦壳睡	to sleep with the head *covered up* by the bed-clothes.
14	壅一大堆人	*surrounded by* a crowd of people.
	HAO².	
壕	城壕	the city *moat*.
	READ HAO⁴.	[marshes.
	水穿了壕	the river has risen till it overflows the
	IA⁴.	
壓	壓倒	*press it* down.
	壓扁了	*crushed* flat.
	欺壓人	to *oppress* people. [the rising.
	官出去親自彈壓	the magistrate himself went out to *repress*
15	壓馬	to *exercise* a horse.
	K'UANG⁴.	
壙	那一天入壙	on what day is he to be laid in the *tomb*?
	LUE³.	
壘	壘墳	to *heap up* earth on a grave.
16	HUAI⁴.	
壞	衣服穿壞了	the clothes are *worn out*.
	木頭朽壞了	the wood is *rotten*.
	乾壞了	*spoiled* with drought.
	娃娃敖壞了	the child is *spoiled*.

(113)

西蜀方言

土 16-21　士 4

	肚子壞了	my stomach is *out of order*.
	壞了瓦心	he has *debased* his conscience.
	壞規矩	to *violate* the rules or customs.
	他把我的事壞了	he has *ruined* my affair.
	那是個壞虫	he is a *bad* fellow.
17 壞 21 壩	牛壞了	the cow is *dead*.
	RANG³.	
	添些壞子在裏頭	to add *matter* to a statement; to add *lies* [to a message.
	PA⁴.	
	平壩	a level *plain*.
	田壩頭	*open fields*.
	河壩	flat land or gravel beds by a river side.
	院壩	the *courtyard* of a house.
	壩壩頭的生意	to keep a stall in a *yard* or on the street.
	扯謊壩	the *liar's yard*; i. e., the *yard* where fortune tellers and others ply their trade.

The 33rd radical. (士)

	SÏ⁴.	
士 4 壯	士農工商各居一業	the *scholar*, farmer, artizan, and merchant, each has his own occupation.
	大紳士	the *gentry*.
	勇士	a *strong man*.
	道士	a Taoist *priest*.
	二居士	a female *Buddhist devotee*.
	CHUANG⁴.	
	強壯	*healthy; strong*.
	年壯的人	a *vigorous* man; one in the prime of life.
	壯班	a *policeman*; a *thief-catcher*.
	酒壯他的膽	wine has *inspired* him with courage.
	田壯	the field is *fertile*.
壳	K'O⁵.	
	小麥壳壳	the *husk* of wheat.
	剝壳的生意	poor trade; lit. like flicking *husks*.

(114)

注 释

【那是个坏虫】坏虫: 坏人。
【牛坏了】牛死了。
壞 [zaŋ³]
壩（坝）[pa⁴]
【院坝】庭院。
【坝坝头的生意】摆摊的小买卖。
【扯谎坝】说谎者聚集的地方。今转指说谎的人。
士 [sʅ⁴]
【二居士】信奉佛教的女信徒。
壯（壮）[tʂuaŋ⁴]
【壮班】警察。
【田壮】土地肥沃。
壳 [kʰo⁵]
【剥壳的生意】现为"薄壳的生意"，利润很低的生意。

注释

【疮壳】痂,疤。
【溜壳子】类似于索道的简易通行工具。
【喜神壳子】小孩玩的面具。
【刘壳子】壳子:骗子,说谎者。
壶(壶)[fu²]
壽(寿)[ṣəu⁴]
【寿期】生日。
夏[çia⁴]
【夏布衫子】夏布:苎麻属,用黄麻或大麻制成的布。用夏布做成的长衫。

士 4-11 夂. 夊 7.

9 壳

核桃壳壳	walnut *shells*.
笋壳	the *sheaths* of the bamboo.
繭壳	the *chrysalis* of the silk worm.
烏龜壳壳	the *carapace* of a turtle.
腦壳	the *skull*; the *head*.
菸袋腦壳	a pipe *head*.
瘡壳	a *scab*.
溜壳子	the sliding (*cylinder*) of a one-rope bridge.
紙壳子	*pasteboard*.
書壳子	the *boards* of a book.
信壳子	an *envelope*.
喜神壳子	a *mask*.
劉壳子	Mr. Liu the *liar*.

11 壺 FU².

茶壺	a tea-*pot*.
水壺	a water *kettle*.
油壺子	a small *lamp* with an iron handle for [carrying
夜壺	a chamber *pot*.
一壺茶	a *pot* of tea. (*N. A.*)

壽 SHEO⁴.

高壽	what is your exalted *age*?
壽期	a birthday.
三歲孩童買壽木遲早都是要的	if a three-year old boy buys a *coffin*, early or late he will need it; i. e., we must all die.

The 34th radical. **夂**

The 35th radical. **夊**

7 夏 SHIA⁴.

夏天	*summer*-time.
夏布衫子	a *summer* gown made of grass-cloth.

夕 2-3

The 36th radical. (夕)

SI⁵.

命在旦夕	his life is not worth a day's purchase; lit. *morning* or *evening*.

UAI⁴.

在外頭	on the *outside*.
你外前人在那裏	where is your husband?
外頭耍的	*vagabonds*.
外面	*exterior, outer side*.
外貌	the *external* appearance of a person.
外科先生	a *surgical* practitioner.
外孫	daughter's children; grand-children of a *different* surname.
外人	an *outsider*; a *stranger*.
口外	*beyond* the frontier.
出外傳道	to go *abroad* to propagate a doctrine.
外國話	*foreign* words.
除此以外	*besides* this.

TO¹.

好兒不要多一個當十個	you do not need *many* good sons, one is as good as ten.
多少	how *much*? how *many*? very *much*: very *many*.
這麽多	so *much*; as *many* as this.
好得多	*much* better.
多用點	use a little *more*.
一千多人	*more than* a thousand people.
多起來	to *multiply*; to *increase in number*.
多大個東西	a *very* big thing.
不多於好	not *very* good; not *very* well.
不要多事	don't be *meddlesome*.
不要多心	don't be *anxious*; don't be *suspicious*.
多半是假的	*probably* it is false.

(116)

注 释

夕 [si⁵]
外 [uai⁴]
【你外前人在那里】外前人：丈夫。
【外头耍的】流浪汉。
【口外】边界以外。
多 [to¹]
【不多于好】不太好。

注释

夜 [ie⁴]
够 [kəu⁴]
夢(梦) [moŋ⁴]
【他是个梦虫】梦虫：婴孩；喜欢做梦或睡觉的人。

夥(伙) [xo³]
【他们自伙子在商量】他们自伙子：他们自己。
【老的伙】我父母。
【我们伙子里】我们兄弟。英文释义应为：we brothers 或 in our group (usu. young people)。

大 [ta⁴] [tai⁴]

夕 5-11 大

5 夜

IE⁴.

| 夜間 | in the *night*-time. |

8 够

KEO⁴.

够不够	is there *enough*?
這個活路够做	this is hard *enough* work indeed!
我自己不够用	I have not *sufficient* for my own use.
不够本	not *equal* to the original cost.
斷不能够	he certainly is not *able*; it will not do.

11 夢

MONG⁴.

做夢	to *dream*.
他是個夢蟲	he is still a baby; lit. a *dreaming* insect.
夢想不及	unexpected; I could not have *dreamt* it.

夥

HO³.

夥黨成羣	to *band together* into a company.
一夥的人	a man of the same *set* or *company*.
找個夥計搭夥	find a *partner* to form a *partnership* with.
夥計讓開些	stand aside, *mate*!
小夥子	a young *fellow*.
他們自夥子在商量	they are consulting among themselves (*plural*).
老的夥	my parents (*plural*).
我們夥子裏	we Mohammedans.

The 37th radical. (大)

大

TA⁴.

大清國	China; lit. the *Great* Pure Kingdom.
一大塊	a *large* piece.
好大的事	how *big* an affair? what a *big* affair!
這雙鞋子大了	these shoes are *too big*.
有兩個那麼大	it is twice the *size* of that.
大路	the *main* road.
大聲喊	to call in a *loud* voice.
他大我一歲	he is a year *older than* I am.
長大了	to grow *big*; to grow to *maturity*.

(117)

大 1

大人娃娃	grown up people and children.
這是我的老大	this is my *elder brother*.
鍾大爺	*old* Mr. Chong.
父母大老爺	his *honour* the district magistrate.
鹿大人	his *excellency* Luh.
天地為大	heaven and earth are *supreme*.
那是個大意人	he is a *careless* fellow.
大家都來	we will *all* come.
大概說	to speak *generally*.
天氣大熱	the weather is *very* hot.
大不同	*very* different.
發大怒	he got *very* angry.
大大方方的	*magnanimous*.
大概點	be more *liberal*.

READ TAI⁴.

大王	a robber *chief*.

FU¹.

老夫子	respected *teacher*; sir.
大夫第	an *official* family; the residence of an [*official* family.]
兩夫婦	husband and wife.
夫頭	head coolie. [*attendants* and horses.]
折夫馬錢	to give travelling expenses; lit. money for
我今天拉你個夫	will you *help* me to-day, please?

T'AI⁴.

這雙鞋子太大	these shoes are *too* large.
太驕傲	*extremely* proud.
他做事太過分	he goes *far* beyond his duty or his rights.
天下太平	the whole country is enjoying *peace*.
太醫	a *good* doctor.
今天出了太陽	the *sun* has come out to-day.
莫在太陽壩頭坐	don't sit in the *sunny* place.
還要幾個太陽	it needs a few more *sunny days*.
太子登基	the *Crown Prince* has come to the throne.
太太	a *lady*.
老太婆	old *lady*.

(118)

注　释

【这是我的老大】老大：哥哥。

【大慨点】慷慨点！大方点！

夫 [fu¹]

【大夫第】士大夫的门第。

【夫头】夫役的头目。

【折夫马钱】夫马：役夫与车马等。清代官员阵亡及在任在差病故者，均给夫马费，专供其雇夫役和车马之用。

【我今天拉你个夫】拉夫：旧谓抓老百姓做杂役；比喻强邀某人做某事。

太 [tʰai⁴]

【莫在太阳坝头坐】太阳坝头：太阳底下，即有阳光照射的地方。

【还要几个太阳】还需要几个晴天。

注释

天 [tʰien¹]

【同天不同地】同父异母。

【五月五日午天师骑艾虎】艾虎：古俗，端午日采艾制成虎形的饰物，佩戴之谓能辟邪祛秽。

【天锅】洞顶呈倒锅底状的溶蚀形态。为洞穴充水时的水汽联合作用的产物，不受基岩节理或层面裂隙影响。

【天河水干了】女性绝经；命运改变。

【天灯】旧时新年前后，民间有在高处悬挂灯盏之俗，此灯彻夜通明，谓之"天灯"。

【天花水】（下雨时直接用器具接来的）雨水。

天 [iao¹]

【收拾得天饶】天饶：即"妖娆"。

天 1

T'IEN¹.

求天老爺下雨	we beseech thee, O God to sent us rain.
下雨天留客天留人不留	It rains, 'tis *providence* detains the guests; 'tis *providence* detains them here, not man.
天大由天	*Heaven* is great—everything depends on *Heaven* (met. parents.).
同天不同地	the same *father* but a different mother.
天下一家	all under *heaven* are one family.
天文	astronomy.
天堂有路你不去 地獄無門闖進來	There is a road to *paradise*, But you choose not to go. There is no door to Hell, and yet You force your way to woe.
五月五日午天師騎艾虎	on the fifth of the fifth month at noon, the *celestial* sage rides on the mug-wort tiger.
天天待客不窮 夜夜做賊不富	Though every *day* you welcome guests, You never will be poor. Though every night you prowl and thieve, You'll ne'er increase your store.
天晴	the *sky* is clear; fair *weather*.
天氣熱	the *weather* is warm.
春天	Spring-time.
天理	truth.
昧盡天良	to deaden one's *conscience*.
天鍋	the condensing pot on the *top* of a still.
天河水乾了	cessation of the menses; change of life.
天燈	a lantern on a post (usually about 33 feet high).
天蓬	an awning.
天花水	rain water caught straight from the clouds.
天平	16 oz. to the pound.

IAO¹.

收拾得天饒	*wantonly* bedizened.
我怕天壽	I am afraid that he will die an *untimely* [death.

(119)

大 2-4

2 失 SHĬ⁵.

失掉東西	to *lose* things.
迷失道路	to *lose* one's way.
失了性的	a lunatic; one who has *lost* his wits.
失身	to *lose* one's virtue (women).
失脚跌倒了	he *slipped* and fell, he *lost* his footing.
謹防失火	take care and not set fire to things; lit. *drop* fire.
作夜失盜	our house was *robbed* last night.
失候	I have *neglected* to entertain you.
這繞失禮	I have *broken* the rules of etiquette.
不要失信	don't *go back on* your word; don't *break* your promise.
失手打倒人	to strike another *accidentally*.
省察自己的過失	search out your own *faults*.
冒失	*rude*.

3 夷 I².

| 夷情房 | the Board of *Barbarian* affairs. |
| 繙夷字 | to translate from the *Tibetan*. |

4 夾 CHIA⁵.

夾扁了	*squeezed* flat.
夾火	to *pick* up fire with the tongs.
夾壁頭	to *plait* bamboo into a wall.
夾板	boards for *pressing* books, etc.
夾尺	a *guage* used in making tubs, pails, etc.
夾剪	*shears* for cutting silver.
線夾	a thread *case*.
螃蠏夾夾	a crab's *claws*.
夾衫子	a *lined* gown.
翻夾了頁	to turn over two leaves of a book at once.
夾生飯	*half-cooked* rice.
那個人夾得很	that fellow is very *close-fisted*.
夾口	*astringent*.
夾舌子	a *stammering* tongue; a *stammerer*.

(120)

注 释

失［ʂʅ⁵］
【失了性的】精神错乱的。
【作夜失盗】昨夜（家里）被盗了。

夷［i²］
【夷情房】清宣统年间曾设有一套管理西藏事务的机构，夷情房为其中之一，主要掌管噶厦公所官员及升补各营官额缺，为蒙古僧人、尼泊尔人发给路照，达木八旗及康属汉族事务，各大活佛掣签等事。
【翻夷字】翻译藏文。

夾（夹）［tɕia⁵］
【夹衫子】犹夹衣，夹衣里一种有面有里、中间不垫絮类的双层衣服。
【翻夹了页】（看书时）同时翻了两页，即多翻了一页。
【那个人夹得很】夹：吝啬。
【夹口】（食物等）让人口嘴发涩。
【夹舌子】口吃者。

注释

奉 [foŋ⁴]
【老奉】普通民众对罗马天主教徒的称呼。
奇 [tɕʰi²]
奄 [ien³]
奈 [lai⁴]
【今年实在奈不过】今年实在熬不住（指谋生困难）。
契 [tɕʰi⁴]
【契友】挚友。
奎 [kʰuei²]
奔 [pən¹]
【効奔走】跑腿。
奓 [tʂa¹]
【奓开口】张嘴；打哈欠。
【墙奓开了】墙裂开了。

大 5-6

5 奉 FONG⁴.

奉差遣	to *be* sent.
奉教	to *receive* instruction; to join the Roman [Catholic church.
老奉.	a Roman Catholic *convert* (said by outsiders).
事奉	to *serve*.
奉養父母	to *attend to* one's parents.
香花供奉	to *offer* incense and flowers to the gods.
我奉承你	I must *praise* you for this piece of work.

奇 CH'I².

奇事	an *extraordinary* affair.
看希奇	to see *strange* sights.
奇奇怪怪	*wonderful*.

奄 IEN³.

for example of use see 悶.

奈 LAI⁴.

把他沒奈何	it puts him in a fix; he has no *resource*.
今年實在奈不過	I really can't *manage* to make a living this year.
我肯幫助你怎奈不得空	I am willing to help you, *but* I have not time.

6 契 CH'I⁴.

| 寫契約 | write out the *title-deed*. |
| 契友 | an *intimate* friend. |

奎 K'UE².

奎星樓   a tower dedicated to the *god of literature*.

奔 PEN¹.

打奔了	*routed*.
効奔走	to *run* errands.
奔奔波波的過日子	to pass one's days in *bustle* and toil.

奓 CHA¹.

把脚奓開	*stretch* open your legs.
奓開口	*open* your mouth; gape.
牆奓開了	the wall is *cracked*.

(121)

大 7-11

TSEO⁴.

奏 皇 上	to *report* to the Emperor.
直 奏 公 曹	Kong Ts'ao the *reporter*; met. a tell-tale.
奏 樂	to *perform* music, as the band does daily in a magistrate's house.

CHUANG³.

| 你 纔 是 個 奘 棒 | you are a *great* lout of a fellow. |

T'AO⁴.

袍 套	a long *overcoat*.
套 褲	wide cloth *leggings*.
書 套 子	a *cover* for a set of books.
一 套 衣 服	a *suit* of clothes.
打 套 頭	to wear a big *turban* like the soldiers.
傘 套 子	an *umbrella case*.
銅 筆 套	a brass pen-*protector*.
挽 個 活 套 套	tie a loose *slipknot*.
安 套 套	to set a *snare*.
套 獐 子	to *snare* the musk-deer.
套 哄 人 家	to *cheat* people.
套 言 不 敍	let us drop *polite* talk and come to business.

SHE¹.

| 銀 錢 難 掙 莫 奢 華 | money is difficult to get; don't be extravagant. |

TIEN⁴.

| 奠 酒 | *libation* of wine. |
| 開 奠 | to *sacrifice* to the spirit of a person who has just died. |

NGAO⁴.

| 奧 妙 的 事 | a *mysterious* affair. |
| 道 理 深 奧 | the doctrine is very *abstruse*. |

LIEN².

| 嫁 奩 | a bride's *trousseau*. |

TO⁵.

| 搶 奪 | to *snatch* violently. |
| 爭 名 奪 利 | to contend for fame (scholars), and *strive* for gain (merchants). |

注 释

奏 [tsəu⁴]
【直奏公曹】公曹：封建衙门中的差吏。

奘 [tʂuaŋ³]
【你才是个奘棒】奘棒：形容人傻或者说话不得当。

套 [tʰao⁴]
【袍套】补服的别称。亦名外褂、外套。
【打套头】打：穿戴。套头：包头巾、缠头布。
【安套套】布设陷阱。
【套哄人家】套哄：哄骗，欺骗。
【套言不叙】客套话不多说了，直奔主题。

奢 [ʂe¹]

奠 [tien⁴]
【奠酒】祭酒。

奥 [ŋao⁴]

奩（奁）[lien²]

奪（夺）[to⁵]

注释

奬（奖）[tsiaŋ³]

奮（奋）[fən⁴]

【奋气不服】奋气：奋发振作。

女 [ny³] [ny⁴]

【你的姑娘女了人没有】女：许配。

奴 [lu²]

好 [xao³]

【他的家屋好】[xao⁴]家屋：家境。

大 11-13 女 3.

13 奬

TSIANG³.

| 褒奬奉承 | to *flatter*. |
| 誇奬自己 | to *boast* of one self. |

FEN⁴.

| 告奮勇 | to volunteer for *active* service. |
| 奮氣不服 | *roused* to opposition. |

The 38th radical. (女)

女

NÜ³.

女人家	*women*.
女流之輩	we *women*.
養女是個禍不養也得過	to rear *girls* is a calamity, we can get on well enough without them.
兒女	sons and *daughters*.
男女老少	male and *female*, old and young.
女老師	a *lady* teacher.

READ Ü⁴.

| 你的姑娘女了人沒有 | is your daughter *betrothed* yet? |

2 奴

LU².

| 小奴才 | you little *slave*! |
| 守財奴 | a miserly *wretch*. |

3 好

HAO³.

做好事	to do *good* deeds.
病好些沒有	are you any *better*?
拿頂好的來	bring the *best* kind.
不學好	not inclined to *goodness*.
好處	*advantage*; *benefit*.
他的家屋好	his family is *rich*.
先生好嗎	are you *well*, Sir?
好比	it may *well* be compared to.
說得好	*well* spoken.
路不好走	the road is not *easy* to travel.

(123)

女 3

你好生聽	listen *carefully*.
飯好了沒有	is the food *ready* yet?
事情弄好了沒有	is the affair *settled*?
好不利害呀	*exceedingly* severe!
天氣好冷	the weather is *very* cold.
好不過意	*very much* ashamed.
我們兩個相好	we two are very *friendly*.
來了好幾囘	he has come a *good* many times.
好久來的	*when* did you come?
有好大	*how* big is it?

READ HAO⁴.

好善惡惡	to *love* good and hate evil.
好喫懶做	he is *fond* of eating, but lazy at working.
好酒貪杯的人	a man who is *addicted to* wine.

如 RU².

如同我們一樣	*like* us.
他不如我	he is not *equal* to me.
這個該如你的意	this ought to *suit* you.
比如說	for *instance*.
口說不如身逢 / 耳聞不如目見	to hear people speak of a thing, is not *equal to* experiencing it; seeing is better than hearing.
如果他不來	*if* he does not come.
假如你不信	*supposing* he will not believe it.
何必如此	*why* so?
死後如何	after death—*how* then?
二四如八	two fours *are* eight.
如今天矮報應甚快	*now* Heaven is near and recompense is swift.
如痛如痛的	*slightly* painful; a dull deep-seated pain.

奸 CHIEN¹.

| 奸巧 | *crafty*. |
| 奸臣賣國 | the *traitorous* official has betrayed his [country. |

妄 UANG⁴.

| 不要妄爲 | don't act in a *disorderly* manner. |

(124)

注 釋

【你好生听】好生: 好好儿地, 认真地, 小心地。

【好不过意】非常惭愧, 不好意思。

【好久来的】好久: 什么时候。

【有好大】有多大?

如 [zu²]

【假如你不信】("你"当为"他", 见803页勘误表。)

【如痛如痛的】一阵一阵地闷疼。

奸 [tɕien¹]

妄 [uaŋ⁴]

注释

妨 [faŋ¹] [faŋ²]
  【你莫妨我】妨：阻碍，妨碍。
妓 [tɕi⁴]
妙 [miao⁴]
妥 [tʰo³]
  【把话说定妥】把事情安排妥当。
  【安顿得停停妥妥的】停妥：停当妥贴。
  【找个妥实人】妥实人：实在人。
妒 [tu⁴]
妖 [iao¹]
姑 [ku¹]

女 4-5

妨

狂妄	silly; crazy.
痴心妄想	he has *foolish* ideas, *wild* notions; building castles in the air.

FANG¹.

你莫妨我	don't *hinder* me.
有妨碍沒得	is there any *hindrance*?

READ FANG².

無妨	no matter.

妓

CHI⁴.

妓女	a *prostitute*.

妙

MIAO⁴.

妙藥難醫冤孽病 / 橫財不富命窮人	a sickness caused by evil deeds, *good* medicine will hardly cure, nor can ill-gotten gains enrich the man who is fated to be poor.
這個東西做得巧妙	this thing is *cleverly* made.
奧妙	*mysterious*.

妥

T'O³.

事情辦穩妥了嗎	is the affair *settled*?
把話說定妥	make a *definite* arrangement with him.
安頓得停停妥妥的	everything is *properly* and *securely* placed.
找個妥實人	seek out a *reliable* man.
慢妥妥的	*slow, dawdling*.

妒

TU⁴.

生煘妒心	to be *envious*.

妖

IAO¹.

妖術	*magic*.
妖言惑衆	*strange* tales to deceive people.
古怪妖精	*fairies* and *elves*.
把觀音菩薩當做妖魔了	to regard the goddess of mercy as a *fiend*: met. to speak ill of a good person.

姑

KU¹.

姑娘	a *damsel*; *daughter*; *father's sister*.
姑爺	*father's sister's husband*.

女 5

小姑子		husband's *younger sister* (unmarried).
新姑娘		a *bride*.
三姑		the three *maids* (as follows)
尼姑		a Buddhist *nun*.
道姑		a Taoist *nun*.
貞姑		an old *maid*. [vicious man.
姑息養奸		*indulge* your child, and he will become a
	CHU⁶, CHO⁵.	
兩妯娌		wives of brothers.
	ME⁴.	
妹妹		a *younger sister*; a *little girl*.
妹夫		*younger sister's* husband.
	SHĬ³.	
無始無終		without *beginning* or *ending*.
始終如一		the same from *first* to *last*; *Semper idem*.
	TS'I¹.	
妻賢夫禍少子孝父心寬		The man whose *wife* is virtuous few ills e'er molest. Pro. 31. 12. The father of a filial son may dwell in perfect rest. Pro. 15. 20.
生人妻		a woman who marries again while her first husband is alive.
	TSIE³.	
姐姐		an *elder sister*.
姐丈		*elder sister's* husband.
小姐		a young *unmarried woman*.
	TSIE⁵.	
討小娶妾		to take a *concubine*.
	TSĬ³.	
親姊妹		sisters.
	UE³.	
我委曲你		I am *wronging* you.
委員		a *deputy*.

(126)

注 释

【新姑娘】新媳妇儿，新娘。
【貞姑】有节操的女子或从一而终的女子。英文释义应为：chaste woman.
妯 [tʂu⁵] [tʂo⁵]
妹 [mei⁴]
始 [sʅ³]
妻 [tsʰi¹]
【生人妻】前任丈夫仍在世而再婚的女人。
姐 [tsie³]
妾 [tsie⁵]
姊 [tsʅ³]
委 [uei³]

注 释

【委缺】委派某人填补空缺。
姓 [sin⁴]
侄（侄）[tṣʅ⁵]
姨 [i²]
姤 [kəu⁴]
【交姤】同"交媾"。
姦（奸）[tɕien¹]
姿 [tsʅ¹]
娃 [ua²] [ua¹]
【私娃子】非婚生子女，私生子。
【贼娃子】小偷，窃贼。

女 5-6

	委缺	deputed to fill a vacancy.
	他的話說得委婉	he speaks in a *conciliatory* manner.

姓 SIN⁴.

	貴姓	what is your honourable *name*?
	僧不問姓道不問名	don't ask a Buddhist priest his *surname* or a Taoist his style.
	百姓	the *people*.

侄 CHIH⁵.

	侄兒子	a *nephew*.
	侄女	a *niece*.

姨 I².

	姨姐	wife's elder *sister*.
	姨夫	wife's sister's husband.
	姨媽	mother's sister; a maternal aunt.
	姨父	mother's sister's husband.
	姨表	cousins whose mothers are sisters.
	姨侄	nephews, children of the wife's sister.

姤 KEO⁴.

	交姤	sexual intercourse.

姦 CHIEN¹.

	姦淫	adultery; fornication.
	拿姦要拿雙，拿賊要拿贓	if you seize *adulterers* you must seize both; if you seize a thief you must seize the plunder also.
	雞姦	men with men working that which is unseemly; *sodomy*.
	強姦	rape.

姿 TSĪ¹.

	幾分姿色	she has a little *beauty*.

娃 UA², ¹.

	娃²娃¹乖	the *baby* is good.
	我的娃娃病了	my *child* is sick (the so-called *child* may be a grown up person).
	帶娃娃	to nurse a *child*; to keep a *catamite*.
	私娃子	a *bastard*.
	賊娃子	a *thief*.

(127)

女 6-8

UE¹.

| 那個像塑得威嚴 | that image is very *majestic*. |
| 老虎死了不倒威 | the tiger is not *terrible* when he is dead. |

IN¹.

| 婚姻爲五倫之一 | *marriage* is one of the five human relationships. |
| 姻緣 | the fate that brings man and wife together; affinity. |

7 NGO².

| 月裏嫦娥 | the lady "Shang-*ngo*" in the moon. |

SO¹.

| 婆娑你 | I have *troubled* you; thank you. |

CHI⁴.

| 媢妬 | *envy*. |

LI³.

| 妯娌 | *wives of brothers*. |

NIANG².

爹娘	*father* and *mother*.
親娘	*mother-in-law*.
張大娘	*Mrs*. Chang.
兩娘母	a *mother* and her child.
娘屋	her *parents'* house; a priest's *parents'* house.
伯娘	father's elder brother's *wife*.
師娘	my master's *wife*.

READ NIANG¹.

| 有幾個姑娘 | how many *daughters* have you? |
| 婆娘蠢笨 | his *wife* is stupid (vulgar). |

8 CH'ANG¹.

| 娼妓 | a *prostitute*. |

LEO².

| 嫛家伙 | a *lazy*, or *weak* workman. |
| 走嫛了 | *tired* with walking. |

(128)

注释

威［uei¹］
姻［in¹］
娥［ŋo²］
娑［so¹］
媢（忌）［tɕi⁴］
娌［li³］
娘［ȵiaŋ²］［ȵiaŋ¹］
【娘屋】婚后女子的婆家或僧人的父母家。
【伯娘】伯母。
娼［tsʰaŋ¹］
嫛（娄）［ləu²］
【娄家伙】懒惰的或虚弱的人。
【走娄了】走累了。

注释

婦（妇）[fu⁴]
婉 [uan³]
婚 [xuən¹]
【婚书】旧时结婚的文约。
婪 [lan²]
婢 [pei⁴]
婆 [pʰo²]
【老人婆】即"婆婆"，丈夫的母亲。
【家婆】外祖母，外婆。
【戏婆子】玩戏法的女人，女魔术师。
【鸡婆】母鸡。
娶 [tsy⁴]
【娶寡妇亲】与寡妇结婚。
婊 [piao³]

女 8-9

	FU⁴.	
婦人		a *woman*; a *wife*.
新媳婦		a *bride*.
	UAN³.	
委委婉婉的話		*pleasant* words.
	HUEN¹.	
婚配		to *marry*.
男大當婚女大當嫁		grown boys should *marry* wives, grown girls should be married out.
婚書		a deed of marriage, given by a woman to her second husband.
	LAN².	
貪婪無厭		very *covetous*.
	PE⁴.	
爲奴作婢的人		*slaves*; *bond servants*.
	P'O².	
老婆婆		an old *woman*.
老人婆		husband's *mother*.
婆家		the husband's family.
兩婆孫		*grandmother* and grandson.
家婆		*grandmother*, i.e., mother's mother.
喫婆婆飯		to live with the parents of the future husband.
媒婆		the *woman* who acts as go-between in arranging a marriage.
婆娘		a *wife* (a disrespectful term).
接生婆		a *midwife*.
巫婆		a *witch*.
戲婆子		a *female juggler*.
鷄婆		a *hen*.
	TSÜ⁴.	
娶妻		to *take* a wife.
娶寡婦親		to *marry* a widow.
	PIAO³.	
婊子		a *prostitute*.

女 9-10

9 媒 ME².

| 那個給你做的媒 | who is acting as *middleman* for you? |
| 買田謝中討親謝媒 | if you purchase a field you must pay the middleman, if you take a wife you must remunerate the *go-between*. |

媚 ME⁴.

| 諂媚小人 | a mean man who *flatters* others for gain. |

婿 SI⁵.

| 女婿 | a *son-in-law*. |
| 兩翁婿 | father-in-law and *son-in-law*. |

10 嫌 SHIEN².

討人嫌	to incur one's *displeasure*.
他犯我的嫌疑	he is *suspicious* of me.
嫌貧愛富	to *dislike* the poor and love the rich.
嫌妻無好妻 嫌夫無好夫	if a husband *despises* his wife (and leaves her), he will never get a good one; if a wife *despises* her husband, she will never get a good one.
窮嫌富不愛	poor and rich alike *hate* it, i. e., a worthless thing.
莫嫌棄	don't *disdain* my small present.

嫁 CHIA⁴.

你的姑娘出嫁沒有	is your daughter *married out* yet?
嫁雞隨雞嫁狗隨狗	if you have *married* a cock follow him, if you have *married* a dog follow him.
不願改嫁	she is not willing to *marry* a second time.
辦嫁奩	to prepare the *bridal* trousseau.

媽 MA¹.

| 媽媽 | mother. |
| 奶媽 | a *wet-nurse*. |

嫂 SAO³.

| 姑嫂 | a man's sisters and *his wife*. |
| 叔嫂 | a man's younger brothers and *his wife*. |

(130)

注 釋

媒 [mei²]
【买田谢中,讨亲谢媒】
　中: 中间人, 介绍人。
媚 [mei⁴]
婿 [si⁵]
【两翁婿】岳父和女婿。
嫌 [ɕien²]
嫁 [tɕia⁴]
媽 (妈) [ma¹]
嫂 [sao³]

注释

媳 [si⁵]
嫉 [tsi⁵] [tsie⁵]
媼（媪）[uən³]
　【媼婆】接生婆，助产士。
嫩 [lən⁴]
　【嫩东东的】幼小而细嫩。
　【嫩宛豆米】宛豆米：即"豌豆米"。
嫖 [pʰiao²]
嫦 [ʂaŋ²]
嬌（娇）[tɕiao¹]
　【娇客】女婿。
　【娇声】假声；娇滴滴的声音。
孏（奶）[lai¹] [lai³]

女 10-14

長哥當爺長嫂當母	}	the elder brother and his wife act the part of father and mother.
嫂嫂		a young married woman.

SI⁵.

媳婦	a daughter-in-law.
新媳婦兒	a bride.

TSI⁵, TSIE⁵.

同行生嫉妒	fellow-craftsmen are envious of each other.

UEN³.

11

媼婆	a mid-wife.

LEN⁴.

嫩東東的	young; fresh; tender.
買個嫩雞	buy a tender chicken.
年輕骨嫩	a young person.
嫩宛荳米	fresh peas.
蛋要羹的嫩	boil the eggs soft.
顏色兒嫩點	mix the colour a little lighter.

P'IAO².

嫖娼	to cohabit with a prostitute.
嫖客	a fornicator.

SHANG².

12

嫦娥	"Shang-ngo," the lady in the moon.

CHIAO¹.

嬌妻	a handsome wife.
嬌客	a son-in-law.
莫把他嬌養慣了	don't spoil him with petting.
嬌聲	a falsetto voice.

LAI¹.

14

孏孏	a woman's breasts and milk.
孏嘴嘴	nipples; teats.

READ LAI³.

請個孏媽餵孏	engage a wet-nurse to suckle the infant.
孏癰	a mammary abscess.
牛孏	cow's milk.

西蜀方言

女 14-17　子 1-3

嬰 15

嬰兒　IN¹.　　an *infant*.

嬸 17

嬸娘　SHEN³.　　*father's younger brother's wife*.

孀

居孀守寡　SHUANG¹.　　to remain a *widow*.

The 39th radical. (子)

子

　　　TSĭ³.
父子　　　father and *son*.
買了一子母牛　　I have bought a cow and a *calf*.
魚子　　　the *roe* of fish.
瓜子　　　melon *seeds*.
花紅子子　　apple *pips*.
子薑　　　fresh ginger.
鐵砂子　　iron *pellets* for fowling pieces.
一子火麻　　a *small bunch* of hemp.
棹子　　　a table.
子　　　a particle attached to many nouns.

孔 1

　　　K'ONG³.
賊娃子來挖孔孔　the thief came and dug a *hole* in the wall.
竈孔　　　the *fire-hole* under a Chinese pot.
只缺孔方兄　I am only short of cash; lit. the square-*holed* brother.
鼻孔　　　the *nostrils*.
毫毛孔竅　the hair and *pores* on the human body.
孔雀翎　　*peacock* plumes, worn by officials.
孔夫子　　Confucius.

孕 2

　　　RUEN⁴.
懷孕　　　to be *with child*.
孕婦　　　a *pregnant* woman.

存 3

　　　TS'EN².
存公道心　*maintain* an upright mind.
把良心存留　*preserve* your conscience pure.
存留他的性命　*spare* his life.

(132)

注　釋

嬰（婴）[in¹]
嬸（婶）[ʂən³]
孀 [ʂuaŋ¹]
子 [tsɿ³]
【鱼子】鱼卵。
【子姜】初生的嫩姜。
孔 [kʰoŋ³]
【灶孔】灶上的烟筒。
孕 [zuən⁴]
存 [tsʰən²]

注释

【没有存的有】没有剩下的。

字 [tsɿ⁴]

【字辈and字派】指名字中用以表示家族辈分的字（多为名字中间的字）。

【守贞不字】字：许配，结婚。指女子守志不嫁。

孝 [ɕiao⁴]

【孝廉公】明、清两代对"举人"的称呼。

季 [tɕi⁴]

孤 [ku¹]

孟 [moŋ⁴]

子 3-5

TSĪ⁴.

存下一點	lay by a little.
沒有存的有	I have uone left.
不知生死存亡	I don't know whether he is *alive* or dead.
你認得字嗎	do you recognise *characters*? can you read?
字輩 and 字派	a set of *characters* used to distinguish the generations of a family.
外國字	foreign *letters*.
敬惜字紙	respect *written* paper.
名字	a name.
字眼子吐得清	he pronounces his *words* clearly.
這個笛子的字眼子清	the *notes* of this flute are clear.
守貞不字	a virgin who does not *marry*.

SHIAO⁴.

萬惡淫為首百行孝為先	of all vices, adultery is the chief; of all virtues, *filial piety* is the foremost.
孝敬父母	*honour* thy father and mother.
孝子	a *dutiful* son; a son *mourning* for his [parents.
孝廉公	a "chü-ren," lit. a *filial* and incorruptible gentleman.
孝衣	the mourning dress worn on the death of [a parent.
披麻戴孝	to wear *mourning*.

CHI⁴.

| 一年四季忙到頭 | busy all the year round, i. e., throughout [the four *seasons*. |
| 栽秧打穀是大季 | planting and reaping *times* are important. |

KU¹.

鰥寡孤獨	widowers and widows, *orphans* and childless.
孤孤單單的	*solitary*; a *lonely* individual.
孤魂野鬼	*friendless* wandering spirits.
孤老院	the *poorhouse*.

MONG⁴.

| 孟夫子 | Mencius. |

(133)

子 6-13

6 孩 SHIAI², HAI².
嬰孩	an *infant*.
小孩子	a *child*.

7 孫 SEN¹.
兒孫滿堂	your sons and *grandsons* fill the house.
外孫	a *daughter's son*.
名落孫山外	my name is below *Sen-shan*, i.e., not among the successful.

猛 MIEN³.
沒得生猛	she has not *borne* any children; barren.

孬 P'IE⁴.
那個東西孬	that article is *bad*.
那是個孬人	he is an *evil* man.

8 孰 SHUH⁵.
到底孰眞孰假	now *which* is true and *which* is false?
這兩個人孰是孰非	*who* is right and *who* is wrong?

9 孱 CH'AN¹.
孱弱不振	*weak*; *spiritless*.

10 孳 TSÏ¹.
沒得一點孳息	there is not the slightest *pecuniary gain*.

13 學 SHIO⁵.
學個手藝	to *learn* a trade.
學文學武	to *study* for the civil and military examinations.
好學	fond of *study*.
學堂	a *school*.
學田	an estate, the income of which is devoted to the maintenance of *scholars*.
學生逃學	the *pupil* plays truant from *school*.
入學	to graduate; to become a "*Siu-ts'ai*"; to enter *school*.
學院	the *literary* president of the province.
學問	*learning*.
化學	the *science* of chemistry.
不要學他	don't *imitate* him.

注 釋

孩〔ṣiai²〕〔xai²〕
孫(孙)〔sən¹〕
猛(娩)〔mien³〕
孬〔pʰie⁴〕
孰〔ṣu⁵〕
（SHUH⁵当为SHU⁵，见803页勘误表。）
孱〔tṣʰan¹〕
孳〔tsɿ¹〕
【沒得一点孳息】没有一点儿金钱上的收获。孳息：繁殖生息。
學(学)〔ɕio⁵〕
【学田】旧时办学用的公田，以其收入作为学校经费。

注 释

孺 [zu³] [zu⁴]
癞 [lai³]
【三癞子】癞：广东、福建方言，指老年所生幼子。排行第三的幼子。
孽 [ɲie⁵]
宄 [kuei³]
【奸宄】坏人。
安 [ŋan¹]
【安一匹亮瓦】亮瓦：一种透明的瓦片，安装在屋顶。亮瓦是融合在中国传统建筑中的快捷计时工具，同时也可加强室内采光。

子 14-17　宀 2-3

14 孺
他在學我　he is *mocking* me.
　　RU³.
黃口孺子　*little children*.
　　READ RU⁴.
老孺人　*wives of officials* of the 9th rank; a term [of respect for old ladies.

癞
　　LAI³.
三癞子　the third *son*.

17 孽
　　NIE⁵.
罪孽深重　the *sin* is very great.
天作孽猶可違 ⎫ if the *retribution* is from Heaven, there
自作孽不可活 ⎭ is still a way of escape; but if you bring it on yourself, you are a dead man.
孽海茫茫　the vast sea of *woe*, i. e., the world.
孽畜　an *evil* beast.

The 40th radical. (宀)

2 宄
　　KUE³.
奸宄　*traitors*.

3 安
　　NGAN¹.
你請萬安我已 ⎫ please keep your mind *at ease*, my affairs
安頓好了　 ⎭ are already *settled*.
平平安安的　*peacefully*.
做到這樣做了 ⎫ having acted in this way are you yet *free*
你心裏安不安 ⎭ *from alarm?*
身體欠安　I am not very *well*.
問李先生安　ask after Mr. Li's *welfare*.
安慰　*comfort*; to comfort.
安閒自在　at perfect *leisure*.
安家樂業　to marry and *settle down* to one's business.
安分守己　to *mind* one's own business.
安理父母　to *lay* one's parents *to rest* in the grave.
安放得好　well *arranged*.
安一匹亮瓦　*place* a glass tile in the roof.

(135)

3-5

安個門	set up a door.
安臟	to put the viscera into an idol—usually [rice, tea etc.
那個地方要安個人	put a man in that place; station a person there.
你那話安不上	what you say cannot be applied to me.
安知非福安知非禍	how do you know it is not a blessing? how do you know it is not a calamity?

SHEO³.

把守關隘	guard the pass.
守夜的	a night watch-man.
守舖子	look after the shop.
他守倒我哭	he wept and importuned me.
守法	to keep the laws.
守本分	to do one's duty.
守寡	to remain a widow.

TS'E⁵.

| 頗有田宅 | he has many fields and houses; a large [property. |
| 陰宅 | a grave. |

HONG².

| 今天開張宏發 | may you have large sales on opening your [shop to-day. |

UAN².

做完喫完算了	when I have done working I have done [eating, that's all.
錢用完了	my cash is all used up.
工夫完畢	the work is finished.
完完全全的	perfect; complete.
哎呀完了	alas! here's a fix!
完糧	to pay taxes.

NGI².

與他相宜的人	one who is in harmony with him.
這個事做得不合宜	this affair is not done properly.
可以便宜行事	you may do it as you find it ought to be done.

注　释

【你那话安不上】你的话不管用。

守［ʂəu³］

宅［tsʰe⁵］

【阴宅】迷信的人称死人安葬之地。

宏［xoŋ²］

完［uan²］

【完粮】上交粮食作为赋税。

宜［ŋi²］

注释

官 [kuan¹]
  【内官子】太监。
  【道官】掌管道教之官。
  【大老官】长兄,哥哥。
定 [tin⁴]
  【定更炮】旧时晚上八时左右,打鼓报告初更开始,称为"定更"。
  【他的话没定准】没定准:不可靠。
  【必定行不去】行不去:行不通。
宗 [tsoŋ¹]

山 5

官

KUAN¹.

但願喫虧少勿占便宜多	may I neither suffer much wrong myself, nor deprive others of their *rights*.
國正天心順官清民自安	an upright prince shall Heaven's favour gain, and *rulers* just the people's peace maintain.
地方官	the local *magistrate*.
官話	the *mandarin* dialect.
內官子	*eunuchs*.
官長	*officials*.
官鹽	*official* salt, i. e., the government monop- [oly salt.
官馬大路	a *main* road.
官司打輸了	the law-suit is lost.
道官	an *official* who rules the Taoists.
堂官	a *waiter*.
官艙	the *passenger* compartment on a boat, a [cabin.
大老官	*elder brother*.
官渡	a *public* ferry.

定

TIN⁴.

沒得一定的地方	there is no *fixed* place.
事情還未定妥	the affair is not *settled* yet.
主意是拿定了的	my mind is *made up*.
打個定心捶	to make up one's mind (accompanied by a thump on one's chest).
定更砲	the gún by which the night-watches are [set.
他的話沒定準	his words are un*reliable*.
必定行不去	it *certainly* will not do.
我一定要	I *must* have it; I *certainly* want it.
你定親沒有	are you *engaged* to be married? (said to men only).
定做一雙鞋子	to make a pair of shoes *to order*.
給幾個定錢	give a little *earnest* money.
秧子長定根了	the young rice is *rooted*.

宗

TSONG¹.

祖宗	*forefathers*.

(137)

山 5-6

宗廟		an *ancestral* temple.
宗族		a *family*; a *clan*.
宗的是那一家?		which sect do you *follow*? what style do [you *copy*?]
宗師大人		the Literary Chancellor.
一宗一宗的		*kind* by *kind*; article by article.
這宗人		this *sort* of man.

TANG⁴.

水宕宕	a *pool* of water.
有些宕宕水	there are a few *puddles*.

HUAN⁴.

官宦人家	*official* people.
宦官	*eunuchs*.

K'E⁵.

	[shopkeeper and *customer*.]
兩主客	laudlord and *tenant*; host and *guest*;
遠來的客	a *stranger* from a distance.
客套	politeness; ceremony.
你纔是個説客	you are a very talkative *person*.
遇倒棒客	to meet with robbers (an affix denoting *persons*).
撞客	a *swindler*; an embezzler.
客商	a *travelling* merchant.
客歲	*last* year.

SHÏ⁵.

宫室	a *mansion*.
正室	the proper *wife*.
側室	a *concubine*.
他有妻室兒女	he has a *wife* and children.

SÜEN¹.

四處宣揚	to *publish* everywhere.
宣講聖諭	to *preach* the Sacred Edict.

IU⁴.

赦宥我的罪過	*forgive* my sins.
請你替我原宥	please *excuse* my fault.

(138)

注 释

【宗的是那一家】宗:遵循,模仿。遵循的是哪一个派别?

宕[taŋ⁴]

【水宕宕】水塘,水池,小水坑。

【有些宕宕水】宕宕水:地上的积水。

宦[xuan⁴]

客[kʰe⁵]

【两主客】房东和房客,主人和客人,店主和顾客。

【遇倒棒客】棒客:帮会组织之一,亦指土匪、强盗。

【撞客】骗子,盗用公款的人。

【客岁】去年。

室[sʅ⁵]

宣[syen¹]

宥[iəu⁴]

【请你替我原宥】原宥:原谅,谅解。请你原谅我的过错。

注 释

害 [xai⁴]
【瘆人的药莫吃,害人的事儿莫做】瘆人:伤人,毒害人体的。英文释义应为: if the drug is poisonous, do not eat it, if something will hurt others, do not do it.

家 [tɕia¹]
【尸家】指诉讼中被谋杀者(被害人)的家庭。
【家门】家族;同姓的亲族。
【这是坐家人户】这是一座家庭住宅。
【他们蛮家】蛮家:粗鲁无礼的人、野蛮人。
【大家攒个劲】大家一起尽力做。

害 7

HAI⁴.

害 人 終 害 己	if you *injure* others, in the end you *injure* [yourself.
瘆 人 的 藥 莫 喫 害 人 的 事 莫 做 }	don't eat poisons, or do things that would *hurt* others.
爲 民 除 害	to benefit the people by suppressing what- [ever is injurious.
他 是 個 禍 害	my son is a great *misfortune*.
有 些 利 害	it is rather *severe*.
我 害 怕 他	I am *afraid* of him.
害 怕 不 得 來	I *fear* he will not come; *perhaps* he will [not come.
害 病	to *contract* a disease.
你 好 不 害 羞 嗎	are you not ashamed?

CHIA¹.

他 在 家 不 在 家	is he at *home*?
囘 天 堂 老 家	to return to the old *home*, i. e., heaven.
家 家 有 長 短 戶 戶 有 高 低 }	every *household* has good points and shortcomings.
一 家 人	one *family*.
尸 家	the *family* of a murdered person (in a [law-suit).
家 鄉 地 方	one's *native* place.
家 門	relatives of the same surname.
家 底 子 勉 强 過 得	their *family* is passably well off.
家 人	*domestic* servants.
家 法	*family* regulations; the bamboo stick, [the rod.
上 親 家 門	to visit the parents-in-law of one's child.
這 是 坐 家 人 戶	this is a dwelling house.
出 家 人	priests and nuns.
男 有 室 女 有 家	men have wives and women have hus- [bands.
我 有 個 家 裏	I have a *wife*.
自 家 的 事	my *own* affair (an affix denoting persons).
我 的 寃 家	my enemy.
他 們 蠻 家	the barbarians.
男 女 兩 家 門 戶 相 當 }	the man's family and the woman's are on terms of equality.
大 家 趲 個 勵	let *us all* put forth an effort.
道 家	the Taoist *religion*; the Taoist *priesthood*.

(139)

宮 宵 宰 宴 容 寄

7-8

天下國家	the *countries* of the world.
猫兒喂家了	the cat is *tamed*, or domesticated.

KONG¹.

宮殿	a *palace*.
子宮	the *womb*.

SIAO¹.

鬧元宵	to enjoy one's self, on the *evening* of the [15th of 1st moon.
今黑了的花宵	to-night is the *night* before their wedding.
耍個通宵	to revel the whole *night* long.

TSAI³.

天上主宰	the *Ruler* of Heaven; God.
宰相	a *Prime Minister*.
宰殺	to *slaughter*; to *butcher* animals.
宰人	to *decapitate* criminals.
宰三合土	to *chop* fresh cement with a knife-like tool.
宰做兩塊	*chop* the silver into two pieces. [shreds.
宰蘿蔔絲	to *chop* or *slice* turnips and carrots into

IEN⁴.

龍門宴	a *feast* given to the new civil and military ["chü-ren."]

IONG².

大度包容	great *forbearance*.
實在難容	very hard to *tolerate*.
人容天不容	men may *tolerate* it, but heaven will not.
放從容點	be more *patient*.
把他太容易了	he has been too *lenient* with him.
看者容易做者難	to look at it is *easy*, but to do it is difficult.
滿臉的笑容	a smiling *countenance*.
面容好看	a beautiful *face*.
容貌端正	an upright *figure*.

CHI⁴.

我在親朋家寄居	I am *lodging* at the house of a friend.
我的東西寄放在成都省	my things are *left* at Ch'en-tu.
寄賣貨物	to *deposit* goods with another to be sold.
寄錢不寄失	*deposited* money may not be lost.

(140)

注 釋

宮 [koŋ¹]
宵 [siao¹]
【今黑了的花宵】今黑:今晚。花宵:结婚的前一天晚上。当晚新郎的至亲要提前来祝贺,新郎要在家里招待至亲及邻里。
宰 [tsai³]
【宰萝卜丝】将胡萝卜或大头菜切成丝。
宴 [ien⁴]
容 [ioŋ²]
寄 [tɕi⁴]

注释

寇（寇）[kʰəu⁴]
密 [mi⁵]
宁（宁）[lin²] [ŋin²]
【已宁再等他一阵】已宁：宁可，宁愿。
【宁绸】丝织品。蚕丝织成，有明显斜纹，绸面平挺，质地结实。织造前预先染色，有素织和花织两类。适于做服装用。因产于南京，故名。
宿 [sio⁵]
寂 [tsie⁵]

山 8

寇 K'EO⁴.

寄生	shrub-like *parasites* on trees.
寄一封信	*send* a letter.
贼寇	*robbers*.
当草寇大王	to become a leader of *highwaymen*.
成了仇寇	they have become *enemies*.

密 MI⁵.

布织得密	the cloth is *finely* woven.
缝密实点	sew it with a *smaller* stitch.
炉桥子要密	make the fire bars *close together*.
密密的包裹	wrap it up *tightly*.
下密密子的雨	*fine, close* rain; a drizzle.
隐密	*secret*.
国家的机密大事	the *hidden* springs of the state.
密室里静坐	keep yourself in a *quiet* room.
二人亲密得很	the two men are very *intimate*.

宁 LIN².

人虽劳苦心是安宁的	although my life is toilsome, my heart is *at peace*.
宁可我饶人莫叫人饶我	I'd *rather* others' faults forgive, than that I others' grace should crave.
已宁再等他一阵	*rather* wait for him a little longer.

READ NIN², LIN².

| 宁绸 | *twilled* silk. |

宿 SIO⁵.

未晚先投宿鸡鸣早看天	put up at your *inn* before night, and rise at cock-crow.
借宿一夜	may I *lodge* with you for the night.
宿冤未报	our *long-standing* wrong is not avenged.
今晚上星宿子明亮	the *stars* are bright to-night.

寂 TSIE⁵.

| 寂寂静静的 | *still; silent*. |

(141)

8-11

ÜEN¹.

遭了冤枉	I have suffered *wrong*.
大老爺伸冤	redress my *grievance*, Your Honour!
冤家宜解不宜結	*enemies* ought to be reconciled.
前世的冤孽	*retribution* for deeds done in a former life.
冤冤枉枉的使些錢	to *needlessly* spend money; to lose on a bargain.

FU⁴.

家業富豪	the family is *wealthy*.
貧不舍命富不舍財	the poor begrudge their lives, and the *rich* their wealth.
學富五車	*very* learned, having swallowed five cart-loads of books.
年富力强	*young* and strong.
身體豐富	*fat* in body.

HAN².

天氣寒冷	the weather is *cold*.
寒暑表	a thermometer.
打寒戰	to have a *cold* shiver.
傷寒病	to catch *cold*.
施寒衣	to give away *winter* clothing.
家業貧寒	the family is *poor*.
地方苦寒	the place is *desolate*, the district is *poor*.
寒士	a *poor* scholar.
離寒舍不遠	not far from my *poor* dwelling.
我實在寒心	I am very *grieved*.

ME⁴.

夢寐無知	ignorant; lit. *sleeping*.

Ü⁴.

貴寓在何處	where is your *lodging*?

CH'A⁵.

自己省察	*examine* yourself.
下細審察	to carefully *investigate*.
察出實情	*search out* the real state of the case.

(142)

注释

冤（寃）[yen¹]
富[fu⁴]
【身体丰富】身体肥胖。
寒[xan²]
寐[mei⁴]
【梦寐无知】同"蒙昧无知"。
寓[y⁴]
察[tsʰa⁵]

注 释

寞 [mo⁵]
寨 [tṣai⁴]
寡 [kua³]
【寡公子】鳏夫，即妻子死后未再结婚的男人。
【称孤道寡】孤、寡：古代王侯的自称。指自封为王。也比喻狂妄地以首领自居。
實（实）[ṣɿ⁵]
【实字眼】具体的、有实在意义的词语。
寢（寝）[tsʰin³]
寬（宽）[kʰuan¹]
【他走得宽】他见多识广。

山 11-12

寞 MO⁵.

| 寂寞得很 | very *lonely*. |

寨 CHAI⁴.

營寨	*barracks*.
搬寨子	to remove to a *hill-fort* in time of danger.
鹿角寨	*cheval-de-frise*.

寡 KUA³.

多寡不一	whether many or *few* (*much* or *little*) is [not certain.
寡婦守寡	the *widow* continues to live in *widowhood*.
寡公子	a *widower*.
寡蛋	an *addled* egg.
稱孤道寡	you style yourself *king* of the castle (ku and kua are used by the Emperor).
好道好寡是少得很	it is fairly good, *but* it is very scarce.
寡淡的	*quite* insipid.

實 SHÏ⁵.

有名無實	having a name without the *reality*.
其實不與我相干	it *really* has nothing to do with me.
實在的事	a *fact*.
說你的實價	state the *actual* price.
老實人說老實話	*honest* men speak the *truth*.
打聽虛實	inquire whether it is false or *true*.
實字眼	a *concrete* word.
這個布結實	this cloth is *strong*.
裝的滿滿實在	it is filled *quite* full.

寢 TS'IN³.

| 我們安寢 | let us *retire* to rest. |
| 廢寢忘餐 | to lose *sleep* and forget to eat. |

寬 K'UAN¹.

移窄就寬	to remove to a more *spacious* place.
他走得寬	he has travelled *widely*.
寬田寬地不如寬量爲人	*wide* fields and *broad* lands, are not to be compared to *magnanimity* of character.

(143)

12-17

寬	寬幾天	*forbear* for a few days.
	寬貸	to *extenuate*.
	你好寬的心	how *easy* you take things.
	請寬章	please *put off* your dress clothes.

SHEN³.

審	審案	to *try* a case.
	審判	to *judge*.
	審的確	to *investigate* thoroughly.
	審聲音	to *discriminate* between voices or musical notes.
	承審官	a *judge*.
	發審局	a *judgment* hall for trying special cases.
	秋審	the autumn *assizes*.

LIAO².

寮	寮房	priests' bedrooms in a temple; lit. comrade's rooms.

SIE³.

寫	他的字寫得好	he *writes* well.
	出名的寫家	a famous *scribe*.
	寫小照	to *sketch* a portrait.
	寫生妙手	clever at *drawing*.
	寫本子書	a *manuscript* book.
	寫房子	to *rent* a house.
	寫挑子	to *hire* coolies.

CH'ONG³.

寵	恩寵	*grace*.
	寵愛	to *love much*.
	納寵	to take a *concubine*.

PAO³.

寶	寶貝	*precious*; valuables.
	寶石	*gems*; jewels.
	珍寶	*pearls*.
	坐在寶坐上	to sit upon the *throne*.
	染得寶色	it is dyed a *good* colour.
	寶號那一天大發	when do you open your *honourable* shop?
	狗寶	dog's *bezoar*.
	一個大寶	a 50 oz. *ingot* of silver.

注释

【请宽章】请宽衣。
審（审）[ʂən³]
【审的确】即彻底调查，追查到底。
寮 [liao²]
【寮房】寺庙中的僧舍。
寫（写）[sie³]
【写挑子】写：租，雇佣。雇佣一个苦力帮助搬运重物。
寵（宠）[tʂʰoŋ³]
寶（宝）[pao³]
【一个大宝】大宝：常称元宝，为状似中国鞋子的金锭或银锭，通常是银锭。旧时在中国当作货币使用。金元宝重五两或十两，银元宝一般重五十两。

注释

寸 [tsʰən⁴] [tsʰuən⁴]
【方寸地】①一平方寸大小的地方,常比喻地方狭小。②心神,心思,心绪。

寺 [sɿ⁴]

封 [foŋ¹]
【收封and放封】现用"收风"和"放风"。收风:指犯人放风后返回牢房。放风:监狱里定时放犯人到牢房外活动。
【七月半烧包封】农历七月十五日是传统的鬼节,四川当地的习俗是将纸钱一叠封成小封,上面写着收受人的称呼和姓名、收受的封数,在屋外焚化。

寸 3-6

The 41st radical. (寸)

TS'EN⁴, TS'UEN⁴.

十寸爲一尺	ten *inches* make one foot.
好大的寸尺	what is the *measurement*?
方寸地	the heart; lit. the square *inch* place.

一寸光陰一寸金
寸金難買寸光陰
失去寸金容易找
失郤光陰難再尋
	A *little* time—an *inch* of gold:
	  For gold the time could ne'er be sold.
	Gold may be lost and found again,
	  But for lost time we search in vain.

SĬ⁴.

| 昭覺寺 | The *monastery* of Refulgent Intelligence |
| 清真寺 | The *mosque* of Pure Truth (a general name for mosques). |

FONG¹.

封官	to *appoint* an official.
封神	to *deify* a person.
封瘡口	to *cover up* a sore; to heal up a sore.
穀子封了林	the rice has *hidden* the water, i.e., it is luxuriant.
封火牆子	a stone or brick fire-wall at the end of a house.
罈子口封得倒 人口封不倒	a jar's mouth may be *stopped up*, but a man's mouth cannot.
封皮	a stamped official paper used to *seal up* doors, boxes, etc.
把信口子封了	*close* the letter.
把他的煙館子封了	the magistrate *closed* his opium den.
收封 and 放封	to put prisoners back into the cells at night, and let them out again in the morning.
封印	to *close* the law-court before the New Year.
封門的雨	a heavy rain which keeps everybody indoors.
封個禮封封	*wrap* up a *present of money*.
七月半燒包封	to burn *packets* of cash paper to ancestors on the 15th of 7th moon.

(145)

寸 6-8

	一封銀子	a *parcel* of silver; 50 oz. of silver. (*N. A.*)
	一封點心	a *packet* of cakes (*N. A.*)
	帶一封信	carry a letter. (*N. A.*)

7 尅 K'E⁵.

	[to the wife.
八字硬有些尅妻	the horoscope is hard, and rather *inimical*

射 SHE⁴.

射箭	to *shoot* arrows.
使冷箭射人	to *back-bite*; to *slander*.
射利之徒	a *scheming* villain.
太陽的光射進來	the rays of the sun *shoot* into the room.

8 專 CHUAN¹.

專心讀書	*devoted* to study.
專的差來	sent *specially*.
專意來的	come on *purpose*.
專門痘科	to make a *speciality* of vaccination.
今年敎的專館	I am teaching a *private* school this year; tutor to a family.
專權舞弊	to *assume* power and work mischief.
不敢自專	I dare not *presume*.

將 TSIANG¹.

將來的事	*future* events.
將近要起身了	we will start *immediately*.
將亮的時候	*near* daylight in the morning.
將就他就是	*conform* to him, that's all; *accommodate* yourself to him.
將就那個木頭用	make it *according to* the wood.
兩將就	the article has two *uses*.
將就過日子	*just managing* to make both ends meet; living from hand to mouth.
將將合式	*just* right, nothing to spare; it will *just* do.
將軍	a Tartar *general*.

READ TSIANG⁴.

	[him; like leader, like men.
強將手裏無弱兵	a strong *leader* has no weak soldier under

(146)

注　釋

尅（克）[kʰe⁵]
射[ʂei⁴]
【射利之徒】谋取财利的人。
專（专）[tṣuan¹]
【专的差来】专门派来。
將（将）[tsiaŋ¹] [tsiaŋ⁴]

注 释

尋(寻) [çyn²] [çin²]
尊 [tsən¹]
對(对) [tuei⁴]

【对襟的马褂】对襟：中装上衣的一种式样。因两襟对开，纽扣在胸前正中，故称。马褂：旧时男子穿在长袍外面的对襟的短褂。以黑色为最普通。原为满族人骑马时所穿的衣服。

【对读】同"校对"。

【你怎么对得住人】英文释义应为：Won't you feel guilty to others?

【小菜对长】蔬菜的价钱翻倍。

【对程钱】钱的一半来路正，另一半来路不正。

【一个对月】两个月。

寸 9-11

9 尋 SHÜIN², SHIN².

找尋	to *seek* for.
尋短路	to commit suicide ; lit. to *seek* a short road.
山中易找千年樹 世上難尋百歲人	Trees that have braved a thousand years, May ou the hills be found, A centenarian who can *find* In all the wide world round ?
尋常人	*ordinary* people.

尊 TSEN¹.

尊敬人	to *honour* people.
閣下尊姓	what is your *honourable* name, Sir ?
尊貴的人	a *noble* person.
尊駕幾時來的	when did you come, *Sir* ?
令尊大人好嗎	is your good *father* well ?
一尊大砲	one cannon. (*N. A.*)

11 對 TUE⁴.

對門子	the *opposite* house.
對襟的禡褂	a riding jacket that buttons down the front.
拿來對筆跡	*compare* the handwriting.
對讀	to correct a copy by the original ; to read proofs.
你怎麼對得住人	how can you *face* people ?
你對得實嗎	can you *confront* him with that story ?
我對他說過	I said it *to* him.
對頭	a *match* ; an *enemy*.
對直走	go *straight on*.
寫一副對子	write a couplet on a pair of *scrolls*.
有對合合的利	the profit is *equal to* the original cost ; cent per cent.
小菜對長	vegetables have *doubled* in price.
對程錢	*half and half* cash, i. e., one-half good cash, and the other half bad.
一個對月	a full month from any given date.
買一對雞	buy a *couple* of chickens, buy a *pair* of fowls.
他做事不對	he does things im*properly*.
你說那個話不對	what you say is not *right*.

(147)

寸 11-13 小 1

13 導 TAO⁴.

對不對	will it *do* or not?
引導	to *lead*.
開導他的心	*enlighten* his mind.

The 42nd radical. (小)

小 SIAO³.

大腳拖累小腳	*natural-footed* persons drag *small* (i. e. bound) footed persons off their feet at work.
說大話使小錢	he speaks "big," but he spends *little*.
你有幾個小的	how many *children* have you?
小姐	a *young* unmarried lady.
我小他兩個月	I am two months *younger*.
小名	the *baby* name.
小衣	trousers; pants.
買小菜	to buy vegetables.
小聲說	speak in a *low* voice.
添幾個小錢	add a little *extra* money, i. e., tea-money [to coolies.
那個人小氣	he is very quick-tempered.
放小跑	to walk quickly.
那個屋頭有小神子	there is a *fairy* in that house; that house is haunted.
小婆子	a concubine.
膽欲大而心欲小 智欲圓而行欲方	*courage* should be great and the mind *careful*, knowledge should be perfect and the mind upright.
小家子	a *selfish* fellow.
大人做事不小 小人做事不大	*magnanimous* men do not act *meanly*, *mean* men do not act *liberally*.
一條小路	a *by-way*.
莫背倒人翻少話	don't talk *slander* behind one's back.
水小了	the water has *subsided*; the river has *fallen*.

1 少 SHAO³.

多種多收少種少收	sow much and reap much, sow *little* and reap *little*. 2. Cor. ix. 6.
少人少世界	*few* people and *few* countries! (ironically).

(148)

注 釋

導（导）[tao⁴]

小 [siao³]

【小衣】内裤，裤子。

【那个屋头有小神子】那个屋子里闹鬼；那个屋子里有神仙。

【小婆子】小老婆，妾，姨太太。

【胆欲大而心欲小，智欲圆而行欲方】心欲小：心思要缜密；智欲圆：指智谋要圆通灵活；行欲方：指行为要方正不苟。做人要气魄宏大，思虑精细，智慧圆融而行为端方。

【莫背倒人翻少话】不要在人的背后造谣中伤。（"少"当为"小"，见803页勘误表。）

少 [ṣao³] [ṣao⁴]

注 释

尖 [tsien¹]
【打尖】行路途中休息一下或吃个便饭。
【把板凳尖紧】用腿把凳子腿用楔子楔紧夹紧。
【这回把我教尖了】尖：伶俐，聪明。

尚 [ṣaŋ⁴]
【尚德不尚力】崇尚道德而不使用武力。

小，1-3

有多少人	how many people? A great many people.
我們少禮	I am *deficient* in politeness; I have not brought a present. [it up.
錢少數要補	the cash is *short* count; you must make
他少到我這裏來	he *seldom* comes here.
這個錢是我少欠他的	I *owe* him this money.
少喫點	eat a little *less*.
少得多不得	you may give *less* but not more.
錢是第一少不得的	money is the in*dispensable* thing.
醜媳婦少不得見公婆	even an ugly daughter-in-law must meet her father and mother-in-law; met., the thing is in*evitable*.
喫少午沒有	have you had your lunch, or dinner?

READ SHAO⁴.

少年人	a *young* man.

3 尖 TSIEN¹.

指尖	the *point* of the finger.
舌尖殺人不見血	the *tip* of the tongue kills without drawing blood. [dictment.
筆尖子	a lawyer's *ability* to write out an in-
樹子尖尖	the *top* of a tree.
鞋尖脚小	the boot is *tapering* and the foot small.
打尖	to take foot; lit. to put in a *wedge*.
竈尖	firewood; lit. stove *wedges*.
把板凳尖緊	*wedge* the stool legs tight.
這回把我敎尖了	being taken in this time has made me *cute*.
他比我還尖	he is *sharper* than I am.
他的耳朶尖	he is *quick* of hearing. [dropping.
尖起耳朶聽	to *prick up* one's ears and listen; eaves-
尖聲尖氣的	to speak with a *shrill* voice.

尚 SHANG⁴.

俗尚奢華	the world *likes* extravagant display.
尚德不尚力	we *esteem* virtuous character, not strength of body. [(Sanscrit).
受戒的和尚	a Buddhist *priest* who has taken orders.

(149)

小 12 尢 3-9

12 殨 TS'AO².
東西用殨了　the thing is *worn out*.
殨成這個樣子　*spoiled* like this!

The 43rd radical. (尢)

尢 IU².
怨天尢人　to *grumble* at Heaven and at one's fellow-men.

3 尥 LIAO².
尥蹶子　to *fling* at; to *kick* against; to *manifest* opposition.
他尥腳尥手的走了　he went off *swinging* his arms and legs, i. e., empty-handed.
尥過去　*throw* it over.
把這個東西拿出去尥了　take this thing and *throw* it away.
尥殼子　a liar; lit. one who *throws* husks.

5 尪 UANG¹.
尪贏做不得活路　*weak* and unable to work.

尨 TSO⁴.
腳有些尨　my foot is a little *crooked*.

9 就 TSIU⁴.
就口的饝饝你都不喫嗎　will you not eat the bread that *comes to* your mouth? Met., will you not seize the opportunity that comes in your way?
事情成就了　the affair is *completed*.
東不成西不就　I am unable to *accomplish* anything in any direction.
你就的那一個的事　for whom are you *working*?
大家將就些　let us all be more *accommodating*.
就來　*just* coming.
就要　I want it *immediately*.
照倒這樣做就好　do it in this way and *then* it will be right.
就是他　it is he; that's the man.
就是了　that's all; very well; all right; just so; let it be so.
就是那個話　just so; quite correct; that's it; just as you say.

(150)

注　释

殨 [tsʰao²]
【東西用殨了】东西用坏了。
【殨成这样子】坏成这个样子。

尢 [iəu²]

尥 [liao⁴]
（LIAO²当为LIAO⁴，见803页勘误表。）
【尥过去】扔过去。
【尥壳子】说谎的人，骗子。

尪（尪）[uaŋ¹]
【尪贏做不得活路】指虚弱而无法干活。

尨 [tso⁴]
【脚有点尨】脚有点跛。

就 [tsiəu⁴]
【照倒这样做就好】照倒：按照。

注 释

尸 [ṣɿ¹]
【扎个尸位】尸：是古代祭礼中的一个代表神像端坐着看而不需要做任何动作的人。尸位：指占着职位却不做事。
【三尸神】道家称在人体内作祟的神有三，称为"三尸"或"三尸神"，每到庚申日便向天帝呈奏人的过恶。

尺 [tṣʰɿ⁵]
【过得倒夹尺】经受得住考验。

尼 [ȵi²]

局 [tɕy⁵]

尿 [ȵiao⁴]

屁 [pʰi⁴]
【打屁】放屁。

尸 1-4

The 44th radical. (尸)

尸

SHÏ¹.

| 扎個尸位 | make an effigy of the *corpse*. |
| 三尸神 | three spirits in the *body* of a man who report his deeds when he is asleep. |

1 尺

CH'Ï⁵.

得尺進丈	give him one *foot* and he will take ten.
拐子尺	a *cubit*.
舉頭三尺有神明	the gods are three *feet* above our heads.
魯班尺	the carpenter's *foot-rule*.
曲尺	a carpenter's *square*. [the *gauge*?]
過得倒夾尺	can you stand the test? lit. can you pass
弓尺	the *bow-foot*, a land measure.
丈尺	*measurement*.
尺寸不够	the *measurement* is short.

2 尼

NI².

| 尼姑菴 | a *nunnery*. |

4 局

CHÜ⁵.

好個格局	what a fine *appearance*! [*undertaking*.
要把大局面顧倒	we must keep up the reputation of the
局外不知局內事	outsiders don't know the internal affairs of the *business*.
搗成騙局	to plan a *trick* to deceive or rob.
怎樣結局	what will be the *outcome*, or *result*, of it?
電報局	a *telegraph office*.
寶川局	the Sï-ch'nau *mint*.
火藥局	a *gunpowder factory*.

尿

NIAO⁴.

| 尿水 | *urine*. |
| 屙尿 | to *urinate*. |

屁

P'I⁴.

| 打屁 | to break *wind*. [*ment*. |
| 打屁股 | to beat on the buttocks, a form of punish- |

(151)

尸 4-5

尾 UE³, I³.

打屁虫	the stinking insect ; a kind of beetle eaten as food in some places.
狗夾起尾巴跑	the dog has run off with its *tail* between its legs. [make *head* or *tail* of it.
摸不倒頭尾	I can't tell beginning from *end* ; I can't.
船尾	the *stern* of a boat.
做到漏尾來	we have come to the *end* of the job.
年尾	the *close* of the year.
還有些首尾	you have still a little debt.
火尾子高	the *flames* were high.
尾子	a *weasel*.
幾尾魚	a few fishes. (*N. A.*)

居 CHÜ¹.

居住	to *dwell*.
居處	a *dwelling* place.
坐居在那裏	where is your *house*, *home*, or *abode*?
分居了	brothers dividing the estate and living in separate *houses*.
結得鄰居好 甚當檢個寶	to have good *neighbours* is like finding precious things.
貧居鬧市無人問 富在深山有遠親	no one asks for the poor man, though he *live* in the market place, but the rich is sought after, though he dwell among the hills.
居孀	to *be* a widow ; to *abide* in widowhood.
官居何職	what office do you { *hold*? *fill*?
居心不要	*determined* not to have it.
弄居一了	arranged ; ready ; finished ; settled.
大居士	a Buddhist devotee (male).
二居士	a Buddhist devotee (female).

屈 CH'Ü⁵, CH'IO⁵.

屈指難數	more than could be counted on the fingers by *bending* them. [is hard.
屈身容易屈心難	to *stoop* the body is easy, to *bend* the will
冤屈	a *wrong*.

注釋

尾[uei³] [i³]

【做到漏尾来】漏尾：收尾。

【尾子】鼬鼠，黄鼠狼。

居[tɕy¹]

【居心不要】居心：下定决心。

【弄居一了】整理好了；准备好了；完成了；解决了。

屈[tɕʰy⁵] [tɕʰio⁵]

注 释

屄 [pʰi¹]
屜 [tʰi⁴]
屍（尸）[ʂʅ¹]
屎 [ʂʅ³]
【推屎爬】蜣螂，俗称屎壳郎。
屌 [tiao³]
屋 [u⁵] [o⁵]
展 [tsan³]
【把衣服熨伸展】用熨斗把衣服熨平。
屌 [tɕʰiəu²]
屑 [sio⁵] [ɕye⁵]
【疯屑】头皮屑。
屙 [o¹]
【屙红白】痢疾。
【肚皮屙】腹泻。

尸 5-8

	P'I¹.	the *vagina*; a word commonly used in cursing.
	T'I⁴.	
鞍屜子		a *saddle-cloth*.
抽屜		a *drawer*.
	SHI¹.	
一副死屍		a *corpse*.
大老爺要來驗屍		the magistrate will come and hold an inquest on the *body*.
	SHI³.	
推屎爬		the *dung* beetle.
屙屎		to evacuate the bowels.
摳鼻甲屎噢的		he would pick the *scabs* off his nose and eat them; disgustingly covetous.
眼屎		*secretions* on the eye-lids.
	TIAO³.	the *penis*.
	U⁵, O⁵.	
房屋田地		*buildings* and fields.
把屋頭掃乾淨		sweep the *house* clean.
我的屋裏		my wife.
親房親屋的弟兄		cousins of the same surname.
	CHAN³.	
把書展開		*open* the book.
把衣服熨伸展		iron the clothes out *smooth*.
鬧不伸展		they cannot *settle* their dispute; lit. *straighten* it out.
心裏舒展		*cheerful* in mind.
	CH'IU².	the *penis*; a word commonly used in cursing.
	SIO⁵, SHÜE⁵.	
鋸木屑		saw-*dust*.
瘋屑		*scurf* on the head.
不屑與他共事		don't *condescend* to act in partnership with him.
	O¹.	
屙紅白		to *pass* blood and mucus; dysentery.
肚皮屙		*diarrhoea*.

(153)

尸 8-18 屮 1

	P'IN².	
屏	屏風	a movable wooden *door-screen*.
	花屏	small ornamental *screens* made of glass, stone or metal.
9	一副屏	a set of 4 or 8 scrolls.
屠	T'U².	
	屠夫	a *butcher*. [count of drought.
11	天乾斷屠	to stop the *slaughter* of animals on ac-
屢	LUE³.	
	我屢次帮你的忙	I *frequently* helped you.
12	屢屢的不聽話	you *constantly* disobey me.
履	LÜ³.	
	夫子履	a gentleman's *shoe*.
	把你的履歷說給我聽	tell me your *antecedents*.
層	TS'EN².	
	兩層石頭	two *layers* of stone.
	兩層高	two *storeys* high. [larly.
	做的有層有次的	done in *sections*, or *gradations*, done regu-
	說話有層次	he speaks with *divisions*, or *heads*.
18		
屬	SHU⁵, SHO⁵.	[me.
	這個地方屬我管	the government of this place *pertains* to
	成都府十六屬	Ch'ên-tu Prefecture contains 16 *depend-ent* districts.
	既屬相好不說套話	we *are* intimate, so may dispense with ceremony.

The 45th radical. (屮)

1	T'EN².	[as in W. Sĭ-ch'uan.
屯	屯兵	military colonists *settled* on the borders
	屯糧食	to *store up* grain.

(154)

注 释

屏 [pʰin²]
【花屏】有雕绘、装饰的屏风。
屠 [tʰu²]
【天干断屠】因为天气干旱而停止了杀戮动物。
屢（屡）[luei³]
履 [ly³]
【夫子履】举止高雅的绅士的鞋子。
層（层）[tsʰən²]
屬（属）[ʂu⁵] [ʂo⁵]
屯 [tʰən²]

注 释

山 [ṣan¹]
【上山】①登山。②埋葬死者。
【官山】公用的坟地。
【浅山】低矮的山。
岔 [tṣʰa⁴]
岸 [ŋan⁴]
【穷奔口岸富奔乡】也作"穷奔码头富奔乡"。意为穷人去人口集中的码头集市求生存,富人去乡下生活。
岫 [siəu⁴]
岳 [io⁵]
峡(峽) [ɕia⁵]
（SHIA¹当为SHIA⁵,见803页勘误表。）
峩(峨) [o²]
島(岛) [tao³]

山 4-5

The 46th radical. (山)

SHAN¹.

上山	to ascend a *mountain*; to bury a person.
上墳山	to visit the *burial-ground*.
官山	a public *graveyard*.
淺山	low *hills*.
這個地方山水好	the *scenery* of this place is fine.
山長老師	principal of the county academy (from the name of the place where Confucius taught).
石山	*stalactites* used in building *rockwork* in [gardens.

CH'A⁴.

| 來到三岔路　須問去來人 } | when you come to *divergent* paths, you must ask the passers-by to direct you. |
| 打岔 | to *change* the subject of conversation. |

NGAN⁴.

把船撐攏岸	pole the boat to the *bank*.
上岸	to go on *shore*. [the rich to the country.
窮逩口岸富逩鄉	the poor go to the *markets*—to live, and

SIU⁴.

| 流水下灘非有意　白雲出岫本無心 } | Without a thought the waters flow Along the river bed. Forth from the *hills* the white clouds go, By no fixed purpose led. |

IO⁵.

| 岳父岳母 | *wife's parents*. |

SHIA¹.

| 船進峽口 | the boat has entered the *gorge*. |

O².

| 峩嵋山 | Mount "*O-me*", west of Chia-tin Fu, Sï-[ch'uan. |

TAO³.

| 海島 | an *island* in the sea. |

(155)

山 8-20 川.

8 崎 CH'I².
山路崎嶇   the mountain roads are *precipitous* or [*dangerous*.

崩 PEN¹.
砲震得山崩地裂   the cannon roars as if it would make the [mountains *fall* and the earth rend.
同治皇崩駕   when the Emperor T'ong-chï *died*.
紅崩   *flooding* in childbirth.

9 嵐 LAN².
嵐炭   *coke*.

嵋 ME², MI².
   for example of use see 峩.

崽 TSAI³.
崽崽   a *child*; the *young* of animals.
狗下了崽崽   the dog has *pups*.

嵌 K'AN¹.
嵌玻璃   to *glaze* a window.
嵌珊瑚珠   to *set* with coral.

11 嶇 CH'Ü¹.
   for example of use see 崎.

14 嶺 LIN³.
大山嶺   great mountain *ranges*.
嶺岡   a mountain *ridge*.
娘子嶺   the Empress *Pass*, near Kuan-shien, Sï-[ch'uan.

嶽 IO⁵.
東嶽治生南嶽治死   the Eastern *Peak* rules life, the Southern *Peak* rules death.

20 巖 NGAI².
山巖   a *precipice*.
巖口   a defile between two *cliffs*.
巖洞   a cave in the *rock*.
巖鷹不打窩下食   the eagle does not kill the things that live [near its eyrie.
乳巖   a mammary *abscess*.

The 47th radical. (川)

川 CH'UAN¹.
四川省   the province of the Four *Streams*.
川流不息的人來   there is a constant *stream* of people com-[ing.

(156)

注　释

崎 [tɕʰi²]
崩 [pən¹]
【红崩】女性大出血称为"红崩"，一般发生在经期或孩子出生时。
嵐（岚）[lan²]
【岚炭】焦煤，焦炭。
嵋 [mei²] [mi²]
崽 [tsai³]
嵌 [kʰan¹]
嶇（岖）[tɕʰy¹]
嶺（岭）[lin³]
【岭冈】山脊。
嶽（岳）[io⁵]
巖（岩）[ŋai²]
【乳岩】乳头溃疡。
川 [tʂʰuan¹]

注释

州 [tʂəu¹]
巡 [syn²]
【巡风】来回侦望监视。
工 [koŋ¹]
左 [tso³]
【我们两个打左】打左：交换。
【左合要回去】左合：一定，必须。
【那是个左性子人】左性子人：倔强的人。
巨 [tɕy⁴]
巧 [tɕiao³]

川 3-4 工 2

州

CHEO¹.

直隸州	an independent *department*, like a "Fu."
單州	a *district*, like a "Shien."
萬國九州	the myriad states and the nine *divisions* of ancient China; met., all the world.

SÜIN².

巡查	to *patrol*; a *patrolling* detective.
巡風	a *spy* (in the Ko-lao-hue.)
巡撫	the Governor of a Province (as Kue-cheo.)

The 48th radical. (工)

KONG¹.

工夫做完了	the *work* is finished.
拜年酒鍾換鍾 / 栽秧打穀工換工	feast for feast at New Year, and *labour* for *labour* at seed-time and harvest.
做了七個工	I have done seven *days' work*.
工匠	an artisan.
工人	a labourer.
開工錢	to pay wages for *labour*.
我沒工本	I have no *capital*.

TSO³.

左手	the *left* hand.
我們兩個打左	let us *change*, or *swap*.
左合要回去	I *must* return.
那是個左性子人	he is a *perverse* fellow.

CHÜ⁴.

| 他是個巨富 | he is a *very* wealthy man. |

CHIAO³.

巧手匠人	a *skilful* workman.
那個女人手面子巧	that woman is *dexterous* at needlework, etc.
他說話做事都靈巧	he is *clever* both at speaking and working.

(157)

工 2-4 己 1

	這個鍾表做得巧	this clock is *ingeniously* made.
	乖巧	*crafty*.
	你來得湊巧	you have come *opportunely*; you are just [in the nick of time.
	輕輕巧巧的	very *light*.

巫 U¹.

巫師	a *wizard*; a *sorcerer*.
巫山峽	the *U*-shan gorges on the *Iang-tsï* west [of *K'ne-fu*.

差 CH'A¹.

一點都差錯不得	there must not be the slightest *mistake*.
差之毫釐失之千里	a small *error* may lead to a great discrepancy.
差不多	not far *wrong*; almost right; nearly.

READ CH'AI¹.

告錯了有原告差錯了有官	if you are wrongly accused, there is your accuser, and if we are wrongly *sent*, there is the magistrate (said by policemen).
差人	official *messengers*; policemen.
當差事	to go on government business.
欽差大臣	an Imperial *commissioner*, an *ambassador*.

The 49th radical. (己)

己 CHI³.

我自己做的	I did it my*self*.
他自己的錢	his *own* money.

巳 I³.

不得巳	no help for it; inevitable; lit., unable to [have *done* with it.
這個事情是可巳而巳的	this affair may be *set aside*; unimportant.
巳經過去的事不要再說	don't mention what is *already* past.
巳後不要再做錯	don't do wrong *hereafter*.

巴 PA¹.

巴心巴肝的朋友	a friend that *sticks* close to one's heart.
巴樹子	to *climb* trees.

(158)

注 釋

巫 [u¹]
差 [tʂha¹] [tʂhai¹]
己 [tɕi³]
巳 [i³]

【这个事情是可巳而巳的】
可巳而巳：可以置之
一旁，不重要。

【巳后不要再做错】巳后：
以后，将来。

巴 [pa¹]

【巴心巴肝的朋友】巴心
巴肝：全心全意，忠
诚地。

【巴树子】爬树。

注释

【巴劝世文】张贴传单。
【把烟巴然】把烟管里的烟吸燃。
【做得巴式】做工考究的。
【嘴巴巴的】亲密的，熟悉的。
【百巴钱】约一百块钱。
巷 [xaŋ⁴]
巾 [tɕin¹]
布 [pu⁴]

己 1-6 · 巾 2

巴勸世文	to *post* tracts.
巴倒牆邊	*near by* the side of the wall.
巴壁燈	a lamp *fixed* against the wall.
我不巴結人	I don't *toady* upon people.
把菸巴然	*suck* the pipe alight.
做得巴式	well made; lit., *after* the pattern.
補個巴	put on a *patch*.
鍋巴	the *crust* of rice off the pot.
打鹽巴	buy a *lump* of salt.
泥巴	mud; *clods*; soil.
嘴巴	the lips.
嘴巴巴的	very intimate; fulsomely familiar.
巴不幸得	would that it were so!
巴豆	croton.
百巴錢	*about* a hundred cash.
打你幾個耳巴子	I will box your ears; I will give you a few slaps on the ear.
打他幾巴掌	beat him a few slaps. (*N. A.*)

6 巷 HANG⁴.

珠市巷	Bead Market *Lane*.
倒街臥巷	to tumble in the streets and sleep in the alleys; drunk.
花街柳巷	places of ill fame; brothels.

The 50th radical. (巾)

巾 CHIN¹.

手巾	a *handkerchief*.

2 布 PU⁴.

本地布	native *calico*.
粗茶淡飯喫得飽 粗布棉衣穿到老	though food be plain, yet one may be satisfied; though the *cloth* be coarse, yet one may be clad even to old age.
竹布	foreign *linen*.
夏布	*grass-cloth*.
口袋麻布	*sackcloth*.
絲瓜布	the *fibre* of Luffa Cylindrica dried and [used as a dishcloth.

巾. 2-5

市

| 布政司 | the Provincial Treasurer (so called because he *dispenses* the funds). |

SHÏ⁴.

米市	the rice *market*.
高抬市價	to raise the *market* price.
市口	prices.
今天米是甚麼行市	what is the *price* of rice to-day?

3 帆 FAN¹.

| 帆篷 | the *sail* of a boat. |

4 希 SHI¹.

[till 70.
人生七十古來希	from ancient times *few* men have lived
看希奇	to see *strange* things.
希罕你	you are a *rarity* indeed!
不要希圖人家的	don't *covet* the things of others.

5 帕 P'A⁴.

搭膴壳帕	a *kerchief*.
網膴壳帕	a *turban*.
露水帕	a bride's *veil*.
洗臉帕	a *cloth* for washing the face.
洗澡帕	a *towel*.
洗碗帕	a *dishcloth*.

帛 PE⁵.

| 財帛 | *wealth*. |

帔 P'E¹.

[ladies.
| 帔肩 | an embroidered *cape* worn by officials and |
| 椅帔 | a *tidy*; an *antimacassar*. |

帖 TIE⁵, T'IE⁵.

下帖子	to send an invitation *card*.
禀帖	a *statement* to an official; a petition.
白頭帖子	an anonymous *placard*.
換帖	to exchange *cards* on entering into a covenant of brotherhood.

(160)

注　释

市[ʂʅ⁴]
【市口】指销路。
帆（帆）[fan¹]
希[ɕi¹]
【不要希图人家的】希图：贪图、图谋，希望达到某种目的(多指不好的)。
帕[pʰa⁴]
【露水帕】土家族新婚的姑娘从轿中被迎亲婆接出，脸上蒙着丝绸帕，称为"露水帕"。
帛[pe⁵]
帔[pʰe¹]
帖[tie⁵][tʰie⁵]
【禀帖】旧时老百姓向官府或官员向上司报告、请示的帖子。
【白头帖子】匿名信；不具名的招帖、海报。

注释

【弄俞帖了】安排好、安顿好，完成。
帝 [ti⁴]
帥（帅）[ṣuai⁴]
帮 [paŋ¹]
【我给你帮补点】我补贴点钱给你。
【大帮信】邮局。
師（师）[sɿ¹]
席 [si⁵]
帳（帐）[tṣaŋ⁴]

巾 5-8

	傳 帖	the servant who carries the *card* case.
	字 帖	a writing *copy*, usually a rubbing from a stone.
	事 情 不 妥 帖	the affair is not *stable* or secure.
	弄 俞 帖 了	*arranged*; *finished*; *settled*.

6 帝 TI⁴.

皇 帝	an *emperor*.
玉 皇 大 帝	the Great *Ruler*; the Pearly Emperor.

SHUAI⁴.

元 帥	a *general*.

7 帮 PANG¹.

請 你 帮 個 忙	please *help* me a little.
大 家 帮 助	let us all *assist*.
我 給 你 帮 補 點	I will *aid* you with a little money.
找 個 帮 手	find a *helper*.
帮 人 的	a *servant*. [van.
一 帮 生 意 人	a *company* of travelling traders; a cara-
一 帮 船	a *flotilla* of boats.
大 帮 信	a general *post office*.
白 菜 帮 帮	the *midrib* of a cabbage leaf.

SĪ¹.

老 師	a *schoolmaster*; Sir.
師 母	the wife of a scholar. [Teacher.
天 地 君 親 師	Heaven, Earth, Prince, Parents, and
師 爺	an official *secretary*.
張 師	*Mr.* Chang (said to a *workman*).
師 娘 子	a *sorceress*; a *witch*.

SI⁵.

擺 酒 席	to spread a *feast*.

8 CHANG⁴.

一 床 帳 子	a set of *bed-curtains*.
搭 個 帳 篷	put up a *tent*, or a *mat-shed*.
老 師 今 年 在 那 裏 設 帳	where have you opened *school* this year, Sir?

(161)

西蜀方言

巾 8

常			
	你纔混帳	you are *stupid* indeed !	
	SHANG².		
	時常	*constantly*.	
	常常記得這個話	*always* remember this.	
	平常的人	*ordinary* people.	
帶	家常飯	our *usual* food ; pot-luck.	
	TAI⁴.		
	腰帶	a *girdle*.	
	緊鬆帶	au elastic *belt*.	
	脚帶	foot *bands*, used by women for binding [their feet.	
	雞腸帶	*tape*.	
	飄帶	hat *strings*.	
	海帶	a kind of *seaweed* used as food.	
	馬肚帶	a horse's *girth*.	
	一帶地方	a *region* or *tract* of country.	
	白帶	leucorrhœa.	
	帶信	to *carry* a letter.	
	帶他一路	*take* him *with* you. [with you ?	
	帶家眷沒有	have you *brought* your wife and family	
	我那天帶了點酒	I had *taken* a little wine that day.	
	天帶黃色有雨 人帶黃色有病	when the sky *bears* a yellow colour, there will be rain ; when a man *has* a sallow complexion, he is sick.	
	搭帶頭	to give bones with the meat to purchasers.	
	說話帶欛子	his speech is interlarded with oaths.	
	找個人給我帶路	find some one to *guide* me.	
	帶個頭	to *take* the lead.	
	帶兵	to *lead* troops.	
	一百帶	*more than* one hundred.	
帷	連本帶利	capital and profit ; principal and interest.	
	UE².		
	帷腰	an *apron*.	
	滿襟帷腰	an *apron* with a bib.	
	口水帷帷	a child's *bib*.	
	桌帷	a *curtain* hung in front of a table.	

(162)

注 释

常 [ṣaŋ²]
带 [tai⁴]
【脚带】旧时妇女用于缠足的带子。
【鸡肠带】用皮、布等做成的窄而长的有弹性的带子,常用来绑扎东西。
【搭带头】把带肉的骨头免费送给买肉者。
【说话带把子】话语中有骂人的字眼。把子:咒骂、诅咒的话。
【一百带】一百多。
帷 [uei²]

注 释

幅 [fu⁵]

帽 [mao⁴]

幕 [mo⁴]
- 【幕宾】私人秘书，古时官员手下的谋士和食客。

㡒 [xua⁵]
- 【扯得㡒㡒的响】扯得哗哗地响。
- 【㡒泐泐一乍雷】轰隆隆的一声惊雷。

幢 [tʰoŋ²]
- 【幢子旛】长条旗。

幟 [tsʰien¹]
- 【贴幟子】在学生的书上贴纸条以标明学习过的内容。

干 [kan¹]
- 【我人不相干】不相干：不舒服。
- 【你有干证人没得】干证人：目击者，证人。

巾 9-17 干

9 幅 FU⁵.
八幅的鋪盖	a bed quilt that requires eight *widths* of [cloth to cover it.
一幅菜園	a *plot* of garden-ground.
一幅地理圖	a map. (*N. A.*)
一幅畫兒	a picture. (*N. A.*)

帽 MAO⁴.
瓜皮帽	melon-skin *cap*; the ordinary small *hat*.
紅冬帽	a winter dress-*hat*.
他愛戴高帽子	he loves to wear the high *hat*, i. e., fond of praise.
風帽	a *hood*.
墻高上做個帽帽	put a *coping* on the top of the wall.

11 幕 MO⁴.
幕賓	a private secretary; anciently one who sat in the *tent* of a military officer.

12 㡒 HUA⁵.
扯得㡒㡒的響	to tear cloth with a *ripping* sound.
㡒霳霳一乍雷	a *crashing* peal of thunder.

幢 T'ONG².
幢子旛	*streamers*, carried in idol processions.

17 幟 TS'IEN¹.
貼幟子	to stick a *slip of paper* on a school boy's book to show how much he has learned.

The 51st radical. (干)

干 KAN¹.
動起干戈	to go to *war*; to stir up *strife*.
與我沒相干	no *concern* of mine.
我人不相干	I am unwell.
牙齒不相干	my teeth are useless.
干係大	the *consequences* are great.
他兩個不得干休	they cannot *settle* their dispute.
你有干證人沒得	have you any *witnesses*?
天干地支	the Heavenly *Stems* and the Earthly [*Branches*.
若干人	a great *many* people.

(163)

平 2-3

平 P'IN².

平壩子	a *level* piece of ground.
平陽大壩	a great *plain*.
平常的事	*common* affairs.
床沒有壩平順	the bed is un*even*.
我兩個平半分	we two will divide it *equally*.
平秧田	to *level* the rice seed-field.
平屋基	to *level* a fonndation for a house.
打平夥	to each pay his share of a meal.
平班的弟兄	brothers and cousins of the *same* genera-[tion].
平銀子的平	*scales* for *weighing* silver.
一平銀子	50 *taels* of silver.
天平稱	16 oz. to the pound.
我來給你們平個中	I will act as middleman and *adjust* your differences.
案斷得不公平	the case was not decided *justly*.
人平不語水平不流	when men are *just* none e'er complain, water is still upon a *plain*.
買賣要公平	business must be done *honestly*.
天下太平	the country is in a state of *peace*.
平平安安的過日子	to pass one's days *tranquilly*.
平時不燒香急時抱佛脚	at *ordinary* times you don't burn incense, but when in distress you embrace the feet of Buddha.
平空捏造的話	a trumped up story.
平生	one's *whole* life.

年 NIEN¹.

今年年成好	the *harvest* is good this *year*.
年年防天乾夜夜防賊盜	*yearly* provide against drought, and nightly beware of thieves.
大年 and 小年	the 1st and 15th of 1st moon.
幫長年	servants engaged for a long term.
好大的年紀	what is your *age*?
他年輕得很	he is very young.

(164)

注 釋

平 [pʰin²]

【平壩子】西南地区常称平地或平原为"坝子"。

【床没有坝平顺】床没有弄平。

【打平伙】聚餐后各付各的账。英文释义应为：to go dutch.

【平班的弟兄】同一辈分的堂兄弟姊妹或表兄弟姊妹。

【我来给你们平个中】平个中：做中间人，以解决分歧。

年 [nien²]

(NIEN¹当为NIEN²，见803页勘误表。）

【帮长年】长期使用的雇工。

注释

幸 [ɕin⁴]
【幸喜得好】非常幸运。

幹(干) [kan⁴]
【肉不贵,我们干得过】肉不贵,我们买得起。
【用银子打干出来的】打干:钻营,活动。通过行贿把某人从监狱里弄出来。

幻 [xuan⁴]
【幻术】戏法,魔术。

幼 [iəu⁴]

幽 [iəu¹]

幾(几) [tɕi³]
【有几多大】①很大。②它有多大?

庀 [pʰei³]
【庀治房子】庀治:修理。

干 5-10　幺 1-9　广 2

5 10 幸幹	SHIN⁴.	
	幸喜得好	very *fortunate*.
	KAN⁴.	
	大能幹	great *ability*.
	幹大事	to *do* great things.
	你幹不幹	*can* you do it or not?
	脥不貴我們幹得過	meat is not dear, we shall be *able* to buy some.
	用銀子打幹出來的	to get out of prison by *bribery*.

The 52nd radical. (幺)

1 幻	HUAN⁴.	
2	幻術	*magic*; sleight of hand.
	IU⁴.	
6 幼	男女老幼	male and female, old and *young*.
	IU¹.	
9 幽	入幽冥	to enter *Hades*.
	涼幽幽的	*cool* and *shady*; *cooling*, as a drink.
	唱得幽雅	to sing *clearly* and distinctly.
	CHI³.	
幾	幾個錢	*how many* cash? (under ten). [ten].
	今天初幾	*which* day of the month is this? (under
	幾個人	*a few* men.
	有幾多大	it was *very* large; *how* large was it?
	前幾年來的	he came *several* years ago.
	幾時起身	*when* will you start on your journey?
	READ CHI¹.	[accident.
	幾乎失事	*almost* made a mistake or met with an

The 53rd radical. (广)

2 庀	P'E³.	
	庀治房子	to *repair* a house.

(165)

广 3-5

3	我要庀治你	I will *thrash* you !
庄	CHUANG¹.	
	做庄稼	to *farm*.
	庄稼漢	a *farmer*.
	茸庄	a deer-horn *depôt* or *market*.
	藥材是大庄	there is a great *trade* in medicines ; medicines are a *staple*.
4	CH'UANG².	
床	一架床	one *bedstead*.
	美人床	a *couch*.
	匠床	a *divan* ; a *lounge*.
	筆床	a *pencil rest*.
	一床鋪盖	one *bedquilt*. (*N.A.*)
	SÜ⁴.	
序	序齒	*precedence* according to age.
	序文	a *preface* ; an *introduction*.
5	一次一序的說	speak in an *orderly* way.
府	FU³.	
	府上在那裏	where is your *residence* ?
	二天我們過府拜望	another day I will come to your *house* and see you.
	府上的人口都清吉嗎	are your folks all well ?
	成都府	the *prefecture* of Ch'en-tu.
	府大老爺	the *Prefect*.
庚	KEN¹.	
	貴庚今年有多少了	how many *years* old are you this year ?
	同年老庚	of the same *age* ; a person of the same *age*.
	開生庚八字	write out the *horoscope*.
底	TI³.	[the top.
	底不合面	the *bottom* goods do not correspond with
	水桶底	the *bottom* of a water-bucket.
	鞋底	the *sole* of a shoe.

(166)

注　释

【我要庀治你】庀治：鞭打，抽打，痛打。

庄 [tʂuaŋ¹]

【茸庄】买卖鹿茸的商铺或存放鹿茸的仓库。

【药材是大庄】①有一大单药材生意；②药材是大头（主要商品）。

床 [tʂʰuaŋ²]

【炕床】旧时大户人家接待宾客的木床，中置矮几，两旁设座位。

序 [sy⁴]

【序齿】也作"叙齿"，即以齿（表年龄）为序，指按年龄大小排序定宴会席次或饮酒次序。

府 [fu³]

【府上的人口都清吉吗】清吉：清平吉祥。

庚 [kən¹]

底 [ti³]

【底不合面】底下的货物与上面的质量不一；表里不一。

注释

【打底子】绘画或油漆家具之前，先用底料涂上底色。

【一吊钱六个底】每一千枚制钱短少六枚。一吊：中国旧时钱币单位，即古时一千个制钱或值一千个制钱的铜币数量。

店 [tien⁴]

【幺店子】路边饭店。

庠 [siaŋ²]

【内庠】庠：学校。已毕业的学生。

【外庠】未毕业的学生。

度 [tu⁴] [to⁵]

库（庫）[kʰu⁴]

年底	the *end* of the year.
打底子	to put on the *first coat of paint*.
說話沒有底	no *foundation* or *ground* for saying so.
在山底下坐家	he lives at the *foot* or *base* of the mountain.
這官的出身是甚麽底子	what was the *origin* of this official's début?
他的家底好	his family *estate* is a rich one.
棹子底下的錢不要	I don't want money *under* the table, i. e., bribes.
在櫃子底下	*underneath* the cupboard.
底下人	*underlings*.
從底下上來的	to come up from *below*.
一吊錢六個底	each 1,000 cash is *short* six.
墊底	to make up a *deficiency* temporarily.
到底你曉不曉得	*after all* do you know or not?

店 TIEN⁴.

官店	an *hotel*.
幺店子	a *wayside inn*.
水食店子	a *restaurant*.
茶房酒店閒話多	there is much idle talk in tea shops and [wine *shops*.

庠 SIANG².

內庠	members of the *academy*; graduates; ["Siu-ts'ai."]
外庠	*under graduates*.

度 TU⁴.

國家的法度	the *laws* of the country.
過度	to overstep *bounds*.
那個人好氣度	he is good-tempered.
用費有度	expenditure is *limited*.
勤儉度日	*pass* your days in diligence and economy.

READ TO⁵.

下細忖度	carefully *consider* it.

庫 K'U⁴.

金銀庫	a *treasury*.
字庫	small towers in which written paper is [burned.

广 7-12

T'IN².
在家庭閒坐	sitting idly at home.

TSO⁴.
蓮花寶座	the Lotus *Throne* of the Goddess of Mercy.
一座山	one hill. (*N. A.*)

K'ANG¹.
康健得好	you are very *hale and strong* for an old man.
恭喜你四季康泰	may you be *happy* all the year through.

SHU⁴.
庶民百姓	the *common people.*
庶出	the children of a *concubine.*

T'O³.
扯一庹雞腸帶	buy a *fathom* of tape.

IONG².
庸庸碌碌的人	a *labouring* man.

SIANG¹.
廂房	the *side rooms* in a courtyard.

LIEN².
沒得一點廉恥的人	a *shame*less fellow.

FE⁴.
把那不好的行爲廢去	*abandon* that evil conduct.
莫做半途而廢的事	don't *discard* a job when it is half done.
成了個廢人	he has become *useless*, through disease, etc.

CH'ANG³. same as 廠.

KUANG³.
廣積陰功	to amass *great* merit.
他的見識廣	his experience is *wide.*
廣大無邊	*boundless.* [*kuang*, i. e., the Lake Province.]
下廣的船	boats that go down river as far as Hu-
廣東人	Cantonese.

(168)

注 釋

庭 [tʰin²]
座 [tso⁴]
康 [kʰaŋ¹]
庶 [ʂu⁴]
庹 [tʰo³]

【扯一庹鸡肠带】庹：中国一种约略计算长度的单位，以成人两臂左右伸直的长度为标准，约合五市尺。鸡肠带：一二厘米宽的白帆布裤腰带。

庸 [ioŋ²]
廂(厢) [siaŋ¹]
廉 [lien²]
癈(废) [fei⁴]
廠(厂) [tʂʰaŋ³]
廣(广) [kuaŋ³]

注释

廟(庙)[miao⁴]
廩(廪)[lin³]
廬(庐)[lu²]
廳(厅)[tʰin¹]
廷[tʰin²]
延[ien²]
廹(迫)[pʰe⁵]
【忙忙廹廹的】急急忙忙的。
建[tɕien⁴]
弄[loŋ¹]

广 12-22　廴 4-6　廾 4

廟

MIAO⁴.

火神廟	the *temple* of the god of fire.
祖廟	an *ancestral hall*.
走土地廟那麼過	go past the *shrine* of the local god.

13 廩

LIN³.

| 廩生 | a selected "siu-tsʻai" who receives a small [*stipend*. |

16 廬

LU².

| 請到茅廬歇憩 | please come to my mean *hut* and rest. |

22 廳

TʻIN¹.

大廳	the open front *hall* of a Chinese house.
松潘廳	the *secondary prefecture* of Song-pʻan.
督捕廳	the district magistrate's *deputy*.

The 54th radical. (廴)

4 廷

TʻIN².

| 朝廷的事 | the affairs of the *government*. |

5 延

IEN².

不要遲延	don't be *dilatory*.
却病延年	to drive away disease and *prolong* life.
延賓待客	to *entertain* guests.

廹

PʻE⁵.

忙忙廹廹的	*hurried*; very busy.
窮廹不堪	unbearably *pressed* by poverty.
受人逼廹	to be *harassed* by people; to be *persecuted*; to be *dunned* for debt.

6 建

CHIEN⁴.

| 建立德行 | to *establish* one's virtue. |
| 建造公館 | to *build* a mansion. |

The 55th radical. (廾)

4 弄

LONG¹.

| 弄不得 | you must not *touch* it. |

(169)

廾 4-12 弋 3-9 弓

把書弄髒了	you have *made* the book dirty.
弄壞了	*spoiled*.
弄假成真	it was *done* in fun, but ended in earnest.
弄巧反拙	to *attempt* to be clever, but only make a fool of one's self.
莫弄險	don't *try* a dangerous experiment.
把他弄出去	*expel* him; *cast* him out.
把他弄來	*conduct* him hither; by exhortation or force *convey* him to this place.
弄船	to *work* a boat.
弄茶飯	to *cook* victuals.
弄刀筆	to *use* the sword-pen, as a writer in the [yamen.
莫戲弄他	don't *make fun of* him.

12 弊 PI⁴.

你莫在中間舞弊	don't *work mischief* between the parties.
說出他的弊病情由他就服了	when I showed up his *roguery* he at once succumbed.

The 56th radical. (弋)

3 式 SHĬ⁴.

格式	a *form* on which to write an indictment.
那個人格式	that fellow is haughty, puts on airs.
欵式	*form; conventionalism*.
樣式都有	there are all *kinds*.
這雙鞋子穿起合式	these shoes just *fit*.
價錢合式	the price is *reasonable*.

9 弑 SHĬ⁴.

臣弑君不赦 子弑父不赦	a *regicide* or a *parricide* may not be forgiven.

The 57th radical. (弓)

弓 KONG¹.

弓箭舖	a *bow* and arrow shop.
操弓箭	to practise *archery*.

(170)

注 释

【弄刀笔】指在衙门里掌管文书或起草诉状,多用作贬义。

弊 [pi⁴]

式 [sɿ⁴]

【那个人格式】格式: 傲慢,装腔作势。

弑 [sɿ⁴]

弓 [koŋ¹] [tɕioŋ¹]

注释

【这个路是过过弓丈的】
弓丈：一种丈量工具。
这条路是丈量过的。

引 [in³]

【作引线】为军队或探险队做向导。

【那个时候发引】发引：指出殡，灵车启行。

【帮人引娃娃】引娃娃：带孩子。

【要不要引子】引子：中医在处方末尾所加的药引，能加强药剂的效力。英文释义应为：ingredient added to the medicinal herbs.

弔（吊）[tiao⁴]
弟 [ti⁴]
弦 [ȼyen²]

弓 1-5

這個路是過過弓丈的	this road has been measured with the *bow* measure.
走弓背背上	to go on the outside of a *curve*.
弓起的	*arched*; *bulging*; *raised* in the middle.

1 引 READ CHIONG¹.

彈棉花的弓   a *bow* for ginning cotton.

IN³. [light.

引路要往亮處引	if you would *lead* people, *lead* them to the [light.]
引水灌田	to *lead* water in courses to water the fields.
勾引好人	to *entice* good people.
作引線	to act as *guide* in any expedition.
那個時候發引	when is the funeral to be? (from the custom of *leading* the coffin of a parent).
進京引見	to go to court and be *introduced* to the Emperor.
那個的引進	who was *middleman* for the job?
引火柴	*kindling*-wood or straw.
帮人引娃娃	to act as nurse or helper with children.
引一句書	to *quote* a passage.
要不要引子	shall I take a *preparatory medicine* before [I take this?

4 弔 弟

TIAO⁴. the same as 吊.

TI⁴.

親弟兄	own *brothers*.
內弟	*wife's younger brother*.
表弟	*cousins* of a different surname (*younger*).
堂弟	*younger cousins* of the same surname.
桃園弟兄	sworn *brothers* (from the story in the "Annals of the Three States.")
弟子	a *pupil* (said by himself when addressing the teacher).
徒弟	an *apprentice*.
師弟	a *younger apprentice*.

5 弦 SHÜEN². [put on; ready for fight.

刀出鞘弓上弦   the sword unsheathed and the *bowstring*

(171)

弓 6-8

6 弭 MIE⁵.
把事情消弭　to *quash* an affair.

7 弱 RO⁵.
身體軟弱　*weak* in body.
筋力衰弱　*enfeebled* with age, etc.
姿質嫩弱　*young* and *delicate* in frame.
胃氣薄弱　my appetite is *poor*.
你縴懦弱得很　you are very *timid* indeed!
弱症病　a *wasting* disease; consumption.

8 弸 PEN¹.
把衣裳弸爛了　to tear one's clothes by *stretching* them.

張 CHANG¹.
張燈掛彩　to *display* lamps and embroidery.
還沒有開張　not yet opened shop (after New Year).
莫張人短　don't *proclaim* the shortcomings of others.
誇張的口氣　*boastful* words.
張張狂狂　*wild*; boisterous.
乖張　*cross-grained*; perverse.
張巴　*rude* in speech; blustering and devoid of [manners.
慢張些　be a little *slower*.
不張識他　take no *notice* of him.
船打張　the boat *rolls*.
買三張紙　buy three *sheets* of paper. (*N. A.*)
一張棹子　one table. (*N. A.*) [misplaced blame, etc.
張冠李戴　you put Mr. *Chang*'s cap on Mr. Li's head;

彌 ÜEN¹.
彌筧　a *semi-circular* basket for carrying earth.
犁彌　the *bent stock* of a plough.

弸 PONG¹.
弸伸展　to *stretch tightly* on a board or frame, as a skin. [skin.
弸針　a tack or pin, used in *stretching* cloth or
匾弸子　a wooden frame for pasting paper on.

(172)

注 释

弭 [mie⁵]

弱 [zo⁵]

弸 [pən¹]
【把衣服弸烂了】弸烂：撕破。

張（张）[tṣaŋ¹]
【莫张人短】不要公开宣扬别人的缺点。
【张巴】说话粗鲁；大惊小怪。
【慢张些】慢点。
【不张识他】张识：搭理，注意，支持。
【船打张】打张：打转，摇晃。

彌 [yen¹]
【彌筧】用来装土的半圆的筐。
【犁彌】犁上的弯曲的树干。

弸 [poŋ¹]

注释

【弸起打】钉住某人的手，把手伸展开来打。
強（强）[tɕʰiaŋ²] [tɕʰiaŋ³]
彀 [kəu⁴]
（K'EO⁴当为KEO⁴，见803页勘误表。）
彈（弹）[tʰan²] [tan⁴]
彌（弥）[mi²]
【弥缝不倒】不能隐瞒坏事。
【弥月之喜】为婴儿满月而办的酒席。

弓 8-14

弸起打	to *pin* a person's hands out and beat him.
上弸子	to put upon the *rack* (a kind of torture).
還弸子	to take *revenge* on.
弸面子	to *assume* airs, or an appearance of respectability.

強 CH'IANG².

好強的人	*overbearing* fellows.
強盗	*thieves*; *robbers*; *burglars*; *highwaymen*.
發憤自強	to *exert* one's self.
人還強壯	I am still *vigorous*.
人強命不強	I am *strong and able*, but my luck is not good.
他的胃口比我強	he is *better* at eating than I am.

READ CH'IANG³.

不要勉強他	don't *compel* him.
富貴在天強求不倒的	*riches and honour* depend on Heaven; they cannot be obtained by *force*.
強勉要得	we will *make* it do; it will have to do; there is no help for it.

彀 K'EO⁴.

| 弔彀失規 | to let the arrow *notch* slip from the string, is to break the rules of archery. |

彈 T'AN².

彈棉花	to *gin* cotton.
彈墨線	to *flick* the carpenter's marking line.
彈琴	to *thrum* on an instrument.
彈壓地方	to *suppress* the disaffected; to *pacify* a district.

READ TAN⁴.

鉛彈子	*leaden bullets*.
砲彈子	a *cannon ball*.
雪彈子	*hail*.

彌 MI².

彌縫不倒	you cannot *conceal* your villainy.
彌月之喜	a feast given when a child is a *full* month old.
阿彌陀佛	*amita* Buddha!!!

(173)

弓 19　彐 8-10　彡 4-8

19 彎

UAN¹.　　　　　　　　　　　　　　　　　　　[line.
彎木頭怕直墨線　a *crooked* stick fears the straight marking-
他的彎拐大　　　his *crookedness* is great; he is a *deceitful* fellow.
手彎子 and 脚彎子　the *inner angle* of the elbow and the knee.
衣彎子　　　　　the *curve* of a garment under the armpit.
轉過彎彎就攏了　when we turn another *corner*, or *bend* of the road, we will reach our destination.

The 58th radical. (彐)

8 彗

HUE⁴.
彗星　　　　　　a comet; lit., a *broom star*.

10 彙

LUE⁴.
字彙　　　　　　a *dictionary*.

The 59th radical. (彡)

4 形

SHIN².
形影相隨　　　　the *substance* and the shadow go together.
形像　　　　　　*appearance*.
人的形容　　　　the *appearance* of a person.
脫了形　　　　　to change the *appearance* through lean-ness; emaciated.
山形　　　　　　the *form* of a mountain.
畫個圖形　　　　draw a *figure* of it; sketch a *picture*.
形容不出來那個樣子　I can't *express* it; I can't *describe* it; unspeakable
這個布織得形　　this cloth is *thin*.
這房子的木料形　the timber of this house is *small and weak*.

8 彩

TS'AI³.
彩畫得好　　　　finely *ornamented*.
雲彩　　　　　　*coloured* clouds.　　　　　　　　[lanterns, etc.
掛彩　　　　　　to hang up *decorations* of figured cloth,
面子上做得光彩　a hypocritical appearance.

(174)

注　釋

彎（弯）[uan¹]
【他的弯拐大】他说话或做事绕了一个大圈。
彗 [xuei⁴]
彙（汇）[luei⁴]
形 [ɕin²]
【这个布织得形】形：薄。
【这房子的木料形】形：小且不牢固。
彩 [tsʰai³]

注释

【抽个彩头】彩头: 吉利、好运气的预兆。

彰 [tṣaŋ¹]

影 [in³]

【唱灯影】灯影: 皮影戏。

彷 [faŋ³]

役 [io⁵]

征 [tṣən¹]

佛(彿) [fu⁵]

彼 [pi³]

往 [uaŋ³]

【往年子】从前,过去。

彡 8-12　彳 4-5

賣彩票	to sell *lottery* tickets.
抽個彩頭	try your *luck!* buy a ticket.
今年子得了個好彩頭	I have met with a good *omen* at the beginning of this year.

11 彰　CHANG¹.

彰顯出來	to *make manifest*.

12 影　IN³.

捕風捉影的	it is like seizing the wind and catching a [shadow.
唱燈影	to perform *shadow* plays.
畫個影子	to sketch the *outline* with charcoal before painting in. [a person.
照得起人影子	it is bright enough to reflect the *image* of
沒得影響	no *hint* of it.
找不倒影響	I cannot find a *trace* of him.

The 60th radical. (彳)

4 彷　FANG³.

彷彿有點像他	*resembling* him.

役　IO⁵.

差役	official *underlings; runners*.

5 征　CHEN¹.

帶兵征勦反寇	to take soldiers and *exterminate* rebels.

佛　FU⁵.

我彷彿看見過	it *seems as if* I had met him before.

彼　PI³.

彼此來往	to have intercourse with one *another*.

往　UANG³.

你來我往	having comings and *goings* with each other; intercourse. [going.
我們沒來往	we have no intercourse; lit., coming and
往那裏去	where are you going *to?*
往年子	*former* years; *past* years.

(175)

彳 5-6

你往往這麼做	you *always* do this!
往後天	*another* day; the third day from now.

6 很 HEN³.

那個人很得很	that fellow is *dreadfully* grasping.
發很些讀書	*exert* yourself more at your studies.
誇自己的很處	to boast of one's own *excellencies*.
你那麼很嗎	are you so *daring*?
很有功夫	there is a *great deal* of work in it.
那個人很聰明	he is *very* wise, or clever.
高很了	*very* tall.
熱得很	*exceedingly* hot.

後 HEO⁴.

後天	the day *after* to-morrow.
悔後遲	too late to repent *afterwards* (an inscription over the jail door).
從今以後	from this time *onward*.
過後再莫題說了	don't speak of the matter *afterwards*.
前後兩天	in about two days.
前前後後的事	all things from first to *last*.
背後的話說得不同	he speaks differently *behind* your back.
在櫃子後頭	*behind* the cupboard.
後頸窩的頭髮摸得倒看不倒	you can feel the hair *at the back of* your neck, but you cannot see it; met., you may guess the future, but you cannot know it.
開個後門	open a *back* door.
後街子	*back* streets.
後房在那裏	where is the privy?
後房妻子	a concubine.
後來居上	the *last* shall be first.
沒得後人	having no *descendants*.
後娘	a *step*-mother.

READ HEO¹. a Ch'en-tu localism.

城後頭	*within* in the city.

(176)

注　釋

很 [xən³]
【那个人很得很】很得很：现常作"狠得很"，意为非常贪心的，贪婪的。
【发很些读书】发很：即"发狠"，下决心，全心投入的，不顾一切的。
【夸自己的很处】很处：长处。
【高很了】非常高。

後（后）[xəu⁴] [xəu¹]
【后房妻子】妾，小老婆。

注　释

律 [lu⁵]
待 [tai⁴]
【请得融念待得薄】请求时恭恭敬敬，实际对待上却显得薄情寡义。请求时是出于尊敬，但对待时却显得粗鲁。
徒 [tʰu²]
得 [te⁵]
【要不得】①不合乎需要的，无用的；②不能那样做，不能容许。
從（从）[tsʰoŋ²] [tsʰoŋ¹] [tsoŋ⁴]

彳 6-8

律　　LU⁵.
犯律法　　to transgress the *laws*.

待　　TAI⁴.
莫待是非來入耳 } ne'er on idle gossip *wait*, former love 'twill
從前恩愛反爲仇 }　turn to hate.
我等待你　　I will *wait* for you.
接待　　to *receive*; to *welcome*.
請得融念待得薄　I asked you out of respect, but I have *treated* [you rudely.

7 徒　　T'U².
幫我找個徒弟　help me to find an *apprentice*.
門徒　　a *pupil*; a *follower*; a *disciple*.
匪徒鬧事　*ruffians* creating a disturbance.
徒然　　in *vain*.

8 得　　TE⁵.
得不倒　　I cannot *get* it.
得福　　to *obtain* happiness.
沒得錢　　I *have* no money.
得病　　to *contract* a disease.
做得倒　　I am *able* to do it.
要不得　　*undesirable*; worthless.
聽得倒　　I *can* hear.
說不得　　it *may* not be said; you must not speak.
多得很　　very many.
隔得遠　　distant.

從　　TS'ONG².
你跟從我來　*follow* me.
順從　　to *obey*. 　　　　　[*comply* with it.
他不依從　　he would not *agree* to it; he would not
從那裏來　　where did you come *from*?
從古至今　　*from* ancient times till now.

READ TS'ONG¹.
來得從容　　to come in in a *dignified* manner.

READ TSONG⁴.
從一品　　*second class* of the first grade of officials.

(177)

彳 8-12

御 9 復	Ü⁴.	[(metaphorical).
御	御駕親征	the *monarch* himself goes forth to war
	西御街	the Western *Imperial* Street (Ch'en-tu).
	FU⁵.	
復	復活	to come to life *again*; *resurrection*.
	反復無常	*changeable*; *inconstant*; *uncertain*.
	回復他一封信	send him a letter in *reply*.
	復不倒原	it is impossible to *restore* the original.
	復興家業	to *restore* the fortunes of the family.
	報復冤仇	to *revenge* a wrong.
徧	P'IEN⁴.	same as 遍.
循	SÜIN⁴.	
	天理循還	providence works in regular *revolutions*.
	循規蹈矩的	one who *follows* the customs.
10 微	循良百姓	*good* people; *tractable* subjects.
	UE².	
	他是個卑微人	he is an *insignificant* person.
	莫嫌輕微	don't despise my *trifling* present.
	微風細雨的	a *little* wind and fine rain; a drizzle.
	些微有點痕跡	it is *slightly* damaged. [slowly.
	微微子的來	move it *little by little*; do it gently or
	天色微明	the grey dawn of the morning.
	你那些隱微的事我曉得	I know your *underhand* tricks.
12 徹	CH'E⁵.	
	徹底清算	reckon it *through* from the beginning.
	徹始徹終我都曉得	I know it *from* beginning *to* end.
	事鬧得透徹	the affair has been *thoroughly* cleared up.
徵	CHEN¹.	
	開徵收糧	to begin to *levy* the taxes.
德	TE⁵.	
	五倫八德	the five relationships and the eight *virtues*.

(178)

注　释

御 [y⁴]
復(复) [fu⁵]
【复不倒原】无法恢复原貌。
徧(遍) [pʰien⁴]
循 [syn³]
（SÜIN⁴当为SÜIN³，见803页勘误表。）
微 [uei²]
【些微有点痕迹】有轻微的损坏。
【微微子的来】微微子：慢慢地，轻轻地。
徹(彻) [tṣʰe⁵]
徵(征) [tṣən¹]
德 [te⁵]

注释

徽 [xuei¹]
【买一定徽墨】一定：同"一锭"。徽墨：中国名墨之一，因产于徽州而得名。

心 [sin¹]
【心慌吃灶心土】灶心土：土灶里柴火烧尽后留下的灰土。
【二心不定】踌躇不定的。
【脑命心】即"囟门"，又叫"顶门"，婴儿头顶前部中间骨头未合缝的地方。
【一尺的过心】过心：直径。直径为一尺。

必 [pi⁵]
【未必然】不一定，不确定。
【今天务必做煞角】做煞角：完成。

彳 12-14　心 1

三從四德	the three obediences and the four *accomplishments* of women.
有德行的人	a *moral* man. [*merit* of it.
做功德道場	to engage priests to chant prayers, for the
這馬的德行好	this horse's *temper* is good.

HUE¹.

買一定徽墨　　buy a stick of *Hue-cheo* ink.

The 61st radical. (心)

SIN¹.

心慌喫竈心土	if your *heart* is out of order, take a dose of mud from the *centre* of the fire-place.
心口子痛	pain in the region over the *heart*.
一心一意	of one *heart* and one mind.
二心不定	undecided, irresolute, unstable.
放心不下	I cannot set my *mind* at rest.
口是心非	his mouth says yes, but his *will* says no ; hypocritical.
㒲心發現	his *conscience* is awakened.
松栢有堅心	the fir and the cedar have hard *heartwood*.
磨心	the *axle* of a mill-stone.
燈心子	a lamp *wick*, sometimes spoken "sin⁴."
腦命心	the *fontanel*.
手板心	the *palm* of the hand.
河心爲界	the *middle* of the river is the boundary.
一尺的過心	a foot in diameter.
一柙點心	a box of *confectionery*.

PI⁵.

他必定要來	he will *certainly* come.
未必然	uncertain ; doubtful.
不可期必	you must not be too *sure*.
可以不必	there is no *need* to.
今天務必做煞角	you *must* finish it to-day.

心 3-4

3 志 CHÏ⁴. [purpose in life.
各有各的志向 each one has his own *bent*, *inclination*, or
沒志氣的人 a man with no *will* or *courage* of his own.

忍 REN³.
忍耐 *patience*.
忍讓 *forbearance*.
我忍不住 I cannot *endure* it.
忍得一時氣 } *restrain* your anger for a little, lest you
免得百日憂 } afterward suffer much sorrow through it.
好忍的心 how *harsh*!

忌 CHÏ⁴. [which an Emperor died.
忌辰 the day to be *avoided*; i. e., the day on
忌日 the anniversary of the death of a parent.
百無禁忌 no superstitious *dread* of anything.
他的忌諱大 he *shuns* many things as being unlucky.
肆行無忌 *reckless*.
不要忌刻人 don't *slight* people.
忌恨人家 to *hate* or *despise* people.
忌鴉片煙 to *abandon* the opium habit.

忙 MANG².
幫忙 to help one when *busy*.
不忙 don't be in a *hurry*.
慌慌忙忙 *flurried*.
他是個不忙的人 he is a slow-coach; a sluggard.

忖 TS'EN³.
忖度 to *reflect* on; to *consider*.

忘 UANG².
忘了根本 to *forget* one's origin, i. e., one's parents.
我忘記了 I have *forgotten*.
我的見忘大 my *forgetfulness* is great.

4 忠 CHONG¹.
忠臣不怕死 } a *loyal* statesman does not fear death; if
怕死不忠臣 } he fears death, he is not a *loyal* statesman; met., an *attached* servant.

(180)

注 释

志 [tʂɻ⁴]
忍 [zən³]
【好忍的心】忍：残酷。
忌 [tɕi⁴]
【不要忌刻人】忌刻：也作"忌克"。指为人妒忌刻薄。
【忌鸦片烟】忌：戒，禁戒。
忙 [maŋ²]
忖 [tsʰən³]
忘 [uaŋ²]
【我的见忘大】见忘：同"健忘"。
忠 [tʂoŋ¹]

注 释

忿 [fən⁴]
忽 [xo⁵]
【做事不要忽略】忽略：粗心，疏忽。
快 [kʰuai⁴]
【快性人】快性：性情爽快，急性子。英文释义应为：Impatient person.
念 [ȵien⁴]
忝 [tʰien³]
【忝在相好】忝：不配，有愧于，常用作谦辞。不配做你的朋友。

心 4

忠信的僕人	a *devoted* retainer.
涼藥苦口利於病 } 忠言逆耳利於行 }	cold medicine is bitter to the mouth, but good for the disease, so *faithful* words are unpleasant, but profitable.
忠厚長者	an *honest* old man.

忿 FEN⁴.

心頭忿不過	inappeasably *angry*.
忿怒	to be *angry*.
忿忿不平	*indignant*.
忿不顧身	*furious*.
忿恨	to *hate*.

忽 HO⁵.

忽然來到	to come *suddenly*.
做事不要忽畧	don't be *careless* at your work.

快 K'UAI⁴.

精神爽快	*healthy* in body; in *good spirits*.
這個屋頭爽快	this house is *pleasant* to live in.
天氣涼快	the weather is cool and *comfortable*.
快樂無邊	exceedingly *happy*.
快些拿來	bring it *quickly*.
快性人	an *active* fellow.
勤快	*active*; diligent.
市口快	sales are *rapid*; the market is *brisk*.
這個活路快不得	this work must not be *hurried*.
牙骨快子	ivory *chopsticks*.
刀子鋒快	the knife is very *sharp*.

念 NIEN⁴.

那個在念嘆我	who is *thinking* of me? (said when one [sneezes, etc.]).
常常記念	to constantly *remember* one.
起個好念頭	cultivate right *thoughts*.
念書	to *read* books.
念經	to *chant* prayers.

忝 T'IEN³.

忝在相好	I am *unworthy* of your friendship.

(181)

心 4-5

	U³.	
忤	忤逆不孝	disobedient and unfilial.
	CH'IE⁵.	
怯	不怯你	I do not *fear* you.
	有些膽怯	rather *timorous*.
	CHIE⁵.	
急	氣性太急	he is too *hasty-tempered*.
	急急廹廹	*hurried*.
	急病請三醫	in a *serious* illness call three doctors.
	緊急的事	an *urgent* affair.
	千急要來	you must come; the matter is very *pressing*.
	救急	to help one in an *extremity*.
	水流得急	the water flows *swiftly*.
	KUAI⁴.	
怪	奇奇怪怪的事	a *strange* affair.
	古怪	a *marvel*.
	難怪	no *wonder*!
	邪魔妖怪	*devils* and *imps*.
	休得見怪	don't be *offended*.
	怪不得我	you cannot *blame* me.
	怪頭怪腦說些	to talk wildly and obscenely.
	LU⁴.	
怒	發怒	to get *angry*.
	怒氣	*anger*.
	P'A⁴.	
怕	孝順父母不怕天 不犯王法不怕官	He who respects his parents well, need not *dread* Heaven's hate; and he who keeps his country's laws, need *fear* no magistrate.
	我怕你不來	I was *afraid* you would not come.
	恐怕是	*perhaps* it is so.
	SIN⁴.	[position.
性	性情不定	an undecided *character*; a vacilating *dis-*

(182)

注释

忤 [u³]
怯 [tɕʰie⁵]
【不怯你】不怕你。
急 [tɕie⁵]
【千急要来】事情非常急迫, 你一定要来。
怪 [kuai⁴]
怒 [lu⁴]
怕 [pʰa⁴]
性 [sin⁴]

注 释

【用定性了】老练，经验丰富。
思 [sɿ¹] [sɿ⁴]
【下细思想】仔细地考虑。
怠 [tai⁴]
【怠惰自甘】非常的懒惰。
怎 [tsən³]
【不怎的】不要担心、害怕；没问题。
怨 [yen⁴]

心 5

男兒無性鈍鐵無鋼 女兒無性爛草無䕺	as blunt iron without temper, so is man without *spirit*; as rotten grass without fibre, so is woman without *will*.
這個馬有點性格	this horse has a bit of a *temper*.
好個天性	how good-*natured*.
他的記性好	his *memory* is good,
保全性命	to preserve one's *life*.
這個木頭硬性	this wood is of a hard *quality*.
藥性	the *properties* of a medicine.
用定性了	seasoned with use, as crockery.

思 SÏ¹.

下細思想	*consider* it minutely.
有些思家	to *think* of one's home.

READ SÏ⁴.

你的意思怎麽樣	what is your *idea* of it?
這一句書的意思	the *meaning* of this sentence.
你有個甚麽意思嗎	what is your *intention*?
我不好意思	I am ashamed.

怠 TAI⁴.

怠慢你	I have treated you *rudely*.
怠惰自甘	inordinately *lazy*.
倦怠得很	very *wearied*.

怎 TSEN³.

這是怎麽樣做法	how is this done?
你有怎麽說的	what have you to say?
你怕他怎的	why do you fear him?

READ TSA⁵.

怎個了	how is this? how will you do?
這是怎樣的話	what sort of talk is this?
不怎的	don't *fear*; no matter.

怨 ÜEN⁴.

怨恨	to *hate*.
口出怨言	to utter *resentful* words.

(183)

心 5-6

	埋怨那一個	against whom do you harbour *ill-will*?
	只怨自己的命	I am only *dissatisfied* with my fate.

CH'I³.

[*money*; avaricious.]
	毫無廉恥	without the slightest *modesty* about taking
	太沒羞恥	too *shameless* altogether.
	惹人恥笑	to provoke people to laugh one to *shame*.

HEN⁴.
	怨恨仇人	to *hate* an enemy.
	恨惡惡事	to *detest* evil.
	懷恨在心	to cherish *spite* in one's heart.
	恨不得咬他兩口	I would not *dislike* biting him.

HEN².
	恆久不變	*constant* and unchanging.
	恆心為善	*steadfast* in doing good.

HUANG³.
	老恍惚了	the mind *confused* with old age; dotage.
	我恍惚聽倒	I have a *dim* recollection of having heard it.
	眼睛是恍的	my eyes are *dim*.
	做生意是恍的	business is an *uncertain* thing.

CH'IA⁵.
	恝然無情	*unsympathetic*; *heartless*.

CH'IA⁵.
	恰恰相會	to meet *opportunely*.
	恰好至當	very *fortunate*; very *suitable*.
	恰合式	*exactly* right; *just* fitting.
	料子要恰點	the material is a little *short* or *deficient*.
	恰倒點用	use it *economically*.

CHIANG⁴.
	犟恀	*wilful*.
	恀拐拐	a *perverse* fellow.
	這個恀遭瘟	this *stubborn* brute!
	事情是恀起的	the affair is at a dead lock.
	走恀了	*stiff* with walking.

(184)

注　释

恥（耻）[tʂʰʅ³]

恨 [xən⁴]

恆 [xən²]

恍 [xuaŋ³]

【老恍惚了】因为年老而变得糊涂了。

恝 [tɕʰia⁵]

【恝然无情】恝然：漠不关心，冷淡的样子。

恰 [tɕʰia⁵]

【恰好至当】非常幸运；很合适。

【恰合式】合式：同"合适"。

【料子要恰点】恰：短，不足。

恀 [tɕiaŋ⁴]

【决恀】同"倔强"。

【恀拐拐】恀：同"犟"。性格倔强的人。

【这个恀遭瘟】遭瘟：得病，遭祸患，惹麻烦，令人讨厌。

注 释

恐 [kʰoŋ³]
恭 [koŋ¹]
恢 [xuei¹]
【恢恢有余】绰绰有余。
　恢恢：宽阔广大的样子。
恩 [ŋən¹]
【恩厚点】恩厚：仁爱，
　慷慨。
恃 [tʂʰʅ⁴]
【不可有自恃的心】自恃：
　过分自信而骄傲。
恕 [ʂu⁴]
息 [si⁵]

心 6

K'ONG³.

| 恐怕他害了病 | perhaps he is taken sick. |
| 恐怕老了喫得做不得 | lest when I am old I should only be able to eat and not to work. |

KONG¹.

恭恭敬敬的	reverently.
恭喜發財	I respectfully wish you may get rich.
十分恭順	perfectly submissive.

HUE¹.

| 恢恢有餘 | and much more than that. |

NGEN¹.

今年皇恩大赦	this year the Emperor of his grace releases [many prisoners.
恩秀才	B.A. degree bestowed on one who has grown too old to try at the examinations.
大老爺開恩	have mercy on me Your Honour!
將恩不報反爲仇	he is not only ungrateful for favours, but becomes an enemy.
沾你的恩	let me be benefitted by your kindness.
是我的大恩人	he is my great benefactor.
恩厚點	be more generous or liberal.
夫妻恩愛	the affection of husband and wife.

CH'Ï⁴.

錢財不足恃	wealth is not trustworthy.
不可有自恃的心	don't be self-reliant.
恃勢	to presume on one's power.

SHU⁴.

| 求你饒恕我 | I beseech you to forgive me. |
| 待人寬恕 | treat people considerately. |

SI⁵.

氣息短	his breath comes short.
嘆息不已	to ceaselessly sigh.
喘息	to pant.
鼻息如雷	his snores are like thunder.

(185)

心 6-7

脚下沒得子息	I have no *offspring*. [un*profitable*]
地土沒出息	the place is un*productive* (and therefore
三分利息	three per cent *interest*.
你們還沒有安息嗎	have you not retired to *rest* yet?
軍務平息了	the war is *ended*. [health.]
你自已要將息	you must *take precautions* about your
莫姑息他	don't *pet* him.

恤 SHIE⁵.

憐恤人	to *pity* people.
體恤窮苦人的心	to *sympathize* with the poor and suffering.

恬 T'IEN².

心裏想恬淡些	be more *contented* in your mind.

恣 TSĬ¹.

恣意橫行	*profligate*.

恙 IANG⁴.

得的甚麼貴恙	what is your honourable *disease*?

患 HUAN⁴.

莫留後患	don't leave *evil results* behind you.
丟個後患	he left *misfortune* behind him, i. e., a family of daughters.
躲避患難	to flee from *difficulties*.
患病	to be *afflicted with* disease.

悍 KAN¹.

悍婦	a *brawling, turbulent* woman; a *virago*.

悔 HUE³.

彌天大罪一悔便消	though your sins fill the universe, re*pentance* will take them away.
賣後悔	to *regret* the past.
長行失悔	always *regretting* the past.
痛悔前非	*remorse* for past misdeeds.
事後反悔	to *change* one's word; to *retract* a promise.

(186)

注 释

【脚下没得子息】子息：子嗣，儿女。

恤 [ɕie⁵]

恬 [tʰien²]

恣 [tsɿ¹]

恙 [iaŋ⁴]

【得的甚么贵恙】恙：病。您生的是什么病？

患 [xuan⁴]

悍 [kan⁴]

（KAN¹当为KAN⁴，见803页勘误表。）

悔 [xuei³]

【长行失悔】一直为过去的事情后悔。

注释

恾 [maŋ¹]
【恾猪】蠢猪。骂人的话。
【生恾子】笨蛋，傻瓜，呆子。
【装恾吃相】通过装疯卖傻利用别人。

悖 [pei⁴]

悄 [tsʰiao¹]

悟 [u⁴]

愳(误) [u⁴]
【误信行】失去信誉，失去好名声。
【误了一点寒】发了一点烧。

悠 [iəu¹]
【往悠远处想】为未来着想。

悦 [ye⁵]

心 7

恾 悖 悄 悟 愳 悠 悦

MANG¹.
恾猪　　　　　a *stupid* pig of a fellow.
生恾子　　　　a *dolt*.　　　　　　　[people.
裝恾喫相　　　to pretend *stupidity* in order to impose on

PE⁴.
悖逆父母　　　to *rebel* against parental authority.
說話悖理　　　his talk is *opposed* to reason.

TS'IAO¹.
靜靜悄悄的　　*still* as a deserted house.
悄悄的　　　　*quietly*; *secretly*; be *quiet*!
悄悄的說　　　to *whisper*.
他悄悄的做了　he did it *secretly*; he did it *on the sly*.

U⁴.
快快醒悟　　　*arouse* yourself at once.
他的悟性好　　he has a quick *perception*.
慢慢悟出來　　to slowly *comprehend*.
大疑大悟小疑小悟　} with great doubts there will come great *understanding* of the subject.

U⁴.
愳不得我的期　you must not *defer* the time I have fixed.
愳了我的大事　you have *hindered* my important business.
愳主顧　　　　to *deceive* one's customers.
愳信行　　　　to *lose* one's reputation.　　[another.
一愳不可再愳　you have made one *mistake*; don't make
愳了一點寒　　I have *caught* a little fever.

IU¹.
往悠遠處想　　think of the *distant* future.
不義之財不得悠久　} ill-gotten wealth will not last *long*.

ÜE⁵.
你喜不喜悅　　are you *pleased* or not?
心中悅服　　　in my heart I *gladly* assent.

(187)

心 8

	HEN³.	
	悻悻自好	*huffed*; *pettish*; a sudden burst of temper.
	HUE⁵.	
	受了迷惑	he was *deceived*.
	心裏疑惑	to *doubt* in one's heart.
	煽惑人心	to *unsettle* men's minds.
	HUE⁴.	
	受人恩惠	to receive *kindness* from people.
	待人賢惠	*gracious* in treatment of others.
	K'ONG⁴.	
	鄉悾子	a *rustic*; a *simpleton*; an *ignoramus*.
	HO⁵.	
	心裏恍惚	*muddled* in mind.
	HUEN¹.	
	心惛意亂	the mind *confused*; *stupid*.
	MEN⁴.	
	憂悶	*sad*. [*melancholy*.
	開遊散悶	to amuse one's-self in order to dissipate
	悶悶奄奄的	*listless*; *languid*.
	你繞是個悶龍	you are a *dull* blockhead indeed!
	大家都悶住了	they were all *silenced*.
	悶菸	tobacco used by robbers to *stupify* people.
	PE¹.	
	大發慈悲	to show great *compassion*.
	悲哭不已	to unceasingly *mourn* and weep.
	離合悲歡一臺戲	the world is full of partings and meetings, *sorrows* and joys, like a play; "all the world's a stage."
	SI⁵.	
	可惜了	to be *regretted*; alas!
	憐惜貧窮人	to *pity* the poor.
	愛惜光陰	be *careful* of your time.

(188)

注 释

悻 [xən³]
【悻悻自好】悻悻：因不如意而怨恨失意的样子。固执己见，自以为是。英文释义应为：Stubborn, obstinate and presumptuous.

惑 [xue⁵]

惠 [xuei⁴]

悾 [kʰoŋ⁴]
【乡悾子】乡下人，笨蛋，没文化的人。

惚 [xo⁵]

惛 [xuən¹]

悶(闷) [mən⁴]
【闷烟】盗贼使用的可以使人昏迷的烟。

悲 [pei¹]

惜 [si⁵]

注 释

悽 [tsʰi¹]
悚 [toŋ³]
【悟悚悚的】指头脑不清醒的样子。也作"昏懂懂"。
惟 [uei²]
情 [tsʰin²]
悴 [tsʰuei⁴]
惡（恶）[u⁴] [ŋo⁵]

心 8

悽 悚 惟 情 悴 惡

TSʻIʼ.

並不吝惜銀錢	I shall certainly not be *sparing* of the money. [a little expense.
成大事不惜小費	in doing important business don't *begrudge*
心中悽慘	*grieved* at heart.

TONG³.

| 悟悚悚的 | *stupid*. |

UE².

| 惟有他不來 | he *only* did not come. |
| 惟願你好 | I *heartily* wish you well. |

TSʻIN².

人情	humane *feelings*.
送個人情	to give a present.
性情和平	of a peaceable *disposition*.
很有才情	he has great *ability*.
不合情理	not according to *reason*.
情慾	*lusts*.
情願讀書	*desirous* of studying; *willing* to study.
說出實情來	state the *facts* of the case.
那個事情我不曉得	I don't know about that *affair*.
情由	*cause*; *origin*.

TSʻUE⁴.

| 顏色憔悴 | a *careworn* appearance; *ghastly*. |

U⁴.

恨惡	to *hate*.
眞是可惡	it is really *detestable*.
你連羞惡都沒得嗎	have you no *shame*?

READ NGO⁵.

| 好善惡⁴惡⁵ | to love good and *hate*⁴ *evil*⁵. |
| 人惡人怕天不怕 | when a man is *vicious*, men fear him, but Heaven does not. |

(189)

心 8-9

兇惡無比		exceedingly *malicious*.
惡言囘答		he answered *truculently*.
那個狗惡		that dog is *fierce*.
面貌醜惡		his face is *ugly*.
	NGEO⁴.	
憑氣		to *grieve*; to *fret*; to be *vexed*.
不要憑他		don't *vex* him.
這纔憑人		this is very *vexing* or *grievous*.
	I⁴.	
我的意思是這樣		my *idea* is this.
我不好意思受		I am ashamed to receive it.
你我的意見相同		your *views* and mine are similar.
我們的意思不是賺錢		our *purpose* (or *intention*) is not to make money.
你的心意如何		what is your *intention*? [obtained his *end*.
得意洋洋		pleased with success; delighted in having
我特意來會你		I came *purposely* to meet you.
固意要去		determined to go.
故意那麼做		*deliberately* done. [a *decision*.
打個主意		make up your *mind*; find a *plan*; come to
我要打你的主意		I will devise a *scheme* to injure you.
這事出人意外		this is beyond one's *expectation*.
意思不同		the *meaning* is different.
做生意		to do *business*; to *trade*.
莫那們大意		don't be so *careless*.
	RE³.	
那個把你惹倒		who *provoked* you? [tated).
那個人惹不得		that fellow must not be *teased* (or *irri-*
惹事生非		to *stir up* trouble.
你莫惹禍		don't *bring* calamity on *yourself*.
天花惹人		small-pox is *contagious*.
把火惹燃		*light* the fire.
惹火燒身		*lighting* a fire to burn one's self.
	Ü⁴.	
病愈了		my sickness is *healed*.

(190)

注 释

憑 [ŋəu⁴]
【憑气】使苦恼,使烦恼。
意 [i⁴]
【固意要去】固意:坚决。
惹 [zei³]
愈 [y⁴]

注释

感 [kan³]
恼(惱) [lao³]
爱(愛) [ŋai⁴]
　【我懒爱给他做得】懒爱: 懒得, 厌恶, 反感。
想 [siaŋ³]
　【丢个想头】想头: 指望, 期望, 英文释义可为: Something memorable or expecting. 留下个纪念物, 令人回忆。
惰 [to⁴]
愁 [tsʰəu²]

心 9

感惱愛想惰愁

KAN³.

感動人心	to *move* people's minds.
感化人心	to *transform* men's hearts.
感恩不淺	very *thankful* for favours.
感謝	to *thank*; *thanks*.

LAO³.

| 惱怒 | to get *angry*. |
| 是非只爲多開口 煩惱皆因强出頭 | all scandal comes of too much tattling, *vexation* is bred by over meddling. |

NGAI⁴.

親愛的朋友	dearly *loved* friends.
愛憐人	to *compassionate* people.
溺愛不敎	*doting* on a child and spoiling him; *petting*.
他偏愛那個娃娃	he shows an undue *preference* for that child.
愛花	*fond* of flowers.
愛耍	he *likes* to play; *fond* of idling.
我懶愛給他做得	I *dislike* doing it for him.
愛惜身體	be *careful* of your body. [ont one's love.
那個花長得愛人	that flower is very *attractive*, i. e., it draws
這是你的令愛嗎	is this your *daughter*?

SIANG³.

想起一個法子	*think* of a plan.
想人家的方子	to *concoct* a scheme to injure another.
慢慢的去想	go and carefully *meditate* on it.
想不出來	I cannot *conceive* (or *comprehend*) it.
想起前頭的事	to *remember* former things. [sake.
丟個想頭	leave a *memento* behind you; leave a keep-
他想得功名	he *wants* to obtain honours.
不想喫	I have no *desire* to eat; I have no appetite.

TO⁴.

| 懶惰 | *lazy*. |

TS'EO².

| 憂愁 | *sorrow*; *sorrowful*. |

(191)

心 9-11

	酒不解真愁	wine cannot dispel real *grief*.
	愁人莫對愁人說 說起愁來愁更多	*sad* ones should not to sad ones speak, for *grief* outspoken greater grows.

Ü².

愚拙人	*ignorant* (or *foolish*) people.
依我的愚見	according to my *humble* opinion.
愚弟	I ; myself.

HUANG¹.

我心慌得很	I am very *nervous* (*faint* or *agitated*).
甚麼事跑得那麼慌	what are you running in such a *hurry* for?

T'AI⁴.

還是那個故態	his *behaviour* is still the same; he has still [the same old way.]

K'UE⁴.

我替他羞愧	I am *ashamed* of him.

T'A⁵.

死心愓地	in utter *despair*.

CH'EN⁴.

你謹慎些	be more *careful*.
慎重其事	to be *attentive* to one's business.

TS'Ï².

慈愛兒女	to *love* one's children.
慈竹	the common bamboo, because it yearly throws up many young shoots.
觀音菩薩大慈悲	the Goddess of Mercy is *very compassionate*.

IN¹.

你要慇懃些	you must be more *careful and diligent*.

ÜEN⁴.

許願	to promise a *thankoffering* to the gods.

HUE⁴.

智慧	*wisdom*.

(192)

注 釋

愚 [y²]
慌 [xuaŋ¹]
態(态) [tʰai⁴]
【还是那个故态】故态：老脾气，老样子，旧日或平素的举止神态。
愧 [kʰuei⁴]
惕 [tʰa⁵]
【死心惕地】即"死心塌地"，打定主意，不再改变。
愼(慎) [tʂʰən⁴]
慈 [tsʰɿ²]
慇(殷) [in¹]
願 [yen⁴]
慧 [xuei⁴]

注释

慨 [kʰai⁴]

慷 [kʰaŋ¹]

怄(怄) [ŋəu⁴]

憩(憩) [tɕʰi⁴]
（K'I⁴当CH'I⁴，见803页勘误表。）

悭(悭) [tɕien¹]
【悭吝】吝啬，小气。

庆(庆) [tɕʰin⁴]
【庆坛】祭拜上天或神祇的祭坛。

虑(虑) [ly⁴]
【当父母的要虑后】做父母的，要考虑孩子的未来，要做长远打算。

慢 [man⁴]
【简慢客】简慢：轻忽怠慢。
【侮慢人】侮慢：轻视。

慕 [mo⁴] [mu⁴]

惭(惭) [tsʰan²]

心 11

	K'AI⁴.	
放慷慨點		be more *liberal*.
慨然應允		to respond *heartily*.
	K'ANG¹.	
慷慨		*magnanimous*.
	NGEO⁴.	
		same as 愿.
	K'I⁴.	
歇憩喝茶		*rest* a little and drink tea.
	CHIEN¹.	
悭吝		*stingy*.
	CH'IN⁴.	
喜慶的事		a *joyful* occasion.
慶壇		to *worship* the gods of the altar.
慶賀你的壽誕		I *congratulate* you on your birthday.
	LÜ⁴.	
當父母的要慮後		parents must *take thought for* the future.
那麼過慮做不成事		you will not be able to do anything for over *anxiety*.
	MAN⁴.	
簡慢客		to be *negligent* to a guest.
侮慢人		to *despise* people.
發生快當慢慢長大		it springs up quickly, but grows *slowly*.
慢慢走		go *slowly*; don't hurry; (a parting salutation).
性子慢		of a *sluggish* disposition.
	MO⁴, MU⁴.	
愛慕父母		to *love* one's parents.
羨慕詩書		to be *fond* of books.
	TS'AN².	
慚愧		to be *ashamed*.

(193)

心 11-12

惨 憎 慰 憂 慾 憤 憨 憲 慣

TS'AN³.

實在悽慘	I am very *wretched*.
我的光景慘	my prospects are *bad*.

TS'AO².

| 憎雜 | *confused* in mind. |

Ü⁴, UE⁴.

| 安慰 | *comfort*; to *comfort*. |

IU¹.

人無遠慮必有近憂	if you don't take thought for the future, you will have present *sorrow*.
時刻犹憂	always *anxious* (or *apprehensive*).
人生不滿百常懷千歲憂	man's age is less than a hundred, but he bears the *sorrows* of a thousand years.
憂愁	*sorrow*.
憂事	a *sorrowful* occasion; a death.

IO⁵.

| | same as 欲. |

12

FEN⁴.

| 發憤讀書 | to *eagerly* study books. |

HAN¹.

你憨鳥了	you are *crazy*; *daft*.
癡不癡憨不憨的	*foolish* looking and yet not a fool.
睡憨了	*dazed* with sleep.

SHIEN³,⁴.

| 文武三大憲 | the three highest civil and military *officers* [in the province. |
| 買本憲書 | buy an *official* calendar. |

KUAN⁴.

慣慣了	*habitually* lazy.
你慣習甚麼買賣	what business are you *accustomed* to or [acquainted with?
喫慣了	*accustomed* to eat it.
習慣成自然	through long practice it becomes natural [to one.
父母把他慣勢了	his parents have *spoiled* him.
慣會扯謊	*addicted* to lying.

(194)

注 釋

慘(惨) [tsʰan³]
憎 [tsʰao²]
慰 [y⁴] [uei⁴]
憂(忧) [iəu¹]
【忧事】令人伤心的场合；死亡。
慾(欲) [io⁵]
憤(愤) [fən⁴]
憨 [xan¹]
【你憨鸟了】憨鸟：癫狂，愚笨。
【睡憨了】睡得昏昏沉沉。
憲(宪) [ɕien³] [ɕien⁴]
【买本宪书】宪书：历书。
慣(惯) [kuan⁴]
【父母把他惯势了】惯势：溺爱。

注释

憍(侨)[tɕiao¹]
憐(怜)[liɛn²]
憫(悯)[min³]
憬[tɕin³]
憑(凭)[pʰin²]
憔[tsʰiao²]
懈[ɕiai⁴]
懇(恳)[kʰən³]
憋[pʰie⁵]
【放憋脱些】快点，敏捷点。
懃(勤)[tɕʰin²]
【慇慇勤勤的】认真地，诚挚地。
懊[ŋao⁴]

心 12-13

CHIAO¹.
莫把娃娃羞憍了 — don't *spoil* the child.

LIEN².
真是可憐 — it is truly *pitiable*.
憐恤人的事 — works of *charity*.

MIN³.
憐憫人 — to *pity* people.
求你可憐我 — I beseech you *pity* me.

CHIN³.
我沒有憬覺得 — I did not *perceive*, I did not *notice*.

P'IN².
有甚麼憑據 — what *evidence* is there?
口說不爲憑 — words alone are not sufficient *proof*.
文憑 — an official's *credentials*.
事憑公事憑中 — matters must be settled according to justice [and equity.

TS'IAO².
形容憔悴 — *haggard* in appearance.

SHIAI⁴.
把工夫懈怠了 — *lazy* at work, *negligent* in business.
把詩書懈怠了 — *inattentive* at study.

K'EN³.
哀懇 — to *supplicate*.
懇求 — to *beseech*.

P'IE⁵.
放憋脱些 — be a little *quicker*; be more *prompt*.
愛憋脱 — to like things done *off-hand*, without delay or inconvenience.

CH'IN².
慇慇懃懃的 — *earnestly*.

NGAO⁴.
你牟全不懊憐他嗎 — are you still unwilling to *relent* (or *pity* him)?

(195)

心 13-15

TONG³.

你的意思我不懂	I don't *understand* what you mean.
不懂事的人	a stupid fellow.
懞懞懂懂的	*confusedly; in a maze.*

IN⁴, ¹.

| 應分該當做的 | what one *ought* to do. |

READ IN⁴.

他沒得話答應	he has nothing to *answer.*
他答應不答應嗎	does he *respond* to the offer or not?
不應承他	don't *respond* to him.
他肯應嘴	he is in the habit of *speaking back.*
這藥叫得應	this medicine is *efficacious*; lit., it *answers* when called.
應許	to *promise.*
我說的那個話應驗了	what I said has been *fulfilled.*
應允	to *grant.*
應酬朋友	to *entertain* friends.

TSAO⁴.

悶燥	*dull; depressed.*
這個娃娃燥人得很	this child *worries* one very much.
囉燥	to *make a row.*

LO⁴.

| 懦弱 | *timid* and *weak.* |

TAI¹.

| 書獃子 | a *pedant.* |
| 老獃子 | a nickname for the *head.* |

HUE¹.

| 莫隳心嗎 | don't be *discouraged* (or *despondent*). |

CH'EN², ³.

| 受懲治的是好兒子 | he is a good son who receives *correction.* |

(196)

注 释

懂 [toŋ³]

應（应）[in⁴] [in¹]

【应分该当做的】应分：分内。该当：应该。分内应该做的。

【这药叫得应】叫得应：有效，灵验。

燥 [tsao⁴]

【闷燥】消沉，迟钝，呆滞。

【啰燥】争吵，吵闹。

懦 [lo⁴]

獃 [tai⁴]

【书獃子】獃：古同"呆"。卖弄学问的人，书呆子。

【老獃子】"脑袋"的别名。

隳 [xuei¹]

懲（惩）[tṣʰən²] [tṣʰən³]

注 释

懩 [iaŋ³]
【口懩懩的要说】指忍不住想说。
悬（悬）[ɕyen²]
怀（怀）[xuai²]
懒（懒）[lan³]
懞 [moŋ³]
【给他一个懞懂大吉】让他在糊里糊涂中碰运气。
【他是个懞的】懞的：无知的,幼稚的。
忏（忏）[tṣʰan⁴]

心 15-17

懩 16

IANG³.
口懩懩的要說　my mouth *itched* to speak.

懸

SHÜEN².
懸梁自盡　to commit suicide by *hanging* one's-self up [to a beam.
懸空空的那麼上去　} how can one go up *suspended* on nothing?
我心裏懸弔弔的　I am in *suspense*.
我懸望他來　I am *anxiously* expecting him.
他的事情懸　his affairs are in a *precarious* condition.
把賬給他懸出來　write out his account and *expose* it to the public.
那個地方懸得很　that place is very *dangerous*.

懷

HUAI².
心懷疑惑　to *cherish* doubt in the heart.
三年懷抱　to *nurse* a child for three years.
懷胎　pregnant.
搵在懷包裏　put it in your *breast* pocket.
心懷不平　my *heart* is not at peace.
加懷加懷　eat a little more (polite).
我忘懷了　I forgot it.

懶

LAN³.
懶得去拿　too *lazy* to go and fetch it.
你又在躱懶　you are *idling* again!
那個人懶散　that fellow is *negligent* and *untidy*.
睡懶覺　to take a nap.

懞

MONG³.
給他一個懞懂大吉　} I will just *blindly* take my chance.
他是個懞的　he is an *ignorant* fellow.

懺 17

CH'AN⁴.
懺悔自己的罪　to *repent* of one's sins.
念經拜懺　to chant prayers and repeat *ritual*.

(197)

心 18-19　戈 2-3

18 懼　CHÜ⁴.
懼怕　　　　　　　to *fear*.
我懼怕你嗎　　　　do you think that I am *afraid* of you?

19 戀　LIEN⁴.
貪戀美色　　　　　to *lust* after women.

The 62nd radical. (戈)

2 戈　KO¹.
內室操戈　　　　　civil *war*; family *strife*; lit., to take up *arms* in one's own house.

成　CH'EN².
那個房子賣成了沒有　　　} have you *completed* the purchase of that house?
謀事在人成事在天　　　} man proposes, but Heaven disposes.
現成的　　　　　　ready-made.
長大成人　　　　　to grow big and *become* a man.
碾成細麵　　　　　grind it *into* powder.
不成器的娃娃　　　a good for nothing fellow.
那個人做不成事　　that man can *accomplish* nothing.
那人老成　　　　　he is an *experienced* man.
沒有說一句成套的話　　} he has not spoken a word of sense.
今年收成好　　　　the *harvest* is good this year.

3 戒　KAI⁴, CHIAI⁴.
以戒下次　　　　　this is to *warn* you not to do it again.
戒殺放生　　　　　to *avoid* killing animals, and to liberate living animals.
除酒戒葷　　　　　to *abstain* from wine and strong meats.
受戒的和尙　　　　a Buddhist priest who has received the *precepts*.
戒鴉片煙　　　　　to *break off* the opium habit.
戒箍子　　　　　　a finger-ring.

(198)

注　釋

懼（惧）[tɕy⁴]
戀（恋）[lien⁴]
戈 [ko¹]
成 [tʂʰən²]
戒 [kai⁴] [tɕiai⁴]

注释

我 [ŋo³]
【我把我自己管倒就是了】我照顾好我自己就行了。

或 [xue⁵] [xua⁵]
【见或有之】"见"应为"间"。间或：表示动作、事情时断时续地发生。有时有，有时没有。
【或上或下二心不定】心里犹豫不决，无法做出决定。

戚 [tsʰi⁵]

戥 [tən³]
【拿戥子称银子】戥子：用以称量微量物品的小型杆秤。最大单位以两计，最小以厘计。

截 [tsʰie⁵]

戰（战）[tʂan⁴]

戲（戏）[ɕi⁴]

戈 3-13

我		NGO³.
	我把我自己管倒就是了	I shall look after *myself*; that's all.
	拿給我	give it to *me*.
	我的東西有個記號	*my* things are marked.
	不是我的	it is not *mine*.
	我們不曉得	*we* do not know.
	我們的房子窄	*our* house is small.
	他給我們一路來的	he came with *us*.
4 或		HUE⁵, HUA⁵.
	或早或晚必要來	I will certainly come *either* early *or* late.
	見或有之	*sometimes* there are.
	或者	*whether*; *perhaps*.
	或二或三	*irresolute*.
	或上或下二心不定	in an *uncertain* state of mind.
7 戚		TS'I⁵.
	親戚家門	relatives of a *different* surname and relatives of the *same* surname.
9 戥		TEN³.
	拿戥子稱銀子	weigh the silver on the *small steelyard*.
10 截		TS'IE⁵.
	截住他不許走	*intercept* and detain him.
12 戰		CHAN⁴.
	下戰書	to declare *war*.
	排兵布戰	to set the *battle* in array.
13	大戰一場	to *fight* a great battle.
戲		SHI⁴.
	一句戲言	a *joke*.
	戲耍成真	from *jest* to earnest.
	唱戲	to act a *play*.

(199)

西蜀方言

戈 13-14 户 4

	戲樓壩壩	the theatre.
	戲臺	the stage.
	戲班子	actors.
	被禪戲	a Punch and Judy *show*.
	耍把戲	*juggling*.
14	調戲人	to *flirt* with women.
戳	CH'O⁵.	
	看戳倒眼睛	take care and not *stick* it into your eyes.
	杵戳記	to affix a *seal* or *stamp* to a document.
戴	TAI⁴.	
	戴帽子	to *wear* a hat.
	戴眼鏡子	to *wear* spectacles.
	穿戴	*clothing* and *hat*.
	找人擔戴	find a man to *undertake* the responsibility.

The 63rd radical. (戶)

戶	FU⁴.	
	大糧戶	a well-to-do country *family*.
	有好多煙戶	how many *families* are there.
	走人戶去了	she has gone visiting.
	戶房	the *Population* and Revenue Office in a [yamen.
	酒行戶	the *headman* among the wine dealers.
	斗戶	a *middleman* who weighs grain in the market.
4	那個的過戶	through whose hands did it pass?
房	FANG².	
	田地房屋	land and *houses*.
	房錢	rent of a *house*.
	油房	an oil *shop*.
	帳房	a Tibetan *tent*.
	站房	an inn.
	碾房	a mill.
	幾間房子	a few *rooms*.
	看個房圈	show us a *room* (in an inn).

(200)

注 释

【戏楼坝坝】戏院。
【被禅戏】"禅"应为"单"。即被单木偶戏,木偶戏的一种。
戳[tṣʰo⁵]
【杵戳记】在文件上盖上印章或标签。
戴[tai⁴]
户[fu⁴]
【有好多烟户】烟户:家庭。
【酒行户】酒商中的头领。
【那个的过户】过户:依照法定手续更换物主姓名。通过谁的手转卖的?
房[faŋ²]
【站房】小酒店。

注 释

【灵房】供奉祖先牌位的房间。
所 [so³]
扁 [pien³]
扇 [ṣan⁴]
【掌扇】古时仪仗的一种，长柄掌形扇。
【排扇】旧时房屋外墙的扇状窗子。
手 [ṣəu³]
【喊个棒手】叫一个空手的苦力。

戶 4-6 手

門房	the porter's *room* in a yamen.
工房	the *Office* of Works in a yamen.
洞房	the nuptial *chamber*.
偏房	a *concubine*.
火房	a *cook*.
我們是二房	we are of the second *branch of the family*.
蜂房	honey-*comb*.
靈房	a *case* for the ancestral tablet.

所 SO³.

公所之地	a public *place*, as a market place.
無所不至	there is nothing *that* he will not do; he will go to any length.
人所共知的	*that which* everybody knows about.
所以	*therefore*; *for that* or *this reason*; *consequently*; *so*.
說不出個所以然	he cannot give a reason.
一所墳	a grave. (*N. A.*)

5 扁 PIEN³.

壓扁了	squeezed *flat*.
扁桶	an *oblong* tub.
扁擔	a coolie's carrying pole (because *flattened* on both sides).

6 扇 SHAN⁴.

一把摺扇	a folding *fan*.
掌扇	a huge *fan* carried in front of officials.
排扇	the transverse *walls* of a house.
雙扇門	a two-*leaved* door. (*N. A.*)
六扇門	a yamen, or magistrate's office. (*N. A.*)

The 64th radical. (手)

手 SHEO³.

兩手不空	both my *hands* are full.
佛手柑	the Buddha's *hand* citron.
喊個棒手	call an empty-*handed* coolie.
打手勢	to make signs with the *hands*.

手 1-2

做手藝		to work at a *handicraft*.
手骭		the forearm.
當下手		to be an *under*helper.
高手匠人		a *skilful* workman.
他的手面子好		*skilful* at needlework; *skilful* at boxing.
東西在我手頭		the things are in my *possession*.
吹鼓手		*trumpeters* and *drummers*.
水手		a boatman; a sailor.
手銃		a revolver; a pistol.
手足弟兄		own brothers.

1 才 TS'AI².

好個人才	what a fine *appearance* he has!
才學滿貫	a man of great *learning*.
既有大才何必推諉	seeing that you have great *abilities*, why refuse to undertake the work.
有口才	he has a *gift* of the gab.
文秀才	a civil graduate.

2 扎 CHA⁵.

找扎舖	a shop where paper designs are *cut out*.
扎鞋底	to *sew* shoe soles.

扑 P'U⁵.

跌個扑爬	to fall *sprawling* on one's face.

打 TA³.

打死人	to *strike* a man dead.
打鑼	to *beat* a gong.
打架	to *fight* (either men or animals).
打板子	to *flog*.
打賊	to *fight against*, or subdue, rebels and robbers.
打雜	to *do* odd jobs.
打濕	to wet.
打牌	to *play* cards or dominoes; to *carry* inscription boards before an official.
撒網打魚	to *catch* fish with a net.

(202)

注 釋

【手骭】前臂。

【他的手面子好】手面子好:针线活技术高超。

才 [tsʰai²]

扎 [tṣa⁵]

【找扎铺】古时一种专做剪纸艺品的店铺。

扑 [pʰu⁵]

【跌个扑爬】张开四肢摔倒,以脸抢地。

打 [ta³]

注释

【这个木头是虫打了的】虫打了：被虫蛀过了。
【那个人不打眼】打眼：显眼，容易引人注意。
【打盘来】把盘子拿来。
【打站房】在旅店住下来。
【百打百斤】大约一百斤。

扠 [tṣʰa³]
扛 [kaŋ⁴] [kaŋ¹]
【哑吧扛】一种由两个苦力抬着的运输货物的机械装置。
【扛头子】扛抬货物的苦力中，处于前面的那个苦力。

手 2-3

各人打掃門前雪 休管他人瓦上霜	each *sweep* the snow from his own door-step; ne'er mind the frost on your neighbonr's tiles; met., mind your own business.
打石頭	to *throw* stones.
打穀子	to *thrash* rice.
打瞌睡	to *nod* with sleep.
這個木頭是蟲打了的	this wood is worm-*eaten*.
昨夜打雷	it *thundered* last night.
打水你要到井邊	if you would *draw* water you must go to the well.
打個轉轉	to *take* a turn round; to go for a walk.
那個人不打眼	that fellow does not *take* my fancy.
打傘	to *carry* an umbrella.
打盤來	*bring* the tray.
打草鞋	to *make* sandals.
打一斤油	*buy* a pound of oil.
打鎗	to *fire* a gun.
打開門	*open* the door.
打聽實在	*inquire* into the facts of the case.
打夥做生意	to *enter into* partnership in business.
打站房	to *put up* at an inn.
三分人才七分打扮	that man is three parts ability and seven parts *clothing*.
百打百斤	*about* a hundred catties.
你打從那裏來	where have you come from?

扠 CH'A³.

把竿子扠上去	*fork up* the clothes rod.

扛 KANG⁴.

扛抬	to *carry on poles* between two.
哑吧扛	a contrivance for transporting goods *carried between two* coolies.
扛頭子	the front coolie of two; a head coolie.
門扛	the large *bar* of a door.
扛門	to *bar* the door.
直扛扛的	*straightforward*; *blunt*.

手 3-4

扣

READ KANG¹.

| 打扛帮 | to *help* another by speaking up for him. |

K'EO⁴. Interchanged with 鈎 in some senses.

門扣子	a door-*latch*.
扣襻	a *button-loop*.
把鈕子扣起	*button* the button.
扣帶	a belt with a *buckle*.
滿算除扣	reckon it all up first and then *deduct*.
扣洋布	the best foreign calico.

READ K'EO¹.

| 一扣線 | a small *hank* of thread. |
| 活拉扣 | a *slip-knot*. |

托

T'O⁵.

不必推托	you need not *decline* (or *excuse* yourself).
托故	an *excuse*; a *pretext*.
托子塼	a large oblong brick, like a *tray*.

抓

CHUA¹.

抓破皮	to *scratch* the skin off.
抓周	reckless *grabbing* (from an old custom).
把他抓住	*seize* him; *clutch* him.
沒得抓頭	there is no *security* or *pledge*.
一把抓子	a flesh *hook* used by cooks.

找

CHAO³.

找個大石頭	*look for* a big stone.
找不倒	I cannot *find* one.
找喫	to *seek* a livelihood.
我要找你	I will *demand* restitution or apology.
他還要找我三百錢	he has still to *make up* 300 cash to me.
我的賬找清楚了	my debt is *paid up*.
袖找子	the *cuff* on a dress-gown.
找袖子	*roll* up your sleeves.
把衣裳找紮起	*tuck* up your gown.

(204)

注 释

【打扛帮】声援某人。
扣 [kʰəu⁴] [kʰəu¹]
【扣襻】扣住纽扣的套。
【满算除扣】先算出总的数量,然后再扣除。
【扣洋布】最好的外国印花布。
【一扣线】一扣:一卷、一束。
托 [tʰo⁵]
【托子砖】一种大的椭圆形的砖。
抓 [tʂua¹]
找 [tʂao³]
【袖找子】长袍的袖口。

注释

抄 [tṣʰao¹]
折 [tṣe⁵]
扯 [tṣʰe³]
　【他两个在扯筋】扯筋：争论，吵架。
　【扯疯】即"抽风"，在医学上称为"惊厥"，是小儿时期常见的急症。
　【扯霍闪】闪电。
承 [tṣʰən²]
　【承发房】古代衙门里的收发室。

手 4

找挑子	to *tie* np a coolie's load.
找扎铺	a shop where paper effigies are *made*.

CH'AO¹.

抄家	to *confiscate* a property.
抄寫	to *transcribe*; to copy out.
一天抄起一雙手	you sit with your *hands* in your *sleeves* all day long. [stalls.
抄手麵	little dumplings sold hot in shops or on

CHE⁵.

折斷了	*broken* asunder.
生意折本	my business is bank*rupt*. [place of cash.
銀子折成錢	to *reduce* cash to silver; to pay silver in
折殀	*discount* in barter.
受折磨	to be greatly *afflicted*.

CH'E³.

扯起風蓬	*haul* np the sail.
扯草	to *pull up* weeds.
把衣裳扯爛了	I have *torn* my clothes.
扯布	to *buy* cloth.
扯胡琴	to *play* on a fiddle.
扯風箱	to *blow* Chinese bellows.
扯露水	to *attract* dew, as plants do.
扯雞毛	to *pluck* chicken feathers.
他兩個在扯筋	they are *quarrelling*.
扯瘋	to have convulsions.
扯謊	to tell lies.
扯霍閃	to lighten.

CH'EN². [yamen.

承發房	the *Receiving* and Despatching Office in a
沒人承受	he has no heirs to *succeed* him.
抱兒承繼後裔	adopt a son to *carry on* the family name.
承當不起	I am in*capable* of undertaking the trust.
不奉承人	don't *flatter* people.
多承你的好意	many *thanks* for your kindness.

(205)

手 4

FU².

扶手板	the *leaning*-board of a sedan chair.
拿竹子綁一路扶手	make a hand-*rail* of bamboo for the bridge.
扶起他走	*support* him along.
扶持	to *uphold*.
極力扶助他	*help* him to the best of your ability.

K'ANG⁴.

| 抗斷不依 | to *rebel* against the decision of the judges. |
| 抗糧不完 | to *resist* taxation and refuse to pay. |

KEO¹.

| 把楂滓抅乾淨 | *scrape* up all that rubbish. |

NIU³.

賊娃子扭了鎖	a thief has *twisted* off the lock.
他總要扭起說	he will certainly *turn* the story about.
扭扭揑揑的樣子	in a *grabbing* and pinching way; *niggardly*.
把他扭倒	*seize* him.

PA³.

把門關倒	shut the door; lit., *take* the door and shut it.
把我當做甚麼人	what do you *take* me to be?
把持公事	to *manipulate* public business.
我們看把戲	let us go and see the *juggling*.
打火把	to carry a *torch*.
拿把憑來	bring your *evidence*.
把守關口	to *guard* a pass.
把細看	look *carefully*.
沒得把柄的人	a man with no *determination* of character.
把總	a centurion.
一把連都要	I want the *whole* lot.
吊把錢	*about* a thousand cash.
一把柴	a *bundle* of firewood. (*N. A.*)
抓把米	take up a *handful* of rice. (*N. A.*)
一把鎖	one lock. (*N. A.*)

(206)

注 釋

扶 [fu²]
抗 [kʰaŋ⁴]
【抗斷不依】不接受法官的判決。
抅 [kəu¹]
扭 [ȵiəu³]
把 [pa³]
【拿把憑來】把凭: 凭证, 证据。
【把細看】仔细地看。
【把总】①动词。总领, 总管。②名词。明清两代镇守某地的武官, 职位次于千总。
【一把连都要】一整堆都要了。

注释

技 [tɕi⁴]
扮 [pan⁴]
（P'AN⁴当为PAN⁴，见803页勘误表。）
【打打扮扮走人户】穿得漂漂亮亮的出门走亲访友。
扼 [ŋɛ⁵]
抛 [pʰao¹]
【抛河】划船渡河。
【多抛点】（购买布匹等需要丈量的物品时，要求卖家）多留点余量。
批 [pʰei¹]
抖 [tʰəu³]
【抖脱】振动，甩动，使散开。
【我要抖你】抖：即"打"。

手 4

| 一把手把他拉住 | he caught him with one grab. (N. A.) |
| 兩把手不夠 | two men are not sufficient. (N. A.) |

CHI⁴.

| 技藝 | mechanical arts; military accomplishments |

P'AN⁴.

| 打打扮扮走人戶 | to *dress up* and go visiting. |
| 外國打扮 | foreign *dress*. |

NGE⁵.

| 扼緊怕扼死
放手怕飛了 | if I grasp it tightly I fear I may *squeeze* it to death, and if I slacken my grip I fear it will fly away. |

P'AO¹.

抛撒五穀	to *fling away* grain.
把前功抛棄了	to *abandon* what one has already wrought.
年輕婦女不可抛頭露面	young women should not *toss* the head and show the face in public.
抛妻別子	to *leave* one's wife and children for a long time.
輕抛抛的	*light* in weight.
抛河	to row a boat across the river.
多抛點	*give* a little extra (said when buying calico).
逢人且說三分話 未可全抛一片心	when you meet a person speak three parts of your mind, it is not necessary to *divulge* everything to him.

P'EI¹.

把賬批清楚	*write out* the account clearly.
候批	to await an *answer* from an *official*.
案批准了	the plea has been *allowed*.
批評他幾句	*reprimand* him.
你批好多	how much do you *offer* for the goods?

T'EO³.

抖灰塵	to *shake off* dust.
抖脫	to take to pieces, as a wooden framework.
我要抖你	I will *beat* you.
身上發抖	to *tremble*.
抖一口氣	to take a breath after hard work.

(207)

手 4-5

挩 T'EN⁴
在路上打個挩	to *delay* on the road.
工夫挩起了	they have *spun out* the work.
兩個人在那裏挩起了	they are *obstructing* each other's progress.
錫壺挩不贏銅壺	a pewter kettle will not *last* as long as a brass one.
挑子不挩頭	the ends of the load are not *balanced*.
他們挩倒做	they *vigorously hurried* the work through.

投 T'EO²
不肯投降	not willing to *yield* to the enemy.
投洋教	to *join* a foreign religious society.
投宿	to *repair* to a lodging for the night.
投明保正	to clearly *inform* the street official.
投不起數	the account does not *tally*.
好話幾句三冬煖 / 話不投機六月寒	a few kind words will warm one's heart even in mid-winter, but one is chilled even in mid-summer if words do not *suit* one's mind.
投榫頭	to *mortise* boards.

挑 TIAO⁴
提心挑膽的	alarmed ; fearful ; lit., to *carry* one's heart [and gall.

挏 ÜE⁵.
打挏了	*dented*, as a pewter pot might be.

READ ÜE¹.
挏個鈎鈎	*bend* the iron into a hook.

5 **招** CHAO¹.
招手	to *beckon* with the hand.
破獄招魂	to break open the earth-prison and *recall* the soul.
招梁子	to *enlist* soldiers.
招留強盜	to *harbour* thieves.
招呼他喫飯	*invite* him to dinner.
給他招呼一聲	go and *tell* him.
不聽招呼	he will not listen to *orders*.

(208)

注释

挩 [tʰən⁴]
【在路上打个挩】打个挩：停留、耽误了一下。
【工夫挩起了】挩起：拖长，消磨。
【两个人在那里挩起了】两个人互相妨碍对方。
【挑子不挩头】担子两边不平衡。
【他们挩倒做】挩倒做：精神旺盛地匆忙赶完工作。

投 [tʰəu²]
【投明保正】清楚地向保长报告。
【投不起数】账目不吻合，对不上账。

挑 [tiao⁴]

挏 [ye⁵] [ye¹]
【打挏了】打瘪了。

招 [tʂao¹]
【招梁子】招募士兵。

注 释

拘 [tɕy¹]
  【拘票】拘留或逮捕犯人时出具的凭证。
抽 [tʂʰəu¹]
  【抽收厘金】厘金：关税。
拙 [tɕye⁵] [tʂua⁵]
  【拙棒】傻瓜，笨蛋。
抹 [mo³] [ma⁵]

手 5

招牌	a *sign*-board.
蚊蟲招扇打 只爲嘴傷人	the mosquito *provokes* one to strike it with the fan, because it seeks to injure one with its mouth.
難得招架	it is difficult to *withstand* him.
不肯招認	he is not willing to *confess* to it.
樹大招風	a high tree *receives* the force of the wind.
招蜂子	to *hive* bees.

CHÜ¹.

莫拘禮	don't strictly *adhere* to etiquette; be free [and easy.
拘票	a warrant for the *arrest* of a person.
拘禁	to *confine* in prison, to put a *constraint* on company.
不拘那一個	no matter who.

CH'EO¹.

拘

抽

把那個木頭抽出來	*pull* that stick out from among the rest.
我抽個空空來	I will *take* a little time and come.
抽不脫身子	I cannot find time; lit., I cannot *pull* myself away.
抽身走了	he *withdrew* and departed.
抽收釐金	to *gather* custom.
抽人丁	conscription.
在抽屉裏頭	in the *drawer*.
我抽你幾鞭子	I will *whip* you a few strokes!

CHÜE⁵ CHUA⁵.

拙

我是個愚拙人	I am a *foolish* man.
拙棒	a *stupid* fellow.

MO³.

抹

抹顔色	to *rub on* colour; to paint.
衣裳抹髒了	you have *smeared* your clothes.
抹頸子	to *cut* one's throat.

MA⁵.

抹樟子	to *wipe* the table.

西蜀方言

手 5

把頭髮抹光生	brush your hair smooth.
抹脫幾十個錢	take a few tens of cash off the string.
抹些	be a little *quicker*.
轉彎抹拐的	turning *corners*.

拐 KUAI³.

拐拐上	at the *corner* of the street or road.
拐脚脚	a *crooked* or *distorted* foot.
車拐拐	a *handle* on a wheel.
倒拐子	the *elbow*.
螺蜥拐	the *ankle*.
做拐了	you have done *wrong*.
拐騙	to *swindle*.
那個娃娃的拐障大	that youngster's *deceitfulness* is great.
拐人妻女	to *kidnap* women.
拐一對鴿子囘來	my pigeon has *decoyed* a pair of pigeous [to my house.

拊 PU⁴.

信步行將去 由天擺拊來	Forward trustingly I go, Heaven *appoints* my fate I know.

拉 LA¹.

拉他起來	*pull* him up.
拉縴籐	to *haul* the tracking rope.
拉倒人	to *seize* a person.
不要拉扯別人	don't *involve* others.
把我們拉扯一 HA	try and get us into the job too.
拉皮條	to *procure* lewd women.
拉賬	to *buy on credit*.

抿 MIN¹.

抿頭髮	to *brush* the hair.
抿泥巴	to *smooth* plaster *with a trowel*.

挐 LA².

挐起走了	he has *taken* it away.
快去挐來	go quickly and *bring* it.
挐不起那麼多	I am not able to *carry* all that.

注 释

【抹些】快一点。
拐 [kuai³]
【倒拐子】手肘的俗称。
【螺蜥拐】足踝骨的俗称。
拊 [pu⁴]
拉 [la¹]
【拉纤藤】拉缆绳。
【拉账】赊账，欠账。
抿 [min¹]
挐（拿）[la²]

注释

拂 [fu⁵]
拈 [nien¹]
拔 [pa⁵] [pʰa⁵]
拜 [pai⁴]
拚（拼）[pʰin¹]
  【拼匀净】平均分配。
拌 [pan⁴]
  【拌钱】小孩子们玩的一种摔纸元宝的游戏。
  【拌嘴巴皮】说长道短，说闲话。
拇 [mu³]
  【指拇子】手指，脚趾。
抱 [pao⁴]

手 5

把東西拏倒	*take hold of* the thing.
拏給他	*give* it to him.
捉拏人	to *apprehend* a person.
拏定主意	*resolve* upon a course of action.

FU⁵.

拂塵	a *duster*, in the form of a coir switch, used [by Taoists.

NIEN¹.

拈菜	to *pick up* food *with chopsticks*.
拈鬮	to *draw* lots.

PA⁵, PʼA⁵.

連根都拔出來	*pull it up* roots and all ; *eradicate* it.
拔膿生肌	*extract* the pus and heal up the sore.
提拔人	to *set up* a man in business, or give him a situation.

PAI⁴.

拜菩薩	to *worship* idols.
拜年	to *greet* one another at the New Year.
行客拜坐客	the traveller first *pays respects* to the resident.
拜客去了	he has gone *visiting*.
我拜托你給我帶一封信	I *respectfully* ask you to carry a letter for me.

PʼIN¹.

拚匀净	*divide* it equally.
我找他拚命	I will find him and *throw away* my life [before him.

PAN⁴.

拌桶	the *separating* tub ; i. e., the thrashing tub [on the harvest field.
把香料拌匀	*mix* the spices evenly.
拌錢	to play *pitch and toss*.
拌嘴巴皮	to gossip.

MU³.

指拇子	*fingers ; toes*.

PAO⁴.

抱娃娃	to *carry* a child *in the arms* ; to *hug* a baby.

手 5

披	抱一抱柴來	bring an *armful* of firewood.
	抱樹子	to *encircle* a tree with the arms.
	抱兒子	to *adopt* a child of the same surname.
	抱愧	to *feel* ashamed.
	P'E¹.	
	披簑衣	to *throw on* a coarse rain-cloak.
	披頭散髮	*dishevelled* hair.
拍	P'E⁵, P'A⁵.	
	拍肩	to *pat* on the shoulder.
	拍灰塵	to *slap* off the dust from clothes, etc.
	一個巴掌拍不響	you cannot *clap* hands with one hand.
	拍門	*knock* at the door.
抬	T'AI².	
	抬轎子	to *carry* a chair *between two*.
	抬盒	an ornamental tray *borne between two*.
	抬起腦壳看	*lift up* your head and look.
	高抬市價	to *raise* the current price.
	抬老營	*insurrection*; to *strike work*.
	抬舉人	to *praise*, or *flatter* people.
	抬頭	a character *raised* above the level of the top line out of respect.
	READ T'AI¹.	
	把那頭抬起	*lift up* that end.
	抬個輕重	*weigh* it in your hand.
抵	TI³.	
	抵住	to *resist*, as an enemy; to *steady*, or *hold*, as against one driving nails.
	抵攏榫	to *drive home* a tenon.
	一命抵一命	to *forfeit* life for life.
	拿地方抵賬	to give land as surety for a debt.
	我抵他幾句	I *withstood* him a little.
	抵攏壁頭	*push* it against the wall.
	把門抵倒	*drop* the door from within.
	事情抵倒了	the affair is *imminent*; the day has arrived.

(212)

注 释

【抱儿子】收养一个孩子。
披 [pʰei¹]
拍 [pʰe⁵] [pʰa⁵]
抬 [tʰai²] [tʰai¹]
【抬盒】古代汉族民间婚娶时所用的一种红色木制礼盒，因其由两人所抬而得名，流行于四川一带。
【抬老营】叛乱，暴动，罢工。
抵 [ti³]
【抵拢榫】使榫卯牢固结合。
【事情抵倒了】抵倒：即将来临。

注 释

担 [tan³]
抑 [liəu³]
【莫把我抑倒】不要死抓着我不放。
拖 [tʰo¹]
【拖账】债务到期不还。
拒 [tɕy⁴]
拆 [tsʰe⁵]
押 [ia⁵]

手 5

TAN³.

雞毛担子	a feather *duster*.

LIU³.

莫把我抑倒	don't *cling* to my shoulder; don't *hang* on [my arm.

T'O¹.

把這個拖開	*drag* this out of the way.
拖鋪蓋	to *drag* the bed clothes over one.
套褲帶拖起了	your legging strings are *trailing down*.
拖石頭	to *trail* heavy stones with a rope. [pit.
一拖炭	a *truckful* of coal, as it is *dragged* out of the
拖蓋房子	to tile a roof as thinly as possible.
拖起兩個娃娃	*embarrassed* with two babies.
莫去拖累別人	don't go and *involve* others.
拖延時候	to *delay*; to *dawdle*.
拖賬	to *delay* the payment of a debt.

CHÜ⁴.

拒絕惡人	to *break off intercourse* with evil men.

TS'E⁵.

拆開書信	*break open* the letter.
我替你拆不出來	I cannot *retail* it; lit., *break* it up for you.
把線縫拆了	*unrip* the seam.
拆乾淨	*pick it all out* clean, as tares from wheat.
拆散人家的婚姻	to *derange* people's marriage appointments.

IA⁵.

畫押	to *sign* a document by marking it with a cross. [ment.
押解犯人	to *escort* prisoners to the capital for judg-
押擔子	to *escort* coolies with goods.
查街的把他押起	the policeman *arrested* or *detained* him.
押租銀	*deposit* money on a house or land.
押歲錢	money given to each member of one's family at the New Year.

(213)

手 5-6

拗 NGAO⁴.

押倒他做	compel him to do it.
小押當	a small *pawn*-shop.
鐵拗	a *lever*; a *crowbar*.
拗刀	a burglar's *jimmy*.
試倒試倒的拗	*lever* it up carefully. [stick.
拗在肩頭上	to *carry* a bundle over the shoulder with a
莫說拗不起的話	don't say that you are not able to *do* it.
那人性拗	that fellow is *obstinate*.
拗不過命	you cannot *wilfully* go beyond your fate.
我們兩個是拗起的	our opinions *differ*; we are working at *cross-purposes*.

挖 CH'A³.

把三脚挖起	*set up* the tripod.
挖個茅蓬	*erect* a straw shed.

指 CHĬ³.

十根指拇有長短	of the ten *fingers* some are long and some [are short.
四指厚的臕	four *finger*-breadths of fat.
大指拇	the *thumb*.
踢倒脚指拇	I have kicked my *toes* against a stone.
連指頭都沒有指過他	I have not even had to *point* the *finger* at him in reproof.
指摘人	to *reprove* one.
望你指示	I look to you to *teach* me.
指路碑	a *sign* post. [me the road.
請你幫我指個路	please *direct* me on my way; please *show*

挌 KO⁵.

他們兩個挌搦	they are *fighting* together.

持 CH'Ĭ².

操持家務	to *manage* one's household affairs.
他一個人就把持了嗎	is he alone to *direct* the business? should he monopolise the affair?
持定主意	to *resolve* on a course of action.

(214)

注　释

拗 [ŋao⁴]

【铁拗】铁质的杠杆，铁橇，起货钩，铁棍。

【拗刀】窃贼的撬棍。

【莫说拗不起的话】不要说大话。

【我们两个是拗起的】我们俩的意见不同；我们俩观点分歧，话不投机。

挖 [tʂʰa³]

指 [tʂɿ³]

挌 [ko⁵]

【他们两个挌搦】挌搦：打斗。

持 [tʂʰʅ²]

注释

拯 [tʂən³]
拷 [kʰao³]
拳 [tɕʰyen²]
拱 [koŋ³]
【拱窑】圆顶的窑。
【拱背背】驼背。
【打拱手】两手抱拳，微微鞠躬，以示恭敬、服从。
挂 [kua⁴]
括 [kua⁵]
拿 [la²]
拏（拿）[la²]
按 [ŋan⁴]
拾 [ʂʅ⁵]

手 6

CHEN³.

| 拯濟百姓 | to *succour* the people. |
| 拯救 | to *rescue*. |

K'AO³.

| 非刑拷打 | to *torture* illegally *in order to extort a confession*. |

CH'ÜEN².

一拳大	as big as my *fist*.
赤手空拳	*empty-handed*, as when one departs this life.
磨拳擦掌	he felt his *fists* and rubbed his palms, as if eager for the fray.
打拳	*fisticuffs*.
打一套拳	to *box* a round.

KONG³.

拱起的	*convex*; *arched*.
一座拱橋	an *arched* stone bridge.
拱窑	a *dome-shaped* kiln.
拱背背	a *hump-back*.
打拱手	to make a slight *bow* with the hands in front of the breast.

KUA⁴. same as 掛.

KUA⁵.

| 括斗 | a *dipper* used for baling a boat. |

LA². same as 拏.

LA². same as 拏.

NGAN⁴.

按跳蛃蛋	to *place the hand on* a jumping flea.
把那頭按倒	*keep down* that end.
按察司	the Provincial Judge.
按律法定罪	to judge one *according to* law.
按月支錢	to pay wages *by* the month.
按時候喫飯	to take meals at a set time.

SHI⁵.

| 收拾行李 | *gather up* the baggage. |

手 6

收 收拾拾走人戶　　to *dress up* and go visiting.
收拾房子　　to *repair* a house.
我要收拾你　　I will *thrash* you.

拴 SHUAN[1].
拴腰帶　　to *bind on* one's girdle.
把牛拴在圈裏　　*fasten up* the cow in the cow-house.
把心要拴倒　　you must *fix* your mind on it.
把脚給我拴倒了　　it *restrains* me from travelling.

挑 T'IAO[1].
喊幾個挑夫挑挑子　　} call a few *coolies* to *carry* the loads.
挑菜喫　　*pick up* some food and eat.
挑選　　to *select*.
挑泥巴　　to *dig up* soil.
挑動是非　　to *stir up* mischief.
挑衣裳　　to *fell* the seams of a garment.
挑花　　to *embroider*.

拶 TSAN[3].
拶手　　to *torture* by wedging pieces of wood be-[tween the fingers.

挖 UA[1].
挖菜園地　　to *dig* a vegetable garden.
挖瓢　　to *hollow out* wooden ladles.
賊娃子挖洞　　the thief has *tunnelled* a hole in the wall.
做事挖根斷苗　　he uses drastic measures; lit., *digs up* the roots and breaks the sprouts.
挖耳子　　an *ear-pick*.
銀挖耳　　a silver hair pin.
恨不得把心挖出來待你　　} would that I could *gouge out* my heart to serve you.
醫得眼前瘡挖去心頭肉　　} it heals the sore but *scoops* my heart out; met., to use capital to pay a debt.
把那個錯字挖補好　　} *erase* that wrong character and re-write it.

(216)

注 釋

拴[ṣuan¹]
挑[tʰiao¹]
拶（拶）[tsan³]
【拶手】旧时一种夹犯人手指的刑罚。
挖[ua¹]
【挖耳子】用来掏耳朵的耳挖勺，耳挖子。
【把那个错字挖补好】把那个错字擦掉再重写上。

注释

挨 [ŋai¹]
　【没得挨靠】没有值得信任的。
　【挨一挨二的来】一个一个地来。
振 [tʂən⁴]
　【地振板】木板地面。
捉 [tʂo⁵]
挟（挟）[tɕia⁵]
　【挟嫌】心怀怨恨。
　【挟床】库存。
捐 [tɕyen¹]
捋 [le⁵]
挬 [pʰao²]
　【挬个沟沟】用锄头挖一条沟。
挪 [lo²]

手 7

NGAI¹.

没得挨靠	I have no one to *trust* to.
我两个的房子挨倒的	our houses are *near* together.
我两个没有挨过手	I have had no *dealings* with him.
挨一挨二的来	come one by one.
挨门求食	to beg from door to door.
挨挨擦擦的	to hang about; to lounge round; to sponge [on people.

CHEN⁴.

地振板	a *boarded floor*; the boards of a *floor*.

CHO⁵.

捉强盗	to *arrest* robbers.
捉黄鳝	to *gripe* eels.
捉鸡	to *catch* a chicken.

CHIA⁵.

挟在夹窝里	he has *clasped* it under his arm.

READ SHIA⁵.

挟嫌	to *cherish* hatred.
不受他的挟制	I will not suffer his *oppression*.
挟床	the stocks.

CHÜEN¹.

捐钱	to *contribute* money.
捐官	to *buy* office.

LE⁵.

捋胡豆叶	to *strip off* bean leaves *with the hand*.
捋肠子	to clean intestines by *drawing* them through the hand.

P'AO².

挬个沟沟	to *dig out* a drill with a hoe.
挬锄	a hoe.
挬饭	to *shovel* rice into the mouth with chop-[sticks.

LO².

把船挪开	*move* the boat *aside*.
官有挪山之计	magistrates have plans for *removing* [mountains.

(217)

手 7

	寬處兌挪	*stand aside* in a wide place (a coolie's call).
	兌挪銀子	to *lend*, or *borrow*, money for a short time without interest.

捕 PU⁴.

	捕班	thief *catchers*.
	螳螂捕蟬豈知黃雀在後	the mantis *clutches* the cicada, but knows not that the yellow bird is behind him.

挺 T'IN³.

	挺脫籬壁	*push out* a piece of wall.
	挺你的牙齒	I'll *knock out* your teeth.
	挺釘子	to *drive out* a nail.
	挺身上前	to go forward *resolutely*.
	硬挺挺的	firm and *unbending*.

挫 TS'O⁴.

	把螺螄骨挫開了	I have *dislocated* my ankle.

捎 SHAO¹.

	捎在挑子上	*tie* it on the top of the coolie's load.
	我們要捎帶一點貨物	I will *lade* my boat with some goods, besides taking you passengers.
	捎一封信	to *carry* a letter.

READ SHAO⁴.

	捎馬子	a long cash bag.

挽 UAN³.

	挽囬不轉	he cannot be *led* back to righteousness; [irreclaimable.
	手挽手的走	to walk hand in hand.
	挽倒他	*hold on to* him; *retain* him as a good friend.
	挽紇縫	to *tie* a knot.
	挽毛辮子	to *twist* the queue round the head.
	挽子	a short string made of palm leaf, used to carry meat.
	挽口	*circumference*.
	把袖子挽起	*turn up* your sleeves.
	花挽袖	embroidered sleeves.

注 释

捕 [pu⁴]

挺 [tʰin³]

【挺脫籬壁】推倒篱笆墙。

挫 [tsʰo⁴]

捎 [ṣao¹] [ṣao⁴]

【捎马子】即马褡子。可搭于肩头或驴、马背上的长形厚布袋，中间开口，两端皆可盛物。

挽 [uan³]

【挽纥缝】打一个结。

【挽子】用棕榈叶做成的短绳，用来带食物。

【挽口】圆周，周长，胸围。

注 释

掌 [tʂuaŋ³]
挣 [tsən⁴]
掣 [tʂʅ⁴]
捧 [pʰoŋ³]
(PO'NG⁴当为PƠNG³，见803页勘误表。)
【捧盒】古代的一种摆件，里面可放杂物。
抡(抡) [lən²]
【我要抡你几锭子】我要打你几拳。
掀 [ɕyen¹]

手 8

CHANG³.

手掌	the *palm* of the hand.
熊掌	bear's *paws*.
鵝掌	a goose's *web-foot*.
釘馬掌	to nail on a horse's *shoe*.
掌大權柄	to *exercise* great authority.
掌櫃	the master of a shop.
二掌櫃	the *manager* of a chair shop. [of another.
打掌子	to act as a substitute ; to do work in place
泥掌子	a plasterer's large square *trowel*.
他掀我一掌	he gave me a push. (*N. A.*)

TSEN⁴.

挣起一個癆病	to *exert* one's self overmuch and cause a [serious illness.
挣錢	to *gain* money by effort.
挣不起來	I cannot *force* it up ; I cannot *lift* it.

CHĪ⁴.

| 我這幾年的事很掣肘 | I have been much *embarrassed* these few years. |

PO'NG⁴.

捧一捧御麥	scoop up a *double handful* of maize.
用手捧盡千江水 難洗今朝滿面羞	though I *lave* up the water of a thousand streams, it will not wash away this one morning's shame.
捧讀書信	to *hold* a letter in the hands and read it.
捧盒	a round box in which presents are *presented*.
大家捧起做這個活路	let us all *unite* and do this job.

LEN².

| 我要抡你幾錠子 | I will *strike* you a few blows with my fist. |

SHÜEN¹.

掀天動地	to *shake* heaven and earth. [in.
掀門簾子進來	he *jerked* aside the door-screen and came
給他一掀	give it a *push*.

(219)

手 8

掮

你們莫掀	don't crowd.
掀他出去	hustle him out.
掀盤	a malt shovel.

T'IEN⁴.

| 捵燈 | to raise the wick of a lamp. |

K'EN³.

勒掯人	to illegally exact money or goods from people.
掯糧不發	to illegally withhold soldiers' rations.
掯節	a time of difficulty or hardship, as a reckoning day.

CH'IA⁵.

掐鼻根	to dig the thumb nail into the root of a fainting person's nose.
你莫掐我	don't pinch me.
掐菜薹	to break off vegetable shoots.
掐草帽子	to plait straw hats.

CHÜEN³.

把門簾子捲起	roll up the door screen.
搭個捲棚	put up an awning that may be rolled back when not sunny.
我還有一捲捲布	I have a small roll of cloth by me.

K'ONG⁴.

| 控告 | to accuse. |

KUA⁴.

掛帳子	to hang up bed-curtains.
掛招牌	to hang out a sign board.
掛麵	vermicelli, made by hanging dough strips on rods.
掛衣裳	to hitch one's clothes on anything by accident.
欠心掛腸	in suspense; anxious about anything.
他把我掛慻了	he keeps putting me off.
掛口不題	patient and silent under obloquy.
掛賬	to enter in an account.
掛個名字	to enroll one's name.
買一掛魚	buy a string of small fishes. (N.A.)

(220)

注 釋

【掀盤】揭老底,揭底牌。
捵 [tʰien⁴]
【捵灯】把灯芯挑高一点。
掯 [kʰən³]
【勒掯人】刁难人,向他人非法勒索钱物。
【掯粮不发】非法扣留士兵的定量配给。
【掯节】艰难困苦的时光。
掐 [tɕʰia⁵]
捲(卷) [tɕyen3]
控 [kʰoŋ⁴]
掛(挂) [kua⁴]
【他把我掛慻了】他一直搪塞我。
【掛口不题】在他人破口大骂时忍耐和保持沉默。

注释

掠 [lio⁵]
捻 [nie⁵]
【捻个手】又叫"摸码儿",旧时农村集市上讨价还价时为避免别人知道,在遮挡物下通过互相捏或感受对方的手来讨价还价的方法。
排 [pʰai²]
掃(扫)[sao⁴]
【扫数还清】还清债务。
【这才扫脸】扫脸:丢面子。
捨(舍)[ʂei³]
授 [ʂəu⁴]

手 8

LIO⁵.

| 掳掠 | to *plunder*. |

NIE⁵.

| 捻個手 | a manner of bargaining by *pinching* or [feeling each other's hands· |
| 捻嘴子了 | dead. |

P'AI².

一排一排的坐	to sit in *rows*.
排行第幾	what is your *rank* in the family?
早些安排	*get ready* beforehand.
排鞋子	to *finish* shoes.
大排場	a *swaggering* dandy.
四排三間	four *partition walls* and three rooms.

SAO⁴.

掃把	a *broom*.
掃把星	a comet.
雞毛掃掃	a feather *duster*.

READ SAO³.

打掃房屋	*sweep* the room.
掃數還清	the debt is *cleared off*.
這纔掃臉	this *puts* one *out of* countenance.

SHE³.

捨得寶來寶掉寶	precious things you will receive if you precious things can *give*; your pearls give *up* then think not strange if you get agates in exchange.
捨得珍珠換瑪瑙	
捨身巖	a cliff over which people throw themselves.
捨不得錢	I cannot *part with* the money; he be-[grudges his cash.

SHEO⁴.

| 男女授受不親 | men and women should not *give* and take [things directly. |
| 傳授 | *precepts* which have been handed down in a family. |

(221)

手 8

T'AN¹.

| 探水淺深 | to *try* in any way, whether water is deep or shallow; to *sound*. |
| 探倒那股病氣 | when I came in *contact* with that contagion. |

READ T'AN⁴.

| 探子 | a *spy*. |

T'IAO³.

掉換銀錢	to *change* money.
掉毛錢	to *change* bad cash for good; to take back bad cash.
左掉	to *swap*.
掉個手	*change* your hand.
打個掉	*turn* it end for end.

READ TIAO⁴.

| 衣裳掉了 | the clothes have *fallen down*. |
| 失掉 | to *lose*. |

T'UE¹.

推車子	to *push* a wheelbarrow.
推橈	to row a boat; to *push* an oar.
推麵	to *grind* flour.
把板子推光生	*plane* the board smooth.
喫不得推個杯嗎	if you can't stand the drink *abstain* from it.
推辭	to *decline* to do anything.

TS'AI³.

| 蜂子探花 | the bees *sip* the flowers. |

TSIE⁵.

接客	to *receive* guests.
接屋簷水	to *catch* the water from the roof in a vessel.
接親	to *marry* a wife.
接線	to *join* a thread.
接桃子樹	to *graft* peach-trees.
接爐橋	to *weld* on a fire-bar.
把索子接起	*splice* the rope.

(222)

注释

探 [tʰan¹] [tʰan⁴]
掉 [tʰiao³] [tiao⁴]
【掉毛钱】将损坏的钱换成好的,收回损坏的钱。
【左掉】交易,交换。
【打个掉】掉个头。
推 [tʰuei¹]
【推桡】划船,推桨。
【推面】磨面粉。
採(采)[tsʰai³]
接 [tsie⁵]
【接炉桥】焊接加热条。

注释

捷 [tsʰie⁵]
捱(挨) [ŋai²]
【情愿在世上捱，不愿在土里埋】宁愿活在世上受苦受难，也不愿死了埋进土里。
【莫在后头尽捱】不要总是在后面磨蹭。
掩 [ien³]
揸 [tṣhaˡ¹]
【一揸钱】一叠钱。
【揸一揸钱】揸：用手指撮东西，拿取。
插 [tṣʰa⁵]
【插不进帮】不被允许加入旅行队。
揣 [tṣʰuai³]

乎 8-9

| 接接連連四天雨 | it has rained for four days *consecutively*. |
| 接倒寫 | write it *after* the last; write it *immediately below* the last. |

TS'IE⁵.

| 報捷 | to announce a *victory*. |
| 捷路 | a *short*-cut; a *near* way; a *bye*-way. |

NGAI². sign of the passive.

捱打	to *be beaten*.
情願在世上捱 / 不肯在土裏埋	I'd rather *suffer* in this world than lie beneath the sod.
實在捱不住了	I really cannot *wait* for it.
莫在後頭儘捱	don't be always *loitering* behind.
捱都捱得脫嗎	do you think that you can get out of it by *procrastinating*?

IEN³.

掩不過衆人的耳目	you can't cover *up* people's ears and eyes.
遮掩	to *hide*, as the face.
把我掩倒了	he *puts* me *in the shade* entirely.
那門是半掩半開的	that door is half *shut* and half open.

CH'A¹.

| 一揸錢 | a *pinch* of cash. |
| 揸一揸錢 | *take up* a *pinch* of cash between the finger and thumb. |

CH'A⁵.

插個草標	to *stick* a twisted straw into anything and expose it for sale
插花戴朶	to wear flowers in the hair.
有意栽花花不發 / 無心插柳柳成陰	a wish to raise flowers will ne'er make them spring; no thought to *plant* willows—a shade they become.
你莫插嘴	don't *intrude* your opinions.
插不進幫	he cannot be *admitted* into the caravan.
扇插子	a fan *case*.

CH'UAI³.

| 揣摩 | to *thoroughly consider*. |

(223)

手 9

CH'ONG⁴.

笋子捅出土	the bamboo shoots have *burst* through the ground.
酒捅了	the wine has *popped* the cork and overflowed.
鎖子捅得開	the lock can be *jerked* open.
把釘子捅出去	*drive* out the nail.
幫我捅一肩	help me to *jog* a shoulder; *i.e.*, help me carry my load.
打手捅	masturbation.
捅殼子	a liar.
捅幾百錢給我	*lend* me a few hundred cash.
大家綁捅捅	all help to *make up the deficiency*.

HUAN⁴.

換銀子	to *exchange* silver.
衣裳換了來洗	*change* your clothes for the washing.
換一根柱頭	*replace* the rotten post with a new one.
換毛	to *cast* hair or feathers; to *moult*.
改心換腸	to *reform* one's self.
換換親	to *intermarry*.
換手摳背	to help each other; lit., to scratch each other's backs.

REO².

| 揉眼睛 | to *rub* one's eyes. |
| 輕輕的揉 | *rub* it gently with the hand as an aching limb. |

K'AI¹.

| 把桌子揩乾淨 | *wipe* the table clean. |

CHIE⁵.

揭帽子	to *take off* the hat.
蓋蓋莫揭早了	don't *lift off* the lid too soon (like, "don't count your chickens before they are hatched").
揭裱	to remount, as scrolls or pictures.
揭二十張紙	*buy* twenty sheets of paper.

CHIEN³. in some senses the same as 揀.

| 揀棉花 | to *pick* cotton. |
| 揀選 | to *select*. |

(224)

注 释

捅 [tʂʰoŋ⁴]

【笋子捅出土】竹笋的幼芽从土里钻出来。

【酒捅了】酒突然冲出软木塞并溢出。

【打手捅】自慰。

【捅殼子】说谎者；骗子。

【大家綁捅捅】綁捅捅：弥补不足。

換（换）[xuan⁴]

揉 [zəu²]

揩 [kʰai¹]

揭 [tɕie⁵]

揀（拣）[tɕien³]

注释

揆 [kʰuei²]
【揆情度理】揆：揣度，揣测。揣测考量是否合情合理。

描 [miao²]

揑（捏）[ȵie⁵]

搝（碰）[pʰoŋ⁴]
【搝倒我连二杆】连二杆：胫骨，也泛指小腿。

提 [tʰi²]

搹 [tʰo⁵]

揪 [tsiəu¹] [tsiəu³] [tsiəu⁴]
【揪痧】民间治疗某些疾病的一种方法。通常用手指揪颈部、咽喉部、额部，使局部皮肤充血。

手 9

剩下的要揆起	*gather* up the remnants.
放賬如捨賬 收錢如揆錢 }	to give credit, is like losing money ; to get your money again, is like *finding* it.
揆一副藥	*buy* a course of drugs.

揆 K'UE².

揆情度理	*consider* the fitness of things.

描 MIAO².

描龍畫鳳	to *sketch* dragons and phœnixes.
描金的磁器	*gilded* China ware.

揑 NIE⁵.

挐泥巴揑個菩薩	to *mould* an idol out of clay.
揑造謠言	to *trump* false reports.

搝 P'ONG⁴.

搝倒我連二扦	it *knocked* me on the shin-bone.
搝腦殼	to *thump* with the head.
搝傷	a *bruise*.
在路上搝倒了	I *met* him on the road.

提 T'I².

提一提籃菜	carry a *basket*ful of vegetables. [law.
他提起腦殼耍	he *carries* his head in his hand, as an out-
提督軍門	a general.
提倒耳朶敎	*take* him by the ear and admonish him.
是那個提起說的	who *suggested* it ?
提醒	to stir up by *reminding* ; to *enlighten*.
時刻提防他	constantly *beware* of him.

搹 T'O⁵.

我是來得搭搹	I have come *uncceremoniously*.

揪 TSIU¹.

揪耳朶	to *seize* one by the ear.
揪着他不放手	he *clutched* him and would not let him go.
揪痧	to *pinch* the throat as a counter-irritant.

READ TSIU³.

把衣裳揪起來	*wring* out the clothes.
拿手揪一 ha⁴.	*twist* it a little.

(225)

西蜀方言

手 9-10

捶揚揮揖援搽撐搥揉搊

READ TSIU⁴.
把手桿捈了　　　I have *sprained* my wrist.
NGANG³, NGAN³.
在那裏捈倒的　　where was he *hiding*?
IANG².
遠近傳揚　　　　to *publish* far and near.
HUE¹.
揮淚　　　　　　to *brush away* tears.
道理發揮得好　　in commenting he *wields* a skilful pen.
I⁵.
作揖　　　　　　to make *the ordinary low bow*.
作過揖的　　　　married.
ÜEN².
我望你救援　　　I look to you to *deliver* me.
CH'A⁵.
搽油　　　　　　to *smear* with oil.
搽胭抹粉　　　　to *rouge* the face.
搽藥　　　　　　to *rub on* medicine.
CH'AN³.
我撐你幾條子　　I'll *beat* you with a stick.
撐灰塵　　　　　to *beat* the dust out of clothes, or off the [articles.
霍閃一撐　　　　the lightning *flashed*.
CH'UE².
搥背　　　　　　to *beat* the back.
打搥　　　　　　to *fight* with the fists.
搥字　　　　　　to take a rubbing of the characters on a [stone.
SANG³.
揉進去　　　　　*wedge*, or *stuff* it into an empty space.
我揉你幾錠子　　I'll *thump* you a bit.
LIU⁴.
把爐子搊通　　　*poke* the ashes out of the grate.

(226)

注　釋

捈[ŋaŋ³] [ŋan³]
揚(扬) [iaŋ²]
揮(挥) [xuei¹]
揖 [i⁵]
援 [yen²]
搽 [tʂʰa⁵]
撐 [tʂʰan³]
【我撐你幾條子】撐：抽打。
【霍閃一撐】闪电闪了一下。
搥(捶) [tʂʰuei³]
【打搥】搥打，敲打。
【搥字】拓印石碑上的字。
揉 [saŋ³]
搊 [liəu⁴]

注释

搋 [tʂʰuai¹]
【拿来搋起】搋：藏物于怀。
携 [ɕi¹]
揌 [tʂan³]
【拿抹揌布揌干】抹揌布：抹布，洗碗布。
搆 [kəu⁴]
【我搆不上他】我难以达到他的水准。
【你莫同我结搆】结搆：结下怨恨，产生敌意。
搬 [pan¹] [pʰan²]
【搬盘人】乱使唤人做无用功。
搧（扇）[ʂan¹]
搜 [səu¹]

手 10

搋　CH'UAI¹.
拿來搋起　　　pocket it in the bosom of your dress.
搋麵　　　　　to *knead* dough.　[*fingers* behind the back.
搋背手　　　　to offer money by *making signs with the*

携　SHI¹.
求你携帶他　　will you kindly *take* him *along with* you.
望你提携　　　I look to you to *assist* me *in my poverty*.

揌　CHAN³.
拿抹揌布揌乾　bring a *dish cloth* and *soak* it up.

搆　KEO⁴.
我搆不上他　　I cannot *reach up to* his level.
你莫同我結搆　don't contract *enmity* with me.

搬　PAN¹.
　　　　　　　　　　　　　　　　　　　[to *flit*.
搬家　　　　　to *remove* from one dwelling to another;
搬兵　　　　　to *transport* troops.　　[for nothing.
搬盤人　　　　to make one run backwards and forwards
搬動是非　　　mischief *making*.
他把我搬不彎　he cannot *bend* me one way or another.
搬來的本錢　　*borrowed* capital.　　　　[rive.
搬開　　　　　to *tear apart*, as a piece of firewood; to

READ P'AN².
搬東西　　　　to *remove* one's goods to another house.
搬木料　　　　to *transport* building materials (wood).
搬靈柩　　　　to *transport* a coffin and corpse to another place.

搧　SHAN¹.
搧扇子　　　　to *fan* with a fan.
搧火　　　　　to *fan* the fire.

搜　SEO¹.
搜贓　　　　　to *search* for stolen property.
搜人家的縫縫　to *scrutinize* people's faults.
搜山狗　　　　a *hunting* dog.

(227)

手 10

SEN³.

損人利己	to *injure* others and benefit one's self.
盆損壞了	the basin is *damaged*.

TA⁵.

搭在肩頭上	to *carry* on the shoulder, as a string of cash.
搭個板板橋	*erect* a wooden bridge.
搭個手拉一把	*give* me your hand and pull me up.
少搭一點骨頭	*give* me less bone with the meat.
搭個梯子	*set up*, or *place*, a ladder.
搭夥做生意	to *form* a joint stock company.
搭鍋煮飯	to boil rice in the same pot; to board together.
搭船	to *take a passage* on a boat.

MIE³.

搣一把下來	*break* off a piece.

NIE⁵.

吵嘴搊搦	*quarrelling* and *fighting*.

T'ANG².

搪縫子	to *stop up* cracks.
亂說些話來搪塞	to talk wildly in order to *screen* one's self.
搪揆	*abruptly*; *unceremoniously*.

U⁵,³.

搗嘴	to *cover* the mouth with the hand.
看搗倒	beware of *smothering* it, as a baby.

T'AO¹.

掏耳朵	to *pick* the ears.
把爐橋掏通	*poke* the ashes out of the grate.
掏陽溝	*clean out* the drain.
掏個過水溝	*dig out* a small water-course among the fields.
掏菸箱	to *lay out* beds for planting tobacco.
掏兩個錢出來	*take* a few cash out of your pocket.

K'O⁵.

搕你的腦殼	I'll *rap* you on the head!
敲搕人家的錢	to *extort* money.

注 释

損（损）[sən³]
搭[ta⁵]
搣[mie³]
【搣一把下来】搣：折断，用手拔。
搦[n.ie⁵]
搪[tʰaŋ²]
搗[u⁵][u³]
【看搗倒】小心窒息。
掏（掏）[tʰao¹]
【掏阳沟】掏：同"掏"。清理排水沟。
【掏烟箱】清理烟嘴里的烟灰。
搕[kʰo⁵]

注 释

搶（抢）[tsʰiaŋ³] [tsʰiaŋ¹]
【打抢人】掠夺，抢劫。
【抢火】从火中抢救物品。
搊[tsʰəu¹]
【搊高帽子】奉承，恭维。
搓[tsʰo¹]
搲[ua³]
【搲一桶水】搲：舀。
摇[iao²]
摺（折）[tṣe⁵]

手 10-11

搶 TS'IANG³.

打搶人	to *plunder* people.
搶犯人	to *rescue* a prisoner.
搶火	to *save things from* a fire.
搶影子	to get hydrophobia from a mad dog who has *stolen through* your shadow.
搶案	a *robbery* case.
搶上不搶下	*hurry* on board; no need to *hurry* on shore.
搶起搶起喫	to *gobble* up one's food.

READ TS'IANG¹.

| 搶白他幾句 | *withstand* him a little. |

搊 TS'EO¹.

搊肩包	to *elevate* the shoulders.
把他搊起來	*lift* him up.
搊猴子上得樹 / 搊狗上不得樹	if you *help* a monkey, he can climb a tree, but if you help a dog, he cannot climb for himself.
搊活人	to *aid* with money or influence.
搊高帽子	to *flatter*.

搓 TS'O¹.

| 搓繩子 | to *twist* a string by rubbing it between the [hands |
| 搓紙撚子 | to *roll* pipe lights. |

搲 UA³.

| 搲兩瓢米出來 | scoop out two ladlefuls of rice. |
| 搲一桶水 | dip up a bucketful of water. |

搖 IAO².

搖頭擺尾	to *shake* the head and wag the tail, as a [dog does.
搖搖擺擺的	a *swaggering* gait.
搖鈴子	to *ring* a hand-bell.
搖色子	to *rattle* the dice.

摺 CHE⁵.

| 摺衣服 | to *fold* clothes. |
| 手摺子 | a small *folded* account book. |

(229)

手 11

摺個角角	*double* down the corner of a book leaf.
摺轉來	to *turn round* and come back.
把書摺倒	*shut* the book.

摩 MO².

for example of use see 攧.

摳 K'EO¹.

摳癢	to *scratch* an itching place.
挖耳子摳進去 釘鈀扯出來	you *grab* it in with an earpick, but it will be torn from you with a rake.
摳腳板心	to *tickle* the soles of one's feet.
害摳心癆	to be afflicted with kleptomania.
多摳兩個錢	give a few cash more.

攧 IN⁴.

攧米	to *measure* rice; to buy rice.
攧布	to *measure* cloth; to buy calico.
攧地基	to *measure* the site for a house.

摟 LEO².

摟轎子	three men *carrying* a two-bearer chair.
幫我摟一把	give me a *lift* here, as with a heavy chair.
摟抱在懷	to *hug* to one's bosom.
拿繩子摟倒	*tie it up* with a string, as something which [is likely to fall.
摟搶人	to *plunder* people.

摞 LO².

摞絲	to *sort* silk.

READ LO⁴.

把書摞起	*pile* up the books.
端起一摞盆	to carry a *pile* of basins.

摸 MO¹.

莫亂摸	don't *touch*.
把錢摸起	*fork out* your money.
摸了幾里路的黑	I *groped* my way a few miles in the dark.
摸脈	to *feel* the pulse.
摸不實在	I don't *know* the facts of the case.
摸魚	to *catch* fish with the hands.

注　释

【把书折倒】合上书。
摩 [mo²]
摳（抠）[kʰəu¹]
【害抠心癆】盗窃成瘾。
攧 [in⁴]
【攧米】①称米。②买米。
【攧地基】测量地基。
摟（搂）[ləu²]
摞 [lo²] [lo⁴]
摸 [mo¹]
【摸不实在】不知道事情的真实情况，搞不清楚。

注 释

【阴倒摸起跑了】暗地里悄悄地跑了,潜逃。
【摸哥】小偷。
摹 [mo¹]
掺(掺) [tsʰan¹]
【掺毛钱】将损坏的钱和好钱混在一起。
摔 [ʂuai³]
【摔的耳屎】("摔的"当为"摔你的"。见803页勘误表。)
挽 [təu¹]
【挽东西】用(衣服的)下摆装东西。
【鞋挽跟】鞋拔子。
搏(抟) [tʰuan²]
摘 [tse⁵] [tsa⁵]
搿 [tsien³]
【搿杆】房屋构架的承重木杆。

手 11

摹	陰倒摸起跑了	to go off *stealthily*; to abscond.
	摸東西	to *pilfer*.
	摸哥	a *thief*.
	MO¹.	
	摹做某人的樣子	to *copy* a certain person.
掺	**TS'AN¹.**	
	鍋頭掺一瓢水	*add* a ladleful of water to the pot.
	掺毛錢	to *mix* bad cash with good.
	藕粉掺的有假	this arrowroot is *adulterated*.
摔	**SHUAI³.**	
	他兩個在摔交子	they are *wrestling*.
	草鞋摔了一背泥巴	your sandals have *splashed* your back with mud.
	摔袖頭子	to disdain one; lit., to *flap* the sleeve.
	摔手	an empty-handed coolie.
	摔的耳屎	I'll *slap* or *box* your ears.
	在手頭摔一摔的	*swaying* loosely in one's hand.
挽	**TEO¹.**	
	挽起衣挽	*lift* up your skirt to make a lap.
	挽東西	to *carry* things *in the lap*.
	鞋挽跟	a shoe-horn.
搏	**T'UAN².**	
	把人搏攏來	*gather* the men together.
摘	**TSE⁵, TSA⁵.**	
	看花莫摘花	look at the flowers but don't *pick* them.
	摘石榴	to *pluck* pomegranates.
	摘脫兩個人	*dismiss* those two men from the job.
	受人指摘	to receive *reproof*.
搿	**TSIEN³.**	
	把他的手搿起	*handcuff* him.
	搿桿	a *prop* used when putting up the frame of a Chinese house.

(231)

手 11-12

摧 TS'UEI¹.

| 摧脚盆箍 | to *drive* on the hoops of a tub. |
| 把馬肚帶摧緊 | *tighten* the horse's girth. |

撐 TS'EN¹.

把窗子撐開	to open the window by *propping* it up.
撐花兒	an umbrella.
撐門面	to *uphold* the honour of the family.
撐持不住	I cannot *sustain* the responsibility.
不是撐船手 休要動篙竿	if you cannot *pole* the boat don't meddle with the boat pole; met., don't attempt to do things that you know nothing about.

READ TS'EN⁴.

撐倒房子	to *prop* up a leaning house.
撐子	a prop.
撐筒	a bamboo tube with a rope through it for [*holding off* a dog.

擎 T'EN³.

| 把心子都擎落了 | this chair *jolts* the heart out of one. |
| 把手給我擎倒了 | it made my hand *tingle*. |

撤 CH'E⁵.

把東西悄悄的撤起走了	he has *removed* his goods to another place secretly (as a bankrupt does).
撤席	*clear away* the dishes (at a feast).
撤囘人馬	to *recall* the troops.

撞 CHUANG⁴.

| 猶如草把撞木鍾 | like *beating* a bell with a bunch of grass; [met., deaf as a post. |

READ CHUANG⁴, CH'UANG³.

把椅子撞倒了	he *knocked* over the chair.
撞背	I will *knock* you on the back (a coolie's cry).
撞騙	to *embezzle*.

READ CH'UANG³,⁴.

| 街上撞倒他 | I *met* him on the street. |
| 撞倒有 | *occasionally* there are (or is) some. |

(232)

注 釋

摧 [tsʰuei¹]
撐 [tsʰən¹]
【撐花儿】伞。
【撐子】支柱。
【撐筒】一种系有绳子的竹筒，用以驱逐恶犬等动物。
擎 [tʰən³]
【把心子都擎落了】重重地往下放。
撤 [tṣʰe⁵]
撞 [tṣuaŋ⁴] [tṣʰuaŋ³] [tṣʰuaŋ⁴]

注释

撫（抚）[fu³]
【抚个儿子】抚：收养，领养。
撬 [tɕʰiao¹] [tɕʰiao⁴]
撽 [kʰuan³]
【事情撽起了】事情遇到阻碍，无法进行下去。
撈（捞）[lao²]
撩 [liao¹] [liao²] [lao¹] [lao²]
【把缝子撩密点】撩：用针缝。用针把开缝的地方缝得密一点。

手 12

撫   FU³.

安撫百姓	to *tranquillize* the people.
撫臺	*Governor* of a province (a little lower in rank than Chï-tʻai).
撫養兒女	to *rear* children.
撫個兒子	to *adopt* a son.

撬   CHʻIAO¹.

賊娃子撬了門	a thief has *prized* open the door.

READ CHʻIAO⁴.

拏撬棒撬緊	take the *rack*-pin and *rack* it up tight, as [a load on a wheelbarrow.

撽   KʻUAN³.

把腦壳撽倒了	his head *stuck* in it.
事情撽起了	the affair is *obstructed*; things have come to a *dead-lock*.
有人撽住他	some men *arrested* him or *hindered* him [from returning.
事情把我撽在城裏頭	matters *detained* me in the city.
鑰匙撽不倒鐍	the key does not *grip* the wards of the lock.

撈   LAO².

撈倒一個死屍	they *dragged* a corpse out of the water.
水裏撈鹽	to *grapple* for salt in water; met., useless labour.
人死如燈滅 猶如湯澄雪 若要還魂轉 水裏撈明月	man dies as flame in darkness quenched, or snow by scalding water drenched, and if his soul you would restore, *haul* that reflected moon ashore; met., impossible.
水撈柴	drift-wood.

撩   LIAO¹,².

把縫子撩密點	*hem* the seam with a smaller stitch.

READ LAO²,¹.

把衣裳撩起	*hold up* your dress.

(233)

手 12

撚　　　NIEN³.
紙撚子　　rolled paper pipe-lights; spills.

撇　　　P'IE⁵.
泡子撇乾淨　　skim off the scum.
撇水灌田　　to lead the water on to the fields.
撇開閒雜人　　to rid one's self of idlers while conversing privately.

播　　　PO⁴.
播弄人家不和睦　to sow discord.

撥　　　PO⁵.
撥字向　　to set the coffin in its proper aspect in the grave.
撥燈　　to trim the lamp while it is burning.
撥開雲霧見青天　when the clouds disperse we will see the clear sky.
撥錢　　to borrow money, to be returned soon without interest.
撥載　　to tranship goods.
撥糧　　to transfer taxes along with land.
刁撥是非　　to stir up mischief.
撥壳壳　　to break off the shell, as of a pea-nut.

撲　　　P'U⁵.
飛蛾撲火自燒身　when the moth flaps against the light, it but burns itself.
灰塵撲進屋來了　the dust flies into the room.
花香撲鼻　　the scent of the flowers is wafted to one's nostrils.

撒　　　SA³,⁵.
撒穀種　　to sow rice broadcast in the seed field.
拿米來撒　　bring some rice and scatter it, to drive away the demons.
撒網　　to spread, or cast, a net.

READ SA⁵.
抓一把撒一把　he grabs a handful and loses a handful; met., prodigal.
撒帖歸一　　tidy up the place.
說那麽撒村的話　what vile words you use!

(234)

注　釋

撚（捻）[nien³]
【紙撚子】捻旧时用来点灯、点烟斗、点火的小纸卷、棉捻。

撇 [pʰie⁵]
【泡子撇干净】把渣滓除去。
【撇水灌田】把水引到田里。

播 [po⁴]

撥（拨）[po⁵]
【拨字向】安放棺木时，调整以选定一个正确的方位。
【拨载】转运（货物）。

撲（扑）[pʰu⁵]

撒 [sa³] [sa⁵]
【撒帖归一】收拾干净。
【说那么撒村的话】撒村：卑鄙可耻的。

注释

撕 [sɿ¹]
　【他两个人撕皮】撕皮：吵架，争论。
撮 [tso⁵] [tsʰo⁵]
　【抓一撮来】一撮：用两三个手指所能拿取者。形容量少。
　【扼个撮撮】旧时两个讨价还价的人将手藏在袖子中，通过手势商讨价格。
　【撮箕】即"簸箕"。一种铲状器具，用以收运垃圾。
擒 [tɕʰin²]
擎 [tɕʰin²]
据（据）[tɕy⁴]
搋 [sai¹]
　【搋背手】行贿。
挡（挡）[taŋ⁴]
擂 [luei²]
掳（掳）[ləu³]
　【掳人】绑架人。
擀 [kan³]

手 12-13

撕 SÏ¹.
衣服撕烂了　　I have *torn* my clothes.
他两个人撕皮　they are *quarrelling*.

撮 TSO⁶.
抓一撮来　　bring a *pinch* of it.
扼个撮撮　　to bargain by feeling each other's hands in [the sleeve.
　　READ TS'O⁵.
撮起　　to *gather* into a dustpan.
撮箕　　a refuse basket.

13 擒 CH'IN².
生擒活捉　　to *capture* alive.

擎 CH'IN².
擎天柱　　a pillar that *upholds* the sky; an atlas; an [indispensable man.

据 CHÜ⁴.
没凭据　　there is no *evidence*.
据我想　　*according* to my way of thinking.

搋 SAI¹.
搋高点　　*wedge* or *prop* it up a little higher.
搋在袖子头　*stuff* it up your sleeve.
搋背手　　to give bribes.

挡 TANG⁴.
abbreviated form of 擋.

擂 LUE².
擂胡椒面　　to *grind* pepper.
莫在我身上擂　don't *roll* about on me (said to a child).

掳 LEO³.
掳人　　to *kidnap* people.

擀 KAN³.
擀面　　to *roll* dough; *rolled* vermicelli.
擀面棒　　a roller for *rolling* dough.
添一盆擀饭　bring a big basin of rice from which to help one's self into the small basin.

(235)

手 13-14

擗	P'IE⁵.	interchanged with 敲.
	擗柴	to *break* sticks for the fire.
	擗倒脚肝	to *fracture* one's leg.
撻	TA⁵.	[the ground or water.
	提起撻	to take up with both hands and *thrash* on
	毛撻兒	the Chinese *queue*.
擔	TAN¹.	
	擔擔⁴子	to *carry* a load with a pole. [sibility.
	千斤擔⁴子要你擔	I want you to *undertake* this great respon-
	不必擔心	you need not *fear*.
	我替你擔心	I am *anxious* about you.
	我擔心他得病	I *fear* he will be sick.
	READ TAN⁴.	
	挑擔子	to carry a *load* on a pole.
	一擔水	two buckets of water.
	脫不倒擔子	you cannot get rid of the *responsibility*.
	擔肩子	the crossbars of a sedan chair, which rest on the bearers' shoulders.
操	TS'AO¹.	
	操兵	to *drill* troops. [don't *worry*.
	不必操心	you need not *exercise* yourself about it;
	操字	to *practise* writing.
	操手藝	to *learn* a trade.
	操持家務	to *manage* one's household affairs.
	操勞你	I have *troubled* you; thank you.
擇	TS'E⁵.	
	選擇	to *select*.
	擇個好日子	*choose* a lucky day.
擁	IONG³.	
	擁擁擠擠	to *crowd* and press upon.
擤	SIN³.	
	擤鼻子	to *blow* the nose *with the fingers*.

(236)

注释

擗 [pʰie³]
（P'IE⁵当为P'IE³,见803页勘误表。）

撻（挞）[ta⁵]
【提起撻】挞：用双手拍打。
【毛撻儿】鸡毛掸子。

擔（担）[tan¹] [tan⁴]。
【脱不倒担子】脱不了干系，应负责任。

操 [tsʰao¹]
【操兵】操练军队。
【操字】练习写字。
【操手艺】学习一门谋生的技术，学做生意。

擇（择）[tsʰe⁵]

擁（拥）[ioŋ³]

擤 [sin³]

注 释

擸 [la⁵] [le⁵]
　【擸鞋底】擸：同"纳"，密密地缝，补缀，缝补。
　【拿帕子擸脑壳】用缠头巾扎在头上。
拧（拧）[ȵin²]
搁（搁）[kʰo⁴] [ko⁵]
拟（拟）[ŋi³]
擡（抬）[tʰai²] [tʰai¹]
挤（挤）[tsi³] [tsi¹]
掷（掷）[tʂʅ⁵]
　【掷色子】色子：即骰子，一种赌具。用骨头、木头等制成的立体小方块，六面分刻一、二、三、四、五、六点。作赌具用。
扰（扰）[zao³]
擂（擂）[luei⁴]
　【擂谷子】用工具捶打，使谷子从谷穗中分离出来。

手 14-15

擸　　　　LA⁵, LE⁵.
　擸鞋底　　　　to *stitch* shoe soles.
　拿帕子擸腦殼　to *bind* up the head with a turban.

拧　　　　NIN².
　手頸頸拧倒了　I have *sprained* my wrist.

搁　　　　K'O⁴.
　搁在桌子上　　*place* it on the table.
　船搁在灘上　　the boat has *grounded* on the shallows.

　　　　READ KO⁵.
　就搁時候　　　to *procrastinate*; to *delay* to *put off* time.

擬　　　　NGI³.
　擬議　　　　　to *deliberate* upon; to *consult* and *decide*.

擡　　　　T'AI², ¹.
　　　　　　　　same as 抬.

擠　　　　TSI³, ¹.
　莫擠　　　　　don't *crowd*.
　擠不進去　　　I can't *push* my way in.
　街上擠得很　　the street is very *crowded*.
　擠奶子　　　　to *milk* an animal.
　擠膿　　　　　to *squeeze* out pus.

15 擲　　　　CHÏ⁵.
　擲色子　　　　to *throw* dice.

擾　　　　RAO³.
　擾亂地方　　　to *disturb* a district, as robbers do.
　又來討擾　　　I have come again to *trouble* you (polite phrase).
　操擾你　　　　I have *inconvenienced* you; thanks.
　心裏煩擾　　　*worried* in mind.

擂　　　　LUE⁴.
　擂鼓　　　　　to *beat* a drum.
　擂穀子　　　　to *hull* rice.

(237)

手 15-16

擺 PAI³.

擺樟子	to *lay* a table for a meal.
擺個攤子	to *spread* out a stall of wares.
擺閒條	to *gossip*; to *chat*.
擺龍門陣	to *talk idle talk*; lit., to *set in order* the "Dragon Gate Tactics."
擺手	to *ware* off with the hand. [negative.
擺腦壳	to *shake* the head when answering in the
打擺了	to be afflicted with *ague*. [tail.
走個龍擺尾	a man strutting, like a dragon *wagging* his
走個風擺柳	a woman strutting like the wind *shaking* the aspens.

撵 NIEN³.

撵他出去	*turn* him out!
撵不走	I cannot *expel* him, as a tenant.
兔子是狗撵出來的 話是酒撵出來的	a rabbit is *started* by a dog, and speech is *set going* by wine.

攀 P'AN¹.

不要攀扯別人	don't *drag* others into it; don't *involve* other [people.

摉 SEO³.

抖摉精神	to *arouse* one's self.

擦 TS'A⁵.

擦乾淨	*rub* it clean.
擦牙齒	to *brush* the teeth.
擦子	a *grater* for grating vegetables.
擦個火	*strike* a match.
我擦身過都沒有看倒他	I *rubbed* shoulders with him, and yet I did not notice him.
擦黑的時候	*dusk*; twilight.

攏 LONG³.

今天要走攏	you must *reach* the place to-day.
沒得人敢攏去	no one dared to *approach* it, or him.
攏在袖子頭	he *put* it into his sleeve.

(238)

注 釋

擺（摆）[pai³]
【摆闲条】闲聊。
【打摆了】因得了疟疾而打冷颤。（"了"当为"子"，见803页勘误表。）
【走个龙摆尾】像龙一样摆着尾巴走。比喻某人走路时昂首阔步、大摇大摆的样子。

撵（撵）[ɲien³]

攀 [pʰan¹]

摉（搜）[səu³]

擦 [tsʰa⁵]
【擦子】一种厨房用具，用于切割少量的蔬菜，使其成丝状或条状。

攏（拢）[loŋ³]

注　释

【拢在一起算】集中到一起计算总价。

搌 [su¹]

攙（搀）[tsʰan¹]

攔（拦）[lan²]

攤（摊）[tʰan¹]

【摊膏药】将膏药展开在纸上。膏药：中医外用药的一种。用植物油或动物油加药熬炼成胶状物，涂在布、纸或皮的一面，可较长时间地贴在患处。

【事情翻了摊】已经解决好的问题又突然出现了。

【摊四】破产程序中债权人需承担40%的风险。

攃 [soŋ³]

【给他几攃】攃：摇动，推动。推他几下。

攢（攒）[tsʰuan²]

手 16-19

攏在一起算	*put* it all together and *reckon* it up.
把榫頭敲攏	*drive* the tenon *home*.
SU¹.	
癢搌搌的	a *tickling* sensation, as when the sole of the foot is tickled.
TS'AN¹.	
把他攙倒	*support* him to his feet.
LAN².	
莫阻攔他	don't *hinder* him.
把路攔倒	to *stop up* a by-path.
要有遮攔	we must have something to *screen* off the place.
攔河網	a *sweep-net*.
扯起攔天網儘說	he draws a net that *sweeps* the heavens— always talking !
T'AN¹.	
攤膏藥	to *spread* a plaster on paper.
攤開曬起	*spread* it *apart* and dry it in the sun, as grain.
把手板攤起	*stretch* open the palm of your hand.
攤屍	to *lay out* a corpse before coffining.
攤還賬目	to *divide up* a bankrupt's stock to pay the creditors.
事情翻了攤	the affair has cropped up again after having been *settled*.
小菜攤子	a *stall* where vegetables are sold.
攤四	a bankrupt *settling* with his creditors at 40 per cent.
很要攤點錢	this is *worth* a good deal.
攤派	to *levy*, or *impose* a subscription.
SONG³.	
給他幾攃	give it a few *shakes*, or *joggles*.
你莫攃	don't *push* me.
TS'UAN².	
把石頭攢攏	*gather* the stones to the place where they are to be used.
把賬攢做一堆	*collect* the accounts into one book ; enter in the ledger.
攢盒	a box with compartments for a *collection* of sweets or meats.

(239)

手 20-21

20 攪

CHIAO³.

攪匀	stir till thoroughly mixed.
攪蛋	to switch eggs.
攪耳朵	to shave the inside of the ear.
攪連點	be a little quicker.
拿來攪了	I used it; I spent the money.
攪用大	the household expenditure is great.
莫在這裏攪擾	don't come bothering here.
打攪你	I have inconvenienced you; thank you.

READ KAO³.

辭攪	to stir carelessly; to act recklessly.
攪拐了	to do a thing wrongly.
攪不贏	unable to do the work in time; too busy.
攪不得	you must not touch it.
他屋頭攪好了	his folks are getting on well; well off.
攪落薄了	to become poor.
我在那裏攪過兩年	I worked there for two years.
攪忘了	I have forgotten it.

攫

TSʻIO⁵, TSO⁵.

| 見了鷹攫兔官都不想做 | to see the falcon seize his prey, is better than office any day. |

攩

TANG⁴.

| 沒得阻攩 | there is no hindrance. |

READ TANG³,⁴.

| 把他攩倒 | intercept him! |
| 抵攩 | to withstand. |

21 攬

LAN³.

[met., to monopolize.

破船多攬載	to engross all the cargo with a broken boat;
攬載子	a small lighter.
包攬詞訟	to undertake to manage a lawsuit.
攬頭子	a contractor; a leading workman.

(240)

注 释

攪（搅）[tɕiao³] [kao³]
【搅连点】快一点。
【搅用大】家庭支出巨大。
【辞搅】做事随意，不用心。
【搅拐了】做错了。
【搅不赢】不能按时完成任务；太忙。
【搅落薄了】落魄了，变得穷困。
攫 [tsʰio⁵] [tsʰo⁵]
（TSO⁵当为TSʻOU，见803页勘误表。）
攩（挡）[taŋ⁴] [taŋ⁴]
攬（揽）[lan³]
【揽载子】小驳船。
【揽头子】承包商，工头。

注释

攞 [pa⁴]
【攞铺】垒砌炕铺或铺开、整理床铺。
【鹊儿攞窝】鸟儿筑巢。

攞 [laŋ³]
【攞楂楂柴】用农具收集地上的枝叶做燃料。

㩆 [tie⁵]

支 [tʂʅ¹]
【拿条子支倒】用杆支撑住。
【把钱子消在那里去了】("子"当为"支",见803页勘误表。)消:同"销",花销,支出。

收 [ʂəu¹]
改 [kai³]
攻 [koŋ¹]

手 21-22 攴. 攴 2-3

攞

PA⁴.
攞铺　　　　　to *make, spread,* or *arrange* a bed.
鹊儿攞窝　　　the birds are *building* a nest.

LANG³.
推推攞攞　　　to *push* one's way through a crowd.
攞楂楂柴　　　to *scrape* up small sticks and leaves for fuel.
攞两堆花生　　*buy* two heaps of peanuts.

TIE⁵.
㩆衣服　　　　to *fold* up clothes.

The 65th radical. (支)

CHĬ¹.
一脉宗支　　　of one *family* or *clan*.
一支兵　　　　a *troop* or *company* of soldiers.
拿条子支倒　　*prop* it up with a pole.
家屋支持不住了　he cannot *support* his family.
把钱子消在那裏去了 } where have you *spent* the money?
支工夫钱　　　to *pay* wages.
莫受别人的支使 don't listen to the *prompting* or *instigation* [of others.

The 66th radical. (攴)

SHEO¹.　　same as 收.

KAI³.
江河易改本性 } a river may easily *change* its course, but
难移　　　　　a man's disposition is hard to alter.
改个日子　　　*alter* the day.
改嫁　　　　　a woman marrying a second time.
改日来拜　　　I will call on you *another* day.
悔罪改过　　　to *repent* of one's sins.

KONG¹.
攻打城池　　　to *assault* a city.
发愤攻书　　　earnestly *apply* yourself to your books.

(241)

攵 3-5

敉 P'IN¹.   same as 別

放 FANG⁴.

放手	let go!
放牛	to *let loose* a cow to feed on pasture land; [to *herd* cattle.
放生	to *liberate* live birds and fishes (a meritorious work).
把船放起走	*unloose* the boat from its moorings and [go.
放學	to *let out* school.
放血	to *let* blood.
放賬	to *lend* money.
放筏子走了	to *abscond*; to *elope*.
太放肆了	you *give* too much *rein* to your passions.
放溜溜馬	to *hire out* ponies by short stages.
放勤快點	be more diligent.
飽了不曉得放碗	he does not know to *set down* his basin when [he is full.
放轎子	*set down* the chair.
我不放心	I am uneasy about it.
放在心上	remember it.
放在桌子上	place it on the table.
沒得放處	there is no place to *put* it.
放點鹽	*put* some salt in it.
這個東西放不得	this cannot be *laid by* for any length of [time.
放一天就臭了	if you *leave* it for a day it will stink.
放痘子	to *inoculate* for small-pox.
放火炮	to *fire* crackers.
放火燒房子	to set fire to houses; arson.
給他放個信	*send* a letter to him.
放活路	to *stop* work.
放風箏	to *fly* a kite.
姑娘放了人戶嗎	have you *betrothed* your daughter?
路上放挑子	a coolie *sub-hiring* another coolie to carry for a short distance.

故 KU⁴.

這是甚麼緣故	what is the *reason* of this?
他故意那麼做	he did it *intentionally*.

(242)

注 释

敉 [pʰin¹]
【敉】发给，发布。

放 [faŋ⁴]
【放账】借钱给别人。
【放筏子走了】潜逃，逃匿，私奔。
【放溜溜马】短时租借马匹。
【没得放处】没有地方放。
【放痘子】接种天花。
【放火炮】放爆竹。
【给他放个信】给他送个信。
【放活路】停止工作。
【姑娘放了人户吗】姑娘订婚了没有？

故 [ku⁴]

注释

啵 [kʰo¹]
【我怕你想挨啵了】啵：敲击。

效 [ɕiao⁴]

致 [tʂɿ⁴]

敕 [tʂʰɿ⁵]

教 [tɕiao¹] [tɕiao⁴]
【做的不落教】做事情不地道，不能让人信服。
【耍的不落教】对人没有礼貌。

啟（启）[tɕʰi³]

攴 5-7

	看故人去了	he has gone to see an *old* friend.
	回到故鄉	to return to one's *native* place.
	仍然如故	just as *formerly*.
	到病故的時候	when you are *dead*.
	亡故了	*dead*.
	故所以我不來	*therefore* I shall not come.
啵	K'O¹.	[knuckles.
6	我怕你想挨啵了	I'm afraid you want to be *rapped* with my
效	SHIAO⁴.	
	效法古人	*imitate* good men.
	我的話應效了	my words are *verified*.
	這個藥效驗如神	this medicine is *efficacious* as a god.
致	CHÏ⁴.	
	致命傷	the wound that *caused* death.
7	大致是這樣子	this is a *general* idea of it.
敕	CH'Ï⁵.	
	受了敕封	the gods have received *royal* appointment.
教	CHIAO¹.	
	教義學	to *teach* a charity school.
	READ CHIAO⁴.	
	教訓人	to *instruct* people.
	聽我的教訓	listen to my *instructions*.
	儒釋道三教	the three *religions*—Confucianism, Buddhism and Taoism.
	教會	a *church*.
	教匪	a *band* of seditions people.
	教師	a *professor* of boxing. [erly joined.
	做的不落教	the seams. of the woodwork are not prop-
	耍的不落教	he is not civil with some people.
啟	CH'I³.	
	不好啟齒	it is not easy to *open* one's mouth; hard to speak about.

(243)

西蜀方言

支 7-8

CHIU⁴.

救命	save life!
救人一命勝造七級浮屠	to save one life is better than building a seven-storied pagoda.
捨死的把他救出來	he rescued him at the risk of his life.
望你打救我	I look to you to help, or succour me.
還有救沒得	is there any remedy?
救火	to extinguish a conflagration.
救生船	a life boat.

MIN³.

| 子弟聰敏 | this lad is clever at his books. |

PAI⁴.

打敗仗	to be defeated in battle.
敗家子	a son who ruins the family.
姑娘敗門風	a daughter has disgraced the family.
敗壞風俗	to demoralize the customs of a place.
胃口敗了	my appetite has failed.
生意敗了	his business has failed.
顏色敗了	the colour is faded.

SÜ⁴.

| 他們正在敘話 | they are talking just now. |

CH'ANG³.

敞壩壩	an open plot of ground.
敞褲脚	wide trousers worn by women.
酒敞子	a wine filler; a funnel.
騎敞馬	to ride a horse bare-backed.
敞不得氣	it must not be exposed to the air.
事情敞出去了	the matter has become public.

P'IE³. interchanged with 撆.

| 敞斷 | to snap through the middle; to break between the hands. |

KAN³.

| 你膽敢這麼做嗎 | how dare you do it? |

(244)

注 释

救 [tɕiəu⁴]

敏 [min³]

敗（败）[pai⁴]

敘（叙）[sy⁴]

敞 [tʂhaŋ³]

【敞坝坝】敞开的拦水建筑物。

【酒敞子】敞子：漏斗。

【骑敞马】敞马：背上秃毛的马。

【敞不得气】不能暴露在空气中。

【事情敞出去了】事情被公开了。

敽 [phie³]

【敽断】用手擘断。

敢 [kan³]

注释

【有加敢没得】敢不敢或能不能（做某事）。

敞 [pi⁴]

散 [san³]

【打一双散裤脚】散：分散，宽松。做一条两个裤腿宽松的裤子。

【吃斋一世不如散事一场】自己吃一辈子的斋不如帮别人解决一场纠纷或者给予经济上的帮助。

【包包散包包散，莫尽婆婆看】肿起的包快点消去，不要让妈妈看见。一般是对受伤的小孩所说。

敦 [tən¹]

敬 [tɕin⁴]

攴 8-9

敞散		
	不敢當	I could not *presume* (polite phrase).
	有加敢沒得	have you the *ability*, or *strength*, to do it?
	PI⁴.	
	敞地在順慶	my *mean* home is in Shuen-ch'in.
	SAN³.	
	爆了箍箍散了架	the hoops have burst and the bucket has *fallen apart*. [women].
	打一雙散褲脚	make a pair of *loose* trousers (worn by
	套褲帶帶散了	your ankle strings are *undone*.
	莫把這個錢打散了	don't *spend* this money.
	那個人懶散	that fellow is very *untidy*.
	READ SAN⁴.	
	會場散了	the fair has *dispersed*.
	喫齋一世不如散事一場	to be a life long vegetarian is not to be compared to *dispelling* one difficulty, as a quarrel, or poverty.
	散勸世文	to *distribute* tracts.
	散心兒	to *dispel* melancholy.
	包包散包包散莫儘婆婆看	may the swelling *disperse* and your mother not see it, said to a child who has hurt itself.
	散兵	to *disband* soldiers.
敦敬 9	**TEN¹.**	
	人長得敦敦篤篤的	he has grown very *stout*.
	CHIN⁴.	
	敬菩薩	to *worship* idols.
	孝敬父母	to *honour* one's father and mother.
	失敬了	I have been wanting in *respect*; I beg your pardon.
	自己要敬重	you must cultivate self-*respect*.
	一點薄敬	a small *token of respect*, i. e., a present.
	恭敬	*respectful, reverent*; to respect, to honour.
	敬盞茶	to *treat* to a cup of tea.

(245)

支 10-12

10 敲 K'AO¹.

敲木魚	to *tap* the wooden fish, an instrument used [by priests.
平生不做虧心事 半夜敲門心不驚	keep all life long a conscience clear, a midnight *rap* will cause no fear.
拏火鐮敲個火	*strike* fire with flint and steel.
敲釘子	to *drive* a nail.
敲釘鎚	to *extort* money.
說些敲打話	to utter a covert sneer.

11 敷 FU¹.

敷壁頭	to *plaster* a wall.
敷藥	to *apply* medicine externally. [clothing.
將敷得倒穿喫	just sufficient to *keep* one in food and
還要給我敷補點	you must *make up* this deficiency to me.

數 SU³.

| 數錢 | to *count* cash. |

READ SU⁴.

總數是好多	what is the *sum* total?
這個錢有少數	this cash is short *count*.
無數的人	people without *number*.
數日前	a *few* days ago.

敵 TI⁵.

仇敵	*enemies*.
這回遇倒敵手	he has met his *match* this time.
敵不敵得住	can you *withstand* him?

12 整 CHEN³.

整治房圈	*set* the room in order.
整齊人馬	to *organize* troops. [(carpenter).
還要整甚麼	what more do you want me to *make*?
把這把椅子整好	*mend* this chair.
莫亂整	don't *do* things recklessly.
整痛了	painful through being *knocked*.
說不贏我們過整	If I cannot reason you down, I'll *fight* you.
整年整月的害病	to be sick the *whole* year round.

(246)

注 释

敲 [kʰao¹]
【拿火镰敲个火】用火石打个火。
【敲钉锤】勒索钱财。

敷 [fu¹]
【敷壁头】壁头:墙壁。涂墙泥。
【将敷得倒穿吃】有足够的吃和穿。

数(数) [su³]

敌(敌) [ti⁵]

整 [tʂən³]
【整治房圈】整理房间。老年人和农村人用语。
【说不赢我们过整】我说不赢你,我们就打。

注 释

敛(斂)[lien⁴]
䥽[tsʰuan⁴]
【䥽米】把米去壳。
斃(毙)[pi⁴]
文[uən²]
斑[pan¹]
斗[təu³]
　【熨斗】熨，同"慰"。
　【枪斗子】烟斗，烟枪。

攴 13-14 文 8 斗

13 斂

LIEN⁴.

| 斂錢 | to *amass* money. |

14 䥽

TS'UAN⁴.

| 䥽米 | to *hull* rice with a foot-pestle. |

斃

PI⁴.

| 吊斃 | *hanged* dead. |

The 67th radical. (文)

UEN².

做文章	to write a *literary* composition, i.e., an essay.
文理	the *classical* style in writing.
文秀才	a *civil* graduate.
文不文武不武	he can do neither one thing nor another; good for nothing.
說話斯斯文文	he speaks in a *genteel* manner.
文書	a dispatch.
勸世文	a moral tract.

8 斑

PAN¹.

斑毛老虎	a *spotted* leopard.
斑竹子	the *mottled* bamboo, used for chair poles.
斑鳩	the turtle dove, from its *markings*.
汗斑	prickly heat; lit., sweat *spots*.
斑疹	scarlet fever, from the *rash*.

The 68th radical. (斗)

斗

TEO³.

一斗米	a *bushel* of rice.
市斗	the market *bushel measure*.
墨斗	the ink *cup* of a joiner's marking line.
熨斗	a clothes iron.
鎗斗子	the *bowl* of an opium pipe.
北斗	the Northern *Bushel*; i.e., part of the Great Bear.

(247)

斗 6-8 斤 4-7

料 6

LIAO⁴.

萬不料成這樣	I would not have *expected* it to come to this.
理料家務	to *manage* one's household.
衣料	*material* for making clothes.
木料	*timber*.
他不是料子	he is not a *useful man*.
馬料	*provender* for horses, excepting grass.
燒料	*coloured glass* ornaments.

斜

SIE².

斜起的	*slanting*.
太陽斜過去了	the sun is *declining*.
斜坡	a gentle *declivity*.
剪一根斜條子	cut a piece of edging *on the cross*.
斜眼睛	*squint*-eyed.
斜紋布	*twilled* cloth.
說斜了	what he says is *beside the mark*; not pertinent, irrelevant.

斟 8

CHEN¹.

sometimes pronounced shen¹ in the first sentence.

| 斟兩盌茶來 | *pour* out two cups of tea. |
| 下細斟酌 | *consider* it carefully. |

The 69th radical. (斤)

斤

CHIN¹.

天平一斤十六兩	"t'ien-p'in" is 16 oz. to a *pound*.
打翻斤斗	to turn a *somersault*.
千斤	an iron *crowbar*.

斧 4

FU³.

斧頭	an *axe*; a *hatchet*.
沾不動就提刀弄斧	on any occasion he will draw a weapon on you.
沒得資斧	I have no money for my *travelling expenses*.

斬 7

CHAN³.

| 斬頭 | to *behead*; to *decapitate*. |

(248)

注　释

料 [liao⁴]

斜 [sie²]

【斜起的】斜的。

【说斜了】所说的不切题，不相关，不得要领。

斟 [tʂən¹]

【下细斟酌】下细: 仔细。

斤 [tɕin¹]

【千斤】铁撬棍。

【沾不动就提刀弄斧】动不动就动刀动枪。

斧 [fu³]

【没得资斧】资斧: 旅费，盘缠。

斩（斩）[tʂan³]

注 释

斯 [sɿ¹]
新 [sin¹]
断（斷）[tuan⁴]
  【断了火烟】穷得无法生火做饭。
方 [faŋ¹]
  【方桌子】方桌。
  【单方】药方，药单。

斤 8-14 方

8 斯

SĪ¹.

斯文人　　　　　a *genteel* person.

9 新

SIN¹.

新年　　　　　　the *New* Year.
新鲜鱼　　　　　*fresh* fish.
新人 and 新郎　　bride and bridegroom.

14 斷

TUAN⁴.

縴籐斷了　　　　the tow-rope has *broken*.
斷屠　　　　　　to *stop* the slaughter of animals during a fast. [ceased to be offered.
香煙斷了　　　　the family is extinct; lit., the incense has
斷了火煙　　　　too poor to light a fire; an uninhabited house.
斷黑的時候　　　dusk, twilight.
斷了氣　　　　　he is dead. [others.
憑衆公斷　　　　to justly *settle* a case in the presence of
斷然不答應　　　I *certainly* will not agree to that.

The 70th radical. （方）

方

FANG¹.

方桌子　　　　　a *square* table.
四四方方一墩　　a *cube*.
一疋方　　　　　a rafter, a plank.
本地方　　　　　this *place*; one's native *place*.
銀子不方便　　　funds are not forthcoming. [plicated.
事情不方便　　　it is not *convenient*; my affairs are com-
我有個好方法　　I have a good *plan*.
單方　　　　　　a prescription.
打比方　　　　　to use an *illustration*.
大大方方的　　　*magnanimous*.
走錯了方向　　　I have gone in the wrong *direction*.
方丈　　　　　　the *judgment-hall* of a Buddhist high priest. [way to pay you out.
我要想你的方子　I will have it out with you; I will find a

(249)

西蜀方言　249

方 4-7

4 於

想方兒	to *scheme* to raise the wind.	
行方便的人少	those who do *things for the benefit of others* are few.	
方人	to make people feel *restrained*.	
我方纔明白	I have *just now* understood.	

Ü².

於今的人	the people *at* the present time.
死於非命	he died *in* an unnatural way.
不多於好	it is not very good; I am not very well.

5 施 SHĪ¹.

施藥不如傳方	*giving away* medicine. to publish a prescription is better than
施恩不望報	to *bestow* favours not expecting any return.
大老爺施恩喇	*grant* me grace, your worship!
施主	a *contributor* to temple lands or funds, etc.
施尿	to incite a child to *pass* water.
這事怎樣施爲	what can we *do* in this case?

旅 LÜ³.

開個旅店	to open an inn for *travellers*.

旄 MAO².

旄牛	the *yak*.

6 旁 P'ANG².

在旁邊	by the *side* of.
站過一旁	stand *aside*.
旁邊人	*bystanders*.
㚢旁	in the *region* of the breasts; the ribs.
字旁	the *radical* of a character.

7 旋 SÜEN².

周圍旋轉	to *revolve* in a circle.
幫我周旋	*speak a good word for* me; *intercede* on my behalf.

READ SÜEN⁴.

旋頭風	a *whirl*wind.
雙旋	a double *crown* on the hair of the head.
腦壳旋暈	my head is *giddy*.

(250)

注 釋

【行方便的人少】为别人好的人太少。

【方人】使人难堪。

於(于)[y²]

【不多于好】不太好；不那么好。

施[ṣʅ¹]

【施尿】把尿。

旅[ly³]

旄[mao²]

【旄牛】牦牛。

旁[pʰaŋ²]

【奶旁】胸部；肋骨。

旋[syen²][syen⁴]

【帮我周旋】帮我说说好话。

【旋头风】旋风。

注释

族 [tsʰu⁵]
旌 [tsin¹]
旒 [liəu²]
旗 [tɕʰi¹]
旛(幡) [fan¹]
既 [tɕi⁴]
日 [zɿ⁵]

【我不知天日】我不知道今天几月几日了。

方 7-12　旡 7　日

族	旋讀旋講	to read and expound *by turns*. [me.
旌	要旋做	you must make it *to order* or *expressly for*
9 旒	TS'U⁵.	
	宗族	the ancestral *clan*.
	TSIN¹.	[the grave at burial.
	銘旌	a memorial *banner*, sometimes placed on
10 旗	LIU².	[actors and idols.
	冕旒	*tassels* on an ancient crown, now worn by
	CH'I¹.	
	旗子	a *flag*. [funeral ceremonies.
	旗旛	*streamers* placed before the door during
	旗人	*bannermen*; the Manchu soldiers.
12 旛	帥字旗	the commander's *standard*.
	FAN¹.	[or to heaven.
	引魂旛	a *streamer* for leading the soul to the grave

The 71st radical. (旡)

7 既	CHI⁴.	
	既是這樣	*since* it is so.

The 72nd radical (日)

日	RĬ⁵.	
	勸君莫睡日頭紅 早起三朝當一工	good gentlemen the *sun* shines red, in bed you should no longer stay; if you three mornings early rise, 'tis equal to another day.
	相聚的日子短 離別的日子長	few are the *days* together spent, but *days* of absence may be.
	白日莫閒過 青春不再來	don't pass the *daytime* thus in vain; your youthful years ne'er come again.
	過好日子	well-off.
	我不知天日	I don't know the *date* of this day.

(251)

日 1-4

1 旦 TAN⁴.
旦夕之間　within a day's time; lit., *morning* and evening.

2 早 TSAO³.
早晨　*dawn*.
一大早晨纔來　when the whole *morning* is gone then you come!
清晨八早的亂說　to use unlucky words in the *early* morning.
喫了早飯沒有　have you had your breakfast?
早栽秧子早打穀　plant *early* and you will reap *early*.
趁早囘頭　repent *betimes*.

旨 CHÏ³.
傳聖旨　to promulgate the *will* of the Emperor.
事奉甘旨　to present *delicacies* to one's parents.

3 旱 HAN⁴.
年歲乾旱　this is a *dry* year.
水旱不一　floods and *drought* are uncertain.
旱路來的　he came over*land*.
起旱　to take to the *road*, after travelling by water.
旱在鍋頭　steam it in the pot.

4 昂 NGANG².
米價昂貴　rice is very *dear*.
那個人志氣昂昂的　} that man is very *steadfast* in purpose.

昌 CH'ANG¹.
大吉大昌　great luck and great *prosperity*.
文昌宮　the temple of the god of literature.

昏 HUEN¹.
黃昏時候　*dusk*; evening twilight; gloaming.
眼睛昏花　my eyes are *dim*.
腦殼昏　my head is *confused*.
昏死了　she has *fainted*.
莫昏說　don't rave; don't talk nonsense.
昏昧無知的人　a *foolish* person.

(252)

注　釋

旦 [tan⁴]
早 [tsao³]
【清晨八早的乱说】一大清早说些不吉利的话。民间风俗清早不能说不吉利的话。
【趁早回头】趁早改变主意。英文释义应为：The early you change mind, the better.
旨 [tʂʅ³]
【事奉甘旨】（给父母）吃好的、喝好的。
旱 [xan⁴]
昂 [ŋaŋ²]
昌 [tʂʰaŋ¹]
昏 [xuən¹]
【莫昏说】不要瞎说。

注释

易 [i⁴]

昔 [si⁵]
【昔年间】早年间，前些年。

昆 [kʰuən¹]
【几昆玉】昆玉：称人兄弟的敬词。你有几个弟兄？

明 [min²]
【明轿子】没有顶蓬的轿子。

旺 [uaŋ⁴]
【猪旺子】旺子：血。猪血。

春 [tṣʰuən¹]

昧 [mei⁴]
【天良不昧】天良未泯。

日 4-5

易 昔 昆 明

I⁴.

莫將容易得 便作等閒看 }	don't lightly esteem what has been *easily* obtained.
便⁴易	*convenient*.
便²易	*cheap*.
出外貿易	to travel and *barter* goods.
公平交易	to do *business* honestly.

SI⁵.

| 昔年間 | in *former* years. |

K'UEN¹.

| 幾昆玉 | how many *brothers* have you? (polite [phrase). |

MIN².

天明的時候	at *dawn* of day.
明天	to-morrow.
明年	*next* year.
明來明去	to come and go *openly*.
明轎子	an *open* travelling chair.
正大光明	*open* and above-board.
我給你說明白	I will tell you *clearly*.
我心裏明白	I *understand* it in my own mind.
聰明人幹糊塗事	he is a *wise* man, but he does foolish things.
高明的人	a very *learned* man.

5 旺 春 昧

UANG⁴.

人還健旺	still hale and *vigorous*.
生意興旺	his business is *prospering*.
豬旺子	pig's *blood*.

CH'UEN¹.

春天	*spring* time.
立春	the *vernal* equinox.
大春 and 小春	summer crops and winter crops.

ME⁴.

| 愚昧無知 | *foolish* and ignorant. |
| 天眞不昧 | conscience *unsullied*. |

(253)

日 5-6

是 SHI⁴.

我是當家人	I *am* the head of the house.
你是那一個	who *are* you?
是不是	*Is* it not so?; *yes* or *no*?
不是魚不是 還是網不牢	it *was* not the fish that was wrong; it *was* the net that was rotten.
是道是個好事寡 是我沒得錢做	it *is* a good business, but I have no money to do it.
不是他幫忙我 就做不贏	had he not helped me, I could not have done it in time.
是人都在說	*all* the people are talking about it.
是非	*right* and wrong; gossip, tittle-tattle.
來說是非者 便是是非人	those who come gossiping, *are* themselves fit subjects for gossip.

皆 TSAN³.

| 那皆 | at that *time*. |
| 我皆不曉得 | I don't know *anything* about it. |

星 SIN¹.

本命星	my natal *star*.
星宿	small *stars*.
掃把星出現	a *comet* has appeared.
過天星	*meteors*.
零星銀子	a *little*, or *small* quantity of silver.

昨 TSO⁵.

昨年	*last* year.
昨天	*yesterday*.
昨回子	the *former* occasion.

晃 HUANG⁴.

亮晃晃的	the sky is *clear*, *brilliant*, like a polished [surface.
霍閃一晃就過了	the lightning goes past with a *flash*.
些微有點太陽 晃晃	there were a few *gleams* of sunshine.
太陽晃眼睛	the sun *dazzles* my eyes.
纔在這裏晃一ha⁴	he *passed* here a while ago; I saw him just [a minute ago.

(254)

注 释

是 [ʂʅ⁴]

【是道是个好事,寡是我没得钱做】好生意是好生意,只是我没有本钱做。

【不是他帮忙我就做不赢】做不赢: 来不及做。

皆 [tsan³]

【我皆不晓得】我对此什么都不知道。

星 [sin¹]

【过天星】流星。

昨 [tso⁵]

【昨年】去年。

【昨回子】上一回。

晃 [xuaŋ⁴]

【才在这里晃一ha⁴】一ha⁴: 一下。刚见到他在这里露了一面。

注释

晌 [ʂaŋ³]
　【吃了晌午没有】晌午：在这里指午饭。吃了午饭没有？英文释义应为：Have you had your lunch?
晒 [ʂai⁴]
时（時）[ʂʅ²]
　【一个时候】时候：与"时辰"同义。相当于两个小时。
　【时兴的衣服】流行款式的衣服。英文释义应为：Fashionable dress.
　【眼时的风俗不同】眼时：眼下，时下。现在的风俗不一样。
晋（晉）[tsin⁴]
　【立志上晋】上晋：即"上进"。
晏 [ŋan⁴]
　【你来晏了】你来晚了。
晨 [ʂən²]
昼（晝）[tʂou⁴]

日 6-7

晌 晒 時

SHANG³.
晌午　　　　　　noon.
小晌午　　　　　just before *midday*.
喫了晌午沒有　　have you had your *dinner*?

SHAI⁴.　　　　　same as 曬.

SHĪ².　　　　　　　　　　　　　　　[English.
一個時候　　　　one Chinese *hour*, equal to two hours
四時　　　　　　the four *seasons*.
莫錯過時侯　　　don't pass the *time* that I have fixed.
這時節不比那時節 } these *days* are not to be compared to former *days*.
時興的衣服　　　the *present* fashion in dress.　　[different.
眼時的風俗不同　the customs of the *present* generation are
事不過當時　　　affairs should not pass the opportune moment.　　[(doctor's talk).
今年的時症少　　*seasonable* sickness is scarce this year,
立時就要　　　　I want it *immediately*.
時時刻刻　　　　constantly.
幾時起身　　　　when do (or did) you start?
年輕的時候　　　when I was young.
時運好　　　　　my *luck* is good.
背時　　　　　　"down on one's *luck*;" wretched; good-for-nothing.

晉

TSIN⁴.
立志上晉　　　　make up your mind to *rise* in scholarship.

晏

NGAN⁴.
你來晏了　　　　you have come *late*.

晨

SHEN².
今早晨　　　　　this *morning*.

晝

CHEO⁴.
晝夜不安　　　　I am distressed *day* and night.

(255)

西蜀方言　255

日 7-8

晦	HUE⁴.	
	滿臉晦氣	sullen features.
	把人的好處背晦了	ungrateful for kindnesses.
眼	LANG⁴.	
	眼衣裳	to *dry*, or *air* clothes in the open air.
	曬眼的地方	a place to *dry* clothes.
晚	UAN³.	
	今晚上	this *evening*.
	夜晚	*night*.
	晚年	*late* in life; in old age.
	晚母	a *step*-mother.
智	CHÏ⁴.	
	聰明智慧	intelligence and *wisdom*.
景	CHIN³.	
	好景緻	a fine *view*.
	光景	*circumstances*.
晷	KUE³,¹.	
	日晷	a sun *dial*.
晾	LIANG⁵.	
	晾衣服	to *air* clothes.
	晾人材	to *exhibit* one's self; to *display* one's talents; to *show off*.
普	P'U³.	
	普天下	*everywhere* under heaven.
晶	TSIN¹.	
	水晶眼鏡子	*crystal* spectacles.
	水晶宮豈由你魚鰕作亂	do you think that we can allow you little fishes and shrimps to come and make a row in Neptune's palace?
晴	TS'IN².	
	今天天晴	the sky is *clear* to-day; *fair* weather.

(256)

注 释

晦 [xuei⁴]
【把人的好處背晦了】背晦：同"悖晦"，糊涂（多指老年人）。对别人的好处不领情，不感激。
眼 [laŋ⁴]
晚 [uan³]
【晚母】继母，后妈。
智 [tʂʅ⁴]
景 [tɕin³]
晷 [kuei³] [kuei¹]
晾 [liaŋ⁴]
（LIANG⁵当为LIANG⁴，见803页勘误表。）
【晾人材】显示出个人的才能。
普 [pʰu²]
晶 [tsin¹]
晴 [tsʰin²]

注释

暇 [ɕia⁴]
暗 [ŋan⁴]
暖 [luan³]
暑 [ʂu³]
【暑天无君子】暑天没有君子，意即天非常热的时候，人们大都不讲究形象而脱了衣服。
晕（暈）[yn⁴] [yn¹]
畅（暢）[tʂʰaŋ⁴]
暴 [pao⁴]
暫（暂）[tsan⁴]
暮 [mu⁴]

日 9–11

暇 暗 暖 暑 晕 10 畅 11 暴 暫 暮

SHIA⁴.
今天閒暇無事 — I am quite at *leisure* to-day.

NGAN⁴.
房子黑暗 — the room is *dark*.
打個暗號 — mark it with a *private* mark.
暗暗的說 — to tell *secretly*.
暗傷 — *internal* injuries.

LUAN³.
天氣暖和 — the weather is *mild*.

SHU³.
　　　　　　　[clothes are put off.
暑天無君子 — there are no gentlemen in *hot* weather,
進山裏頭避暑 — to go to the mountains to escape the *summer heat*.

ŪIN⁴,¹.
腦売暈 — my head is *giddy*; vertigo.　[sea-sickness.
暈船 — sickness caused by the motion of a boat;

CH'ANG⁴.
心裏快暢 — joyous; in good spirits.
他這個話說得通暢 } he states the matter *clearly*.

PAO⁴.
暴躁 — *fierce*.
烏風暴雨 — a great wind and *violent* rain.
暴虐百姓 — to *violently* oppress the people.

CHAN⁴.
天有不測的風雲
人有暫時的禍福 } heaven is sometimes overcast by an unexpected blast; happiness and evil thus oft come *suddenly* to us.
暫時的 — *temporary*; for a *brief* space.

MU⁴.
年近歲暮 — at the *close* of the year.

(257)

日 12-19　曰 2-6

12 曉 SHIAO³.
| 雞報曉 | the cock heralds the *dawn*. |
| 我不曉得他的 | I don't *know* anything about his affairs. |

曆 LI⁵, LIE⁵.
| 15 買本皇曆 | buy an Imperial *calendar*. |

曠 K'UANG⁴.
| 19 曠野地方 | a *wilderness*; *waste* land. |

曬 SHAI⁴.
曬衣服	to *dry* clothes *in the sun*.
曬太陽	to *bask* in the sun.
臉曬黑了	your face is sunburnt.

The 73rd radical. (曰)

2 曲 CH'Ü⁵, CH'IO⁵.
灣灣曲曲的	*crooked*.
你受了委曲	you have suffered *wrong*.
分曲直	to discriminate between right and *wrong*.
唱曲子	to sing *songs*.

3 更 KEN¹.
把冷酒更了	*change* the cold wine for hot.
沒得更改的	*unchangeable*; *unalterable*.
打更	to beat the *night-watches*.

READ KEN⁴.
| 更好 | *much* better. |
| 更要小心 | you must be *more* careful. |

6 書 SHU¹.
一本書	a *book*.
那個事情上了書	that matter is recorded in *books* or history.
書信	a *letter*.
跑文書	to carry *dispatches*.
讀書人	a scholar; the literati. [for others.
代書	a writer; one who *writes* indictments, etc.,

(258)

注　释

曉（晓）[ɕiao³]
曆（历）[li⁵] [lie⁵]
曠（旷）[kʰuaŋ⁴]
曬（晒）[ʂai⁴]
曲 [tɕʰy⁵] [tɕʰio⁵]
更 [kən¹]
【把冷酒更了】更：换。把冷酒换成热的。
【没得更改的】无法更改的，不能更改的。英文释义应为：this cannot be changed.
書（书）[ʂu¹]
【跑文书】递送政府公文。
【代书】代人写状告书的人。

注 释

【御书】皇帝书写的字。英文释义应为：Characters written by the emperor.

【八行书】旧式信笺每页八行，因此代称信件。

曹 [tsʰao²]

【进一曹出一曹】来一批走一批。

替 [tʰi⁴]

【请个人替倒】请个人替一下。

曾 [tsʰən²] [tsən¹]

【曾孙】"曾"，音为[tsən¹]。

最 [tsy⁴] [tsuei⁴]

【最小胆】胆子小。

會（会）[xuei⁴]

【茶钱某人会了】会茶钱，又称"开茶钱"，即付茶钱。

【请个会】请会：旧时民间一种经济互助活动。当遇到困难急需用钱时，约请亲朋，议定每人出资金额、会期长短等。由发起人充当"会首"，得头份会金，并负责收齐各家应出资金。

書 6-9

	書辦	*writers*; *scribes* (a self-depreciatory term).
	御書	the Imperial *autograph*.
	八行書	*writing-paper* ruled with eight spaces.
	書館	a *school-room*.
	書名	the *school* name, given to a boy.

7 曹 TS'AO².

	陰曹地府	the *nether-world*; *Hades*.
8	進一曹出一曹	one *company* of people came and another left.

替 T'I⁴.

	我願替你做	I am willing to do it *for* (or *instead of*) you.
	請個人替倒	engage a *substitute*; get some one to take your place.

曾 TS'EN². [*past tense*].

	何曾有那些事	how could there be such things? (sign of
	不曾	not *yet*.
	曾孫	*great-grandson*.

READ TSEN¹.

	曾祖	*great-grandfather*.

最 TSÜ⁴, TSUE⁴.

	最要緊	*most* important.
9	最小膽	*very* timid.

會 HUE⁴.

	聚會	to *assemble*.
	會朋友	to *meet* a friend.
	茶錢某人會了	Mr. So-and-So has *paid* for your tea.
	趕會	to go to a *festival* or *fair*.
	請個會	to form a *mutual benefit society*.
	你會做些甚麼	what are you *able* to do?
	我會意了	I *comprehend* your meaning.
	心中理會	I *comprehend* it; I *understand* it.
	這是個好機會	this is a good *opportunity*.
	等一會	wait a *little*.

(259)

曰 9 月 2-4

今天會要下雨	it is *likely* to rain to-day.
會生病	it *may* cause disease; *likely* to bring on illness.
房子會倒	the house is *likely* to or *about to* fall.

The 74th radical. (月)

月 ÜE⁵.

月亮	the *moon*.
一年十二個月	there are twelve *months* in one year.
月月開	the *monthly* rose.
月經	menstruation.
小月	an abortion.
坐月	lying in; confinement.
月宮門	a *round* doorway.

²有 IU³.

一切所有的	all that I *possess*.
有茶有酒多兄弟 / 急難何曾見一人	when tea and wine are plentiful what wealth of brothers true, when troubles great beset you round kind friends are very few.
水有源頭木有根	a river *has* a source, and a tree *has* a root.
你有幾歲	how old are you? (said to a child).
有了有了	*enough! enough!* (no more, thank you).
頭上有青天	*there is* a blue heaven above us, i. e., heaven takes notice.
不怕的有我	Don't be afraid, I will be responsible.
有些不同	*some* are different; *there are* some differences.

⁴服 FU⁵.

衣服	*clothes*.
守服	to observe *mourning*.
不服水土	not *accustomed* to the climate.
給他服禮	*confess* yourself in the wrong and beg his pardon.
心裏服不下去	I cannot *submit* to it in my mind.
不服王化	not *submitting* to the rule of the sovereign.

(260)

注　釋

月 [ye⁵]
【小月】流产。
【坐月】又称"坐月子",妇女产后一个月里调养身体。英文释义应为: Confinement after childbirth.

有 [iəu³]
【有了有了】够了够了（带有感谢的意思）。

服 [fu⁵]
【守服】同"守孝"。
【给他服礼】向他道歉,请他原谅。

注 释

朋 [pʰoŋ²]
朔 [so⁵]
朗 [laŋ³]
望 [uaŋ⁴]
【望起脑壳】抬起头向上。
【莫望倒我】别向我看。
意为别指望我会帮你。
朝 [tsao¹] [tsʰao²]
【清朝起来】清朝：大早上。大早上起床。

月 4-8

朋	有錢的人人服事 無錢的人服事人	men *serve* the rich, the poor *serve* men.
	服藥不效	*taking* medicine does no good.

P'ONG².

6 | 是我的好朋友 | he is my good *friend*.

SO⁵. [month.

7 朔 | 朔望日喫素 | to fast on the *first* and the fifteenth of the

LANG³.

朗 | 明明朗朗的念 | read *distinctly*.

UANG⁴.

望 | 望起腦壳 | to *lift up* the head.
| 望板 | thin ceiling boards.
| 他望倒塔子去了 | he went *towards* the pagoda. [long distance.
| 站高望遠 | if you stand on a high place you can *see* a
| 莫望倒我 | don't *look* at me!
| 我仰望先生幫助 | I *look* to you to help me, Sir.
| 我望你好 | I *wish* you well.
| 沒指望 | no *hope* or *expectation*. [to come.
| 請客望客來 | when one invites guests, one *expects* them
| 大名望先生 | a scholar or doctor with a great *reputation*.

CHAO¹.

8 朝 | 清朝起來 | rise at *dawn*.

READ CH'AO². [with the Emperor.

| 朝君 | to *pay court* to a prince; to have an audience
| 朝山拜佛 | to *visit* a sacred high place and worship
| | Buddha. [present dynasty).
| 清朝 | the "Pure *Dynasty*" (the name of the
| 朝鞋 | dress shoes with rounded toes.
| 朝左邊走 | go *towards* the left. [bearer's call).
| 朝寬處讓 | yield the road at a wide place (chair-
| 朝上頭推 | to place the responsibility on one's
| | superiors.

(261)

月 8-14　木 1

期　CH'I¹.

約定日期	to agree on a *set* day.
喜期	the *date fixed* for a wedding.
不期而遇	to meet by chance; to meet without previous *arrangement*.
今天期大	this is a lucky day; there are many marriage or funeral *fixtures*.
那是期必不倒的	you cannot be *certain* about that.

朦　MONG².

| 他只圖朦混過去 | he simply seeks to *impose upon* people. |

The 75th radical. (木)

木　MU⁵.

一根木頭	a piece of *wood*. [lit., *wooden* heads.
木腦壳	puppets used in Punch and Judy shows;
樹木	*trees* (while yet growing).
木廠	a *timber* yard.
木匠	a carpenter.
木渣滓	chips.
木花兒	shavings.
獨木橋	a foot bridge made of a single *plank* or *tree*.
老木	a *coffin*.
手脚麻木	hands and feet *benumbed*.

末　MO⁵.

始末緣由	the reason of it from first to last.
研成細末	grind it to a fine *powder*.
末末蚊	gnats; midges (from their small size).

本　PEN³.

莫忘根本	don't forget your *origin*, i.e., your parents.
本人沒話說	I have nothing to say about it.
本縣	I, the district magistrate.
守本分	to attend to one's *own* duty. [place.
本地人	the people (or natives) of *this* (or *that*)

(262)

注　释

期 [tɕʰi¹]
【今天期大】今天是个大日子或好日子（指适合婚丧嫁娶的）。
【那是期必不倒的】那事不确定。

朦 [moŋ²]

木 [mu⁵]
【木渣滓】即"木渣子"，木屑。
【老木】棺材。

末 [mo⁵]
【末末蚊】小蚊子。

本 [pən³]

注释

【手本】明清时谒见上司或贵官时所用的名帖。

未 [uei⁴]

【你未必说那个话】未必：不必，不需要。你不必说那个话。

【还在未定之天】（事情）何时发生没有定数。

朱 [tʂu¹]

朽 [ɕiəu³]

杞 [tʂʅ³]

朶（朵）[to¹] [to³]

杈 [tʂʰa⁴]

【搬杈枝子】修剪掉（树木的）侧枝、旁枝。

杖 [tʂaŋ⁴]

木 1-3

未	本色人	a simple man, a guileless chap.
	有本事	he has ability.
	本錢	*capital* in business. [into?
	一部有幾本	how many *volumes* is this work divided
	手本	an official's *visiting card*.
	UE⁴.	
	你未必說那個話	you need *not* say that.
	未滿三十歲	he is *not* yet thirty.
	未曾勤工先打算	count the cost before you begin the work.
	你未免太過分了	you certainly overstep your duty (ue-mien, two *negatives*).
2 朱	還在未定之天	it is very *uncertain* when that will happen.
	CHU¹.	
	朱紅緞	*scarlet* satin.
	朱唇	*red* lips. [uses it.
	朱筆	the *vermilion* pencil; the secretary who
朽	**SHIU³.**	
	木頭朽爛了	the wood is *rotten*.
	爛朽朽的	*broken; torn; spoiled*.
杞	**CHI³.**	for example of use see 枸.
朶	**TO¹.**	
	耳朶	the *ear*.
	READ TO³.	
	摘一朶花	pluck a flower. (*N. A.*)
	一朶黑雲	a black cloud. (*N. A.*) [(*N. A.*)
3 杈	拏火鏡照一朶火	kindle a flame with the burning glass.
	CH'A⁴.	
	樹枝開杈	the trees are putting forth *branches*.
	搬杈枝子	pinch off the *side shoots*.
杖	**CHANG⁴.**	
	枴杖	a *staff*.
	杖四十	to *beat* a prisoner 40 blows *with a rod*.

西蜀方言

木 3

杏 HEN⁴.
杏子　　apricots.
杏仁　　apricot kernels, commonly called *almonds*.

杆 KAN¹.
桅杆　　a *mast*.
欄杆　　a *fence*; a *balustrade*; *parapet*.
金線欄杆　yellow *ribbon*.
燈杆　　a *lamp post*.

杠 KANG⁴.
燒杠槓　to burn *small baskets full of paper cash* and [boxes full of paper ingots.

READ KANG¹
杠炭　　*charcoal* (from the name of a tree from [which it is made).

李 LI³.
李子　　a *plum*.
一挑行李　a coolie load of *luggage*.

呆 TAI¹.
你纔是個癡呆漢　you are a *stupid* dolt.

杉 SHA¹.
杉木板子　*pine* boards.

束 SU⁵, SHU⁵.
束手無策　I have no resource, as if my hands were [bound.
管束　　to *restrain*.
給先生送束脩　take the *school fees* to your teacher.

杜 TU⁴.
杜後患　to *prevent* evil conseqnences.
寫個杜賣約據　write an argument in order to *avoid* after [expenses.
杜鵑花　the *azalea*.

材 TS'AI².
好材料　good *materials*.
藥材　　crude medicines.
不成材　a worthless fellow.
鋸成三材　saw it into three *lengths*.
身材高大　he is tall in *person*.

(264)

注　釋

杏 [xən⁴]
杆 [kan¹]
杠 [kaŋ⁴][kaŋ¹]
【燒杠槓】燒紙錢。
李 [li³]
呆 [tai¹]
杉 [ṣa¹]
束 [su⁵][ṣu⁵]
杜 [tu⁴]
【寫個杜賣約據】杜賣約據：也叫杜賣契，買賣田園租業的契約。
材 [tsʰai²]
【鋸成三材】（把木材）鋸成三段。

注 释

村 [tsʰən¹] [tsʰuən¹]
【说话村吃饭也村】说话和吃饭的样子都土里土气的。
【莫说撒村的话】撒村：村野的粗鲁话。不要说粗鲁的话。

杌 [o⁵] [u⁵]
枕 [tṣən³]
枝 [tṣʅ¹]
扭 [tṣəu³]
杵 [tṣʰu³]
【打杵】山区人背重物时用木棍支撑得以休息。
【打杵拜会】拜会时不从轿椅上下来，意为当众给人难堪。
【短杵杵的】杵杵的：形容词后缀，多用以表示状态。
【稳杵】支稳当。
【杵图章子】盖图章。
【他说话来杵我】杵：顶撞，使人难堪。

果 [ko³]

木 3-4

村
TSʻEN¹, TSʻUEN¹.

蒲 村	the *village* of Pʻu.
鄉 村 地 方	*country* districts. [and manner of eating.
說 話 村 喫 飯 也 村	he is *countrified* (i.e., *coarse*) both in speech
那 個 人 村	that fellow is *rude* or *savage*.
莫 說 撒 村 的 話	don't use *vile* language here.

杌
O⁵, U⁵.

| 杌 凳 兒 | a high *stool*, either round or square. |

枕
CHEN³.

| 枕 頭 | a *pillow*. |
| 枕 子 | the *beams* under a wooden floor. |

枝
CHĪ¹.

	[and myriad leaves.
千 枝 萬 葉	a luxuriant tree; lit., thousand *branches*
三 枝 箭	three arrows. (*N. A.*)
一 枝 筆	a pencil. (*N. A.*)

扭
CHEO³.

| 腳 鐐 手 扭 | fetters and *manacles*. |

杵
CHʻU³.

	[by water.
碓 杵	the *head of a pestle* worked by the foot or
打 杵	a *prop* used by coolies to rest their carrying-poles on. [the chair.
打 杵 拜 會	to call at the door without descending from
短 杵 杵 的	short and *stumpy*.
掃 把 掃 得 光 杵 杵	the broom is worn to a *stump*.
穩 杵	*prop* the load or chair firmly.
杵 圖 章 子	to *stamp* with a seal.
杵 攏 壁 頭	*push it against* the wall.
杵 攏 看	to *put forward* the head and look.
他 說 話 來 杵 我	he *affronted* me; he *retorted* on me.

果
KO³.

| 五 穀 百 果 | the five grains and the hundred *fruits*. |
| 功 果 | *merit* obtained by subscribing to temples, bridges, or other good works. |

(265)

木 4

	京果茶食	confectionery.
	果然應驗了	it has *really* come to pass.
	果敢有爲	*very courageous* and resourceful.
	LIN².	
林	樹林	a *forest*; a *wood*; a *grove* of trees.
	竹林	a *clump* of bamboos.
	ME².	
枚	猜枚兒	to play at odds and evens (a *N. A.* like 個).
	PA¹.	
杷	枇杷枇杷隔年開花	O *loquat* tree, O *loquat* tree, you flower at the end of the year I see.
	PAN³.	
板	分板子	thin *boards*.
	牆板	the *boards* used in ramming a mud wall.
	板板橋	a *plank* bridge.
	雕印板子	to cut wooden *blocks* for printing.
	打板子	to flog with a *rod* of bamboo or wood.
	板鞋	*clogs*.
	花板	a *coffin* of fancy wood.
	火板板	a beggar's *coffin*.
	石板	*flag* stones.
	手板	the *palm* of the hand.
	脚板痛	the *soles* of my feet ache.
	皮板薄	the *skin* of this fur is thin.
	板鴨	dried ducks.
	板栗子樹	a chestnut tree. [etc.
	老板	the *captain* of a boat; the *master* of a shop.
	睡在地下板	to *writhe* on the ground in anger.
	魚板得很	the fish *wriggles* a great deal.
	死板板的	*inert; stupid and obstinate.*
	P'I².	
枇	枇杷樹	the *loquat* tree (*Eriobotrya japonica*).
	PE¹.	
杯	茶杯	a tea-*cup* without a lid.

(266)

注 释

林 [lin²]

枚 [mei²]

【猜枚儿】一种游戏，多用为酒令。其法是把瓜子、莲子或黑白棋子等握在手心里，让别人猜单双、数目或颜色，猜中者为胜，不中者罚饮。

杷 [pa¹]

板 [pan³]

【鱼板得很】板：用力跳跃、扭动。鱼跳动得很厉害。

枇 [pʰi²]

杯 [pei¹]

【茶杯】英文释义应为：teacup.

注释

柿[ʂʅ⁴]
松[soŋ¹]
東(东)[toŋ¹]
【我们办个甚么东道】
  東道：准备的宴席或物品。我们该准备点什么？
枋[faŋ¹]
【穿枋】大梁。
【枋子】棺材。
柱[uaŋ³]
杳[miao³]
【杳杳冥冥】混沌、迷茫的样子。
查[tṣʰa²]

木 4-5

	玻璃杯子	a glass *tumbler*.
	一杯茶	a *cup* of tea.
	SHĬ⁴.	
柿	柿子	*persimmons*.
	SONG¹.	
松	松樹	the Chinese *pine* tree.
	羅漢松	the *yew* tree.
	鐵甲松	a *cycad* (Encephalartos cycadifolius).
	松香	*rosin*.
	松兒石	*turquoise* stones.
	TONG¹.	
東	日出東方	the sun rises in the *east*.
	東家	a *capitalist*; the parents who invite a school master (i. e., the host who sits on the *east* side).
	大財東	a *wealthy* man.
	我們辦個甚麼東道	} what *provisions* shall we purchase?
	東西	a *thing*.
	FANG¹.	
枋	買一疋枋	buy a *plank*; buy a piece of *squared* timber.
	門枋	a door-*post* (squared).
	穿枋	a cross-*beam* (squared).
	枋子	a *coffin*.
	枋料	*coffin* timber.
	UANG³.	
柱	大寃柱	a great *wrong*.
	走些寃柱路	to go some *needless* errands.
	柱費了我的心	I have spent myself *in vain*.
	MIAO³.	
杳	杳杳冥冥	in a *trance-like* state; *semi-conscious*.
	CH'A².	
查	巡查地方	to *patrol* a district.
	查街的	a *policeman*.
	清查數目	*examine* and see if the number is correct.

(267)

木 5

柴 CH'AI².
燒柴 — to burn *firewood*.

柘 CHE⁴.
柘樹 — a small thorny tree (*Curandia triloba*), the leaves are fed to silkworms.

栅 CHA⁴.
開栅子 — open the *street-gate*.
栅門子 — the *gate* of a farmyard.
砍栅子 — to cut down the *brushwood* round fields.

柱 CHU⁴.
柱頭 — a *post*; a *pillar*.

染 RAN³.
染布 — to *dye* cloth.
染水 — *dye*; the *price for dyeing* an article.
染匠 — a *dyer*.
不消染手 — don't *meddle* with this business.
我一點都沒有沾染 — I have had nothing whatever to do with the matter.
瘟疫到處傳染 — the pestilence is very *infectious*.

柑 KAN¹.
橘子柑 — the loose jacket *orange*.
黃柑 — the thick-skinned *orange*.
蜜佛手柑 — the sweet Buddha's-hand *citron*.

柔 REO².
有剛有柔 — he is both firm and *gentle*.
性情溫柔 — he has a *mild* (or *kind* disposition).
優柔不斷 — too *meek* and lacking in decision.
話來得溫柔 — his words were very *kind* or *gentle*.
牀舖柔軟 — this coverlet is nice and *soft*.
身體柔弱 — *feeble* in body.

枸 KEO³.
枸杞子 — the fruit of *Lycium chinense*, dried and used as a medicine.

(268)

注 释

柴 [tʂʰai²]
柘 [tʂei⁴]
栅 [tʂa⁴]
柱 [tʂu⁴]
染 [zan³]
【不消染手】不消: 不用, 不需要。不需要插手。
柑 [kan¹]
柔 [zəu²]
【话来得温柔】说话很温柔。
枸 [kəu³]

注释

枷 [tɕia¹]
架 [tɕia⁴]
【朒架子】朒，同"肉"，屠夫挂肉的架子。
【莫架起架起的说】不要编造谎言。
柬 [tɕien³]
【下一封全柬】仝柬：即请柬。
柩 [tɕiəu⁴]
枯 [kʰu¹]
枴（拐）[kuai³]
【拐耙子】背负重物休息时起支撑作用的T型木制工具。
【三丁拐】三个人抬的轿子。

木 5

枷架柬柩枯枴

CHIA¹.

披枷帶鎖	to wear the *wooden collar* and fetters.
把他枷起	put the *cangue* on him; *cangue* him.
枷擔	an ox's *yoke*.
枷牛	*yoke* the ox; to start ploughing in the spring.

CHIA⁴.

立起架子	to put up the *frame-work* of a house.
搭個花架子	put up a *trellis* for flowers.
衣架	a clothes-*horse*.
書架子	a book-*case* without doors.
朒架子	a butcher's *stall*, where meat is hung up for sale.
肘架子	to stand with *arms* set a-kimbo.
瘦得光架子	as lean as a *skeleton*.
招架不住	I am unable to *withstand* him.
打架	to *fight* (either men or animals).
架花	to *embroider*.
把轎子架起	*hang* the chair up on the rafters.
莫架起架起的說	don't *invent* lies in that fashion.
一架筏子	one *raft*. (*N. A.*)
一架車子	one *wheelbarrow*. (*N. A.*)

CHIEN³.

| 下一封全柬 | to send an *invitation card*. |

CHIU⁴.

| 搬靈柩 | to transport a *coffin containing a corpse*. |

K'U¹.

樹子枯了	the tree is *withered*.
枯骨	*dry* bones.
形容枯槁	*cadaverous* looking.
生意枯得很	business is very *dull*.

KUAI³.

杵枴杖	to use a *staff*, as an old person does.
枴耙子	a short *prop* to rest a burden on.
三丁枴	a three-bearer chair.

(269)

木 5-6

LIU³.
| 柳樹 | the *willow* tree. |
| 身子柳柳的 | tall and *slender* in person. |

MONG³.
| 某人 | a *certain* person. |

PIN³.
| 權柄 | *authority*. |
| 留個話柄 | to drop a *hint*. |

PE⁵.
| 柏樹 | *cedar* and *cypress* trees. |
| 卷柏 | grey *lichen* (*Selaginella involvens*). |

IU⁴.
| 柚子 | the *pumelo*. |

HE⁵.
| 核桃 | the *walnut*, so named because of its large [*kernel*. |

READ HU¹, FU¹.
| 桃子核核 | peach *stones*. |

CH'IANG¹.
| 眼鏡子的框框 | spectacle *frames*. |

HUAN².
| 盤桓幾天 | to *wander about* for a few days to see the [sights of a place. |
| 心裏盤桓幾到 | to *ponder* over a few times. |

KEN¹.
樹根根	the *root* of a tree.
六根不全	deformed in body.
根本	*origin*.
根基	*foundation*.
根底	*antecedents*.
說出根由來	tell us the *reason*.
山根	the *bridge of the nose*.
一根樹子	one tree. (*N. A.*)
一根索子	a rope. (*N. A.*)

(270)

注 釋

柳 [liəu³]

【身子柳柳的】形容身材高而修长。

某 [moŋ³]

柄 [pin³]

柏 [pe⁵]

柚 [iəu⁴]

核 [xe⁵] [xu¹] [fu¹]

框 [tɕʰiaŋ¹]

桓 [xuan²]

【心里盘桓几到】几到：几次。心里反复考虑了几次。

根 [kən¹]

【山根】鼻梁，此处是以山比喻鼻。

【一根树子】一棵树。

注释

株 [tṣu¹]
校 [tɕiao⁴]
格 [ke⁵]
【一间两格】一间房被分成了两部分。
【我才失格】失格：言行不当，有失规矩或身份。我刚才言行失礼。
桂 [kuei⁴]
栗 [li⁵]
案 [ŋan⁴]
【白案上的师傅】面点师。
栢（柏）[pe⁵]
桑 [saŋ¹]

木 6

CHU¹.
幾株樹子　　a few trees. (N. A.)

CHIAO⁴.　　same as 較.

KE⁵.
字格子　　guiding *spaces* used under the paper when [writing.
寫個格子　　write a school boy's *copy*.
一間兩格　　one room with two *divisions* separated by a partition wall.
不拘一格　　we are not forced to follow one *pattern* or [way.
我纔失格　　I have broken the *rules of etiquette*; I have made a mistake.
格外　　besides; over and above; lit., outside the [*custom or limit*.
講格言　　to discourse *moral precepts* to the people.

KUE⁴.
桂花樹　　the *Osmanthus fragrans* which flowers in the eighth month.
肉桂　　*cinnamon*.
桂圓　　the dried fruit of the *longan*.

LI⁵.
板栗子　　*chestnuts*.

NGAN⁴.
案板　　a kitchen *table*.
案子　　a tailor's *bench*.
案棹　　a butcher's *block*.
白案上的師傅　　a baker.
開口案賬　　to pay *board* at an inn.
公案　　the *table* before a judge.
審案　　to judge a *case*.
入鱉案　　the first B. A. on the list.

PE⁵.　　same as 柏.

SANG¹.
桑樹　　the *mulberry* tree.
桑蔴　　*silk* and linen.

(271)

木 6

桃 T'AO².

桃子	a *peach*.
烏桃	a *nectarine*.
桃花水	*peach* blossom water; i. e., turbid flood water in spring time from its colour.
買二十個核桃	buy twenty *walnuts*.
櫻桃子貴	the *cherries* are dear.

條 T'IAO².

樹條子	fir tree *trunks* felled and trimmed; *timber*.
鐵條子	an iron *rod*.
使牛條子	a *stick* for driving a buffalo at the plough.
鎗條子	a *ramrod*.
紙條子	a *strip* of paper.
石條子	a long hewn stone.
羊條	*serge*.
打條	to plan an *expedient* for raising money.
條規	*rules*.
幾條街	a few streets. (*N. A.*)
一條河	a river. (*N. A.*)
一條狗	a dog. (*N. A.*)
一條蛇	a snake. (*N. A.*)
一條命	a life. (*N. A.*)

桐 T'ONG².

| 桐子樹 | *Aleurites cordata*, from the nuts of which an oil is extracted. |
| 桐油 | the oil of the "*t'ong*" tree. |

栽 TSAI¹.

栽秧子	to *plant* out rice.
絆一個倒栽蔥	to tumble a *somersault*; lit., an onion *planted* upside down.
栽個樁樁	to *set* a post in the ground.
栽培兒孫	to *rear* and educate one's children and grand-children.

READ CHUAI¹.

栽倒了	to *tumble*.
栽瞌睡	to *nod* with sleep.
栽倒我買	he *forced* me to buy it of him.

(272)

注 释

桃 [tʰao²]

【桃花水】也作"桃华水",即春汛。

條（条）[tʰiao²]

【使牛条子】赶牛用的细长木棍。

【打条】为急需用钱而想办法。

桐 [tʰoŋ²]

栽 [tsai¹]

【栽倒我买】栽:硬给安上。强迫我买。

注释

桅 [uei²]
栀(栀) [tʂʅ¹]
梓 [tsɿ³]
桴 [fu¹]
桿(杆) [kan³]
梗 [kən³]
【买个梗的】梗：完整，整个。买个完整的。
梜(筴) [tɕia⁵]
桷 [ko⁵]
【屋桷子】屋椽。
梨 [li²]
梁 [liaŋ²]

木 6-7

UE².
- 起桅 — to step the *mast* of a boat.
- 較場壩的桅杆 — the *flagstaff* on the parade ground.

CHĪ¹.
- 栀子花 — the *Gardenia* (the seed pods are used to stain wood yellow).

TSĪ³.
- 梓檀木 — the wood of *Rottlera japonica*.

FU¹.
- 桴炭子 — *charcoal* made from twigs and burned in hand stoves.

KAN³.
- 秤桿 — the *beam* of a steelyard.
- 一桿秤 — a steelyard. (*N. A.*)

KEN³.
- 菜子梗 — the dry *stems* of the oil plant.
- 那個人梗直 — he is an *upright* man.
- 頑梗難化 — *obstinate*.
- 梗塞不通 — *obstructed*, as a drain, river, road, etc.
- 一吊梗錢 — a *full* thousand cash.
- 買個梗的 — buy a *whole* one.
- 做了一天梗的 — I worked for an *entire* day.

CHIA⁵.
- 梜棍板子 — an instrument of torture, used to *squeeze* the wrists or the body.

KO⁵.
- 屋桷子 — the small *rafters* on which the tiles are laid.

LI².
- 梨兒 — *pears*.
- 梨園弟子 — actors; lit., apprentices of the *pear* garden.

LIANG².
- 屋梁 — the *ridge pole* of a house.
- 橋梁 — the *girders* of a bridge.
- 斗梁子 — the *handle* of a bushel measure.

(273)

木 7

山梁子		the *ridge* of a mountain.
雙梁子鞋		shoes with two *seams* or *bands* of leather [over the toes.
鼻梁		the *bridge* of the nose.
帶一匹梁子		to lead a regiment of *soldiers*.

SHIAO¹.

梟首　　to *expose* the heads of criminals *in cages*.

ME².

梅花　　several varieties of *plum tree* grown for the [beautiful flowers.
酸梅子　a kind of sour *plum* used in dyeing.
楊梅瘡　a bubo.

CHIAI⁴, KAI⁴.

器械　　*weapons*; *arms*.
連械　　a broad *flail* for thrashing beans.

PANG¹.

梆梆　　a *rattle* made of a hollow piece of wood, [with a slot at one side.

SHAO¹.

樹梢梢　*twigs*.
要有個好下梢　desire a good *end*.
梢長大漢　a *tall* and stalwart person.
梢公多了打破船　too many *steersmen* wreck the boat (like "Too many cooks, etc.")

SU¹.

梳子　　a *wide-toothed comb*.
梳頭　　to *comb* the hair.

SO¹.

梭子　　a *shuttle*.

T'I¹.

梯子　　a *ladder*.
石梯子　stone *steps* or *stairs*.

T'ONG³.

水桶　　a water *pail* or *bucket*.
箍桶匠　a *cooper*.

(274)

注　释

【双梁子鞋】鞋面上有两条带子的鞋。
梟（梟）[ɕiao¹]
梅 [mei²]
械 [tɕiai⁴] [kai⁴]
梆 [paŋ¹]
梢 [ʂao¹]
【要有个好下梢】期待好的结局。
【梢长大汉】高大健壮的人。
梳 [su¹]
梭 [so¹]
梯 [tʰi¹]
桶 [tʰoŋ³]
[箍桶匠]制作桶的匠人。

注 释

椮(槮)[tsan³]
梧[u²]
棧(栈)[tṣan⁴]
植[tṣʅ⁵]
棹(桌)[tṣo⁵]
椅[i³]
【一堂椅子】一套椅子（八个椅子为一套）。
棋[tɕʰi²]
萁(棋)[tɕʰi²]
棄(弃)[tɕʰi⁴]
棘[tɕie⁵]

木 7-8

	一桶 水	a *bucketful* of water.
	蜂桶	a *bee-hive*.
	袖桶子	the *sleeve* of a gown.
	韤桶子	the *leg* of a sock.
	TSAN³.	[of prisoners.
	椮子	*strips of wood* used in torturing the hands
	U².	
	梧桐樹	*Sterculia platanifolia*; a tall straight tree.
	CHAN⁴.	same as 站 in the sense of "inn" only.
	CHÏ⁵.	
	培植	to *cultivate*, either plants or people.
	CHO⁵.	
	棹子	a *table*.
	一棹客	a *tableful* of guests, i. e., eight. [of feast.
	擺三棹席	to lay three *tables* at a feast; lit., *tablefuls*
	I³.	
	一堂椅子	a set of eight *chairs*.
	CH'I².	
	下棋	to play *chess* and similar games.
	棋子塊	*checkered*; *diamond-shaped*.
	CH'I².	same as last.
	CH'I⁴.	
	舍不得丢棄	he begrudges *giving it up*.
	當棄絕不好的行為	} you ought to *abandon* evil courses.
	棄邪歸正	to *renounce* the corrupt and revert to the correct.
	棄世	to die.
	CHIE⁵.	
	荆棘	*thorny bushes*.

(275)

西蜀方言

木 8

	CHIE⁵.	
極	天邊地極	to the *utmost bounds* of heaven and earth.
	南極 and 北極	the south *pole* and the north *pole*.
	無極 and 太極	the immaterial and the material in nature.
	極多	*very* many.
	我們的命極苦	our lot is *extremely* bitter.
	KUAN¹.	
棺	棺材	a *coffin*.
	KUEN⁴.	
棍	棍棍棒棒	a *club*; a *stick*.
	光棍	a *rascal*; lit., a *bare-stick*.
	MIEN².	
棉	棉花	*cotton*.
	棉馬掛	a *wadded* coat.
	PANG⁴.	
棒	君子點頭便知 愚人棒打不醒	if you but nod your head, a wise man will know; if you flog a fool with a *stick*, he will still be stupid.
	棒客	robbers.
	P'ONG².	
棚	棚匠	a *bamboo mat* maker.
	帳棚	a *tent*.
	考棚	examination *booths*.
	一棚十個人	ten soldiers in one *mess*.
	SEN¹.	
森	森嚴	*majestic*; *severe*.
	綠森森的	*bright* green.
	白森森的	*pure* white.
	TS'I.	
棲	沒得棲身的地方	I have no *resting* place.
	棲流所	a beggar's house; lit., a place where wanderers may *rest*.

(276)

注 释

極（极）[tɕie⁵]
棺[kuan¹]
棍[kuən⁴]
【光棍】①还没有结婚的男子。英文释义应为：unmarried man。②无赖。
棉[mien²]
棒[paŋ⁴]
【棒客】土匪，强盗。
棚[pʰoŋ²]
森[sən¹]
【绿森森的】明亮的绿色。
棲（栖）[tsʰi¹]
（TS'I 当为 TS'I¹，见803页勘误表。）
【栖流所】乞丐或无家可归之人的容身之所。

注 释

棠 [tʰaŋ²]
棣 [ti⁴]
棟（栋）[toŋ⁴]
棗（枣）[tsao³]
椒 [tsiao¹]
棕 [tsoŋ¹]
椏（丫）[ia¹]
　【买的椏子】比喻便宜买来的赃物。
楂 [tṣa⁴]
楚 [tsʰu³]
　【账交清楚】清账，还清欠款。
楔 [sie⁵]
樤 [pʰao⁴]
　【一樤钱】以十计的整数钱，如10, 100, 1000, 10000等。
椿 [tṣʰuən¹]

木 8-9

T'ANG².
海棠花　　Pyrus spectabilis.

TI⁴.
棣棠花　　Kerria japonica.

TONG⁴.
棟梁之材　one who is a pillar in a community.

TSAO³.
紅棗　　　red jujubes, commonly called dates.

TSIAO¹.
海椒　　　capsicum.
花椒　　　red pepper.

TSONG¹.
棕樹　　　a palm tree; Chamaerops excelsa.
棕竹　　　a small palm which grows in clumps like [bamboo.
棕繩子　　coir ropes.

IA¹.
枝枝椏椏　branches and forks.　　　　[cheaply.
買的椏子　to buy stolen property, and therefore to buy

CHA⁴.
山楂　　　a small red fruit; a species of haw.

TS'U³.
苦楚　　　suffering; distress.
聽清楚　　to hear clearly.
賬交清楚　the debt is cleared off.

SIE⁵.
砍個楔子　make a wedge.
楔緊　　　wedge it tight.

P'AO⁴.
一樤錢　　10 cash; tens of cash as 100, 1,000, 10,000.

CH'UEN¹.
　　　　　　　　　　　　　　　　　　[a vegetable.
椿芽　　　young shoots of Cedrela odorata, used as

(277)

木 9-10

CH'UAN².
椽 椽子 — the small *rafters* on which the tiles are laid.

FONG¹.
楓 楓木樹 — a kind of *plane*-tree.

SHÜEN⁴.
楦 楦頭 — a *last* for shoes.
楦鞋 — to *stretch* shoes *with a last*.

TS'IU³.
楸 刺楸樹 — a tall spinous tree with palmate leaves and [soft wood.

K'AI³.
楷 楷書 — the *plain, square* style of writing Chinese [character.

LAN².
楠 楠木 — *Machilus nanmu*, a tree with fine hard [wood.

IANG².
楊 楊柳樹 — the common *willow*.
白楊 — the *aspen*.
黃楊 — the *box*-tree.

NIE⁵.
業 各找執業 — each one should find some *employment*.
掙個事業 — to follow a *calling* or *business*.
祖業 — an ancestral *estate*.
我業已說過 — I have *already* said.

CHA⁴.
榨 油榨 — an oil-*press*.
榨板 — a board for *pressing* things; a rat trap.
拿個東西榨倒 — get something and *press* it down.
雪把菜子榨斷了 — the snow has *crushed* the oil-plants.

T'A⁵.
榻 那在裏下榻 — where are you lodging; lit., where have you [got a *bed*.

CH'UE².
槌 鼓槌 — a drum-*stick*, usually a wooden *mallet*.
槌衣裳 — to *beat* clothes with a stick when washing.

(278)

注 释

椽 [tʂʰuan²]
楓（枫）[foŋ¹]
楦 [ɕyen⁴]
【楦头】鞋楦，做鞋用的模型。
楸 [tsʰiəu¹]
（TS'IU³当为TS'IU¹，见803页勘误表。）
楷 [kʰai³]
楠 [lan²]
楊（杨）[iaŋ²]
業（业）[ȵie⁵]
【各找执业】执业：从事的行业。各自找从事的行业。
榨 [tʂa⁴]
【拿个东西榨倒】榨：压。拿个东西压一下。
榻 [tʰa⁵]
【那在里下榻】("那在里"当为"在那里"，见803页勘误表。）
槌 [tʂʰuei²]

注释

槐 [xuai²]
榦（干）[kan⁴]
【那个人枝干】人像树的枝干已经长成，比喻人知识渊博，充满智慧。
槁 [kao³]
榔 [laŋ²]
榪（杩）[ma³]
榴 [liəu²]
槓 [loŋ³]
【买一百个槓子】买一百扎纸钱。
榜 [paŋ³]
槃 [pʰan²]
榫 [sən³]
【说话不对榫】比喻说话不对题或互相不认同。
榮（荣）[yn²]
樟 [tsaŋ¹]

木 10-11

槐	HUAI².	
	槐子樹	Sophora japonica; the flower buds are [used to dye yellow.
榦	KAN⁴.	
	那個人枝榦	a well-formed person; lit., like a tree with [trunk and branches complete.
槁	KAO³.	
	漸漸枯槁	gradually *wasting away*, as with sickness.
榔	LANG².	
	檳榔	the *betel-nut*.
榪	MA³.	
	榪桶	a *commode*.
榴	LIU².	
	石榴	the *pomegranate*.
槓	LONG³.	
	買一百個槓子	buy a hundred *baskets of paper money*.
榜	PANG³.	
	發榜	to issue the *list* of successful competitors [after an examination.
	榜樣	an *example*.
槃	P'AN².	
	掌槃	a large *tray*.
	棋槃	a chess *board*.
榫	SEN³.	
	榫頭	a *tenon*; a *dovetail*.
	公榫 and 母榫	*tenon* and *mortise*.
	說話不對榫	their words do not agree.
榮	ÜIN².	
	榮華富貴	*splendour*, wealth and honour.
	好榮耀	great *glory*!
樟	CHANG¹.	
	香樟木	the wood of the *camphor-tree*, used for [making boxes, etc.

(279)

木 11

CHUANG¹.

椿 椿	a *stob*; a *stake* set in the ground.
寄 馬 椿	a *post* to tie a horse to.
半 椿 子	a *hobbledehoy*; a *low house, fence,* etc.; [lit., a half *post*.
樹 椿 椿	the *stump* of a tree.
穀 椿	rich *stubble*.
椿 子 穩	he is firm on his feet.
一 椿 事	an affair. (*N. A.*)

HUAN⁴.

| 槵 子 | *soap-berries*. |
| 槵 子 珠 | *soap-berry* beads, used in rosaries. |

K'AI⁴.

大 概 相 像	the *general* appearance is similar.
說 個 大 概 的 樣 子	to speak *generally*; on the whole.
一 概 不 准	*all* are forbidden.

CHIN³.

| 木 槿 花 | *Hibiscus syriacus*. |

KUE⁵.

| 棺 槨 | the inner and *outer coffins*, the latter is [made of planks set in the grave. |

LEO².

天 樓	a *loft*; an *upper story*.
望 樓	a *look-out platform*.
鼓 樓	a *drum-tower*.
戲 樓	the *stage* of a theatre.
樓 板	*floor-boards*.
橋 樓 子	a wooden bridge, large or small.

TEO¹.

| 白 菜 槻 槻 | the *root*, or *stock* of a cabbage. |

TSIANG³.

| 槳 脚 | the *row-locks* of a boat, i. e., where the [*oar* rests in rowing. |

IO⁵.

| 奏 樂 | let the *music* begin! |
| 樂 器 | *musical* instruments. |

注 释

椿(桩)[tʂuaŋ¹]
【寄马桩】拴马的桩子。
【半桩子】(呆头呆脑的)小伙子；低矮的房屋、围墙。

槵 [xuan⁴]

概 [kʰai⁴]

槿 [tɕin³]

槨(椁) [kue⁵]

樓(楼) [ləu²]

槻 [təu¹]
【白菜槻槻】白菜根部。

槳(桨) [tsiaŋ³]

樂(乐) [io⁵] [lo⁵]

注释

模 [mu²]
标（标）[piao¹]
　【估标】一种类似于买彩票的游戏。
　【插标】①旧时于物品上或人身上插草作为出售的标志；②给犯人增加罪名。
　【提标】兵制名。清制，各省提督直辖的绿营官兵，称为"提标"。
槽 [tsʰao²]
样（样）[iaŋ⁴]
　【样起手要打】举起手装做要打的样子。
樘（撑）[tsʰən¹]
横 [xuən²] [xuan²]
　【横人】蛮横之人。

木 11-12

	READ LO⁵.	
	快樂	joy; pleasure.
	樂得的	lucky! lit., pleased to get it!
模	MU².	
	模樣	a pattern.
	模子	a mould. [ment.
	脚模手印	the print of a hand and a foot on a docu-
標	PIAO¹.	
	估標	to buy a lottery ticket. [criminal.
	插標	to attach the accusation to a condemned
	提標	the General's standard.
	長得標緻	a fine figure!
槽	TS'AO².	
	馬槽	a horse trough; a manger.
	打個槽槽	make a groove in it.
	猪出得槽了	the pig is fat enough to be killed.
	槽門子	an outer gate.
樣	IANG⁴.	
	全不像樣	utterly unlike what it ought to be.
	做走了樣	you have not followed the pattern.
	裝模做樣	to copy the manner of another.
	怎麽樣	in what way? how?
	各樣的書	all kinds of books.
	都是一樣	all are alike.
	一樣大的	the same size; as big as this or that.
	樣起手要打	to feint or menace with the hand as if about to strike.
12 樘	TS'EN¹.	
	樘弓架子	a bracket under a shelf.
橫	HUEN², HUAN².	
	橫起的	transverse; crosswise; at right angles.
	橫順都是一樣	it is the same in any case.
	橫人	a perverse fellow.
	滿口橫話	his words are utterly unreasonable.

(281)

木 12

HUA⁴.
樺皮	the bark of a kind of *birch*.

RAO².
搬橈	to work an *oar*; to steer with a broad *oar*.
小橈片	a *paddle*.
加兩把橈	add two *oars*.
推橈	to row.

CHI¹.
機頭	a *loom*.
機房	a *weaver's shop*.
機匠	a *weaver*.
機骨轉兒	a *hinge-joint*.
機器	a *machine*.
機關	*machinations ; artifices ; designs*.
商量的甚麼機密事	what *secrets* are you talking ?
機會	an *opportunity*.

CH'IAO².
一道橋	a *bridge*.
爐橋	the *bars* of a grate.
這個板子是橋起的	this board is *warped*.
學算盤要記倒橋數	in learning the abacus you must remember the number of the *rows*.
事情橋了盤	there is a hitch in the transaction.
我是橋的	I am *unacquainted* with that kind of work.

CH'ÜE⁵.
鋸一檓下來	saw off a *piece*.

KAN³.
橄欖	the Chinese *olive*.

CHÜ⁵.
橘子	the loose-jacket *orange*.
金橘	the small cumquat *orange*.

(282)

注　釋

樺（桦）[xua⁴]
橈（桡）[ʐao²]
【搬橈】摇船桨。
【小橈片】小船桨。
【推橈】推桨。
機（机）[tɕi¹]
橋（桥）[tɕʰiao²]
【这个板子是桥起的】桥起：像桥一样拱起。
【事情桥了盘】在事情或交易中有障碍。
【我是桥的】桥：不熟悉。我对那事不熟悉。
檓（檅）[tɕʰye⁵]
橄 [kan³]
橘 [tɕy⁵]

注释

橙 [tsʰən²]
樸(朴) [pʰu⁵]
榫 [tɕʰien⁴]
【楼榫】屋顶椽架。
樹(树) [ʂu⁴]
橡 [siaŋ¹]
橐 [to⁵]
樵 [tsʰiao²]
檢(检) [tɕien³]
【检起来】检: 同"捡"。
【我给你检账】检账: 付账。
【检房子】修房子, 更换屋顶散落的瓦片。
檎 [tɕʰin²]
檑 [luei⁴] [luei¹]

木 12-13

TS'EN². [pumelo.
橙子   the common *orange*; in some places the

P'U⁵.
穿得樸素   *plainly* dressed.
樸實   *sincere; simple-minded.*

CH'IEN⁴.
樓榫   the *rafters* which support the floor of a loft.

SHU⁴.
一根樹子   a *tree*.

SIANG¹.
栗橡子樹   the Chinese *oak*.
栗橡子   *acorns*.

TO⁵.
囊橐空虛   I have no money; lit., the *bag* is empty.

TS'IAO².
漁樵耕讀   fishing, *wood-cutting*, farming and study; four ancient occupations.

CHIEN³.   in some senses the same as 揀.
刮骨檢驗   to scrape the bones and *examine* them; a form of inquest. [erty.
到處搜檢   to *search* everywhere, as for stolen prop-
檢點   be very careful; beware!
檢起來   *pick* it *up*.
檢柴   to *gather* sticks for firewood.
我在街上檢的   I *found* it on the street.
檢菜盆   *gather up* the vegetable dishes.
我給你檢賬   I will pay the bill for you.
檢房子   to *replace* dislodged tiles on the roof.

CH'IN².
林檎   the *cherry-apple*.

LUE⁴. [wall on an enemy.
滾木檑石   wood and stones which are *hurled* from a

(283)

木 13-17

	READ LUE¹.	[wall.
一橹就下去了		he came down with a *tumble*, as from a
	CH'IN².	[hall.
檠凳		long *benches*, sometimes placed in the main
	LIN³.	[cepting the ridge pole).
檁子		the cross *beams* that support the roof (ex-
	T'AN².	
檀香		*sandal-wood*.
	TANG⁴.	
床檔頭		the *end* of a bed.
在屋檔頭		at the *gable* end of the house.
	KUE⁴.	
盌櫃		a *cupboard*.
書櫃		a *book-case*.
櫃臺		a shop *counter*.
錢櫃		a shop *till*.
	PIN¹.	
檳		for example of use see 榔.
	T'AI².	[spread.
檯子辦得好		the feast *tables* were well supplied; a good
	TEN⁴.	
櫈		same as 凳.
	HUAN⁴, HUANG⁴.	
桌子擴樌		the *crossbars* of a table.
	ÜEN².	
香櫞菓		a large kind of *citron*.
	LONG¹.	
囚櫳		a prisoner's *cage*.
櫳門子		the *outer gate* of a mansion.
	LAN³.	
木欄杆		a wooden *railing*.
石欄杆		a stone *parapet*.
牛欄		a cow-house, or *pen*.

(284)

注释

【一橹就下去了】一个跟头就跌下去了。

檠 [tɕʰin²]

【檠凳】长凳。

檁（檩）[lin³]

檀 [tʰan²]

檔（档）[taŋ⁴]

櫃（柜）[kuei⁴]

檳（槟）[pin¹]

檯（台）[tʰai²]

櫈（凳）[tən⁴]

樌 [xuan⁴] [xuaŋ⁴]

【桌子擴樌】桌子边框。

櫞（橼）[yen²]

櫳（栊）[loŋ¹]

欄（栏）[lan³]

注 释

【栏杆辫子】衣服上装饰用的丝带。
樱(櫻) [in¹] [ŋən¹]
槚 [pʰin²]
【槚果】苹果。
权(權) [tɕʰyen²]
欗(把) [pa⁴]
【锄头把把】把把：器物上的手柄。
【话把把儿】话柄。
【说话带把子】说话带脏字。
揽(欖) [lan³]
欠 [tɕʰien⁴]
次 [tsʰɿ⁴]

木 17-21 欠 2

欗 | 櫻 | 18 | 權 | 21 | 欗 | 欖 | 欠 | ²次

欄 菜 園 子 — to *fence* a vegetable garden. [etc.
欄 杆 辮 子 — Chinese *ribbon* used for trimming dresses,
　IN¹, NGEN¹.　second sen., read "in¹" only.

櫻 桃 — *cherries*. [hip.
金 櫻 子 — the fruit of *Rosa laevigata*; a kind of large
　P'IN².

槚 菓 — the *apple*.
　CH'ÜEN².

從 權 — to act as *expediency* demands. [cumstances.
權 且 應 酬 — we must entertain him under the cir-
專 權 — to monopolize *power*.
沒 得 那 個 權 柄 — I have not that *authority*.
　PA⁴.

鋤 頭 欗 欗 — the *handle* of a hoe.
刀 欗 子 — the *hilt* of a sword or knife. [speaker.
話 欗 欗 兒 — a word that is a *handle* against the
說 話 帶 欗 子 — to use *obscene* language.
　LAN³.　for example of use see 橄.

The 76th radical. (欠)

CH'IEN⁴.

銀 錢 欠 缺 — I am *deficient* in money.
德 行 欠 缺 — *wanting* in virtue. [unwell.
我 這 幾 天 欠 安 — I have been *out of sorts* these few days;
欠 賬 — to *owe* a debt.
寫 個 欠 字 — write an I. O. U.
我 名 下 他 還 有 欠 項 } he still owes me a *debt*.
我 心 裏 墨 欠 我 的 兒 子 } I am *longing* to see, or hear from my son.
　TS'ɿ⁴.

次 日 — the *next* day.
這 個 布 要 次 點 — this cloth is *inferior* to that.

欠 2-10

6 欸	要依個次序		it must be done in proper *order*.
	下次		the next *occasion*.
7 欸		K'E⁵.	same as 咳.
		K'UAN³.	
	欸待客		to be *courteous* to guests. [*bric-a-brac*, etc.]
	玩欸式		to delight in *formality*, *fanciful etiquette*,
	公欸		a *public affair*.
	議條欸		to discuss the *articles of a treaty*.
	籌欸		to consult about *ways and means*.
	欸起了		*detained*; *arrested*; *hindered*.
8 欲		IO⁵.	
	私欲		evil *desires*; *lusts*.
欺		CH'I¹.	
	欺哄人		to *cheat* people.
	不要自欺		don't *deceive* yourself.
	欺人是禍饒人是福		to *delude* brings misery, to forgive brings happiness.
	佔欺頭		to gain an *advantage*.
	這個東西買得有欺頭		I have bought this article very cheaply.
欽		CH'IN¹.	
	欽差		an *imperial* commissioner.
9 歇	這是欽定		this is by *royal* order.
		SHIE⁵.	
	歇憩		to *rest*.
	歇個手		*rest* from labour for a little.
	這裏不歇客		we do not *lodge* strangers here.
	歇站房		to *lodge* in an inn.
	一歇做起		do it *instantly*; to do a thing *hurriedly*.
10 歉	説了一歇		he talked for a *while*.
		CH'IEN⁴.	
	年歲歉收		there is a *scanty* harvest.
歌		KO¹.	
	唱歌		to sing *songs*.
	歌詩		to *chant* ditties.

(286)

注　釋

欸[kʰe⁵]

欸（款）[kʰuan³]

【款起了】阻挡，扣留。

欲[io⁵]

欺[tɕʰi¹]

【占欺头】占便宜。

欽（钦）[tɕʰin¹]

歇[ɕie⁵]

【说了一歇】歇：量词，次，回。说了一会儿。

歉[tɕʰien⁴]

歌[ko¹]

注 释

歎（叹）[tʰan⁴]
歡（欢）[xuan¹]
止 [tʂʅ³]
【止住他】拦住他。
正 [tʂən¹] [tʂən⁴]
【这是你的正分】正分：责任。
【正字】楷书。
【正天平】校准天平。
此 [tsʰʅ³]

欠 11-18 止 1-2

11
歎
18

T'AN⁴.   same as 嘆.

HUAN¹.

滿心歡喜   full of *joy*.
歡歡喜喜的   *joyfully*.
我不喜歡他   I am dis*pleased* with him.

The 77th radical. (止)

止

CHǏ³.

止住他   *stop* him !
謠風止息了   the rumours have *ceased*.
在那裏止   where does it *end ?*
不止一吊錢   more than 1,000 cash.
止痛   to *allay* pain.
禁止賭博   to *prohibit* gambling.

1 正

CHEN¹, ⁴.

正月   the *first* month.

READ CHEN⁴.

端正   *straight*.
那個人正直   he is an *upright* man.
正經人   a *moral* man.
根深不怕風搖動 } deep-rooted, fear not if the wind does blow,
樹正何愁月影斜 } *straight*-stemmed, why grieve though moon bent shadow throw ?
要正自己   you ought to *reform* yourself.
這是你的正分   this is your *duty*, or *lot*.
正命夫人   the *proper* wife.
正房   the *principal* building in a Chinese house.
正字   the ordinary *square style* of Chinese characters.
正天平   *exactly* 16 oz. to the pound.
正在說話的時候   *just* as he was speaking.

2 此

TS'Ĭ³.

如此   like *this*; thus.
彼此幫助   help one another.

(287)

步 3-12

3 步 PU⁴ [to worship at a shrine.
- 三步一拜 — to bow every three *paces* when on the way
- 矮子上樓梯步步升高 — like a dwarf ascending a ladder, he rises *step by step*.
- 步行 — to go *on foot*.
- 步兵 — *foot* soldiers.
- 請留步我有話說 — please wait a little, I have something to say.
- 萬不諳到那個地步 — no one expected him to come to this *position* or *condition*.
- 三步水 — a roof with 4 rafters on one side (3 *spaces* between the rafters.).

4 武 U³.
- 武官 — a *military* official.
- 行武出身 — risen to office through the *army*.
- 動武 — to use *violence*.

歪 UAI¹.
- 歪起的 — *awry; askew; crooked*.
- 楊歪嘴兒 — Mr. Iang with the *wry* mouth.
- 歪人 — a *wicked* fellow.

READ UAI³.
- 把脚歪了 — I have *sprained* my ankle.
- 船歪得很 — the boat *rolls* terribly.

8 歲 SUE⁴.
- 辭歲 — to take leave of the old *year*.
- 好大歲數 — what is your *age*?
- 今年年歲孬 — the *harvest* is bad this year.
- 值年太歲犯不得 — the *cyclic symbols* for this year must not be infringed (in burying, etc.).

12 歷 LIE⁵, LI⁵.
- 閱歷得多 — I have *passed through* much in my time.
- 問明他的來歷 — inquire into his *antecedents*.
- 歷代以來就有的 — it has been the same through many *successive* generations.

(288)

注 释

步 [pu⁴]
【万不谙到那个地步】万万没想到会到如此地步。

武 [u³]

歪 [uai¹] [uai³]

岁（岁）[suei⁴]
【今年年岁孬】年岁孬：收成不好。

历（历）[lie⁵] [li⁵]

注 释

歸（归）[kuei¹]
歹 [tai³]
死 [sɿ³]
　【死巷子】死胡同。
歿 [mo⁵]
殀 [iao¹]
殄 [tʰien³]
　【暴殄】任意浪费, 糟蹋。
　英文释义应为: to waste.

止 12-14　歹 2-5

14 歸　KUE¹.

歷年都是這麼興起的 } it was always done in this way in *former* years.

樹高千丈葉落歸根 } though a tree be 10,000 feet high, the leaves will *return to fall back to* the root.

歸老家去了　he has been *gathered to* his fathers.
不歸他管　it does not *belong to* his jurisdiction; none of his business.
事情說歸一沒有　is the affair *settled*, or arranged?
做歸一了　*finished; completed.*

The 78th radical. (歹)

歹　TAI³.

不知好歹　he does not know good from *evil.*
為非作歹　to work *wickedness.*
心腸歹毒　*depraved.*

2 死　SI³.

人不怕三十而死 只怕死後無名 } a man does not fear to *die* at the age of 30, but fears that after he is *dead*, no one will speak well of him.

死生有命　*death* and life are decreed.
這個天氣熱死人　this weather is hot enough to *kill* one.
打個死紇縺　tie a *hard* knot.
死巷子　a *blind* alley, a cul-de-sac.
死水　*stagnant* water.
把門釘死　nail the door up; nail the hinges so that it [cannot be unhinged.

4 歿　MO⁵.

歿世不忘你的恩　till *death* I will not forget your kindness.

殀　IAO¹.

你不怕殀壽嗎　do you not fear an *untimely* end?

5 殄　T'IEN³.

暴殄　*wasteful.*

(289)

西蜀方言　289

歹 5-16 殳 5

6 殃	IANG¹.	
	遭了殃	I have met with a *great misfortune*.
	災殃	a *calamity*.
8 殊	SHU¹.	
	殊不知	*nevertheless*.
	殊不可解	I *really* do not understand it.
12 殘	TS'AN².	
	殘害百姓	to *injure* the people.
	殘忍刻薄	*cruel* and mean.
	眼睛殘	his eyes are *greedy*, or *covetous*.
	殘廢人	an *infirm* and helpless person.
	殘年難過	the *end of the year* is difficult to pass.
	帶殘疾	to have an *infirmity*.
	喫殘了的	to eat *leavings*, like a beggar.
13 殨	K'UE⁴.	
	瘡殨爛了	the abscess has *burst*.
14 殮	LIEN⁴.	
	沒得人收殮他	there is no one to *enshroud* the corpse.
	入殮沒有	is he *coffined* yet?
14 殯	PIN⁴.	
	寄殯在外	to have a *coffin* containing a corpse above [ground.
	殯菜秧子	to *plant* a lot of young plants together for a time.
16 殱	TS'IEN¹.	
	用火殱化	to *destroy* a corpse by cremation.

The 79th radical. (殳)

5 段	TUAN⁴.	
	分做兩段	to divide into two *lots*, as a piece of land
	一段書	a *paragraph*.
	手段高	his *skill* is great, as a mechanic.

(290)

注 释

殃 [iaŋ¹]

殊 [ṣu¹]

殘（残）[tsʰan²]

【殘年難過】殘年: 年终。一年最后的日子难以度过。

殨（殨）[kʰuei⁴]

殮（殓）[lien⁴]

殯（殡）[pin⁴]

【殯菜秧子】培育菜苗。

殲（歼）[tsʰien¹]

段 [tuan⁴]

注释

殷 [in¹]
殺（杀）[ṣa⁵]
【故杀】故意杀害。
殽 [ɕiao²]
【今天吃的甚么殽馔】今天吃的什么菜肴？
毁 [xuei³]
殿 [tien⁴]
毆（殴）[ŋəu³]
毋 [u²]
母 [mu³]

殳 6-11 毋 1

6 殷 IN¹.
殷實之家 — a *wealthy* family.

殺 SHA⁵.
殺傷 — to *wound* with a knife.
殺死 — to *slay*.
殺雞 — to *kill* a chicken by cutting its throat.
殺豬 — to *slaughter* pigs.
誤殺 — accidental *manslaughter*.
故殺 — wilful *murder*.
自殺 — *suicide*.
一把好殺手 — a brave *fighter*.
那個人有殺氣 — he is a *fierce* fellow.

8 殽 SHIAO².
今天喫的甚麼殽馔 — what *viands* did you have at the feast to-day?

9 毀 HUE³.
拆毀房屋 — to *destroy* a house.
約據毀了 — the agreement has been *destroyed*.
毀壞東西 — to *smash up* things.
毀謗人 — to *slander* people.

殿 TIEN⁴.
金殿 — the golden *palace* of the Emperor.
正殿 — the main *hall* of a Buddhist temple.

11 毆 NGEO³.
鬬毆 — to *fight*.
毆打生員 — to *beat* a graduate.

The 80th radical. (毋)

毋 1 U².
毋庸掛慮 — *don't* be anxious about it.

母 MU³.
父母 — father and *mother*.
老丈母 — wife's *mother*.

(291)

母 1-5 比

國母	the Empress.	
父母官	the parent ruler, i. e., the district magistrate.	
母牛	a *cow*.	
母豬	a *sow*.	
母狗	a *bitch*.	
雞母	a *hen*.	
字母子	the *radicals* of the Chinese language; an *alphabet*.	
醋母子	*mother* of vinegar.	

3 每 ME³.

每逢出門	*each* time you go on a journey.
每每說的話不好聽	he is *constantly* using obscene language.

5 毒 TU⁵.

毒藥	*poison*.
毒死人	to *poison* people.
毒蛇	a *venomous* snake.
毒氣	*noxious* matter; *hate*.
瘋狗毒	*hydrophobia*.
以毒攻毒	to oppose *evil* with *evil*.
那個人手毒	that man is *cruel*.

The 81st radical. (比)

比 PI³.

拏來比一比	*compare* them together.
貨怕比	goods won't stand *comparison*.
比不上	cannot be *compared* with; not *equal* to.
他比我好過	he is better off than I am (sign of the *comparative*).
比銀子	to *weigh* silver.
比大小	*measure* the size.
比子	a little board used by gamblers to *measure* cash.
比方說	to *illustrate*; for *instance*; for *example*.

READ PI⁴.

你不消阿比他	don't *associate* with that fellow.

(292)

注 释

【鸡母】母鸡。

【字母子】即字母,常指汉语拼音字母。

【醋母子】用来做醋的酵母。

每 [mei³]

毒 [tu⁵]

比 [pi³] [pi⁴]

【比子】赌博时量钱的板子。

【你不消阿比他】不消:不用。阿比:附和。你不用附和他的意见。

注释

毛 [mao²]
【闲毛】汗毛。
【眼眨毛】眼睫毛。
【活路做得毛】毛：粗糙，不细致。工作做得不细致。
【毛钱】毛：不纯净的。来路不干净的脏钱。

毡 [tṣan¹]
【京毡窝】北京毡帽。

毫 [xao²]

毬（球）[tɕʰiəu²]

毛 5-7

The 82nd radical (毛)

MAO².

闲毛	the *hair* on the body (usually pronounced ["han² mao"]).	
嘴上没得毛 做事情不牢	} if a man has no *hair* on his upper lip, he is not stable enough to manage anything.	
长毛	the T'ai-p'in rebels.	
眼眨毛	the *eye-lashes*.	
下毛毛雨	to rain a *fine* rain; *drizzle*.	
毛狗	a wild *hairy* dog; a fox.	
紮毛人	to make a straw effigy.	
羊毛	*wool*.	
鸡毛	chicken *feathers*.	
毛脚毛手	a coarse, *vulgar* fellow.	
活路做得毛	the work is *coarsely* or *roughly* done.	
毛钱	*bad* cash.	
毛病	a *disease*; a *defect*.	

CHAN¹.

毡子	a *felt* rug.
京毡窝	a Pekinese *felt* cap.

HAO². [Pecco.

白毫茶	a white *downy* kind of tea, commonly called
买卖争釐毫	in business we reckon to the *10,000th* part of a tael.
一毫之恶勸人莫作 一毫之善與人方便	} exhort people not to do the *least* evil; the smallest good is beneficial to men.
不差分毫	not a *fraction* wrong; perfectly correct.
毫无二心	without the *least* guile; sincere (a *superlative*).
毫光闪闪	the *reflected rays* of light dart about.

CH'IU².

繡毬花	the hydrangea, from the *globular* form of the flowers.

(293)

毛 8-13 氏 1 气 6

8 毯

T'AN³.

| 毯子 | a *woven rug*. |
| 毛毯 | yak hair *cloth* from 6 in. to 8 in. wide. |

CHIEN⁴.

| 踢毽子 | to kick the *shuttle-cock*. |

TSO⁵.

| 一粒毛 | a *patch* of hair on the body. |

12 毢

RONG²,³, IONG²,³.

| 毢毢毛 | *down* on birds; *fine hair* on animals. |
| 這個床舖毢和 | the coverlet is *soft*. |

13 氊

CHAN¹.

| | same as 氈. |

The 83rd radical. (氏)

氏

SHÏ⁴.

| 楊門趙氏 | Mrs. Iang *née* Chao. |

1 民

MIN².

爲官不與民作主 枉食朝廷俸祿高 }	if a magistrate does not rule the *people*, he receives his pay in vain.
頁民	loyal *subjects*.
民間的風俗	*popular* customs.

The 84th radical. (气)

6 氣

CH'I.

蒸上氣沒有	has the *steam* risen in the steamer yet?
濕氣	watery *vapours*; damp.
臭氣	bad *odours*; stench.
出氣不贏	to pant for *breath*; short-winded.
要落氣了	he is about to die.
看他的口氣何如	see what his *answer* will be.
他的氣力大	his *energy* is great.
發氣	to show *temper*; to get angry.

(294)

注 释

毯 [tʰan³]
毽 [tɕien⁴]
粒 [tso⁵]
毢 [zoŋ²] [zoŋ³] [ioŋ²] [ioŋ³]

【毢毢毛】毢：鸟兽身上的细软毛。绒毛。

【这个床铺毢和】这个床很软。

氊(毡) [tsan¹]
氏 [ʂɿ⁴]
民 [min²]
（CH'I当为CH'I⁴, 见803页勘误表。）
氣(气) [tɕʰi⁴]

【出气不赢】不赢：来不及。气喘吁吁，上气不接下气。

【发气】生气，发脾气。

注释

水 [ṣuei³]
【水药】以水为剂的药物。
【水糖】粗砂糖。
【水菜】泡菜，腌菜。
【下水】猪大肠。
【送个水礼】酒食之类的普通礼品。
【水脚】水路运输的费用。

气 6 水

脾氣不好	his *temper* is bad.
怒氣	*anger*.
沾不動就使氣	constantly giving way to *anger*, short-tempered.
遣繞氣人	this is *vexing*.
和氣	harmony; harmonious.
沒志氣的人	a man without purpose.
正氣	straightforward.
臉上的氣色好	the *expression* of his face is good.
天氣冷	the *weather* is cold.
各處風氣不同	the *customs* of each place are different.
福氣	happiness.
運氣	luck.
節氣	a semi-monthly solar period.

The 85th radical. (水)

水 SHUE³.

井水	well *water*.
水煙	cut tobacco smoked in the *water*-pipes.
水藥	*liquid* medicine.
眼淚水	tears.
口水	spittle.
汗水	perspiration; sweat.
露水	dew.
墨水	ink.
水糖	coarse brown sugar; *moist* sugar.
水柿子	ripe persimmons, because *juicy*.
水菜	pickles.
下水	pig's intestines.
送個水禮	to give a present of *eatables*.
水路	a *river* journey, or route.
趕下水	to go down *river*.
水腳	passage money on a boat; freightage.
山水	*scenery*.
水土好	the *climate* is good.

水 1-3

	暗地裏進了水	he has given *bribes*. [bnsiness silver.
	扣銀水	to deduct the difference between good and
1 氷永	PIN¹.	same as 冰.
	ÜIN³.	
	永遠	for *ever*; *everlasting*; *eternal*.
	永不食言	I will *never* go back on my word.
2 汁求	CHĪ⁵.	
	熬出汁來	boil the *juice* or *essence* out of it.
	CH'IU².	
	求雨	to *pray* for rain.
	求人不如求神	it is better to *ask* of gods than of men.
	哀求	to *beseech*.
	苛求	to *importunate*; to *dun*.
	求噢	to *beg* for food. [granted.
	有求必應	if there is a *request* it will certainly be
	求官不倒連秀才都貼了	I *aimed* at being a magistrate, but failed, and even lost my degree.
3 汊池汗江	CH'A⁴.	
	汊河	*divergent* streams, *bifurcated* rivers.
	CH'Ï².	[of fire.
	太平池	a stone *cistern* where water is stored in case
	蓮花池	a lotus *pond* or *tank*.
	城池	the city *moat*.
	糞池	a dung *pit*.
	墨池	an ink-*well*.
	HAN⁴.	
	出汗	to *perspire*.
	盜汗	night *sweats*.
	汗衣	an inner jacket or shirt.
	CHIANG¹.	
	楊子江	the Iang-tsī *River*.
	皇上的江山	the empire.

注释

【暗地里进了水】背地里收受贿赂。
氷（冰）[pin¹]
永 [yn³]
汁 [tʂʅ⁵]
求 [tɕʰiəu²]
【求官不倒连秀才都贴了】想谋求官职不成功，连秀才都丢了。
汊 [tʂʰa⁴]
池 [tʂʰʅ²]
汗 [xan⁴]
江 [tɕiaŋ¹]

注释

【你才不江湖】你太年轻，没有阅历，不谙世事。

汛 [syn⁴]

【汛部厅】防汛处。

污（汚）[u¹]

沉 [tṣʰən²]

沈 [tṣʰən²]

决（決）[tɕye⁵]

没 [mu⁵] [mo⁵]

沐 [mo⁵]

杳（原文错误，当为"沓"）[tʰa⁵] [ta⁵]

【在这个沓沓】在这个地方。

【吊沓墨在纸上】在纸上滴一滴墨。

沙 [ʂa¹]

水 3-4

汛 汚 ₄沉 沈 決 没 沐 杳 沙

江湖	travelling traders, peddlers, tramps, etc.
你纔不江湖	you are very inexperienced.
SÜIN⁴.	
汛部廳	the captain of a district city *guard*.
U¹.	
染污濊	to contract *moral defilement*.
受污辱	to receive an *insult*.
CHʻEN².	
沉底	to *sink* to the bottom.
沉香木	Aquilaria agallochum, so called because it [sinks in water.
免墮沉淪	to escape *eternal destruction*.
病越發沉重	his disease is much worse; he is *sinking*.
那個話深沉	that is a *profound* saying.
CHʻEN².	same as last.
CHÜE⁵.	same as 決.
MU⁵, MO⁵.	
沒有	I have *not*; I did *not*.
沒得人來	no one has come.
我沒得話說	I have *nothing* to say.
MO⁵.	
沐浴淨身	to *wash* a corpse.
TʻA⁵, TA⁵.	
在這個杳杳	in this *place*.
READ TA⁵.	
吊杳墨在紙上	to drop a *blot* of ink on the paper.
SHA¹.	interchanged with 砂.
河沙	river *sand*.
沙石	*sand*-stone.
沙漠之地	a *sandy* desert.
落黃沙	fine yellow *sand* falling on plants (said to be sand storms from the north).

西蜀方言

水 4-5

沙 鍋	very coarse black *earthen-ware* pots.
鐵 沙 子	iron *pellets* used in fowling pieces.
沙 鑭	a *filter*.
沙 虫	the larvae of musquitoes.

沌 TEN⁴.

| 混 沌 | *chaos*. |

汪 UANG¹.

汪 洋 大 海	the *vast* ocean.
這 個 樹 子 好 汪	what a *great* tree !
這 塊 朕 汪 幾 帶 肥	this piece of meat is *very big* and fat.
清 汪 汪 的 水	*clear* water.
衣 裳 還 是 水 汪 汪 的	the clothes are still *soaking* wet.

沾 CHAN¹.

衣 裳 沾 了 油	my clothes are *stained* with oil.
沒 有 沾 過 他 的 恩	I have not *received* favours from him ; I am not obliged to him.
毫 無 沾 染	I have not *meddled with* the matter ; nothing to do with it.
你 不 消 沾 絆 我	you need not come *toadying* and hindering me.
沾 不 動 就 罵 人	he curses people on the slightest provocation.

治 CHÏ⁴.

處 治	to *chastise*.
我 要 醫 治 你	I'll *punish* you ; I'll give you a beating.
那 個 醫 生 善 會 治 病	that doctor is good at *healing* diseases.

注 CHU⁴.

| 他 注 意 在 那 個 地 方 | his heart is *set upon* that place. |

法 FA⁵.

律 法	*laws*.
禮 法	*rules* of politenes.
方 法	a *plan* ; a *way* ; a *method*.

(298)

注　釋

【沙鑭】鑭：同"缸"。过滤器。

沌 [tən⁴]

汪 [uaŋ¹]

【这个树子好汪】汪：分量多，足。这棵树很茂盛。

【这块肉汪几带肥】这块肉大且肥。

沾 [tṣan¹]

【你不消沾绊我】你不用谄媚和阻碍我。

治 [tṣʅ⁴]

注 [tṣu⁴]

【他注意在那个地方】他的心思在彼处。

法 [fa⁵]

注 释

泛 [fan⁴]

河 [xo²]

【做山河里头的买卖】做山区里的买卖。

泣 [ɕie⁵]

沽 [ku¹]

泥 [ɲi²]

泮 [pʰan⁴]

泡 [pʰao⁴]

【长得泡酥酥的】泡酥酥，同"泡舒舒"，形容又健康又胖（多形容婴儿）。

【泥巴霜打泡了】泡：松软，不紧实。泥巴被霜弄得松软了。

泑 [iəu⁴]

【盂碗的泑子好】泑子，同"釉子"。

水 5

泛 FAN⁴.

沒法子	there is no help for it.
效法	to *imitate*.
浮泛的話	*trivial* talk; *light* gossip.
泛泛之交	a *casual* acquaintance.

河 HO².

丟在河頭連魚都瘆得死	if you should throw—that placard—in the *river*, even the fishes would be poisoned.
做山河裏頭的買賣	to trade in a mountainous district.

泣 SHIE⁵.

哭泣	to *weep*; to *cry*.

沽 KU¹.

沽點酒來	*buy* some wine.
沽名釣譽	to fish for praise.

泥 NI².

same as 坭.

泮 PʻAN⁴.

泮池	a semi-circular *pool* in front of a literary temple.

泡 PʻAO⁴.

打泡子	to skim off *froth* or *scum*.
起水泡	to raise a *blister*.
膿泡瘡	*pimples*.
魚泡	the *air-bladder* of a fish.
泡衣服	*soak* the clothes.
泡盌茶	*infuse* a cup of tea.
泡菜	*pickled* vegetables.
發得泡酥酥的	well raised, as bread; *spongy*.
長得泡酥酥的	*plump*, as a baby.
泡炭	*soft* charcoal.
泡木頭	*soft* wood.
泥巴霜打泡了	the frost has rendered the soil *friable*.

泑 IU⁴.

盂盌的泑子好	the *glaze* on this earthen-ware basin is good.

西蜀方言

水 5

	FU¹.	
熱沸沸的		boiling hot.
	READ P'U⁵.	
飯鍋沸了		the rice pot is boiling over.
好生看沸出了		beware and not fill it to overflowing.
	PE⁵, PO⁵.	
淡泊人		a poor man.
	PO¹.	
波浪		waves.
平地起風波		to raise waves on level ground, i. e., to stir up trouble without cause.
	SĬ⁴.	
連泗紙		a kind of fine white paper (evidently from the name of a place).
	T'AI⁴.	
恭喜你否去泰來		I congratulate you that the trouble is past and peace restored.
	T'O².	
落在沱裏頭		he has fallen into a deep pool in the river.
	TS'ÜEN².	
井泉		a well of spring water.
黃泉		the grave.
	KAN¹.	
米泔水		water in which rice has been washed; lit., rice-sweetened water.
	ÜEN².	
沿河兩岸的人		the crowds along both banks of the river.
沿途保護		to protect one by the way.
	IU².	
豬油		pork fat; lard.
牛油		beef suet.
羊油		tallow.
菜油		vegetable oil.
梳頭油		hair oil.

(300)

注 釋

沸 [fu¹] [pʰu⁵]

【好生看沸出了】不要让水溢出。

泊 [pe⁵] [po⁵]

波 [po¹]

泗 [sɿ⁴]

【连泗纸】又叫"连四纸"、"连史纸",素有"寿纸千年"美称。早在元代即被誉为"妍妙辉光,皆世称也"的精品。原产于福建省邵武。

泰 [tʰai⁴]

沱 [tʰo²]

【落在沱里头】沱:水中较深的潭。

泉 [tsʰyen²]

泔 [kan¹]

【米泔水】即淘米水。

沿 [yen²]

油 [iəu²]

注释

洪 [xoŋ²]
洄 [xuei²]
【洄水沱】江河中可以停船的较深的水湾。
活 [xo⁵]
派 [pʰai⁴]
洒 [sa³]
洗 [si³]

水 5-6

洋油	kerosene.
油漆	paint.
荳油	bean-*soy*.
打酥油	to churn *butter*.
油紙	*oiled* paper; water-proof paper.
菸油	tobacco *juice*.
油嘴滑舌	*voluble*; a *garrulous* person.

HONG².

洪水	a *deluge*; a *flood*.
寬洪大量	*magnanimous*.

HUE².

洄水沱	a *whirlpool*.

HO⁵.

不得活	he cannot *live*.
是活的嗎	is it a *living* thing? is it *alive*?
活鮮鮮的魚	*live* fish.
沒得活路做	I have no *work* to do; I have no *occupation*.
放活動點	be more *active*; look *spry*!
過快活日子	to pass one's days in *pleasure*.
活水	*running* water; *living* water.
窗子是活的	the window is *movable*.
活像他	*very* like him.
說得活現	he speaks *confidently*.

P'AI⁴.

支派	a *branch* of a family.
派差護送	to *appoint* an escort.
分派他們做工夫	*allot* to each one his work.
一派的謠言	a *lot* of lying stories.
正正派派的人	an *upright* man.

SA³.

洒水	to *sprinkle* water.
洒脫	*free* from cares or work; *liberal* with [money.

SI³.

洗臉	to *wash* the face.

(301)

水 6-7

洗澡	to *bathe*.
洗心	to *cleanse* the heart *from evil*; to *reform*.
洗漿衣裳	to *starch* clothes.

TONG⁴.

巖洞	a *cave* in a cliff.
煤炭洞	the *horizontal shaft* of a coal mine.
三洞拱橋	a stone bridge with three *arches*.
耗子洞	a rat *hole*.
衣裳爛了一個洞	I have worn a hole in my clothes.
挖個洞子	dig a *hole*.
黑洞洞的	*dark*; a dim light, as in a cavern.

TSIN¹.

| 關津渡口 | guard houses and custom houses at *fords* and *ferries*. |
| 口頭沒得津液 | I have no *saliva* in my mouth; I am parched. |

IANG².

東洋大海	the great eastern *ocean*, i.e., the Pacific Ocean.
洋布	*foreign* calico.
洋錢	dollars; rupees.
西洋景	a panorama; a peep show.
洋洋得意	*fully* satisfied; *greatly* pleased.

FU².

浮在水面上	to *float* on the water.
浮橋	a *floating* bridge; a pontoon bridge.
我會浮水	I can *swim*.
放浮鴨	to feed *ducks*.
輕浮	*light and giddy* in character.
莫聽他的浮言	don't listen to his *silly* talk.
手脚浮腫	my hands and feet are *swollen*.

HAI³.

漂洋過海	to cross the *sea*.
海賊	pirates.
海角	conch shells.
海子	a small *lake* or mountain *tarn*.

注 释

洞 [toŋ⁴]
津 [tsin¹]
洋 [iaŋ²]
浮 [fu²]
海 [xai³]
【海子】山间小湖。

注释

【耍得四海】在四海之内都能玩得开。形容一个人性格开朗和蔼，善于交际。

浩 [xao⁴]

浪 [laŋ⁴]

【浪使浪用】挥霍无度。

流 [liəu²]

【赶流流场】一个市场接一个市场地赶。

【和而流】跟从邪恶的做法，沉迷酒色。

【痞子流神】痞子流氓。

涉 [ʂʅ⁵] [ʂe⁵]

消 [siao¹]

水 7

浩 浪 流 涉 消

HAO⁴.

海盌	a *large* basin.
誇海口	to boast *inordinately*.
耍得四海	he is very *genial*.
請你替我海涵	please *intercede* for me.
工程浩大	the work is *great*.
事情浩繁	my affairs are *multitudinous*.

LANG⁴.

長江後浪催前浪 一輩新人趕舊人	as on the Long River the *waves* follow fast, so each generation displaces the last.
在水裏浪來浪去	*drifting* about in the water.
浪出來了	it *splashed* over the side, as water out of a [basin.
浪使浪用	to spend *extravagantly*.
浪子收心一片寶	if a *prodigal* repents he becomes a worthy [man.

LIU².

[economy money lasts.

細水長流	small streams *flow* long; met., with
流水賬	a day-book.
船放流	let the boat *float* with the current.
趕流流場	to go from market to market.
流鼻血	to *bleed* at the nose.
流淚	to *shed* tears. [dissipated.
和而流	to *follow* every evil impulse or example;
下流人	the *vulgar* classes.
痞子流神	a *roving* vagabond.
九流	nine kinds of people who can *travel* anywhere in pursuit of their business.
入流	to enter the Ko-lao Hue.
我們女流輩	we women (a self-depreciatory term).

SHI⁵, SHE⁵.

[and *fording* rivers for me.

有勞跋涉	I have troubled you, crossing mountains
毫無干涉	it is not the slightest *concern* of mine.

SIAO¹.

消化	to *melt*; to *digest*. [the evening.
消夜	the evening meal, because taken to *pass*

(303)

西蜀方言

水 7-8

	消脫一點	reduce it a little.
	那個地方消得貨	one can *dispose* of goods in that place.
	消氣	to *allay* one's anger.
	水消了	the water has *receded*.
	怎樣開消	how is this affair to be *settled*?
	賬開消不清	I cannot *pay up* my debts.
	走漏消息	the *news* has got abroad; to let the cat out [of the bag.
	不消說	you *need* not speak about it.
浸	TS'IN⁴.	
	汗浸透了衣裳	the perspiration has *soaked* through my clothes. [run.
	字寫浸了	the writing is blurred through ink having
	缸子有點浸水	the water-jar is *leaking* a little.
浴	IO⁵.	for example of use see 沐.
涵	HAN².	
	涵養得好	you are very *patient* or *forbearing*.
	海涵	*indulgent*; *leniency*.
涸	K'O⁵.	
	餅子乾涸涸的	the cakes are *dry and hard*.
浮	FU⁴.	[a bucket.
	浮水	to *lave* water with the hands; to *bale* with
	浮斗	a vessel used for *baling* a boat.
	浮筧	a bucket for *raising water*, worked by two men with ropes.
混	HUEN⁴.	
	混鬧一場	to wrangle *confusedly* for a while.
	混沌的時候	*chaos*.
	混來財	*unjust* or *dishonest* gains.
	男女混雜	men and women *promiscuously* mixed.
	你這麼混賬	O! you *stupid*.
	你莫濛混我	don't try to *deceive* me.
	有個混名	he has a *nick*-name.

(304)

注 释

【消脱一点】减少一点。

浸 [tsʰin⁴]

浴 [io⁵]

涵 [xan²]

涸 [kʰo⁵]

浮 [fu⁴]

【浮水】浮在水面。

【浮斗】捆在船身上的一种容器，类于浮标，但体积比浮标大。

【浮筧】用来引水的水桶。

混 [xuən⁴]

【混来财】来路不明的财物，不当所得。

注 释

【混过光阴】虚度光阴。
泪(泪)[luei⁴]
凉(凉)[liaŋ²]
淋[lin²]
渝(沦)[lən²]
深[ṣən¹]
【毛病害得深沉】病的很重。
【头发长深了】头发长长了。
涡[o¹]
淑[ṣu⁵]
淌[tʰaŋ³]
【淌起淌起的来】像下雨后的洪流一样喷涌。

水 8

涙凉淋渝深	混過光陰	to pass one's life in idleness and uselessness.
	混飯喫	to get a meal with the crowd at a feast, or work on a big job, though unskilled.
	LUE⁴.	
	流眼淚	to shed *tears*.
	LIANG².	same as 凉.
	LIN².	
	晴乾不肯去 直待雨淋頭	he will not go when the weather is good, but waits till the rain *drops* down on his head; procrastination.
	雨淋淋的	*rainy* weather.
	血淋淋的一個腦壳	his head was *dripping* with blood.
	淋茄子	to *water* brinjals.
	LEN².	for example of use see 沦.
	SHEN¹.	
	親恩深似海 子罪重如山	the grace of a parent is *deep* as the sea, the sin of a son is heavy as a mountain.
	有好深的水	how *deep* is the water?
	道理深奧	the doctrine is *profound* or *abstruse*.
	深深的作個揖	make a *low* bow.
	毛病害得深沉	his malady is *deep-seated*; met., his covetousness is great.
	指甲子深	*long* finger-nails; grasping.
	頭髮長深了	his hair has grown *long*.
	深藍	*dark* blue.
	夜深了	*late* at night.
涡淑淌	**O¹.**	
	漩兒渦	a whirl*pool*.
	SHU⁵.	
	賢淑	*virtuous*.
	T'ANG³.	
	淌起淌起的來	*gushing* down, like a torrent after rain.
	淌眼淚	to *shed* tears.

(305)

水 8

淳

| 拿去淆乾淨 | take this basin and *rinse* it clean. |
| 淆一身大汗 | to *perspire* profusely. |

SHUEN².

那個地方的人淳樸	the people of that place are *honest* and *simple*.
那個馬淳善得好	that horse is very *gentle*.
這地方的風俗淳厚	the customs of this place are *good*.

涮

SHUAN⁴.

| 拿水涮一涮 | *rinse* it out with water. |

淬

TS'Ü¹.

| | [the sound of *fizzing*]. |
| 搁在水頭一淬 | put it in the water and temper it (from |

淡

TAN⁴.

淡而無味	*tasteless*; *insipid*.
性情恬淡	*indifferent*; *lackadaisical*.
生意冷淡	trade is *dull*.
交情冷淡	the friendship has grown *cold*.
淡淡泊泊的過日子	to pass one's days in *poverty*.
淡淡的題了幾句	he just *casually* mentioned it.
淡紅	*light* red.

淘

T'AO².

淘米	to *scour* rice before cooking it.
淘金	to *wash* sand for gold dust.
淘井	to *clean out* a well.
淘灘	to *deepen* a river bed.
淘了幾個字	I have *picked up* a little learning.
這事情淘神	how *troublesome* this affair is!
這些娃娃淘氣	the children *worry* one.

添

T'IEN¹.

添錢	*add more* money; *raise* the price.
添飯	*bring more* rice.
又添了一個人	they have had an *increase* in their family.

(306)

注　釋

淳 [ʂuən²]
涮 [ʂuan⁴]
淬 [tsʰy¹]
【搁在水头一淬】淬：用冷水把物品的极热状态突然改变。
淡 [tan⁴]
淘 [tʰao²]
【淘滩】加深河床。
【这事情淘神】淘神：耗费精神。
添 [tʰien¹]

注 释

凄（淒）[tsʰi¹]
涎 [syen²]
  【起了涎】发霉了。
  【涎 ta⁵ta⁵的】慢吞吞,拖拉的样子。
  【他长行在这里涎】他长时间在这里流浪。
浅（淺）[tsʰen³]
  【浅毛子】短毛衣服。
  【浅学浅学】我的学识浅薄,常用于自谦。
净（淨）[tsin⁴]
  【净银子】纯银。
  【净钱】干净的、来路正当的钱。
清 [tsʰin¹]

水 8

凄 TS'I¹. same as 淒.

涎 SÜEN².
涎口水 — spittle; slavers.
起了涎 — it has become *mouldy*.
涎 ta⁵ ta⁵ 的 — *slow*.
他長行在這裏涎 — he is always *loafing* about the place.

淺 TS'IEN³.
水淺 — the water is *shallow*.
山地淺薄 — the soil on the hills is *thin*.
淺毛子 — a garment of *short* fur.
這個顏色淺了 — this colour is rather *pale*. [lite).
淺學淺學 — my accomplishments are *superficial* (po-
見識淺 — he has *little* experience.

淨 TSIN⁴.
不乾淨 — it is not *clean*.
那個人手脚不乾淨 — that fellow is not *honest*; he is light-fingered.
淨銀子 — *pure* silver; silver without alloy.
淨錢 — *clean* cash, without small cash.
東西賣乾淨了 — the things are sold out.

清 TS'IN¹.
　　　　　　　　　　　[seen; truth will out.
水清石自現 — when the water is *clear* the stones will be
清油 — *clear* oil, i. e., the oil of the Chinese rape.
流清鼻子 — a *clear* running at the nose.
清早 — the early morning.
清茶 — the tea is *weak* (polite).
寫個清單 — write out a *clear* list.
說清楚沒有 — did you tell him *clearly*? [again.
錢要清數 — count the money *correctly*; count it over
清板子 — to *plane and fit* the edges of boards.
清刨 — a long plane. [eye-lashes and pretty eyes.
長得眉清目秀的 — what a handsome child! lit., *well-formed*
清淨 — *quiet*, as a place.

(307)

水 8-9

涯
清風雅淨　　a *quiet* secluded spot.
清閒
　　　IA².
奔走天涯　　to travel to the *ends* of the earth.
作何生涯　　what is your *trade*?

淹
　　　NGAN¹, IEN¹.
淹死了　　*drowned*.
水淹齊腰髁　　the water was up to my waist.　[fields.
水大把田都淹了　the river has risen and *inundated* the
　　　READ IEN².
病淹淹穩穩的好久了 } I have had a *long* and *tedious* illness.

液
　　　IE⁴.
津液　　*saliva*.

淫
　　　IN².
犯姦淫　　to commit *adultery*.
那個地方淫風大　that place is very *licentious*.
淫書　　*obscene* books.

淵
　　　ÜEN¹.
肚子裏淵博　　his learning is *profound*.

渣
　　　CHA¹.
　　　　　　　　　　　　　[bean-curd.
豆渣　　the *dregs* left from the process of making
渣渣柴　　*refuse* used as fuel.
我的眼睛打不得渣滓 } you can't throw *dust* in my eyes.
木渣兒　　*chips* of wood.
瓦渣兒　　*pot*sherds; broken tiles.

湛
　　　TSAN⁴.
金湛湛的　　*glittering* with gold.

湖
　　　FU².
湖廣　　the *Lake* Provinces.
江湖上的人　　travelling mountebanks of all sorts.
湖縐　　a thin kind of silk originally brought from
　　　　　　the *Lake* Provinces.

(308)

注　释

涯[ia²]
【作何生涯】生涯：从事某种职业或活动。你从事什么职业？

淹[ŋan¹][ien¹][ien²]
【病淹淹缠缠的好久】淹淹缠缠：拖延好久。英文释义应为：The illness has lasted for long, or the illness has been chronic.

液[ie⁴]

淫[in²]

淵（渊）[yen¹]

渣[tṣa¹]
【我的眼睛打不得渣滓】我的眼睛容不得沙子。比喻不能接受不公平或不完善的事物，不迁就姑息。

湛[tsan⁴]

湖[fu²]

注 释

浑(渾)[xuən¹][xuən²]
　　[kʰuən²]
【生得浑厚】浑厚：(人)
　　纯朴，没有恶意。
【浑浑全全的】浑：全。
　　全部的。
渴[kʰo⁵]
渺[miao²]
涽[ʂuən²]
汤(湯)[tʰaŋ¹]
【汤猪】用滚烫的水烫猪
　　（去掉猪毛）。
【这个才汤水】这个真是挺
　　麻烦的，让人烦恼的。
【在背后添汤】在别人背
　　后传播流言。
渡[tu⁴]
溻[toŋ³]
【浑溻溻的水】浑浊的水。

水 9

渾	HUEN¹.	[fish; stealing when there is confusion.
	趁渾水好捉魚	taking advantage of *muddy* water to catch
	渾渾濁濁惹些事	to *stupidly* go and stir up mischief.
	生得渾厚	a *simple and inoffensive* man.
	READ HUEN².	
	渾身	the *whole* body.
	READ K'UEN².	
	煮渾的	boil it *whole*.
	渾渾全全的	*entire; complete*.
	渾吞家產	he has usurped the *whole* patrimony.
渴	K'O⁵.	
	口渴	*thirsty*.
	噢茶解渴	drink tea to allay *thirst*.
	渴想	to *long for*.
渺	MIAO³.	
	都是些渺茫的話	it is all mere *vague* talk.
涽	SHUEN².	the same as 渾.
湯	T'ANG¹.	
	雞脧湯	chicken *broth*.
	湯瓢	an iron ladle for lifting *soup*.
	湯丸子	balls of rice flour containing a pinch of sugar boiled in *water*.
	湯豬	to *scald* a pig.
	湯衣裳	to *scald* clothes with boiling water. [fire
	踏湯步火	to go through *scalding water* and through
	這個繞湯水	what a *bother*! how *troublesome*.
	在背後添湯	to spread tales behind one's back.
渡	TU⁴.	
	渡船	a *ferry* boat.
溻	TONG³.	
	渾溻溻的水	*turbid* water.
	醱溻溻的湯	*thick* soup.

(309)

西蜀方言

水 9-10

測	TS'E⁵.	[of characters.
	測字先生	a fortune teller who *estimates* the value
	不可測度	*unfathomable*; *incomprehensible*.
	如果有不測	supposing something should *unexpectedly* happen.
湊	TS'EO⁴.	same as 凑.
溫	UEN¹.	[months.
	二八月天氣溫和	the weather is *mild* in the 2nd and the 8th
	溫熱水	*lukewarm* water.
	溫柔的人	a *kind* person; a *gentle*man.
	你要喫個溫補的藥	you must take a *tonic* medicine.
	溫書	to *revise* a book, to *re-read* a book.
湮	IEN¹.	[person.
	湮沒不彰	*lost* to view among other men; an ordinary
游	IU².	same as 遊.
湧	IONG³.	
	湧進去	to *rush* in; to *burst* in suddenly.
渵	MAO⁴.	
	水渵出來	the water *bubbles* up; the water *spurts* out.
	渵火	to suddenly get angry.
	渵出一股賊	a band of robbers *appeared* on the scene.
準	CHUEN³.	similar to 准.
	這個藥有準頭	this medicine of *proved efficacy*.
	說話沒得個定準	he speaks in an *undecided* way.
	貨物準折	to make *up* a deficiency with goods.
滑	HUA⁵.	
	路滑溜溜的	the road is very *slippery*.
	蹚滑了脚	my foot *slipped*.
滙	HUE⁴.	
	滙兌銀錢	to *transmit* money, as a bank does.
	滙票	a *draft* on a bank.

(310)

注 釋

測（测）[tsʰe⁵]
湊（凑）[tsʰəu⁴]
溫 [uən¹]
湮 [ien¹]
游 [iəu²]
湧（涌）[ioŋ³]
渵 [mao⁴]
【渵火】光火，发脾气。
準（准）[tʂuən³]
【这个药有准头】有准头：有效果。
【货物准折】用货物补足，补偿差额。
滑 [xua⁵]
滙（汇）[xuei⁴]

注释

溝(沟)[kəu¹]
溪[tɕʰi¹]
溜[liəu¹] [liəu⁴]
　【路溜得很】溜: 光滑, 平滑, 无障碍。路很滑。
　【溜跟】鞋拔。
　【抹溜些】利索些, 快一点。
　【放溜溜马】短时期租马。
滅(灭)[mie⁵]
溺[mie⁵]
滂[pʰaŋ²]
滔[tʰao¹]
濕[ta⁵]

水 10

溝 KEO¹.

過水溝	water *courses* among the fields.
河溝	the *bed* of a torrent.
漕溝	the *channel* of a river.
城壕溝	a city *moat*.
陰溝	a covered *drain*.

溪 CH'I¹.

| 山溪水 | a mountain *stream*. |

溜 LIU¹.

路溜得很	the road is very *slippery*.
溜跟	a shoe horn.
抹溜些	be a little *quicker*.

READ LIU⁴.

溜索	the *sliding* rope, i. e., a single rope bridge.
溜牲口	to *exercise* a horse.
馬溜了韁	the horse has *broken loose*.
一溜烟兒走了	he was off like a *puff* of smoke.
放溜⁴溜¹馬	to hire horses for short stages.

滅 MIE⁵.

勦滅	to *exterminate*.
把燈滅了	*extinguish* the lamp.
消滅了	*dispelled*, as a difficulty or a rumour.

溺 NIE⁵.

| 溺女 | to *drown* girl babies. |
| 溺愛不敎 | *doting* on and spoiling a child. |

滂 P'ANG².

| 大降滂沱 | it fell a *great* rain. |

滔 T'AO¹.

| 萬惡滔天 | his wickedness *reaches up* to heaven. |

濕 TA⁵.

| 衣裳還是濕濕的 | the clothes are still *wet*. |

(311)

水 10-11

	TSÏ¹.	
地土滋潤		the soil is *moist*.
頂好的滋味		a delicious *flavour*.
不許在那裏滋事		no one is allowed to *stir up* mischief there.
把縫子滋倒		*calk* the seam; *stop up* the crack.
	TSÏ³.	
渣滓		*refuse*; *rubbish*.
鴉片煙渣滓		the *dregs* of opium.
	ÜEN².	
水有個源頭		water has a *source*.
根源		an *origin*; a *reason*.
	CHANG³.	
河頭漲大水		the river has *risen* very high.
水漲了沒有		has the water *boiled*?
	CHʽÏ⁴, CHÏ⁴.	
滯塞不通		*obstructed*.
	LAN³.	
㴭脺		to *cure* meat.
㴭菜		to *pickle* vegetables.
	UA¹.	[*wet*.
稀滒滒的		*puddly*; *muddy* as a road; *sloppy* as food;
	Ü².	
他在中間漁利		he *fishes* for gain between the parties.
	HAN⁴.	
漢人		a *Chinese*.
老漢		an old *man*; my father.
大漢子		a tall, stout *fellow*. [guage.
不懂漢話		he does not understand the *Chinese* lan-
羅漢堂		the Hall of the Disciples of Buddha (from the Sanscrit).
	KUEN³.	
滾水		*boiling* water.

(312)

注　釋

滋 [tsɿ¹]
【把縫子滋倒】滋：用膏狀物將縫隙封住並抹平。把縫封住。

滓 [tsɿ³]

源 [yen²]

漲（涨）[tṣaŋ³]

滯（滞）[tṣʰɿ⁴] [tṣɿ⁴]

㴭 [lan³]
【㴭脺】㴭：用盐腌渍（生的蔬菜、鱼、肉等）。脺，同"肉"。

滒 [ua¹]
【稀滒滒的】泥土泥泞的，稀烂的。

漁（渔）[y²]

漢（汉）[xan⁴]
【汉人】汉族人。英文释义应为：the Han people; the Hans.

滾（滚）[kuən³]

注释

【到处都滚过】许多地方都去过。
漏[ləu⁴]
　【捻水不漏的人】指做事滴水不漏的人。
　【漏厘】走私。
滷（卤）[lu³]
满（滿）[man³]
　【骄傲满假的人】骄傲自满的人。
漫[man⁴][mən⁴]
漠[mo⁴]
漚（沤）[ŋəu⁴]

水 11

打滾	to *roll over*, as a horse does.
滾出去	get out of this! begone! bundle out!
石頭滾下來了	the stone came *bounding* down.
到處都滾過	I have *travelled* everywhere.
滾過大浪來的	I have met with some strange adventures.

LEO⁴.

房子漏雨	the roof *leaks*.
漏瓢	a strainer; a colander.
捻水不漏的人	one who could hold water in his hand and not *lose* any; close-fisted.
漏網的魚	a fish which has *escaped* the net; a scape-gallows.
漏釐	to *smuggle*.
不可洩漏機關	you must not *disclose* this matter; don't let the cat out of the bag.

LU³.

鹽滷	*brine* as pumped up from the salt wells.
滷脥	meat cooked in a *salt* condiment.

MAN³.

裝滿了	filled *full*.
滿心滿意	*sa*tisfied.
滿出來了	it has overflowed; too full.
滿任	to *complete* a term of office.
期限滿了	the time is *fulfilled*; the set time has come.
滿身的瘡	his *whole* body is covered with sores.
滿到處都有	there are some *everywhere*.
驕傲滿假的人	a very *proud* man.
滿州人	the *Man*chus.

MAN⁴, MEN⁴.

水漫過來了	the river has *overflowed* its banks.

MO⁴.

	read mo⁵ in conjunction with 沙.
漠不相關	he is quite *indifferent* to me.

NGEO⁴.

漚壞了	spoiled with *damp*.
漚起霉霉了	it has gone *mouldy*.
漚麻	to *steep* hemp.

(313)

水 11

漂 P'IAO¹.

漂海	to cross the sea; lit., to *float over* the sea.
拏錢打漂漂	to play ducks and drakes with cash; met., to go to law.
漂皮曉得一點	to have a *slight*, or *superficial* knowledge [of a thing.
擔子漂不漂	will you *sub-hire* a coolie to carry your load?

READ P'IAO⁴.

漂白布	to *bleach* calico.

READ PIAO¹.

漂布衫子	a *light-coloured* gown.
水漂出多少遠	the water *spurted* to a great distance.

滲 SEN⁴.

有些滲水出來	the water *soaks* out of it.

漱 SU⁴.

漱個口	*rinse out* your mouth.

漩 SÜEN⁴.

水起漩	the water *swirls*.

滴 TI⁵, TIE⁵.

滴五滴藥	*drop* five *drops* of medicine.
滴水簷	the eaves of a house.

漕 TS'AO².

當漕	to obstruct the *channel* of the river.

漿 TSIANG¹.

漿衣裳	to *starch* clothes.
泥漿漿	*mire*.
桑樹漿漿	the *milky juice* of the mulberry tree.
荳漿	a milky *liquid*, consisting of ground beans and water from which bean-curd is made.
痘子長漿	the small-pox pustules are full of *virus*.

(314)

注 釋

漂 [pʰiao¹] [pʰiao⁴] [piao¹]
【拿钱打漂漂】浪费钱，把钱打了水漂儿。
【漂皮晓得一点】知道一些表面的、肤浅的知识。
渗（渗）[sən⁴]
漱 [su⁴]
漩 [syen⁴]
滴 [ti⁵] [tie⁵]
漕 [tsʰao²]
【当漕】阻塞河道。
漿（浆）[tsiaŋ¹]

注 释

渐（漸）[tsien⁴]
漆 [tsʰi⁵]
演 [ien³]
渍（漬）[tsie⁵]
潮 [tʂʰao²]
【检潮】清理船底的污水。
【潮泥】河水冲击形成的泥层。
潷（滗）[pi⁵] [pie⁵]
【滗米汤】滗：挡住液体中的东西，把液体倒出。挡住米，倒出米汤。
溃（潰）[kʰuei⁴]
润（润）[zuən⁴]
浇（浇）[tɕiao¹]
澄 [tʂʰən²] [tʂən⁴]

水 11-12

TSIEN⁴.

| 漸漸多起來 | to *multiply* little by little. |
| 天氣漸熱 | the weather is *gradually* getting hot. |

TS'I⁵.

漆樹	the *lacquer* tree.
給我漆個黑漆檯子	I want you to *varnish* this table with black *varnish*.
油漆匠	a *painter*.
漆墨黑	as dark as *varnish* and ink.

IEN³.

| 操演兵丁 | to *drill* troops. |

TSIE⁵.

| 痕漬 | a *stain*. |

CH'AO².

地氣潮濕	the ground is *very damp*.
檢潮	to bale the *bilge-water* out of a boat.
潮泥	a rich *alluvium*.

PI⁵, PIE⁵.

潷米湯	*drain off* the water from the rice.
潷油	*skin off* the fat.
燈裏頭潷點油	*pour* a little oil into the lamp.

K'UE⁴.

| 匪徒潰散 | the robbers have *dispersed*. |

RUEN⁴.

地土潤	the soil is *moist*.
衣裳還有點潤	the clothes are still *damp*.
顏色光潤	his complexion is *fresh*.

CHIAO¹.

| 澆水 | to *sprinkle* water with the hand. |
| 澆蠟 | to *dip* candles. |

CH'EN², CHEN⁴.

| 澄清 | to *purify* or *clarify*, as water with alum. |

(315)

水 12-13

CHIE⁵.

洗得潔白	it is washed *perfectly clean*.
愛潔淨	to love *cleanliness*.
把自己的心打掃潔淨	*purify* your own heart.

P'O⁵.

一潑雨	a *shower* of rain.
潑糞	to *sprinkle* liquid manure on the fields.
心頭潑煩	*troubled* in mind, *worried*.
他來潑我	he came and *insulted* me.
放潑	to become *reckless* and *ungovernable*.
潑婦	a *virago*; a *termagant*.

READ PO⁵.

| 活潑潑的 | *lively*, as a fish in the water. |

HUANG².

| 裝潢 | *ornamented*, as a temple roof. |

SE⁵.

摸起澀手	it is *rough* to the touch.
有些澀口	it is slightly *astringent*.
眼睛澀	eyes *smarting* from tiredness.

CH'O⁵, CHO⁵.

不分清濁	he does not distinguish between pure and *impure*, or good and *evil*.
一股濁氣	a *foul* smell.
這個渾渾濁濁的世道	this *confused* or *chaotic* world.

CHIE⁵.

| 激怒 | to *excite* anger. |
| 感激你 | I thank you. |

LONG².

| 不濃不淡的 | neither *rich* nor insipid; neither *familiar* nor distant. |
| 他兩個人情濃 | they are very *intimate* or *fond*. |

(316)

注 释

潔（洁）[tɕie⁵]
潑（泼）[pʰo⁵] [po⁵]
【一潑雨】一场雨。
【心头泼烦】泼烦: 烦躁。心里烦躁。
【放泼】无人约束, 肆意胡为。
潢 [xuaŋ²]
澀（涩）[se⁵]
濁（浊）[tʂʰo⁵] [tʂo⁵]
激 [tɕie⁵]
濃（浓）[loŋ²]

注释

澀 [se⁵]
澡 [tsao³]
澤（泽）[tsʰe⁵]
濠 [xao²]
濶（阔）[kʰue⁵]
濫（滥）[lan⁴]
濛 [moŋ²]
濕（湿）[sʅ⁵]
濤（涛）[tʰao²]
【惹波涛】惹麻烦。
濟（济）[tsi⁴] [tsi³]
瀝（沥）[lie⁵]
【沥米】一种做饭的方法，将米在锅里煮至大半熟，滤去米汤，再放在甑子里蒸熟。

水 13-14

澀	SE⁵.	same as 澁.
澡	TSAO³.	
	下河洗澡	to *bathe* in the river.
	澡塘子	a *bathing* establishment.
	洗澡盆	a *bath* tub.
澤	TS'E⁵.	
	恩澤	*grace*; *favour*.
	臉上潤澤	a *fresh* complexion.
	HAO².	same as 壕.
濠		
14		
濶	K'UE⁵.	same as 闊.
濫	LAN⁴.	
	濫使濫用	to spend *prodigally*.
	莫濫交	don't be "hail-fellow-well-met" with [every-body.
	開濫條	to concoct a *villainous* scheme to make money between parties.
濛	MONG².	
	下濛濛雨	*drizzling* rain.
濕	SHÏ⁵.	
	打濕了	it has got *wet*.
	濕氣重	very *damp*.
	水濕貨	goods which have been damaged by water.
濤	T'AO².	
	惹波濤	to stir up *trouble*.
濟	TSI⁴.	
	賙濟窮人	to *aid* poor people.
	這點銀子不濟事	this silver is in*sufficient* for the purpose.
	他不濟事	he is *incapable*.
	READ TSI³.	
	衣冠濟濟	a *fine* array of dress hats and clothes! as [at a feast.
瀝	LIE⁵.	
	瀝米	to *strain* rice.

(317)

西蜀方言

水 15-22 火

15 濾 LI⁴.
濾飯 — to *strain* boiled rice before steaming it.

瀑 P'O⁵.
瀑布 — a *waterfall*.

瀉 SIE⁴.
肚皮瀉 — *diarrhœa*.
瀉痢 — *dysentery*.
瀉藥 — a *purgative*.

18 灌 KUAN⁴.
放水灌田 — to *irrigate* the fields.
挈水灌花 — *water* the flowers.
灌藥 — to *pour* medicine down a person's throat.
酒灌醉了 — he has *filled* himself drunk.
灌膿 — to *suppurate*.

灑 SA³.
same as 洒.

灘 T'AN¹.
陡灘 — a swift *rapid*.
沙灘 — a sand *bank*.
石灘灘 — a *bed* of rocks by the side of a river.
跑灘兒 — a vagabond; a roving adventurer.

19 瀿 TSAN⁴.
水瀿起來了 — the water *splashed* up.

22 灣 UAN¹.
河灣灣 — a *bend* on a river.
灣船 — to *moor* a boat.

The 86th radical. (火)

火 HO³.
燒火沒有 — have you lighted the *fire* yet?
敲個火 — strike a *light* with flint and steel.

(318)

注 释

濾(滤)[li⁴]

瀑 [pʰo⁵]

瀉(泻)[sie⁴]
【肚皮泻】拉肚子。

灌 [kuan⁴]
【灌脓】化脓,人或动物的身体组织因细菌感染等而生脓。

灑(洒)[sa³]

灘(滩)[tʰan¹]

瀿 [tsan⁴]
【水瀿起来了】瀿:溅。水溅起来了。

灣(湾)[uan¹]
【湾船】停船,停泊。

火 [xo³]
【敲个火】利用钢铁和打火石的敲击来取火。

注释

【火草】火绒，一种引火用的绒棉。
【火纸】纸钱。
【找开火】想办法弄钱。
【火重】中医称的内火旺盛。
【火鐵】紧急委任状。
灰 [xuei¹]
灯 [tən¹]
灵 [lin²]
　（LIN⁴当为LIN²，见803页勘误表。）
炸 [tʂa⁴]
灾（灾）[tsai¹]

火 2-3

火房	a cook.
打個火把	carry a torch.
火鏡	a *burning* glass.
洋火	foreign *matches*.
火草	tinder.
火紙	coarse brown paper used for making spills.
火油	kerosene.
火器	*firearms*.
開火	to open *fire*; to *fire* a cannon; to light a [smelting *furnace*.
找開火	to think of a plan to raise some cash.
火食在内	*firing* and food included.
急得火煋子潰	irritated till he flew into a passion; lit., till [*sparks* flew.
他冒了火	he got *angry*.
火性子人	a *quick*, or *fiery*-tempered man.
火重	the internal *heat* is great (of a sick person).
火鐵	an *urgent* warrant.

灰 HUE¹.

柴灰	wood *ashes*.
石灰	lime.
灰磨兒	bean-curd (from the *gypsum* or *lime* used [in making it.
灰塵大	the *dust* is great.
吞煙灰	to swallow opium *ash*.
灰麵	*flour*.
灰色	ashen; gray.
心灰了	*weak* with old age.

灯 TEN¹.　same as 燈.

灵 LIN⁴.　same as 靈.

炸 CHA⁴.

| 打了一個炸雷 | a *sudden loud* peal of thunder. |

灾 TSAI¹.

天灾	divine *judgments*.
遇着灾難	he met with a *calamity*.
水灾 and 火灾	flood and fire.

(319)

火 3-5

灾灶炒   TSAI[1].   same as last.

     TSAO[4].   same as 竈.

     CH'AO[3].

炒茶葉子   to *roast* tea leaves in a pan.
炒菜   to *fry* vegetables.

     IEN[1].

天氣炎熱   the weather is *very hot*.

     K'ANG[4].

拏來炕起   hang it over the fire to *dry*. [over a fire.
炕籠子   a bamboo frame or cage for *drying* clothes
炕床   a brick bed heated by a flue (used in the North). [smoked.
在炕上薰起   hang it up over the kitchen *fire* to be
天氣炕陽   the weather is *roasting* hot.

     LU[2].   same as 爐.

     CHA[4].

曬炸了   *cracked* or *burst* with the sun.

     READ CHA[5].

油炸糕   cakes *fried* in oil.

     CHU[4].

清早起來一炷香 } at daybreak rise, a *stick* of incense burn,
謝天謝地謝三光 } thank heaven, thank earth and thank the three great lights.

     P'AO[2].

在子母灰裏頭炮   *roast* it among the hot ashes.

     T'AN[4].

黑炭   coal.
炭廠   a *coal* mine.
過爐炭 or 二炭   cinders.

注释

灾 [tsai¹]
灶 [tsao⁴]
炒 [tṣʰao³]
炎 [ien¹]
炕 [kʰaŋ⁴]
【拿来炕起】炕：（烟）熏烤。拿来挂着熏烤。
【炕笼子】用来烤干衣服的笼子。
【天气炕阳】天气像炙烤般热。
炉 [lu²]
炸 [tṣa⁴] [tṣa⁵]
炷 [tṣu⁴]
炮 [pʰao²]
【在子母灰里头炮】（将食物）放在热灰烬中烘烤。
炭 [tʰan⁴]

注释

点 [tien³]
 (TIEN¹当为TIEN³，见803页勘误表。)
烔 [toŋ¹]
 【红烔烔的】红彤彤的。
烝 [tsən¹]
 【烝饭】烝，同"蒸"。
烛 [tʂu⁵]
烘 [xoŋ¹]
 【烘锅魁】锅魁，又叫"锅盔"，一种干馍，是陕西关中地区城乡居民喜食的传统风味面食小吃。
烤 [kʰao³]
烈 [lie⁵]
烙 [lo⁵]
烹 [pʰoŋ¹]
乌(烏) [u¹]
烟 [ien¹]
 【房子烟】房子里冒烟。

火 5-6

	TIEN¹.	same as 點.
点	TONG¹.	
烔 6	紅烔烔的	of a *flaming* red colour.
	CHEN¹.	
烝	烝飯	to *steam* rice.
烛	CHU⁵.	same as 燭.
烘	HONG¹.	
	烘衣服	to *dry* clothes *over a fire*. [winter.
	烘籠	*hand stoves* carried by all poor people in
	烘鍋魁	to *bake* scones.
烤	K'AO³.	
	烤餅子	to *bake* cakes.
	燒烤猪	to *roast* a sucking pig.
	烤衣裳	to *dry* clothes *at the fire*.
	烤火	to *warm* oneself *at* the fire.
烈	LIE⁵.	
	那個馬烈	that horse is *fiery*.
	性烈如火	his temper is *fierce* as fire.
	烈女	a *chaste* virgin.
烙	LO⁵.	
	烙猪頭	to *singe* a pig's head with a hot iron.
	烙鐵	a small *smoothing* iron used by tailors.
烹	P'ONG¹.	
	拿醋來烹	to *cook* with vinegar, as fish.
烏	U¹.	
	烏鴉	a *crow*.
	烏龜	a *black* turtle.
	化爲烏有	to be resolved into *nothing*.
烟	IEN¹.	for other examples see 煙.
	烟子	*smoke*; soot.
	房子烟	the room is *smoky*.

(321)

火 6-8

刷烟子	to paint *black*, usually with pine-*soot*.	
清烟戶	take a census of the *families*.	
烟霧	*fog*.	

8 然 RAN².

那個自然嗎	that's *of course*! *naturally* so!
始而勉强久之自然	put forth effort at first, and afterwards it will become *natural*.
果然不錯	*truly* that is so!
不然	on the contrary; if not so. [*real*.
不以爲然	he does not deem it *important, necessary* or
然後	thereupon; forthwith.

燌 SHIN⁴.

菜放在鍋頭燌起	put the food back into the pot and *warm* it up a bit.
地方的陰燌大	the place is very much *shaded* with trees.
老毛病燌天晴落雨	a chronic disease *foretells* fair or foul weather.

焚 FEN².

焚香	to *burn* incense.

焙 PE⁴.

火焙紙	brown paper that has been *fire dried*.

烤 K'ONG³.

烤飯	to *steam* rice in the pot instead of in a steamer.

焦 TSIAO¹.

炒得焦黑	*scorched* in the frying.
飯焦臭了	the rice is *burned* in the cooking.
焦乾 and 焦濕	*very* dry and *very* wet.
這個事情焦人	this is very *annoying*.

無 U².

無限無量	*without* bounds; *limitless*.
一無所有	he had *not* anything.
無法可免	there is *no* way of escape.
無中生有的事情	they have made trouble out of *nothing*.

(322)

注　释

【刷烟子】用松树的烟灰来刷黑。
【清烟户】烟户：人户。清点人口。
然 [ẓan²]
燌 [ɕin⁴]
【菜放在锅头燌起】燌：炙，烧。菜放在锅里热一热。
【地方的阴燌大】这个地方的树荫大。
【老毛病燌天晴落雨】身上的老毛病能预知天晴还是下雨。
焚 [fən²]
焙 [pei⁴]
【火焙纸】用火烘烤过的纸。
烤 [kʰoŋ³]
【烤饭】用炒锅煮饭。
焦 [tsiao¹]
無（无）[u²]

注释

焰 [ien⁴]
　【今黑了月亮戴焰】今晚的月亮边缘有光圈。
照 [tʂao⁴]
　【一对高照】高照: 灯笼。
　【手照子】手里拿的烛台。
　【照子蛋】臭蛋, 变质的蛋。
　【莫照闲】不要多管闲事。
煇 (辉) [xuei¹]
煌 [xuaŋ²]
煮 [tʂu³] [tsu³]
煳 [fu²]
煩 (烦) [fan²]

火 8-9

焰
9
照

	IEN⁴.	
	今黑了月亮戴焰	there is an *areola* round the moon to-night.
	CHAO⁴.	
	照個亮來	*shine* a light here! bring a lamp.
	一對高照	a pair of official *lanterns* on poles.
	手照子	a *candlestick* to carry in the hand.
	照子蛋	an *addled* duck egg, so called because tested by the light.
	照壁	the *screen* wall of a mansion.
	好生照管倒	*look after* the things carefully.
	莫照閒	don't *concern* yourself with our business.
	現錢照顧	to *patronize* a shop with ready money.
	照鏡子	to *look in* a mirror.
	照像	to *photograph* a person.
	護照	a *passport*.
	照倒這個樣子做	make it *according to* this pattern.
	照倒這個話說	speak *as* I tell you.

煇

	HUE¹.	
	好生煇煌出來	take pains and *brighten* up the place.
	我把你煇煌起	I will *trim* you up and make you look respectable.

煌

	HUANG².	
		for examples of use see last.

煮

	CHU³, TSU³.	
	煮飯	to *boil* rice.

煳

	FU².	
	烤煳了	*burned* in the baking.
	煳鍋粑	the crust of rice on the bottom of the pan.
	衣服烘煳了	the clothes have been *scorched* in the drying.
	燒得煳焦焦的	*charred*.

煩

	FAN².	
	耐煩	patient amid *troubles*.
	煩勞你	may I *trouble* you to—; I would be obliged to you if—.
	我心裏煩燥得很	I am very *worried*.

(323)

火 9

煖 LUAN³.

飽煖思淫慾 } full and *warm*, men become lustful; hungry
饑寒起盜心 } and cold, they are driven to thieve.

煉 LIEN⁴.   [the fire.

眞金不怕火來煉   true gold is not afraid of being *tried* in

煋 SIN¹.

火煋子濆   the *sparks* fly.

煤 ME².

煤炭   coal.
紙煤子   tinder.

煏 PI⁵, PIE⁵.

炭火煏出來的   *roasted* before a charcoal fire.

煞 SHA⁵.   [or not?

墳站不站煞   will this grave be subject to *evil influences*
工夫煞角了   the work is *finished*.
煞角那一本   the *last* volume.

煎 TSIEN¹.

煎蛋   to *fry* eggs.

READ TSIEN⁴.

煎白蠟   to *melt* white wax in a pan.

揫 TS'IU¹.

揫臘膥   to *smoke* hams.
揫蜂子   to *smoke* bees; to *fumigate* bee-hives.
烟子揫眼睛   the smoke hurts one's eyes.

煨 UE¹.

煨薑   to *roast* ginger in the embers.
煨肉   to *stew* meat in a jug.

煙 IEN¹.

鴉片煙   *opium*.   same as 烟.

(324)

注 释

煖（暖）[luan³]
煉（炼）[lien⁴]
煋 [sin¹]
煤 [mei²]
【纸媒子】引火纸。
煏 [pi⁵] [pie⁵]
【炭火煏出来的】煏：用火烘干。用炭火烘出来的。
煞 [ṣa⁵]
【坟站不站煞】这座坟会不会受到凶神的影响？
【工夫煞角了】煞角：完成。重庆地区多山，农民开荒种地必须因地制宜，做成梯田，梯田都不规则，小块错落，狭长弯曲，田地两头往往形成尖角。在梯田里犁田、插秧，通常的顺序便是从一个角开始，到另一个角结束，因此叫做"煞角"。
【煞角那一本】最后那一本。
煎 [tsien¹] [tsien⁴]
揫 [tsʰiəu¹]
【揫蜂子】烟熏蜂巢。
煨 [uei¹]
煙（烟）[ien¹]

注释

熏 [ɕyn¹]
熿 [xuaŋ⁴]
燆 [ɕie⁵]
熊 [ɕioŋ²]
　【人熊】学名称作"罴"，姿态五官似人，性猛力强，可以掠取牛马而食，所以叫做"人熊"。
煽 [ṣan¹]
熨 [yn⁴]
熄 [si⁵]
熱（热）[ẓe⁵]
　【看热了】看后觉得羡慕或嫉妒。
熛 [pʰiao³]
　【一熛就过了】熛：闪光。一闪就过了。
　【拿在火上熛】熛：燃烧。拿到火上烧。
熰 [ŋəu⁴]
　【天气熰热】熰：天旱而且非常热。
　【熰个火】熰：燃烧柴草让火不旺只冒烟。

火 10-11

10 熏 SHÜIN¹.
熏臘肉　to *smoke* hams.

熿 HUANG⁴.
熿眼睛　to *dazzle* the eyes.

燆 SHIE⁵.
火大了燆人　the fire is great; it *scorches* one to go [near it.

熊 SHIONG².
人熊　the brown *bear*.

煽 SHAN¹.
謠言煽惑人心　the rumours *excite* people's minds.

熨 ÜIN⁴.
熨衣服　to *iron* clothes.
熨斗　a *smoothing* iron.

熄 SI⁵.
吹熄燈　*extinguish* the lamp.
把火打熄了　to *extinguish* a conflagration.

11 熱 RE⁵.
熱水　*warm* water.
熱起來了　the weather is getting *hot*.
熱病　a *fever*.
熱心熱腸的人　a *zealous* person. [marriage or a funeral.
辦得鬧熱　*grandly* or *ostentatiously* conducted, as a
看熱了　moved to *desire* or *envy* by the sight of.
親熱　*warm* friends.

熛 P'IAO³.
　　　　　　[house.
一熛就過了　one *blaze*, and it is all over, as a thatched
拿在火上熛　*singe* it over the fire.
火熛熛的痛　smarting, stinging pain, as from a burn.

熰 NGEO⁴.
天氣熰熱　the weather is *very close and warm*.
熰個火　keep a fire burning slowly.

(325)

火 11-12

TSAO¹.

燸		
花生燸得好	the peanuts are *roasted crisp* or *brittle*.	

NGAO².

熬猪油	to *boil* down lard.
熬藥	to *decoct* medicine.
這個柴熬火	this firewood burns a long time.
昨晚些熬夜	I had a *restless* night last night.

READ NGAO¹.

受不盡的煎熬	my *sufferings* are endless.
我實在熬不過了	I really cannot *bear* it.
熬價錢	to *keep up* the price.

SHU⁵.

穀子熟了	the rice is *ripe*.
飯熟了	the rice is *properly cooked*.
賣幾畝熟土	buy a few acres of *arable* land.
這是我的一個熟路	this is a *well-known* road to me; a *familiar* route.
遠賊必有熟脚	a thief from a distance must have an accomplice *acquainted* with the house.
勇操練熟了	the soldiers are *thoroughly* drilled.
熟人	an *acquaintance*.
書要念熟	you must read the book till you *know* it [*thoroughly*.
這是他的熟手	this is his trade; lit., what he is *skilled* at.
睡熟了	*sound* asleep.

12

RAN².

燃	
點燃	to *light*; to *set fire to*.
房子燃起來了	the house is *on fire*.
吹燃	blow it *alight*; blow it to a flame.

SÜEN².

煸	
煸雞毛	to *scald* the feathers off a chicken.

SHAO¹.

燒	
燒香	to *burn* incense.
火燒不燃	the fire will not *burn*. [*burned*.
燒會	to enter the Ko-lao Hue when incense is

(326)

注 释

燸 [tsao¹]
【花生燸得好】这花生烘烤得很松脆。

熬 [ŋao²]
【这个柴熬火】熬：持久。这个木柴耐烧。
【熬价钱】抬高价格。

熟 [ʂu⁵]

燃 [zan²]

煸 [syen²]
【煸鸡毛】煸：把已宰杀的猪、鸡等用开水烫后去毛。

烧（燒）[ʂao¹]
【烧会】上寺庙烧香。

注释

【烧阴阳火】当面说好话，背地里做坏事。
烫（烫）[tʰaŋ⁴]
燈（灯）[tən¹]
燋 [tsiao⁴]
【蜂燋】蜜蜂蜇伤。
燉（炖）[tən⁴]
燕 [ien⁴]
燭（烛）[tʂu⁵]
【毛蜡烛】香蒲，又名"火烛"。英文释义应为：Cattail, bulrush reed mace.

火 12-13

燒盡了	*burned* away.
燒火老	one who commits adultery with his daughter-in-law.
燒陰陽火	to speak good to one's face but evil behind [one's back.
火燒天	a red sky.
燒窰	to *fire* a brick or tile kiln.
燒菸	to *smoke* tobacco.
把鐵燒紅	*heat* the iron red hot.
燒烤席	a feast at which a *roast* pig is provided.
燒開水	to *boil* water.
燒酒	*ardent* spirits.
燒坊	a distillery where *ardent* spirits are made.
燒白	a sweet pudding of glutinous rice and sugar eaten at feasts.
發燒	*feverish*.
耳朵燒	ears *burning*.
瘡燒得很	the ulcer is much *inflamed*.
走很了燒當	to walk too much and get *fired* between [the legs.

T'ANG⁴.

看燙手	beware of *scalding* your hand.
燙酒	to *heat* wine.

TEN¹.

一盞燈	a *lamp*.
掛燈彩	to hang up *lanterns* and decorations at a [festival.

TSIAO⁴.

燒艾燋	to burn *moxa* as a counter-irritant.
蜂燋	a hornet's *sting*.

TEN⁴.

燉雞	to *steam* a chicken.

IEN⁴.

燕子	the *swallow*; the *sand-martin*.

CHU⁵.

蠟燭	*candles*.
毛蠟燭	*bulrushes*.

(327)

燙 燈 燋 燉 燕 燭
13

火 13-24

燥	TS'AO⁴.		
	這個藥燥辣	this medicine is very *pungent*.	
	我就燥火了	I will *get angry* in a minute!	
	READ TS'AO⁴, SAO⁴.		
	高燥地方	a high and *dry* place.	
	READ SAO⁴.		
	泡燥	*friable*, as soil; *crumby*, as bread.	
營	IN², ÜIN².		
	營盤	*barracks*; a camp.	
15	買賣營生	to *get a living* by trade.	
爆	PAO⁴.		
	桶箍爆了	the hoops of the pail have *burst*.	
	竹子曬爆了	the bamboos are *cracked* with the sun.	
	爆穀花兒	the *pop* rice for making sweetmeats.	
熬	NGAO¹.		
16	熬胺	to *stew* meat.	
爐	LU².		
	茶爐子	a *stove* for boiling kettles on.	
17	高爐	a refining *furnace*.	
爛	LAN⁴.		
	打爛了	it is *broken*.	
	煮爛了	*boiled* to shreds.	
	爛衣裳	*ragged* clothes.	
	菓子爛了	the fruit is *rotten*.	
	爛瘡	an open sore.	
	爛肉的藥	a *caustic*.	
	路爛	the road is very *muddy*.	
	吃得爛醉	he is dead drunk.	
	爛事情是難事情	a *ruined* business is a difficult business.	
	爛子秀才	a pettifogging B. A.	
	賬放爛了	bad debts.	
24 爨	TS'UAN¹.		
	分爨	to *board* separately.	

(328)

注 釋

燥 [tsʰao⁴] [sao⁴]
【我就燥火了】我就要发火了。
【泡燥】(像土壤、面包)干燥松散的。
營(营)[in²] [yn²]
爆 [pao⁴]
熬 [ŋao¹]
【熬肉】熬:熬,煮。炖肉。
爐(炉)[lu²]
爛(烂)[lan⁴]
爨 [tsʰuan¹]
【分爨】分家。英文释义,应为: To break up the family and live apart.

注 释

爪 [tʂao³]
  【狐爪】狐爪。
  【手爪】手指甲。
  【一双爪爪】一双手。
爬 [pʰa²]
  【爬草】用耙子耙草。
争（爭）[tsən¹]
  【争数】短缺，计数不足。
  【争不多】差不多。
為（为）[uei²] [uei⁴]
  【为我说个方便】为我说说好话。

爪 4-8

The 87th radical. (爪)

CHAO³.

狐爪	foxes' *claws*.
鷹爪子	eagle's *talons*.
手爪	finger *nails*.
一雙爪爪	a pair of *hands*.

P'A².

爬草	to *rake* grass.
一歲常在娘懷裏 二歲就在地下爬	the first year an infant plays in its mother's bosom, the second year it *crawls* on the ground.
爬起來	*scramble* to your feet! get up!
矮爬爬的	*dwarf*, as a plant or tree.

TSEN¹.

爭氣	to *exert* one's self.
爭先	to *strive* for precedence.
紛爭	to *wrangle*.
爭鬬	to *fight*.
爭數	*short* count.
爭一顆米	one grain *short*; nearly.
爭不多	not far out; almost.

UE².

為好人	to *be* a good man.
無所不為	there is nothing that he will not *do*.
行為不好	his *conduct* is bad.
以為	to *deem*; to *consider* as.

UE⁴.

為的甚麼事	what was the *reason* of it?
為我的事	*because* of my affairs.
為甚麼不來	*why* did you not come?
為我說個方便	speak a good word *for* me.

(329)

The 88th radical. (父)

FU⁴.

父親	a *father*.
寄父	a kind of *father*; an adopted *father*.
伯父 and 叔父	*uncles* on the father's side.
繼父	a step-father.
祖父	grand-*father*.
舅父	maternal *uncles*.
神父	a Roman Catholic priest.

PA², ¹.

| 爸²爸¹ | father. |

TIE¹, TI¹, TIA¹.

| 爹媽 | father and mother. |

IE².

爺兒父子	*father* and son; the whole clan of them.
親爺	*father*-in-law.
爺爺	grand-*father*.
大爺	old *man*.
老爺	*gentleman*.
大老爺	His Worship, the district magistrate.
老太爺	the *father* of a graduate or an official.
少爺	a gentleman's son.
冒頂兒大爺	the *head* of a seditious band.
劉三爺	the third brother of the Liu family (so called when old).
副爺	*soldier* (direct address).

The 89th radical. (爻)

SHUANG³.

爽快	*comfortable*; *cheerful*; in good health and [*spirits*.
爽口	*agreeable* to the taste.
定然不爽	there will be no *mistake* about it.

(330)

注 释

父 [fu⁴]
【寄父】义父,养父,干爹。
爸 [pa²] [pa¹]
爹 [tie¹] [ti¹] [tia¹]
爺(爷)[ie²]
【亲爷】岳父。
【冒顶儿大爷】指爱出风头,好挑事的人。
【副爷】将领的属僚,官阶较低的武官。
爽 [ṣuaŋ³]
【定然不爽】一定不要出差错。

注 释

爿（床）[tʂʰaŋ²]
牆（墙）[tsʰiaŋ²]
片 [pʰien⁴] [pʰien³]
版 [pan³]
牌 [pʰai²]
　【粉牌】涂有白漆的木牌，用以记事。
　【耳牌子】耳坠子。
牙 [ia²]
　【牙猪】被阉的公猪。

爿 4-13　片 4-8　牙

The 90th radical. （爿）

爿 4-13

CH'UANG². same as 床.

TS'IANG². same as 墙.

The 91st radical. （片）

片 4-8

P'IEN⁴.

布片子　　　scraps of cloth; rags.
一張片子　　a gentleman's card.
換片子　　　to change a baby's napkins.

READ P'IEN⁴, ³.

瓦片　　　　pieces of broken tile; potsherds.
切成片片　　cut it into slices.
雪片　　　　snow flakes.

PAN³. same as 板.

版 **牌**

P'AI².

操籐牌　　　to practise the use of the shield.
靈牌子　　　the spirit tablet.
門牌　　　　a register of the inmates of a house, hung [up at the door.
招牌　　　　a sign-board.
把招牌打爛了　he has spoilt his reputation.
粉牌　　　　a white writing-board.
界牌　　　　a boundary stone.
紙牌　　　　playing-cards.
骨牌　　　　dominoes.
耳牌子　　　ear-pendants.

The 92nd radical. （牙）

牙

IA².

四牙六齒　　the cow has four molars and six incisors.
牙猪　　　　a hog.

(331)

牙 牛 3-4

牙靶骨	the jaw-bone.
牙祭	meat allowed to servants, usually on the 2nd and 16th of the month.
牙齒	teeth.
牙齒痛	tooth-ache.
牙骨	ivory.
四牙八橫	a table with four brackets under the corners, [and eight cross-bars.

The 93rd radical. (牛)

NIU².

黃牛	cattle; cows; oxen.
水牛	water buffaloes.
騷牛 and 牸牛	bull and cow.
牛兒子	calf.
牛肉	beef.
牛蚊子	the cleg; the gad-fly.
地牯牛	the ant-lion.

K'EO³.

| 牲牰 | a domestic animal. |

LAO².

監牢	a prison.
你要牢牢謹記	you must steadily bear it in mind.
拴牢靠點	tie it up securely.
做得牢實	strongly made.

MU³.

| 牡丹花 | the peony. |

MU⁵.

| 牧牛童兒 | a boy who tends cattle; a cow-herd. |

U⁵.

萬物	all things.
好個物件	that's a fine article!
不要畫人物子的	I don't want those ornamented with human [figures.
好個人物子	what a fine figure!

(332)

注 释

【牙靶骨】颌骨。
牛 [ȵiəu²]
【骚牛】未阉割过的公牛。
牰 [kʰəu³]
牢 [lao²]
牡 [mu³]
牧 [mu⁵]
物 [u⁵]

注释

牯 [ku³]
牲 [sən¹]
牴 [ti³]
牮 [tsiən⁴]
  【牮房子】用柱子斜着撑起房子。
  【牮杆】支撑物,支柱。
特 [tʰe⁵]
牸 [tsʅ⁴]
  【牸牛】母牛。
牵(牽) [tɕʰien¹]
  【他牵长在这里】他经常来这里。
  【把口袋牵起】把口袋打开。
犁 [li²]
㸺 [ṣa¹]
  【㸺牛】母牛。
犏 [pʰien¹]
犒 [kʰao⁴]
犧(牺) [ɕi¹]

牛 5-16

5 牯	KU³.	
	牯牛	a *bull*; the male of cattle.
牲	SEN¹.	[(chicken, fish, and pig).
	獻個三牲	to *offer* the three *sacrificial animals*—
	牲畜	*domestic animals*.
牴	TI³.	
	牴觸父母	to *oppose* one's parents.
牮	TSIEN⁴.	
	牮房子	to *prop up* a house.
	牮桿	a *prop*.
6 特	T'E⁵	
	特意	on *purpose*; specially.
牸	TSÏ⁴.	
7	牸牛	a *cow*; the female of cattle.
牽	CH'IEN¹.	
	牽牛	to *lead* a cow.
	他牽長在這裏	he is *constantly* coming about.
	把藤牽上架子	*train* the creeper on to the trellis.
	牽藤	a *tow*-rope.
	把口袋牽起	*hold open* the sack.
	牽連	to *implicate*.
犁	LI².	
	犁頭	a *plough*.
	犁田	to *plough* a field.
㸺	SHA¹.	
9	㸺牛	a *cow*; the female of cattle.
犏	P'IEN¹.	
	犏牛	a *cross-breed* between the yak and the cow.
10 犒	K'AO⁴.	
	犒勞	to *reward* workmen with meat or money [beyond their wages.
16 犧	SHI¹.	
	犧牲	*sacrificial animals*.

(333)

犬 2-5

The 94th radical. (犬)

CHʻÜEN³.

看家犬	a watch *dog*.

FAN⁴.

犯王法	to *transgress* the laws of the country.
犯罪	to *sin*; to *trespass*.
犯姦淫	to *commit* adultery.
冒犯人家	to *offend* people.
犯上	to *offend* one's superior in word or deed.
犯人	a *criminal*.
是個老犯	he is a long-term *prisoner*.

CHUANG⁴.

形狀	the *appearance* of persons or things.
狀紙	an *indictment*.
寫認狀	write an *agreement* or *acknowledgment*, to [give a *receipt*.
狀元	the highest literary honour in the empire; senior wrangler.

KʻUANG².

癲狂了	*mad*; *daft*; *wild and frolicsome*.
發狂	*delirious*.
狗狂要下雨	when the dog is *frisky* there will be rain.
那個人輕狂	that fellow is *light-headed*, or *giddy*; not serious.

NIU³.

狃於風俗	*confirmed* in the evil practices of the place.

FU².

狐皮袍子	a *fox*-skin gown.

SHIA⁵.

狎愛	to love *fondly*; to *dote* upon.

KEO³.

一條狗	a *dog*.
藏狗	a Tibetan *mastiff*.

(334)

注 释

犬 [tɕʰyen³]
犯 [fan⁴]
【是个老犯】老犯：羁押了很久的犯人。
狀（状）[tʂuaŋ⁴]
狂 [kʰuaŋ²]
狃 [n̠iəu³]
【狃于风俗】狃：因袭，拘泥。拘泥于风俗。
狐 [fu²]
狎 [ɕia⁵]
【狎爱】溺爱。
狗 [kəu³]
[藏狗] 即藏獒。

注释

【天狗吃太阳】即日食。
狠 [xən³]
狡 [tɕiao³]
狭（狹）[ɕia⁵]
狼 [laŋ²]
狸 [li³]
猖 [tʂʰaŋ¹]
【吐血猖起猖起的来】大口大口地吐血。
【猖坟】打开坟墓（多指盗墓、毁墓）。
猝 [tsʰu⁵] [tsʰo⁵]
猛 [moŋ³]
猜 [tsʰai¹]

犬 5-8

	京狗	a Pekinese pug-dog; small dogs generally.
	牙狗 and 母狗	dog and bitch.
	豺狗	a wolf.
	天狗喫太陽	the heavenly dog eating the sun; an eclipse.
	狗兒子	a pup.
6 狠	狗肉	dog-flesh.
	HEN³.	same as 很.
	CHIAO³.	
7 狡	狡猾	crafty; greedy.
	SHIA⁵.	
狹	房子窄狹	the house is small and cramped.
	肚皮窄狹	narrow-minded.
	LANG².	
狼	豺狼	the wolf.
	狼心狗肺	cruel.
	LI³.	
8 狸	狐狸	the fox.
	CH'ANG¹.	
猖	猖狂	violent.
	吐血猖起猖起的來	to spit blood copiously.
	猖墳	to open a grave.
猝	TS'U⁵, TS'O⁵.	
	倉猝	impetuous; abrupt.
	MONG³.	
猛	兇猛	cruel.
	濕柴怕猛火	wet firewood cannot withstand fierce fire.
	我猛然想起來了	I have suddenly thought of it.
	發猛財	to get rich suddenly.
猜	TS'AI¹.	
	猜謎子	to guess riddles.

(335)

犬 8-10

	猜疑	to *suspect*.
	人心難猜	it is difficult to *divine* a man's mind.
9	**CHU¹.**	
猪	脚猪	a *boar*.
	母猪	a *sow*.
	猪兒	a *pig*.
	刺猪	the *porcupine*.
	拉肥猪兒	to kidnap a *rich man* in order to extort a [ransom.
	HEO².	
猴	猴子	a *monkey*.
	猴兒包	goiter, (from the resemblance to a *monkey's* [throat).
	MAO¹,², MIAO¹,².	
猫	猫兒	a *cat*.
	木猫兒	a wooden rat-*trap*.
	水猫子	the *otter*.
	SHIEN⁴.	
献		same as 獻.
	SIN¹.	
猩	猩猩氈	rugs dyed with the blood of a species of [monkey.
	IU².	
猶	事情猶未定	the affair is *still* undecided.
	利刀割人瘡猶合 惡語傷人恨不消	knife wounds may *yet* be healed, harsh words breed endless hate.
10	猶如親生的	*as though* the child were his own.
	HUA⁵.	
猾	奸猾	evil and *crafty*.
	TAI¹.	
獃		same as 呆.
	SÏ¹, SHÏ¹.	
獅	獅子	a *lion*.
	IO⁵.	
獄	牢獄	a *prison*.
	地獄	hell.

(336)

注 釋

猪 [tṣu¹]
【脚猪】公猪。
【刺猪】豪猪,箭猪。
【拉肥猪儿】绑架富人以勒索赎金。
猴 [xəu²]
【猴儿包】甲状腺肿。
猫 [mao¹] [mao²]
　　[miao¹] [miao²]
【水猫子】水獭。
献 [ɕien⁴]
猩 [sin¹]
猶(犹) [iəu²]
猾 [xua⁵]
獃(呆) [tai¹]
獅(狮) [sɿ¹] [ʂɿ¹]
獄(狱) [io⁵]

注释

獐 [tʂaŋ¹]
獨(独) [tu⁵]
【一条独路】一条没有岔路口的路。
獲(获) [xo⁵]
獵(猎) [lie⁵]
獸(兽) [ʂəu⁴]
獻(献) [ɕien⁴]
獺(獭) [tʰa⁵]
玄 [ɕyen²]
【玄妙没测】玄妙莫测。
率 [so⁵]
玉 [y⁴]
【玉色】浅绿色，浅蓝色。

犬 10-16　玄 1-6　玉

獐 12	CHANG¹.	same as 麏.
獨	TU⁵.	
	獨一無二	only one and no other.
	獨子	an only son.
	孤獨	orphans and childless, or lonely.
14	一條獨路	a single road with no branch roads.
獲	HO⁵.	
15	拏獲了沒有	have they arrested him or not?
獵	LIE⁵.	
	打田獵	to hunt for game.
獸	SHEO⁴.	
	野獸	wild animals.
	獸頭兒	a cat.
	人面獸心	beastly; having a man's face but a beast's [heart.
16 獻	SHIEN⁴.	
	獻雄雞	to offer a cock as a sacrifice.
獺	TʻA⁵.	
	水獺子	the otter.

The 95th radical. (玄)

1 玄	SHUEN².	
	玄妙沒測	abstruse and incomprehensible.
6 率	SO⁵.	
	統率	to command; to lead.
	做得草率	carelessly done.

The 96th radical. (玉)

玉	Ü⁴.	
	玉石	jade-stone; gems.
	玉皇大帝	the Immaculate Emperor and Great Ruler [(Taoist God).
	玉色	a light blue or light green colour.

玉 3-5

	UANG².	
君王		a *king*.
王法		the *king's* laws.
蜂王		a *queen* bee.
	ME².	
玫瑰花		a *scented red* rose.
	UAN².	
玩耍		to *amuse* one's self, *diversion*.
	READ UAN⁴.	
玩花		to *enjoy* the flowers.
古董玩器		*antique* articles.
	CHEN¹.	
珍珠		*pearls*.
山珍		*delicacies* from the mountains.
看得珍重		to *esteem* very highly.
自己珍重		you must exercise self-*respect*.
	TIEN⁴.	
玷辱父母		to *dishonour* one's parents.
	LIN².	
鏨得玲瓏		*finely* chased, as silver ornaments.
那個子弟玲瓏		that lad is *smart*.
	PO¹.	
玻璃瓶子		a *glass* bottle.
	P'E⁵.	
琥珀圈子		*amber* bracelets.
	SHUAN¹, SHAN¹.	
珊瑚		*red coral*.
	TAI⁴.	
玳瑁		*tortoise-shell*.

(338)

注 释

王 [uaŋ²]
玫 [mei²]
玩 [uan²] [uan⁴]
珍 [tʂən¹]
【看得珍重】珍视。
玷 [tien⁴]
玲 [lin²]
【鉴得玲珑】在银饰上镶嵌得很好看。
【那个子弟玲珑】那个小伙子伶俐聪明。
玻 [po¹]
珀 [pʰe⁵]
珊 [ʂuan¹] [ʂan¹]
玳 [tai⁴]

注释

珠 [tṣu¹]
班 [pan¹]
【大班头】对抬轿子的人的尊称。
【老班子 and 小班子】家庭里的老一辈和小一辈。
现（现）[ɕien⁴]
理 [li³]
【文理字眼子】文绉绉的字眼。

玉 6-7

6 珠 CHU¹.

念素珠	to tell the *beads*, as Buddhist devotees do.
珍珠瑪瑙	*pearls* and agates.
一個滴水珠	a small *nodule* of silver.
眼珠子	the *pupil* of the eye.

班 PAN¹.

一班人	a *class* of persons; a *shift* of workmen.
七里爲一班路	seven "li" is a *shift* with an official's chair-bearers.
大班頭	chair-bearer (a respectful term).
加班	a *coolie* hired on the road to help.
班上的	*policemen*; *yamen runners*.
班房	the small prison in a yamên, the jail.
班子上的人	*actors*.
老班子 and 小班子	the older and younger *generations* of a [family.

7 現 SHIEN⁴.

現出來	to *display*.
這些字都現	the characters are all *distinct*.
現今	*at present*.
現在的事	*present* affairs, the things that *now* are.
現成的東西	*ready*-made things.
現錢	*ready* money.

理 LI³.

管理	to *govern*.
辦理事情	to *manage* affairs.
道理	*reason*; *doctrine*; *right*.
不講理的人	an *unreasonable* fellow.
是個不合理的事	it is an *unreasonable* affair.
天理良心	Heaven-bestowed *reason* and conscience.
各理各的事	let each one *attend to* his own business.
又來理起說	he came and *brought up* the matter again.
你不理會嗎	do you not *comprehend*?
文理字眼子	*classical* characters.

(339)

玉 7-11

琉₈ 琥 琴 琶 琵₉ 瑕 瑚 瑁 瑙 瑞₁₀ 瑰 瑪₁₁ 璋		
	LIU².	
琉璃瓦		glass tiles.
	FU³.	
琥珀珠		amber beads.
	CH'IN².	
彈琴		to play on a lute.
二胡琴		the two-stringed fiddle.
脺胡琴		sounds made with the throat in imitation [of the fiddle.
風琴		foreign organs, melodeons, etc.
	PA¹.	
琵琶		the Chinese guitar.
	P'I².	
		for example of use see last.
	SHIA².	
白玉無瑕		a white jade-stone without flaw.
	FU².	
		for example of use see 珊.
	MAO⁴.	
玳瑁框子		tortoise-shell spectacle rims.
	LAO³.	
瑪瑙		precious stones like agate, bloodstone, etc.
	SHUE⁴.	
祥瑞之兆		an auspicious omen.
	KUE⁴.	
刺玫瑰		a thorny kind of rose.
	MA³.	
		for example of use see 瑙.
	CHANG¹.	
弄璋		to bear a son, (from the jade plaything anciently given to a boy).

(340)

注 释

琉 [liəu²]
琥 [fu³]
琴 [tɕʰin²]
【肉胡琴】嗓子模拟胡琴发出的声音。
琶 [pa¹]
琵 [pʰi²]
瑕 [ɕia²]
瑚 [fu²]
瑁 [mao⁴]
瑙 [lao³]
瑞 [ʂuei⁴]
瑰 [kuei⁴]
瑪（玛）[ma³]
璋 [tʂaŋ¹]
【弄璋】古时人们生下男孩，就会把一种玉"璋"给他们玩。引申为生男孩。

注 释

璃 [li²]
環（环）[xuan²]
瓊（琼）[tɕʰyn²]
瓏（珑）[loŋ²]
瓜 [kua¹]
【瓜娃子】傻瓜，笨蛋。
瓢 [pʰiao²]
瓣 [pan⁴]
瓤 [zaŋ²]
【没瓤子的人】没有智慧和勇气的人。

玉 11-16　瓜 11-17

璃 13	LI².	for example of use see 玻 and 琉.
環	HUAN².	
	耳環子	ear-rings.
	玉環	a jade bracelet.
	環繞	to encircle.
	連環	swivel-hooks, used by butchers to hang [meat on.
瓊 15	CHʻÜIN².	
16	瓊漿	excellent wine; nectar; wine of the gods.
瓏	LONG².	for example of use see 玲.

The 97th radical. (瓜)

瓜	KUA¹.	
	西瓜	the melon.
	瓜子	melon-seeds.
	黃瓜	the cucumber.
	南瓜	the squash.
	苦瓜	the bitter gourd.
	木瓜	the quince.
	戴瓜皮子	to wear the common round cap.
	我們拿來瓜分	let us divide it equally.
11	瓜娃子	a fool; a stupid fellow.
瓢	PʻIAO².	[a calabash.
	水瓢	a ladle for lifting water, sometimes made of
14	一瓢水	a ladleful of water.
瓣	PAN⁴.	
	花瓣瓣	the petals of a flower.
	柑子瓣	the divisions of an orange.
17	胡豆瓣	pickled bean lobes.
瓤	RANG².	
	南瓜瓤	the pulp of a squash.
	絲瓜瓤	the fibre of the Loofah, used as a dish-cloth.
	沒瓤子的人	a man with no grit or gumption.

(341)

瓦 6-13　甘 4-6

The 98th radical. (瓦)

UA³.
盖瓦　to roof with *tiles*.
打瓦　in reduced circumstances.

P'IN².
花瓶子　a *vase* for flowers.
藥瓶子　a medicine *bottle*.

T'ONG².
瓴瓦　long *semi-circular tiles*, used on temples.

TIEN⁴.
把桌子甎稳　*wedge* something under the table leg to [steady it.

CHUAN¹.
泥甎　unburnt *brick*.
甎牆　a *brick* wall.

TSEN⁴.
甑子　a wooden *rice-steamer*.

ONG⁴.
甕子鍋　a *deep* iron boiler.

The 99th radical. (甘)

KAN¹.
甘草　*liquorice*; lit., *sweet* grass.
喫甘蔗　to chew *sugar*-cane.
甘心願意　*delighted* and willing.

SHEN⁴.
刑罰甚重　the punishment is *very* heavy.
你做甚麼事　what are you doing?

T'IEN².
人好水也甜　when a person is in good health even water [is *sweet*.
口甜如蜜心黑似漆　his mouth is *sweet* as honey, but his heart is black as varnish.
嘴巴子甜　*soft*-tongued.

(342)

注　释

瓦 [ua³]
瓶 [pʰin²]
瓴 [tʰoŋ²]
【瓴瓦】同"筒瓦"，用于大型庙宇、宫殿的窄瓦片，制作时为筒状，成坯为半，经烧制成瓦。一般以黏土为材料。
甎 [tien⁴]
【把桌子甎稳】地不平时在桌腿下垫上木片等使桌子平稳。
甎（砖）[tsuan¹]
甑 [tsən⁴]
【甑子】炊具，主要用于蒸米饭，外部略像木桶，但底部为竹篾编成的向内、向上略拱的圆锥，因此有许多小孔，放于鬲或锅上蒸食物。
甕（瓮）[oŋ⁴]
【瓮子锅】铁制深煮锅。
甘 [kan¹]
甚 [şən⁴]
甜 [tʰien²]

注释

生 [sən¹] [sən⁴]
【种子发生了】发生：萌发，滋长。种子发芽了。
【书生得很】对于课业很生疏。
產（产）[tsʰan³] [tʂʰan³]
甥 [sən¹]
【生产一个女子】生了一个女儿。

生 6-7

The 100th radical. (生)

生

SEN¹.

生娃娃	to *bear* children.
生日	a *birth*day.
龍生龍鳳生鳳 耗子生兒會打洞	the dragon bears a dragon and the phœnix *produces* phœnix, and the offspring of a rat knows how to gnaw a hole.
一位先生	a gentleman.
門生	a follower; a disciple.
生命	*life*.
種子發生了	the seed has *sprung up*.
平生爲人	all my *lifetime* as a man.
人生在世	people *living* in this world.
生理	a *livelihood*.
發生茂盛	to *grow* luxuriantly.
生病	to *contract* a disease.
不必生氣	you need not *get* angry.
惹事生非	to *stir* up mischief.
生蘿蔔	*raw* turnips.
生飯	*half-boiled* rice.
書生得很	he is very *ignorant* of his lesson.
你好生做	do it carefully.

READ SEN¹,⁴.

生蛋	to *lay* eggs.

6 產

TS'AN³, CH'AN³.

生產一個女子	to *bear* a daughter.
小產	an *abortion*.
今年子出產好	the *crops* are good this year.
那個地方出甚麼土產	what are the *natural productions* of the place?
產業	an *estate*; *property*.

7 甥

SEN¹.

外甥	a *sister's son*; a nephew of a different surname.
外甥女	a *sister's daughter*.

生 7 用 2 田

甦	SU¹.	
	甦醒	to *revive*, as from a swoon.
	一身都麻甦甦的	I feel *limp* and weak.

The 101st radical. (用)

用	IONG⁴.	
	閒時做來懣時用 / 急時做來不中用	make it at your leisure, use it in your need; things made just when wanted are very poor indeed.
	我信用那個人	I like to *employ* that man.
	用費大	the *expenses* are great.
	錢用過足了	the money is all *spent*.
	請多用點	*eat* a little more.
	用火燒	*burn* it *with* fire.
	用心讀書	*study with* all your heart; give attention [to reading.

甩	SHUAI³.	
	甩石頭	to *throw* stones.
	甩脫	to *cast* off.
	莫說甩話	don't *revile*.

甫	FU³.	
	請問閣下的臺甫	what is your *style*, Sir ?

The 102nd radical. (田)

田	T'IEN².	
	墵田	*rice-fields* on the plain.
	心田	the heart.
	硯田	an ink-slab.

甲	CHIA⁵.	
	滿了六十花甲子	reached the age of 60; completed the *cycle*.
	甲長	the *headman* of a ward.
	甲於天下	the *first* man in the empire; in scholarship, [wealth, etc.
	身懷六甲	enceinte.

(344)

注 釋

甦（苏）[su¹]
用 [ioŋ⁴]
【我信用那个人】信用：雇佣，聘用。
甩 [ʂuai³]
【莫说甩话】不要谩骂。
甫 [fu³]
【请问阁下的台甫】台甫：即表字，又称字，敬辞，古代的中国人在名字外，为自己取的与本名意义相关的别名。请问阁下的字是什么？
田 [tʰien²]
甲 [tɕia⁵]

注　释

【疮甲甲】伤口结的痂。
申[ṣən¹]
由[iəu²]
男[lan²]
【侄男】侄儿。
【外男】外甥。
界[tɕiai⁴]

甲 2-4

我們的官是個科甲班子	our magistrate is a *literary* man.
頭戴盔身穿甲	to wear helmet and *armour*.
鱉甲	a turtle's *shell*.
穿山甲	the *pangolin*.
指甲	finger *nails*.
指甲花	balsam (Impatiens) from the appearance [of the seed pods.
魚鱗甲	the *scales* of a fish.
瘡甲甲	*scabs*.

SHEN¹.

申明出來	to *state* a case clearly.
官受了申飭	the magistrate has been *reprimanded*.

IU².

說出根由	explain the *origin* of it.
是個甚麼情由	what is the *cause* of it?
不曉得他的來由	I don't know about his *antecedents*.
由不得我	it does not *depend upon* me.
萬事不由人作主一生都是命安排	nothing is ordered by man, all is decreed by fate.
自由自在	*independent* and at ease.
由成都下重慶	to go *from* Ch'en-tu down to Ch'ongk'ing.
由隨你	*as* you please.
由他去罷	*let* him go that's all.

LAN².

男女	*man* and woman; *male* and female.
男子漢不在屋頭	the *husband* is not at home.
侄男	a brother's *son*, nephew.
外男	a sister's *son*, nephew.
親男色	*sodomy*.

CHIAI⁴.

邊界	a *boundary*; a *frontier*.
界牌	a *boundary* stone between two counties.
界石	a *landmark*.

(345)

田 4-7

	說話莫犯江界	don't talk about other people's business.
	世界上的風俗	the customs of this *world*.
	UE⁴.	
畏	畏懼	to *dread*.
吵₅	CH'AO¹,⁴.	same as 炒.
畜	SHIO⁵.	[sheep, hen, dog and pig.
	六畜	the six *domestic* animals, i. e., horse, cow,
留	LIU².	
	留客不如早打發	it is better to send visitors away early than to *detain* them. [about leaving.
	請留步	please *stay* a little; don't be in a hurry
	把這個菜留倒	*lay by* this food *for future use*.
	你要留心	you must *pay attention*. [dulgent.
	做事要留情	in managing matters be considerate or in-
	MONG³.	
畝₆	八十畝田	eighty *acres* of rice fields.
異	I⁴.	[a *different* surname.
	異姓亂宗	to confuse the family by adopting a son of
	那個人有異心	his heart is *estranged*.
	那是個異人	that's a *strange* fellow.
	異邦人	*foreign* peoples.
略	LIO⁵.	
	我大略曉得	I have a *general* knowledge of it.
	不可忽略	you must not be *careless*.
畧	LIO⁵.	same as last.
畢	PI⁵.	
	我的話說畢了	I have *finished* speaking.
	畢竟不同	*after all* they are not the same.
番₇	FAN¹.	
	三番兩次的說	I have spoken of it *time* after *time*.

(346)

注　釋

【说话莫犯江界】不要说他人是非。

畏 [uei⁴]

吵 [tṣʰao¹] [tṣʰao⁴]

畜 [ɕio⁵]

留 [liəu²]

畝（亩）[moŋ³]

異（异）[i⁴]

略 [lio⁵]

畧（略）[lio⁵]

畢（毕）[pi⁵]

番 [fan¹]

注 释

畫（画）[xua⁴][xua⁵]
　【写倒画笔】笔画顺序写错了。

當（当）[taŋ¹][taŋ⁴]
　【应分该当的】应该这样的。
　【当中人】中人：居间介绍或作证的人。
　【给个当头】当头：在当铺借钱用的抵押品。
　【说停当了】（事情）说定了，就绪了。

田 7-8

費了一番心	I expended some thought on the matter. (N.A.)
西番 會說番話	Western *barbarians*, i. e., hill tribes and able to speak *Tibetan*. [Tibetans.

HUA⁴.

畫畫兒	to *draw* a picture.
畫山水	to *sketch* or *paint* scenery.
畫虎畫皮難畫骨 知人知面不知心	it is easy to *sketch* a tiger's skin, but not its bones; you may know the face of a man, but you do not know his heart.
畫個十字	to *sign* a document by making a cross.
畫匠	a fresco-*painter*.
畫眉子	the Chinese thrush.

READ HUA⁵.

寫倒畫筆	to write the *strokes of a character* in the [wrong order.

TANG¹.

應分該當的	what *ought* to be.
當中人	to *act as* middleman.
當兵	to *be* a soldier.
當家人	the *head* of a house.
當不起	I am un*worthy*!
在當中	in the *middle*.
當面說	say it *to* his face.

READ TANG⁴.

當衣服	to *pawn* clothes.
把我當做甚麼人	whom do you take me to *be*?
當真的	it *is* true.
給個當頭	give a *pledge*.
當鋪	a *pawn*-shop.
當個房子	to *mortgage* a house.
我上了他的當	I have been taken in by him.
穩當	steady; secure.
在床當頭	at the *end* of the bed.
說停當了	the affair is *settled*.

(347)

田 14-17　疋 7·9　疒 2

14 疆

CHIANG¹.

| 分疆界 | to distinguish the *boundaries*; to understand the *limits* of a thing. |
| 福壽無疆 | may your happiness and your years be *boundless* (birthday wish). |

17 疊

TIE⁵.　　same as 叠

The 103rd radical. (疋)

P'I⁵.

一疋布	a *piece* of cloth. (*N. A.*)
一疋草	a *blade* of grass. (*N. A.*)
一疋毛	a *feather*. (*N. A.*)

7 疏

SU¹.

我去的稀疏	I have *seldom* gone there.
種的稀稀疏疏的	sown *thinly*.
莫疏虞了	don't be *careless*.
生疏	to grow *distant* towards anyone.
把話疏通	to *clear up* a dispute.

疎

SU¹.　　same as last.

9 疑

NGI².

疑人不用　用人不疑	if you *suspect* a man don't employ him, if you employ a man don't *suspect* him.
疑心生暗鬼	a *suspicious* heart raises demons of darkness.
避嫌疑	avoid *suspicious* conduct; abstain from all appearance of evil.
心裏生了疑惑	there are *doubts* in my mind about it.

The 104th radical. (疒)

2 疘

CHIAO³.

| 疘腸痧 | *colic*; *enteritis*. |

(348)

注释

疆 [tɕiaŋ¹]
疊（叠）[tie⁵]
疋（匹）[pʰi⁵]
疏 [su¹]
【我去的稀疏】我去的次数少。
【莫疏虞了】不要疏忽了。
疎（疏）[su¹]
疑 [ŋi²]
疘 [tɕiao³]
【疘肠痧】肠绞痛, 疝气。

注释

疔 [tin¹]
【羊毛疔】羊毛痧,羊毛疔瘤,西医学名炭疽热。

疙 [ke⁵]

疝 [ʂuan⁴]

疥 [tɕiai⁴]

疤 [pa¹]

疫 [io⁵]

疹 [tʂən³]
【一泼疹候】一种流行病。

症 [tʂən⁴]

痱(痹) [fei⁴]
【漆痱子】新鲜漆引起的皮疹。

疳 [kan¹]
【疳积】以神萎、面黄肌瘦、毛发焦枯、肚大筋露、纳呆便溏为主要表现的儿科病症。英文释义应为: Infantile malnutrition.

疱 [pʰao⁴]

疲 [pʰi²]

病 [pin⁴]
【我的病翻了】我的病复发了。

疒 2-5

	TIN¹.	
疔瘡		very painful *boils*.
羊毛疔		a violent *colic*.
	KE⁵.	
疙瘩		*wens*; *sebaceous tumours*.
	SHUAN⁴.	
疝氣		*scrotal hernia*; *hydrocele*.
	CHIAI⁴.	
疥瘡		*itch*.
	PA¹.	
瘡疤子		a *scar* left after a sore is healed.
	IO⁵.	
瘟疫		a *pestilence*.
	CHEN³.	
發出一身疹子		a *rash* coming out all over the body.
	CHEN⁴.	
一潑症候		an *epidemic*.
	FE⁴.	
熱痱子		*prickly heat*.
漆痱子		a *rash* caused by fresh lacquer.
	KAN¹.	
疳積		a *wasting disease* of children—*consumption*.
	P'AO⁴.	
腳上走起疱		I have raised a *blister* on my foot with [walking.
	P'I².	
精神疲倦		*wearied*; *tired*.
	PIN⁴.	
我的病翻了		I have had a relapse of my *sickness*.
病了幾天		*sick* for a few days.
他有個心病		he has a *fault*, or a *moral defect*.

(349)

疒 5-7

疼 T'EN².
肚皮疼痛 — my stomach aches.
疼愛 — to love much.

疴 T'O².
疴背子 — a humpback.

疾 TSI⁵, TSIE⁵.
痢疾 — a dysenteric disorder.
疾速回去 — to return hastily.

疽 TSÜ¹.
附骨疽 — a deep-seated abscess.

疵 TSÏ¹.
沒得一點瑕疵 — without the slightest flaw or failing.

痔 CHÏ⁴.
痔瘡 — piles.

痕 HEN².
傷痕 — a wound; a scar.
痕跡 — a trace of anything; a stain.

痊 TS'ÜEN².
病痊愈了嗎 — have you recovered from your illness?

痨 LAO³.
乾癆痨 — itch.

痣 CHÏ⁴.
黑痣 — moles; freckles; black-heads.

痢 LI⁴.
紅白痢 — dysentery.

痧 SHA¹.
痧症 — cholera.

痠 SUAN¹.
痠痛痠痛的 — painful.
走得腿痠 — I have walked till my legs ache.

(350)

注 釋

疼 [tʰən²]
疴 [tʰo²]
【疴背子】駝背。
疾 [tsi⁵] [tsie⁵]
疽 [tsy¹]
【附骨疽】毒氣深沉，結聚於骨而發生的深部膿瘍，又稱"骨癰"、"貼骨癰"。
疵 [tsʅ¹]
痔 [tʂʅ⁴]
痕 [xən²]
痊 [tsʰyen²]
痨 [lao³]
【乾癆痨】疥瘡。
痣 [tʂʅ⁴]
痢 [li⁴]
痧 [ʂa¹]
【痧症】痧子、瘴氣。
痠 [suan¹]

注释

痘 [təu⁴]
【放痘子】种痘，接种疫苗。
瘏 [tʰu⁵] [tʰo⁵]
痞 [pʰi³] [pʰi⁴]
【痞骗人】强求，胡搅蛮缠。
【长行把人痞倒】总是依赖某人。
痛 [tʰoŋ⁴]
痴 [tʂʰɿ¹]
痼 [ku⁴]
痳 [lin²]
【痳症】麻疹。
蔴 [ma²] 应为"麻"。
【蔴猫儿】灰猫。
痿 [uei¹]
【人痿得很】痿：中医指身体某些部分萎缩或丧失机能。人十分羸弱。

疒 7-8

痘 TEO⁴.
放痘子 — to inoculate with *small pox*.
牛痘 — vaccine.
痘科先生 — a vaccinator.

瘏 T'U⁵, T'O⁵.
瘏頭瘡 — *scalled* head.

痞 P'I³.
痞騙人 — to *importunate*; to *beg persistently*.
斯文痞子 — a genteel *beggar*.
刁痞 — to stir up *mischief*.
痞棍 — a *pettifogging* blackguard.

READ P'I⁴.
長行把人痞倒 — he is constantly *sponging* on one.

痛 T'ONG⁴.
腦壳痛 — my head *aches*.
傷心痛哭 — to grieve and weep *bitterly*.
我心痛他 — I *pity* him.
我實在痛快 — I am really *extremely* pleased.

痴 CH'Ï¹.
same as 癡.

痼 KU⁴.
成了痼疾 — the disease has become *incurable*.

痳 LIN².
痳症 — *stone*, *gravel*, and similar *urinary diseases*.

蔴 MA².
出蔴子 — to have *measles*.
大蔴瘋 — *leprosy*. [do.
蔴嘴 — to *benumb* the lips, as some kinds of pepper
手蔴木了 — my hand is *benumbed*.
蔴猫兒 — a *gray* or *tabby* cat.

痿 UE¹.
人痿得很 — my body is very *weak*.

(351)

疒 8-10

痰 T'AN².
吐痰　　　to cough up phlegm.
痰盒子　　a small spittoon.
林痰　　　crazy Mr. Lin.

瘀 Ü⁴.
瘀血　　　extravasated blood in a bruise, or abscess; [clots of blood.

瘋 FONG¹.
半邊瘋　　partial paralysis.
瘋子　　　a lunatic.
母豬瘋　　epilepsy.
瘋狗　　　a mad dog.
瘋癲了　　he is mad.
害頭瘋　　to have a severe head-ache.
中了瘋　　to have a fit of apoplexy.
扯臍瘋　　infantile convulsions.
酒瘋子　　a person who is wild with drink.

瘷 TSIU⁴.
痲瘷了　　distorted with small-pox scars.

瘍 IANG².
九子瘍　　scrofulous sores.

瘡 CH'UANG¹.
長了一身的瘡　to have sores all over the body.
瘡熟了　　the abscess is ripe.
坐板瘡　　boils on the buttocks.

痦 KE⁵.   properly kao³. For examples of use see 疳.

瘧 NIO⁵.
瘧疾　　　ague.

瘙 SAO⁴.
周身發瘙　itching all over the body.

瘦 SEO⁴.
面黃肌瘦　cadaverous and lean.
割瘦肉　　buy lean meat.

(352)

注　釋

痰 [tʰan²]
瘀 [y⁴]
瘋(疯) [foŋ¹]
【扯脐疯】婴幼儿惊厥。
瘷 [tsiəu⁴]
【痲瘷了】天花疤痕。
瘍(疡) [iaŋ²]
【九子疡】生于颈部的一种感染性外科疾病，俗称"疬子颈"或"老鼠疮"。
瘡(疮) [tʂʰuaŋ¹]
痦 [ke⁵]
瘧(疟) [ȵio⁵]
瘙 [sao⁴]
瘦 [səu⁴]

注 释

瘊 [suei¹]

瘩 [ta⁵]

【瘊疙瘩】瘙痒的疙瘩。

瘟 [uən¹]

瘺（瘘）[ləu⁴]

瘢 [pan¹]

痨（痨）[lao²]

癀 ⌈xuaŋ²⌉

【癀肿病】黄疸病。

療（疗）[liao²]

【療病】治疗疾病。

癡（痴）[tʂʰʅ¹]

癤（疖）[tsie⁵]

【癤子疮】小脓包。

癢（痒）[iaŋ³]

疒 10-15

瘊瘩瘟瘺瘢痨癀療癡癤癢		
	田地瘦薄	the fields are very *poor*.
	鞋襪子要瘦點	make the shoes a little *tighter*.
	SUE¹.	
	痿痿蔫蔫的	*feeble*, as after sickness.
	TA⁵.	
	瘊疙瘩	an itching *wen* or *swelling*.
	UEN¹.	
11	今年豬發瘟	the *plague* has broken out amongst the [pigs this year.
	LEO⁴.	
	痔瘺	*piles*.
	PAN¹.	
	發出一身瘢	to have a *rash* all over the body.
12	臉上起瘢點	black *spots* (*black heads*) coming out on the [face.
	LAO².	
	痨病	*consumption*.
	READ LAO⁴.	
	痨倒了	to be *poisoned*.
	痨人的	*poisonous*.
	HUANG².	
	癀腫病	*jaundice*.
	LIAO².	
14	療病	to *cure* a disease.
	CHʻI¹.	
15	癡蠢	*foolish*; *stupid*.
	TSIE⁵.	
	癤子瘡	small *abscesses*.
	米癤子	*pimples*.
	IANG³.	
	發癢	to *itch*. [etc.
	手癢	one's hand *itching* to strike, touch, gamble,

(353)

西蜀方言

疒 16-25　癶 7

16 瘝		
	HO⁵.	
	瘟亂症	Asiatic *cholera*.
癩	LAI⁴.	
	巴骨癩	*leprosy*.
	狗癩了	the dog has *mange*.
	癩子瓜	the squash—from the *mottled* appearance.
	癩格包	the toad.
17 癬	SHÜEN³, SÜEN³.	
	銅錢癬	*ringworm*.
	牛皮癬	crusted *ringworm*.
癮	IN³.	
18	上了癮	he has a *craving* for it, as opium.
癰	IONG¹.	
19	癰疽	an *abscess*.
癱	T'AN¹.	
	癱瘋病	*paralysis*.
25	瘋癱了	*palsied*.
癲	TIEN¹.	
	瘋瘋癲癲的人	a *crazy* fellow; a *daft* man.
	癲狗	a *mad* dog.
	老癲悚了	in second childhood.

The 105th radical. (癶)

7 登	TEN¹.	
	登高望遠	when you *ascend* high you can see far.
	幾時登程	when will you *start* on your journey?
	隨手登簿	*enter* the item in the account at once.
	登他走	*pay* him off.
	纔在打登登	the child is just *bobbing* on its feet, not yet able to walk.
	長登了	*full-grown*.

(354)

注　釋

瘝（霍）[xo⁵]
癩（癩）[lai⁴]
【巴骨癩】麻风病。
【癩格包】蟾蜍，癩蛤蟆。
癬（癬）[çyen³][syen³]
癮[in³]
癰（癰）[ioŋ¹]
癱（癱）[tʰan¹]
癲（癲）[tien¹]
【老癲悚了】指老年人像儿童似的有点疯癲癲的。
登[tən¹]
【登他走】打发他走。
【才在打登登】（孩子）双脚才在摆动（意为还不能走）。
【长登了】登：成熟。长成熟了。

注 释

發（发）[fa⁵]
  【要发很些】发很：发狠。要更努力些。
  【这个子弟没得发变】这个年轻人没有什么发展和变化。
  【没有发起】（面团）没有发起来。
  【发面】发酵面团。
  【尸发了】尸体肿胀了。
  【发体】身体发胖。
  【发客】成批贩卖，批发。
  【颜色发了】褪色。

白 [pe⁵]
  【出个告白】告白：告示。

癶 7 白

發 FA⁵.

發芽芽	to *shoot forth* buds ; to *sprout*.
要發很些	*exert* yourself a little more.
這個子弟沒得發變	this youth is not going to *develop* much ability.
發兵救援	to *send* more soldiers to help.
打發一個人去問	*send* a man to enquire.
打發女	to *send forth* a daughter, i. e., to be married.
發藥	to *dispense* medicines.
發醋	to *ferment* vinegar.
沒有發起	it has not *risen*, as dough.
發麵	*leavened* dough.
屍發了	the corpse is *swollen*.
昨夜河頭發了水	the river *rose* in the night.
發病的東西喫不得	you must not eat things that would *cause* sickness.
今年纔發蒙	he has just *commenced* to go to school this year.
他的癮發了	his craving has *come on*.
我的病又發了	my malady has *broken out* again.
天在發白	it will soon be light ; day is *breaking*.
發財	to *become* rich.
發體	to *get* fat.
他發了氣	he *got* angry.
發餉銀	to *pay* the troops.
發客	to *sell* wholesale.
顏色發了	the colour is *faded*.

The 106th radical 白

白 PE⁵.

白紙	*white* paper.
白契	an *unstamped* document.
白天	*day*-time.
白白的跑一遍路	to *vainly* run an errand, or take a journey.
出個告白	to post a *notice*.
說白話	to tell *lies*.

(355)

白 1-4 皮

1 百 PE⁵.
白人	a *common* person ; an undergraduate.
明白	to *understand* ; *clear* ; *perspicuous*.
白菜	*cabbage*.
一百錢	one *hundred* cash.
百姓	the *people* ; lit., *many* names.
百長	a *centurion*.
百貨釐金	custom on *all* kinds of goods.

2 皂 TSAO⁴.
皂班	*lictors* who are dressed in *black*.
皂角	the beans of the *soap-tree*.
皂礬	*sulphate of iron*.

3 的 TI⁵.
不的確	not *certain*.
我的帽子	my hat (*possessive*).
花是紅的	the flower is red (*adjectival*).
剃頭的	a barber (*relative*).
說話的時候	when he was speaking (*relative*).

4 皇 HUANG². see also under 亼.
皇上	an *emperor*.
買本皇曆	buy an *Imperial* calendar.
皇木林	*royal* forests.

皆 CHIAI¹, KAI¹. for example of use see 俱.

膘 P'IAO⁴.
收飾得膘亮	tied up *white* and clean.
顏色染得膘亮	the colour is dyed *bright* and clean.

The 107th radical. (皮)

皮 P'I².
揉皮子	the *skin* on the human body.
肚皮	the *stomach*.
山裏頭的人皮厚	the mountaineers are hospitable.

(356)

注 釋

【白人】普通人。
百 [pe⁵]
皂 [tsao⁴]
【皂班】旧时州县衙役三班中的一班,其职掌站堂行刑。也泛指差役。
【皂礬】硫酸亚铁。
的 [ti⁵]
皇 [xuaŋ²]
皆 [tɕiai¹] [kai¹]
膘 [pʰiao⁴]
【收饰得膘亮】收拾得白净整齐。
皮 [pʰi²]
【揉皮子】人的皮肤。

注 释

【做活路皮】皮,同"疲",疲沓、拖沓。干活很慢。
【生意皮】皮,同"疲",货物销售不畅。

皲 [tsʰe⁵]
【脸上起鸡爪皲】脸上起了皱纹。

奣 [ta⁵]
【瘦的一奣皮】瘦得皮肤起皱松弛。形容衰老憔悴。

皱(皱)[tsoŋ⁴]

皿 [min³]

皮 5-10 皿

剝皮	to flay ; to peel.
牛皮子	an ox *hide*.
皮袄子	a *fur* coat.
皮匠	a tanner, currier, or leather merchant.
皮鞋	*leather* shoes.
橘子皮	orange *peel*.
樹皮子	the *bark* of a tree.
口皮	the *lips*, the *flap* of an envelope.
眼皮子	the *eye-lids*.
除皮	weight without the *basket* or *wrapper* ; net weight.
打個封皮	to paste on a *strip* of paper slantwise across [a door or box.
銅皮子	a *thin sheet* of brass.
喫麪皮子	to eat *thin sheets* of dough boiled in gravy.
地皮錢	*ground* rent.
皮紙	a *tough* kind of paper.
做活路皮	he is *slow* at work.
生意皮	business is *dull*.
皮蛋	pickled eggs.
皮老漢 and 皮兒子	step-father and step-son.

5 皲 TS'E⁵.

臉上起雞爪皲	getting *wrinkles* on the face.
手上凍起黃瓜皲	my hands are *chapped* with the cold.
田開了皲	the soil in the fields is *cracking* with the drought.

6 奣 TA⁵.

| 瘦的一奣皮 | wasted to a *wrinkled* skin, emaciated. |

TSONG⁴.

| 臉上起皱皱了 | his face is *wrinkled* with age. |

The 108th radical. (皿)

10 皿 MIN³.

| 器皿兒 | a *utensil* of any kind. |

(357)

皿 3-6

3 盂	Ü².		
	盂鉢		brown, glazed basins of various sizes.
4 盆	P'EN².		
	脚盆		a tub.
	洗臉盆		a washhand basin.
	一盆水		a basinful, or tubful, of water.
	臨盆		parturition.
	火盆		a fire-pan on a frame, a brasier.
	花盆		a flower pot.
盈	IN².		
	惡貫滿盈		the measure of his iniquities is full.
盃	PE¹.		
			same as 杯.
5 盌	HAI³.		
	酒盉		a large wine jar.
盌	UAN³.		
	飯盌		a rice bowl.
	菜盌		a vegetable basin.
	茶盌		a tea-cup.
	一盌飯		a basin of rice.
	盌櫃		a cupboard.
	橡盌盌		acorn cups.
益	I⁵.		
	沒得益處		there is no benefit or advantage in it.
6 盒	HO⁵.		
	帽盒		a hat box.
	眼鏡盒子		a spectacle case.
	粉粧盒		a rouge pot.
	幾架抬盒		a few present trays (carried by two bearers [each).
盖	KAI⁴.		
	鍋盖		a pot lid.
	盖子		a cover.

(358)

注 释

盂 [y²]
盆 [pʰən²]
盈 [in²]
盃（杯）[pei¹]
盉 [xai³]
【酒盉】大酒罐子。
盌（碗）[uan³]
【橡碗碗】橡木杯或碗。
益 [i⁵]
盒 [xo⁵]
【几架抬盒】抬盒: 旧时喜庆时常用的一种装礼品的木盒子, 由两人抬着。
盖 [kai⁴]

注 释

【盖面子】涂清漆。
【盖得过人】超过别人。
盔 [kʰuei¹]
　【毡盔盔】毡帽。
　【盔头】即"头盔"。
　【红盔盔】粗陶盆。
　【沙盔儿】粗陶臼。
盗 [tao⁴]
盗（盗）[tao⁴]
盛 [ʂən⁴]
　【盛德人】盛德：品德高尚。品德高尚之人。
盏（盏）[tʂan³]
盟 [min²]
塩（监）[ien²]
監（监）[tɕien¹]

皿 6-9

鋪蓋		a *coverlet*.
蓋倒		*cover* it.
蓋瓦		to *roof* with tiles.
遮蓋不倒		you cannot *conceal* the matter.
蓋面子		to *lay on* the outer coat of varnish.
說蓋面子話		to talk *hypocritically*.
蓋得過人		to *surpass* others.
盛	K'UE¹.	
盔甲		*helmet* and cuirass.
氈盔盔		a felt *cap*.
盔頭		a block for making *caps* on.
紅盔盔		a coarse earthenware *basin*.
沙盔兒		a coarse earthenware *mortar*.
盗	TAO⁴.	same as the next.
盗	TAO⁴.	
遇倒强盗		to meet with *robbers*.
盗案		a *robbery* case.
盗寶		to *steal* the treasures of a place, as foreigners are said to do.
盛	SHEN⁴.	
長得茂盛		it has grown *luxuriantly*.
生意茂盛		business is *prosperous*.
盛德人		a *virtuous* man.
盞	CHAN³.	
燈盞子		the *oil-cup* of a Chinese lamp.
盆盞		*crockery*.
盟	MIN².	
結盟		to swear a *covenant*.
塩	IEN².	same as 監.
監	CHIEN¹.	
坐監		to be in *prison*.

(359)

皿 9-11

READ CHIEN⁴.

監察	to *inspect*.
太監	an *eunuch*.
監工	to *oversee* workmen, to *superintend* a work.
監試	the Governor-General *overseeing* the examinations.
監生	a degree bought for Tls. 108.

TSIN⁴.

喫不盡的虧	I have *endless* grievances.
我的命盡了	my life is *ended*!
自盡	to *end* one's life; to commit suicide.
無窮無盡	*inexhaustible*.
話不可說盡	don't push the matter to the *extreme*.
柴盡是濕的	the firewood is *all* wet.
他盡是罵人	he is *always* cursing people.

P'AN².

七寸盤	a seven inch *plate*, i. e., an ordinary tea plate.
平盤子	the *scales* of a balance.
臉盤子	the face.
錢盤子	a cash-*tray*.
打算盤	to *reckon* on the abacus.
盤買賣	to *transact* business.
盤纏	*travelling* expenses.
盤算人家	to *overreach* people.
一盤現交	pay the *whole amount* over in ready money.
兒女難盤	children are difficult to *rear*.
路上盤短	to take a chair for short stages when travelling.
盤活路	*massage*.
一個活盤盤	a *clique*; a number of persons working into each other's hands.
盤問	to *question*; to *interrogate*.

KU³.

銅盬子	a *shallow* copper *pot* with a cover.
磁器盬子	*shallow* vegetable *dishes* with covers.

(360)

注 釋

盡（尽）[tsin⁴]
盤（盘）[pʰan²]
【一盘现交】全盘交付现钱。
【儿女难盘】养育儿女很艰难。
【盘活路】按摩。
【一个活盘盘】一个小圈子、小集团。
盬 [ku³]
【铜盬子】铜质的带盖锅。

注释

目 [mu⁵]
【眼目】眼睛。
直 [tṣʰʅ⁵]
【对直走】笔直走。
盲 [maŋ²]
【青盲眼】青光眼。英文释义应为：Glaucoma.
看 [kʰan⁴] [kʰan¹]

目 3-4

The 109th radical. (目)

MU⁵.

眼目	the *eyes*.
眼目下的事	*present* affairs.
數目	a *number*.
題目	a *theme* ("t'i" is properly the subject, and "mu" the *heads*).
目錄	the *contents* of a book; an *index*.

CHĬ⁵.

對直走	walk *straight* on.
山中有直樹 / 世上無直人	there are *straight* trees on the mountains, but there are no *upright* men in the world.
莫信直中直 / 須防仁不仁	don't believe that all is *straight* that appears *straight*, beware of the unkindness behind the kindness.
我是個心直口快的人	I am a *blunt* out-spoken fellow.

MANG².

青盲眼	*blindness* from paralysis of the optic nerve; [amaurosis.

K'AN⁴.

看不見	I cannot *see*.
看穿了	I *see* through the affair.
看他那座答應	*see* how he answers.
試看	try and *see* if it will do.
聽看	hark! listen and *see*.
好看	beautiful; lit., good to *look* at.
看守莊稼	to *guard* the crops from thieves.
看門的	a *doorkeeper*.
看房子	to *look* for or at a new house; to *look* after the house.
看不看脈	do you *feel* the pulse?
看病	to *examine* a sick person, as a doctor does.
看書	to *read* a book.

(361)

目 4

看成孬的了	to *regard as* bad, or worthless.
看不起他	I don't *esteem* him.
求你看成我	please *favour* me.
你看這個豬有好多斤	how heavy do you *estimate* this pig to be?
看跌倒	*beware* of falling.

READ K'AN[1].

看牛	to *tend* cattle.
一樣看待	*treat* all alike.
看司	the lay *keeper* of a temple, door-*keeper* of a [college.

MIAO[2].

好生眇	*look* at it carefully.
我沒有眇見	I have not *seen* it.

MI[5].

眉毛	the *eyebrows*.

P'AN[4].

沒人顧盼	there is no one who *cares for* me.

SEN[3].

四川省	the *province* of Sï-ch'uan.
成都省	Ch'en-tu, the *provincial capital*.
省察自己	to *examine* one's self.
減省	to *reduce* expenditure; to be sparing.

SIANG[1].

那兩個人相像	these two persons are like each other; [*resembling*.
沒相干	no *concern*.
田地相連	*adjoining* fields, or property.
不相生	*mutually* discordant.
這個東西相因	this article is *cheap*.
買得相因	*cheaply* bought.

READ SIANG[4].

丞相	a *minister of state*.

眇眉盼省相

注 释

【求你看成我】请你支持我,请你帮助我。
【看跌倒】注意别摔倒。
【看司】看守,看门人。
眇 [miao²]
【好生眇】仔细看。
眉 [mi⁵]
盼 [pʰan⁴]
【没人顾盼】顾盼:照顾,看护。
省 [sən³]
相 [siaŋ¹] [siaŋ⁴]
【不相生】相互不协调。
【这个东西相因】相因:价钱便宜。

注释

【大相公】相公：旧时对成年男子的敬称。

盹 [tən⁴]

眨 [tsa⁵]

眞（真）[tʂən¹]

【病顶了真】病情变得严重了。

【传个真子】画肖像。

眛 [mei⁴]

【盲眛无识】盲眛：不明事理。

眠 [mien²]

【把桅子眠起】眠：横放。

眩 [ɕyen⁴]

【烂眼眩】眼睑发炎。

衆（众）[tʂoŋ⁴]

眷 [tɕyen⁴]

目 4-6

| 大相公 | the eldest *boy* in a family. |
| 看相的 | a *physiognomist, phrenologist* and *pathognomist* in one. |

TEN⁴.

5 盹

| 打盹兒 | to *nod* with sleep. |

TSA⁵.

眨

| 擠眉眨眼做過場 | to *wink* at each other and play tricks. |
| 眨個眼就沒有見 | he disappeared in the *twinkling* of an eye. |

CHEN¹.

眞

眞神面前燒不得假香	don't try to deceive me ; lit., you may not burn false incense before the *true* gods.
眞麝香	*genuine* musk.
眞是不錯	*truly* it is right.
認眞	to be in *earnest*.
病頂了眞	the sickness has become *serious*.
傳個眞子	to draw a *portrait*.

ME⁴.

眛

| 盲眛無識 | *almost blind* and unable to recognise anybody. |

MIEN².

眠

蠶子有三眠	silkworms take three *sleeps*.
瞌睡睡眠了	he is *sleeping* soundly.
把桅子眠起	unstep the mast and *lay* it *alongside*.

SHÜEN⁴.

眩

| 腦殼昏眩 | *giddy, dizzy*. |
| 爛眼眩 | inflamed eyelids. |

CHONG⁴.

6 衆

| 衆人 | *all* men ; the people ; the public. |
| 衆位朋友 | *all* you good friends. |

CHÜEN⁴.

眷

| 無娘兒子天眷顧 | Heaven will *care for* the orphan boy. |
| 帶家眷沒有 | have you brought your *family* with you ? |

(363)

目 6-8

眶 K'UANG¹.
眼眶子 — the *socket* of the eye.

眯 MI¹.
眯一眯的 — *blinking* the eyes, as when dust has gone [into them.
眼睛腫眯了 — the eyelids swollen and *closed*.

眼 IEN³.
一雙眼睛 — the *eyes*.
獨眼龍 — a one-*eyed* person.
莫當人家的眼睛 — don't tell tales on others (especially [thieves).
眼前的事 — present affairs.
眼不見心不煩 — what the *eye* does not see the heart does [not grieve for.
這個巴巴打眼得很 — this patch is very *noticeable*.
鍼鼻眼 — the *eye* of a needle.
猫兒眼 — cat's-*eyes* (stones).
毛眼 — *pores* of the body.
鑽幾個眼眼 — bore a few *holes*.
衣裳爛了個眼 — there is a *hole* in the garment.
三隻眼 — a pair of pants.
拿給我看一眼 — let me have a look at it. (*N.A.*).
一眼倉 — one granary. (*N.A.*)
一眼牛圈 — one cow-house. (*N.A.*).

睜 FONG⁴.
眼睛合睜了 — eye-lids *heavy* or *closed* with sleep.

睏 K'UEN⁴.
他在那裏睏着了 — he has *fallen asleep* there.
睏倒放 — lay it *on its side*.

瞍 SO².
陰倒瞍 — to secretly *watch*; to spy.

脹 CHANG⁴.
眼睛脹痛 — my eyes are *swollen* and sore.
那個東西有些脹眼睛 — that article is very *attractive*.

(364)

注释

眶 [kʰuaŋ¹]

眯 [mi¹]
【眯一眯的】眼睛一睁一闭的。

眼 [ien³]
【莫当人家的眼睛】不要搬弄是非,揭人隐私。
【这个巴巴打眼得很】巴巴:实为"疤疤",补丁。打眼:惹人注目。
【针鼻眼】针眼。
【钻几个眼眼】眼眼:小孔。
【一眼仓】眼:量词。一个粮仓。

睜【foŋ⁴】

睏 [kʰuan⁴]
【他在那里睏着了】睏:睡。
【睏倒放】躺着放。

瞍 [so²]
【阴倒瞍】偷偷地看,监视。

脹 [tʂaŋ⁴]
【那个东西有些脹眼睛】脹:吸引。

注释

睖 [lən²]
  【睖他一眼】睖：睁大眼睛注视，表示不满。
睁（睁）[tsən¹]
  【睁光瞎】睁眼瞎。
腚 [tin²]
  【好生腚倒】小心，当心。
睦 [mu⁵]
  睡 [ʂuei⁴]
  【放睡倒】平躺。
督 [tu⁵]
  睬 [tsʰai³]
  睛 [tsin¹]
  【眼睛珠珠】眼球。
瞀 [mu⁴]
  【那个娃娃的眼睛瞀】瞀：愚笨，反应慢。
睹 [tu³]

目 8-9

睖 LEN².
睖他一眼 — he *glared*, or *frowned*, at him.

睁 TSEN¹.
把眼睛睁開 — *open* your eyes.
睁光瞎 — amaurosis.

腚 TIN².
好生腚倒 — *attend* carefully! *look* ont; *look* at it atten- [tively.

睦 MU⁵.
他一家人和和睦睦的 — his family lives in great *harmony*.

睡 SHUE⁴.
睡着了 — he is *asleep*.
睡不着 — I cannot *sleep*.
睡倒好幾天 — he has been *lying down* for a few days with [sickness.
放睡倒 — lay it *flat* on its side, as a beam.

督 TU⁵.
督率工人 — to *oversee* workmen.
督隊 — to *lead* troops; to be *a ringleader* in any- [thing.
督辦軍務 — to *direct* a campaign.

睬 T'SAI³.
沒得人睬我 — no one *entertained* me.
不睬識他 — took no *notice* of him; not *pleased with* him.

睛 TSIN¹.
眼睛珠珠 — the *eyeball*.

瞀 MU⁴.
那個娃娃的眼睛瞀 — that child is slow at learning; lit., his eyes are *dull*.

睹 TU³.
拏給我睹睹 — let me *look* at it.

(365)

西蜀方言

目 10-12

10 瞎

SHIA⁵.

| 瞎子 | a *blind* person. |
| 打瞎眼摸兒 | to play *blind*man's buff. |

MIN².

| 我死都不瞑目 | I will not *close* my eyes even when I die. |

K'O⁵.

| 瞌瞌睡 | to *sleep*, as from weariness. |
| 早晨的瞌唾香 | *sleep* is very sweet in the morning. |

11 瞀

MA².

| 眼睛看字是瞀的 | my eyes are *blurred* when I try to read. |
| 打瞀子眼的時候 | at dusk. |

MAN².

| 瞞得過人瞞不過天 | you may *conceal* a thing *from* man, but you cannot *conceal* it *from* heaven. |

P'IAO³.

| 瞟眼睛 | *squint*-eyed; *cross*-eyed. |
| 瞟竊看一 ha | to steal a *glance* at. |

LIAO³.

| 一看就瞭然 | as soon as you see it you *understand* it. |

K'UEI⁴.

| 兩眼昏瞶 | both my eyes are *dim*; my vision is *blurred*. |

12 瞧

TS'IAO².

| 拏給我瞧一瞧 | let me *look* at it. |
| 瞧見他沒有 | have you *seen* him? |

P'U³.

| 眼睛瞀瞨瞀瞨的 | my eyes are *dim*. |

T'ONG².

| 瞳眼人兒 | the *pupil* of the eye. |

(366)

注 释

瞎 [ɕia⁵]

【打瞎眼摸儿】一种小儿游戏。先在地上画一个圈，作为游戏的范围，众小儿"识拳儿"决出输家为"瞎子"，其余小儿为"(团)鱼"。"瞎子"用手绢蒙上眼睛，在游戏圈中乱摸，"团鱼"则在圈中躲闪。谁被摸到，谁就改当"瞎子"。

瞑 [min²]

瞌 [kʰo⁵]

瞀 [ma²]

【眼睛看字是瞀的】瞀：模糊，看不清楚。

【打瞀子眼的时候】打瞀子眼：傍晚。

瞞(瞒) [man²]

瞟 [pʰiao³]

瞭(了) [liao³]

瞶(瞆) [kʰuei⁴]

瞧 [tsʰiao²]

瞨 [pʰu³]

【眼睛瞀瞨瞀瞨的】瞀瞨瞀瞨：模糊，看不清楚。

瞳 [tʰoŋ²]

【瞳眼人儿】瞳孔。

注 释

瞅（瞅）[tʂʰəu³]
　【好生瞅倒】好生：好好儿地；认真，仔细。（你）好好看着。
瞻 [tʂan¹]
矛 [mao²] [miao²]
矜 [tɕin¹]
知 [tʂʅ¹]
矩 [tɕy³]
短 [tuan³]

目 13　矛 4　矢 3-7

13 瞅

CH'EO³.

好生瞅倒　　watch carefully; be on the look out.
這回把你瞅倒了　I have seen (caught) you this time.

CHAN¹.

瞻　觀瞻　　splendid, as a building or an affair.

The 110th radical. (矛)

MAO².

矛　自相矛盾　　he confounds the *spear* and the *child*, i. e, [contradicts himself.

READ MIAO².

4　矛桿子　　a long *lance*.

CHIN¹.

矜　矜孤恤寡　　to *compassionate* orphans and widows.
　　矜誇　　to *brag*.

The 111th radical. (矢)

CHĪ¹.

3 **知**
不知道　　I don't *know*.
知心的朋友　an intimate friend; lit., a friend who *knows* [one's heart.
知府　　a prefect, i. e., one who *understands and manages* the affairs of a prefecture.
明知故犯　　to *knowingly* and wilfully transgress.
不知事的　　ignorant fellows.
知識　　*knowledge* of a thing; *experience*.
先給我們一個知會　} give us *notice* beforehand.

CHÜ³.

5 **矩**　守規矩　　to observe the *rules* or *customs*.

TUAN³.

7 **短**
大路旁邊打草鞋有的說長有的說短 } like making sandals by the road side, some say they are long and some say they are *short*; opinions differ.

(367)

西蜀方言

矢 7-12 石

	人窮志短馬瘦毛長	man poor—purposes *limited*; horse lean—hair long.
	莫說人家的長短	don't speak of the virtues and *failings* of others; don't criticise.
	短倒	*intercept* him!
	短尖子	to *stop* a shoot by pinching out the point.
	本錢短	my capital is *insufficient*.
	你要短價錢	you must *abate* the price.
	短擺子	to *cure* ague.

矬 8 CH'O⁵.

	衣裳短矬矬的	the garments are *very short*.
	矮矬矬的	*dwarfish*; *dumpy*.

矮 NGAI³.

	矮胖矮胖的	a *short* stout man.
	矮子	a *dwarf*.
	板凳矮	the stool is *low*.
	價錢矮	the price is *low*.
	價錢矮不下來	he will not *abate* the price.
	銀子程分矮	this silver is *inferior*.

矯 12 CHIAO³.

	說矯強的話	to talk *obstinately*.

The 112th radical. 石

石 SHÏ⁵.

	石頭	a *stone*.
	火石	*flint*.
	石膏	*gypsum*.
	石厰	a *quarry*.
	石橋	a *stone* bridge.

READ TAN⁴.

	十斗爲一石	ten bushels make a *picul*.

(368)

注释

【短倒】短：拦。倒：用在动词或表示程度的形容词后面，加强命令或嘱咐的语气。

【本钱短】短：缺少。

【你要短价钱】短：减少，降低。

【短摆子】治疗疟疾。

矬 [tsʰo⁵]

【衣裳短矬矬的】矬矬：形容词后缀，形容不好的状态。

矮 [ŋai³]

【价钱矮】矮：低。

矯（矫）[tɕiao³]

【说矫强的话】矫强：矫情。指强词夺理，无理取闹。

石 [ʂʅ⁵] [tan⁴]

注释

矺 [ta⁵]
  【矺家拌伙】一怒之下摔了碗碟。
  【看矺倒】当心跌倒。
砍 [kʰan³]
砒 [pʰei¹]
砂 [ʂa¹]
砌 [tsʰi⁴] [tɕʰy⁴]
砦（寨）[tsai⁴]
砧 [tʂən¹]
  【砧墩】厚而结实的砧板。
砱 [toŋ³]
砲（炮）[pʰao⁴]
  【火炮子】爆竹。
破 [pʰo⁴]
  【破梦】破：解释。

石 3-5

3 TA⁵.
| 矺家拌伙 | to *smash* the dishes in a rage. |
| 看矺倒 | beware of *falling*. |

4 K'AN³.
砍做兩節	*chop* it into two lengths.
砍竹子	to *cut down* bamboos.
砍傷人	to *wound* a person with a sword.

P'E¹.
| 紅砒 | red *arsenic*. |

SHA¹.
| 硃辰砂 | *cinnabar*. |

TS'I⁴, CH'Ü⁴.
| 砌階簷 | to *pave* a walk under the eaves. |
| 砌甎牆 | to *build*, or *lay* a brick wall. |

CHAI⁴.
| | same as 寨. |

CHEN¹.
| 砧板 | a butcher's *block*. |
| 砧墩 | a blacksmith's *anvil*. |

TONG³.
| tin³ tin³ 砱砱的 | the sound of falling stones, etc. |

5 P'AO⁴.
一門砲	one *cannon*.
砲船	a *gun* boat.
火砲子	fire *crackers*.

P'O⁴.
破衣裳	*ragged* garments.
破城	to *take* a city.
破地獄	to *break open* hell.
破夢	to *interpret* a dream.
看破了	I see *through* it all.

(369)

石 5-7

T'O².
秤砣	the *weight* of a steelyard.
一砣泥巴	a *lump* or *clod* of earth.
結砣起的菓子	bearing fruit in *clusters*.

TSA⁵.
| 砸碎 | to *crush* into fragments. |
| 砸核桃 | to *crack* walnuts. |

CHU¹.
| 銀硃 | *vermillion*. |

HANG¹.
硈城牆	to *ram* the earth when building a city wall.
你硈倒我	you *oppress* or *force* me.
這馬我硈不住	I cannot *manage* this horse.

LAO².
| 硇砂 | *hydrochlorate of ammonia*. |

NIEN², NGAN², NGAI².
| 研成細末 | *triturate* it. |
| 研墨 | to *rub* ink on the ink-slab. |

LIU².
| 硫磺 | *brimstone; sulphur*. |

SIAO¹.
| 火硝 | *saltpetre*. |
| 硝皮子 | to *tan* hides. |

NIEN⁴.
| 硯臺 | an *inkslab*. |

NGEN⁴.
心硬如鐵	his heart is *hard* as iron; *obdurate*.
嘴硬	his talk is *perverse*.
硬擔承	one who acts as *surety*.
硬是不錯	*really it is true*.
硬功名	a degree that has been honestly wrought [for.

(370)

注释

砣 [tʰo²]

砸 [tsa⁵]

硃（朱）[tʂu¹]
【银朱】朱红。

硈 [xaŋ¹]
【硈城墙】夯实城墙。
【你硈倒我】你把我难住了。
【这马我硈不住】硈：控制。

硇 [lao²]

研 [ȵien²] [ŋan²] [ŋai²]

硫 [liəu²]

硝 [siao¹]
【火硝】硝酸钾的俗称。
【硝皮子】用草灰泡水后把晒干的皮子"烧"熟，然后把皮子阴干使之变软，毛在皮子上也就比较结实了。

砚（砚）[ȵien⁴]

硬 [ŋən⁴] [ŋən³]

注释

【树有三尺绵头,人有几句硬话】硬:(态度)坚决或执拗。

【石头硬脚】硬:挫伤。

碁(棋)[tɕʰi²]

碌(碌)[lu⁵]

碍[ŋai⁴]

硼[pʰoŋ²]

碑[pei¹]

碎[suei⁴]

【碎娃娃】小孩子。

【零碎活路】打零工。

石 7-8

我人還硬梆	I am still *hale* in body.
冷硬了	*stiff* with cold, as food or a dead body.
樹有三尺綿頭 人有幾句硬話	} any tree has three feet of tough wood at the root, and any man has a few *decided* words, i. e., a little will of his own.
我過硬要	I am *determined* to have it.

READ NGEN³.

石頭硬腳	the stones *bruise* my feet.
枕頭硬腦壳	the pillow *hurts* my head.
摸起硬手	*hard* to the touch.
把牙齒硬了	to *hurt* the teeth on a hard thing in the [food.
蛋硬破了	the eggs are broken by *contact with hard things*.

8 碁

CH'I². same as 棋.

碌

LU⁵.

勞勞碌碌的過日子	} to pass one's days *laboriously*.

碍

NGAI⁴. same as 礙.

硼

P'ONG².

硼砂	*borax*.

碑

PE¹.

石碑	stone *tablets* of all kinds.
修路碑	a "road repairs *tablet*."
填碑	a *gravestone*.
指路碑	a *fingerpost*.

碎

SUE⁴.

打碎了	broken into *fragments*.
碎銀子	*small pieces* of silver.
碎娃娃	a *little* child.
零碎活路	*odd* jobs.
零碎東西	*odds and ends*.

(371)

石 8-10

碉	牛雜碎	ox *tripe*. [bose.
碇	嘴巴零碎	his conversation is *disconnected and ver*-
碓		TIAO¹.
	碉房	*stone* houses of the tribesmen and Tibetans.
		TIN⁴.
	下碇	let down the *anchor*.
		TUE⁴.
	碓窩	a large stone *mortar*.
	水碓	a *mortar* worked by a water wheel.
碗		UAN³.
碰		same as 盌.
碟		P'ONG⁴.
		same as 撞.
		TIE⁵.
	碟子	small *plates* like *saucers*.
	醬油碟子	small *platters* for sauce.
確		CH'IO⁵.
	確確可憑	it is *certain* and may be proved.
	這是的的確確的	this is very *certain*, or *sure*.
		K'O⁵. [person.
磕	磕頭	to *knock* one's head on the ground to a
碼	山路磕絆大	on mountain roads the *obstacles* are great.
		MA³.
	法碼	the *weights* of a balance. [or shoes).
	好長的尺碼	what is the size, or *measure*, (of garments
	碼字	*figures*.
	打碼號	*number* them.
碾		NIEN³.
	碾米	to *hull* rice.
	碾甘蔗	to *crush* sugar cane between rollers.
	碾輥子	a mill roller.
	碾房	a mill. [medicines.
	藥碾子	an iron trough and wheel for powdering

(372)

注 释

【嘴巴零碎】说话唠叨。

碉 [tiao¹]

碇 [tin⁴]

【下碇】放下锚。指船只停泊或靠码头。

碓 [tuei⁴]

【碓窝】用石头做成的舂米的器具。

【水碓】又称"机碓"、"水捣器"、"翻车碓"、"斗碓"或"鼓碓"、"水碓",一种舂米用具。

碗 [uan³]

碰 [pʰoŋ⁴]

碟 [tie⁵]

確(确) [tɕʰio⁵]

磕 [kʰo⁵]

【山路磕绊大】磕绊大:不好走。

碼(码) [ma³]

【码字】数字。

【打码号】计数。

碾 [ȵien³]

【药碾子】中医碾药用的工具,由铁制的碾槽和像车轮的碾盘组成。

注　释

磉 [saŋ³]
【磉凳】柱下的石磴凳子。
磋 [tsʰo¹]
【他磋磨我】磋磨：考验。
磁 [tsʰɿ²]
【磁器】同"瓷器"。
碜（硶）[tsʰən³]
【牙碜碜的】碜：食物里夹着沙子。
磚（砖）[tṣuan¹]
磬 [tɕʰin⁴]
磨 [mo²] [mo⁴]
磺 [xuaŋ²]
磽（硗）[ɕiao¹]
磹 [ṣan⁴]
【白磹泥】"磹"，古同"墡"。白土。

石 10-12

磉	SANG³.	[rest.
磋	磉凳	the *plinths* on which the posts of a house
磁	TS'O¹.	
	他磋磨我	he *grinds* me down; he *oppresses* me.
11	TSʻĬ².	
碜	磁器	*Chinaware*; *porcelain*.
磚	磁石	*loadstone*.
磬	TS'EN³.	
磨	牙碜碜的	*gritty*, as sand in food.
	CHUAN¹.	
		same as 磚.
	CH'IN⁴.	
		[ping idols.
	敲磬	to strike the *inverted bell* when worship-
	MO².	
	打磨光生	*polish* it well.
	刀鈍石頭磨	⎫ a blunt knife may be *sharpened* on a stone,
	人蠢沒奈何	⎭ but if a man is stupid there is no help for it.
	磨墨	to *rub* ink on an inkslab. [carrying pole.
	把肩膀磨痛了	I have *rubbed* my shoulder sore with the
	磋磨人	to *test* a man with a difficult job.
	READ MO⁴.	
	手磨	a hand-*mill*; a *quern*.
12	HUANG².	[brimstone.
磺	放磺烟	to make a dense yellow smoke by burning
磽	SHIAO¹.	
磹	地土磽薄	the soil is *barren* or *poor*, and shallow.
	SHAN⁴.	
	白磹泥	a kind of *white* porcelain *clay*.

(373)

西蜀方言

石 14-15　示 1-4

14 礙 NGAI⁴.

礙難	a *hindrance*. [thing?
有妨礙沒有	is there any *objection* to my saying some-
有些礙口	there are *restraints* on my speech.

15 礮 P'AO⁴.　same as 砲.

攀 FAN².

青礬	*sulphate of iron*.
白礬	*alum*. [with *alum*.
礬連泗	a fine white paper which has been treated

礦 KONG³.

| 鐵礦 | *iron ore*. |

READ KUANG³.

| 礦子灰 | *unslaked lime* ; *fresh lime in the lump*. |

The 113th radical. (示)

示 SHÏ⁴.

請官出示	ask the official to issue a *proclamation*.
大老爺分示的	the magistrate *ordered* it.
求你指示	please *point it out* to me ; please *explain*.
打手示	to make *signs* on the fingers.

礼 LI³.　same as 禮.

社 SHE⁴.

| 社稷壇 | an altar to *Earth*, or the *Gods of the Land*. |
| 春社 | a spring festival when the people worship at the tombs (May 16). |

祀 SÏ⁴.

| 祀祖先 | to *sacrifice* to ancestors. |
| 春秋的祭祀 | *sacrifices* in spring and autumn. |

祈 CH'I².

| 祈求 | to *beseech*. |

(374)

注 释

祝 [tṣu⁵]
神 [ṣən²]
祟 [suei⁴]
祖 [tsu³]
祠 [tsʰɿ²]
票 [pʰiao⁴]
【差票子】旧时地方官派差役传人的凭证。
【钱票子】纸币。
【银票子】银行汇票。
【票号】旧时指山西商人所经营的钱庄，以汇兑为主要业务。也叫"票庄"。
祧 [tʰiao⁴]
【一子双祧】祧：承继先代。俗称"两房合一子"，旧时大家族中一子继承两家。
祥 [siaŋ²]
【没祥】犹不祥，没有好处。
祭 [tsi⁴]
【烧牙祭】做丰盛的饭食。

示 5-6

5

CHU⁵.
祝壽　　　I *wish* you many happy returns of the day [(birthday).

SHEN².
敬神　　　to worship *gods*.
小神子　　the *fairies*; a pettish person.
家神　　　the domestic *divinities* whose names are written upon a sheet of paper.
家鬼弄家神　strife in the family.
神主牌　　the *spirit* tablet.
心神不安　not in good *spirits*; out of sorts.

SUE⁴.
野鬼作祟　an evil spirit is bringing *calamity* upon us.

TSU³.
敬祖宗　　to worship *ancestors*.
祖業田地　the *ancestral* estate.
我們的家祖　our *grandfather*.

TSʼƗ².
楊家祠堂　the *ancestral* hall of the Iang family.

6

PʼIAO⁴.
差票子　　a policeman's *warrant* to arrest a person.
錢票子　　a cash *ticket*.
銀票子　　a bank *draft*.
票號　　　a bank.

TʼIAO⁴.
一子雙祧　a son who *inherits* the estates of both father [and uncle.

SIANG².
這個兆頭不祥　this omen is un*lucky*.
沒祥　　　no *good*; worth*less*; un*desirable*.

TSI⁴.
祭物　　　*sacrifices*.
燒牙祭　　to give meat to servants on the 2nd and [the 16th of each moon.

(375)

示 8-13

8 禁 CHIN⁴.
禁止宰殺	to *forbid* the slaughter of animals as during a drought.
三尺禁地	three feet of *forbidden* ground outside city [walls.
禁子頭	a *jailor*.

9 祿 LU⁵.
| 喫俸祿 | to receive government *pay*. |
| 他的衣祿好 | his *income* is good. |

10 稟 PIN³.
稟官	to *state* a case to an official.
稟帖	a *petition*; a *statement* of a case.
稟性	*temperament*.

11 福 FU⁵.
| 福不在財多
財多不是福
福在子孫賢
子孫賢是福 | true *happiness* consists not in great wealth, great wealth is not true *happiness*, *happiness* depends on your children being virtuous, when children are virtuous that is *happiness*. |
| 受福氣 | to enjoy *good fortune*. |

12 禍 HO⁴.
福來要曉得接 禍來要曉得避	when good comes be prepared to receive it, but when *evil* comes be wise to avoid it.
把禍根除脫	to root out the cause of *misery*.
惹天禍	to bring a *judgment* on one's self.

13 禪 SHAN².
| 禪師 | a Buddhist priest; lit., one who *meditates*. |

禮 LI³.
家無常禮	the ordinary *etiquette* is not practised in [the family circle.
沒禮信的人	a person with no *manners*.
送個禮信	to give a *present*.
禮房	the Board of *Rites* in a yamên.
脈禮	*fees* to a doctor for diagnosing a case.

(376)

注 释

禁 [tɕin⁴]
【禁子头】狱卒。

禄(祿) [lu⁵]
【他的衣禄好】衣禄：即俸禄，指收入。

稟 [pin³]

福 [fu⁵]

祸(禍) [xo⁴]
【惹天祸】闯了大祸。

禅(禪) [ʂan²]

礼(禮) [li³]
【没礼信的人】礼信：礼仪，礼节。
【送个礼信】礼信：礼物。
【礼房】明清时知县衙门办理祭祀、考试等事务的下属机关。
【脉礼】诊费的敬称。

注释

祷（祷）[tao³]
禳[zaŋ²]
【请端工禳解】请巫师祈祷消除灾殃。
【禳星拜斗】礼拜北斗星，祈祷消除灾殃。
禽[tɕʰin²]
禾[xo²]
秀[siəu⁴]
私[sɿ¹]
【打私娃子】人工流产私生子。
秃[tʰu⁵][tʰo⁵]
秉[pin³]

示 14-17　禸 8　禾 2-3

14
祷
17
禳

TAO³.
祷告　　　　to *pray*.

RANG².
请端工禳解　invite a sorcerer to *beseech the gods* to avert [calamity.
禳星拜斗　　to *worship* the Northern Bushel.
没得一点禳解　there is no *abatement* in the terms.

The 114th radical. (禸)

8
禽

CH'IN².
禽兽　　　　*birds* and *beasts*.

The 115th radical. (禾)

禾
2
秀
私

HO².
禾苗茂盛　　the *young rice* is growing well; the *braird* [is good.

SIU⁴.
长得俊秀　　a *handsome* person.
秀才　　　　a *graduate*; B.A.; lit., *cultivated* talents.

SĪ¹.
我有点私事　I have a *private* affair to attend to.
打私交　　　to do business with.
起私心　　　to act *selfishly*.
私欲　　　　*secret* lusts.
私盐　　　　*smuggled* salt.
打私娃子　　to destroy *illegitimate* children (the in- [variable rule).

秃
3
秉

T'U⁵, T'O⁵.
秃子　　　　a *bald-headed* person.

PIN³.
秉公办理　　to *maintain* righteous principles.

(377)

禾 3-5

SIEN¹.
秈米　　ordinary rice as distinguished from "ho³ [mi."

TIAO⁴.
穀豹豹兒　　ripe ears of rice.
蔴柳豹豹兒　　pendant seed pods of the "hemp willow."

K'O¹.
科場　　the examination of "siu-ts'ai" for "chü-ren" degree.
科派人家　　to extort money for many things, as runners do.
內外科　　medical and surgical practice.
眼科　　an eye-specialist.

P'I³.
秕壳　　unfilled husks of rice.

TS'IU¹.
秋天　　autumn.
秋分　　the autumnal equinox.
秋收　　the harvest.

CH'EN⁴.
一把秤　　a steelyard.
一秤杠炭　　10 lbs. of charcoal.

TSU¹.
收租喫飯　　to live on the rents of one's property.
租房子　　to rent a house.
壓租　　the deposit money on house or land.
租牛　　to hire an ox.

IANG¹.
秧田　　the seed field in which the young rice is raised.
秧毡　　mattress made of young rice.
菜秧子　　seedling plants of vegetables.
樹秧子　　young trees.

(378)

注　释

秈 [sien¹]
豹 [tiao⁴]
【谷豹豹儿】稻穗。
【蔴柳豹豹儿】豹豹：穗状物。
科 [kʰo¹]
【科派人家】科派：谓摊派力役、赋税或索取（钱财）。
秕 [pʰi³]
秋 [tsʰiəu¹]
秤 [tʂʰən⁴]
租 [tsu¹]
【压租】押金。
秧 [iaŋ¹]
【秧毡】嫩谷穗制成的软床垫。

注 释

移 [i²]
程 [tʂʰən²]
【程色银子】程色：成色。含有一定合金比例的银子。
稀 [ɕi¹]
程（秆）[kan³]
稍 [ʂao¹]
【某人出的稍】稍：资本，资金。
税 [ʂuei⁴]
【过税】纳税。

禾 6-7

6 移 I².

移開些	*move* it out of the way a little.
你遷移在甚麼地方	where have you *removed* to? where do you live now?
把東西移出去	*remove* your furniture.
辦移文	a dispatch asking if a prisoner should be *transferred* to his native place.
辦移交	to *hand over* or *transfer* a charge to one's successor.
請老爺移縣	I appeal (from the "T'in") to the "Shien" [magistrate.
沒得趲移	there can be no *change* made; unalterable.
許人一物千金不移	when your word is given let not untold wealth *alter* it.

7 程 CH'EN².

有好多路程	how long is the *road*? how far is it? [fore him.
他是甚麼前程	what is his degree? lit., the *road* that lies be-
工程浩大	the *work* is great, as building a house.
定個章程	to lay down *rules*.
程色銀子	silver with a *certain percentage of alloy*.

稀 SHI¹.

不稀不密	neither *sparse* (or wide) nor crowded.
這個布織得稀	this cloth is *loosely* woven.
弄稀點	make it *thinner*, as porridge.
稀飯	congee.
稀泥巴	mire.
路稀爛	the road is very *muddy*.

秆 KAN³.

菜子秆	the *dried stems* of the oil plant.

稍 SHAO¹.

稍稍喫得一點飯	he can eat but *very little* food.
某人出的稍	a certain person supplied the *capital*.

税 SHUE⁴.

過税	to *pay duty* on.
税契	to *pay dues* on a legal document.

(379)

禾 8-10

8 稠 CH'EO².

人稠地密	densely populated.
稠湯	to thicken soup.
稠水	kitchen slops.

稜 LEN².

| 三稜子的柴花子 | a piece of firewood with three edges. |

稞 K'O¹.

| 青稞 | a kind of wheat. |

稗 PAI⁴.

| 稗子 | tares. |

9 稱 CH'EN¹.

那麼稱呼他	[should we address him. what name should we call him by? how
稱讚	to commend; to praise.
稱炭	to weigh coal on the steelyard.

READ CH'EN⁴.

| 不稱意 | it does not suit my mind. |

種 CHONG³.

| 撒穀種 | to sow rice seed. |
| 這又是一種 | this is a different kind or species. |

READ CHONG⁴.

| 種蔴得蔴種荳得荳 | if you sow hemp, you will reap hemp; if you sow beans, you will reap beans. Gal. vi. 7. |
| 泥色孬不出種 | the soil is bad; it will not produce a crop. |

10 稨 PIEN³.

| 稨荳 | a thin broad kind of runner bean. |

稿 KAO³.

稿薦	a straw mattress.
草個稿稿	write out a rough draft of anything.
稿爺	a military official's secretary.

(380)

注 释

稠 [tʂʰəu²]
稜 [lən²]
【三稜子的柴花子】稜子：指物体的边角。柴花子：木柴。
稞 [kʰo¹]
稗 [pai⁴]
稱(称) [tʂʰən¹] [tʂʰən⁴]
種(种) [tʂoŋ³] [tʂoŋ⁴]
稨 [pien³]
【稨豆】扁豆。
稿 [kao³]
【稿荐】稻草编的垫子。
【稿爷】军官的秘书。

注 释

稽 [tɕi¹]
稼 [tɕia¹] [tɕia⁴]
【今年庄稼出重】出重：丰收。
穀（谷）[ku⁵]
【包谷】玉米。
稷 [tsi⁵]
穈 [mi²]
積（积）[tsi⁵] [tsie⁵]
穢（秽）[xuei⁴] [uei⁴]
【秽气秽气】形容难闻的味道，或难听的话。
穩（稳）[uən³]
穪 [ie⁵]
【穪米米】有点瘪不饱满的果仁。
【打穪了气】无精打采的。

禾 10-14

CHI¹.
稽察來歷不明的人 } examine suspicious characters.
我在那個地方稽留了幾天 } I was *detained* a few days at that place.

CHIA¹, ⁴.
今年莊稼出重 *farming* is good this year.

KU⁵.
五穀雜糧 all kinds of *grain* and pulse.
穀子 *rice* in the ear; also, the *grain before it is hulled*.
包穀 *maize*.

TSI⁵.
江山社稷 the whole empire with the gods thereof. [(*Earth and her products*)].

MI².
穈子 a small variety of *millet*.

TSI⁵, TSIE⁵.
堆積 to *pile up*; to *accumulate*.
積土成山積水成河 } *heaped* up soil becomes a mountain, *accumulated* waters become a river.

HUE⁴, UE⁴.
污穢 *filth*.
穢氣穢氣 what a *vile* smell! what *obscene* talk!

UEN³.
桌子不穩 the table is not *steady*.
站不穩 he cannot stand *firmly*.
那個事怕不穩當 I am afraid that affair is not *safe*, or reliable.
話說三道穩篾綑三道緊 } a thrice told tale is true, a thrice twined tie is tight.
耍得穩重 he acts in a *decorous* manner.

IE⁵.
穪米米 *undeveloped* seeds of grain or pulse.
打穪了氣 knocked *insensible*.

(381)

穴 2-4

The 116th radical. (穴)

SHIE⁵.

| 不入虎穴焉得虎子 | if you do not enter the tiger's *den* how can you catch her cubs. |
| 買一穴地 | to buy ground for a grave. (*N. A.*) |

CHIU⁴.

講究	*proper* or *thorough* in etiquette or surroundings; *conventional*. [unconventional.
不講究	to dispense with form; to set no store by;
沒講究的人	an ill-bred fellow. [case.
請官追究	ask the official to proceed to *investigate* the
究竟是怎樣	*after all* how is it?

K'ONG¹.

| 打空手 | to go *empty* handed. |
| 空中 | the *vault of heaven*; the *sky*. |

READ K'ONG⁴.

空¹口說空⁴話	an *empty*¹ mouth speaks *idle*⁴ words.
樟子是空起的	the table is *not in use*.
不得空	I cannot find *leisure*.
找個空地方	find a *vacant* space.
身不空	enceinte.
銀錢空乏	my money is *exhausted*.

CH'UAN¹.

鑽穿了	it is bored *through*.
把錢穿起	*string* the cash.
穿針	to *thread* a needle.
穿連子	rats.
看穿了	to see *through* a matter.
穿透事	to *negotiate* business.
穿了幾個眼	the sore has *broken out* in several places.
穿衣裳	to *wear* clothes, i. e., such as the head or the limbs are put *through*.

注 释

穴 [ɕie⁵]
【买一穴地】穴地: 坟地。
究 [tɕiəu⁴]
空 [kʰoŋ¹] [kʰoŋ⁴]
【身不空】怀孕。
穿 [tʂʰuan¹]
［穿透事］谈生意。

注释

窃 [tsʰie⁵]
穽（阱）[tsin³]
　【打金穽】金阱：墓穴或骨瓮。挖一个坟墓。
窌（窖）[kao⁴]
窄 [tse⁵]
　【银钱窄逼】钱快用完了。
怱（窗）「tsʰaŋ¹」「tʂʰuaŋ¹」
　【戴个窗窗】戴一副眼镜。
窗 [tsʰaŋ¹]「tʂʰuaŋ¹」
窖 [kao⁴]
　【疮窖口了】疮愈合了。
　【事情窖不倒口】事情完成不了。
窣 [so⁵][sio⁵]
窟 [kʰu⁵]
窨 [in⁴]
　【地窨子】地窖,地下室。
　【窨酒】在地窖里藏过的酒。指陈酒。
窝（窩）[o¹]
　【一窝花】窝：量词。英文译义应为：a cluster of flowers.

穴 4-9

窃	TS'IE⁵.	same as 竊.
穽	TSIN³.	
打金穽		to dig a *grave*.
⁵窌	KAO⁴.	same as 窖.
窄	TSE⁵.	
路窄		the road is *narrow*.
這個房子窄		this house is *small*.
銀錢窄逼		money is *scarce*. [*narrow*.
心頭想得窄		his experience is *limited*; his plans are
⁶怱	TS'ANG¹, CH'UANG¹.	
怱子		a *window*.
天怱眼		a *skylight* made by arching the tiles.
戴個怱怱		to wear *spectacles*.
窗	TS'ANG¹, CH'UANG¹.	same as last.
⁷窖	KAO⁴.	
地窖		a *cellar*; an underground *storehouse*.
窖紅苕		to *pit* or *store* sweet potatoes.
瘡窖口了		the sore is *healed up*.
事情窖不倒口		the transaction cannot be *completed*.
窣	SO⁵, SIO⁵.	for example of use see 窸.
⁸窟	K'U⁵.	
打地窟寵		to dig a *hole* under a wall, as a thief does.
⁹窨	IN⁴.	
地窨子		a *cellar*. [*cellar*.
窨酒		old wine; wine that has been stored in a
窩	O¹.	
燕子窩		a swallow's *nest*.
一窩猪兒		a *litter* of pigs. (*N. A.*)
一窩花		one flowering plant. (*N. A.*)

穴 9-11

心窩子	the *hollow* on the breast-bone.
挾腳窩	the *arm-pits*.
銀窩子	a *mould* for casting silver ingots.
鐵窩子	a small iron *mortar*.
燈窩子	a small native lamp.
挖窩窩	scoop out a small *hollow*.
窩起的	concave.
轉窩子	the *offspring* of parents of different coun-tries or provinces.
私窩子	a secret *brothel*.
窩戶	a *resetter*.
窩盜	to *harbour* thieves.
窩贓	to *receive* stolen property.

10 窮 CH'IONG².

窮要窮得硬健 餓要餓得新鮮	if you are *poor*, be independent; and if you are hungry, don't show it.
貧窮的人	a *destitute* person.
無有窮盡	without *limit*; inexhaustable.
我把他問窮了	I questioned him till he was speechless, or at his wit's end.

窰 IAO².

甎瓦窰	a brick *kiln*.
窰貨圈子	a *pottery* yard.
逛窰子	to frequent a *brothel*.

11 窸 SI⁵.

窸窸䆒䆒	a *rustling* sound.

窺 K'UE¹.

窺看	to *spy* out.

寫 TIAO⁴.

衣裳寫角	the corner of the garment *projects* too much.
寫了一隻角在他業內	my land *juts* into his property.
寫做	to farm land at some distance from one's dwelling.
離城寫遠	a *long distance* from the city.

(384)

注 释

【转窝子】父母不同乡或省，其后代被称为"转窝子"。
【私窝子】隐密的妓院。
窮（穷）[tɕʰioŋ²]
窰（窑）[iao²]
【窑货圈子】陶器厂子。
【逛窑子】逛妓院。
窸 [si⁵]
窺（窥）[kʰuei¹]
寫（鸢）[tiao⁴]
【衣裳寫角】衣角凸起。
【寫做】到离自己住处很远的地方劳作。
【离城寫远】距离城市很远。

注释

竅(窍)[tɕʰiao⁴]
竄(窜)[tsʰuan⁴]
【味道竄】味道浓重。
窿(窿)[loŋ²]
【他的窟窿太多】窟窿：负债,亏空。
竈(灶)[tsao⁴]
【打灶】用砖石砌成灶台。
【井灶】四川、云南等地煎制井盐的工场。
竊(窃)[tsʰie⁵]
立[li⁵][lie⁵]
竒(奇)[tɕʰi²]
站[tʂan⁴]
【站倒】倒：表示状态的持续。站着。

穴 13-17 立 4-5

13 竅	CH'IAO⁴.	
	一竅不通	not one of his *heart holes* is open; very [stupid.
	訣竅	the *key* to a parable; the *solution* of a difficulty.
竄	TS'UAN⁴.	
	逃竄	to escape and go *into hiding*.
	味道竄	the flavour is *strong*, or *penetrating*.
16 窿	LONG².	
	你有天大的窟窿 我有地大的補釘	though you have a *hole* as large as heaven, I have a patch as big as the earth.
	他的窟窿太多	he has got into *scrapes* all round.
竈	TSAO⁴.	
	打竈	to build a *cooking-range*.
	竈房	a kitchen.
	井竈	salt*pans*.
17 竊	TS'IE⁵.	
	偷竊	to *thieve*.

The 117th radical. (立)

立	LI⁵, LIE⁵.	
	立碑	to *set up* a stone tablet.
	立起的	*standing upright*.
	都成立了	they are all *grown up* now.
	立規矩	to *establish* a custom.
	立約據	to *settle and write out* an agreement.
	立後嗣	to *adopt* a son.
	立定主意	*make up* your mind; *determine* on a course [of action.
	立刻	*immediately*.
4 竒	CH'I².	same as 奇.
5 站	CHAN⁴.	
	站起來	*stand* up.
	站倒	*stand* still.

(385)

立 5-9

在那裏站	where are you *lodging*?	
站客	to *lodge* people.	
站房	an inn.	
四季荳站站	*stakes* for kidney beans.	
一站路	a *stage*; a day's journey. (*N. A.*)	
PIN⁴.	same as 並.	
CHANG¹.		
文章	an *essay*.	
一章書	a *chapter* of a book.	
圖章	a *seal*.	
CHIN⁴.		
他竟自去了	he *finally* went off in spite of me.	
他竟不曉得	*after all* he did not know.	
SONG³.		
竦動人心	to *excite* people's minds.	
毛骨竦然	*horrified*.	
長行咳咳竦竦的	continually *coughing* and *shaking*.	
T'ONG².		
童子娃兒	a *boy*.	
童生	a *young student*.	
童貞女	Roman Catholic *nuns*.	
CHÜIN⁴.		
工完告竣	to report the *completion* of a work.	
CHIE⁵.		
盡心竭力	to *exert* all one's mind and strength.	
TUAN¹.		
筆竿端	as *straight* as a pencil.	
端走	go *straight forward*.	
樹子端正	this tree is *straight*, or *upright*.	
端飯來	*bring* some rice!	

注 释

【站客】安置客人入住客栈。

【站房】驿站。古时专供传递文书者或来往官吏中途住宿、补给、换马的处所。

【四季豆站站】立在地上支撑云豆植物的棍子。

竝（并）[pin⁴]

章 [tṣaŋ¹]

竟 [tɕin⁴]

竦 [soŋ³]

【长行咳咳竦竦的】一直不停地咳嗽且浑身抖动。

童 [tʰoŋ²]

【童贞女】天主教中的修女。

竣 [tɕyn⁴]

竭 [tɕie⁵]

端 [tuan¹]

【笔杆端】像笔杆一样直。

注 释

【摆端】安排妥当。
【看他怎样开端】看他怎么样打开这个物体。
【端工】也作"端公",以装神弄鬼、替人祈祷为职业的男巫。
竹 [tṣu⁵] [tṣo⁵]
竿 [kan¹]
【吃竿叶子烟】用烟筒抽一口烟。
笆 [pa¹]
【编笆子】编竹席。
笑 [siao⁴]
笋 [sən²]
符 [fu²]

立 9 竹 3-5

品行端方	his conduct is *upright*.
擺端	to arrange *properly*.
看他怎樣開端	see how he opens the *subject*.
異端邪說	heterodox *subjects*.
端工	a sorcerer.

The 118th radical. (竹)

竹 CHU⁵, CHO⁵.

| 竹子 | *bamboos*. |
| 竹筒筒 | a *bamboo* tube. |

竿 KAN¹.

竹竿子	bamboo *poles*.
釣魚竿	a fishing *rod*.
菸竿	a pipe *stem*.
喫竿葉子菸	to smoke a *pipe* of tobacco. [cattle driver].
掌竿竿	a pettifogger; (lit., to hold the *stick* like a

笆 PA¹.

編笆子	to make *bamboo* mats.
夾籬笆	to make *fence*. [bed.
床笆子	the bamboo *frame* on the bottom of a coolie

笑 SIAO⁴.

莫笑我	don't *laugh* at me!
實在好笑	*laugh*able.
賠個笑臉	to put a *smiling* face on the matter.
他們在說笑	they are *jesting*.
冷笑	to *sneer*.
惹人笑罵	to provoke people to *ridicule*.

笋 SEN³.

| 笋子 | bamboo *sprouts*. |
| 蒿笋 | lettuce *stalks*. |

符 FU².

| 前言要符後語 | what you said before and what you say [now ought to *agree*. |

(387)

西蜀方言

竹 5-6

笠	筆跡不符	the writing is not like his writing.
笨	畫符	to write a charm.
	LI⁵, LIE⁵.	
	斗笠	a bamboo rain-hat worn by coolies.
	PEN⁴.	
	蠢笨	stupid.
	穿多了是笨的	if you have too many clothes on, you are awkward at work. [fellow.
	生得粗笨	he has grown up awkward; a big ungainly
第	做得笨	clumsily made.
	TI⁴.	
	有次第	in regular order; there is a sequence.
	第一好	first-class (denotes the ordinal).
	第一個字	the first character.
	大夫第	the residence of an official family.
箈	**T'IAO².** [W. Sï-ch'uan).
笛	箈篲	a broom (a name used in mountains of
6	**TI⁵, TIE⁵.**	
筏	吹笛子	to play the flute.
筋	**P'A².**	
	紮筏子	to make a raft.
	CHIN¹.	
	鹿筋	deer sinews.
	筋力大	his strength is great.
	腳轉筋	cramp in the legs. [it.
	紙筋 or 草筋	paper or grass used in plaster to strengthen
	太陽筋痛	my temples ache.
	扯筋	to scold, wrangle or quarrel. [road.
	筋絆絆的	bickering, as coolies behaving badly on the
筐	**K'UANG¹, CH'IANG¹.**	
	提筐子	a hand-basket.
	籮筐	large baskets for carrying grain.
	一筐綫	a hank of thread. (N. A.)

(388)

注 释

笠 [li⁵] [lie⁵]

笨 [pən⁴]

【穿多了是笨的】衣服穿太多了干活会笨拙，不方便。

第 [ti⁴]

【大夫第】封建社会官僚贵族的大宅子。

箈 [tʰiao²]

笛 [ti⁵] [tie⁵]

筏 [pʰa²]

筋 [tɕin¹]

【脚转筋】转筋：抽筋。

【太阳筋痛】太阳筋：太阳穴。

【筋绊绊的】事情不顺利，理不清。

筐 [kʰuaŋ¹] [tɕʰiaŋ¹]

注 释

笄 [tɕi¹]
 【年已及笄了】笄,同"筓"。及笄：古时指女子十五岁可以盘发插笄的年龄，即已经成年可以婚嫁了。
筆（笔）[pi⁵]
筍（笋）[sən³]
答 [ta⁵]
等 [tən³]
 【等做一路】结伴一起走。
筒 [tʰoŋ²]
 【诗筒】也作"诗筩"。一种竹制文房用具，用于插放诗笺或书籍。
策 [tsʰe⁵]
筧（笕）[tɕien³]
 【做个筧】筧：横安在屋檐上承接雨水的长竹管。

竹 6-7

CHI¹.
| 年已及笄了 | she is now of *marriageable* age. |

PI⁵.
一枝筆	a *pencil*; a *pen*.
親筆寫的	written with one's own hand.
筆直的走	walk *straight* on.
好筆墨	good *composition*.
寫一筆賬	write out an account. (*N. A.*)

SEN³.
same as 笄.

TA⁵.
| 他不答應 | he will not *answer*; he will not *agree* to the [bargain. |
| 答不出來 | unable to *reply* to a question. |

TEN³.
一切等等	all *sorts* of things.
不是等閒的人	he is not the same as an *ordinary* person.
等做一路	*wait* and let us go together.
不等他哭	don't *allow* him to cry.

T'ONG².
筒車	a wheel fitted with bamboo *tubes* for raising [water.
吹火筒	a blow *pipe* for blowing the fire.
筆筒	a pencil *point* protector.
花筒	fireworks.
鑲鐵筒子	a tin *canister*.
詩筒	the smallest size *envelopes*.
樹子要鋸兩筒	cut the tree into two *lengths*.

TS'E⁵.
| 請你幫我畫個策 | help me to think of a *plan*. |

CHIEN³.
| 做個筧 | make a *gutter* on the edge of the roof. |
| 筧筒 | a bamboo *water pipe* or *spout* from the roof to the ground. |

(389)

竹 7-8

箔　　P'A².
箔箔兒　　a bamboo *rake*.
線箔子　　a frame for winding thread on.
箔兒哥　　a thief.

　　SHAO¹.
筲箕　　a *basket* used to strain rice.

　　SUAN⁴.　same as 算.

　　T'ONG³.
箭筒　　a *quiver*.
蜂筒　　a bee-*hive*.
書筒子　　large red *envelopes* for invitation cards.

　　IEN².
筵席　　a *feast*.

　　TSEN¹.
放風箏　　to fly *kites*.

　　CHEO³.
掃箒　　a *broom*.
蚊箒子　　a mosquito *switch*.

　　CHI¹.
簸箕　　a large winnowing *basket*.

　　KO⁴.　same as 個.

　　K'U¹.
箍箍　　bamboo *hoops*.
菜箍　　oil *cake*.
一箍　　as large round as a *circle formed by the* [thumb and forefinger.
戒箍子　　a finger *ring*.
把他箍緊點　　rule the child more strictly; *hoop* the tub [tightly.
箍脚盆　　to *hoop* a tub.

　　CHA⁵.
在那裏駐劄　　where do you *lodge*?

(390)

注 释

笆 [pʰa²]
【笆笆儿】搂柴草的竹制器具。
【笆儿哥】小偷。
筲 [ʂao¹]
【筲箕】一种盛饭用的竹筐。
筭（算）[suan⁴]
筩（筒）[tʰoŋ³]
【书筒子】专门用来装邀请函的大红信封。
筵 [ien²]
筝（筝）[tsən¹]
箒（帚）[tʂəu³]
箕 [tɕi¹]
箇（个）[ko⁴]
箍（箍）[kʰu¹]
【菜箍】（饲养牲畜的）油渣饼。
【戒箍子】戒指。
劄 [tʂa⁵]
【在那里驻劄】驻劄，同"驻扎"。

注释

管 [kuan³]
【管带兵了】("了"当为"的",见803页勘误表。)
【把他管不倒】我管不了他。
【经管匠人】负责管理工人,即监管。
算 [suan⁴]
箋(笺) [tsien¹]
【花粉箋】装饰用的墙纸。
箸 [tṣu⁴]
築(筑) [tṣu⁵]
【鼻子筑了气】鼻子堵住了。
【筑倒脚】落地太猛以致脚扭伤。

竹 8-9

管

KUAN³.
翎管子 — the *tube* on an official hat into which the [feather is stuck.
筆管子 — a pencil *point protector*.
管帶兵了 — to *command* troops.
四川管的 — *governed* by Sï-ch'uan.
當總管 — to act as an *overseer*.
把他管不倒 — I cannot *control* him.
不管他的 — I do not *manage* his affairs, never mind [him.
只管做 — just *make it your business* to do it; never mind anything else. [of hearing.
耳朶不管事 — my ears do not do their work; I am dull
管事的人 — a *manager*.
狗不管事 — the dog is *useless*.
經管匠人 — to *oversee* workmen.
管得一兩年 — it will *last* a year or two.
扯過收管 — to get a *receipt*.

算

SUAN⁴.
算盤 — an *abacus*.
算法 — *arithmetic*.
算賬 — to *reckon* accounts; to dismiss a servant.
不上算 — it does not matter; of no *account*; futile.
這個不算好 — this does not *reckon* good; this is not the best.
算我錯 — *regard* it as my mistake.
算了就是 — there's an end of it then!
算命 — to tell *fortunes*.

箋

TSIEN¹.
花粉箋 — flowered *wall-paper*.

箸

CHU⁴.
動箸 — take up your *chopsticks* and begin (polite).
重用一箸 — take another *pinch* of food (polite).

築

CHU⁵.
築牆 — to *ram* an earth wall.
鼻子築了氣 — the nose *obstructed*.
築倒脚 — to *stub* the foot against anything, to *sprain* [the ankle.

(391)

西蜀方言

竹 9

FAN⁴.

說得圓範	well said; lit., said after a perfect *pattern*.
做得圓範	well done.
鬭不圓範	I cannot bring the affair to a happy con-[clusion.

CHUAN⁴.

篆字	*seal* characters.
官篆	your honourable *style*?

CHIA⁵.

線篋	a thread *case*.

P'IEN¹.

一篇書	a *leaf* of a book.

SIANG¹.

板箱	a wooden *box*.
皮箱	a leather *trunk*.
風箱	*bellows*.
豆腐箱	a *frame* in which bean-curd is set.

TSIE⁵.

節巴	*joints* in bamboo; *knots* in wood.
鋸一節下來	saw off a *piece*.
手指節	the *joints* of the fingers.
一節書	a *verse* of a book.
時節	a semi-lunar *period* of time.
過節	to keep a *festival*.
守節	to be *continent* after the death of a hus-[band.
節儉點	be more *economical*.

READ KE⁵.

節巴	*joints* in bamboo; *knots* in wood.
樹節樴	the *base of the trunk* of a tree.

TSIEN⁴.

指路不明猶如暗箭傷人	to direct one on the wrong road is like secretly shooting one with an *arrow*.
馬箭	mounted *archers*.
挿耳箭	to stick a small *dart* through the ears [(punishment).

(392)

注 釋

範（范）[fan⁴]
【斗不圓范】不能圆满完成任务。
篆 [tʂuan⁴]
篋（箧）[tɕia⁵]
【线箧】盛线用的纸夹。
篇 [pʰien¹]
箱 [siaŋ¹]
節（节）[tsie⁵] [ke⁵]
【树节樴】樴：指树木的根和靠近根部的茎。树干，即树木的主体部分，树身。
箭 [tsien⁴]
【马箭】骑射手。
【插耳箭】耳箭：旧时重犯示众时插在颈后耳旁的箭牌。

注释

篡 [tsʰuan⁴]
篙 [xao²]
篦（箆）[pi⁴]
　【箆虱子】将虱子梳掉。
紤 [la⁵]
　【紤篾】驯牛的竹条。
篩（筛）[ʂai⁴]
　【罗筛】细网筛。
　【筛灰面】灰面：面粉。
筬（筘）[kʰəu⁴]
　篓（篓）[ləu³]
篱 [li⁴]
　【篱子】即篱笆。
篾 [mie⁵] [mi⁵]
篷 [pʰoŋ²]
笯 [təu¹]
　【提笯】笯：盛东西用的竹器，也有用藤或柳条做成的。

竹 10-11

10　TS'UAN⁴.
篡位　　　　to *usurp* the throne.
　　HAO².
篙竿　　　　a *boat pole*.
　　PI⁴.
篦子　　　　a *fine toothed comb*.
牛篦子　　　a *curry-comb*.
篦虱子　　　to *comb* out lice.
　　LA⁵.
紤篾　　　　*bamboo ropes* used for harnessing oxen.
　　SHAI¹.
筛子　　　　a *riddle*.
羅筛　　　　a hair *sieve*.
筛石灰　　　to *riddle* lime.
筛灰麵　　　to *sift* flour.
11　K'EO⁴.
　　　　　　　　　　　　　[regular order).
絲絲入筬　　every thread goes through the *reed* (met.,
　　LEO³.
　　　　　　　　　　　　　[with paper.
油篓子　　　an oil *basket* made of bamboo and covered
　　LI⁴.
　　　　　　　　　　　　　[celli.
篱子　　　　a bamboo *ladle*, used when cooking vermi-
　　MIE⁵, MI⁵.
篾條　　　　*split bamboo*.
篾匠　　　　a *bamboo-mat maker*.
　　P'ONG².
天篷　　　　*mat* for the ceiling of a room.
船篷　　　　*mat roof* of a boat.
涼篷　　　　*mat awning*.
蓮篷　　　　the *seed-pod* of the lotus.
　　TEO¹.
提笯　　　　a hand *basket*.

竹 11-13

12 簡	坐箯子	a mountain *chair*.
	一箯白菜	one *head* of cabbage. (*N. A.*)
	CHIEN³.	
	簡慢你	I have been *negligent to* you (polite).
	他做事簡便	he does things *quickly*, i. e., *off-hand*.
	簡直不說	to *curtly* shut up; I won't argue the matter.
	他簡直走了	he *straightway* departed.
簫	**SIAO¹.**	
	吹簫	to play on a *whistle*.
箪	**TAN¹.**	
	掛箪	to hang up the *food-basket*, i. e., a Buddhist [priest lodging at a temple.
簪	**TSAN¹.**	
	簪子	a broad *clasp* for the hair, worn by women.
	簪花掛紅	to *stick* flowers in a bridegroom's hat and tie a red sash round his shoulder.
	玉簪花	a liliaceous plant with white flowers—Pancratium?
簟	**TIEN⁴.**	
13	晒簟	a large *mat* for drying grain on.
簳	**KAN³.**	
	箭簳子	the *shaft* of an arrow.
簾	**LIEN².**	
	門簾子	a door *screen*.
	轎簾子	a chair *blind*.
	草簾子	a thin straw *mattress*.
簸	**PO³.**	
	簸米	to *winnow* rice.
	剩得些簸籮貨	I have only a few of the worst goods left.
	船簸得很	the boat *pitches* very much.
簿	**PU⁴.**	
	賬簿	an *account book*.

(394)

注 释

【坐箯子】箯子: 走山路坐的竹轿, 一般用竹椅捆在两根竹竿上做成。

【一箯白菜】一棵白菜。

簡(简) [tɕien³]

【簡慢你】簡慢: 多用作表示招待不周的谦词。

【他做事簡便】簡便: 快。

【簡直不說】簡直: 表示干脆如此, 相当于"索性"。

簫(箫) [siao¹]

箪(箪) [tan¹]

【挂箪】箪: 古代盛饭的圆竹器。

簪 [tsan¹]

簟 [tien⁴]

【晒簟】晒谷子的大席子。

簳 [kan³]

簾(帘) [lien²]

【草帘子】细草垫。

簸 [po³]

【剩得些簸籮货】簸籮货: 垫底货, 即品质差的货物。

簿 [pu⁴]

注 释

簽(签) [tsʰien¹] [tsʰien⁴]
【木头签了】木头裂开或粗糙,如未刨光的木材。
【签田】用锄头犁田。
【倒签皮】又称"倒刺"。指甲附近翘起的小片表皮。

簷(檐) [ien²]
【檐老鼠】蝙蝠。

籃(篮) [lan²]

籍 [tsie⁵]

籌(筹) [tsʰəu²]
【一根筹】筹:计数的用具,多用竹子制成。

籐(藤) [tʰən²]

籠(笼) [loŋ²] [loŋ³]

竹 13-16

簽

TS'IEN¹.   interchanged with 籖.   [papers.
簽押   to *sign* a document; a clerk who *stamps*
牙簽   a tooth-*pick*.

READ TS'IEN⁴.   [planed wood.
木頭簽了   the wood is *splintered*, or rough, as un-
簽田   to *break up* clods with a hoe.
簽箆子   to *clean* a comb with a pointed stick.

READ TS'IEN¹,⁴.   [finger nails.
倒簽皮   *agnail*; loose strips of skin behind the

簷 14

IEN².
屋簷   the *eaves* of a house.
來在矮簷下怎敢不低頭   when you come under low *eaves* why do you not bow your head?
簷老鼠   a bat.   [the top of mosquito curtains.
罩簷子   an embroidered piece of cloth hung along

籃

LAN².
菜籃   a vegetable *basket*.
搖籃   a baby's *cradle*.

籍

TSIE⁵.
書籍   *books*.
祖籍   one's *native place*.

籌 15

CH'EO².
一根籌   a *tally*.   [means.
先要籌個欵   we must first *deliberate* on the ways and

籐

T'EN².
籐籐   a general name for *creepers*.
筋剛籐圈子   bracelets made of a tough *creeper*.
籐床   a *cane*-bottomed bedstead.

籠 16

LONG².
鵲兒籠   a bird's *cage*.
雞籠   a chicken *coop*.

(395)

西蜀方言

竹 16-19

裝籠子	to confine a criminal in a *cage*.
燈籠	a *lantern*. [etc.
蒸籠	a *steamer* for steaming vegetables, meat,
牛嘴籠	an ox's *muzzle*.
把他嘴籠倒	*muzzle* it.
烤烘籠子	to warm one's self with a *fire-basket*.
籠鞋	a woman's *overshoes*.
手籠子	*mittens*.
籠哄人家	to *cheat* people.
一籠罩子	a *set* of bed curtains. (*N. A.*)

READ LONG³.

編竹籠	to plat very long bamboo *baskets* to retain [the river banks.
巴籠	a fisher's *creel*.
籠子	an *eel trap*.

17 籆 Ü⁴.

| 籆子 | a *bobbin*; a *spool*. |
| 籆線 | the *woof* of cloth. |

籤 TS'IEN¹.

interchanged with 签.

打籤子	to stick up a *slip of bamboo or wood* with a notice on it. [ing of the gods.
靈籤	*bamboo tallies* used in temples when inquir-
火籤	an urgent official *warrant*.
手上劃個籤子	a *splinter* has run into my hand.
籤子門	an onter gate of upright *slats* or *bars*.

19 籬 LI².

| 籬笆子 | a *fence*. |
| 籬壁 | lath and plaster *walls* of houses. |

籮 LO².

| 籮筻 | grain *baskets*. |
| 皮籮子 | a coarse, square *basket* with a cover, used for transporting goods. |

(396)

注 释

【装笼子】旧时惩罚囚禁犯人的一种方式。即把囚犯装到囚笼里。

【把他嘴笼倒】把他嘴套住(不让说话)。

【笼鞋】一种女式套鞋。

【手笼子】手套。

【笼哄人家】笼哄：欺骗。

【一笼罩子】一套床帷。

【巴笼】钓鱼人的鱼篮。

籆 [y⁴]

【籆子】线轴。

【籆线】织布中的纬线。

籤（签）[tsʰien¹]

【打签子】即做扦子。使竹片或木片成尖锐细长杆状物。

【灵签】卜具。

【火签】旧时官署紧急拘传人犯的一种签牌。

【签子门】直立式栅栏门，或一条条门板插入槽中组成的活门，旧时临街商铺常用。

籬（篱）[li²]

【篱壁】刷墙。

籮（箩）[lo²]

注 释

米 [mi³]
　【米沙沙】米粉。
　【桃子米米】桃核。
粉 [fən³]
　【襄王粉】漂白土。
　【粉蝶】白色的蝴蝶。
秒 [ʂa¹]
　【红秒糖】红蔗糖。
　【喂米秒秒】喂婴儿吃粥。
粘 [tʂan¹]
粒 [li⁵]
粗 [tsʰu¹]

米 4-5

The 119th radical. (米)

MI³.

買米	to buy *rice*, i. e., *hulled rice*.
米沙沙	ground *rice*; *rice* meal.
南瓜米	squash *seeds*.
豌豆米	shelled peas.
桃子米米	peach *stones*.
鰕米	shrimps.

FEN³.

花粉	*powder* used to paint the face.
粉條	vermicelli made from pea *flour*.
打的粉碎	broken to *fragments*.
襄王粉	fuller's-*earth* (first character read siang¹).
粉箋紙	paper for ceilings, *whitened* with fuller's-earth.
鉛粉	*white* lead.
粉板	a *white-painted* board for writing on.
粉紅	pink; lit., *white*-red.
粉壁牆	a *white-washed* wall.
粉蝶	*white* butterflies and millers.

SHA¹.

| 紅秒糖 | coarse brown *sugar*. |
| 喂米秒秒 | to feed an infant with rice meal *gruel*. |

CHAN¹.

| 拿漿子來粘起 | bring the paste and *paste* it. |
| 使膠來粘 | *stick* it together with glue; *glue* it. |

LI⁵.

| 一粒米 | one *grain* of rice. (*N. A.*) |

TS'U¹.

| 鍼線粗糙 | the needlework is *coarse*. |
| 粗中有細 | good properties under a *rough* exterior. |

(397)

米 5-9

	線要用粗點	use a *thicker* or *coarser* thread.
	粗心膽大	*rude* and *daring*.
	說話粗俗	*vulgar* in speech.
6 粧	**CHUANG¹.**	
	梳粧	to *dress*; used of women only.
	辦嫁粧	to prepare a bride's *trousseau*.
	假粧	to *pretend*.
粟	**SIO⁵.**	[for food.
	狗尾粟	a kind of *grass* cultivated in some parts
	ÜE⁵.	
粵	粵東人	*Cantonese* people.
7 粱	**LIANG².**	
	高粱	*millet*.
8 精	**TSIN¹.**	
	精兵	the *finest* troops.
	精細人	a *clever* and thorough man.
	遺精病	involuntary loss of *semen*.
	好精神	in good *spirits*.
	精痛	*very* painful.
粿	**KO³.**	
	糖粿子	*cakes*; *confections*.
粽 9	**TSONG⁴.**	[in leaves.
	粽子	*dumplings* made of glutinous rice wrapped
糊	**FU².**	
	漿糊	*paste*.
	裱糊房屋	to *paste* paper on the walls of a room.
	糊窗子	to *paper* a window.
	糊壁頭	to *plaster* a wall with mud or lime.
	糊裏糊塗的	*stupidly*; *carelessly*; *heedlessly*.
糍	**TS'Ï¹.**	
	糍巴	*cakes* of *glutinous* rice.

(398)

注　釋

粧（妆）[tṣuaŋ¹]
【假妆】假装。

粟 [sio⁵]
【狗尾粟】即粟，又称"小米"。

粵 [ye⁵]

粱 [liaŋ²]

精 [tsin¹]
【精痛】很痛。

粿 [ko³]
【糖粿子】一种由白糖和面粉做成的糕点。

粽 [tsoŋ⁴]

糊 [fu²]

糍 [tsʰɿ¹]
【糍巴】又称"糍粑"，糯米做的一种小吃。

注　释

糕 [kao¹]
糖 [tʰaŋ²]
糞（粪）[fən⁴]
糠 [kʰaŋ¹]
糟 [tsao¹] [tsʰao²]
【糟房】酒厂。
糙 [tsʰao⁴]
漿（浆）[tsiaŋ⁴]
【打一碗浆子】浆子：浆糊。
糧（粮）[liaŋ²]
【点粮食】播种谷物。
【吃粮】指参军（有配给的口粮）。

米 10-12

10 糕　KAO¹.

雞蛋糕	sponge *cakes*.
涼糕解渴	*blanc-mange* allays thirst.

糖　T'ANG².

白糖	white *sugar*.
花生糖	pea-nut *candy*.
糖涼水	*sugared* cold water used in hot weather.
蜂糖	*honey*.

11 糞　FEN⁴.

馬糞	horse *dung*.
糞塘	a *manure* pit.
灌糞	to *manure*.
糞草	*leaf-mould*.

糠　K'ANG¹.

米糠	*chaff* of rice.

糟　TSAO¹. [various ingredients.

醪糟	*freshly fermented glutinous rice* boiled with
酒糟	*draff*.
醋糟	*sediment* of vinegar.
亂糟糟的	*untidy; disorderly; confused*.
我的事情糟	my business is in a *muddle*.

READ TS'AO².

糟房	a *distillery*.

糙　TS'AO⁴.

米糙	the rice is *badly cleaned*.
做得粗糙	*coarsely* made; *clumsily* done.

漿　TSIANG⁴.

打一盆漿子	make a basin of *paste*.
打成漿漿	knocked into a *paste-like* mass.

12 糧　LIANG².

點糧食	to sow *cereals* (rice excepted).
喫糧	to be a soldier; lit., to eat *rations*.

米 12-14　糸 1-3

14 糯	上糧	to pay *taxes*.
	大糧戶	a wealthy landed proprietor.
糰	LO⁴.	
	糯米	*glutinous* rice.
	T'UAN².	
	飯糰糰	a *ball* of cooked rice.

The 120th radical. 糸

1 系	SHI⁴.	
	說得沒譜系	to speak in a *disconnected* manner.
2 糾	CHIU¹.	
	這個官司把我糾纏倒了	this lawsuit *embarrasses* me.
	兩個糾住打	they are *wrestling* and fighting; they have come to *grips*.
	糾衆斂錢	to *collect* a crowd in order to make money, [like a quack.
3 紇	KE⁵.	
	打個死紇縫	tie a hard *knot*.
紅	HONG².	
	紅顏色	*red* colour.
	紅葉	a go-between ; a match-maker.
	紅花	the safflower.
	朱紅	*vermilion*.
	土紅	*red* ochre.
	吐紅	to spit *blood*.
	紅船	the *red* boat, i. e., the lifeboat.
	掛紅	to hang *red* drapery in honour of any one.
	穿紅衣的犯人	a *red* coat criminal, i. e., one condemned [to die.
	紅契	a *stamped* document.
	紅銅水壺	a *copper* kettle.

(400)

注　釋

【上粮】纳税。

糯[lo⁴]

糰(团)[tʰuan²]

系[ɕi⁴]

【说得没谱系】说话没有系统性和条理。

糾(纠)[tɕiəu¹]

【纠众敛钱】纠：集合。

紇(纥)[ke⁵]

【打个死纥縫】纥縫，同"疙瘩"。打个死结。

紅(红)[xoŋ²]

【红叶】唐代有"红叶题诗"的佳话，后因以"红叶"为传情的媒介，借指媒人。

【吐红】吐血。

【穿红衣的犯人】指死囚。

注 释

【红黑两党】指在白天和黑夜出没的盗匪。
【他红黑要去】他死活要去,他一定要去。
纪(纪)[tɕi³]
纡(纡)[y¹][y²]
　【纡椅子】摇椅,圈椅。
　【把他脾气纡好】纡:改正。
紂(纣)[tʂəu⁴]
約(约)[io⁵]
　【邀邀约约的赶会】搭伴赶赴庙会。
紙(纸)[tʂʅ³]
紛(纷)[fən¹]
紡(纺)[faŋ³]

糸 3-4

燒紅了	*red* hot.
紅黑兩黨	*day* robbers and night robbers.
他紅黑要去	he will go by hook or by crook.
臉就紅了	he *blushed* with shame; he *flushed* with [anger.
花紅	crab-apples.

紀 CHI³.

好大的年紀	what is your *age*?
給別個當經紀	to be *middleman* in business transactions.

紆 Ü¹,².

紆椅子	round-backed chairs made of *bent* wood.
紆端	to *straighten* a bent tree.
把他脾氣紆好	*correct* his temper.

紂 CHEO⁴.

不要助紂為虐	do not assist a *wicked* man in his wicked-[ness (from Emperor *Cheo*).

約 IO⁵.

約期	to *agree* to a time.
寫個約據	to write out an *agreement*.
條約	a *treaty*.
邀邀約約的趕會	to *band together* and go to a festival.
好生約束	*control* or restrain him.
拿秤約一 ha⁴	*try* it on the steelyard.
儉約	*economical*.
大約	speaking *generally*.

紙 CHÏ³.

人情似紙張張薄	men's feelings are like sheets of *paper*—[all thin.
寫一張紙	write out an *agreement*.

紛 FEN¹.

紛爭	to wrangle *confusedly*.

紡 FANG³.

紡線子	to *spin* cotton.

(401)

糸 4

CHIE⁵.

加三級	to be promoted three *steps*.
降級留任	to degrade an official but leave him in office.
取首級	to *be*head a person.

LA⁵.

納稅	to *pay* custom.
恭喜你新春納福	may you *enjoy* happiness in this New Year.
納妾	to *marry* a concubine.

SHA¹.

| 紗帕 | a black *crape* turban. |
| 紗褂 | a *gauze* coat, worn in summer. |

UEN⁴.

| 賬目紊亂 | the account is *confused*. |

SHUEN².

| 純良的百姓 | *loyal* subjects. |

SO⁵.

索子	a rope; a cord.
索橋	a bamboo *cable* bridge.
我要索你的命	I will *seek* your life by committing suicide [and haunting you.
勒索	to *extort*.
索性做完	let us *exert* ourselves and finish this.

SU⁴.

素打扮	*plain* dress.
素起一雙手	I have brought no present; lit., I am [empty-handed.
喫素	to live on *vegetable* diet; to fast on 1st and 15th of each month.
素來沒有見過他的面	I have not met him *heretofore*.
平素	*usually*; *ordinarily*.

TIAO⁴.

| 綢牛 | to *tie* up an ox. |
| 綢命 | to *sustain* life for a time. |

(402)

注释

级（级）[tɕie⁵]
纳（纳）[la⁵]
纱（纱）[ʂa¹]
紊 [uən⁴]
纯（纯）[ʂuən²]
索 [so⁵]
素 [su⁴]
【素起一双手】空手（没带礼物）来访。
绸 [tiao⁴]
【绸牛】将牛绑牢。
【绸命】维持生命。

注释

纹(紋)[uən²]
【纹银】纯银,指成色最好的银子。
【罗纹】在编织中用正反针相间编织以形成回旋的花纹。
【看经纹】医生通过检查手纹来判断病情。

紮(扎)[tʂa⁵]
【扎脚带子】指中国古代妇女缠足。
【扎堰】筑堤坝。
【一扎炮】一捆爆竹。

终(終)[tʂoŋ¹]
絃(弦)[ɕyən²][siən²]
累[luei³][luei⁴]
绊(絆)[pʰan⁴]
绅(紳)[ʂən¹]
（SHEN⁴当为SHEN¹,见803页勘误表。）
【烂绅士】讼棍,骗人的律师。

糸 4-5

紋

UEN².

紋路	lines ; marks.
紋銀	pure silver.
羅紋	muslin.
看經紋	a doctor examining the lines on a child's [fingers.
波紋	ripples.

紮

CHA⁵.

紮脚帶子	to *bind on* ankle bands (women).
把衣裳紮起	*tuck* up your gown.
紮營	to *pitch* a camp.
紮水桶	to *calk* a bucket.
紮堰	to dam a river or canal.
路上紮雨	we were *delayed* on the road by rain.
一紮砲	a *bundle* of fire crackers. (*N. A.*)

終

CHONG¹.

有始有終	having a beginning and an *end*.
臨終	to come to one's *end*; to die.
是非終日有 不聽自然無 }	though slander be spoken the *whole* day to me, if I will not hear it, it ceases to be.

絃

SHÜEN², SIEN².

| 一根絃 | a *string* for a musical instrument. |
| 三絃子 | a three-*stringed* guitar. |

累

LUE³,⁴.

| 帶累 | to *involve*. |
| 累贅 | to *embarrass*. |

絆

P'AN⁴.

絆脚索	a *hindrance*; an *encumbrance*.
繩子絆倒脚	the rope has *tripped* me up.
絆舌	tongue-*tied* (literally).

紳

SHEN⁴.

| 紳士 | the *gentry*. |
| 爛紳士 | a *pettifogger*. |

(403)

糸 5-6

SHAO⁴.

| 我們在那裏會紹 | where shall we *meet* again? |
| 紹酒 | *wine* from *Shao*-shing, or an imitation [of it. |

SI⁴.

細盌	*fine* China basins.
細茶	*good* tea.
細故事	a *small* matter.
喫得細	you eat *little*.
下細看	look at it *minutely*; consider it *in detail*.
你要細心	you must be *careful*.

TSĨ³.

| 紫色 | *purple*. |

RONG².

| 絨鞋 | *velvet* shoes. |
| 織絨 | coarse *woollen cloth*, made to imitate lamb-[skin. |

CHIE⁵.

帽結子	a cap *knot*.
頭髮結了餅	his hair is *knotted* into a cake.
肚子結起了	bowels *constipated*.
結親	to *contract* a marriage.
交朋結友	to *contract* a friendship.
巴結人	to *curry favour* with people.
結案	to *wind up* a lawsuit.
下去具結	go and *settle* it according to my judgment.
結賬	to *settle* a bill.
結局	*results*.
結菓子	to *bear* fruit.
結實	*durable*.

KE¹.

拏給他	*give* it *to* him.
給他說	*say* it *to* him; tell him.
我給你買	I will buy it *for* you.

(404)

注 释

绍（紹）[ʂao⁴]
【我们在那里会绍】会绍：会合。
细（細）[si⁴]
【细碗】精致的碗。
【细茶】好茶。
【吃得细】吃得少。
【下细看】仔细看。
紫（紫）[tsɿ³]
绒（絨）[zoŋ²]
结（結）[tɕie⁵]
【肚子结起了】便秘。
给（給）[kei¹]，[tɕie⁵]

注 释

【办搅给】搅给：开支，开销。
络(络)[lo⁵]
【络丝】络：缠绕。
絮[sy⁴][suei⁴]
【张棉絮】从蚕茧中抽丝。
绞(绞)[tṣiao³]
丝(丝)[sʅ¹]
统(统)[tʰoŋ³]
【统共是好多】一共是多少？
【一统碑】一块石碑。
【统在袖子头】塞在袖子里。
绝(绝)[tsye⁵]

糸 6

絡 絮 絞 絲 統 絕

READ CHIE⁵.

辦攪給	to purchase *provisions* for the house.

LO⁵.

絡絲	to *reel* silk.
到處聯絡	everywhere *connected*, as a secret society.
周身的經絡	the *blood vessels* of the body.
他把我籠³絡了	he *deceived* me.

SÜ⁴, SUE⁴.

棉絮	*bowed cotton*; *cotton wool*.
張棉絮	*bowed silk* made from the remains of silk [cocoons.

CHIAO³.

絞蔴繩	to *twist* ropes.
定絞罪	to condemn to be *strangled*.

SÏ¹.

取絲	to wind *silk* from the cocoons.
一絞線	a small *hank* of thread.
蛛絲網	a spider's *web*.
銅絲	brass *wire*.
篾絲	very *narrow strips* of bamboo.
朘絲	meat *shreds*.
一絲絲都不要	I don't want *the least bit* of it.

T'ONG³.

天下一統	the whole country is under one *ruler*.
統領官	a *commander* of troops.
沒得統率	there is no *head* in that house.
統共是好多	what is the *total*?
一統碑	a stone tablet. (*N. A.*)
統在袖子頭	*tuck* it up your sleeve.

TSÜE⁵.

我兩個絕交	our friendship must be *broken off*.
棄絕	to *reject*.
罵不絕口	to curse without *interruption*.

糸 6-7

	絕了口糧	hard up; lit., food supplies are interrupted.
	絕種	to exterminate utterly.
	絕氣	to die.
	走了絕路	to be put to an extremity.
	絕色	very beautiful.
	生絕了	it has grown extremely well.
	絕不可行	it certainly will not do.
7 經	CHIN[1].	
	經過多少風霜	I have passed through many trying experiences.
	經手	to negotiate a matter; to pass through [one's hands.
	經侑	to serve; to attend to.
	好生經管倒	look after this business carefully.
	正經人	an upright man.
	經得儴	he can endure tiredness.
	經年	throughout the year.
	經血	the menses.
	經事	durable; serviceable.
	五經	the five classics.
	念經	to chant a liturgy.
	不經䃽	not easily soiled, as certain colours of cloth.
	這柴不經燒	this kind of firewood does not burn long.
	開水燙不得怕經	you must not pour boiling water on it; it may crack as glass.
絹	CHÜEN[4].	
	絹子	raw silk cloth.
綑	K'UEN[3].	
	綑人	to bind a person with cords.
	綑做一綑	bind it into one bundle.
	布綑子	a cloth seller's pack.
	一綑柴	a bundle of firewood.
綁	PANG[3].	
	綁緊	to bind tightly.
	綁腿兒	leggings, sometimes worn by women.

注 釋

【绝气】断气。指死亡。
經（经）[tɕin¹]
【经侑】服务；出席。
【好生经管倒】好好管理。
【经得儴】儴：疲惫、颓丧的样子。能忍受疲劳。
【经年】全年；经过一年或若干年。
【经事】顶事；耐用。
【开水烫不得怕经】不能用开水烫。
絹（绢）[tɕyen⁴]
綑（捆）[kʰuən³]
綁（绑）[paŋ³]

注 释

绣（绣）[siəu⁴]
维（维）[uei²]
绸（绸）[tʂʰəu²]
绰（绰）[tʂo⁵] [tʂʰo⁵]
　　　[tsʰao²]
绯（绯）[fei¹]
　【绯好吃】绯：形容程度高。很好吃。
抡（纶）[lən²] [lən¹]
　【纶线】在手指间绕线。
绽（绽）[tʂʰan⁴] [tsan⁴]
　【绽了线】衣缝脱线，引申为裂开。
緌 [uei¹]
　【帽緌子】帽穗，帽缨子。
纲（纲）[kaŋ¹]
紧（紧）[tɕin³]
　【手紧】指不随便花钱或给人财物。形容吝啬。

糸 7-8

绣	SIU⁴.	same as 繡.
維	UE².	
	維持世道	to *uphold* right doctrine as preachers of the [Sacred Edict do.
綢	CH'EO².	
	綢緞舖	a *silk* and satin shop.
綽	CHO⁵, CH'O⁵.	
	綽號	a *nickname*.
	READ CH'AO².	
	寬綽	*wide; spacious*.
緋	FE¹.	
	緋紅	*bright* red.
	緋好喫	*very* good to eat.
	緋惡的一個人	*exceedingly* wicked man.
	緋燙的	*scalding* hot.
綸	LEN²,¹.	
	綸綫	to *twist* a thread between the fingers.
	綸紙撚子	to *roll* spills between the fingers.
	綸藥丸子	to *roll* pills between the fingers.
綻	CH'AN⁴.	
	破綻大	the garment is much *torn*.
	READ TSAN⁴.	
	綻了綫	the thread is broken and the seam un-[ripped.
緌	UE¹.	
	帽緌子	the red *tassel* on a dress hat.
綱	KANG¹.	
	沒綱常	neglectful of the great *principles* of hu-[manity.
緊	CHIN³.	
	細緊	to tie *tight*.
	手緊	*close*-fisted.

(407)

糸 8

	口 緊	*cautious* in speech.
	我 緊 得 很	I am in great *straits* for necessities.
	水 緊	the river is *swift*.
	不 要 緊	it is not *important*.
	緊 憽 事	an *urgent* matter.
	趕 緊 做	do it *at once!* do it *quickly!*
綾	LIN².	
	板 綾	silk *damask*.
	羽 綾	linen *damask*.
	綾 邊 子	*sarcenet* borders on scrolls, etc.
綹	LIU³.	
	割 包 剪 綹	to cut *purses*.
	綹 婊 子	a *pickpocket*.
綠	LU⁵.	
	綠 顏 色	a *green* colour.
	銅 綠	*verdigris*.
綿	MIEN².	
	綿 軟	*soft*. [used for lining garments.
	張 綿	the silk of cocoons stretched on a frame,
	這 個 脟 是 綿 的	this meat is *tough*.
	壽 數 綿 長	a *long* life.
	下 綿 𩃬 雨	rain falling a *long* time.
	事 情 攪 綿 𩃬 了	the affair is *protracted*.
	他 經 得 綿	he is *persevering*.
	綿 扯 扯 的	*dilatory; tardy*.
	老 綿 筋	a *procrastinator; a slow-coach*.
綳	PEN¹.	
	戴 個 綳 綳	to wear a *pinafore*.
綵	TS'AI³.	same as 彩.
網	UANG³.	
	一 鋪 網	a *net*.
	網 子	a *net* for the hair.
	難 逃 法 網	it is difficult to escape the *meshes* of the law.

(408)

注 释

【水紧】水势急。

绫(綾)[lin²]

【板绫】绸缎。

【羽绫】亚麻锦缎。

【绫边子】丝织品的边角。

绺(綹)[liəu³]

【割包剪绺】划包偷窃。

【绺婊子】扒手，小偷。

绿(綠)[lu⁵]

绵(綿)[mien²]

【这个脟是绵的】这个肉有点老，嚼不动。

【他经得绵】他能持之以恒。

【绵扯扯的】拖拖拉拉的。

【老绵筋】磨磨蹭蹭的人。

绷(綳)[pən¹]

【戴个绷绷】绷绷：围裙。

绱(彩)[tsʰai³]

網(网)[uaŋ³]

【一铺网】一张网。

【网子】头发网套。

注 释

【受人家的网罗】网罗：指使。
缓（缓）[xuan³]
練（练）[lien⁴]
【练丝】未染色的熟丝。
【练勇】清代地方武装团练、乡勇等的统称。
緬（缅）[mien⁴]
編（编）[pien¹]
【编毛鞑子】编辫子。
【编布】织布。
【尽是编起的】编起：捏造。
【莫来编我】不要来诱惑我。
縭（缏）[pien³]
線（线）[sien⁴]

糸 8-9

網倒了	caught in a net.
一網打盡	to take all at one haul.
受人家的網羅	caught in men's *evil devices*.
蜘蛛網	a spider's *web*.

9 緩 HUAN³.

稍緩兩天	*delay* for a few days.
緩急相通	helping each other in *ease* or *urgency*.
緩緩的來	come *slowly*; don't be in a hurry about it.
緩一口氣	*wait* till I take a breath.

練 LIEN⁴.

練絲	to *boil* and *rub* raw silk with soap in order [to soften it.
打練	to *roll about* on the ground like a dog.
操練	to *drill* troops.
練勇	*drilled* troops.
團練	local volunteers.

緬 MIEN⁴.

緬甸國	Burmah.

編 PIEN¹.

編號	to *arrange* according to number or mark.
編毛辮子	to *braid* or *plait* the queue.
編毛韈子	to *knit* woolen socks.
編布	to *weave* cloth.
盡是編起的	the stories are pure *inventions*.
莫來編我	don't try to *entice* me.

縭 PIEN³.

縭子	a *hem*.
把袖子縭起	*tuck* up your sleeves.

線 SIEN⁴.

一根線	one *thread*; a straight *line*.
墨線	a carpenter's marking *line*.
針線活路	needlework.
引線	a *match*; a *fuse*; a *guide*.

(409)

糸 9-10

緒
SÜ⁴.
摸不倒頭緒　　I cannot find the *clew*; I cannot make head [or tail of it.

緞
TUAN⁴.
緞子　　*satin*.
洋線緞　　*Italian cloth*.
羽緞　　*camlet*.

緯
UE⁴.
緯線　　the *woof* of cloth.

緣
ÜEN².
千里姻緣一線牽　a thread will draw together those who are *decreed* for each other, though separated a thousand miles.
有緣撞著無緣錯過　} if it is in my *fate* I will obtain my desire, if not I will miss it.
無緣無故　　without *cause* or reason.

READ ÜEN⁴.
緣衣裳　　to trim a dress.
緣一炷香　　to *hem* with a narrow hem.

10
緻
CHÏ⁴.
生得標緻　　*handsome*.
做得細緻　　*finely* made; of *delicate* workmanship.

縋
CHUE⁴.
縋下來　　to *let down* as by a rope; to *suspend*.

縣
SHIEN⁴.
知縣　　a *district* (or *county*) magistrate.

絛
T'AO¹.
絲絛子　　silk *cords* and *tapes*.

縐
TSONG⁴.
縐起的　　*wrinkled*.
燒縐了　　*shrivelled* with fire.

(410)

注　釋

緒（绪）[sy⁴]
緞（缎）[tuan⁴]注：原文字头"緞"疑为打印错误。
【洋线缎】一种棉织品。表面光洁，像缎子。
【羽缎】亦称"羽毛缎"。像缎子一样光滑的棉织品。用于做大衣、外套的里子。
緯（纬）[uei⁴]
【纬线】纬纱编织品上编织的横线。
緣（缘）[yen²] [yen⁴]
【缘衣裳】修剪衣服。
【缘一炷香】烧一炷香。
緻（致）[tʂʅ⁴]
縋（缒）[tʂuei⁴]
縣（县）[ɕien⁴]
絛（绦）[tʰao¹]
【丝绦子】用丝线编成的带子。
縐（绉）[tson⁴]
【绉起的】起皱的。
【烧绉了】烧瘪了。

注 释

繁 [fan²]
【这个地方繁】繁：兴盛，繁荣。
【这个娃娃甚么繁法】这个小孩非常调皮。

縫（缝）[foŋ²][foŋ⁴]
【他一点缝隙都没得】他没有一点儿破绽。

縴（纤）[tɕʰien¹][tɕʰien⁴]
【纤索】拉牲口的绳索。
【拉纤】用绳子在岸上拉船前进。英文释义应为：to pull the towline of a boat.

繀 [suei⁴]
【繀儿】线轴。

縹（缥）[piao¹]
【缥布衫子】淡蓝色的上衣。

縮（缩）[so⁵]

績（绩）[tsʰie⁵],[tsie⁵]
【绩麻】搓麻织布。

縱（纵）[tsoŋ⁴]

糸 11

繁 FAN².

這個地方繁	this is a *turbulent* place.
這個娃娃甚麼繁法	this child is very *troublesome*, or *mischievous*.

縫 FONG².

縫衣裳	to make clothes; lit., to *sew* clothes.

READ FONG⁴.

縫子	a *seam*; a *crack*; a *crevice*.
他一點縫隙都沒得	he has not the least *fault*.

縴 CH'IEN¹.

縴籐	a tow-*line*.

READ CH'IEN⁴.

縴索	an ox's *traces*.
拉縴	to pull the *traces* in front of a mandarin's [chair.

繀 SUE⁴.

繀兒	a *bobbin*; a *spool*.

縹 PIAO¹.

縹布衫子	a *light blue* gown (*azure*).

縮 SO⁵.

縮頭	to *draw in* the head, like a tortoise.
縮短點	*shorten* it a little.
人老縮了	he is *shrunken* with age.
新衫子下水要縮	a new gown will *shrink* when it is washed.

績 TS'IE⁵, TSIE⁵.

績蔴	to *splice* hemp threads for weaving.

縱 TSONG⁴.

縱容匪徒	to *allow* bad men to live under one's jurisdiction; to *connive at*.
放縱情欲	to *give rein to* one's lusts, to *indulge* one's [passions.

糸 11-12

	一個縱步就過去了	he went across it at one *jump*.
	這個縱是好那個還是要不得	*although* this is good that is worthless.

TSONG³.

總爺	a *centurion*; a *chiliarch*.
客總	a *justice of the peace*, elected for life.
總而言之	to *sum up* the matter.
共總是好多	what is the *sum total*?
我總不信	I *certainly* don't believe it.

CHI⁵.

織布	to *weave* cloth.

TSO⁵.

布織得結繖	the cloth is *firmly* woven.
這個做得結繖	this article is *strongly* made.

FAN¹.

繙出中國話來	*translate* it into Chinese.

RAO³.

圍繞	to *surround*; to *environ*.
把我𢲶繞倒	it *embarrasses* me.
旗子繞	the streamer *waves* in the wind.

LIAO².

心思繚亂	my mind is *confused*.

SIU⁴.

繡花舖	an *embroidery* shop.
繡鞋	*embroidered* shoes.

TA⁵.

紇縫	a *knot*.
撞個青紇縫	to get a *bruise*.
木頭紇縫	a *knot* in wood.
澀紇縫	a sour plum, or pear.

(412)

注 释

總（总）[tsoŋ³]
【总爷】①明清时对总兵的尊称。②旧时对武职人员的尊称。
【客总】治安法官，太平绅士。

織（织）[tʂʅ⁵]

繖 [tso⁵]
【布织得结繖】结繖：扎实，牢固。

繙（翻）[fan¹]

繞（绕）[zao³]
【旗子绕】绕：飘扬。

繚 [liao²]

繡（绣）[siəu⁴]

縫 [ta⁵]
【木头纥缝】木头结节。英文释义应为：Node: tubercle.
【涩纥缝】味酸未熟的李子或梨子。

注 释

繫（系）[ɕi¹]
繪（绘）[xuei⁴]
繳（缴）[tɕiao³]
【繳票】移交委任状。
繮（缰）[tɕiaŋ¹]
繭（茧）[tɕien³]
繩（绳）[ʂuən²]
【火绳】①古代枪炮的引火绳。②用艾草等搓成的绳，燃烧发烟，用来驱除蚊虫或引火。
繼（继）[tɕi⁴]
繻[sy¹]
【布口子繻了】布的边缘快磨破了。
辮（辫）[pien⁴]
纂[tsuan³]
【自己纂起说的】自己炮制故事。
【纂饮食吃】抢别人东西吃。
【安纂纂】设置陷阱。

糸 13-14

13 繫

SHI¹.

| 提 筐 繫 | the *handle* of a basket. |
| 背 筐 繫 | the *shoulder straps* of a creel. |

繪

HUE⁴.

| 繪 個 圖 形 | to *draw* the plan of a place. |

繳

CHIAO³.

| 繳 票 | to *deliver up* a warrant to an official. |

繮

CHIANG¹.

| 馬 繮 繩 | a horse's *halter*. |

繭

CHIEN³.

| 繭 壳 | the *cocoon* of the silk-worm. |

繩

SHUEN².

蔴 繩 子	a hemp *string*.
火 繩	a *rope* of bamboo fibre used as a match for guns, or pipes, and as a clock.
紅 頭 繩	the red *cord* worn on the hair by both sexes before marriage.

14 繼

CHI⁴.

| 繼 母 | a step-mother; lit., one who *succeeds* a [mother. |
| 繼 兒 子 | a step son. |

繻

SÜ¹.

| 布 口 子 繻 了 | the cut edge of the cloth is *frayed*. |

辮

PIEN⁴.

| 梳 辮 子 | to comb out the *queue*. |
| 絲 辮 子 | narrow silk *braid*. |

纂

TSUAN³.

自 己 纂 起 說 的	they *concocted* the story themselves.
纂 飲 食 喫	to get food by *sponging* on others.
安 纂 纂	to set *eel-traps*.

(413)

西蜀方言

糸 15-19 缶 3

15 纏 CHʻANˆ2.

纏腳	to *bind* the feet, as women do.
蛇是纏人的	snakes *entwine* people.
我纏不贏他	I cannot beat him at *importunity*; I cannot get rid of him.
屋頭沒得攪纏	I have no money in the house for *ordinary* expenditure.

SHIO⁵, SIO⁵.

續絃	to marry a second wife; lit., to *mend* or *join* the lute string.
陸續有來的	there are some *continually* coming.

MIE⁵.

纖釘兒	*small* nails; tacks.

TSʻAI².

他是纔來的	he has *just* arrived.
這樣做纔好	do it thus, *then* it will be right.

IN¹.

帽纓子	the *tassel* on a dress hat.

TU⁵.

坐纛旗	the general's *standard*.

The 121st radical. (缶)

KANG¹.

水缸	a large water *jar*.
一缸水	a *jarful* of water (N. A.).
茶缸	a tea *bowl* with a cover.
缸鉢	a large earthenware *basin*.
石缸	a stone water-*tank*.
謹防小石頭打爛你的大缸缸	beware that a small stone break not your big *jar*; met., beware of insignificant persons.

(414)

注　释

纏（缠）[tʂʰan²]
【屋头没得搅缠】家里没有钱开支了。
續（续）[ɕio⁵][sio⁵]
纖[mie⁵]
【纖钉儿】小钉子，大头钉。
纔（才）[tsʰai²]
纓（缨）[in¹]
纛[tu⁵]
【坐纛旗】古时军队中的大旗。
缸[kaŋ¹]

注释

缺 [tɕʰye⁵]
　【田缺口】农田里放水的出口。
　【缺唇】上唇缺损, 也称"兔唇"。
　【缺牙巴】指门牙掉了的人。
餅(瓶)「pʰin²]
銚 [tʰiao⁴]
　【沙銚子】沙锅。
罃 [in¹]
罄 [tɕʰin⁴]
罈(坛) [tʰan²]
甕(瓮) [oŋ⁴]
罐 [kuan⁴]
罕 [xan³]

缶 4-18　网 3

4 缺 CH'ÜE⁵.

缺角的不要	we don't want *broken* cornered ones, as the basin is *chipped*. [tiles, etc.
盆打缺了	the basin is *chipped*.
刀砍缺了	the edge of the knife is *hacked*. [water.
田缺口	an opening in a field dike to let off surplus
缺唇	hare-lip; malformed *fissure* of the lip.
缺牙巴	a person who has lost some front teeth.
缺少人力	*deficient in* helpers; undermanned.
補好缺	to fill a good *official* post; lit., vacancy.

6 餅 P'IN².　same as 瓶.

銚 T'IAO⁴.

沙銚子	coarse earthenware *pots* used for cooking.

10 罃 IN¹.

罃粟壳	poppy heads, so called from their resemblance to small *jars*.

11 罄 CH'IN⁴.

賣得罄盡	*entirely* sold out, as a poor man's furniture.

12 罈 T'AN².

菜罈子	a pickle *jar* with a rim for holding water and a cover.

13 甕 ONG⁴.　same as 甕.

18 罐 KUAN⁴.

罐子	a *jar*; a *jug*; a *saucepan*.
打火罐	dry *cupping*.

The 122nd radical. (网)

3 罕 HAN³.

希罕	rare; scarce.
罕有呀罕有	one *seldom* hears of such conduct!
我希罕你來	I am surprised at you coming! (ironical).

(415)

网 6-10

6 罣 KUA⁴.
interchanged with 掛.
我罣念你	I *constantly* think of you.

8 罩 CHAO⁴.
雞罩	a chicken *coop* without a bottom.
烘罩	a bamboo *frame* for drying clothes over a fire.
燈罩子	a lamp *shade*; a lamp *chimney*.
喪罩	a large *covering* over a coffin; a *pall*.
日罩子	a large red sun-*shade* carried before officials.
掛罩子	to hang up *mosquito curtains*.
罩子散了	the *fog*, or *mist*, has dispersed.
罩魚	to *catch fish* by putting a *basket* over them.

置 CHĪ⁵.
安置一個地方	to *appoint* one to a station.
這事怎樣安置	how shall we *decide* this affair?

罪 TSUE⁴.
犯罪	to commit a *trespass*, to *sin*.
認罪	to confess one's *faults*.
定罪	to adjudge the *punishment*.
罪人	a *criminal*.
我得罪你	I have *offended* you; I beg your pardon.

9 罰 FA⁵.
受了重刑罰	he has received a heavy *punishment*.
罰跪	to *punish* a child by causing him to kneel.
父母責罰兒女	parents *chastise* their children.
罰了他一吊錢	*fined* him 1000 cash.

署 SHU⁴.
署任官	a magistrate who is appointed to office *temporarily*.

10 罵 MA⁴.
不罵人	don't *revile*, *curse*, or *scold* people.

罷 PA⁴.
不肯罷休	unwilling to *desist*.
罷了罷了	*enough! enough! stop! stop!*

注 释

罣（挂）[kua⁴]
罩 [tṣao⁴]
【喪罩】覆盖棺材的东西。
【日罩子】古时官员出行时用来遮阳的用具。
【罩子散了】雾散了。
【罩鱼】用竹笼子捕鱼。
置（置）[tṣʅ⁵]
罪 [tsuei⁴]
罰（罚）[fa⁵]
署 [ṣu⁴]
【署任官】代理官员，临时委派的官员。
罵（骂）[ma⁴]
罷（罢）[pa⁴]

注 释

【李子罢市了】罢市:下市。
罾[tsən¹]
【搬罾】罾:古代一种用木棍或竹竿做支架的方形渔网。搬罾:升起渔网。
羅(罗)[lo²]
【春罗】丝织品的一种。
【罗柜】一种筛面粉用的工具。
羁(羁)[tɕi¹]
羊[iaŋ²]
【劚羊】淘羊。
【地羊子肉】地羊:犬的别称。狗肉。
美[mei³]
羔[kao¹]

网 10-18 羊 3-4

	李子罢市了	the plum season is *past*.
	去罢	go! *(imperative)*.
12	不是的罢	surely not?
罾	TSEN¹.	
14	搬罾	to raise the *square lifting net*.
羅	LO².	
	自投羅網	he got himself into the *net*.
	羅紋罩子	*muslin* bed-curtains.
	春羅	a thin silk fabric used for summer clothing.
	買個羅篩	buy a *hair-sieve*.
	羅櫃	a *bolter* for sifting flour.
	羅盤	the *compass*.
18	十八羅漢	the 18 disciples of Buddha (a transliteration from the Sanscrit).
羁	CHI¹.	
	把我羁留幾天	he *detained* me for a few days.

The 123rd radical. (羊)

羊	IANG².	
	羊子	*sheep*; *goats* (general).
	公羊 and 母羊	a *ram* and a *ewe*.
	綿羊 and 山羊	*sheep* and *goats*.
	羊兒子	a *lamb*.
	劚羊	a *wether*.
	羊肉	*mutton*.
3	地羊子肉	*dog*-flesh.
美	ME³.	
	美味	a *delicious* flavour.
	美人	a *beautiful* woman.
	我是一片美意	my intention is *good*.
4	讚美	to *praise*.
羔	KAO¹.	
	羔羊子	a *lamb*; a *kid*.

(417)

西蜀方言

羊 5-13

5 羞 SIU¹.
羞人	to *shame* one.
羞羞	*shame! shame!*
不怕羞	*shame*less.

6 着 CHO⁵.
你們要着意	yon must *fix* your mind upon it; pay attention to duty.
說個着落	give one a *definite* idea.
不着實	un*trust*worthy; un*stable*.
說不着	I *could* not say that.
找不着	I *can*-not find it.
睡着了	asleep (a particle attached to some verbs).
還不曉得着忙	he does not even know to *hurry*.
着一個人去	send a man.

義 NGI⁴.
義氣	*righteousness*.
義學	a *charity* school.
一吊錢打不齊脚後跟,財短仁義長	a string of cash hung over the shoulder will not reach to the heels, the benefits of money are temporary, of *righteous*-ness lasting.

羣 CH'ÜIN².
一羣羊	a *flock* of sheep.
一羣猪兒	a *herd* of swine.
一羣人	a *crowd* of people.

群 CH'ÜIN². same as last.

9 羹 KEN¹.
| 御麥羹 | a kind of maize *porridge*. |
| 調羹 or 瓢羹 | a *spoon*. |

赢 LUE². for example of use see 㾾.

13 羶 SHAN¹.
| 有一股羶氣 | it has a *rank* smell, like beef or mutton. |

(418)

注 释

羞 [siəu¹]
着 [tʂo⁵]
【你们要着意】着意：用心,仔细。
【说个着落】着落：确实的根据,可靠的来源。
【不着实】着实：踏实,切实,符合实际。
义(义) [ŋi⁴]
【义学】旧时一种面向贫寒子弟的免费学校,资金来源为地方公益金或私人筹资。
羣(群) [tɕʰyn²]
群 [tɕʰyn²]
羹 [kən¹]
【御麦羹】玉米粥。
赢 [luei²]
羶(膻) [ʂan¹]

注释

羽 [y³]

舡 [koŋ⁴]
【一舡就攏來了】一下子就聚拢过来了。
【乱舡】闯入，侵入。

翅 [tṣʅ⁴]

翁 [oŋ¹]

翎 [lin²]
【箭翎花】指箭羽。

習（习）[si⁵]

翡 [fei³]

翠 [tsʰuei⁴]
【翠雀】即翡翠鸟。

翦 [tsien³]

翰 [xan⁴]

羽 3-10

The 124th radical. (羽)

Ü³.
羽扇　　　　　a *feather* fan.
羽毛　　　　　a strong rough kind of cloth.
羽緞領架子　　a *camlet* waistcoat.

KONG⁴.
一舡就攏來了　it came upon me with a *rush*.
亂舡　　　　　to *intrude*; to *rudely rush* into a place.
舡起雨走　　　to *run with head bent down* against the rain.

CHÏ⁴.
翅膀　　　　　*wings*; *fins*.
一翅飛多少遠　it flies a long distance with one *flap of the* [*wings*.

ONG¹.
老翁　　　　　*old gentleman* (respectful).

LIN².
花翎　　　　　peacock *plumes* worn by officials.
箭翎花　　　　the *feather* on an arrow.

SI⁵.
學習　　　　　to *practise*.
習慣成自然　　*habit* makes it natural.

FE³.
翡翠玉　　　　*kingfisher* jade (a valuable kind).

TS'UE⁴.
翠雀　　　　　the *kingfisher*.

TSIEN³.
　　　　　　　same as 剪.

HAN⁴.
多承你的翰墨　thanks for your letter; lit., *pencil* and ink.
翰林院　　　　the National Academy.

(419)

羽 11-14 老

11 翳 I⁴.
| 翳子 | a disease of the eyes. |

12 翼 I⁴.
| 毛翼還沒有長齊 | all its *feathers* have not grown yet. |
| 左右的羽翼 | *accomplices*; *confederates*. |

翻 FAN¹.
翻書	to *turn* over the leaves of a book.
翻牆	to *climb* over a wall.
翻山	to *cross* over a mountain.
打翻觔斗	to perform a somersault; to *retract*.
病又翻了	he has had a *relapse*.
翻轉穿起	*turn* it *outside* in and wear it.
翻臉	to *change* countenance.
事情又翻了生	the affair has cropped up *again*.
翻倉	to *turn* out grain to dry.
翻了船	the boat was *upset*.
翻煙	to *re-*smoke opium.

14 耀 IAO⁴.
| 滿身的榮耀 | covered with *glory*. |

The 125th radical. (老)

老 LAO³.
老的伙	the *old* couple; parents.
凡事要好須問三老	if you want to have all your work well done, you must ask advice of three wise *old* men.
人老癲悚樹老心空	an *old* man is silly, as an *old* tree is hollow.
老人家	*old* man.
還沒有把老房子找倒	I have not yet managed to get a coffin.
老吳	Mr. U. (respectful way of addressing coolies).

(420)

注　釋

翳[i⁴]
【翳子】眼睛角膜病变后遗留下来的疤痕组织，影响视力。眼疾的一种。英文释义应为：Cataract.

翼[i⁴]

翻[fan¹]
【病又翻了】旧病复发。
【事情又翻了生】意外又发生了。
【翻仓】晾晒谷物。
【翻烟】复吸鸦片。烟瘾又犯了。

耀[iao⁴]

老[lao³]
【老的伙】老年夫妇；父母。
【凡事要好须问三老】三老：泛指年长有声望的老人。
【人老癫悚，树老心空】人老了易糊涂，树老了易中空。
【还没有把老房子找倒】还没有准备棺材。

注释

【谷子老了】谷物成熟了。
考 [kʰao³]
【过考】通过考试。
【考金石】试金石。
者 [tṣei³]
耆 [tɕʰi²]
而 [zʅ²]
耐 [lai⁴]
崅 [tṣuan¹]
耍 [ṣua³]
【做了耍的】做得很有乐趣。
【转耍】转悠玩耍。
【我这几天耍起在】我这几天空闲着。

老 3-4 而 3

	范大老爺	His Honour District Magistrate Fan.
	老成人	an *experienced* person.
	穀子老了	the grain is *ripe*.
	菜長老了	the vegetables have grown *old and tough*.
	蛋煮老了	the eggs are *hard* boiled.
	老實話	*honestly* speaking.
	老早就收了工	he stopped work *very early*.

3 考　K'AO³.

考試	to *examine* students.
過考	to pass an *examination*.
考察	to *investigate* a matter.
考金石	a stone for *testing* silver with; *touch*-stone.

者　CHE³.

我撞倒一個老者　I met an old man, lit., *one who* is old.

耆　CH'I².

報耆老　to report *age* to the Emperor, who grants [a button·

The 126th radical. (而)

4 而　RI².

照着書上的話而行　} act according to the book (conjunction; and).

3 耐　LAI⁴.

沒得忍耐	he has no *patience*.
你這麼耐煩	how *patient* you are!
我實在耐不過	I really can't *endure* it.

崅　CHUAN¹.　same as 專.

耍　SHUA³.

耍泥巴	to *play with* mud.
做了耍的	it was done in *fun*.
轉耍	to knock round *seeking amusement*.
我這幾天耍起在	I am *idle* these days; out of work.

(421)

而 3 耒 4

耍一陣	rest a little; stay a while.
二天請來耍	come another day and pay us a visit.
耍龍燈	to parade with a dragon lantern.
耍刀	to fence with a sword.
耍錢	to gamble.
好⁴耍	fond of idleness.
耍脾氣	to give rein to one's disposition.
外頭耍的	vagabonds.
耍秤	to play tricks with the steelyard; to cheat.
耍書	light literature.

The 127th radical. (耒)

⁴耖 CH'AO¹, ⁴.

耖田	to plough fields a second time.

READ CH'AO⁴.

把菜耖一 ha	turn the vegetables over in the pan.
自己耖起出來的事	he stirred up the trouble himself.
耖窩子	to raid a thief's den.

耗 HAO⁴.

耗費大	the expenditure is great.
莫把精神耗散很了	don't expend your energies or strength too much.
錢財耗散了	his money is all squandered.
耗子	rats; mice.

耕 KEN¹.

耕田	to plough fields, to cultivate land.
耕牛	a plough ox.
舌耕	to teach school for a living.

耙 P'A².

耙子	a harrow.

READ PA⁴.

耙田	to harrow the fields.

注 释

【耍钱】赌钱。
【好耍】懒惰的。
【外头耍的】游手好闲者。
【耍秤】欺骗。
【耍书】通俗读物,消遣读物。

耖 [tṣʰao¹] [tṣʰao⁴]
【耖田】犁地后用再把耖弄细土块打碎,使地平整。
【自己耖起出来的事】自己搞出来的麻烦事。即庸人自扰。
【耖窝子】搜捕窃贼老巢。

耗 [xao⁴]
【莫把精神耗散很了】很了: 很多。

耕 [kən¹]
【舌耕】在学堂授徒教书以谋生。

耙 [pʰa²]

注释

耘 [yn²]
【耘萝卜秧】耘：间苗。

枷（柫）[tɕia¹] [tɕia⁴]
【连枷儿】拍打谷物、使籽粒脱落下来的农具，由一个长柄和一排竹条或木条构成。

耳 [ʐʅ³]
【取耳】挖除耳垢。
【灌耳心】耳朵里长脓。
【没耳性的人】耳性：记性，记忆力。
【不耳他】不听他，不理他。
【耳子】木耳菌的一种，生长在腐朽的树干上，形状如人耳，黑褐色，胶质，外面密生柔软的短毛，可供食用。

耻 [tʂʰʅ³]
聊 [liao²]
聒 [kua⁵]
聘 [pʰin⁴]

耒 4-5　耳 4-7

耘　ÜIN².
耘蘿蔔秧　to *thin* young turnips.

枷　CHIA¹,⁴.
連枷兒　a *flail*.

The 128th radical. (耳)

耳　RÏ³.
取耳　to clean out the *ears*.
灌耳心　an abscess in the *ear*.
那是耳邊風的話　that is a mere rumour.
打耳巴子　to box the *ears*.
沒耳性的人　one who is utterly inattentive to exhortation or advice. [to him.
不耳他　don't *listen* to him; don't pay any attention
草鞋耳子　*loops* on the sides of sandals.
邊耳子草鞋　sandals of the common pattern.
耳朵帽　a cap with *flaps* to cover the ears.
耳鍋　a shallow pan with two *handles*.
耳房　a *side* room. [ears).
耳子　edible *lichen* (so called because it resembles

耻　CHʻÏ³.　same as 恥.

聊　LIAO². [idle scamp.
無聊的人　a person with no *means of support*; an
寫得聊草　*badly* or *hurriedly* written.

聒　KUA⁵.
聒聒的叫　*croaking*, like frogs.
聒聒聒不歇憩　incessant *gabbling*.

聘　PʻIN⁴. [teach school.
聘個老師　to *invite* a school-master to come and
自幼聘定的　she was *betrothed* in her childhood.

(423)

耳 7-11

SHEN⁴.

聖人	sages.
聖廟	a *Confucian* temple.
聖門弟子	*Confucianists*; literati.
講聖諭	to discourse on the *Sacred* or *Imperial* [Edict.

TSÜ⁴.

| 聚會 | to *assemble*. |

UEN².

耳聞是虛眼見是實	what the ear *hears* is false, what the eye sees is real.
有甚麼新聞	what *news* is there?
聞倒一股香氣	to *smell* a fragrance.

T'IN².

| 灌聤耳 | a *running* ear. |

LIEN².

筋骨聯絡	the sinews and bones of the body are *knit* [together.
寫一副對聯	write a *couplet* for a pair of scrolls.
辮聯子	a false queue.
聯一件衣裳	to *make*, or *sew* a garment.

SHEN¹.

聲音	a *sound*; a *tone*.
聲氣	a *voice*.
不做聲	to be silent.
給他説一聲	tell him.
打個響聲	make a *noise*.
回聲	an *echo*.
風聲不好	the *rumours* are bad.
名聲	*reputation*.

SONG³.

| 高聳聳的 | *high*, as a mountain, *tall*, as a man. |
| 黑聳聳的 | *dim* and dark, as an object in the moon- [light. |

(424)

注 釋

聖（圣）[ʂən⁴]
聚 [tsy⁴]
聞（闻）[uən²]
聤 [tʰin²]
【灌聤耳】耳朵流脓。
聯（联）[lien²]
【辮联子】假发辫子。
【联一件衣裳】缝制一件衣服。
聲（声）[ʂən¹]
聳（耸）[soŋ³]

耳 11-16 聿 5-8 肉

聰 12

TS'ONG¹.

| 聰明 | clever; sharp-witted. |

職 16

CHĬ⁵.

| 職分 | an *office*; a *duty*. |

聾

LONG¹, ².

| 聾子 | a *deaf* person. |

聽

T'IN¹, ⁴.

聽見風就是雨	he *hears* the wind and says it is rain; to add to stories.
聽嫌話	to *listen* to idle talk.
你要聽話	you must *obey* orders; be obedient.

READ T'IN⁴.

再去打聽	go again and *inquire*.
藥聽了	the medicine has proved *efficacious*.
要聽其自然	you must *follow* nature; let it come naturally.

The 129th radical. (聿)

聿 5

I⁴.

| 在那裏聿業 | where are you *studying*? |

肆 8

SĬ⁴.

| 放肆 | *dissolute*; *licentious*. |

The 130th radical. (肉)

肉

RU⁵.

割肉	to buy *butcher's meat*.
猪肉, 牛肉, 羊肉	*pork, beef* and *mutton*.
親骨肉	of the same parents; lit., bones and *flesh*.
肉身	the *body*.
這個桃子的肉頭厚	the *flesh* of this peach is thick.
核桃肉	the *kernels* of walnuts.

(425)

注　释

聰（聪）[tsʰoŋ¹]
職（职）[tsʅ⁵]
聾（聋）[loŋ¹] [loŋ²]
聽（听）[tʰin¹] [tʰin⁴]
【药听了】药物有效。
聿 [i⁴]
【在那里聿业】聿，同"肄"。在什么地方求学？
肆 [sʅ⁴]
肉 [zu⁵]
【割肉】买肉。

肉 2-4

2 肋 LE⁵.
肋巴骨	the *ribs*.
割肋條	to buy a *rib* of beef.

肌 CHI¹.
肌瘦得很	*fleshless*; very lean; skinny.
肌巴	the *penis*.

3 肘 CHEO³.
砍個肘子	buy a *hind-leg* of pork.
肘起來	to *raise above the head with the hands*.
那個把他肘起	who is *backing*, or *supporting* him?
唱木肘肘	to act with *puppets*.
硬肘	*firm*; *strong*; *durable*.
受了他的掣肘	he *restricted* me.

肝 KAN¹.
肝子	the *liver*.

肛 KANG¹.
肛門	the *anus*.
脫肛	*prolapsus ani*.

肖 SIAO⁴.
不肖的子孫	degenerate sons, i. e., not *like* their fathers.

肚 TU⁴.
肚皮巴了背	my *belly* clings to my back; I have no *stomach*.
肚皮痛	*stomach* ache.
肚量大	his *patience* is great.

READ TU³.
小肚子	the *bladder*.
脚肚子	the *calf* of the leg.

4 腑 CHÜIN⁴.
雞腑子	a fowl's *crop*.

胖 PANG⁴.
水打胖	*swollen* by water, as the body of a drowned *person*.

(426)

注　释

肋 [le⁵]
【肋巴骨】肋骨。
肌 [tɕi¹]
【肌巴】阴茎。
肘 [tʂəu³]
【肘起来】用手把头托起。
【那个把他肘起】谁在支持他？
【唱木肘肘】演木偶戏。
【硬肘】硬朗，结实。
肝 [kan¹]
肛 [kaŋ¹]
肖 [siao⁴]
肚 [tu⁴] [tu³]
【肚皮巴了背】没有胃口。
腑 [tɕyn⁴]
胖 [paŋ⁴]
【水打胖】浮肿。

注释

肢 [tṣɻ]
  【四肢百体】人体的各个部分。泛指全身。
肥 [fei²]
胘 [kuən³]
肺 [fei⁴]
肯 [kʰən³]
  【肯害病】易生病。
肩 [tɕien¹]
  【一肩跑拢】扛着东西往目的地跑,中间不休息。
  【砍肩子】背心。
股 [ku³]
  【一股生意】一笔生意。
  【一股地方】一块地方。
  【三股子】三股线。
育 [io⁵]

肉 4

肢 CHĪ¹.
四肢百體　　the four *limbs* and the hundred members, [i. e., the body.

肥 FE².
肥猪　　a *fat* pig.
肥土　　*fertile* land.
拉肥猪兒　　to kidnap *rich* persons.
只顧肥己　　he only seeks to *benefit* himself.

胘 KUEN³.
股胘大臣　　the chief officers of a prince; lit., legs and [arms.

肺 FE⁴.
心肺　　heart and *lungs*.
這是我肺腑的話　　these are my honest intentions.

肯 K'EN³.
肯不肯　　are you *willing*?
肯看書　　he *likes* to study.
肯害病　　*subject* to sickness.

肩 CHIEN¹.
肩膀　　the *shoulder*.
一肩跑攏　　to carry the load to the stopping place [without resting.
砍肩子　　a waistcoat (because the sleeves are cut off at the *shoulders*).

股 KU³.
屁股　　the *buttocks*.
幾股水　　a few *streams* of water. (*N. A.*)
一股生意　　a *share* in a business. (*N. A.*)
一股地方　　a *plot* of ground.
三股子　　a three-*ply* thread. (*N. A.*)
一股酸氣　　a sour smell. (*N. A.*)

育 IO⁵.
養育　　to *nurture*.
沒得生育　　having no children; barren. [children.
育嬰堂　　an orphanage and home for destitute

(427)

肉 5

FU².
胡荳	*Tartar* beans.
胡椒	*foreign* pepper, i. e., black pepper.

ME⁵.
血脉	the *blood* in the veins.
看脉	to feel the *pulse*.
脉理錢	a doctor's fees.
這座山從那裏發脉	what mountain range does this hill spring from?

LU³.
胬肉	*proud flesh*.

P'ANG⁴.
胖子	a *fat* person.

PAO¹.
衣胞	the *placenta*.
胞弟	own younger brother.

PE¹.
背¹在背⁴上	to *carry*¹ things on the *back*⁴.
背¹背⁴子	*carry*¹ a *load*⁴ on the back.
兒子替父親背案	the son pleads guilty in place of the father.
背了賬	to be in debt.
背不住	I cannot *endure* it; unbearable.
背山鄰近	we live on the same mountain (either the same or opposite sides).

READ PE⁴.
手背	the *back* of the hand.
背起手	to *place* the hands *behind* the back.
背書	to *repeat* by heart (from the custom of turning the *back* on the teacher).
背約	to *renounce* an agreement.
背街	a *back* street.
地方背靜	the place is quiet.

(428)

注 釋

胡 [fu²]
【胡豆】①蚕豆的别名。②古时豌豆亦别称"胡豆"。

脉 [me⁵]
【脉理钱】脉理: 医道, 医术。诊费。

胬 [lu³]
【胬肉】一种眼病, 中医指眼球结膜增生而突起的肉状物, 即翼状胬肉。英文释义应为: A triangular mass of mucous membrane growing from the inner corner of the eye.

胖 [pʰaŋ⁴]

胞 [pao¹]
【衣胞】在分娩胎儿之后, 由子宫排出的胎盘和胎膜。

背 [pei¹] [pei⁴]
【背背子】背子: 用来背东西的长背篓。
【地方背静】背静: 偏僻, 安静。

注释

【背了亮】从天黑坐到天亮。

胚 [pʰei¹]

【身胚大】身胚：也作"身坯"。身材魁梧。

胎 [tʰai¹]

胆 [tan³]

胃 [uei⁴]

脂 [tʂʅ¹]

胵 [tʂʰʅ¹]

【鸡胵子】鸡用于贮存食物的器官。

胁（胁）[ɕie⁵]

【胁挟窝】腋窝。

【软胁】腰。

胸 [ɕioŋ¹]

胰 [i²]

【胰子】肥皂。

胯 [kʰua³]

【大胯胯】大腿。

脉（脉）[me⁵]

能 [lən²]

肉 5-6

胚胎胆胃

背了亮	to sit with *back to the light*.
背篼	a *basket for carrying on the back*.
耳朵有些背	I am a little *deaf*.
背时	out of *luck*.
背光	a *reflector*.

P'E¹.

| 身胚大 | stout in *body*. |

T'AI¹.

| 怀胎 | to be with child; *pregnant*. |

TAN³.

| | same as 膽. |

UE⁴.

胃上的病	a disease of the *stomach*.
胃口不强	my *appetite* is poor.
脾胃不好	his *temper* is bad.

CHĬ¹.

| 胭脂 | *rouge*. |

6 脂胵胁胸胰胯脉能

CH'Ĭ¹.

| 雞胵子 | a chicken's *crop*. |

SHIE⁵.

| 胁挟窝 | the *armpits*. |
| 软胁 | the *loins*. |

SHIONG¹.

| 胸膛 | the *chest*; the *breast*. |

I².

| 胰子 | *soap*. |

K'UA³.

| 大胯胯 | the *thigh*. |

ME⁵.

| | same as 脉. |

LEN².

| 能幹 | *ability*. |

(429)

肉 6-7

	無能之輩	an incompetent person.
	能做那一行	what work are you *able* to do?
	能說不能行	he *can* speak, but he cannot act.

TSI⁵.

	背脊骨	the *back* bone.
	屋脊	the *ridge* of a house.

TS'UE⁴.

	脆萵笋	*crisp* lettuces.
	乾脆	they are dried *brittle*.

IEN¹.

	胭侯	the *throat*.
	胭脂蘿蔔	*red* turnips.

CHIN⁴.

	脚脛骨	the *shin-bone*.

CHIO⁵.

	一雙脚	the *feet*.
	他的脚頭重	he walks with a heavy *step*.
	山脚	the *foot* of a hill.
	板凳脚	the *leg* of a stool.
	三脚	a *tripod*.
	脚子	a *coolie*.
	脚錢	a *coolie's* hire; carriage of goods.
	好脚色	a fine fellow, i. e., a good worker.
	千脚虫	*millepedes*.
	地脚石	*foundation* stones laid under the lowest [cross beams.
	牆脚	the *base* of a wall.
	靛脚子	dyers' *dregs*.

ME².

	脢子頭兒	*brisket* of pork, beef, or mutton.

P'AO¹, PAO¹.

	尿脬	the *bladder*.
	氣脬卵	scrotal hernia.

(430)

注 釋

脊 [tsi⁵]
脆 [tsʰuei⁴]
胭 [ien¹]
【胭侯】咽喉。
【胭脂萝卜】红萝卜。
脛（胫）[tɕin⁴]
脚 [tɕio⁵]
【他的脚头重】脚头：脚步。
【脚子】脚夫。
【脚钱】付给脚夫或搬运工的报酬。
【地脚石】大梁的垫石。
【靛脚子】沉在染缸底部的颜料。
脢 [mei²]
【脢子头儿】胸部的肉。
脬 [pʰao¹] [pao¹]
【尿脬】膀胱。
【气脬卵】阴囊疝，指腹腔脏器经腹股沟环脱出并下降至阴囊鞘膜腔内，又称为腹股沟阴囊疝。

注释

脖 [po⁵]
【他有个臂脖】他有个靠山或担保人。
脩（修）[siəu¹]
脱 [tʰo⁵]
【把字脱下来】把字影印或描绘下来。
胀（胀）[tsaŋ⁴]
【胀臌病】水肿；浮肿。
腐 [fu³]
腒 [kʰu²]
【腒倒】蹲下。
【在成都腒了几年】在成都住了几年。
【房子腒下去了】房子倒塌了。
【矮腒腒的】矮墩墩的。
腑 [fu³]

肉 7-8

脖　　　PO⁵.
　臂脖子　　　the *back of the shoulder*. [*friend at court.*
　他有個臂脖　he has a *surety*, or an *advocate*; he has a

脩　　　SIU¹.
　束脩　　　a schoolmaster's *fees*.

脱　　　T'O⁵.
　脱衣服　　　to *undress*.
　脱一層皮　　to *cast* a skin, as after a fever.
　頭髮脱了　　my hair is *coming out*.
　放脱　　　to *liberate*.
　解脱　　　to *unloose*.　　[an apprentice.
　還脱不得手　he cannot be trusted to do it alone yet, as
　跑不脱　　　he cannot *escape*.
　推脱　　　to *retract*; to *back out of*.
　瓦脱了節　　the tiles have slipped out of place.
　脱俗　　　*uncommonly* kind, liberal, clean, tidy, etc.
　把字脱下來　to *copy* good writing by tracing.

8 胀　　　CHANG⁴.
　泡胀　　　to soak a thing until it *swells*.
　肚子胀　　　*distended* stomach.
　胀臌病　　　*dropsy*.

腐　　　FU³.
　腐肉　　　*proud flesh*.
　荳腐　　　*bean-curd*.
　腐儒　　　a *bad* scholar.

腒　　　K'U².
　腒倒　　　to *crouch down*, to *squat*.
　在成都腒了幾年　he *dwelt* in Ch'en-tu a few years.
　房子腒下去了　the house has *collapsed*.
　矮腒腒的　　*squat; dumpy*.

腑　　　FU³.
　　　　　　　　[lungs and *intestines*.
　不知肺腑　　I don't know his private opinion; lit,.

(431)

西蜀方言

肉 8-9

CH'IANG¹.

滿腔的怒氣	his *breast* was full of anger.
不開腔	don't open your *mouth!* shut up!
十里不同腔	the *dialect* is different every 10 li.

T'IE⁵.

| 連睇 | the *spleen* of a hog. |

P'I².

脾胃弱	my *appetite* is poor; lit., *spleen* and [stomach.
脾寒	*fever* and *ague*.
脾氣	*temper*; *disposition*.

UAN³.

| 手腕腕 | the *elbow*. |

SHEN⁴.

| 腎子 | the *testicles*. |

TSIN¹.

| 腈肉 | *lean* meat; the *lean* parts of an animal. |

IE⁵.

| 鹽腌子 | *salted fish*. |

IE⁴.

| 腋翅 | the *wings* of a bird. |

CH'ANG².

腸子	the *intestines*.
熱心熱腸	warm *affections*.
貫腸	*sausages*.

LAN².

| 腩揉 | to *cure* or *salt* meat. |

CHONG³.

| 腳腫了 | my feet are *swollen*. |
| 浮腫 | *puffy*. |

(432)

注 釋

腔 [tɕʰiaŋ¹]
睇 [tʰie⁵]
【連睇】猪内脏。
脾 [pʰi²]
腕 [uan³]
【手腕腕】肘关节。
肾 [ʂən⁴]
【肾子】睾丸。
腈 [tsin¹]
【腈肉】瘦肉，也叫"赤肉"。和肥肉、白肉相对。
腌 [ie⁵]
【盐腌子】咸鱼。
腋 [ie⁴]
腸（肠）[tsʰaŋ²]
腩 [lan²]
【腩揉】加工或腌制肉类。
腫（肿）[tsoŋ³]

注释

腹 [fu⁵]
【贪口腹】贪吃，嘴馋。
脵 [zəu⁴]
【脵眼睛】分不清好坏。
【脵皮子】皮肤。
【脵莲花儿】指身体上被打留下的手掌印。
【脵头厚】（树叶、花朵等）厚、茂密。
胴（胴）[lo²]
【十胴全中状元】胴：手指纹。
腮 [sai¹]
腦（脑）[lao³]
【望起脑壳】抬起头。
【潮脑】即樟脑。
腥 [sin¹]
腯 [tʰən²]
腰 [iao¹]
【腰子会】屠夫会。

肉 9

腹	FU⁵.	
	肚腹	the *belly*; the *abdomen*.
	贪口腹	sponging on others for food.
	心腹人	an intimate friend.
脵	REO⁴.	
	喫脵	to eat *butcher's meat*.
	脵眼睛	one who cannot distinguish between good [and bad; *lit.*, *flesh* eyes.
	脵皮子	the skin.
	脵莲花儿	an imitation of clappers, made by slapping [the body.
	脵头厚	thick in *substance*, as leaves, flowers, etc.
胴	LO².	
	十胴全中状元	if you have *circular striæ* on the points of your fingers you will become "chuang-üen."
腮	SAI¹.	
	泪流满腮	the tears ran down his *cheeks*.
腦	LAO³.	
	腦臓	the *brain*.
	望起腦壳	lift up your *head*.
	沒得個頭腦	there is neither *head* nor *tail* to it.
	潮腦	*camphor*.
腥	SIN¹.	
	一股腥氣	a *rank* smell like meat or fish.
腯	TʻEN³.	
	肥腯腯的	*fat*, like a pig.
腰	IAO¹.	
	猪腰子	pig's *kidneys*.
	腰子會	pork butchers, because they give the kid-[neys to the guild.
	腰桿	the *small of the back*; the *loins*.
	一腰桿深的水	*waist* deep water.
	拴腰帶	tie on your *girdle*.

(433)

肉 9-11

	帶 帷 腰	to wear an *apron*.
	腰 板	*wainscot* reaching about *waist* high.
	說 到 半 中 腰	we had just got to the *subject*.
	山 腰 腰 上	*half-way* up a hill.
	腰 店 子	a *half-way* house; a *wayside* inn.

10 膏 KAO¹.

	膏 藥	plasters prepared from various *oils*.
	膏 火	a student's stipend; lit., *oil* and *fire*.
	石 膏 豆 腐	bean-curd made with *gypsum*.

膈 KE⁵.

	膈 子 朕	the *midriff* of a pig.
	膈 食 病	loss of appetite.
	打 膈 噔 兒	to *hiccough*.

READ KE³.

	打 膈	to *belch*.

膀 P'ANG³.

	割 一 個 膀	buy a *small leg of pork* (not more than two [or three pounds weight].

腿 T'UE³.

	腿 桿	the *leg*.
	大 腿	the *thigh*.
	火 腿	a cured *ham*.

臃 ONG⁴.

11	臃 臭 臃 臭 的	*stinking*, as vegetables that have gone bad [in a jar.

膚 FU¹.

	皮 膚 作 癢	an itching *skin*.

膠 CHIAO¹.

	牛 膠	ox *glue*.
	拏 膠 來 膠 起	*glue* it with *glue*.
	膠 蠟	to *dip* candles.

(434)

注　釋

【腰店子】半路上的房子；路旁的旅馆。

膏 [kao¹]

【膏火】①照明用的灯火。②指供学习用的津贴。

膈 [ke⁵] [ke³]

【膈子朕】猪腹部的肉。

【膈食病】中医称具有下咽困难、胸腹胀痛、吐酸水等症状的病。

膀 [pʰaŋ³]

腿 [tʰuei³]

臃 [oŋ⁴]

【臃臭臃臭的】非常臭。

膚（肤）[fu¹]

膠（胶）[tɕiao¹]

【胶蜡】制蜡烛。

注释

膝 [si⁵]
　【磕膝头】膝盖。
膛 [tʰaŋ²]
　【眼膛子深】眼膛子：眼窝。
膆 [tsʰao²]
　【心里膆得很】（由于饮食粗劣导致的）肠胃不好。
膨 [pʰən¹]
腻 [n̠i⁴]
膳 [şan⁴]
　【父母的养膳】养膳：赡养。
臌 [ku³]
　【气臌革】气臌：中医指由于气不通而引起的水肿，浮肿。
臂 [pʰei⁴]
䏓 [toŋ³]
　【肥䏓䏓的】很胖。
　【这个橘子䏓块】这是一个大橘子。
膁 [tɕʰien³]
　【狐膁】狐狸侧腹的白毛。
膾（脍）[xuei⁴]
臁 [lien²]
　【臁疮】小腿溃疡。
　【猪臁䐑】猪内脏。

肉 11-13

膝	SI⁵.	
	磕膝頭	the *knee*.
膛	TʻANG².	
		[self; to be surety.
	拍起膛子説	to slap one's *chest* when referring to one's
膆	眼膛子深	deep *eye-sockets*.
	TSʻAO².	
		[poor food.
12 膨	心裏膆得很	my stomach is *weak*, through living on
	PʻEN¹.	
腻	喫得膨脹	the stomach *distended* with eating.
	NI⁴.	
		[stand.
	起了油腻	it has got *oily* or *greasy*, like a dirty lamp-
	肥得腻人	it is fat enough to *sicken* one.
膳	腻得很	*grudging*.
	SHAN⁴.	
		[children.
13	父母的養膳	*provisions* supplied to parents by their
臌	KU³.	
	氣臌革	*dropsy*.
臂	PʻE⁴.	
䏓		for example of use see 膝.
	TONG³.	
	肥䏓䏓的	*very fat*.
	這個橘子䏓塊	this is a *large* orange.
膁	CHʻIEN³.	
	狐膁	the white fur on the *flank* of the fox.
膾	HUE⁴.	
	雜膾	a basin of *mixed* meats; *hodge-podge*.
臁	LIEN².	
	臁瘡	sores on the *calf of the leg*.
	豬臁䐑	a pig's *spleen*.

(435)

西蜀方言

肉 13-18

臉	LIEN³.	[to disguise.
	打臉掛鬚	to paint the *face* and put on a moustache;
	沒臉見人	out of *countenance*; no *face* to meet people.
	他厚起臉儘說	he hardens his face and keeps on speaking; shameless.
	不要臉	regardless of one's *reputation*; shameless.
膿	LONG².	
	流膿	to exude *pus*.
臊	SAO¹.	
	臊臭	*stinking*, as the smell of a urinal.
	臊甲子	the cockroach (on account of its *smell*).
膽	TAN³.	
	苦膽	the *gall*.
	龍膽草	gentian (lit., dragon's *gall* grass).
	膽子大	his *courage* is great.
14 臍	TS'I².	
	肚臍眼	the *navel*.
	臍帶子	the *navel* string.
腝	RU².	
	手桿腝了	my arms are *weak*. [swampy ground.
	這個木頭是腝的	this wood is *soft*, as that grown in low
15 臘	LA⁵.	[old custom.
	臘月	the 12th month; lit., *sacrificial*, from an
	臘脒	*cured* meat (because cured in winter).
膘	PIAO¹.	
	三指寬的膘	three finger-breadths of *fat*. [districts).
	猪膘	*cured* pork (a name used in the mountain
18 臟	TSANG⁴.	[*entrails* put into him.
	沒有安臟的人	a stupid person; lit., one who has had no

(436)

注 释

臉（脸）[lien³]
【打脸挂须】画脸描胡子。
【他厚起脸尽说】他厚起脸皮不停地说；不知羞耻。
膿（脓）[loŋ²]
臊 [sao¹]
【臊甲子】蟑螂。
膽（胆）[tan³]
臍（脐）[tsʰi²]
腝 [zu²]
【手杆腝了】手软了。
臘（腊）[la⁵]
膘（膘）[piao¹]
臟（脏）[tsaŋ¹]
【没有安脏的人】愚蠢的人；没心没肺的人。

注释

臣 [tʂʰən²]
　【爱臣儿】最喜欢的。
卧(卧) [o⁴]
　【卧龙带】又作"卧龙袋"，额隆袋，是满族男子的一种服装，马褂的一种。
临(临) [lin²]
　【临凡】谓天仙降临尘凡。
自 [tsɿ⁴]
臬 [ɲie⁵]
臭 [tʂʰəu⁴]
　【他出气臭酒】他呼出的全是酒气。
　【臭话】下流话。
　【两个臭了】两个人关系闹僵了。

臣 2-11　自 4

The 131st radical. (臣)

CH'EN².

| 君臣 | prince and *statesman*. |
| 愛臣兒 | a *favourite*. |

O⁴.

坐臥不安	no rest either sitting or *lying down*.
臥房	a *sleeping* room.
臥龍帶	an outer jacket with loug sleeves and but- [toning down the front.

LIN².

臨凡	to *descend* into this world.
臨時纔來忙	when the time has *come* then you hurry.
臨終的時候	when you *come to* die.

The 132nd radical. (自)

TSÏ⁴.

自古以來	*from* ancient times downward.
自從婚配以後	*since* he was married.
由不得你自己	it does not depend on *yourself*.
自家人	the people of my *own* family.
自然	*naturally* so; *of course*.
我很不自然	I am far from well; lit., not in a *natural* [state of health.
安然自在	in peace and *at ease*.

NIE⁵.

| 臬臺 | the provincial judge (so called from the [batons at his door). |

CH'EO⁴.

臭氣	a *stench*.
他出氣臭酒	his breath *smells of* wine.
臭子	*musk*.
臭話	*obscene* talk.
臭聲名	a *bad* reputation.
臭虫	bed bugs; lit., the *stinking* insect.
兩個臭了	they have become *unfriendly*.

(437)

至 8 臼 4-8

The 133rd radical. (至)

CHÏ⁴.

無所不至	[is nothing he will not *come to*. abandoned; he will *do* anything; lit., there
至到如今	*until* the present.
至誠	*very* sincere.
孬到至極	*extremely* bad.
至於這一切	*as for* all these things.

T'AI².

	[the *lookout-loft*.
不得下臺	in a fix; lit., unable to come down from
講臺	a *platform*; a *pulpit*.
土臺打坐	let us sit down on the *bank*.
燈臺	a *lampstand*.
制臺	Governor General of a province (a *title of respect* to officers).

The 134th radical. (臼)

IAO³.

舀舀	a *ladle*; a *spoon*.
舀一盌飯來	*ladle* out a basin of rice for me.

CH'ONG¹, CHONG¹.

舂鹽	to *pound* salt in a mortar.
舂他一頓	*hit* him a blow.

CHIU⁴.

舅舅	*maternal uncles*.
舅子	*wife's brothers*.

Ü³.

與我無干	it has nothing to do *with* me.
與我無益	it is no advantage *to* me.

(438)

注 释

至 [tʂʅ⁴]
【孬到至極】坏到极点。
臺（台）[tʰai²]
【土台打坐】坐在河边。
舀 [iao³]
【舀舀】勺子。
舂 [tʂʰoŋ¹] [tʂoŋ¹]
【舂他一頓】打他一拳。
舅 [tɕiəu⁴]
與（与）[y³]

注 释

興（兴）[ɕin¹] [ɕin⁴]
【这个兴得宽】兴得宽：广泛发生，实行。
【你们那边兴不兴】兴：举办，实行。
【时兴样】流行的风尚。

舉（举）[tɕy³]
【不受人的抬举】抬举：称赞；提拔。

舊（旧）[tɕiəu⁴]
【辛苦钱过得旧】越是辛苦赚来的钱，越会珍惜。

臼 8-12

9 興 SHIN¹.

與人不同	different *from* other men.
與其走路不如騎馬	walking is not so nice as riding (denotes *comparison*).
十年興敗多少人	in ten years' time many men *prosper* and many are ruined.
與旺	*flourishing*.
那一天興工	on what day will you *commence* work?
這個興得寬	this is *done* in many places; widely *practised*.
你們那邊興不興	do you *practise* these things in your country?
時興樣	the present fashion.

READ SHIN⁴.

說得高興	to speak *elatedly*.

11 舉 CHÜ³.

舉目觀看	to *raise* the eyes and look.
萬事勸人休瞞昧 舉頭三尺有神明	we exhort you to practise no deception in anything; the gods are but three feet *above* our heads.
我舉薦你	I will *recommend* you.
舉人	a Master of Arts.
不受人的擡舉	he cannot stand *praise*, he becomes proud.
還沒有舉動	they have not yet *commenced* work.
一舉兩便	killing two birds with one stone.

12 舊 CHIU⁴.

舊的不去新的不來	if the *old* does not go the new does not come.
衣是新的好 人是舊的好	clothes—new ones are good; servants—old ones are best.
我們是舊交	we are friends of *long standing*.
辛苦錢過得舊	hard-earned money lasts a *long time*.
舊年	last year.
顏色舊了	the colour is *faded*.
照舊	as *before*.

(439)

舌 2-10 舛 6

The 135th radical. (舌)

SHE⁵.

| 舌頭 | the *tongue*. |
| 耍舌頭 | to *squabble*. |

SHE⁴.

| 離塞舍不遠 | not far from my *humble abode*. |
| 舍弟 | my *younger brother*. |

SHU¹.

| 舒舒服服的 | *easy; comfortable*. |

P'U⁴.

開舖子	to open *shop*.
崇義舖	the *village* of Ts'ong-ngi.
床舖	a *bed*.

KUAN³.

公舘	a *mansion*.
會舘	*guild-halls*.
學舘	a *school*.
茶舘	a *tea shop*.
開醫舘	to open a *dispensary*.

TA⁵.

| 㗳嘴 | to *smack* the lips. |

The 136th radical. (舛)

U³.

跳的跳舞的舞	*jumping* and *dancing*.
亂舞	to *fence* about recklessly.
屋頭的東西亂舞起	the things in the house are all *higgledy-piggledy*.
給他一歇舞起	do it in a *rough and ready* fashion.

(440)

注 释

舌 [ṣe⁵]
【耍舌头】花言巧语，耍嘴皮子。
舍 [ṣei⁴]
舒 [ṣu¹]
舖（铺）[pʰu⁴]
舘（馆）[kuan³]
㗳 [ta⁵]
【㗳嘴】吃东西嘴唇出声。
舞 [u³]

注释

般 [pan¹]
　【般般不少】一样都不少，即种类齐全。
船 [tʂʰuan²]
　【茶船子】飞碟。
舵 [to⁴]
艙（舱）[tsʰaŋ¹]
　【火舱】船上做饭的场所。
艞 [tʰiao⁴]
　【搭艞板】跳板，置于船、岸之间供人上下的长板。
艭 [ʂuaŋ¹]
　【艭飞燕的船】艭飞燕：一种小型桨船。
良 [liaŋ²]
艱（艰）[tɕien¹]

舟 4-18　艮 1-11

The 137th radical. (舟)

⁴ 般　PAN¹.

| 般般不少 | there are all *sorts* of things. |
| 莫給他一般的見識 | don't make yourself the same *kind* of man as he is; answer not a fool according to his folly. |

⁵ 船　CH'UAN².

一隻船	one *boat*.
火輪船	a *steamer*.
茶船子	a *saucer*.

舵　TO⁴.

| 船載千金主舵一人 | though the boat carries 1,000 catties, there is but one man at the *helm*. |

¹⁰ 艙　TS'ANG¹.

| 火艙 | the cooking *compartment* in a boat. |

¹² 艞　T'IAO⁴.

| 搭艞板 | to put out a *landing plank* from a boat to [the shore. |

¹⁸ 艭　SHUANG¹.

| 艭飛燕的船 | a small *two-oared* boat. |

The 138th radical. (艮)

¹ 艮　LIANG².

艮心	the conscience; lit., *good* heart.
善艮的百姓	*loyal* people.
艮馬比君子六畜與人同	a *gentle* horse is like a prince, all other animals are like the common people.

¹¹ 艱　CHIEN¹.

| 銀錢艱難 | money-making is *distressing*. |

(441)

The 139th radical. (色)

SE⁵.

顏色配得好	the *colours* are well matched.
秋色	the *hues* of autumn.
好氣色	a good *complexion*.
女色	female *beauty*.
酒不醉人人自醉 色不迷人人自迷	it is not wine that intoxicates people, they intoxicate themselves, nor do *women* beguile men, men beguile themselves.
出色的人	a *notable* person.
孬脚色	a useless *fellow*.
這個高一個色	this is of better *quality*.
色子	*dice*.

IEN⁴.

艷粧	to dress *gaudily*.
你莫在這裏妖艷兒	don't come here with your *seductive ways*.
艷陽天氣	the *genial but enervating* weather of spring.

The 140th radical. (艸)

NGAI⁴.

陳艾	*mugwort*.

SHIONG¹.

川芎	*angelica*, grown in Sï-ch'uan.

SHO⁵.

芍藥花	a small variety of *peony*; the *dahlia*.

Ü⁴.

芋兒	the young tubers of the *taro*.
洋芋	*potatoes*.

注 釋

色 [se⁵]
【这个高一个色】这个质量好一些。
艷（艳）[ien⁴]
艾 [ŋai⁴]
【陈艾】艾叶。
芎 [ɕioŋ¹]
芍 [ʂo⁵]
芋 [y⁴]
【芋儿】芋头。
【洋芋】马铃薯。

注 释

芝 [tṣɻ¹]
芬 [fən¹]
芳 [faŋ¹]
芙 [fu²]
花 [xua¹]

【石花】钟乳水的花状凝结物,即碳酸钙。
【买一个钱的刨花】刨花:刨木料时刨下来的薄片,多呈卷状。
【花马】斑马。
【岔花田】邻近田地(属于不同人)。
【游花街】花街:妓院。

艸 4

芝芬芳芙花

CHĪ¹.
芝蔴 — sesamum.

FEN¹.
草木長得芬芳 — plants are growing *luxuriantly*.

FANG¹.
留芳百世 — to leave a *good name* to a hundred generations.

FU².
芙蓉花 — *Hibiscus mutabilis*.

HUA¹.
一朵花 — one *flower*.
一窩花 — one *flowering-plant*.
花園 — a *flower* garden.
花生 — peannts.
天花 — small-pox.
石花 — *lichens* on stones.
棉花線子 — *cotton*, thread.
蔥花兒滿撒 — a pinch of leek *shreds* on every dish; to flatter all round.
買一個錢的刨花 — buy a cash worth of *shavings*.
柴花子 — split firewood.
繡花 — to embroider *flowers*.
花布 — *figured* cloth.
花馬 — a *piebald* horse.
花狗兒 — a *spotted* dog.
染花了 — unevenly dyed.
岔花田 — adjacent fields all belonging to different owners.
花轎子 — a bride's chair, which is profusely ornamented.
花錢 — to *spend* money; the red paper ornaments hung on door lintels at New Year.
花費不多 — the *expense* is not great.
遊花街 — to go to a *brothel*.
眼睛花了 — *blurred* vision.
把心耍花了 — his mind is *absorbed* in his vicious pleasures.

(443)

艸 4-5

	CHIAI⁴.	
芥末		ground *mustard*.
	CH'IEN⁴.	
下荋粉		put in some *thickening*, usually pea-flour.
	CHIE⁵.	
白芨兒		a beautiful orchid found on the sandy [banks of rivers.
	FEN¹.	
草木長得芬芳		the plants are growing *luxuriantly*.
	CH'IN³.	
芹菜		*celery*.
水芹		*water-cress*.
	PA¹.	
芭蕉		the *banana*.
	IA².	
荳芽		bean *sprouts*.
發芽芽了		*budding; springing; germinating*.
	ÜEN².	
芫荽		*coriander*.
	CHU⁴.	
苧蔴		*china-grass; Boehmeria nivea*.
	I³.	
苡仁米		the seeds of *Job's-tears (Coix lachryma)*.
	RO⁵.	
若是不好		*if* it is bad.
假若		*supposing*.
	MU⁵.	
馬苜蓿		a small *trefoil* used as a vegetable, and [also for fodder.

(444)

注 释

芥[tɕiai⁴]
荋[tɕʰien⁴]
芨[tʂie⁵]
芬[fən¹]
芹[tɕʰin²]
（CH'IN⁴当为CH'IN²，见803页勘误表。）
芭[pa¹]
芽[ia²]
芫[yen²]
【芫荽】香菜。
苧[tʂu⁴]
苡[i³]
若[zo⁵]
苜[mu⁵]

艸 5

	KEO³.	
苟	苟合爲婚	living in *fornication* with a woman.
	CH'IE².	
茄	茄子	the *brinjal* or egg-plant.
	茄色	the colour of brinjals, shades of purple and [violet.
	K'O¹.	
苛	苛刻人	to *annoy* or *oppress* people.
	K'U³.	
苦	苦藥	*bitter* medicine.
	勞勞苦苦得來的	obtained through much toil and *suffering*.
	受苦	to endure *affliction*.
	下苦	a person in *distressing* circumstances; the [destitute.
	MAO².	
茅	茅草	a tall grass (*Imperata arundinacea*).
	笆茅草	reed-grass (*Erianthus japonicus*).
	茅房	a *thatched* shed; a privy.
	茅茅柴	*dry grass* used for firewood.
	MONG⁴.	
茂	草木茂盛	*luxuriant* vegetation.
	財源茂盛	your business is *prospering*.
	人丁茂盛	his family is *large and flourishing*.
	MIAO².	
苗	菜苗苗	*seedling* vegetables.
	後代根苗	*descendants*.
	苗子	a race of aborigines in W. China.
	MO².	
茉	茉莉花	the white *jessamine* (*Jasminium sambac*).
	PAO¹.	
苞	花苞苞	flower *buds*.

(445)

注 释

苟 [kəu³]
【苟合为婚】男女间不正当的结合。

茄 [tɕʰie²]

苛 [kʰo¹]

苦 [kʰu³]
【劳劳苦苦得来的】辛勤劳作得来的。
【下苦】贫苦人。

茅 [mao²]
【笆茅草】芦苇草。
【茅茅柴】用作柴火的干草。

茂 [moŋ⁴]

苗 [miao²]
【菜苗苗】正在成长的蔬菜。
【后代根苗】根苗：子孙。

茉 [mo²]

苞 [pao¹]

西蜀方言

艸 5-6

	CHAN¹.	
秧苫		a *mattress* made of young rice.
	T'AI².	
蒼苔		*moss* on stones.
青苔		*mossy growth* on stones under water.
	SHAO².	
田茗		a kind of *vetch*, grown as a field crop.
江西茗		a kind of *clover*.
紅茗		*sweet potatoes*.
脚板茗		foot-shaped *yams*.
	IN¹.	
英雄		a *leader* among men.
	CH'A².	
喫茶		to drink *tea*.
茶食		*confectionery*.
打茶尖		to take a small lunch.
茶錢		*tea* money; extra cash given to coolies.
茶花		the *camellia*.
	HUANG¹.	
開荒		to break up *waste land*.
茨荒荒		thorny *undergrowth*.
收荒的		a dealer in *second-hand* articles.
丟荒疏了		*neglected*, as a handicraft; out of practice.
荒年		a year of *dearth*.
	HUE².	
茴香		*fennel*; *dill*, and *anise*.
	RONG².	
鹿茸		*young antlers* of the deer, used as medicine.
煮茸了		boil it till it is *soft*.
把穀草打茸		beat the straw till it is *pliable*.

(446)

注 释

苫 [tṣan¹]
【秧苫】用青水稻制成的床垫。
苔 [tʰai²]
【苍苔】青色苔藓。
茗 [ṣao²]
【江西茗】一种三叶草。
【红茗】红薯。
【脚板茗】脚形山药,甘薯。
英 [in¹]
茶 [tṣʰa²]
【打茶尖】吃一点午饭。
荒 [xuaŋ¹]
【茨荒荒】荆棘。
【丢荒疏了】指学业、技术因不常习用而致生疏。
茴 [xuei²]
茸 [zoŋ²]
【煮茸了】煮至细软。
【把谷草打茸】把稻草打至柔韧。

注 释

荆 [tɕin¹]
苳 [ko⁵]
【苳葱】洋葱。
荔 [li⁴]
茫 [maŋ²]
茼 [tʰoŋ²]
茨 [tsʰɿ⁴]
草 [tsʰao³]
【草字】草书。
莊（庄）[tʂuaŋ¹]
莧（苋）[xan⁴]
【冬苋菜】一种青菜，四川地区常用来做咸菜或盐干菜。

	CHIN¹.	
黃荆子		a kind of thornless *thorn* tree.
紫荆花		the Judas tree (*Cercis sinensis*).
拙荆在看屋		my wife (lit., stupid *thorn*) is keeping the house.
	KO⁵.	
苳葱		*onions*, especially *Allium victoriale*.
	LI⁴.	
荔枝		the *lichee* (*Nephalium litchi*).
	MANG².	
渺渺茫茫的		*vague*.
	T'ONG².	
茼蒿菜		*Chrysanthemum segetum*, used as a vegetable.
	TS'ɿ⁴.	
		same as 刺.
	TS'AO³.	
割草		to cut *grass*.
穀草		rice *straw*.
花草		*flowering plants*; *flowers* real or artificial.
燈草		the *pith of rushes*, used as lampwick.
今年的布草貴		*calico* is dear this year.
草房子		a *thatched* house.
草地		wild *pasture* lands.
草紙		coarse brown paper made from *straw*, etc.
做得聊草		*roughly* done.
草字		the *running hand* in writing.
	CHUANG¹.	
莊重		*respectful and proper* in conduct.
	HAN⁴.	
莧菜		a species of *Amarantus* used as a vegetable.
冬莧菜		*Malva verticilata*, used as a vegetable.

(447)

西蜀方言 447

艸 7-8

	HO².	
荷葉		lotus leaves.
荷包蛋		poached eggs.
荷包兒		a *purse* carried at the girdle.
	LI¹.	for example of use see 茉.
	SÜ¹.	for example of use see 茪.
	MO⁵.	
莫亂説		don't talk nonsense.
莫非是某人		I wonder if it is so-and-so.
	TEO⁴.	
胡荳米兒		horse *beans*, shelled fresh *beans*.
四季荳		kidney *beans*.
豌荳		peas.
	CH'ANG¹.	
菖蒲		the *calamus* or *sweet flag*.
	FE³.	
菲薄得很		a very *mean* gift (polite).
	HUA².	
中華國		China; lit., the *Glorious* Central Kingdom.
光華		brilliant.
花開得華麗		the plant has flowered *gorgeously*.
榮華富貴萬萬年		*glory* and wealth to all generations.
虛華世界		this *vain* world.
	CHÜIN¹.	
菌子		mushrooms, toadstools, etc.
	KU¹.	
慈菇		the *arrowhead*, grown as a vegetable.
摩菇		a variety of *mushroom*.

(448)

注 释

荷 [xo²]
莉 [li⁴]
（LI¹当为LI⁴，见803页勘误表。）
荽 [sy¹]
莫 [mo⁵]
荳（豆）[təu⁴]
菖 [tṣʰaŋ¹]
菲 [fei³]
【菲薄得很】菲薄：微薄，形容礼物，常作谦词。
華（华）[xua²]
【光华】光彩明亮。
菌 [tɕyn⁴]
（CHÜIN¹当为CHÜIN⁴，见803页勘误表。）
菇 [ku¹]
【摩菇】蘑菇。

注 释

菊 [tɕy⁵]
菓（果）[ko³]
【果木子】可以吃的果实。
菱 [lin²]
【铁菱角】菱角状的尖锐铁器。战时置于路上或水中，用以刺伤敌方人马。
菉（菉）[lu⁵]
【菉豆】扁豆。
莽 [maŋ³]
菴（庵）[ŋan¹]
【茅菴草舍】对自家房子的谦称。
菢（抱）[pao⁴]
【菢蛋】孵蛋。
【菢房】孵化家禽的场所。
【一菢猪儿】菢：量词，窝。
萆（蓖）[pi¹]
萍 [pʰin²]
菠 [po¹]
菩 [pʰu²]

艸 8

	CHÜ⁵.	
菊 花		chrysanthemums.
六 月 菊		asters.
洋 菊 花		dahlias.
	KO³.	
菓 木 子		edible *fruits*.
	LIN².	
菱 角		water-chestnuts (Trapabispinosa).
鐵 菱 角		caltrops.
	LU⁵.	
菉 荳		lentils.
	MANG³.	
太 粗 莽 了		he is too *rude*.
	NGAN¹.	
茅 菴 草 舍		my mean *hut* (polite).
菴 觀 寺 院		*temples* of all kinds.
尼 姑 菴		a *nunnery*.
	PAO⁴.	
菢 蛋		to *hatch* eggs.
菢 房		an *incubator*.
一 菢 猪 兒		a *litter* of pigs. (N. A.)
	PI¹.	
萆 麻 油		castor-oil.
	PI'N².	
浮 萍		duckweed.
	PO¹.	
菠 菜		spinach.
	P'U².	
菩 薩		an *idol* (from the Sanscrit word "*Bodhi-sativa*").

艸 8-9

	T'AO².	
葡萄	葡萄	the *vine*; *grapes*.
	TS'AI⁴.	
菜	小菜	*vegetables*.
	葷菜	*strong meats*.
	海菜	*food* from the sea; *seaweed, etc.*
	鹹菜	*pickles*.
	請菜	please partake of the *food* (includes everything but rice).
	沒得菜	the *dishes of meat* are very poor (polite).
	菜子	Chinese *rape*, from which the vegetable oil is extracted.
	UE¹.	
萎	曬萎了	*drooping* or *flagging* with the sun, as plants [do].
	IEN¹.	
菸	葉子菸	*tobacco*.
	FU², K'U².	
葫	葫蘆	the *bottle-gourd*.
	SHÜEN¹.	
萱	椿萱並茂	are your parents both well? lit., cedrela and *daylily* (polite).
	HUEN¹.	
葷	不喫葷	to fast from *strong meats*.
	大葷	*pork*.
	小葷	*beef*.
	葷素點心	confectionery made *with* or without *lard*.
	KO⁵.	
葛	葛蔴布	summer cloth made from the fibre of *Pueraria Thunbergiana*.
	瓜葛親	distantly connected relatives (like creepers).
	K'UE².	
葵	向日葵	the *sunflower*.

(450)

注 释

萄 [tʰao²]
菜 [tsʰai⁴]
【请菜】分享食物（但不包括米饭）。
萎 [uei¹]
菸（烟）[ien¹]
葫 [fu²] [kʰu²]
萱 [ɕyen¹]
【椿萱并茂】喻父母健在。
葷（荤）[xuən¹]
【大荤】谓肥腻的肉食，有时特指猪肉。
【小荤】牛肉。
葛 [ko⁵]
【瓜葛亲】远房亲戚。
葵 [kʰuei²]

注释

落[lo⁵]
【太阳落坡】太阳下山了。
【轿子落平】放下轿子。
【胎落了】流产了。
【落个数】统计个数。
【落薄了】落薄：同"落魄"。
【心子落不下】放心不了。
萹[pien³]
葡[pʰu²]
蒂[ti⁴]
【花蒂蒂】花萼。
董[toŋ³]
葬[tsaŋ⁴]
葱[tsʰoŋ¹]
【葱子】洋葱。
【办一根葱】贿赂考官。

艸 9

落	LO⁵.	
	落葉子	the *fall* of the leaf; trees *dropping* their [leaves.
	落雨	to *rain*.
	落到地獄	to *descend* into hell.
	太陽落坡	the sun is *setting*.
	轎子落平	*set down* the chair.
	胎落了	*abortion*.
	生意落盤	the transaction is *completed*.
	落頭髮	to *cast* the hair.
	落了魂	to *lose* one's wits; scared.
	黑的落在白的上	*written down* in black and white.
	落個數	*note* the number; make an inventory.
	不至落空	it will not be *in vain*.
	落薄了	*reduced* to poverty.
	沒得下落	there is no trace of him; I cannot find him.
	你座落在那裏	where do you *live*?
	有着落沒得	is anything *definite* done yet?
	心子落不下	I cannot be *at rest* about it.
萹	PIEN³.	
	萹竹葉	*flags*.
葡	P'U².	
	葡萄架	a *vine* trellis.
	北葡萄	dried *grapes*.
蒂	TI⁴.	
	花蒂蒂	the *calyx* of a flower.
董	TONG³.	
	古董舖	*antique* shops, old *curiosity* shops.
	古董人	an *old-fashioned* person.
葬	TSANG⁴.	same as 塟.
葱	TS'ONG¹.	
	葱子	*onions*. [degree.
	辦一根葱	to bribe the officials *all through* for B. A.

(451)

西蜀方言

艸 9-10

萬 UAN⁴.
十千爲一萬 — 10 thousand make one *myriad*.
萬人 — all men.
萬事皆已定 / 浮生空自忙 } all things are decreed, it is vain to hurry.
萬歲牌 — an *emperor's* tablet.
萬萬不能 — certainly not.

萵 O¹.
萵笋尖 — the top leaves of overgrown *lettuce*.

葉 IE⁵.
樹葉子 — a *leaf* of a tree.
金葉子 — gold *leaf*.
茶葉子 — tea (before it is infused).
葉子菸 — *leaf* tobacco, smoked like cigars.
車葉子 — the boards on the endless chain of a pump.
肝葉子 — the *lobes* of the liver.
紙葉子 — playing *cards*.

蒸 CHEN¹.
蒸嘗田 — entailed property, the proceeds of which [are used for ancestral *sacrifices*.

蓄 SHIO¹.
積蓄起來的 — *accumulated*.

蒿 HAO¹.
苦蒿 — *southern-wood* (artimisia).

蓋 KAI⁴.
same as 盖.

蒙 MONG².
蒙童子 — pupils; lit., *ignorant* lads.
發蒙 — to begin to go to school.
寫蒙格 — to trace characters over a copy.
蒙頭蒙尾 — to *darken* counsel.
蒙恩 — to *receive* favours.
蒙古 — *Mongolia*.

(452)

注 释

萬(万)[uan⁴]
【万岁牌】御赐的牌匾。
萵(莴)[o¹]
葉(叶)[ie⁵]
【金叶子】宋代出现的一种黄金货币。
蒸[tʂən¹]
【蒸尝田】田里的收成用来祭祀祖先，故称。
蓄[ɕio⁵]
（SHIO¹当为SHIO⁵，见803页勘误表。）
蒿[xao¹]
蓋(盖)[kai⁴]
蒙[moŋ²]
【蒙童子】学生。
【写蒙格】先生写一张字模，学生把白纸盖在上面，按照白纸映出的字影描摹。
【蒙头蒙尾】添乱，使更加混乱、困难。

注释

蒲 [pʰu²]
  【石菖蒲】观赏植物的一种，茎可入药。
蓆（席）[si⁵]
襄 [so¹]
蒜 [suan⁴]
蓉 [ioŋ²]
蔗 [tṣei⁴]
蔻 [kʰəu⁴]
  【肉豆蔻】一种植物，可作香料。
  【蔻肉】一种肉类做法，类于扣肉。
蔫 [ien¹]
  【蔫蔫缠缠】不舒服的，不愿意的。
蓼 [liao³]
蓮（莲）[lien²]
蔴（麻）[ma²]
蔔（卜）[pu⁴]

艸 10-11

蒲	P'U².	
	蒲草蓆子	rush mats.
	蒲團	a hassock.
	石菖蒲	a small leaved *flag (Typha latifolia)*.
蓆	SI⁵.	
	曬蓆	large *mats* on which grain is dried.
襄	SO¹.	
	襄衣	a *palm-fibre rain-cloak*.
蒜	SUAN⁴.	
	大蒜	*garlic*.
蓉	IONG².	
		for example of use see 芙.
蔗	CHE⁴.	
	甘蔗	*sugar-cane*.
蔻	K'EO⁴.	
	肉豆蔻	the *nutmeg*.
	蔻肉	a dish of meat sometimes provided at [feasts.
蔫	IEN¹.	
	白菜曬蔫了	the cabbages are *flagging (drooping)* with [the sun.
	蔫蔫趣趣	*indisposed*.
蓼	LIAO³.	
	蓼子草	*smartweed*.
蓮	LIEN².	
	蓮花	the *lotus*.
	唱蓮花閙	beggars chanting to an accompaniment of [clappers.
	蓮花白	cabbage, the round hard-headed sort.
蔴	MA².	
		same as 麻.
蔔	PU⁴.	
	白蘿蔔	*turnips*.
	紅蘿蔔	*carrots*.

(453)

西蜀方言 453

艸 11-13

	SU¹.	
蔬菜		vegetable diet.
	T'ONG¹.	
蓪草		Fatsia papyrifera (the pith is used for making artificial flowers).
泡蓪樹		a tree with soft, light wood, Pauloowia imperialis.
	IN⁴.	
蔭生		son of a person who died in defence of his country.
	CH'IAO².	
蕎子		buckwheat.
	MA³, MAI³.	
苦蕒菜		the sow-thistle; the dandelion.
	TANG⁴.	
漂流浪蕩		idle and dissipated.
放蕩無禮		reckless and unreasonable.
蕩子		prostitute.
把盌蕩乾淨		rinse the basin.
掃蕩乾淨		to make a clean riddance of.
蕩刀子		to hone a knife.
	TSIAO¹.	
芭蕉扇		fans shaped like a banana leaf.
	HAO¹.	
薅田		to weed rice fields.
把毛辮子薅倒		seize him by the queue.
	HAI⁴.	
薤子		a small variety of globe onion.
	CHIANG¹.	
生薑		fresh ginger.
薑黃		a yellow dye used to dye paper, turmeric.

(454)

注　释

蔬[su¹]
蓪[tʰoŋ¹]
蔭(荫)[in⁴]
　【荫生】为保卫国家而死的烈士之子。
蕎(荞)[tɕʰiao²]
　【荞子】荞麦。
蕒(荬)[ma³] [mai³]
　【苦荬菜】蒲公英。
蕩(荡)[taŋ⁴]
　【荡子】娼妓。
　【把碗荡干净】把碗洗干净。
蕉[tsiao¹]
薅[xao¹]
　【薅田】耘田。
薤[xai⁴]
薑(姜)[tɕiaŋ¹]

注 释

薄 [po⁵]
薩（萨）[sa¹]
薪 [sin¹]
薦（荐）[tsien⁴]
【草荐】草垫子，草席。
藁 [kao³]
藍（蓝）[lan²]
藐 [miao³]
【小藐人】卑鄙的、品行低下的人。
藻 [pʰiao²] [pʰiao¹]
【浮藻子】浮萍。
薹 [tʰai²]
藏 [tsʰaŋ²] [tsaŋ⁴] [tsaŋ³] [tsan³]

艸 13-14

薄 PO⁵.
厚薄不均　thick and *thin* are unevenly mixed.
穿得單薄　*thinly* clad.
命薄　my fate is *poor*.
做事刻薄　he does things *meanly*.
一點薄禮　a small present.
薄荷油　oil of *peppermint*.

薩 SA¹.
　　for example of use see 菩.

薪 SIN¹.
薪水　a teacher's wages; lit., *fuel* and *water*.

薦 TSIEN⁴.
寫封薦書　write a letter of *introduction*.
是那個舉薦的　who *recommended* him?
草薦　a straw *mattress*.

14 藁 KAO³.
藁篾子　thin *straw* mats.

藍 LAN².
藍靛　*indigo*.
藍布　*blue* cloth.

藐 MIAO³.
藐視人　to *disdain* people.
小藐人　a mean man; one who *haggles* about trifles.

藻 P'IAO², ¹.
浮藻子　*duckweed*.

薹 T'AI².
白菜薹　the *flower-stalk* of cabbages.

藏 TS'ANG².
隱藏　to *conceal* one's self.
收藏　to *store away* goods.

(455)

艸 14-16

READ TSANG⁴.

西藏	Tibet; lit., the *Treasure-house* of the West.
總爺打藏	the centurion invites his friends to a paying feast.
藏婆子	a *Tibetan* woman.

READ TSANG³, TSAM³.

| 藏巴 | *meal* made of various grains used by the [Tibetans. |

FAN².

| 藩臺 | Treasurer of a province; lit., one who *fences* [about—the money. |

NGI⁴.

武藝	military *accomplishments*.
手藝	a *trade*, a *handicraft*.
藝多不養家	a jack-of-all-*trades* cannot support his [family.

NGEO³.

| 藕粉 | flour made from *lotus-root*; *arrowroot*. |

IO⁵.

草藥	herb *remedies*.
喫藥	to take *medicine*.
火藥	*gunpowder*.

MO².

| 口摩 | *mushrooms* from beyond the frontiers. |

LU².

| 茅蘆桿 | dry *reed* grass, used for fuel. |

HO⁵.

| 藿香 | *betony*. |

SU¹.

蘇蔴子	*Perilla ocymoides* (a bird-seed).
你纔不蘇氣	you are very im*proper*.
做得姑蘇	*well* made.

(456)

注 释

【总爷打藏】打藏：赴盛宴。
【藏婆子】西藏妇女。
【藏巴】西藏人民用各种谷物制成的食物。
藩 [fan²]
藝（艺）[ŋi⁴]
藕 [ŋəu³]
藥（药）[io⁵]
摩 [mo²]
【口摩】国外进口的磨菇。
蘆（芦）[lu²]
藿 [xo⁵]
蘇（苏）[su¹]
【你才不苏气】苏气：态度大方，打扮漂亮。
【做得姑苏】做得很好。

注释

蘭(兰)[lan²]
蘸[tsan⁴]
【蘸盃】放调料的小碟子。
蘿(萝)[lo²]
虎[fu³]
虐[nio⁵]
虔[tɕʰien¹]
處(处)[tʂʰu³][tʂʰu⁴]

艸 17-19　虍 2-5

17 蘭　LAN².

蘭草花　orchidacious plants, such as *cymbidium, maxalaria*, etc. [used to scent tea.
株蘭　*chloranthus inconspicuous*, the flowers are
19 玉蘭　*magnolia yulan*.

蘸　TSAN⁴.

蘸點墨　*take a dip* of ink on your pencil.
蘸盃　small sauce dishes in which food is *dipped* when eating.

蘿　LO².

白蘿蔔 and 紅蘿蔔 *turnips* and *carrots*.
蘿蔔子　*turnip* seed.

The 141st radical. (虍)

2 虎　FU³.

老虎　a *tiger*.
母老虎　a *tigress*; a virago.
虎將　a *brave* general.
明知山有虎 } if you know there is a *tiger* in the moun-
莫向虎山行 } tain, don't go to the mountain.

3 虐　NIO⁶.

暴虐百姓　to *tyrannize* over the people; to *oppress*.

虔　CH'IEN¹.

5 要虔心　you must be *devout* when worshipping the [gods.

處　CH'U³.

我要處治你　I will *chastise* you!
我爲你的事很 } I met with great *blame* on your account.
受處分
處不下去　I will not be *appeased*.

(457)

虛 5-7

READ CH'U⁴.

別處不同	other *places* are different.
貴處在那裏	where is your honourable *place* of abode?
有那些用處	what are the *uses* of it?
有甚麼好處	what is the *benefit*? where is the advan-[tage?]

6 虛

SHÜ¹.

虛空中	in *space*; in the *vault of heaven*.
他屋頭是空虛的	his house is *empty*.
虛度光陰	to pass one's days in *vain*.
虛假	*false*.
踹虛了脚	I took a *false* step; put my foot into a hole.
虛字眼	an *abstract* word; a particle.
外實內虛	an appearance of wealth without the [reality.]
太謙虛	you are too *humble-minded*.
做賊人心虛	a thief is always *apprehensive*.
人虛弱	I am *weak* in body.
脉虛	the pulse is *weak*.
牆脚虛了	the wall is *undermined*; the base of the [wall is broken down.]
你莫虛華	don't be *extravagant*.
虛華世界	this *vain* world.

7 號

HAO⁴.

打個記號	put a *mark* on it to remember it by.
約個暗號	to fix on a private *signal*.
掛號	to register one's *name*.
國號	the *name* of a dynasty.
年號	the *style* of a reign.
你是甚麼大號	what is your *style*?
號令不行	his *commands* are not obeyed.
號衣	*regimentals*; uniform.
是甚麼寶號	what is your honourable *business*, or [shop sign?]
大字號	a large wholesale firm; a large business with nothing exposed for sale, as a pawn-shop.
號筒	a *trumpet*.

(458)

注　釋

虛 [ɕy¹]
【虛字眼】虛字或虛詞。
【你莫虛華】你不要浮華不实。

號（号）[xao⁴] [xao²]
【你是甚么大号】什么是你的风格？
【大字号】大型批发公司。

注 释

【号头儿】新郎。
【讨赏号】赏号：赏金。
虞（虞）[y²]
【不虞故得】出乎意料。
虧（亏）[kʰuei¹]
虫 [tṣʰoŋ²]
【生虫】生蛆。
虱 [se⁵]
虰 [tin¹]
【虰虰猫儿】蜻蜓。
虼 [ke⁵]

號 7-10　虫 2-3

號頭兒	a *groom*.
頭號子	the best *kind*.
討賞號	to claim a *reward*.

READ HAO².

| 號哭 | to *weep* and *wail*. |

虞 Ü².

| 我自己疏虞了 | I was not *careful*; I was remiss in my duty. |
| 不虞故得 | un*expectedly*. |

10 虧 KʻUEI¹.

說虧欠	to speak of people's *shortcomings* towards [one's self.
喫虧	to suffer *wrong*.
莫虧人	don't *overreach* people.
填虧空	to make up a *deficit*.
虧心	to *violate* one's conscience.
虧省很了	he is very much *debilitated* by excesses.
草鞋虧脚	the sandals *hurt* my feet.

The 142nd radical. (虫)

虫² CHʻONG².

虫喫了的	eaten by *insects*.
生虫	to breed *maggots*.
虫子	the white wax *insect*.

虱² SE⁵.

| 虱子 | a *louse*. |
| 竹虱子 | bamboo *bugs*. |

虰 TIN¹.

| 虰虰猫兒 | the *dragon-fly*. |

虼³ KE⁵.

| 虼蚤 | a *flea*. |

(459)

虫 3-5

	MONG².	
蛋₄	牛䖟蚊	clegs; gad-flies.
	FU².	
蚨	青蚨	copper cash (from a species of water-beetle).
	PANG⁴, PAN⁴.	
蚌	蚌壳	clam shells.
	KONG¹.	for example of use see 蜈.
蚣		
	TSAO³.	
蚤	蛇蚤籠	flea traps.
	P'A².	
蚆	海蚆子	cowry shells.
	海蚆狗兒	pug-dogs.
	UEN².	
蚊₅	蚊子	mosquitoes; gnats.
	CHU⁴.	
蛀	虫蛀了	eaten by insects; worm-eaten.
	KU¹.	
蛄	叫蛄蛄	grasshoppers.
	SHE².	
蛇	一條毒蛇	a venomous snake.
	四脚蛇	large lizards.
	蛇苞兒	Fragaria japonica.
	CHA³.	
蚱	油蚱貓兒	a kind of edible locust.
	TAN⁴.	
蛋	雞蛋	hen's eggs.
	魚蛋	fish roe.

(460)

注 释

䖟 [moŋ²]
蚨 [fu²]
【青蚨】传说中的一种母与子分离后必会聚回一处的虫;比喻金钱。
蚌 [paŋ⁴] [pan⁴]
蚣 [koŋ¹]
蚤 [tsao³]
蚆 [pʰa²]
【海蚆子】即贝子,软体动物的一种。
【海蚆狗儿】哈巴狗。
蚊 [uən²]
蛀 [tʂu⁴]
蛄 [ku¹]
蛇 [ʂei²]
【蛇苞儿】野草莓。
蚱 [tʂa³]
【油蚱猫儿】油炸蝗虫。
蛋 [tan⁴]
【鱼蛋】鱼卵。

注释

蛆 [tsʰy¹]
蛛 [tṣu¹]
蜂 [kaŋ⁴]
【东蜂日头晒蜂雨】(晒，应为"西"，见803页勘误表。东边日出西边雨。)
【蜂带】彩虹。
蛔 [xuei²]
【蛔食虫】肠道蠕虫。
蛟 [tɕiao¹]
蚰 [tɕʰy⁵] [tɕʰio⁵]
蜂 [foŋ¹]
蜀 [ṣu⁵]
蛹 [ioŋ³]
蛾 [o²]
【涨水蛾】春天里黑蚂蚁聚居的场景。
蜈（蝛）[u²]

虫 5-7

蛆
  TSʻÜ¹.
6 生了蛆   it has bred *maggots*.
蛛
  CHU¹.   for example of use see 蜘.
蜂
  KANG⁴.   an unauthorized character used for 虹 [hong².
東蜂日頭晒蜂雨   a *rainbow* in the east betokens sun, and in the west rain.
蜂帶   *rainbow-coloured* bands used for foot- [binding.
蛔
  HUE².
蛔食虫   *intestinal worms, tape-worm*.
蛟
  CHIAO¹.
出蛟   a *water-dragon* has come forth, said when [there is a great flood).
蚰
  CHʻÜ⁵, CHʻIO⁵.
蚰蟮   *earthworms*.
蜂
  FONG¹.
蜜蜂子   *bees*.
泥蜂子   mud *wasps*.
牛角蜂   a large species of *hornet*.
蜀
  SHU⁵.
西蜀   the ancient kingdom of *Shu* (the present [Sĭ-chʻuan).
蛹
  IONG³.
蠶蛹兒   the *pupa* of the silkworm.
蛾
  O².
飛蛾   *butterflies; moths*.
漲水蛾   black ants hiving in the spring.
喉嚨長了蛾子   he has *diphtheria*.
蜈
  U².
蜈蚣虫   a *centipede*.

(461)

虫 8-10

8 蜘蜇蝱蜜

	CHÏ¹.	
蜘蛛		a *spider*.
	MA².	for example of use see 蜇.
	MONG³.	
草蝱子		a kind of edible *locust*.
	MI⁵,¹.	
蜂蜜糖		*honey*.
甜蜜蜜的		*sweet*.

9 蝠蝮蝴蝦蝲蝗蝙蝕蝶

	FU⁵.	for example of use see 蝠.
	FU⁵.	
土蝮子蛇兒		venomous *snakes*; *vipers*.
	FU².	
花蝴蝶		*butterflies*.
CH'IE², K'E², CH'I².		
蝦蟆兒		a *frog*.
蝦蟆兒館		a boy's school (from the sound of the boys [at lessons).
	LA⁵.	
蠶蝲子 or 羊蝲子		large poisonous *caterpillars*.
	HUANG².	
蝗虫		*locusts*.
	PIEN³.	
夜蝙蝠		*bats*.
	SHÏ⁵.	
日蝕		an *eclipse* of the sun.
	TIE⁵.	for example of use see 蝴.

10 螞

	MA³.	
螞蟥		a *leech*.
螞蟻子		*ants*.

(462)

注释

蜘 [tṣʅ¹]
蜇 [ma²]
蝱 [moŋ³]
蜜 [mi⁵] [mi¹]
蝠 [fu⁵]
蝮 [fu⁵]
蝴 [fu²]
蝦(虾) [tɕʰie²] [kʰei²] [tɕʰi²]
【虾蟆儿】蛤蟆。
【虾蟆儿馆】男童学校。
蝲 [la⁵]
蝗 [xuaŋ²]
蝙 [pien³]
蝕(蚀) [ṣʅ⁵]
蝶 [tie⁵]
螞(蚂) [ma³]

注释

蝽 [koŋ³]
【猪蝽嘴】猪嘴。
【猪把地蝽烂了】猪把地都拱烂了。
【蝽猪子】野猪。
螃 [pʰaŋ²]
螌 [pan¹]
【螌蝥】同"斑蝥",昆虫,身体黑色,鞘翅上有黄黑色斑纹,关节处能分泌黄色毒液。
螢(萤) [yn²]
蛳(螄) [sʅ¹]
蹌 [tsʰaŋ¹]
融 [ioŋ²]
【他两个融念得很】他两个很亲密。
螺 [lo²]
【螺蛳骨】脚踝骨。
蟆 [ma³]
螬 [tsʰao²]
【螬虫】肠道蠕虫。
蟒 [maŋ³]

虫 10-11

蝽	KONG³.	
	猪蝽嘴	a pig's snout.
	猪把地蝽爛了	the pig has *rooted* up the ground.
	蝽猪子	a wild pig.
	毛虫黑聳黑聳 走路一蝽一蝽 }	the caterpillar is black and *arches* his back as he walks.
螃	PʻANG².	
	螃蟹	*crabs*.
螌	PAN¹.	
	螌蝥	Chinese *cantharides*.
螢	ÜIN².	
	螢火虫	*fireflies*.
蛳	SÏ¹.	
	螺蛳	*spiral-shelled* snails, etc.
蹌	TSʻANG¹.	
	蹌蠅	*flies*.
融	IONG².	
	大家通融	let us all *combine*, i. e., *help* each other with [money.
	他兩個融念得很	they are very *intimate*.
螺	LO².	
	田螺蛳	*spiral* shells found in the rice fields.
	吹海螺	to blow the *conch* shell.
	螺蛳釘	*screw* nails (foreign).
	螺蛳骨	the ankle-bone.
蟆	MA³.	for example of use see 蝦.
螬	TSʻAO².	
	螬虫	*intestinal worms*.
蟒	MANG³.	
	蟒蛇	a large *serpent*.

(463)

虫 11-15

	SI⁵.	
蟋蟀		crickets.
	SO⁵.	for example see last.
	HUANG².	for example of use see 蟥.
	CH'ONG².	same as 虫.
	CHI³.	
蟣子		nits of lice.
	P'AN².	
梳個蟠蟠頭		to do the hair up in a coil, as Chinese [women do.
蟠毛蓋子		to wind the queue round the head.
蟠香		spiral incense.
蟠花		to train, or twist, a plant into a fantastic [shape.
	SHAN².	
蟬子		cicadas.
	SHAN⁴.	for example of use see 蚰.
	SHIAI⁴,³, HAI⁴,³.	for example of use see 螃.
	NGI⁴.	
白螞蟻		white ants.
	SHIE⁵.	
蠍子		a scorpion.
	SHAN².	
蟾酥		a milky secretion extracted from the eye- [brows of the toad (medicine).
	CH'UAI⁴.	
倚老撒薑		he depends on his old age to bully others, [or importune.
	IN².	for example of use see 蝽.
	CH'UEN³.	
愚蠢		foolish.

(464)

注 释

蟋 [si⁵]

蟀 [so⁵]

蟥 [xuaŋ²]

蟲（虫）[tʂʰoŋ²]

蟣（虮）[tɕi³]

【虮子】虱的卵。常比喻微细的事物。

蟠 [pʰan²]

【梳个蟠蟠头】梳一个盘状发型。

【蟠毛盖子】将辫子绕在头上。

蟬（蝉）[ʂan²]

蟮 [ʂan⁴]

蟹 [ɕiai⁴] [ɕiai³] [xai⁴] [xai³]

蟻（蚁）[ŋi⁴]

蠍（蝎）[ɕie⁵]

蟾 [ʂan²]

薑（疌）[tʂʰuai⁴]

【倚老撒疌】仗着年长欺凌弱小。

蠅（蝇）[in²]

蠢 [tʂʰuən²]

注 释

蠚[xo¹][xo²]
【毛虫蠚人】毛虫咬人。
蠟(蜡)[la⁵]
【黃蠟】即蜂蜡，色黄，故称。
【牛油蠟】蜡烛。
蠱(盅)[ku³]
【放蠱】下毒。
蠶(蚕)[tsʰan²]
【蚕子】蚕茧。
【土蚕子】甲虫和毛虫。
蠻(蛮)[man²]
【蛮子】旧时北方人对南方人的讥称。
【在他屋头当蛮】在他的房子里时我像个奴隶。
血[ɕie⁵]
衆(众)[tʂoŋ⁴]

虫 15-19　血 6

蠚	HO¹,².	
	蠚蔴	stinging nettles.
	毛虫蠚人	hairy caterpillars sting people.
蠟	LA⁵.	
	白蠟	white wax.
	黃蠟	bees' wax.
17	牛油蠟	tallow candles.
蠱	KU³.	
	放蠱	to put poison in a person's food.
	蠱惑人	to delude people.
18		
蠶	TS'AN².	
	蠶子	silkworms.
	土蠶子	grubs and caterpillars.
19		
蠻	MAN².	
	蠻子	barbarians, i. e., the aboriginal tribes and the Tibetans.
	在他屋頭當蠻	I am like a slave in their house.
	蠻悍	vigorous; overbearing; daring.

The 143rd radical. (血)

血	SHIE⁵.	
	吐血	vomiting blood. [long.
	血汗錢萬萬年	money gained by bloody sweat will last
	臉上沒血色	he has no colour in his face.
	血氣之勇	a lusty fellow.
	親血表	cousins, i. e., mother's brother's sons.
	血性子的人	an earnest person.
6	出不起血	he has no money to give.
衆	CHONG⁴.	same as 衆.

(465)

行

The 144th radical. (行)

SHIN².

行路	to *walk* on the road.
步行嗎坐轎子	are you *walking* on foot or going by chair?
沒得行李	I have no *baggage*.
行權	to *act* on expediency.
不行	it will not *do*.
走路不得行	walking will not *do*; I cannot walk.
行善	to *do* good.
行個禮	*make* a bow.
行為	*conduct*.
品行不好	his *conduct* is bad.
盡行要不得	all are *undesirable*.
概行壞了	all are *spoiled*.
他在行醫	he is *practising* as a doctor.
生意行時	business is *prospering*.
五行	the five *elements*.
木匠的行頭	a carpenter's *tools*.

READ SHIN⁴.

好個德行	what a good *disposition*!
這個馬的德行好	this horse's *temper* is good.

READ HANG².

八行書	note paper ruled with eight *spaces*.
行綿襖	to *baste* a wadded gown; to *quilt*.
行伍	the *ranks*; the *army*.
排行第幾	what is your *rank* in the family?
不在行	not obedient to the parents' behests; a greenhorn.
洋行	a foreign *warehouse*.
同行生忌妒	people in the same line of *business* are envious of each other.
行市	the *current* price.
七十二行	the seventy-two *trades*.
行斗	the *official* bushel measure.

(466)

注　释

行 [ɕin²] [ɕin⁴] [xaŋ²]

【走路不得行】走不动了。

【尽行要不得】全部不受欢迎。

【概行坏了】全都变质了。

【生意行时】生意兴旺。

【木匠的行头】木匠的工具。

【好个德行】道德品行好。

【行绵袄】缝棉袄。

【行伍】军队。

注释

【轿行】出租轿子的营业机构。

【不成行的子弟】一无是处的家伙。

【那个人行势】那是一个有能力的人。

【行势溜了】你太自负了。

衍 [ien³]

術（术）[ṣu⁴] [ṣu⁵]

街 [kai¹]

【正街】主要街道。

【街市银子】质量低劣的银子。

衕 [tʰoŋ²]

衙 [ia²]

衚（胡）[fu²]

衛（卫）[uei⁴]

【你卫护他吗】你要偏袒他吗?

衣 [i¹]

行 3-9 衣

3 衍	轎行	a chair *shop*.
	不成行的子弟	a good-for-nothing lad.
	那個人行勢	that is a man of ability.
	行勢溜了	you are too boastful.
	IEN³.	
5 術	子孫繁衍	his descendants are *numerous*.
	SHU⁴,⁵.	
	心術好	his *purposes* are good.
	藝術	a *craft*.
	邪術	*necromancy*.
6 街	KAI¹.	
	正街	the main *street*.
	上街	to go on the *street*; to go in to *town* from [the country.
	街市銀子	*business* silver; silver of inferior quality.
	街坊	the *inhabitants of a street*; neighbours.
7 衕 衙	TʼONG².	for example of use see 衚.
	IA².	
	衙門八字開,有理無錢莫進來	the *courthouse* gate is like the character eight, with only right on your side and no money don't enter here.
9 衚 衛	FU².	
	衚衕	a *street* in a Tartar city.
	UE⁴.	
	你衛護他嗎	do you *defend* him? how can you speak in [his favour.
	READ UE².	
	衛隊	a military mandarin's body-*guard*.

The 145th radical. (衣)

衣 I¹.

一件衣裳	one *garment*.
換衣裳	to change one's *clothes*.

(467)

表 3-5

	小衣 and 汗衣	trousers and shirt.
	老衣	grave-clothes.
	出門求衣食	to work for a living (lit., clothing and food).
	披蓑衣	to wear a rain-cloak of palm fibre.
	衣架子好	a fine figure (lit., clothes-horse).
	傘衣子	an umbrella cover.
3 表	PIAO³.	
	表裏都是一樣	it is the same outside and inside.
	一表人材	a handsome person.
	聽我表明	listen and I will make it clear to you.
	姑表親	cousins of a different surname.
	鐘表舖	a clock and watch shop.
衩	CH'A³.	
	衩衩褲	children's pants open behind.
衫	SHAN¹.	
	布衫子	a calico gown.
衾	CH'IN².	
4 衮	衣衾都齊備了	the funeral clothes and coverlet are all [prepared.
	KUEN³.	
	衮衣裳	to trim a woman's jacket with a broad hem.
	衮身子	a short outer jacket, made like a gown with the skirts cut off.
衲	LA⁵.	
	衲陀	a patched garment worn by priests.
衰	SHUAI¹.	
	漸漸的衰老	gradually growing old and feeble.
	衰敗	to decline, as a family or a state.
5 袍	P'AO².	
	袍子	an outer gown worn by men and some- [times by women.
	袍哥	the Ko-lao Hue; a member of the secret society, from having clothes in common.

(468)

注 释

【小衣and汗衣】衬裤和汗衫。

【老衣】殓衣的俗称。

【衣架子好】身材好。

表[piao³]

衩[tʂha³]

【衩衩裤】小孩子穿的开裆裤。

衫[ʂan¹]

衾[tɕhin³]

【衣衾都齐备了】衣衾：指装殓死者的衣服与单被。

衮（衮）[kuən³]

衲[la⁵]

【衲陀】打补丁的僧服。

衰[ʂuai¹]

袍[phao²]

【袍子】表示或标志某一行业、等级或职务的装束。

注释

被 [pi⁴]
【单被子】被单。
袚 [fu⁴]
【袚膝】古代衣裳前的蔽膝，用熟皮制成。形制、图案、颜色按身份、等级不同而有区别。
袖 [siəu⁴]
袈 [tɕia¹]
袋 [tai⁴]
靿 [iao⁴]
【靴靿子】半长统靴。
袱 [fu⁵]
【手袱子】手帕。
【烧袱子】汉族祭拜死者的信仰习俗，流行于四川各地，由烧纸钱演化而来。
裂 [lie⁵]
裁 [tsʰai²]

衣 5-6

被袚袖袈袋靿袱裂裁

PI⁴.
單被子　　　a *coverlet*; *bed-sheets*.
人善被人欺 } a good man is cheated *by* others, and a
馬善被人騎 } gentle horse is ridden *by* men.
昨夜被了盜　last night I was robbed *by* burglars.

FU⁴.
袚膝　　　　knee-*pads* made of embroidered silk.

SIU⁴.
衣袖　　　　the *sleeve* of a garment.
領袖　　　　a *head-man*.

CHIA¹.
　　　　　　[tion from Sanscrit).
袈裟　　　　a Buddhist priest's gown (a translitera-

TAI⁴.
裝在口袋裏頭　put it into a *sack*.
菸袋　　　　a tobacco *pipe*.

IAO⁴.
靴靿子　　　*half-top* boots.

FU⁵.
　　　　　　[bundle in.
包袱　　　　a *square piece of cloth* for wrapping a
手袱子　　　a *handkerchief*.
燒袱子　　　to burn *packets* of cash paper.

LIE⁵.
　　　　　　[drought.
田都乾裂開了　the rice-fields are *cracking* with the

TS'AI².
裁衣裳　　　to *cut* clothes.
裁縫　　　　a *tailor*.
裁尺　　　　tailor's measure.
裁紙　　　　to *cut* paper into sheets.
　　　　　　[troops.
裁去老弱　　to *discard* the old and feeble among the
裁奪　　　　to *plan*.

(469)

衣 7

7 裝 CHUANG¹.

裝枕頭	to *fill* a pillow.
裝水菸	to *sell smokes* from a Chinese hookah.
裝貨	to *lade* goods.
裝在樻子頭	*store* it in the cupboard.
裝板壁	to *fit in* boards in a partition wall.
蟠個裝頭	to *train* a plant into a *fantastic* shape.

READ CHUANG³.

裝數	to *make up* a deficit.

裔 I⁴.

後裔	*posterity*.

裟 SHA¹.

裟裟布	*very coarse* native calico.

裙 CH'ÜIN².

裙子	a lady's *skirt*.
包裙	a large square cloth for wrapping a baby in [to carry on the back.

裏 LI³. often pronounced "i³" before "t'eo" as in second son.

裏子	the *lining* of a garment.
在裏頭	*within*; on the *inside*.
在城裏	*in* the city.
這裏	*here*; in this place.

裕 Ü⁴.

家資富裕	*abundant* possessions; a. wealthy person.

補 PU³.

家財萬貫補補 釘釘有一半	though a family be wealthy yet half of their clothes are *patched* and darned.
補壁頭	to *mend* a partition wall.
補路	to *repair* roads.
補藥	a *tonic* medicine.
補少數	to *make up* short count.

(470)

注 释

裝（装）[tʂuaŋ¹] [tʂuaŋ³]
【蟠个装头】将植物修剪成一个有趣的形状。
【装数】弥补赤字。
裔 [i⁴]
裟 [ʂa¹]
【裟裟布】粗布。
裙 [tɕʰyn²]
裏（里）[li³]
裕 [y⁴]
補（补）[pu³]
【补壁头】修补隔墙。
【补路】修补马路。
【补少数】弥补短缺。

注释

【补服】明清时的官服。因其前胸及后背缀有用金线和彩丝绣成的补子以表示品级，故称。

袿 [kua⁴]

裹 [ko³]

【裹肚子】口袋。

【算裹起了】（计账时）算糊涂了。

製（制）[tṣʅ⁴]

裱 [piao³]

【裱褙铺】裱褙：把布或纸一层一层地粘在一起。提供裱褙、安装卷轴等服务的商店。

裳 [ṣaŋ²]

襃 [pao¹]

褙 [pei⁴]

褊 [pien³]

衣 7-9

8 袿裹製裱裳

	READ PU³, P'U³.	
	補服	the insignia of rank on the front and on [the back of an official's robe.
	KUA⁴.	
	大袿子	an outer *robe*.
	馬袿	a short riding *jacket*.
	汗袿子	a *shirt* or inner *jacket*.
	號袿子	regimental *jacket*.
	領袿子	a *waistcoat*.
	袿個緞面子	*sew on* a satin facing to the gown or jacket.
	KO³.	
	把對子拿來裹起	*roll up* the scrolls.
	裹纏子	bands used by coolies to *wrap round* their [ankles.
	裹肚子	a Chinese pocket.
	算裹起了	our reckonings are *confused*.
	CHĬ⁴.	
	連衣裳都沒有 製一件	} I have not even *made* an article of clothing for myself.
	PIAO³.	
	裱一副對子	to *mount* a pair of scrolls.
	裱褙鋪	a shop where scrolls are *mounted*.
	SHANG².	
	衣裳	clothes.

9 襃褙褊

	PAO¹.	
	襃獎奉承的話	*flattering* words.
	PE⁴.	
	褙殼子	*pasteboard*, made of paper and old rags.
	PIEN³.	
	房屋褊窄	the house is *small*.
	心裏褊窄	*irascible*.

(471)

西蜀方言

衣 9-12

複	FU⁵.	
	說重複話	to reiterate; lit., to speak *repeated* words.
褳	IAO¹.	
	褲褳	*waistband* of trousers.
褥	RU².	
	褥子	a bed *mattress*.
	馬褥子	a saddle *rug*.
褟	T'A⁵.	
	汗褟子	an inner *jacket*; a *shirt*.
褲	K'U⁴.	
	褲子	*trousers*.
	腿褲	wide cloth *leggings*.
褡	TA⁵.	
	褡褳子	a long *pocket* or *purse* with a slot at the side; a cash bag.
褳	LIEN².	for example of use see last.
縵	MAN².	
	褸褶褲	pants made *close* behind.
褸	LEO³.	
	穿得褸 k'ua³ k'ua² 的	clad in *filthy* and *ragged* garments.
褻	SIE⁵.	
	言語褻瀆	his language is *profane*.
襌	TAN¹.	
	被襌戲	a Punch and Judy show; lit., a *sheet* show.
	臥襌	a bed-cover.
	挖襌	an *apron* with a bib.

(472)

注释

複（复）[fu⁵]
褳 [iao¹]
褥 [zu²]
【马褥子】马鞍毯。
褟 [tʰa⁵]
【汗褟子】贴身的衣衫。
褲（裤）[kʰu⁴]
褡 [ta⁵]
【褡褳子】长方形口袋，中间开口，两头缝合，一般挂在腰带上或搭在肩上。
褳（裢）[lien²]
縵 [man²]
褸（褛）[ləu³]
褻（亵）[sie⁵]
襌（禅）[tan¹]
【被襌戏】皮影戏。
【卧襌】床罩。
【挖襌】带围嘴的围兜。

注释

襟 [tɕin¹]
【绅襟人户】具有家学渊源的人家。
襖（袄）[ŋao³]
裆（裆）[taŋ¹]
褴（褴）[lan⁴]
襯（衬）[tsʰən⁴]
襴（斓）[lan²]
【入了学穿襴衫】襴衫：古代士人之服。
褶（褶）[tʂe⁵]
襻 [pʰan⁴]
【纽襻】扣住纽扣的套。
【帽襻】帽带，可以扣住下巴，固定帽子。
西 [si¹]

衣 13-19 西

13 襟 CHIN¹.
大衣襟 — the large *lapel* of a gown.
連襟弟兄 — the husbands of two sisters; lit., connected *lapels*.
胸襟闊大 — very good-natured; lit., his breast *lapel* is very wide.
紳襟人戶 — a scholar's family; literati.
一身襟襟吊吊的 — your clothes are *flapping* untidily about you; slatternly.
衣裳襤襟襟 — his clothes are *ragged*.

襖 NGAO³.
綿襖 — a wadded *gown*.

裆 TANG¹.
褲裆 — the *seat* of the pantaloons.

16 褴 LAN⁴.
穿得襤褸 — clad in tattered and *filthy* garments.

17 襯 TS'EN⁴.
一個光棍十個幫襯 — every blackleg has ten others to *assist* him.

18 襴 LAN².
入了學穿襴衫 — when a man graduates he wears a *trimmed* gown.

褶 CHE⁵.
褶子裙 — a *plaited* skirt.
打個褶子 — put a *tuck* in it.

19 襻 P'AN⁴.
鈕襻 — a button *loop*.
帽襻 — a hat *strap* which comes round under the chin.

The 146th radical. 西

西 SI¹.
西門 — the *West* Gate.
西天 — the *Western Heaven*.

西 3-12 見

西洋景	a *foreign* panorama.
買東西	to buy *things*.

3 要 IAO⁴.

不要	I don't *want* it.
要得緊	urgently *required*; important.
要不倒那麽多	I do not *need* as much as that.
要不得	worthless; bad; disgraceful; un*desirable*.
你要曉得	you *ought* to know.
不要說	don't speak.
要不要又發脾氣	off and on he gets in a temper.
你去問他要	go and *demand* it.
險要地方	*important* passes and strongholds.
我定要來	I certainly *will* come.
要攏了	*about* to arrive.
這個要粗點	this kind *is* coarser.

12 覆 FU⁵.

一反一覆	back and *forth*; unstable.

The 147th radical. (見)

見 CHIEN⁴.

沒有見人	I did not *see* him.
一見如故	as soon as they *met* they were like old acquaintances.
看見	to *see*.
當見証	to be a *witness*.
得見面	to be *admitted* to the presence of.
事大事小見官便了	whether big or little an affair is settled when you have gone before the magistrate.
我的書不見了	my book is lost.
莫見我的過	don't *regard* my offence.
我見不得風	I must not be *exposed* to the wind.
他見不得我	he is displeased with me; he cannot bear the sight of me.

(474)

注　釋

【西洋景】民间一种供娱乐用的装置，匣子里装着画片，匣子上有放大镜，可见放大的画面。因最初画片多西洋画，故名。

要［iao⁴］

【要拢了】就要到了。

覆［fu⁵］

见（見）［tɕien⁴］

【莫见我的过】请原谅我的冒犯。

注释

规（规）[kuei¹]
【房子没得个规栏】房子周围没有篱笆或围墙。

视（视）[sɿ⁴]

觑（睹）[tu³]

亲（亲）[tsʰin¹]
【亲爷】岳父。

見 4-9

我做得孬見不得人	I have done it badly, it is not fit to be *seen*.
聽見	to hear, i. e., to *perceive* by the ear.
不見得熱	the warmth is not *perceptible*.
不見得好	there is nothing *perceptibly* good about it.
還沒有見到	you don't *understand* it yet.
見識	*experience*.
做事短見	he manages matters in a selfish and short-*sighted* way.
意見不同	*opinions* differ.
拿個主見出來	form some *plan* of your own.

4 規 KUE¹.

規矩	a *rule*; *custom*; *manners*; *orderly*.
房子沒得個規欄	there is no *fence* round the house.

5 視 SHÏ⁴.

近視眼	short-*sighted*; lit., eyes that *see* near at hand.
他坐視不理	to *look* on without interfering.
他藐視我	he lightly *esteems* me.

9 覷 TU³. same as 睹.

親 TS'IN¹.

親熱	*attached* to each other; very *intimate*.
雙親	my *parents*.
親姊妹	*own* sisters.
親人	*kindred*.
遠水難救近火 遠親不如近鄰	distant water will hardly extinguish a fire near at hand, so near neighbours are better than distant *kin*.
人親財不親 財帛要分明	though the persons are *related* the goods are not so, they must be evenly divided.
親戚	*relatives* of a different surname.
親家	my son-in-law or daughter-in-law's father.
親爺	my wife's father.
親自動手	I will begin my*self*.
親筆寫的	it is his *own* handwriting.

(475)

見 13-18　角 6

13 覺

CHIO⁵.

| 不憬覺得 | before I was *aware* of it; I did not *notice*. |
| 覺得有些痛 | I *feel* it aching a little. |

READ CHIAO⁴, KAO⁴.

| 睡覺 | to *sleep*. |
| 睡了一覺好瞌睡 | he had a good sound sleep. (N. A.) |

18 觀

KUAN¹.

房子修得觀瞻	the house is *splendidly* built.
求你觀切我	please *favour* me.
觀看	to *look at*; to *regard*.
觀音菩薩	the Goddess of Mercy; lit., the goddess who is *attentive* to cries.

READ KUAN⁴.

| 伏龍觀 | the *temple* of the cronching Dragon. |

The 148th radical. (角)

角 KO⁵.

牛角	an ox's *horns*.
葫荳角	bean *pods*.
在角角裏頭	in the *corner*.
口角	the *corners* of the mouth; *quarrelling*.
三尖角	a *triangular* piece of ground.
十角為一升	10 *ko* make 1 *shen*, corn measure.

6 解

KAI³, CHIAI³.

解腰帶	*unloose* your girdle.
解錢串子	*untie* the cash string.
解板子	to *saw* timber into boards.
還有解沒得	is there any *remedy*?
解毒的藥	an *antidote*.
解渴	to *allay* thirst.
解手	to *ease* nature.

(476)

注　釋

覺（觉）[tɕio⁵] [tɕiao⁴] [kao⁴]

【不憬觉得】没有注意到。

觀（观）[kuan¹] [kuan⁴]

【房子修得观瞻】房子盖得很漂亮。

【求你观切我】请多多关照。

角 [ko⁵]

【在角角里头】在角落里。

解 [kai³] [tɕiai³] [kai⁴] [tɕiai⁴]

【解板子】把木材锯成板子。

注 释

【积金千两不如明解经书】积攒千金不如读懂儒家经典。
【解粮饷】将给养分发给官兵。

觸（触）[tʂo⁵]
言 [ien²]
訃（讣）[pʰu⁵]
訂（订）[tin⁴]
計（计）[tɕi⁴]
訓（训）[ɕyn⁴]

角 6·13　言 2-3

解愁散悶	to *dissipate* sorrow and melancholy.
講解	to *explain*.
積金千兩不如明解經書	to clearly *expound* the classics is better than to amass a thousand ounces of gold.
註解	a *commentary*.
解不透	I cannot *interpret* it; I do not comprehend [the meaning.

KAI⁴, CHIAI⁴.

解犯人	to *transfer* prisoners to another court.
解地丁	to *transmit* revenue.
解糧餉	to *forward* supplies to the army.
解元	first of the "chü-ren" graduates.

13 觸　CHO⁵.

抵觸父母	to *oppose* one's parents.
把他觸了怒	it *irritated* him.

The 149th radical. (言)

言 2　IEN².

言語行為	*words* and actions.

訃　P'U⁵.

訃書	an *intimation* card announcing a parent's [death.

訂　TIN⁴.

訂日期	to *fix* a day.

計 3　CHI⁴.

不計其數	unable to *reckon* the amount.
定個計策	settle upon a *plan*.
中了他們的計	he fell into their *trap*.

訓　SHÜN⁴.

教訓兒孫	to *teach* one's children and grandchildren.
訓練兵丁	to *instruct* and drill troops.
聽教訓	listen to *instruction*.

(477)

言 3-4

記 CHI⁴.

你記不記得	can you *remember*?
不要忘記	don't *forget*.
記念父母的恩	*remember* your parent's goodness.
記性孬	my *memory* is bad.
要記個賬	*note it down* in the account.
記號	a *mark*; a *sign*; a *signal*.

訕 SHUAN⁴.

| 訕笑 | to *bandy* jokes. |

討 T'AO³.

討一個錢	I *beg* one cash.
討口子	a *beggar*.
要個人討保	you must find a person to *plead* and be surety for you.
討賬	to *dun* for payment.
討菜	to *look for* wild vegetables.
討親	to *seek for* a wife.
討人嫌	to *induce* people to dislike one; hateful; annoying.
自己討賤	you have *brought* poverty upon yourself.

訊 SÜIN⁴.

| 案訊了沒有 | has your case been *tried* yet? |

託 T'O⁵.

| 我拜託你 | I will *commission* you to do a job for me. |
| 託你的福 | I *depend* on you for happiness (like "by your grace"). |

訛 O².

| 說訛了 | *altered* in pronunciation; *mispronounced*. |

吵 CH'AO¹.

| 吵擾你 | I have *troubled* you (polite). |

訪 FANG³.

| 訪朋友 | to *inquire* of a friend. |

注 释

記（记）[tɕi⁴]
訕（讪）[ʂuan⁴]
討（讨）[tʰao³]
【讨口子】乞丐。
【讨菜】寻找野菜。
【讨亲】娶亲。
【自己讨贱】不识好歹，自讨苦吃。
訊（讯）[syn⁴]
【案讯了没有】案子审了没有？
託（托）[tʰo⁵]
訛（讹）[o²]
【说讹】发音改变，发音错误。
吵（吵）[tʂʰao¹]
訪（访）[faŋ³]

注释

【采访局】问询处。
許(许) [ɕy³]
訣(诀) [tɕye⁵]
【挽诀】(佛教徒或道教徒所用的)神秘的手势。
訥(讷) [la⁵]
設(设) [ʂe⁵]
【设帐】设立学校授徒。
訟(讼) [soŋ⁴]
【停讼牌】停止诉讼的公告。
【讼棍】挑唆别人打官司,借以从中牟利的人。
詐(诈) [tʂa⁴]
【打诈冒】假冒领取。
證(证) [tʂən⁴]
【放干证】干证:诉讼双方的有关证人。让证人出庭。

言 4-5

許 SHÜ³.

暗暗的訪察	to *examine* into a matter privately.
採訪局	an *inquiry* office.
不許他進來	don't *allow* him to come in.
許人望許神 人望神望	*promise* to a man—he expects fulfilment, *vow* to the gods—they look for performance.
許親	to *betroth* in marriage.
許久沒有見面	we have not met each other for a *very* [long time.
有許多人	how *many* people are there? there are *many* people.

訣 CHÜE⁵.

挽訣	to make *mysterious* signs on the *fingers*, as Buddhists and Taoists do.

訥 LA⁵.

訥喊一聲	*shout* aloud.

設 SHE⁵.

設帳	to *establish* a school.
設席	to *spread* a feast.
設法	to *devise* a plan.
設有不測	*supposing* that the unexpected should [happen.

訟 SONG⁴.

停訟牌	a notice forbidding *litigation*.
訟棍	a *pettifogger*.

詐 CHA⁴.

打詐冒	to *impose* upon; to *pretend*.
奸詐	*deceptive*.

證 CHEN⁴.

有甚麼憑據為證	what have you to bring forward as [evidence?
作見証	to bear *witness*; to *testify*.
放干証	to produce *witnesses*.

(479)

言 5-6

	TS'I².	[the original *accusation*.
詞	久告不離原詞	in a protracted law-suit you must hold to
	衆口一詞	all people *say* the same; the public are of one mind.
	CHU⁴.	
註	註子	a *commentary*.
	閻王註定三更死	} if Nien Uang (King of Hades) *decrees* that you should die in the third watch, he
	不肯留人到五更	will not leave you to the fifth.
	P'IN².	
評	品評	to *discuss* the merits of anything.
	說評書	to tell stories and *discuss* the merits of the dramatis personæ.
	批評	to *criticize*; to *revise*; to *comment on*.
	SU⁴.	
訴	訴寃枉	to *state* one's grievance.
	遞訴呈	to hand in one's *defence* in a law-suit.
	CH'A⁴.	
詫	很詫異	very *strange*; *amazing*.
	CHU¹.	
誅	遭天誅	to suffer a divine *judgment*.
	HUA⁴.	
話	說幾句話	to speak a few *words* or *sentences*.
	同君一夜話	} to *converse* for one evening with a scholarly
	甚讀十年書	man is equal to ten years of study.
	不懂他的話	I don't understand his *talk*.
	中國話	the Chinese *language*.
	你不聽話	you don't obey *orders*.
	KAI¹.	
該	我該欠他的	I *owed* him a debt, in a former existence.
	不該我說	it is not *right* for me to say.

注释

詞（词）[tsʰɿ²]
註（注）[tsu⁴]
【注子】①古代酒壶。金属或瓷制成。英文释义应为：A kind of decanter in ancient times. ②赌博时所押的钱。Stake; wager. ③量词。用于款项。
評（评）[pʰin²]
訴（诉）[su⁴]
詫（诧）[tʂʰa⁴]
誅（诛）[tʂu¹]
話（话）[xua⁴]
該（该）[kai¹]

注释

夸(夸)[kʰua¹]
诓(诓)[kʰuaŋ¹]
【诓娃娃】哄骗小孩子。
诡(诡)[kuei³]
诗(诗)[ʂʅ¹]
试(试)[ʂʅ⁴]
【试倒试倒的】试试看。
详(详)「siaŋ²」
【话怕详】说话最怕的是曲解。
诚(诚)[tʂʰən²]
誓[ʂʅ⁴]

言 6-7

應該做的	what *ought* to be done.	
今天該攏	he *should* arrive to-day; he is *due* to-day.	
該不怕的嗎	there is no *need* to fear, is there? will it be all right?	

K'UA¹.

誇海口	to *boast* inordinately.
自己不誇那個誇	if he did not *brag* of himself, who would do it for him?
不是娘誇女 根本女兒乖	it is not a case of the mother *praising* the daughter, the girl herself is good (used metaphorically).

KU'ANG¹.

誆娃娃	to *cajole* children.

KUE³.

詭詐的人	a *deceitful* person.
詭計	*treacherous* schemes.

SHĬ¹.

做一首詩	to write a *poem*.
詩經	the Book of *Poetry*.

SHĬ⁴.

鄉試	the provincial *examination* of B.A. for M.A. degree.
試來嘗點	taste and *try*.
試倒試倒的	*experimenting*; *feeling one's way*; to *test* and see.

SIANG².

不曉得詳細	I don't know the *particulars*.
說得詳細	to speak *in detail*.
話怕詳	words are in danger of being *wrested*.

CH'EN².

誠實	*sincere*; *real*.
誠心	*sincerely*.

SHĬ⁴.

對天鳴誓	to take an *oath* before Heaven.

(481)

言 7

誦 SONG⁴.
誦經 — to *recite* or *chant*, prayers.

誌 CHÏ⁴.
加冠誌喜 — to cap a young man *in honour of* his [wedding.

認 REN⁴.
認不得 — I don't *recognize* it, or him.
認錯 — to *confess* one's fault.
認眞 — to *acknowledge* the importance of; to act [in earnest.

說 SHO⁵.
說話 — to *speak*.
誰個背後無人說 }
那個人前肯說人 } behind whose back will no one *talk scandal*? to whose face will any one *speak evil*?
說他幾句 — *scold* him a little.
說了親沒有 — have you *bespoken* a wife yet?
四書上說 — the Four Books *say*.

誕 TAN⁴.
壽誕 — a *birthday*.

誚 TS'IAO⁴.
譏誚 — to *ridicule*.

誨 HUE⁴.
敎誨 — to *teach*; to *admonish*.
慢藏誨盜冶容誨淫 } negligent storage *induces* thieves, and a bedizened face *invites* lewdness.

誣 U¹.
誣賴人 — to *throw blame on* another, to *implicate* [another *falsely*.

誤 U⁴.
— same as 悮.

誘 IU³.
引誘 — to *entice*, to either good or evil.

(482)

注 釋

誦（诵）[soŋ⁴]
誌（志）[tsʅ⁴]
認（认）[zən⁴]
說（说）[ṣo⁵]
誕（诞）[tan⁴]
誚（诮）[tsʰiao⁴]
誨（诲）[xuei⁴]
誣（诬）[u¹]
誤（误）[u⁴]
誘（诱）[iəu³]

注 释

語（语）[y³]
諂（谄）[tsʰan³]
諕 [fu³]
諉（诿）[uei³]
　【没得推诿】没有借口。
課（课）[kʰo⁴]
　【磨课】给磨工的碾磨工钱。
　【国课】国家税收。
　【占课】一种占卜方法。
諒（谅）[liaŋ⁴]
　【替我原谅】替我设身处地想想。
論（论）[lən⁴]
誰（谁）[ṣuei²]
　【谁个说的】谁说的。

言 7-8

語 Ü³.
言語　　　　　words; speech.
俗語說得好　　the *proverb* well says.
人間私語天聞若雷 } Heaven hears men's private *conversation* as plainly as thunder. [do.
說隱語　　　　to utter obscure *words*, as Taoist prophets

諂 CH'AN³.
諂媚人　　　　to *flatter* people.
不喜人家的諂媚　I am not fond of *flattery*.

諕 FU³.
諕嚇人　　　　to intimidate people with *loud talk*.

諉 UE³.
沒得推諉　　　without *excuse*.
我諉託你　　　I *intrust* this matter to you.

8 **課** K'O⁴.
一天的工課　　the *work* of the day.
磨課　　　　　a miller's *fee* (either in money or in kind).
國課　　　　　*taxes* of a country. [sponses.
占課　　　　　to divine by inquiring in a *book of re-*

諒 LIANG⁴.
我諒想他不應允　I *guess* he won't agree to it.
替我原諒　　　put yourself in my place and *imagine your feelings*; excuse me.

論 LEN⁴.
　　　　　　　[two vols.
兩論　　　　　the *discourses* of Confucius arranged in
議論　　　　　to *discuss*.
議論人　　　　to *criticize* people.
不論那一個　　no matter who.

誰 SHUE².
誰個說的　　　*who* said so?

(483)

言 8-9

談 TʻAN², TAN⁴

| 誰人能夠 | what man is able? [will blame another. |
| 誰不怪誰 | this one will not blame that one; no one |

READ Tʻan²

談話	to chat; to converse; to talk.
幾句笑談	a little playful talk.
談匠	a gossip.
四川的鄉談	the dialect of Sï-chʻuan.
談駁人	to criticize people.

調 TʻIAO²

調勻	mix it thoroughly.
調一筆墨	take up a pencilful of ink.
兩個錢的調和	two cash worth of mixed spices.
調戲	to inveigle women.
調理病人	to nurse the sick.

READ TIAO⁴

唱調子	to sing a tune.
調兵	to move troops from one place to another.
調署	to transfer to another post.
他的調度甚好	his managing ability is great.
好才調	great ability.

請 TSʻIN³

請客	to invite guests.
請坐	please sit down.
請問一個話	may I ask you a question.
請個火房	to engage a cook.
請罪	to confess one's fault. [in all ceremonies.
請請	please! please! an indispensable phrase

諱 HUE⁴

| 忌諱 | to avoid, as the use of certain words in the [early morning. |

諫 CHIEN⁴

| 諫勸 | to remonstrate with. |

(484)

注　釋

談（谈）[tʰan²] [tan⁴]

【谈匠】爱说长道短的人，只说不练的人。

【四川的乡谈】乡谈：方言。

【谈驳人】谈驳：非议，批评。

调（调）[tʰiao²] [tiao⁴]

【两个钱的调和】很便宜的调味品。

【调署】调动职位。

【好才调】好文才。

请（请）[tsʰin³]

【请问一个话】我想问一下。

【请个火房】火房：通"伙房"，厨师。

諱（讳）[xuei⁴]

諫（谏）[tɕien⁴]

注释

谋（谋）[moŋ²]
　【谋衣食】谋生。
谙（谙）[ŋan²]
　【清丝谙缝】严丝合缝，缝隙严密闭合。
　【谙墨】研墨。
　【你打谙那一天起身】你打算哪一天出发。
　【这里有好多钱你谙一ha】这里有多少钱你猜一下。
　【谙倒使】小心使用。
诺（诺）[lo⁴]
谕（谕）[y⁴]
䜣 [xa²][ɕia²]
　【䜣说了的】瞎说的。
　【说䜣话】说瞎话。
谎（谎）[xuan³]
　【谎壳】无籽的谷物。
　【谎架子】惯于说谎的人。

言 9-10

谋	MONG².	
	谋衣食	to *plan* how to get a living.
	谋人妻子不顾家}	Who *schemes* his neighbour's wife to take, For his own house does trouble make.
	谋人田地水推沙}	Who *plots* to steal his neighbour's land, His own will go like shifting sand.
	谋反	to *plot* against the government.
谙	NGAN².	
	清絲谙縫	to *fit* tightly ; to *put together* exactly.
	筲箕 k'ang⁴ 鍋萬 不谙}	a rice strainer would never *fit* a pot (a play on the word *ngan*); I did not *expect* you.
	谙墨	to *rub* ink on an ink-slab.
	你打谙那一天 起身}	on what day do you *think* you will start?
	這裏有好多錢 你谙一 ha⁴}	*guess* how much money there is here.
	谙倒使	use it carefully, i. e., *reckoning* how long it should last.
諾	LO⁴.	
	一呼百諾	when he calls a hundred respond; an in- [fluential man.
	輕諾寡信	seldom believe light *promises*.
	一諾千金	his *word* is as good as a thousand of money.
諭	Ü⁴.	
	上諭	an Imperial *edict*.
	請官出示曉諭	may it please your honour to *notify* the [people.
10 䜣	HA², SHIA².	
	䜣說了的	*recklessly* spoken.
	說䜣話	to speak *wild* words.
谎	HUANG³.	
	谎壳	*empty* husks on grain.
	莫扯谎	don't tell *lies*.
	谎架子	an inveterate *liar*; lit., a *lie* frame.

(485)

言 10-12

CHIANG³.

你莫講	don't you *talk!* shut up!
講書	to *explain* a book; to *preach*.
講價	to *bargain* about a price; to *haggle*.
講理	to *discuss* the rights and wrongs of a quarrel with one's opponent.

CHIEN³.

| 他說話有些謇 | he speaks with a *stutter*. |
| 謇吧郎 | a *stammerer*. |

CH'IEN¹.

| 謙虛 | *modest; meek*. |
| 莫作謙 | don't be *backward*; don't be *over polite*. |

MI⁴.

| 燈謎子 | *riddles* written on lanterns. |

PANG⁴.

| 毀謗 | to *vilify*. |

SIE⁴.

| 多謝 | many *thanks*. |
| 謝中 | to *fee* middlemen. |

T'EN².

| 謄書 | to *copy; to transcribe*. |
| 謄羅幾個人 | to *transfer* a few workmen to another job. |

IAO².

| 布散謠言 | to spread *evil rumours*. |

CHIN³.

| 謹慎 | *careful; heedful*. |
| 謹防 | *beware!* |

CHEN⁴. same as 証.

CHI¹.

| 譏笑 | to *ridicule; ridicule*. |

(486)

注 释

講（讲）[tɕiaŋ³]
謇 [tɕien³]
【他说话有些謇】謇：结巴，口吃。
【謇吧郎】口吃的人。
謙（谦）[tɕʰien¹]
【莫作謙】别谦虚。
謎（谜）[mi⁴]
謗（谤）[paŋ⁴]
謝（谢）[sie⁴]
【谢中】支付报酬给中间人表示感谢。
謄（誊）[tʰən²]
【誊罗几个人】把几个人转移到其他工作上岗位。
謠（谣）[iao²]
謹（谨）[tɕin³]
證（证）[tʂən⁴]
譏（讥）[tɕi¹]

注 释

識（识）[sɿ⁵]
議（议）[ŋi⁴]
警[tɕin³]
　【警戒下次】警告不得再有下一次，下不为例。
譬[pʰei⁴]
　【比譬】举例说明。
譜（谱）[pʰu³]
　【说得不巴谱】说话不靠谱，荒谬。
　【谙一百银子的谱谱】估计一百两银子左右。
　【算个毛谱子】估算一下，毛估估。
　【晓得个大谱子】知道个大概。
譟（噪）[tsʰao³]
護（护）[fu⁴]
　【打保护】邀请巫师寻求保佑。

言 12-14

識 SHĪ⁵.
不 識 字　I do not *know* letters.
不 認 識 他　I do not *recognize* him.
我 兩 個 是 舊 相 識　we are old *acquaintances*.
不 識 好 歹　unable to *distinguish* between good and [evil.
學 個 見 識　to gain some *experience*.
相 識 滿 天 下 } one's *acquaintances* would fill the land, but
知 心 能 幾 人 } those who know one's heart are very few.

13 議 NGI⁴.
議 價　to *discuss* the price; to bargain.
議 論 紛 紛　to *debate* and dispute.
公 議 尺 子　the *common* foot-measure.

警 CHIN³.
警 戒 下 次　I *warn* you not to do it again.

譬 P'E⁴.
比 譬　to *illustrate*.
譬 如　*supposing*.

譜 P'U³.
族 譜　a clan *register*.
畫 譜　a *treatise* on drawing. [*received standards*.
說 得 不 巴 譜　nonsensical talk; lit., not according to
諳 一 百 銀 子 的 } I reckon *about* 100 taels.
譜 譜 }
算 個 毛 譜 子　reckon *approximately*.
曉 得 個 大 譜 子　I have a *general* idea of it.

譟 TS'AO³.
14 譟 擾 你　I have *troubled* you (polite).

護 FU⁴.
保 護　to *protect*. [of the gods for a sick person.
打 保 護　to invite a sorcerer to beseech the *protection*
護 送　to *escort*; an *escort*.

(487)

言 14-19

	惜錢休送子 護短莫從師	if you begrudge the money, don't bring your son to school, and if you would *screen* his faults, don't let him have a school master.
	衛護	to *screen* a person's faults.
	護書	a card case.
	護心油	fat round the heart.

15 譽 Ü².

	面譽小人	a mean man who *flatters* people to their [face.

讀 TU⁵.

	有田不耕倉廩虛 有書不讀子孫愚	he who has fields and does not till them, will have empty barns, and he who has books and does not *study* them, will have ignorant children.
	讀書人	scholars; literati.

READ TEO⁴.

16	要讀⁵個句讀出來	read it in *sentences*; mind your pauses.

變 PIEN⁴.

	變化	to *transform*; metamorphosis.
	改變	to *change*; to *alter*.
	兵變了	the soldiers have *mutinied*.
17	發變	a person's *adroitness* in business.

讒 TS'AN².

	讒謗人	to *slander* people.
	讒言敗壞君子 冷箭射死賢人	*slander* will ruin a princely man as a secret arrow would slay a sage.

讓 RANG⁴

	謙讓	*yielding*; humble; compliant; complaisant.
	讓路	to *yield* the road; to stand aside.
	讓價	to *abate* the price.

READ RANG³.

19	讓他幾句	*reprove* him.

讚 TSAN⁴.

	讚美	to *praise*.

(488)

注 釋

【卫护】护短。
【护书】官员用的公文夹，主要用于放置各种札、谕、批等公文。
【护心油】心脏旁边起保护作用的油脂。
譽（誉）[y²]
【面誉小人】面誉：当面谄媚说好话。当面说好话的小人。
讀（读）[tu⁵] [təu⁴]
變（变）[pien⁴]
【发变】应变。
讒（谗）[tsʰan²]
讓（让）[zaŋ⁴] [zaŋ³]
讚（赞）[tsan⁴]

注释

豁 [xo⁵]
豈(岂) [tɕʰi³]
豇 [tɕiaŋ¹] [kaŋ¹] [tʂaŋ¹]
豉 [sʅ¹]
豌 [uan¹]
豐(丰) [foŋ¹]
【家屋丰厚】家庭富裕。
【待人丰厚】待人大方。
象 [siaŋ⁴]
豪 [xao²]

谷 10　豆 3-11　豕 5-7

The 150th radical. (谷)

10 豁 HO⁵.
放豁達些　　be more *magnanimous*.

The 151st radical. (豆)

3 豈 CH'I³.
豈敢　　　　how dare I? (polite).
豈有此理　　was there ever such a thing? (strong negative).

CHIANG¹, KANG¹, CHANG¹.
4 豇
豇豈　　　　a variety of *kidney* bean, *Vigna sinensis*.

SHĪ¹.
8 豉
豈豉　　　　*pickled* beans.

UAN¹.
11 豌
豌豈尖　　　the tender points of *pea* shoots, used as a vegetable.

FONG¹.
豐
豐收年歲　　an *abundant* harvest.
家屋豐厚　　his family is *affluent*.
待人豐厚　　to treat people *liberally*.

The 152nd radical. (豕)

SIANG⁴.
5 象
象鼻子　　　an *elephant's* trunk.
象牙快子　　ivory chopsticks.
象皮　　　　India-rubber.

HAO².
7 豪
英雄豪傑　　a *leader* among men.
是個有豪氣的人　he is a man of some *boldness* in standing up for the right.

(489)

豕 7-9 豸 3-8 貝 2

9 豫	惡棍土豪	a *ringleader* in mischief in the district.
	莫耍橫豪	don't play the *bully*, or *tyrant*.
	Ü⁴.	
	豫先打個主意	make up your mind *beforehand*.
	豫備歸一了	*ready*; *prepared*.

The 153rd radical. (豸)

CH'AI².

3 豺 豹	豺狗	a *wolf*.
	PAO⁴.	
5	豹子	a *leopard*.
	TIAO¹.	
貂	貂皮褂子	a *sable* fur robe.
	黃鼠貂	a *weasel*.
	貂翎子	the *squirrel*.
8 貌	MAO⁴.	
	好個像貌	what a fine *figure*!
	外貌	outward *appearance*.

The 154th radical. (貝)

PE⁴.

貝	山裏頭有寶貝沒得	are there *precious things* among the mountains?
	活寶貝	a live *valuable*, i. e., a son.
	CHEN¹.	
2 貞 貟	貞節婦	a *chaste* widow.
	FU⁴.	
	皇天不負苦心人	Heaven will not *disregard* the afflicted.
	負心人	an *ungrateful* person.

(490)

注 释

【莫耍橫豪】不要恃强凌弱。
豫[y⁴]
【豫备归一了】准备好了。
豺[tʂʰai²]
豹[pao⁴]
貂[tiao¹]
【黄鼠貂】黄鼠狼。
【貂翎子】松鼠。
貌[mao⁴]
【好个像貌】长得多漂亮啊。
貝(贝)[pei⁴]
貞(贞)[tʂən¹]
負(负)[fu⁴]

注释

贡（贡）[koŋ⁴]
财（财）[tsʰai²]
贩（贩）[fan⁴]
　【遇倒贩子手】碰到棘手难对付的对手。
货（货）[xo⁴]
　[荒货摊子] 荒货：旧货。
贯（贯）[kuan⁴]
　【说得不贯气】不贯气：不连贯。
贫（贫）[pʰin²]

贝 2-4

³贡 财 ⁴贩 货 贯 贫

宁可负人 莫我切 负人	I would rather be *slighted* than *slight* others.
负了重债	I *owe* a heavy debt.
辜负人的恩	to *abuse* one's kindness.
他欺负我	he *defrauded* me.

KONG⁴.

进贡	to pay *tribute*.
贡茶	*tribute* tea.
贡生	*presented* graduates; superior "siu-ts'ai."

TS'AI².

钱财如粪土 仁义值千金	*money* is like dung, benevolence and righteousness are worth a thousand of gold.
大财主	a *wealthy* man.
财神菩萨	the god of *wealth*.
人无浑财不富 马无夜草不肥	without ill-gotten *gains* a man will not grow rich, as a horse will not fatten unless fed on pasture.
讲财礼	to bargain about a bride's *dowry*.

FAN⁴.

牛贩子	a cattle *dealer*.
遇倒贩子手	to meet one's match at knavery.

HO⁴.

货物	*merchandise*.
乾货铺子	a dry *goods* store.
荒货摊子	a stall for the sale of second-hand *articles*.

KUAN⁴.

万贯的家财	a wealthy family; lit., possessing a myriad [strings of cash.
说得不贯气	*disconnected* talk.
他们都是贯通了的	they are all in league with one another.

P'IN².

贫穷	*destitute*.
家贫不算贫 路贫贫坏人	to be *poor* at home is not *poverty*, but to be *poor* on the road is starvation.

(491)

貝 4-5

貪 T'AN¹.

貪財	to *covet* riches.
貪心大	very *avaricious*.
好酒貪杯	*fond* of wine.
壅壁上畫個貪	paint a dragon on the screen wall (a warning to the *avaricious*).

責 TSE⁵.

責人之心責己 恕己之心恕人	if you would *reprove* others, *reprove* yourself, and if you would excuse yourself, excuse others.
責備	to *reprove*.
責罰	to *punish* by imposing a fine.
這是我的責任	I am *responsible* for this job.

費 FE⁴.

家中的用費	household *expenses*.
月費	a teacher's wages.
幫行費	to pay the trade *fees*.
費心	to *expend* one's mind; thank you.
莫費事	don't *put yourself* to so much *trouble*.
費手	*troublesome* to do, or make.
淘神費力	troublesome and toilsome.
很費些工夫	it has taken a lot of work.
費錢	it uses up the money.

貯 CHU⁴.

黃泥巴田貯水	a clay rice field *holds* or *retains* the water.

貳 RI⁴.

same as 二.

賀 HO⁴.

恭賀你	I *congratulate* you.
送賀禮	to send *congratulatory* presents.
朝賀	a national *rejoicing*, as at an emperor's birthday.

貴 KUE⁴.

貴國是那一國	what is your *honourable* country?
新貴人	a bridegroom; a successful student.

(492)

注 释

貪（贪）[tʰan¹]
責（责）[tse⁵]
費（费）[fei⁴]
【月费】教师月薪。
【帮行费】交易费。
【莫费事】别自找麻烦。
【费手】费事，麻烦。
貯（贮）[tṣu⁴]
貳（贰）[zɿ⁴]
賀（贺）[xo⁴]
貴（贵）[kuei⁴]
【贵国是那一国】您是哪国人？
【新贵人】①新郎。②科举中第者，学业优异的学生。

注 释

【自己耍耍得尊贵】要自尊自重。

買（买）[mai³]

【买活民心】得到民心支持。

【把官买活了】买通官员。

貿（贸）[moŋ⁴]

貶（贬）[pien³]

貸（贷）[tai⁴]

貼（贴）[tʰie⁵]

【替人体贴】换位思考，将心比心。

資（资）[tsɿ¹]

【取了你的资财】您破费了。

【好个资质】真帅气。

賄（贿）[xuei⁴][xuei³]

【贿他一个日子】许诺一个付钱的准确日子。

貝 5-6

買	自己耍耍得尊貴	be more *dignified*; have more self-*esteem*.
	價錢貴	the price is *dear*.
	MAI³.	
	買活民心	to *purchase* the good-will of a business.
	買米	to *buy* rice.
	自買自賣	to *buy* one's own goods; met., to act double.
	大買賣	a big *business*.
	買賣人	a *business* man.
	買主	the *buyer*.
	把官買活了	to *bribe* the official.
貿	**MONG⁴.**	
	貿易	to *barter*.
貶	**PIEN³.**	
	貶官職	to *degrade* an official.
貸	**TAI⁴.**	
	向人借貸的	*borrowed* from another.
	定責不貸	I will certainly punish you and not *let* you [off].
貼	**TʻIE⁵.**	
	貼勸世文	to *paste up* tracts.
	貼膏藥	to *stick on* a plaster.
	貼心的好朋友	an *attached* friend.
	事情辦妥貼了	everything is properly *settled*.
	貼補了	*supplied*; *made up*, as a deficiency.
	替人體貼	to be *considerate*; to put one's self in the place of another.
資	**TSƗ¹.**	
	取了你的資財	I have deprived you of your *money* (polite).
	藥資	*fees* to a doctor who gives medicine.
	好個資質	what a fine *figure* that lad has.
賄	**HUE⁴.**	
	受賄	to take *bribes*.
	READ HUE³.	
	賄他一個日子	*promise* to pay him on a certain day.

(493)

西蜀方言

貝 6-7

賂	LU[4].	賄賂	bribes ; to bribe.
賃	LIN[4].	賃一套衣服	to hire a suit of clothes.
賠	SHE[5].	賠本不賣貨	I will not sell if I am to lose by it.
		帶話帶長帶錢帶賠	if he carries a message it grows, if he carries money it diminishes.
		賠了聲氣	he has lost his voice.
		這個屋裏肯賠東西	things are liable to be stolen in this house.
		水煮賠了	the water has evaporated in the boiling.
臟	TSANG[1].		same as 贓.
賊	TSE[5].	做賊	to be a thief.
		水賊	pirates.
		木賊	horse-tail rushes, used for polishing wood.
	READ TSUE[2].	賊娃子	thieves ; burglars.
		老賊	an old black-guard.
賑	CHEN[3].	賑濟百姓	to relieve the poor in time of distress.
賓	PIN[1].	賓客相待	I treated him as a guest.
		西賓	a tutor, so called by his employer (the guest who sits on the west side).
賓	PIN[1].		same as last.
賒	SHE[1].	不賒賬	we don't give credit at this shop.

(494)

注 釋

賂（赂）[lu⁴]
賃（赁）[lin⁴]
賠 [ṣe⁵]
【賠了聲气】没底气了。
【这个屋里肯賠东西】这屋里易遭贼，经常被偷。
【水煮賠了】水开了。
脏（脏）[tsaŋ¹]
賊（贼）[tse⁵] [tsuei²]
【水贼】海盗。
【木贼】一种多年生草本蕨类植物。
【贼娃子】窃贼。
賑（赈）[tṣən³]
賓（宾）[pin¹]
【西宾】旧时宾位在西，故称。常作为对家塾教师或幕友的敬称。
賓（宾）[pin¹]
賒（赊）[ṣei¹]

注释

賬（账）[tṣaŋ⁴]
【打烂账】穷困潦倒。
賙（赒）[tṣəu¹]
質（质）[tṣʅ⁵]
賦（赋）[fu⁴]
賢（贤）[ɕien²]
賣（卖）[mai⁴]
【卖气力】干体力活儿。
【得钱卖放】收受贿赂后偷偷放走囚犯。
【那个地方卖得过】那个地方不用进去，可以走过去。
賠（赔）[pʰe²]

貝 8

8 賬 CHANG⁴.

| 到處都有賬 | he has *debts* or *accounts* everywhere. |
| 打爛賬 | utterly impoverished and homeless; reduced to beggary. |

賙 CHEO¹.

| 賙濟人 | to *bestow alms* on the poor. |

質 CHÏ⁵.

| 對質 | a face to *face* discussion; to confront. |

賦 FU⁴.

| 靈魂是天老爺賦的 | the soul is *bestowed* on us by God. |
| 賦稅 | to *pay* taxes. |

賢 SHIEN².

如今世上人眼淺只重衣冠不重賢	at the present day men are shortsighted, they only regard the outward appearance as important, not the *virtue*.
家有賢妻男兒不遭橫事	if the wife is *virtuous* the husband escapes trouble.
那個人賢惠	that is a *worthy* and a generous man.
聖賢	*sages*.

賣 MAI⁴.

價錢賣得好	you have *sold* it at a good price.
賣氣力	to do manual labour for a living.
得錢賣放	to take a bribe and let a prisoner escape.
賣主	the *seller*.
賣主求榮	to *betray* one's master in hope of honour.
那個地方賣得過	you can *pass by* that town *without entering* it.

賠 P'E².

照數賠還	to *repay* in full.
養女是個賠錢貨	to bring up daughters is a *losing* game.
賠不是	to *confess* one's self in the wrong.

(495)

貝 8-10

賞 SHANG³.

賞功勞	to *reward* merit.
賞號	a *reward*.
獎賞	a *prize*.
出賞格	to offer a *reward* by proclamation.
月半節賞孤	to *offer* to the orphan spirits on the 15th of 7th moon.
不賞臉	I will not *regard* your intercession.
賞花	to *enjoy* the flowers.

賜 T'SĬ⁴.

| 賞賜 | to *bestow* upon; to *reward*; a *reward*. |

賤 TSIEN⁴.

貨賤人夾疑	if goods are *cheap* people are suspicious.
作賤人	to *disesteem* people; to *depreciate* others.
貧賤	poor and *ignoble*.
賤姓楊	my *mean* name is Iang (polite).
賤內	my wife; lit., the *mean interior*.
那個花賤	this flower is *common*, or *easily cultivated*.

賴 LAI⁴.

我依賴你	I *rely* on you.
無賴之徒	a vagabond with no visible *means* of sup-[port.
自己錯了賴別人	to *accuse* another of the wrong you have done yourself.

賭 TU³.

賭輸贏	to *gamble*.
賭咒	to *risk* an oath on.
我賭你摸我	I *defy* you to touch me.

賺 CHUAN⁴.

| 賺錢 | to *gain* money in business. |

賽 SAI⁴.

賽穿戴	to *emulate* another in display of clothing.
迎神賽會	*rivalry* in idolatrons display.
賽過一切	she *excelled* them all.

(496)

注 釋

賞（赏）[ṣaŋ³]

【月半节赏孤】赏孤：旧时成都人在七月十五除了向祖先烧祭袱子外，还祭奠无名英烈，以及客死他乡或无人祭祀的可怜人。七月半祭孤魂。

赐（赐）[tsʰɿ⁴]

贱（贱）[tsien⁴]

【那个花贱】那种花很普通，易培植。

赖（赖）[lai⁴]

赌（赌）[tu³]

赚（赚）[tṣuan⁴]

赛（赛）[sai⁴]

【迎神赛会】旧俗把神像抬出庙来游行，并举行祭会，以求消灾赐福。

注 释

贽(贽) [tʂʅ⁵]
【贽见礼】学生第一次上学时送给老师的见面礼。
赘(赘) [tʂuei⁴]
【莫赘渎我】不要吹捧我。
赢(赢) [in²]
赎(赎) [tu⁵] [ʂu⁵]
赃(赃) [tsaŋ¹]
【贼在当面坐,无赃不定罪】指没有证据就不能妄下结论。
赤 [tʂʰʅ⁵]
赦 [ʂei⁴]

贝 11-18 赤 4

11 贽

CHI⁵.
贽見禮　　　a *present* given to a teacher by a pupil on [first going to school.

CHUE⁴.
我的累贅大　my *encumbrances* are great.
莫贅瀆我　　don't *toady* me; I don't want fulsome flat-[tery.
招贅過門　　to go and live with one's wife's parents.

13 贏

IN².
輸錢只爲贏錢起　losing money is the result of *winning* [money.
做不贏　　　I am not able to *overtake* the work.
出不贏氣　　panting for breath; short-winded.
我說不贏他　I cannot *beat* him at talking.

15 贖

TU⁵, SHU⁵.
把房子贖回來了　he has *redeemed* his house from the mort-[gagee or tenant.
一行偶乖百行沒贖　if in one action you should err, a hundred acts will not *atone* for it.

18 贓

TSANG¹.
賊在當面坐無贓不定罪　though a thief should live just over the way, having seen no *booty* I dare not say.
贓官　　　　an official who take *bribes*; an unjust judge.

The 155th radical. 赤

4 赤

CHʻI⁵.
赤身露體　　*naked*.
打赤脚　　　to go *bare*-foot.
一片赤心　　*earnest*; *sincere*.

赦

SHE⁴.
赦罪　　　　to *forgive* sins.
大赦天下　　a general *pardon*.

(497)

走 2-3

The 156th radical. 走

TSEO³.

走路	to *walk*; to *travel on foot*.
出去走一轉	to go out for a *walk*.
他們都走了	they are all *gone*.
走脚	to *elope*.
走人戶	to *visit* a friend; to go *visiting*.
肚皮走	*diarrhœa*.
走氣	to *leak* air, as at a crack.
事情走了風	the affair has *leaked* out; the news has become public.

FU⁴.

| 赴席 | to go to a *feast*. |

CHIU¹.

| 雄赳赳的 | a *martial* bearing. |

CH'I³.

起來	*get up! rise!*
生起來了	it has *sprung* up, as seed.
李子起了灰	the plums are ripe, i. e., the bloom is on the skin.
起心好久了	I have had this determination for some time.
起身	to *start* on a journey.
起一堂學	to *start* a school.
起脚錢	coolie hire paid before *starting* on a journey.
起旱路	to *take* to an overland route after having travelled by water.
起火	to *raise* a conflagration.
起房子	to *build* a house.
從那裏起	where shall I *commence*?
纔題起說	we had just *begun* to speak of it.
起頭	at the *beginning*.
起坎	to go on shore; to disembark.
起載子	to *unload* cargo.
把他起起走	*eject* the tenant from the house.
起子	a *parer* for paring knives.

(498)

注 释

走 [tsəu³]

【走脚】跑腿。英文释义应为: to run errand.

【走人户】串门。

【肚皮走】拉肚子, 腹泻。

【走气】漏气。

赴 [fu⁴]

赳 [tɕiəu¹]

起 [tɕʰi³]

【生起来了】雨后春笋般涌现。

【李子起了灰】李子熟了。

【起心好久了】有此决心很久了。

【起一堂学】设立一所学校。

【起脚钱】出发前给苦力的报酬。

【从那里起】从哪里着手。

【才题起说】刚说到。

【起坎】上岸。

【起载子】卸货。

【把他起起走】把房客赶走。

注释

【起刀子】开刀锋。
【起猪肉皮子】剥猪皮。
【做起没有】做好没有。
趿 [tɕʰie⁴]
【走路趿一趿的】走路一瘸一拐的。
趁 [tʂʰən⁴]
（CHʻIE¹当为CHʻIE⁴，见803页勘误表。）
超 [tʂʰao¹]
越 [ye⁵]
【越见好】越来越好。
赶(趕) [kan³]
【要赶拢省】赶拢：赶到。（疑有误，可能"省"后缺"上"）
【赶活路】赶着去工作。
【赶不起】规定时间内完不成。
【赶场】赶集。
【赶船】乘船。
【我赶不倒你】我比不上你。
趖 [so¹]
【慢慢的趖】趖：移动，滑行。
【趖针子】蛇。

走 3-7

	起刀子	to *pare* the edge of a knife thin.
	起猪肉皮子	to *cut* the skin *off* pork.
	起一层泥巴	to *shovel off* the top layer of soil.
	穿起	put it on ; wear it (*present time*).
	做起没有	have you done it yet ? (*past time*).
	买不起	I cannot *afford* to buy it.
5	都是一起的	they all belong to the same *class* or *com-[pany*.
趿	CHʻIE⁴.	
	走路趿一趿的	to *limp* with pain.
趁	CHʻEN¹.	
	趁早	*take advantage of* the earliest opportunity.
超	CHʻAO¹.	
	超群出众	to *surpass* ordinary men.
越	ÜE⁵.	
	越礼犯分	to *overstep* the bounds of propriety and *[duty.*
	越见好	*still* better.
7	越快越好	the quicker the better (*comparative*).
趕	KAN³.	
	赶出去	to *expel* ; to *drive out.*
	赶鱼	to *drive* fish into a net.
	要赶拢省	I must *press on* till I reach the capital.
	赶快些	*hurry up !*
	赶活路	to *hurry* on work.
	赶不上	I cannot *overtake* him.
	赶不起	I cannot *overtake* the work in that time.
	赶场	to *attend* a market.
	赶船	to *take passage on* a boat.
	我赶不倒你	I cannot *equal* you.
	今年赶不倒往年	this year is not *equal to* former years.
趖	SO¹.	
	慢慢的趖	*glide* along gently.
	趖针子	a snake ; lit., *gliding* needle.

走 8-19 足 4

8 趣 TS'Ü⁴.　　　　　　　　　　　　[as a slight.
這繚沒趣　there is no *fun* in this; rather *unpleasant*,
不知趣　not noticing what is *pleasing* to others.
說趣話　to *joke*; to *jest*.
那個人趣　he is a *jocular* fellow.
這個事情趣得很　this is a *droll* affair.

趁 NIEN³.
快把他趁轉來　*pursue* him quickly and bring him back.
趁不上他　I cannot *overtake* him.
把他趁出去　*expel* him; turn him out.
趁山狗　a *hunting-*dog.

19 趲 TSAN³.
趲開　*move* it to one side; stand out of the way. [price.
沒得走趲　there can be no *change* made; fixed, as a
一步一趲　a step and a *limp*, like a lame man.
趲家　to *remove* to another house; to *flit*.
趲肥猪　to *fatten* a pig for market.
趲圓子　a secret language.

The 157th radical. (足)

足 TSU⁵, CHÜ⁵, TSIO⁵.
不知飽足　you never know when you have had *enough*.
衣食豐足　*abundance* of food and clothing.
人心不足　men's hearts are never *satisfied*.
力錢要足數　coolie money must be paid *in full*.
足足走了半個月　I walked for a *full* fortnight.
足色銀子　*pure* silver.

4 爬 P'A³.
爬倒　to *sprawl* on all fours.

(500)

注　释

趣 [tsʰy⁴]
【说趣话】开玩笑。
【那个人趣】趣：爱开玩笑的，打趣的。
趁 [nien³]
【快把他趁转来】追上去把他带回来。
【趁不上他】赶不上他。
【把他趁出去】把他赶出去。
【趁山狗】一种猎犬。
趱（趲）[tsan³]
【趱开】移到一边。
【没得走趱】没有变化。
【一步一趱】一瘸一拐地走。
【趱家】搬家。
【趱肥猪】把猪养肥卖。
足 [tsu⁵] [tɕy⁵] [tsio⁵]
爬 [pʰa³]
【爬倒】伸开手足躺卧。

注释

跩 [sa⁵]
【跩半节鞋】穿起半截鞋。
跑 [pʰao³]
【跑文书】送信函公文。
跋 [pa⁵]
跛 [po³]
跍 [ku¹]
【跍倒起】蹲下。
【跍堆堆】在墓地野餐。
趾 [tsʰη¹]
【把鞋子趾干净】趾：擦。
【把鞋子趾烂了】趾：磨。
【趾起走】慢腾腾地走。
【把毛虫趾死】趾：踩。

足 4-5

跩 SA⁵.

| 跩起一雙鞋 | to *tread down* the heels of one's shoes. |
| 跩半節鞋 | to *wear* shoes without heels, like a beggar. |

跑 P'AO³.

快些跑	*run* quickly.
跑馬射箭	to shoot arrows when the horse is *galloping*.
牛跑了	the ox has *run away*.
跑不脫	he cannot *escape*.
跑文書	to *carry* dispatches.
雲跑東雨不凶 雲跑南雨成團 雲跑北雨沒得 雲跑西騎馬披蓑衣	when the clouds *go* eastward there will be little rain, when the clouds *drive* to the south there will be heavy showers, when the clouds *drift* northward it will be fair weather, but when the clouds *fly* to the west you had better mount and put on your waterproof.

跋 PA⁵.

| 跋山涉水 | to *cross* mountains and ford rivers. |

跛 PO³.

| 瘸腳跛手的 | *cripple* in hands and feet. |

跍 KU¹.

| 跍倒起 | *squat* down. |
| 跍堆堆 | to *picnic* at the tombs. |

趾 TS'Ɪ¹.

把鞋子趾乾淨	*wipe* your shoes clean.
把鞋子趾爛了	you have *rubbed* your shoes into holes.
趾起走	to walk with a *shuffle*.
在地下趾起走	to *trail* one's body along on the ground.
把毛虫趾死	to *crush* a caterpillar with the foot.
踏一腳還要 趾兩ha	he is not content with treading me down, he must *grind* me under his feet.

足 5-6

CH'IA², K'A².

跨過去	stride across it.
還要大跨一步	you must give a higher price; lit., take a big *stride*.
鑽衙門如跨竈房門一樣	he goes into the court-house like *stepping* into the kitchen.

TIE⁵.

| 看跌倒 | beware of *falling*. |
| 銀子跌了價 | silver has *fallen* in price. |

KEN¹.

脚後跟	the *heel*.
跟倒轎子走	*follow* the chair.
跟官的	one who *attends* on an official.
跟倒我讀	read it *after* me.
跟倒這個樣子做	do it *according to* this pattern.
跟倒做	do it *immediately*.
跟倒幾天的雨	rain for a few days *together*.
在這跟前	*here*.
在父母跟前	in the presence of your parents.
栽冒兒跟斗	to turn a somersault.

KUE⁴, K'UE⁴.

| 跪倒起 | *kneel* down. |

CHIEN³.

| 修跰巴 | to pare *corns*, or *hard lumps of skin* on the [feet or hands. |

LU⁴.

對直一條大路	the main *road* straight in front of you.
這一節路相因	coolie hire is cheap on this part of the *jour*-[ney.
走水路	to travel by water.
他們是一路來的	they came *together*.
找不倒活路	I cannot find *work*, i.e., a *way* to make a [living.
我沒得路	I have no *resource*.
格字路路	the *lines* on ruled paper.
讀幾路書	to read a few *lines* of a book.

(502)

注 释

跨 [tɕʰia²] [kʰa²]
【跨过去】跨过去。
【还要大跨一步】还要大提价。
【钻衙门如跨灶房门一样】指进衙门要低头。

跌 [tie⁵]

跟 [kən¹]
【跟倒轿子走】跟着轿子走。
【栽冒儿跟斗】翻筋斗。

跪 [kuei⁴] [kʰuei⁴]
【跪倒起】跪下。

跰 [tɕien³]
【修跰巴】跰巴：茧子。

路 [lu⁴]
【这一节路相因】相因：便宜。这段路雇苦力的价格便宜。
【我没得路】我没有门路。
【格字路路】方格纸。
【读几路书】读几行书。

注 释

跳 [tʰiao⁴]
　【跳端工】又称"跳端公",民间举行祭祀仪式时巫师跳舞蹈以驱邪。
　【心子跳】心悸。
跡（迹）[tsie⁵]
　【收脚迹】迷信认为人死后魂魄会到生前的地方。
蹮（蜷）[tɕyen¹]
　【大家蜷个脚】大家各退一步。
踏 [tʰa⁵]
踢 [tʰi⁵] [tʰie⁵]
踐（践）[tsien⁴]
　【莫践踏字纸】敬惜字纸。
　【不践言】说话不算数。
踪 [tsoŋ¹]
蹅 [tṣʰa¹]
　【看蹅虚脚】当心踩空。

足 6-9

跳	T'IAO⁴.	
	跳過去	leap across.
	把我嚇一跳	it made me *jump* with fright.
	跳巖	to throw one's self over a cliff.
	跳端工	to call in a sorcerer to *perform* his incantations.
	心子跳	*palpitation* of the heart.

跡 TSIE⁵.
有形跡　　there are *traces*.
看脚跡　　to look at a thief's *foot-prints*.
收脚跡　　gathering his *foot-prints*, as the soul of a dead person is supposed to do.

蹮 CHÜEN¹.
蹮倒睡　　to sleep with the legs *drawn up* in bed.
大家蹮個脚　both yield a little; lit., *draw in* your legs.
蹮起指拇兒算　*double up* your fingers and reckon.

踏 T'A⁵.
踏青　　　to visit the graves; lit., *tread* the green.
一脚踏兩隻船　a foot *planted* on two boats.
踏板兒　　a long *footstool*, or *step*, in front of a bed.
踏踏實實的　*trustworthy*; *reliable*.
踏起一雙鞋　to wear shoes down at the heel.

踢 T'I⁵, T'IE⁵.
馬把我踢一脚　the horse *kicked* me.

踐 TSIEN⁴.
莫踐踏字紙　don't *tread* on written paper.
不踐言　　he did not *fulfil* his promise.
作踐人　　to *oppress* people.

踪 TSONG¹.
無踪無影　not a *trace* of it.

蹅 CH'A¹.
看蹅虚脚　beware of taking a false *step*.
一脚蹅在陽溝頭　I *stepped* into a drain with one foot.

(503)

足9-12

蹀 TIE⁵.
氣得蹀脚　stamping with rage.

踹 CH'AI³.
看莫把東西踹倒了　} take care and not tread on things.
踹高脚　to walk on stilts.
踹左　keep to the left (a chair-bearer's call).
踹界　to walk round the boundaries.
踹水過去　to wade across a stream.
踹橋　to open a new bridge.
踹一乘轎子　to make a sedan chair.
踹布　to mangle cloth after having been dyed.
踹石　a dyer's mangle.

蹄 T'I².
馬蹄子　horse's hoofs.
豬蹄子　pig's feet.
羊蹄子　sheep's trotters.
油蹄子　a small bamboo ladle for measuring oil.

蹩 P'AN².
蹩脚打坐　to sit cross-legged and meditate, as Buddhists do.
打毽蹩毽　to kick the shuttle-cock with the soles of the feet alternately.

蹺 CH'IAO¹.
莫把脚蹺起　don't sit with your legs crossed.
看板凳蹺　beware of the stool tilting up.
踹蹺　to wear wooden heels in shoes, as some women do.
蹺假　to feign modesty when offered anything.

READ CH'IAO⁴. interchangable with 虭.
蹺起脚走　to walk on the heels as women with bound feet do.

蹨 LIEN⁴.
路蹨得稀爛　the road is trodden into mire.
把麥子蹨死了　the wheat has been stamped to death.

(504)

注　释

蹀 [tie⁵]
踹 [tʂʰai³]
【踹界】沿着边界走。
【踹水过去】踹水：涉水。
【踹桥】新桥的落成仪式。
【踹一乘轿子】制作一乘轿子。
【踹布】布料染完后滚压。
【踹石】染布后用于滚压的石头。
蹄 [tʰi²]
【油蹄子】油提子，一种竹制长柄的量油器具。
蹩（盘）[pʰan²]
【打毽盘毽】踢毽子。
蹺（跷）[tɕʰiao¹] [tɕʰiao⁴]
【蹺假】假装客气。
蹨 [lien⁴]
【路蹨得稀烂】路被踩踏成泥坑。
【把麦子蹨死了】麦子被踩踏死了。

注释

蹈 [tao⁴]
蹶 [tɕye⁵]
　【那个马打蹶子】打蹶子：跳起来用后腿向后踢。
蹬 [tən⁴]
　【事情犯蹭蹬】蹭蹬：路途险阻难行。比喻事情不顺利。
蹭 [tsʰən⁴]
　【走蹭了腿】蹭：因摩擦而破。
　【说话硬蹭】硬蹭：严厉。
　【他们都说蹭起了】他们吵起来了。
蹰 [tʂʰu²]
蹉（跶）[ta⁵]
　【看跶倒】当心跌倒。
躁 [tsʰao⁴]
躍（跃）[iao⁴]
　【那个子弟跳跃】跳跃：活跃，活泼。
躊（踌）[tsʰəu²]
身 [ʂən¹]

足 12-14 身

	TAO⁴.	
蹈	赴湯蹈火都要去	he will go, though he should have to face [hot water and *tread on* fire.
蹶	CHÜE⁵.	
	那個馬打蹶子	that horse *kicks*.
蹬	TEN⁴.	
	蹬一脚	to *stamp* one's foot.
	事情犯蹭蹬	the affair is *unsuccessful* and very tiring.
蹭	TS'EN⁴.	
	走蹭了腿	my legs *ache* with walking.
	說話硬蹭	to speak *harshly*.
	那個人蹭得很	he is very *quarrelsome*.
	他們說蹭起了	they have come to *wrangling*.
13 蹰	CH'U².	for example of use see 躇.
蹉	TA⁵.	
	看蹉倒	beware of *falling* down.
躁	TS'AO⁴.	
	性子躁	*hasty*-tempered.
躍	IAO⁴.	
	那個子弟跳躍	that youth is *active*, or *spry*.
躊	CH'EO².	
	心裏躊躇不定	very *undecided* in one's mind.

The 158th radical. (身)

身	SHEN¹.	
	身體	the *body*.
	沒得身家有性命	I have no *family* to think of, but I have my life to take care of.
	終身大事	a *life*-long affair, as marriage.

(505)

身 3-8

	身上沒得錢	I have no money on my *person*.
	好大個身分	what is his *position* in life?
	身價	wages.
	身後的事我不管了	I don't concern myself with what may happen after I am dead.
	有一身的賬	over head and ears in debt.
	上了身	enceinte.
	身子不空	enceinte.
	正身身	the main *trunk* of a tree.
3 躬	KONG¹.	
	打躬	to make a slight *bow*.
	出躬	to pass water.
4 耽	TAN¹.	
	多耽擱兩天	*stay* two days longer.
	路上沒得耽擱	there will be no *delay* on the road.
	耽悮工夫	to *retard* work by procrastination.
6 朓	TIAO⁴.	
	單單朓朓的	a slender and *tall* person.
躲	TO³.	
	躲避一時	to *hide* for a time; to keep out of the way.
	躲煞	to *avoid* the spirit of a dead person returning to the tablet.
	躲肩	to *shirk* work.
	扯躲子的話	to tell lies.
7 䝗	LANG¹.	
	䝗䝗朓朓的人	a *tall* and *slender* person.
8 矮	NGAI³.	same as 矮.
躺	T'ANG³.	
	躺覺	to *lie down* and sleep.
	躺在板凳上	*lay* him over a form and thrash him.

(506)

注　释

【上了身】怀孕了。
【正身身】树干。
躬 [koŋ¹]
【打躬】弯下身行礼。
耽（耽）[tan¹]
朓 [tiao⁴]
【单单朓朓的】身材又高又瘦的人。
躲（躲）[to³]
【躲煞】旧俗以人初死的鬼魂为煞，举家出门躲避。
【躲肩】逃避工作。
【扯躲子的话】说谎。
䝗 [laŋ¹]
【䝗䝗朓朓的人】又高又瘦。
矮 [ŋai³]
躺 [tʰaŋ³]

注 释

軀（躯）[tɕʰy¹]
軃 [tʰo³]
【軃起袖子】让袖子垂下。
【事情还是軃起的】軃起：悬而未决，含糊不定。
車（车）[tʂʰei¹][tɕy¹]
【天车】一种吊车。
【车水】抽水。
【车车匠】在木制车床车削圆形木器的工匠。
【车得转】转得动。
【二马车】指烟管与贮烟筒分开的水烟袋。
軍（军）[tɕyn¹]
【打军务】上战场。

身 11-12 車 2

11 軀

CH'Ü¹.

身軀高大　　　　tall in person.

12 軃

T'O³.

軃起袖子　　　　to let the gown sleeves *dangle* down.
事情還是軃起的　the affair is still *in suspense*.

The 159th radical. (車)

車 CH'E¹.

車子　　　　　　a *wheel-barrow*.
紡花車　　　　　a *spinning-wheel*.
車盤　　　　　　a *water-wheel*.　　　　　　[up heavy pillars.
天車　　　　　　a kind of *crane*, or *windlass* used for setting
風車　　　　　　*fanners*.
水車　　　　　　a *pump* with an endless chain.
車水　　　　　　to *pump* water.
車架子　　　　　a *turning-lathe*.　　　　　　　[things.
砍的沒得車的圓　chiselled things are not so round as *turned*
車車匠　　　　　a *turner*.
車得轉　　　　　it can be *turned* round on its axle.
一車就是一碗　　he swallows a basin of rice at one *turn* of
　　　　　　　　　his chopsticks.
車前草　　　　　the plantain.

CHÜ¹.
　　　　　　　　　　　　　　　　　　　　　　[tached.
二馬車　　　　　a water-pipe, with box for tobacco at-

2 軍

CHÜIN¹.

投軍　　　　　　to enlist in the *army*.
軍裝　　　　　　*army* stores.
打軍務　　　　　to go to *war*; to *campaign*.
軍功　　　　　　*military* prowess.
軍犯　　　　　　banishment; exile.

(507)

西蜀方言　507

車 3-7

3 軒 SHÜEN¹.

| 茶軒 | a tea-*shop*. |
| 氣宇軒昂 | a *lofty* bearing. |

4 軟 RUAN³.

穿一身細軟衣服	clad in *soft* raiment; richly dressed.
軟弱	*weak*; *feeble*.
脾氣柔軟	*mild* tempered; *pliant*.
把我心說軟了	he got round the *soft* side of me.
喫個軟飽	to take a moderate meal.
這個平軟	this balance is a little *short* of the standard.
軟辦	the district magistrate settling a bad case without reporting it.

6 較 CHIAO⁴.

| 把這兩個東西比較 | *compare* the two things. |
| 不與他計較 | don't *measure* strength with him; don't condescend to *argue*. |

READ KAO⁴.

| 平不一要較過 | the scales require to be *adjusted*. |

載 TSAI³.

| 一年半載 | in half a *year* or a year. |

READ TSAI⁴.

破船多攬載	to *load* a lot of cargo in a broken boat.
裝一載	to take one *boat-load* of goods.
載書	to *bind* a book.
載在書上	*recorded* in a book.

7 輕 CH'IN¹.

輕巧活路	*light* work.
輕輕的放	set it down *softly*.
脚輕手快	*active*.
輕輕狂狂的	of a *light* or *giddy* disposition.

(508)

注 釋

軒（轩）[ɕyen¹]
軟（软）[ʐuan³]
【吃个软饱】吃到适度饱。
【这个平软】平软：离标准还差一点点。
較（较）[tɕiao⁴]
【平不一要较过】天平需要校正。
載 [tsai³] [tsai⁴]
【装一载】装一船货。
【载书】装订书。
輕（轻）[tɕʰin¹]
【轻巧活路】轻松的活儿。

注释

【轻容易】非常容易。
【年轻骨嫩】不成熟。
【看得轻】轻视。
【人口轻省】家里人口少。
【轻粉】药材，为片状结晶，状似雪花。色白，有银色光泽。

辅（辅）[fu³]
辊（辊）[kuən¹]
轮（轮）[lən²]
辈（辈）[pei⁴]
输（输）[ʂu¹]
辗（辗）[tʂan³]
辖（辖）[ɕia⁵]

車 7-10

輕容易	very easy.
年輕骨嫩	young in years and tender in body; im-to disesteem. [mature.
看得輕	
輕生	regardless of one's life.
人口輕省	there are *few* people in the family.
輕粉	calomel.

輔 FU³.

8
| 輔助 | to *aid*; to *assist*. |

輥 KUEN¹.

輥子	a stone *roller*; a *millstone* for hulling rice.
輥筒	the *rollers* of a dyer's mangle.
車輥子	the *wheel* of a barrow.

輪 LEN².

車輪	the *wheel* of a barrow.
耳輪	the outer *rim* of the ear.
輪班看守	to mount guard in *rotation*.

輩 PE⁴.

一輩子	a *lifetime*.
一輩強一輩	every *generation* is better than the last.
老前輩	forefathers; progenitors.

9
輸 SHU¹.

上捐輸	to pay extra taxes, called the "People's [offering."
贏了官司輸了錢	you win the lawsuit but *lose* your money.
輸家 and 贏家	the family of the bride, and the family of the bridegroom.

10
輾 CHAN³.

| 輾轉難忘 | what you have *turned over and over* in your [mind, is easy to remember. |

轄 SHIA⁵.

| 管轄 | to *govern*. |
| 轄制 | to *tyrannize* over. |

(509)

輿 10-15 辛

輿 Ü².

for example of use see 堪.

ÜEN².

東轅門 — the eastern *side door* of a yamên.

轉 CHUAN³.

三天打回轉 — to *return* in three days.
悔不轉來 — impossible to *turn* back; no room for re-[pentance.
看得不轉眼 — to stare steadily at, never *turning* away the eyes.
轉個手 — give a little more money.
他心裏的轉折大 — he is a *shifty* fellow.
轉佃 — to *sublet* a house.

READ CHUAN⁴.

鐘停了不轉 — the clock has stopped; it will not *turn* or [go.
轉轉骨 — the wrist bone.
團轉 — all *around*; everywhere.
走轉路 — to go by a *circuitous* route.
打個轉轉 — to take a *turn* round; to go for a walk.
他反轉不依 — he, on the *contrary*, would not comply.

12 轎 CHIAO⁴.

轎子 — a *travelling* chair.
轎舖子 — a *chair*-shop.

14 轟 HONG¹.

雷聲轟轟 — the *rumbling* of thunder. [conntry.
轟轟烈烈的 — uproariously; famous, as a flourishing

15 轡 P'E⁴.

馬轡頭 — a horse's *bridle*.
一轡頭就跑了 — he bolted *instantly*.

The 160th radical. 辛

辛 SIN¹.

辛辛苦苦掙的 — gathered with much *bitterness* and suffer-[ing, as money.

(510)

注 釋

輿（舆）[y²]
轅（辕）[yen²]
【东辕门】衙门的东门。
轉（转）[tṣuan³] [tṣuan⁴]
【悔不转来】后悔也没用。
【转个手】过个手赚差价。
【他心里的转折大】转折大：诡计多端。
【转佃】转租出去。
【转转骨】腕骨。
【团转】到处。
【走转路】绕行。
【打个转转】散步。
【他反转不依】他无论如何不依从。
轎（轿）[tɕiao⁴]
轟（轰）[xoŋ¹]
轡（辔）[pʰei⁴]
【一辔头就跑了】立刻就跑了。
辛 [sin¹]

注 释

辜 [ku¹]
【辜负材料】浪费材料。
辞 [tsʰɿ²]
辣 [la⁵]
【辣嘴】说话尖刻。
【锅烧辣了】锅烧烫了。
【火辣了点】火太猛了。
【他的手辣】他很凶。
办（辦）[pan⁴]
【这么横要办你】你这么无法无天，我要惩罚你。
辨 [pien⁴]
辭（辞）[tsʰɿ²]
【不辞劳】不逃避辛苦的工作。
辯（辩）[pien⁴]
（PIEN²当为PIEN⁴，见803页勘误表。）
辰 [ʂən²] [tʂʰən²]

辛 5-14 辰

5 辜　KU¹.
無辜受累　involved though *guilt*less.
辜負大恩　*ungrateful* for great favours.
6 辭　辜負材料　to *waste* materials in the making of any-[thing.
　　TSʻƗ². same as 辭.
7 辣　LAƗ⁵.
辣子　*capsicum*.
辣嘴　*pungent*.
鍋燒辣了　the pan is *hot*.
火辣了點　the fire is too *fierce*.
他的手辣　he is very *severe*.
9 辦　PAN⁴.
辦事　to *manage* an affair. [by an official).
這麽橫要辦你　you are perverse, I will *punish* you (said
辦酒席　to *prepare* a feast.
辦嫁奩　to *provide* a bride's trousseau.
辦的甚麼貨　what goods are you *trading* in.
12 辨　PIEN⁴.
辨別眞假　to *distinguish* between true and false.
　　TSʻƗ².
再三推辭　to *refuse* repeatedly.
不辭勞　he does not *shirk* work.
辭行　to *take leave of*; to say good-bye.
14 辯　PIEN².
辯明白　to *state* clearly, to *explain*.
還在强辯　do you still obstinately *dispute*?
辯駁　to *argue*; to *contradict*.

The 161st radical. **辰**

辰　SHEN², CHʻEN².
一個時辰　one Chinese *hour* (two English hours).

(511)

辰 3-6 辵 3-4

	那些年辰好	those were good *years*.
	時辰表	a watch, or a clock.
	日月星表	sun, moon and *stars*.

3 辱 6　RU⁵.

不可凌辱他	you may not *insult* him.
把老子玷辱子	you have *disgraced* your parents.

農　LONG².

九九八十一農夫老兒田中犁	eighty-one days after the winter solstice the *husbandman* begins to plough the rice fields.

The 162nd radical. (辵)

3 巡　SÜIN². same as 巡

迃　Ü¹.

你纔是個迃老夫子	you are very *perverse*, or *obstinate*.

4 近　CHIN⁴.

近水知魚性 近山識鳥音	if you live *near* the river you will know the habits of the fishes, if you live *near* the hills you will know the notes of the birds.
看路程遠近	it depends on the *distance*.
街坊鄰近	*neighbours*.
親近好人	*make friends* with good men. [(polite).
少親近	I have seldom been *in your company*
將近要黑	it will *soon* be dark.

返　FAN³.

往返得好久	how long will it take you to go and *return*?
我往返了幾回	I went and *came* several times.

迎　IN².

迎接	to *receive*, as a guest.
迎春	to *welcome* spring (a festival).

(512)

注释

【那些年辰好】年辰：岁月。

【时辰表】手表，闹钟。

【日月星表】（"表"当为"辰"，见803页勘误表。）

辱 [zu⁵]

【把老子玷辱子】辱没了自己的父母。

農（农）[loŋ²]

巡 [ɕyn²]

迃 [y¹]

近 [tɕin⁴]

【少亲近】很少交往。

【将近要黑】马上天黑了。

返 [fan³]

迎 [in²]

注释

迥 [tɕyn³]
迫 [pʰe⁵]
追 [tsuei¹]
迷 [mi²]
逆 [n̠ie⁵]
迸 [pin¹]
【田开了迸缝】迸缝：因干旱而裂缝。
送 [soŋ⁴]

辵 4-6

迥 迫 追 迷 逆 迸 送		
	在家不會迎賓客 出路方知少主人	if you cannot *entertain* strangers you will find few who will welcome you.
	CHÜN³.	
	迥不相同	*very* unlike.
	P'E⁵.	same as 迫.
	TSUE¹.	
	追趕不上	I cannot *overtake* him.
	追賬	to *press* the payment of a debt; to *dun*.
	追悔不及	no place for *repentance*.
	MI².	
	迷惑人	to *delude* people.
	醉得迷迷沉沉的	*dazed* with drink.
	NIE⁵.	
	忤逆的兒子	a *disobedient* son.
	逆理犯分	*contrary* to reason and duty.
	PIN¹.	
	田開了迸縫	the fields are *cracked* with drought.
	板子迸了	the board is *split*.
	脚上凍起迸口	my feet are *chapped* with the cold.
	SONG⁴.	
	送君千里終需一別	if I would *accompany* you a thousand miles there would still be a parting.
	不送不送	don't trouble to *accompany* me (polite).
	眼睛送他多少遠	I *followed* him with my eyes for a long distance.
	送貨上船	*deliver* the goods at the boat.
	是送給我的	it was *presented* to me.
	千里送毫毛 禮輕仁義重	if a man *brings* a hair a thousand miles *as a present*, his gift is small, but his love is great.
	送喪	to *attend* a funeral.

(513)

辵 6-7

T'AO².

逃走	to *run away*; or *abscond*.
逃營	to *escape* from camp; to *desert*.
逃兵	a *deserter*.
逃荒	to *flee* from a famine-stricken district.
逃學	to *play truant*.

T'UE⁴.

退兵	to *withdraw* troops; to *retreat*.
退開些	*stand back* a little.
退後一步自然寬	*yield* a little and the dispute will settle itself.
把我嚇了幾個倒退	it scared me a few *steps backward*.
官退了堂	the magistrate has *retired* from the court.
水退了	the water has *receded*.
退房子	to *give up* a house.
下半天退了涼	the weather becomes cooler in the afternoon.
不退燒	the fever does not *abate*.
用不得包退	what you cannot use I will *take back*.
退光漆	varnish that *reflects* the light; lacquer work.
顏色退了	the colour has *faded*.
退個牛兒子	to *calve*.

SIAO¹.

| 逍遙得好 | to *ramble at leisure*. |

CHE⁴.

| 這個地方 | *this* place. |
| 這些東西 | *these* things. |

TS'EN³.

| 逞他的能 | *confident* in his power, *presumptuous*. |

CHO⁵.

| 把他逐出去 | *expel* him; *eject* him. |
| 巴個逐條 | to put out a notice *disowning* a son. |

(514)

注 释

逃 [tʰao²]
【逃营】从营地逃跑，当逃兵。

退 [tʰuei⁴]
【用不得包退】用不得：不能用。
【退个牛儿子】生小牛。

逍 [siao¹]
【逍遥得好】闲逛。

這（这）[tṣei⁴]

逞 [tsʰən³]

逐 [tṣo⁵]
【巴个逐条】声明脱离父子关系。

注 释

逢 [foŋ²]
【要相逢难相逢除非纸上画真客】("客"当为"容",见803页勘误表。)
【那一天逢场】逢场:按照当地约定赶集的日子。
【逢二五八】指几个相邻的集市都不安排在同一天,你如逢"一四七",我就逢"二五八",他就逢"三六九"等。这样就能方便商贩有更多的交易机会。

逛 [kuaŋ⁴] [kaŋ⁴]
【酒把他逛起了】喝醉了。
【张逛李逛驾云扯谎】东家长西家短胡扯。
【打逛子】聊天。

连(连) [lien²]
【连乡会】哥老会,近代中国一个民间秘密结社组织。
【事情太留连了】留连:拖延。
【一把连】全部,全数。

走 7

逢 FONG².

要相逢難相逢除非紙上畫眞客	if we desire to *meet* each other but cannot we had better exchange portraits.
那一天逢場	when is market day?
逢二五八	each 2nd, 5th, and 8th is market day.
難逢難遇的	very hard to *meet* with; rare.

逛 KUANG⁴, KANG⁴.

| 出去逛一轉 | let us go for a *ramble*. |
| 在麥田裏逛⁴來逛⁴去 | to *walk about* in a person's wheat field. |

READ KANG⁴.

| 酒把他逛起了 | he is *beside himself* with drink; *drunk*. |

READ KUANG³.

| 張逛李逛駕雲扯謊 | to *wander* idly from house to house telling lies. |
| 打逛子 | to *idly talk*; to *gossip*. |

連 LIEN².

連鄉會	the "*United* Regions Society"—the "Ko-Lao Hue" in W. China.
連界的	*bordering* on each other, as farms or countries.
接接連連的客來了	a *continuous* stream of guests.
事情太留連了	the affair is too *protracted*.
連倒幾天的雨	rain for several days *together*.
連年都是這個規矩	year *by* year the custom has been the same.
一把連	the *whole lot*.
連腔都不敢開	one dares not speak *even*.
連兒帶母	the cow *and* the calf.
不要連累人	don't *implicate* others. [met., to *involve*.
痛脚連累好脚	the aching foot *implicates* the sound foot;

(515)

辵 7

SHIO⁵, SIO⁵.

| 即速去 | go *quickly!* make *haste!* |

TEO⁴.

| 莫在路上逗遛 | don't *delay* on the road; don't *loiter* by the way. |

T'EO⁴.

看透了	I see *through* it; I *comprehend*.
說透人情	to *convince* people; to *move* their feelings.
一點亮光透進來了	there is a little light coming *through* the window.
濕透了衣裳	my clothes were wet *through*.
透紅	red *through* and *through*.
透爐子	*poke* the fire.

TI⁴.

| | same as 遞. |

T'U².

| 沿途平安 | peace by the *way*. |

T'ONG¹.

通行天下	to *pervade* the empire.
通使通用	used *everywhere*.
通省都曉得	the *whole* province knows of it.
這條路不通	this road is not *open* to traffic; no *thoroughfare*.
大便不通	*constipated*.
要通知他	you must *notify* him.
他們是通的	they are in *communication*.
通不得風	the secret must not be *made known*.
通氣的朋友	an *intimate* friend.
通商	business *intercourse*.
通事	an *interpreter*.
不通亮	not *transparent*.

TS'AO⁴.

| 造團冊 | to *make* a record of the inhabitants of a parish. |

(516)

注 释

速 [ɕio⁵] [sio⁵]
【即速去】马上去。
逗 [təu⁴]
透 [tʰəu⁴]
【说透人情】以情感来打动人。
【透炉子】捅炉火。
遞（递）[ti⁴]
途 [tʰu²]
通 [tʰoŋ¹]
【通使通用】各地都可用。
【通不得风】秘不可宣。
【通事】旧时指翻译人员。
【不通亮】不透明。
造 [tsʰao⁴] [tsao⁴]
【造团册】制作教区的居民册。

注 释

【大造主】造物主。
【两造】有关争讼的双方当事人。
週（周）[tʂəu¹]
迯（奔）[pən⁴]
【索子奔断了】绳子拉断了。
【你筋奔些】筋奔：活跃，敏捷。
進（进）[tsin⁴]
【进教】入教。
【进水】行贿。
【会进】考中进士。

是 7-8

起造房屋	to *build* houses.
恩同再造	your kindness has as it were *recreated* me.
好造化	a happy *transformation*! good fortune!
大造主	the Great *Creator*.
私造謠言	to secretly *fabricate*, or *propagate* vile [rumours.
兩造	the two *parties* in a case.
不敢造次	I dare not be *disorderly* (polite).

READ TSAO⁴.

造反	to *rebel*.
造孽得很	*suffering* grievous evil.
木匠戴枷自作自造	the carpenter is wearing the wooden collar, he made it and he is *bearing* it.
你又在造事	you are *stirring up* mischief again?

8 週

CHEO¹.

| 週流不息 | to *revolve* unceasingly, as the seasons. |
| 三週年 | three *whole* years. |

迯

PEN⁴.

迯命的跑	to *run* as for one's life.
投迯	to *flee* to for succour.
索子迯斷了	the rope was broken through being *jerked*.
你筋迯些	be *active*; look *spry*.

進

TSIN⁴.

進退兩難	it is difficult either to *advance* or to recede.
進屋來	*enter* the house.
進教	to *enter* a religion; to *join* a church.
進香	to *offer* incense.
進水	to *give* bribes.
進貢	to *pay* tribute.
沒有長進	he has made no progress in learning, or skill.
那個房子有幾進	how many *divisions* are there in that house [from front to back?
會進	to attain to the "*tsin-sï*" degree.

(517)

卷 8-9

逸	I².	
	安逸自在	at *ease* and quiet, as a wealthy man.
	我人不安逸	I am not *well*.
逾	Ü².	
	莫做過逾了	don't *overstep* your duty.
過	KO⁴.	
	經過我的手	it *passed through* my hands; I *transacted* the business.
	過年	to *pass* from the old year to the new; the [New Year festival.
	過了期	it is *past* the set time.
	過路的人	a *passer*-by.
	忍耐過日	to *spend* one's days patiently.
	他屋頭好過	his family is well-off.
	過午沒有	have you had your lunch?
	過不去	im*passable*, as road or river; unable to get *through* the year from poverty.
	過河	to *cross* a river.
	過了世	*passed* from this world; dead.
	沒有過火	the rice is only half-cooked.
	過心	*diameter*; *across* the centre.
	過天星	a meteor.
	拿過來	bring it *over*.
	過那裏去	where are you going *to*?
	過秤	to *weigh* on the steelyard.
	長子不過房	the eldest son may not be *adopted* into [another family.
	肚子過	*diarrhœa*.
	不過三百錢	not *more than* 300 cash.
	做事過分	to *overstep* one's duty.
	我心頭難過	I am ill at ease (either mentally or phys-[ically).
	很不過意	very much ashamed.
	過錢	to *pay* money.
	米有甚麼過頭	what is the *price* of rice?
	多少過場	he has a great many *tricks* or *feints*.
	我有甚麼過錯	what *fault* have I?

(518)

注 释

逸 [i²]
【我人不安逸】我身体欠佳。

逾 [y²]
【莫做过逾了】不要越职。

過（过）[ko⁴]
【他屋头好过】他家里日子过得好。
【没有过火】米饭夹生没有做熟。
【过心】直径。
【过天星】流星。
【过那里去】去哪儿?
【长子不过房】过房:无子而以兄弟或同宗之子为后嗣。旧时风俗,长子不能过继给人家。
【肚子过】拉肚子。
【很不过意】不好意思。
【过钱】付钱。
【米有甚么过头】米价多少?
【多少过场】计谋、鬼点子多。

注释

遍 [pʰienˇ]
【遍地都撒起】撒了一地。
逼 [pie¹] [pi⁵]
遂 [sy⁴]
趟（遖）[tʰaŋ⁴]
【那个马的遖子好】那是一匹好赛马。
【他一遖子跑了】他跑着离开了。
【把我很跑了几遖子】我来回跑了好多趟。
達（达）[ta⁵]
【家务发达】他的家业很成功。
道 [tao⁴]
【同行道】同业，同行。

足 9

	人非聖賢焉能無過	if a man is not a sage how can he be without *transgression*?
遍	沒有見過	I have not seen it *(past time)*.

P'IEN⁴.

逼	遍地都撒起	it is scattered on the ground *everywhere*.

PIE¹·, PI⁵.

	你莫逼我	don't *annoy* or *harass* me.
	緊防逼出人命	beware lest you drive him to an *extremity*.

READ PIE⁵.

	逼嫁	to *compel* a widow to marry again.
	威逼	*imperious*.

SÜ⁴.

遂	百般順遂	everything goes *smoothly*; all is according [to one's mind.

T'ANG⁴.

趟	那個馬的趟子好	that horse is a good racer, i. e., he can run [many *heats* on the parade ground.
	他一趟子跑了	he went off at a *run*; he bolted.
	把我很跑了幾趟子	I had to go and come a great many *times*.

TA⁵.

達	通達人情	*thoroughly acquainted with* human nature.
	家務發達	his family is *advancing* in the world; *successful* in life.
	報達父母的恩	to *recompense* one's parent's goodness.

TAO⁴.

道	道路	a *road*.
	街道窄	the *street* is narrow.
	門道兒	a *doorway*.
	道臺	an intendant of *circuit*.
	同行道	of the same *craft*.
	講道理	to discuss *reason*; to settle the *rights* of a [case in the tea-shop.
	傳道	to propagate a *doctrine*.
	道人	a *Taoist*; a devotee of *Reason*; a Rational-[ist.

(519)

西蜀方言

	知道	to *know*.
	說道讀書	*talking* of study.
	道謝	I *express* my thanks; thank you.
	走了幾道	I have gone a few *times*.
	喫三道藥	take three *doses* of medicine.
	一道橋	one bridge. (*N. A.*)
遁	TEN⁴.	[earth! I cannot find him.
	我肯信他會土遁	I believe he is able to *vanish* into the
	他學了奇門遁的	he has studied the *mysteries* of the "ch'i" and the "men."
違	UE².	[one's back.
	陽奉陰違	to flatter to one's face but *oppose* behind
遊	IU².	
	周遊天下	to *travel* all over the country.
	到處遊玩	to *ramble* about seeking amusement.
	遊擊	a lieutenant-colonel whose duty is to keep down robbers.
	遊學	a *wandering* scholar.
	遊街	to *parade* the streets with a bride's trousseau or an idol procession.
	打遊火	to *follow* an army for plunder.
	遊手好閒	*idle* and fond of doing nothing.
遇	Ü⁴.	
	沒有遇見過	I have not *met* him.
	遇着有事就擱了	I *happened* to be busy and was delayed.
	這個事情不遇緣	this is an unfortunate affair; lit., it does not *meet* with luck.
	來得不遇時	he came in*opportunely*.
運	ÜIN⁴.	[limbs.
	運動手脚	to *move* the arms and feet; to *exercise* the
	運起走	to *carry* two loads alternately; alternately lifting the ends of a heavy weight.

(520)

注 释

【走了几道】走了几回。
遁 [tən⁴]
違(违) [uei²]
遊(游) [iəu²]
【游街】游行。
【打游火】跟随军队抢掠。
遇 [y⁴]
【来得不遇时】不遇时；不凑巧。
運(运) [yn⁴]
【运起走】运走。

注 释

【今年我交运脱运】交运脱运：运气一个接着一个。

遣 [tɕʰien³]
  【遣发】流放。

遛 [liəu²]
  【逗遛】闲荡。

逊（逊）[syn⁴]

遢 [tʰa⁵]

递（递）[ti⁴]

遥 [iao²]
  【他到逍遥府享福去了】逍遥府：天堂。

远（远）[yen³] [yen⁴]
  【这里走成都有好远】这里离成都有多远？
  【远年】多年前。

卷 9-10

	運糧	to *transport* rations for troops.
	人走時運馬走臕	a man succeeds when in *luck*, and a horse goes when well fed.
10 遣	今年我交運脫運	my *fortunes* have taken a turn for the better this year.

CH'IEN³.

差遣	to *depute*; to *commission*.
遣發	*banishment*.
沒得消遣的地方	there is no place where I can *dispel* my sorrow or care.

LIU².

逗遛	to *loiter*.

SÜN⁴.

謙遜	*humble*; *meek*.

T'A⁵.

那個人不愛乾淨邋遢	he hates cleanliness—*filthy* fellow!

TI⁴.

遞給我	hand it to me.
遞呈子	to *send in* an indictment.

IAO².

路遙知馬力 事久見人心	a *long* road tests a horse's strength, and a tedious affair proves a friend's heart.
他到逍遙府享福去了	your departed friend has gone to enjoy blessedness in the Hall of *Ease*.

ÜEN³.

這裏走成都有好遠	how *far* is it from here to Ch'en-tu?
遠走不如近爬坡	better surmount difficulties at home than travel *far* in search of wealth.
離得遠	*far* off.
日子不遠了	the day is not *far* distant.
遠年	many years ago.

(521)

辵 10-12

READ ÜEN⁴.

不曉得遠近	I don't know the distance.
永永遠遠的	eternally; for ever.
走了遠路	I have gone a *round-about* road.

SHĬ⁵.

適值他沒有在屋頭	it *happened* that he was not at home.

CHE¹.

一手遮天	you can *cover* the sky with one hand (sarcastic).
遮太陽	to *shade* from the sun.
莫遮倒亮	don't stand in the light.
我不要你遮風遮雨	I don't need you to *shield* or *protect* me.
沒得一點遮攔	there is no *fence* on that side of the house.
遮醜	to *screen* one's faults.

CH'Ï².

遲慢	slow; dilatory; procrastinating.
來得太遲慢	you have come too *late*.
遲鈍	dull; stupid.

TSAO¹.

遭殃	to *incur* a divine judgment.
屋漏又遭連夜雨 行船正遇打頭風	when the roof leaks it *happens* to rain night after night, and just when we set sail there is an adverse wind.
遭塌人	to *illtreat* people.
遭塌飲食	to *waste* or *misuse* food.
我親自走一遭	I will go myself one *time*.

I².

父母遺留的	that which has been *handed down* by parents; inherited property.
父母的遺體	the body *bequeathed* to me by my parents.
留下遺囑	to leave a *will*.

(522)

注釋

適(适)[sɻ⁵]
遮[tʂei¹]
【莫遮倒亮】別把亮擋住。
遲(迟)[tʂʰɻ²]
【迟慢】拖拉。
遭[tsao¹]
遺(遗)[i²]

注释

遶（绕）[zao³]
遼（辽）[liao³]
（LIAO⁴当为LIAO³，见803页勘误表。）
【辽叶壳】竹叶斗笠。
選（选）[syen³] [syen⁴]
遷（迁）[tsʰien¹]
【改过迁善】忏悔。
遵[tsən¹]
【遵断】默许，同意。
還（还）[xuan²]
【还阳】从恍惚中苏醒。
邁（迈）[mai⁴]

罡 12-13

	遺腹兒	a *posthumous* child.
	我的遺忘大	my *forgetfulness* is great.
	遺精病	seminal *emissions*; spermatorrhœa.
	遺尿	wetting the bed.
遶	RAO³.	same as 繞.
遼	LIAO⁴.	
	遼葉壳	rain hats made of *broad-leaved bamboo*.
選	SÜEN³.	
	選擇	to *select*; to *pick out*.
	READ SÜEN⁴.	
	候選	to await *appointment* to office.
遷	TSʻIEN¹.	
	遷移	to *remove*; to *change* one's residence.
	改過遷善	to *repent* and *reform*.
	遷延日子	to *put off* the day; to *procrastinate*.
遵	TSEN¹.	
	遵命	I *obey* your commands.
	遵斷	I *acquiesce* in the decision of the judge.
還	HUAN².	
	還家	to *return* to one's home.
	還個價錢	to *offer* a price.
	還陽	to *revive* from a trance.
	還賬	to *repay* a debt.
	還原	to *restore* the original article.
	還禮	to *exchange* courtesy.
	還在下雨	it is *still* raining.
	還有不有	have you any *more*?
邁	MAI⁴.	
	年高老邁	waxing *old and feeble*; *aged and infirm*.
	邁開大步	to walk with *rapid and energetic strides*.

(523)

辵 13-19 邑 4

避 PI⁴.

| 避難 | to *flee* from danger or difficulty. |

邀 IAO¹.

邀個同伴	*invite* a comrade to go with you.
給他告邀	*beg* his pardon.
邀父母官的恩	we *beseech* the magistrate to grant him [grace.
邀牛	to *drive* an ox.
邀邀約約踏青	to go to the graves in *company*.

邋 LA⁵.

| 邋裏邋遢的 | *filthy*; *slovenly*. |

邊 PIEN¹.

在這邊	on this *side*; in this country.
分半邊	take the *half* of it. [associates, etc.
身邊的人	people who live *beside* one, as domestics,
邊哭邊笑	to cry and laugh *by turns*, or *at once*.
褢邊	to trim a dress; *trimming*.
邊界相連	*bordering* on each other.
在邊邊上	on the *margin*.

邏 LO¹.

| 車得邏邏轉 | to work up a *brisk* business. |
| 哄得邏邏轉 | to cheat people. |

The 163rd radical. (邑)

那 LA⁵.

那一個	*who*?
這是那個的書	*whose* book is this?
那一樣好	*which* kind is best?
那一年的事	in *what* year did it happen?
從那裏來	*where* did you come from?

(524)

注　释

避 [pi⁴]
邀 [iao²]
【给他告邀】请求他原谅。
【邀父母官的恩】乞求审判官法外施恩。
【邀牛】赶牛。
邋 [la⁵]
边（边）[pien¹]
【分半边】分一半。
逻（逻）[lo¹]
【车得逻逻转】逻逻转：不停地转动。
【哄得逻逻转】骗人。
那 [la³] [la⁴]
（LA⁵当为LA³，见803页勘误表。）

注 释

【那么晓得】怎么知道的?
【那话不消说】不消说:不值一提。
邦 [paŋ¹]
邪 [sie²]
【邪法】魔术。
【莫把话说邪了】别曲解我的意思。
邨(村) [tsʰən¹] [tsʰuən¹]
郎 [laŋ²]
【两郎舅】郎舅:男子与其妻兄弟的合称。
部 [pu⁴]
都 [tu¹]
鄉(乡) [ɕiaŋ¹]
【乡坝里】乡下。

邑 4-10

那個時候喫的	*when* did he swallow it ?
那麼曉得	*how* do you know ?
READ LA⁴.	
那話不消說	you need not mention *that*.
那些人來得不善	*those* people are up to no good.
是那個時候做的	it was done *then*.
過那邊去	go over *there*; to go to your country.
PANG¹.	
和睦鄰邦	to be at peace with neighbouring *countries*.
SIE².	
改邪歸正	to turn from *heresy* to orthodoxy.
邪法	*sorcery*.
遇了邪	he has met with an *evil spirit*, he has been [bewitched.
莫把話說邪了	don't put an *evil* meaning into my words.
邪淫的念頭	*impure* thoughts.
TS'EN¹ TS'UEN¹.	same as 村.
LANG².	
張郎殺猪登仙去 } 李郎看經被虎傷 }	*Mr.* Chaug killed pigs, yet he became an immortal, while *Mr.* Li, who studied the liturgy, was killed by a tiger.
有幾個令郎	how many *sons* have you?
新郎	a *bridegroom*.
兩郎舅	brothers-in-law.
PU⁴.	[many. (*N. A.*)
一部書	a complete book either in one volume or
TU¹.	
都是好的	they are *all* good.
我都勸過他	I *too*, or *also* exhorted him.
胖都都的	fat and *large*.
SHIANG¹.	
鄉壩裏	in the *country*.

邑 10-12　酉 2-3

	趕 鄉 場	to attend a *country* market.
	鄉 攞 老	a *country*man.
	家 鄉 人	fellow-*villagers*; natives of the same place.
	你 曉 不 曉 得 四 鄉	do you know the customs of the place?
	鄉 約	a justice of the peace.
11	鄉 試	the *Provincial* examinations.

11 鄙 P'I³.

	卑 鄙 的 人	a mean *vulgar* fellow.

鄰 LIN².

	隔 壁 鄰 居	*neighbours*.
12	鄰 國	*adjacent* countries.

12 鄭 CHEN⁴.

	人 要 鄭 重	a man ought to be *circumspect*.

The 164th radical. 酉

2 酊 TIN¹.　for example of use see 酩.

3 配 P'E⁴.

	配 成 對	to *match* in pairs.
	配 不 上	not *equal* to; unable to *match*.
	不 配	un*worthy*.
	配 鑰 匙	to *fit* a lock with a key.
	還 沒 有 婚 配	they are not *married* yet.

酒 TSIU³.

	酒 館 子	a *wine* shop.
	酒 米	glutinous rice from which *wine* is made.
	發 酒 瘋	mad with *drink*.
	辦 酒 席	to spread a *feast*.
	若 要 斷 酒 法　醒 眼 看 醉 人	if you want to know how to abstain from *drink*, arouse yourself and look at a drunken man.

(526)

注　释

【赶乡场】赶集。
【你晓不晓得四乡】你知道那个地方的风俗习惯吗?
鄙 [pʰi³]
鄰（邻）[lin²]
鄭（郑）[tʂən⁴]
【人要郑重】郑重: 慎重, 细心。
酊 [tin¹]
配 [pʰei⁴]
酒 [tsiəu³]
【酒米】糯米。

注 释

【他过了酒没有】他结婚了吗?
【酒钱】原指饮酒或买酒的钱。借指赏钱、小费。
酥 [su¹]
酩 [min²]
酬 [tʂʰəu²]
【没得人应酬】没有人款待我。
【酬客】收到礼物后设宴款待对方。
醻(酬) [tʂʰəu²]
酵 [tɕiao⁴]
醇 [ʂuən²]
酷 [ku⁵]
【挖酷人】挖酷：欺侮，压迫。
酸 [suan¹]
【老酸】学究。
醋 [tsʰu⁴]
醉 [tsuei⁴]

酉 3-8

5 酥	他過了酒沒有	is he married yet?
	酒錢	a bonus; letter money; extra money given [to coolies.
	SU¹.	
	酥油	butter.
6 酩	酥餅子	crisp cakes.
	MIN².	
	酩酊大醉	very drunk; intoxicated.
酬	CH'EO².	
	沒得人應酬	no one entertained me.
醻	酬客	to make a feast in return for presents re- [ceived.
	CH'EO².	same as last.
酵	CHIAO⁴.	
	酵水	yeast; barm.
醇	酵頭	leaven for making wine.
	SHUEN².	
酷	這個酒的味道醇	this wine has a rich flavour.
	KU⁵.	
	挖酷人	to oppress people.
酸	SUAN¹.	
	酸醋	sour vinegar.
	酸菜	pickled vegetables.
	老酸	a scholar; one who interlards his talk with [high-flown words.
8 醋	忍氣吞酸	to swallow an affront.
	TS'U⁴.	
	燅醋	vinegar.
	兩個喫醋	the two friends are soured.
醉	TSUE⁴.	
	喫得醉如泥	dead drunk; lit., drunk as mud.
	烟醉倒了	sick from smoking tobacco or opium, as a [beginner.

(527)

西蜀方言

酉 8-14

醃 9 IEN¹.
醃個腿子	*salt* a leg of pork.
今年醃肉沒有	have you *pickled* any pork this season?

醒 SIN³.
醒起的	*awake*.
喊醒他	*wake* him up.
醒砲	the *morning gun* fired at the yamên.
提醒他	*exhort* him.
他不曉得醒悟	he won't be *aroused*.
蛋醒了	the eggs are *stinking*.
10 漿子放醒了	the paste is *sour*.

醜 CH'EO³.
長得醜	*ugly*.
說醜話	to talk *vile* scandal.
丟個醜	to get a *bad reputation*.
11 家醜不可外傳	a family *disgrace* should not be spoken of [abroad].

醫 I¹.
醫病	to *heal* diseases.
行醫	to practice the *art of healing*.
醫生	a doctor.
醫館	a dispensary.

醪 LAO².
醪糟蛋	freshly *fermented glutinous rice* with eggs.

醋 TSAO¹.
	same as 糟.

醬 TSIANG⁴.
12 醬油	*soy*; *sauce*.

醮 TSIAO⁴.
打醮	to observe a *thanksgiving festival*.
14 再醮	a widow *marrying again*.

醺 SHÜIN¹.
醉醺醺的	*intoxicated*.
酒氣醺醺	the smell of wine *pervades* the place, or [the man.

(528)

注　釋

醃（腌）[ien¹]

醒 [sin³]

【醒起的】醒着的。

【醒炮】旧时衙门头门外每天都要定时"放炮"，黎明时的一炮叫做"醒炮"。炮响后，家家户户就要起床，一天的劳作也就开始了。

【蛋醒了】醒：发臭。

【浆子放醒了】醒：酸。

醜（丑）[tʂʰəu³]

醫（医）[i¹]

醪 [lao²]

【醪糟蛋】酒酿（酒米）煮鸡蛋。

醋（糟）[tsao¹]

醬（酱）[tsiaŋ¹]

醮 [tsiao⁴]

【打醮】教徒设坛念经做法事。

【再醮】寡妇改嫁。

醺 [ɕyn¹]

注释

醾 [moŋ²]
醸（酿）[ȵiaŋ²] [ȵiaŋ⁴]
【酒酿酿】发酵酒。
【甜得酿人】太甜了。
釁（衅）[ɕin⁴]
【找不出他的衅隙】衅
　隙：破绽。
釅（酽）[ȵien⁴]
【熬酽汤】酽汤：浓汤。
释（释）[sʅ⁵]
里 [li³]
重 [tsʰoŋ²] [tʂoŋ⁴]
【重起】再加倍；堆起，
　堆叠。
【说重皮子话】重申。
【有好重】有多重？

酉 14-20 釆 13 里 2

醾 MONG². [vinegar.
17 起了白醾醾　it has gathered a white *scum* on it, as
醸 NIANG².
　酒酿酿　*fermented liquor*.
　READ NIANG⁴.
　甜得酿人　sweet enough to *sicken* one.
18 酿酒　to *ferment* liquor.
釁 SHIN⁴.
　找不出他的釁隙 I cannot find any *fault* in him.
20 爲甚麼事起釁　what was the cause of the *quarrel*?
釅 NIEN⁴.
　釅茶　*strong* tea.
　熬釅湯　make some *strong*, or *thick* soup.

The 165th radical. **(釆)**

13 **释** SHĬ⁵.
　释放　to *liberate*.
　註释　a *commentary*.

The 166th radical. **(里)**

里 LI³.
2 一百二十里　120 Chinese *miles*.
重 CH'ONG².
　重起　to *redouble*; to *pile* one thing on another.
　說重皮子話　to *reiterate*.
　重修　to *rebuild*.
　READ CHONG⁴.
　有好重　how *heavy* is it?

(529)

里 2-6. 金

恩重如山	his grace is *great* as a mountain.
看得貴重	to regard as honourable and *important*.
重重的說他兩句	he reprimanded him *severely*.
病體沉重	his sickness is *severe*; beyond hope of recovery.
君子自重	a gentleman should have self-respect.
那個人心重	that fellow is very *covetous*.

4 野 IE³.

打野歇	to camp on the *wilds*.
野人	*savages*.
野草	*weeds*.
猫兒放野了	the cat has run *wild*.
野獸	*wild* beasts.
他心野得很	he has a *restless* disposition.
撒野	*reckless*; rude.

5 量 LIANG².

沒商量	I will not *consult* about it; I will not discuss the matter.
平生只會量人短 何不囘頭把自量	you do nothing but *discuss* the failures of others, why not *consider* your own?

READ LIANG⁴.

下細酌量	*consider* it carefully.
量體裁衣	cut the clothes to your measure; met., consider your means.
不自量	he did not *estimate* his own abilities.
飯量大	his *capacity* for rice is great; a good appetite.
力量	*strength*; ability; means.
大量人	a *magnanimous* person.
膽量大	his *courage* is great; lit., "*measure* of his gall."

6 釐 LI².

same as 厘.

The 167th radical. 金

金 CHIN¹.

眞金不怕火來燒	*true gold* does not fear the fire.
金黃色	*golden*.

(530)

注 释

【看得贵重】看得很重。
【那个人心重】心重：贪婪，爱财。
野 [ie³]
【打野歇】露营。
【猫儿放野了】放野：不听话。
量 [liaŋ²] [liaŋ⁴]
【大量人】宽宏大量的人。
釐（厘）[li²]
金 [tɕin¹]

注释

【恩金儿】富裕而慷慨的人。

【泥金】赤陶土。

針(针) [tʂən¹]

【学针㸁】针㸁：针线。

【钱针】用于串钱的长针。

釘(钉) [tin¹] [tin⁴]

【钉封】旧时一种用特殊方法封合的文书。它用钉子先在文书上扎眼，而后用纸捻子穿上，以示文书的机密和紧要。一般用于寄递处决囚犯的公文。

【钉石头】投掷石头。

釵(钗) [tʂʰai¹]

【裙钗】指女子。

釧(钏) [tʂʰuan¹]

【银钏子】银手镯。

金 2-3

金銀花	honey-suckle; lit., *gold* and *silver* flower.
金針花	*golden*-needle flower, the day-lily.
打釐金	to gather *custom*.
添個千金	they have got a *daughter*.
恩金兒	a wealthy and benevolent person.
金鉑	*tinsel*.
泥金	*terra-cotta*.

²針

CHEN¹.

積錢猶如針挑土 退財好似水推沙	making money is like picking up earth with a *needle*, but spending it is like water washing away sand.
學針黹	to learn *needle*-work.
錢針	a long *needle* for stringing cash.
銀針	silver *hair-ornaments*.
穿針引綫	to act as go-between or match-maker; lit., to thread the *needle*.

釘

TIN¹.

釘子	a *nail*.
釘鞋	*nailed* boots.
竹釘子	bamboo *pegs*.
眼中釘	he is like a *spike* in my eye.
釘封	a letter from the Emperor containing a criminal's death-warrant.

READ TIN⁴.

拿釘子釘起	*nail* it with *nails*.
釘書	to *bind* books.
釘飄帶	to *sew on* hat strings.
釘石頭	to *throw* stones.

³釵

CH'AI¹.

釵環首飾	*hair pins*, earrings, and head gear.
裙釵	a female.

釧

CH'UAN¹.

銀釧子	a silver *bracelet*.

(531)

金 3-4

釬 HAN⁴.
- 釬一把壺 — to *solder* a teapot.
- 銅釬 — to *weld* with brass.

鈕 K'EO⁴. — interchanged with 拘 in some senses.
- 鈕子 — a *button*.
- 鈕帶 — a belt with a *clasp*.
- 鈕起 — *button* it.

READ K'EO¹. — may be 鈎.
- 鍊子鈕鈕 — the *links* of a chain.

釣 TIAO⁴.
- 釣魚 — to *angle*.
- 釣竿 — a *fishing* rod.
- 魚不上釣 — the fish do not take the *bait*.

鈔 CH'AO⁴.
- 太費鈔 — too lavish an expenditure of *money*.

鈎 KEO¹.
- 吊魚鈎 — a fishing *hook*.
- 帳鈎 — bed-curtain *hooks*.
- 鈎出來 — *hook* it out.

鈕 NIU³.
- 鈕子 — a *button*.

鈀 PA⁴, P'A². — same as 耙.

鎙 SA⁵.
- 一鋸子鎙開 — to *saw* a piece of wood *lengthways*.

鈍 TEN⁴.
- 刀子鈍 — the knife is *blunt*.
- 口鈍 — *slow* of speech.
- 蠢鈍 — *stupid*.

(532)

注 释

釬（焊）[xan⁴]
【釬一把壺】焊：焊接。
【銅焊】用銅焊接。
鈕（扣）[kʰəu⁴] [kʰəu¹]
【扣帶】有扣头的腰带。
【扣起】扣好。
釣（钓）[tiao⁴]
鈔（钞）[tʂʰao⁴]
【太费鈔】太花钱。
鈎（钩）[kəu¹]
鈕（钮）[ȵiəu³]
鈀（钯）[pa⁴] [pʰa²]
鎙 [sa⁵]
【一鋸子鎙开】用锯子把木头纵向锯开。
鈍（钝）[tən⁴]

注　释

钳（钳）[tɕʰien²]
【嘴钳子好】口才好。
铃（铃）[lin²]
铂（铂）[po⁵]
钵（钵）[po⁵]
钹（钹）[po⁵]
【搧钹】敲击铙钹。
铁（铁）[tʰie⁵]
铅（铅）[yen³]
铳（铳）[tʂʰoŋ⁴]
衔（衔）[xan²] [ɕien²]
铰（铰）[tɕiao³]
【铰耳朵】掏耳朵。用一把细长的绞刀伸进客人耳孔,轻轻铰动,将耳孔的汗毛铰光,耳屎掏尽。

金 5-6

5 鉗　CH'IEN².
火鉗　　　a pair of *tongs*.
帶狗鉗鉗　to wear an iron *collar*, as a felon.
螞蟥鉗　　an iron *staple*.
嘴鉗子好　he has a gift of the gab.

鈴　LIN².
搖鈴　　　to ring a *handbell*.
響鈴子　　horse *jingles*.

鉑　PO⁵.
金銀鉑　　gold and silver *tinsel*.

鉢　PO⁵.
鉢子　　　an earthenware *basin*.

鈸　PO⁵.
搧鈸　　　to play *cymbals*.

銕　T'IE⁵.　same as 鐵.

鉛　ÜEN³.
黑鉛　　　lead.

6 銃　CH'ONG⁴.
鐵銃子　　a *petard*.

銜　HAN².
馬銜口　　a horse's *bit*.
銜很在心　to *harbour* illwill; to *retain* anger.

READ HAN², SHIEN².
一品銜　　the highest *rank* of officials.

鉸　CHIAO³.
鉸一節下來　*clip* off a piece.
鉸耳朵　　to *shave* the inside of the ear.

(533)

金 6-7

	MIN².	
銘旌		a *memorial* inscription put in, or on the [grave.
	CHU¹.	for example of use see 鐳.
	T'ONG².	
黃銅		*brass*.
紅銅		*copper*.
	IN².	
漂銀		the best *silver*.
一個銀子		an ingot of *silver* (about Tls. 10).
銀花		*silver* hair-ornaments.
水銀		*mercury*.
	CH'U², TS'U².	
鋤頭		a *hoe*; a *mattock*.
尖鋤		a *pick*.
	T'IN².	
車鋌子		the *spindle* of a spinning wheel.
	FONG¹.	
刀子鋒快		the knife is *very sharp*.
前部先鋒		the *vanguard* of an army.
	RUE⁴.	
精銳的兵		*valiant* soldiers. [slaught.
一股銳氣		an *impetuous* charge; a *desperate* on-
	CHIA⁵, KA⁵.	
鐵鋏		iron *tongs*.
鋏一把柴		*take up* some fire-wood *with the tongs*.
京鋏子		spectacle *legs*.
螃蟹鋏鋏		crab's *claws*.
	P'U¹.	
鋪曬簟		*spread out* the drying mats.
去鋪排他		go and *instruct* him.

(534)

注 释

銘（铭）[min²]
【銘旌】竖在灵柩前标志死者官职和姓名的旗幡。
銖（铢）[tʂu¹]
銅（铜）[tʰoŋ²]
銀（银）[in²]
【漂银】最好的银子。
【银花】银簪。
鋤（锄）[tʂʰu²] [tsʰu²]
鋌（铤）[tʰin²]
【车鋌子】纺车的车轴。
鋒（锋）[foŋ¹]
銳（锐）[ʐue⁵] [ʐuei¹] [ʐuei²] [ʐuei³] [ʐuei⁴]
鋏（铗）[tɕia⁵] [ka⁵]
【京铗子】眼镜腿。
鋪（铺）[pʰu¹]
【去铺排他】铺排：指导。

534 西蜀方言

注 释

【他的铺排大】他喜欢指使别人。

【一套铺陈】铺陈：寝具。

銷（销）[siao¹]

【倾销银子】浇铸银锭。

【销差】旧指向上级汇报已完成差遣任务。

銹（锈）[siəu⁴]

【水把脚锈了】水田里的水使脚皲裂。

銼（锉）[tsʰo⁴]

錐（锥）[tsuei¹] [tsy¹]

【茨把脚锥了】荆棘刺伤了脚。

鋼（钢）[kaŋ¹]

【过不过得钢板】这事牢靠吗？

錦（锦）[tɕin³]

鋸（锯）[tɕy⁴]

金 .7-8

他的鋪排大	he is fond of *ordering* others about.
鋪葢	a Chinese *bed-quilt*.
一套鋪陳	a full set of *bedding*.
鋪起一層灰	*covered* with dust.

銷 SIAO¹.

傾銷銀子	to *cast* silver ingots.
一筆勾銷	*cancelled* by one stroke of the pen.
開銷	to *dismiss* from service. [thereon.
銷差	to *complete* a commission by reporting

銹 SIU⁴.

刀起了銹	the knife is *rusted*. [feet.
水把脚銹了	the water of the rice fields has *chapped* my

銼 TS'O⁴.

銼子	a *file*.
銼鋸子	to *file* a saw.

錐 TSUE¹.

錐子	an *awl*.
錐個眼眼	*bore* a hole with an awl.

READ TSÜ¹.

茨把脚錐了	a thorn has *pricked* or *pierced* my foot.
蜂子錐人	bees *sting* people.

鋼 KANG¹.

這個刀子鋼火好	the *steel* of this knife is good.
金鋼鑽	*diamonds*; a glazier's *diamond*.
過不過得鋼板	is the affair *solid*, *secure*, or *real*?

錦 CHIN³.

錦緞邊子	a kind of *brocade* border on scrolls.
錦繡文章	an *elegant* essay.

鋸 CHÜ⁴.

鋸子	a *saw*.

(535)

金 8

鍿		TSI¹.
	銅鍿	a fret-*saw* made of notched brass wire.
	鍿做兩節	*saw* it into two pieces.
	沒得鍿銖	I have no *coppers*.
錈		CHÜEN³.
	刀子錈了口	the edge of the knife is *turned*.
錨		MAO².
	拿來下錨	throw him into the river; lit., drop the [*anchor*.
錫		SI⁵.
	錫蠟臺	*pewter* candlesticks.
	釺錫	*solder*.
錛		PEN¹.
	錛鋤	an *adze*.
錠		TIN⁴.
	一錠銀子	an *ingot* of silver.
	一錠墨	a *stick* of ink.
錢		TS'IEN*.
	三十個錢	thirty *cash*.
	錢舖子	a *cash* shop.
	錢紙	*cash* paper, which is burned to the dead.
	寡母子錢	ancient *coins*.
	工錢	*wages*.
	學錢	school *fees*.
	本錢 and 利錢	*capital* and *interest*, or *profit*.
	二兩三錢銀子	two and three-*tenths* taels of silver; 2 3/10 oz.
	錢把眼睛打瞎了	*money* has blinded him.
	有錢的人	a man of *wealth*; a man of *means*.
錯		TS'O⁴.
	我錯了	I am *wrong*. [*to suffer*.
	認錯不該死	if a man confesses his *fault* he ought not

(536)

注　释

鍿（锱）[tsɿ¹]
【沒得鍿銖】没有铜钱。
錈（锩）[tɕyen³]
錨[mao²]
【拿来下锚】把人扔进河里。
錫（锡）[si⁵]
錛（锛）[pən¹]
【錛鋤】扁斧。
錠（锭）[tin⁴]
錢（钱）[tsʰien²]
（TS'IEN⁴当为TS'IEN²，见803页勘误表。）
【钱纸】冥币。
【寡母子钱】古代钱币。
錯（错）[tsʰo⁴]

注释

鍫（锹）[tsʰiao¹]

鍾（钟）[tsoŋ¹]

【茶钟】一种无盖的小茶杯。

鍋（锅）[ko¹]

鍊（炼）[lien⁴]

【做得结鍊】结鍊：结实耐用。

鋥 [sin⁴]

【铁鋥了】铁生锈了。

鏤（镂）[ləu⁴]

【要鏨鏤明的】要鏨上丰富的纹饰。

鍍（镀）[tu⁴]

鎮（镇）[tsən⁴]

【镇台】总兵。

金 8-10

9 鍫 鍾 鍋 鍊 鋥 鏤 鍍 10 鎮

TS'IAO¹.

人有失错马有漏蹄　　men all make *mistakes*, horses all stumble.
不错　　quite right; quite true.
我們兩個錯過了　　we *missed* each other; we *passed* each other [without seeing.
窩鍫　　an agricultural implement used for digging small round holes.
鍫一鏨糖　　*scoop* out a lump of brown sugar.

CHONG¹.

茶鍾　　a small tea *cup* without a cover.

KO¹.

米還沒有下鍋　　the rice has not been put into the *pot* yet.
燒一鍋水　　boil a *potful* of water.

LIEN⁴.

地頭鍊熟就好了　　when you get *accustomed* to the place it will be all right.
做得結鍊　　*strongly* made; *durable*.
鐵鍊子　　an iron *chain*.

SIN⁴.

鐵鋥了　　the iron is *rusted*.

LEO⁴.

鏤菸竿　　to *bore* a bamboo for a pipe-stem.
鏤條　　a *borer*.
要鏨鏤明的　　sculpture the figures in bas-relief or like fret-work.

TU⁴.

鍍金耳環　　gold *plated* ear-rings.

CHEN⁴.

鎮守地方　　to *guard* a place.
鎮臺　　a brigadier-general.

(537)

金 10-11

CH'UE².

| 鐵鎚 | an iron *hammer*. |
| 沒有鎚得好 | it has not been well *hammered*. |

SO⁵.

| 鐵鎍橋 | a suspension bridge constructed of iron [*rods*. |

K'AI³.

| 鎧甲 | *armour*. |

SO³.

一把鎖	a *lock*.
鎖門	*lock* the door.
自開鎖	one who blurts out secrets.
把他鎖起	put him in irons.

SEO¹.

| 鏤鋸 | a *mortising* saw. |
| 鏤他兩鋸 | to pass a saw through a joint to make it [fit closer. |

TS'IANG¹.

營鎗	a *musket*; a *rifle*.
鳥鎗	a *fowling-piece*.
手鎗	a *pistol*; a *revolver*.
水鎗	a small *syringe*.
煙鎗	an opium *pipe*.
打彎鎗	to sell smokes from a water *pipe*.
當鎗桿子	to write an essay for another at an examination.

IONG².

| 鎔化 | to *melt*; to *smelt*. |

CH'UAN³.

鍋鏟	a small *shovel* used in cooking.
鏟鋤	a kind of wide *hoe*.
鏟平	*shovel* or *hoe* it level.

(538)

注 釋

鎚（锤）[tʂʰuei²]
鎍（索）[so⁵]
鎧（铠）[kʰai³]
鎖（锁）[so³]
【自开锁】比喻守不住秘密的人。
鏤（镂）[səu¹]
【镂锯】一种用于镂空的锯子。
鎗（枪）[tsʰiaŋ¹]
【营枪】步枪。
【水枪】注射器。
【打弯枪】卖水烟。
【当枪杆子】考试时帮别人代写文章；代考。
鎔（镕）[ioŋ²]
鏟（铲）[tʂʰuan³]

注 释

鏇（镟）[syen⁴]
鏖 [ŋao⁴]
鏡（镜）[tɕin⁴]
　【千里镜】望远镜。
　【火镜】可以用来取火的凸透镜。
鏝（镘）[man⁴]
　【拌镘儿】掷钱游戏。
鏨（錾）[tsan⁴]
　【没得个断錾】态度不明确。
鐘（钟）[tʂoŋ¹]
鏵（铧）[xua²]
鐧（锏）[tɕien³]

金 11-12

SÜEN⁴.

油鏇餅	flaky cakes made in *whorls*.
鏇個洞	*turn* a hole in the wood.
鏇子	a little utensil for cutting blanc-mange [into fine strips.

NGAO⁴.

| 鏖盤 | a *griddle*; a Chinese *oven*. |

CHIN⁴.

鏡子	a *mirror*.
眼鏡子	*spectacles*.
千里鏡	a *telescope*.
顯微鏡	a *microscope*.
火鏡	a burning-*glass*.
護心鏡	a *breast-plate*.

MAN⁴.

| 拌鏝兒 | to play pitch and toss; the player wins the coins which fall with the *obverse* side up. |

TSAN⁴.

鏨子	a *chisel*.
鏨字	to *chisel* letters on china.
鏨花	to *emboss* flowers on metal.
鏨紙花	patterns of flowers *cut* in paper.
沒得個斷鏨	not *precise*; without *decision*.

CHONG¹.

打鐘	to strike a large *bell* with a mallet.
自鳴鐘	a *striking clock*.
三點鐘	three *o'clock*.

HUA².

| 換鏵 | to change a *ploughshare*. |

CHÜEN³.

| 操一對鐧 | to practise with the *rapier*. |

(539)

金 12-16

	LIAO².	
脚鐐		fetters.
	RAO².	
鐃鈸		small *cymbals*.
	TEN⁴.	
馬鐙		stirrups.
	HUAN².	
門鐶		a pair of iron rings used for door *handles*.
	LIEN².	
鐮刀		a *sickle*; a *reaping hook*.
火鐮		the *steel* used for striking fire from flint.
	TANG⁴,¹.	
鐺⁴鐺¹		a *peddler's gong*.
	READ TANG¹.	
鐺鐺的響		a *twanging sound*, like a peddler's gong.
響鐺鐺的		*famous*.
	T'IE⁵.	
毛鐵		*pig iron*.
鐵絲		*iron* wire.
鐵匠		a blacksmith.
鐵打的心腸		hard-hearted, lit., bowels made of *iron*.
做得鐵實		*strongly* made.
鐵面無私		*firm* and upright.
	SÜ¹.	
鎖鑐		the *wards* of a lock.
	PIN¹.	
鑌鐵		*tin*.
	CHA⁵.	
鍘草		to *chop* straw for fodder.
鍘刀		a *straw-cutter*.

(540)

注释

鐐（镣）[liao²]
鐃（铙）[ʐao²]
鐙（镫）[tən⁴]
鐶（镮）[xuan²]
鐮（镰）[lien²]
【火鐮】旧时一种取火工具，由于形似弯弯的镰刀，与火石撞击能产生火星而得名。
鐺（铛）[taŋ⁴][taŋ¹]
【铛铛】小贩的锣。
鐵（铁）[tʰie⁵]
【毛铁】生铁。
【做得铁实】铁实：扎实，结实。
鑐[sy¹]
【锁鑐】鑐：锁中的簧片。
鑌（镔）[pin¹]
【镔铁】古代的一种钢，把表面磨光再用腐蚀剂处理，可见花纹。
鍘[tʂa⁵]

注释

鑪（炉）[lu²]
【化钱炉】用于烧纸钱的三脚容器。

鑲（镶）[siaŋ¹]
【镶不起】无法修补。
【三镶桌子】由三块木板拼成的桌子。

鐵（尖）[tsʰien¹]

鑰（钥）[io⁵]
【通关钥匙】万能钥匙。"关"应为"开"。

鑷（镊）[nie⁵]

鑼（锣）[lo²]

鑿（凿）[tsʰo⁵]

鑽（钻）[tsuan¹][tsuan⁴]
【缝一件钻钻】做一件背心。
【钻花】手摇曲柄钻。

長（长）[tsʰaŋ²][tṣaŋ²]
【长起的】纵长地，纵向地。

金 16-19 長

鑪 LU².

檀香鑪	a brass *censer*.
化錢鑪	large tripod vessels in temples, in which cash paper is burned.
銅手鑪	a brass hand-*stove*.

17 **鑲** SIANG¹.

鑲不起	it cannot be *pieced together* (as a broken basin).
三鑲棹子	a table made of three boards *fitted together* at the edges.
三鑲蒜苗子	three *beds* of garlic.

鐵 TS'IEN¹.

| 鐵擔 | a long *carrying pole* pointed at both ends for carrying straw. |

鑰 IO⁵.

| 通關鑰匙 | a *key* that will open all locks. |

18 **鑷** NIE⁵.

| 鑷子 | *nippers* used to pull hairs out of pork. |

鑼 LO².

| 打鑼 | to beat a *gong*. |

鑿 TS'O⁵.

| 鑿子 | a carpenter's *chisel*. |

鑽 TSUAN¹.

| 鑽進去 | to *push* one's way into. |
| 縫一件鑽鑽 | make a *waistcoat*. |

READ TSUAN⁴.

鑽子	an *awl*; a brad-awl.
鑽花	a *brace-bit*.
鑽個眼眼	*bore* a hole with a brad-awl.

The 168th radical. 長

19 **長** CH'ANG².

| 八尺長 | eight feet *long*. |
| 長起的 | *length*wise. |

長門

這個路長	this road is long, i. e., the miles are long.
長生不老	to live long and never grow old.
長買主	a constant customer.
生意做不長久	that business will not last long.
做長工	domestic servants.
各有所長	each has that wherein he excels.
家家都有長短	in every family there are merits and de- [merits.
生意不長錢	the business does not gain me any money.

READ CHANG³.

長牙齒	to grow teeth.
長得高	he has grown tall.
長子	the eldest son.
他長我兩歲	he is my senior by two years.
長了虫	it has bred maggots.
長進	to improve at work; to advance in learning.
米長了價	rice has risen in price.
給他長臉	keep him in countenance; don't put him [to shame.
家長	the head of a family.
甲長	a village elder or head-man.
堰長	the head-man of a dam.
山長	principal of an academy.

The 169th radical. (門)

門 MEN².

大門	the front door.
釘活門神	to crucify a criminal on a door; lit., a live [door-god.
城門	a city gate.
出門人	a traveller.
門上大爺	a magistrate's porter.
窗子門	a window shutter.
敎門	a sect, usually denotes Mohammedans.
入沙門	to enter the Buddhist religion.
門生	a disciple; a scholar; a follower.

注 释

【生意不长钱】长钱：生利，赚钱。
【堰长】小型水利工程的负责人。
【山长】历代对书院讲学者的称谓。
门(門)[mən²]
【钉活门神】把罪犯活活钉在门板上。
【出门人】旅行者。
【教门】宗教派别，常指伊斯兰教。
【入沙门】出家，皈依佛教。

注 释

【门前人没有在屋头】丈夫不在家。
【大有门面】很风光。
【这是个门头】门头：赚钱的计划。
【你会甚么门路】你做什么工作？
【门门都有】样样都有。
闩（闩）[ṣuan⁴][ṣuan¹]
闪（闪）[ṣan³]
【闪不得劲】不能松开手。
【闪不得火】警惕火情。
【霍闪】闪电。
闭（闭）[pi⁴]
【闭倒眼睛】闭上眼睛。
【经闭不通】月经不调。
閒（闲）[ɕien²][xan²]

門 1-4

1 門	門風不正	the reputation of the *family* is bad.
	還沒有過門	the girl has not yet gone to live with her betrothed's *family*.
	門前人沒有在屋頭	my husband is not at home.
	大有門面	he has a great *reputation*.
	這是個門頭	this is only a *scheme* to raise some money.
	找個門路	to look for a *means of livelihood*.
	你會甚麼門路	what is your *occupation*?
	鈕門子	a button-*hole*.
	引門	the *touch-hole* of a gun.
	門門都有	there are all *kinds*.
	定一門親	to bespeak a wife. (*N. A.*)
	一門大砲	a cannon. (*N. A.*)

SHUAN⁴,¹.

2 閂	門閂	the large cross-*bar* of a front door.
	閂門	*bar* the door.

SHAN³.

3 閃	閃開	*stand aside*.
	閃出一個大壩	the mountains *open out* into a great plain.
	把腳閃了	I have *slipped* my foot; *sprained* my ankle.
	閃不得勁	you must not *relax* your hold; keep a firm [grip.
	閃不得火	you must not let the fire *slacken*.
	閃一閃的	*wriggling*; *swaying* up and down.
	霍閃	*lightning*.

PI⁴.

4 閉	閉倒眼睛	*close* your eyes.
	閉口	*shut* up!
	把火閉了	*cover* up the fire with dross.
	經閉不通	*obstruction* of the menses.

SHIEN², HAN².

閒	閒暇無事	at *leisure*.

(543)

西蜀方言

閒 閏 開

閒 4

人閒長指甲 心閒長頭髮	when the body is *unoccupied* the nails grow, when the mind is *at rest* the hair grows.
閒不慣	I am not accustomed to *idleness*.
喫閒飯的	daughters; *idlers* about the house.
閒房媳婦	the future daughter-in-law who has already been received into the family.
閒場冷淡	when there is no market the streets are deserted.
管人閒事受人磨	if you meddle with the *petty* affair of others you will get yourself into trouble.
說閒話	to gossip.

IA¹.

門是閒開的	the door is *ajar*.

RUEN⁴.

閏五月	an *intercalary* fifth month.

K'AI¹.

開門	*open* the door.
開了年來	come after the New Year has *begun*.
開頭沒有做好	in the *beginning* he did not do it well.
開賬	to *open* shop after the New Year.
把賬開出來	*write out* my account.
開錢	to *pay* money.
開炭廠	to *start* a colliery.
開船	to *unloose* a boat from its moorings.
一百要開	less than 100 cash.
不得開交	I cannot *get out of* this business.
求大老爺開恩	I beseech Your Worship to *grant* me grace.
分開	to *separate*.
離開這個地方	*leave* this place.
人都散開了	the people have *dispersed*.
開荒山	to *bring* waste land *under cultivation*.
開山子	a hatchet.
開花	to *bloom*.

(544)

注 释

【闲房媳妇】没过门的媳妇。
【闲场冷淡】市场不开市时,街道上很冷清。
闲 [ia¹]
【门是闲开的】门半开着。
閏(闰)[ʐuən⁴]
開(开)[kʰai¹]
【开了年来】明年年初来。
【开账】春节后店铺开张营业。
【开钱】付钱。
【一百要开】不足一百元。
【不得开交】没法打发,摆脱不了。
【开山子】短柄小斧。

注 释

間（间）[tɕien¹] [kan¹]
　　[tɕien⁴]
【中中间间】正中心。
【间或间来】有时。
閘（闸）[tʂa⁴]
【千斤闸】吊闸。
鬧（闹）[lao⁴]
【闹房】闹洞房。
【闹嘴】吵架。
【闹酒】喝酒并喧闹。
閣（阁）[ko⁵]
閫 [kʰan³]
【门閫】门槛。
閶 [tɕʰiaŋ¹]

門 4-6

開花砲	a mortar for firing bombs.
胃口不開	my appetite does not *increase*.
走開	stand *aside*; get out of the way.
開水	*boiling* water.

CHIEN¹.

中中間間	in the *middle*.
天地間	*between* heaven and earth; everything in [the world.
這三年間	*during* these three years.
忽然間	*in* an instant.

READ CHIEN¹, KAN¹.

| 幾間房子 | a few rooms. (*N. A.*) |

READ CHIEN⁴.

間或間來	he comes *sometimes*.
無有間斷	without *intermission*.
反間計	a scheme to *separate* friends.

5 閘 CHA⁴.

| 千斤閘 | a *portcullis*. |

LAO⁴.

鬧熱	*busy*; *noisy*.
鬧房	a kind of house-warming at a wedding.
鬧嘴	to *quarrel*.
鬧事	to *stir up trouble*; to *make a row*.
鬧酒	*noisy* over wine.
6 鬧成了	the affair is *settled*; lit., the *squabbling* is [ended.

閣 KO⁵.

| 閨閣 | the women's *apartments*. |
| 閣下 | Sir. |

閫 K'AN³.

| 門閫 | a door-*sill*; a *threshold*. |

閶 CH'IANG¹.

| 門閶 | the door-*frame*, i. e., lintel and door-posts. |
| 閶闔門 | a door with *frame* and panels. |

(545)

門 6-10

	KUE¹.	
閨門		the *female* apartments.
閨女		a *virgin*; an *unmarried female*.
	K'UEN³.	[*apartments*.
莫說人家的閨閫		don't speak of the affairs of people's *inner*
都閫府		a *captain* commanding 250 or 500 men.
	IO⁵, ÜE⁵.	
閱邊		to *inspect* the boundaries.
閱操		to *review* troops.
少閱歷		he has little *experience*.
	READ IE⁵.	
閱門		a *doorkeeper* in a yamên.
	LANG⁴.	
房子起得高閬		a high and *spacious* house.
	NIEN².	
閻王		the King of Hades.
	HUEN¹.	[at the *palace gate*.
叩閽		to appeal to the Emperor ; lit., to knock
	K'UE⁵.	
地方寬闊		the place is *wide*.
銀錢廣闊		his money is very *plentiful*.
	UE².	
大人入闈		the officers enter the *examination* halls.
	CH'UANG³.	[*cry*).
看闖倒		beware of getting *knocked* (chair bearer's
闖道		to rudely *push ahead* when a superior is coming the other way.

(546)

注　释

閨(闺) [kuei¹]

閫(阃) [kʰuən³]

【莫说人家的闺阃】不要谈论人家的隐私。

【都阃府】清代正四品武官都司的别称。

閱(阅) [io⁵] [ye⁵] [ie⁵]

【阅边】巡视边境。

【阅门】衙门的看门人。

閬(阆) [laŋ⁴]

【房子起得高阆】又高又宽敞的房子。

閻(阎) [ȵien²]

閽(阍) [xuən¹]

【叩阍】百姓到朝廷向皇帝诉冤。

闊(阔) [kʰue⁵]

【银钱广阔】富有。

闈(闱) [uei²]

【大人入闱】科举考试时监考官进入考场。

闖(闯) [tʂʰuaŋ³]

【看闯倒】当心碰到(轿夫说的话)。

注释

阖（阖）[xo⁵]
【阖家人等】全家。
闕（阙）[tɕʰye⁵]
【朝京阙】对着皇宫方向鞠躬。
關（关）[kuan¹]
【关书】教师的聘书。
闡（阐）[tʂʰan³]
闢（辟）[pʰie⁴]
防 [faŋ²]
阻 [tsu³]

門 10-13　阜 4-5

閡	HO⁵.	
	闔家人等	the *whole* family.
闕	CH'ÜE⁵.	
	朝京闕	to bow towards the *Emperor's palace.*
關	KUAN¹.	
	關門	*shut* the door.
	田裏頭關水	to *dam* water in a rice-field.
	關口	a *customs' barrier.*
	事不關己莫勞心	if the affair does not *concern* you don't trouble yourself about it.
	關書	a letter *engaging* a school teacher.
	關照	to *patronize.*
	關係大	the *consequences* are great.
	關乎人的生死	*involving* life or death.
12 闡	CH'AN³.	
13 闢	闡明	to clearly *explain*; to *enlarge* upon.
	P'IE⁵.	
	開天闢地	the *unfolding* of the universe; creation.

The 170th radical. (阜)

4 防	FANG².	
	養兒防老積穀防饑	rear a son to *provide against* old age, store up grain to *ward off* famine.
	防備	to *guard against*; to *prepare* for an emergency.
	謹防火	*beware* of fire!
	恐防跌着	*beware* of stumbling.
	守口如瓶防意如城	*guard* your mouth like a bottle and your thoughts like a city.
5 阻	TSU³.	
	阻隔	to *impede*; to *obstruct*, as an obstacle would.
	阻攔	to *hinder*; to *oppose*, as a person would.

(547)

西蜀方言　547

阜 5-6

附	FU⁴.	
	附近地方	the *adjacent* country.
	長了附骨	diseased bone; lit., to grow a *supplementary* bone.
陀	T'O².	
	活像普陀巖樣	crowded just like P'u-*t'o* cliff.
阿	O¹, A¹.	
	是阿	all right! just so!
	希客阿	you are a great stranger!
	阿意逢迎	to *pander* to the wishes of another.
	阿我忘記了	*oh!* I have forgotten it.
限	HAN⁴, SHIEN⁴.	
	限個日子	*set* or *appoint* a day.
	夫妻本是同林鳥 大限來時各自飛	Like birds in one grove are husband and wife, but they each fly their ways at the *limit* of life.
	無有限量	*limit*less; boundless.
降	CHIANG⁴.	
	降臨	to *descend*; *come down* to my mean abode.
	降災	the gods *send down* calamity.
	降級留任	to *degrade* an official but leave him in office.
	READ SHIANG².	
	投降	to *submit*, as rebels to authority.
	我降不著他	I cannot *subdue* him.
	降魔	to *exorcise* demons.
陋	LEO⁴.	
	是我們那個地方的陋俗	it is a *vile* custom of our place.
	十分醜陋	very *ugly*.
陛	PE⁴.	
	制臺進京陛見	the Governor-General has gone into the capital to *have an audience with* the Emperor.

(548)

注 释

附 [fu⁴]
【长了附骨】附骨：骨质增生。
陀 [tʰo²]
阿 [o¹] [a¹]
限 [xan⁴] [ɕien⁴]
降 [tɕiaŋ⁴] [ɕiaŋ²]
【我降不著他】我镇不住他。
陋 [ləu⁴]
陛 [pei⁴]

注释

阵（陣）[tʂən⁴]
  【吃饭好一阵】吃过饭以后多长时间了?
除 [tʂʰu²]
  【除服】脱去丧服。
  【除留倒】留下一部分。
陕 [ʂan³]
  【老陕】地道的陕西人。
陞（升）[ʂən¹]
  【哪一天高升】哪天出发?
  【升炮】燃放爆竹或烟花。
陡 [təu³]
  【陡胆的话】大胆的讲话。
  【他那个话来得陡】陡：唐突。
  【那个人的气性陡】陡：轻率的，急躁的。

阜 7

7 陣 CHEN⁴.

擺陣勢	to set a *battle* in array.
纔走了一陣陣	it is just a *little while* since he left.
喫飯好一陣	how long is it since you had your rice?
下了一陣雨	there has been a *shower* of rain.

除 CH'U².

賊盜該除良民宜保	thieves ought to be *eradicated* and good people protected.
除服	to *put off* mourning clothes after 27 months.
除夕	the last night of the year, when all rubbish is *cleared out* of the house.
除留倒	to *lay by* part of anything.
除這個以外	*besides* this.
除非是	*without* doubt it is.
除一百八十個錢	*subtract* 180 cash.

陝 SHAN³.

老陝	a native of the province of *Shan*-si.

陞 SHEN¹.

聯陞三級	to *rise* three steps in rank at once.
高陞一點	*raise* the price a little; give a little more.
那一天高陞	what day will you *start* on your journey?
把轎子陞起	*lift* the chair poles at one end to let the occupant get out.
陞砲	*fire* the petards!

陡 TEO³.

這個路陡	this path is *steep*.
壁陡的路	a road as *steep* as a wall.
山陡上不去	the hill is *precipitous*, we cannot ascend it.
陡然富貴	to *suddenly* become wealthy and honourable.
陡膽的話	a *bold* speech.
他那個話來得陡	that was an *abruptly* spoken word.
那個人的氣性陡	his temper is *hasty*.

(549)

阜 7-8

ÜEN⁴, UAN⁴.

院子	a *courtyard* in a house.
書院	an *academy*.
學院	the commissioner who examines under-gradnates.
娼妓院	a *brothel*.

CH'EN².

鋪陳	*bed and bedding*.
陳衣鋪	*old* clothes shop.
陳飯	rice *left* after a meal.
陳蛋	*stale* eggs.
陳古八十年的話	*out of date* talk; *irrelevant*.

HAN⁴.

陷下去多少深	to *sink* deeply in the mud.
陷坑	a pit for *trapping* animals in.
陷害好人	to *implicate* good people.
雨把我陷了幾天	the rain *delayed* me a few days.

LU⁵.

| 陸續不斷 | *constant; uninterrupted*. |

P'E².

| 陪客 | to *entertain* a guest. |

IN¹.

陰涼地方	a *shady* cool place.
陰乾的	dried in the *shade*.
陰黃	rhubarb, because dried in the *shade*.
陰陰天	a *dull* day.
各人陰倒	all *keep it secret*.
陰倒做	to do *secretly*.
作陰功	to *privately* do good deeds.
損了陰德	you have *injured your virtue*.
混過光陰	to pass one's *time* in vicious ways.
買一棺陰他	buy a *burial-ground* or *a site for a grave*.

(550)

注 释

院 [yen⁴] [uan⁴]

陳(陈)[tʂʰən²]

【铺陈】床和寝具。

【陈蛋】不新鲜的蛋。

【陈古八十年的话】老话，不着边际、不切题的话。

陷 [xan⁴]

【雨把我陷了几天】陷：耽搁。

陸(陆)[lu⁵]

陪 [pʰei²]

陰(阴)[in¹]

【阴黄】大黄。英文释义应为：a kind of herb.

【阴阴天】阴暗天。

【各人阴倒】大家保密。

【阴倒做】秘密地做。

【作阴功】做好事不声张。

【买一棺阴他】给他买一块地安葬。

注释

【阴人】女人。
隍 [xuaŋ²]
階(阶) [kai¹]
隆 [loŋ²]
隄(堤) [tʰi²]
隊(队) [tuei⁴]
【归不倒队】不能重新归队；亏本。
陽(阳) [iaŋ²]
【平阳地方】开阔地带。
【阳沟】露出地面的排水沟。
【做阳面子】做秀，做表面文章。
隘 [ŋai⁴]
碼(码) [ma³]

阜 8-10

	陰溝	a *covered* drain.
	陰間	*Hades*.
	陰陽先生	a geomancer, one who discusses the male [and *female principle*.
	下陰	the male *genitals*.
	陰物	the female *genitals*.
	陰人	a woman.
9	HUANG².	
隍	城隍廟	the Temple of the Wall and *Moat*.
階	KAI¹.	same as 堦.
隆	LONG².	
	生意興隆	business is *prosperous*.
	隆冬天氣	*extremely* cold weather.
隄	TʻI².	same as 堤.
隊	TUE⁴.	
	歸不倒隊	unable to rejoin the *ranks*; to lose capital.
	隊伍	the *army*.
陽	IANG².	
	太陽	the *sun*.
	向陽地方	a *sunny* place.
	陰陽	the female, hidden or passive, and the *male*, [*open* or *active* principles.
	平陽地方	a level and *open* space.
	陽溝	an *open* drain.
	陽間	in *this* world.
	做陽面子	to put on a fair *outward* appearance.
	陽物	the *male* genitals; the penis.
10	NGAI⁴.	
隘	守隘口	to guard a *pass*.
碼	MA³.	
	一碼柴	a *pile* of firewood.
	碼起一堆柴	pile up a heap of firewood.

(551)

阜 10-14

SHIE⁵.
他二人有隙	there is a *quarrel* between them.

KE⁵.
隔門	*partition* doors behind a shop.
櫃子分四隔	the cupboard has four *compartments* or [shelves.
隔壁子	the *neighbour's* house, the *neighbours*.
隔教	of a *different* religion.
隔山容易隔水難	to be *separated* by a hill is easy, but by a [river, difficult.
隔得遠	*far apart*.
隔一天發	to come on every second day, as ague.
夫婦沒得隔夜仇	husband and wife's quarrels do not last over night.
隔菢	to keep a hen from sitting on eggs by tying [it up.
兩弟兄是隔起的	the brothers are at *variance*.

13 SHIEN³.
好險	very *perilous*.
毛病凶險	the sickness is *dangerous*.
病人險了一回	the sick man had a *severe* turn.
險些把我捉倒	he *nearly* caught me.

SUE², SHUE².
跟隨	to *follow*.
隨身帶的有表	to carry a watch on his person.
拿個隨手來	bring a dish cloth to wipe the table (tea-[shop).
隨時都來得	you can come *at* any time.
隨便	*at* your convenience; *as* you please.
事不隨心	the affair does not *suit* my mind.
隨寓而安	to rest *wherever* one can find lodgings.
隨後就沒有來	he did not come *afterwards*.

14 IN³.
隱藏不住	it cannot be *concealed*.
莫隱瞞我	do not *deceive* me.
隱痛隱痛的	a *dull* pain.

(552)

注　释

隙 [ɕie⁵]
【他二人有隙】有隙：有裂痕，有矛盾。

隔 [ke⁵]
【隔壁子】隔壁邻居。
【隔菢】通过捆绑来阻止母鸡孵蛋。
【兩弟兄是隔起的】两弟兄不和。

險（险）[ɕien³]

隨（随）[suei²] [ʂuei²]
【拿個隨手來】随手：擦布，抹布（茶馆用语）。

隱（隐）[in³]

注 释

隶（隷）[li⁴]
　【皂隷】衙门里的差役。
隻（只）[tʂʅ¹]
　【一只眼儿】独眼龙。
雀 [tsʰio⁵]
雄 [ɕioŋ²]
　【雄子and母子】雄鸟和雌鸟。
　【雄鸡公】公鸡。
　【他的心雄】雄：胆量大。
　【雄势】宏伟壮观；仪表堂堂。
　【太阳不雄】阳光不强烈。
集 [tsi⁵]

隶 9　隹 2-4

9 隶

The 171st radical. **(隶)**

LI⁴.

隷字　　　an ancient style of writing, first used by [underlings.
皂隷　　　lictors; out-runners.

2 隻

The 172nd radical. **(隹)**

CHĬ¹.

一隻鷄　　one chicken. (N. A.)
一隻羊　　one sheep. (N. A.)
一隻鞋　　one shoe. (N. A.)
一隻船　　one boat. (N. A.)
一隻手　　one hand. (N. A.)
一隻眼兒　a one-eyed person. (N. A.)

3 雀

TS'IO⁵.

雀兒　　　a *bird*.

4 雄

SHIONG².

雄子 and 母子　the *male* and female of *birds*.
雄雞公　　　a *cock*.
他的心雄　　he is *courageous*; brave.
英雄好漢　　a *leader*; a hero.
雄勢　　　　*imposing* in appearance.
太陽不雄　　the sun is not *strong*.
今天我這個人不雄　　}I am not feeling *strong* to-day.
這兩年我都雄不起了　}these two years I have been unable to *make a show*; (too poor).
奸雄　　　　treacherous.

集

TSI⁵.

聚集　　　　to *assemble*.

隹 4-10

IA³.

收拾得雅緻	elegantly fitted up, as a house.
長得秀雅	handsome, as a person.
唱得幽雅	to sing harmoniously.
你們雅靜些	be a little quieter there!

NGAN⁴.

| 雁鵝 | the wild goose. |

TS'Ṛ².

| 一雌一雄 | a male and a female bird. |
| 決個雌雄 | try which is the weaker or the stronger. |

TIAO¹.

雕個板子	to engrave a block for printing.
雕花草人物	to carve figures in wood.
雕匠	a carver.

SÜ¹.

| 雖然是 | although it is. |

CHI¹.

雞母 and 雞公	a hen and a cock.
劇雞	a capon.
雞眼睛	corns on the feet; lit., hen's eyes.
雞冠花	the cock's-comb flower.
雞兒	chickens.
野雞	pheasants.
田雞	frogs.
灶雞子	crickets.
雞皮子	"chicken-skin," the appearance of the skin [when cold.

SHUANG¹.

一雙鞋子	a pair of shoes. (N. A.)
生一對雙	to bear twins.
雙關二意的話	a double-entendre.

(554)

注 释

雅 [ia³]

【唱得幽雅】幽雅：与环境和谐。

雁 [ŋan⁴]

雌 [tsʰɿ²]

雕 [tiao¹]

雖（虽）[sy¹]

雞（鸡）[tɕi¹]

【鸡儿】小鸡。

【灶鸡子】蟋蟀。

【鸡皮子】(天冷或受惊吓时身上出的)鸡皮疙瘩。

雙（双）[ʂuaŋ¹]

【生一对双】生一对双胞胎。

【双关二意的话】一语双关。

注 释

雜（杂）[tsa⁵]
離（离）[li²] [li⁴]
【离书】休书。
難（难）[lan²] [lan⁴]
【把我很作难】让我非常为难或陷入困境。
【十七是我的母难】我的母难：我的生日。

佳 10-11

雜 TSA⁵.

雜貨舖	a fancy goods store; lit., *mixed* goods.
打 雜	to do *odd* jobs; a man of all work.
閒 雜 人	*nondescripts*; *idlers*.
雜 種	*bastard*!
雜 書	books, outside of the classics, on *various* subjects.
雜 木	woods of *various* kinds, excepting pine or [cedar.
羊 雜 碎	a sheep's *entrails*.

11 離 LI².

離開這個地方	*leave* this place.
分 離	to *take leave* of; to *part* from.
離 書	a bill of *divorce*.
離 開 了	it has *come apart*.
離 不 得	*in*dispensable.

READ LI⁴.

| 煮 離 了 骨 | the meat is boiled *off* the bone. |
| 離 得 近 | not far *off*. |

難 LAN².

那個路難走	that road is *hard* to travel; a bad road.
難道他不曉得嗎	is it possible that he does not know? lit., *hard* to say.
難 得 做	*difficult* to do.
難 看	*repulsive*; not nice to look at.
難 為 你	I have *troubled* you; thank you.
把 我 很 作 難	it put me to great *inconvenience*; put me in [a fix.
艱 難 困 苦	*distress* and poverty.

READ LAN⁴.

災 難	*calamities*.
十磨九難成好人	perfected through *suffering* or *adversity*.
落 難	to fall into *difficulties*.
十七是我的母難	the 17th is my *birthday*.

(555)

西蜀方言

雨 3-5

The 173rd radical. (雨)

Ü³.

下雨	to *rain*.
打白雨	a sunny *shower*.
雨衣	water-proof clothing.
雨傘	an umbrella.

SÜE⁵.

下雪	to *snow*.
雪山	*snowy* mountains.
雪花白	*snowy* white.
雪讎	to *wipe out* an injury; to be revenged.

ÜIN².

烏雲接日	a black *cloud* receives the setting sun, it [will be rain.
雲抬司	a chair-bearer; lit., *cloud*-bearer.

LUE².

打雷	to *thunder*.
打雷同	to imitate another; to hit upon the same idea.
雷公虫	a centipede (the *thunder* is supposed to [kill them).
喫雷	a servant taking commission on purchases.

LIN².

零頭錢	the money *remaining* over.
一千零三十	1,030—one thousand *and* thirty.
零碎東西	*odds and ends*.
做零工	to do *odd* jobs.
零賣花生	to *retail* pea-nuts.
不賣零的	we do not sell in *small quantities*; we do [not *retail*.

TIEN⁴.

電氣	*electricity*.
暗室虧心神目如電	when you secretly sin the gods see it like a *lightning flash*.
電線	*telegraph* wires.

(556)

注 释

雨 [y²]
【打白雨】一边有阳光一边还下太阳雨。
雪 [sye⁵]
雲(云) [yn²]
【乌云接日】快下雨的天象。
【云抬司】轿夫。
雷 [luei²]
【打雷同】模仿别人；想法一致。
【雷公虫】蜈蚣。
【吃雷】佣人购物时拿回扣。
零 [lin²]
電(电) [tien⁴]

注释

需 [sy¹]
震 [tʂən⁴]
【震手】因肘部被撞击而使手有刺痛感。
霄 [siao¹]
霉 [mei²]
【人霉了】霉：失势。
霆 [tʰin²]
霍 [xo⁵]
霶 [la⁵]
霎 [sa⁵]
霞 [ɕia²]
霜 [ʂuaŋ¹]

雨 6-9

6 需 SÜ¹. interchanged with 須.
需要的 that which is *needful*.
只要些需 I only want a *very little*.

7 震 CHEN⁴.
地皮都震了 the very earth did *shake*.
震手 to make the hand *tingle*, as a knock on the [elbow.

霄 SIAO¹.
飛入雲霄 to fly up into the *clouds*.

霉 ME².
起了霉 *mildewed*.
長了毛霉 covered with *mould*.
一股霉氣 a *damp* smell.
人霉了 come down in the world; *shabby* genteel.

霆 T'IN².
雷霆火發 angry like *thunder* and lightning.

8 霍 HO⁵.
扯霍閃 *lightning*.

霶 LA⁵.
嘩霶霶的雨 a *splashing* rain (from the sound).

霎 SA⁵.
下了一霎雨 there has been a *shower* of rain. (*N. A.*)

9 霞 SHIA².
早晨發霞等水燒茶 when in the morning a *red sky* you see, wait and get water to boil for your tea.

霜 SHUANG¹.
打白頭霜 *hoar-frost*.

(557)

雨 11-16 青

11 霧 U⁴.
烟霧　　　fog; mist.
眼睛霧了　my eyes are *dim*; my sight is *beclouded*.

13 露 LU⁴.
一苗露水一苗草　"ilk a blade o' grass keps its ain drop [o' dew."
眼露水　tears.
白花露　scent; eau-de-cologne, etc.
露出醜來　to *expose* one's shame.

霹 P'IE⁵, P'I⁵.
霹靂一聲　the sound of a *clap* of thunder.

靂 LIE⁵, LI⁵.
　　for example of use see last.

霸 PA⁴.
霸佔人家的　to *usurp* or *appropriate* the things of [others.
稱霸王　a *petty tyrant*; a leader of banditti.

16 靈 LIN².
靈牌子　the *spirit* tablet.
抬靈柩　to carry out a coffin with a corpse in it.
菩薩靈聆　the idol is *responsive*.
這個藥靈聆　this medicine is *efficacious*.
不靈變　not *clever*.

The 174th radical. 青

青 TS'IN¹.
割青草　to cut *green* grass for fodder.
青菓　olives (canarium pimela).
蛋青　the *white* of an egg.
青天白日　in the clear light of day; lit., *azure* sky and [white sun.
青布　*black* or *dark-coloured* cloth.
臉青面黑　a *scowling* countenance.

(558)

注 释

霧（雾）[u⁴]
【眼睛霧了】雾：看不清，模糊。
露 [lu⁴]
【眼露水】眼泪。
【白花露】香水、雪花膏之类。
霹 [pʰie⁵] [pʰi⁵]
靂（雳）[lie⁵] [li⁵]
霸 [pa⁴]
靈（灵）[lin²]
【不灵变】不聪明。
青 [tsʰin¹]

注 释

靛 [tien⁴]
【打靛】制作蓝靛染料。
静 [tsin⁴]
非 [fei¹]
【这才非礼】非礼: 不合礼仪。
靠 [kʰao⁴]
【这个树子是靠的】靠: 嫁接。
【靠实没法】确实没办法。
面（面）[mien⁴]

靑 8　非 7　面

8 靛　TIEN⁴.

打靛　to beat *indigo* leaves to extract the dye.

静　TSIN⁴.

地方清静　the place is *quiet*; a *secluded* spot.
好静　fond of *solitude*.
街上人都静了　the streets are *deserted*.
看他的動静　watch his conduct.

The 175th radical. (非)

非　FEI¹.

非分的事　it is *not* his duty.
無非是　*doubt*less.
誰是誰非　who is right and who is *wrong*?
這纔非禮　this is certainly *improper*.
爲非作歹　to work *wickedness*.
非常的人　an *uncommon* person.

7 靠　K'AO⁴.

靠天吃飯　we *depend* on Heaven for our food.
靠不住　*un*trustworthy.
拴牢靠點　tie it more *securely*.
把船靠攏岸　bring the boat in to the bank; *moor* the boat by the shore.
這個樹子是靠的　this tree is *grafted*.
靠實沒法　there is *really* no help for it.

The 176ht radical. (面)

面　MIEN⁴.

臉面　the *face*.
會過一面　I have met him once.
打照面　to see one *face* to *face*; to pay a visit.

(559)

面. 革 2-4

當面說	say it to my *face*.
你的臉面大	your *cheek* is great.
他的門面寬	his *reputation* is great.
臉臉面面的	in *handsome* style.
辦得體面	*grandly* or *stylishly* conducted.
體面人	a *stylish* person; *grand* folk.
面子	the *front* or *outside* of a thing.
皮面光	good only on the *surface*.
桌面子	the *top* of a table.
一面的話	one *side* of the question.
面一層泥巴	lay the surface with mud.
開舖面	to open a shop *front*.
眼面前	*before* your eyes.
前面走	go in *front*.
一面說一面哭	he talked and wept at the same *time*.
老面	Mohammedans (so called by others because of the resemblance between 回 and 面).

The 177th radical. (革)

革 KE⁵. [*change* the face.

洗心革面	to *reform*; lit., to wash the heart and
禁革煮酒	to *prohibit* the making of wine.
功名是革了的	he has been *deprived* of his degree.
革職	to *degrade* from office.
革奶奶	to *wean* a child.

靪 TIN¹.

打補靪	to fill a servant's place in his absence.

靴 SHÜE¹.

靴子	*top-boots*.
隔靴子搔癢	to scratch an itching place through the *top-boot*; met., unavailing.

注 释

【他的门面宽】门面宽: 名望高。
【脸脸面面的】外表体面。
【面一层泥巴】面: 涂在外面。
【老面】伊斯兰教徒。
革 [ke⁵]
【禁革煮酒】禁止酿酒。
【革奶奶】给孩子断奶。
靪 [tin¹]
靴 [ɕye¹]

注 释

靶 [pa³]
鞋 [xai²]
【板板鞋】木屐。
【鸡婆鞋】高帮靴子。
鞍 [ŋan¹]
鞘 [siao⁴]
鞔 [man²]
【鞔鞋底】把布蒙在鞋底。
鞜 [tʂaŋ³]
【鞜鞋】也作"上鞋"。把鞋帮和鞋底缝合成鞋。
鞭 [pien¹]
鞦 [tsʰiəu¹]
【打鞦】荡秋千。
【后鞦】马屁股。
鞓 [oŋ⁴]
【鞋鞓子浅了】鞋帮子太矮了。

革 4-10

靶 PA³.
6 靶子 — a *target*.

鞋 HAI².
鞋子 — *shoes*.
鞋舖 — a *shoe shop*.
草鞋 — *sandals*.
板板鞋 — *clogs*.
雞婆鞋 — winter *boots* with high uppers.

鞍 NGAN¹.
7 馬鞍子 — a horse's *saddle*.

鞘 SIAO⁴.
刀鞘子 — a *sheath* for a knife; a *scabbard* for a [sword.
銀鞘子 — small *cases* for transporting silver, containing about 500 taels each.

鞔 MAN².
8 鞔鞋底 — to *cover* shoe soles with cloth.

鞜 CHANG³.
9 鞜鞋 — to *patch* shoes *with leather*.

鞭 PIEN¹.
馬鞭子 — a horse *whip*.
竹鞭子 — *rattans*.
鞭他的背 — *scourge* his back.

鞦 TS'IU¹.
打鞦 — to play on a *swing*.
10 後鞦 — a horse's *crupper*.

鞓 ONG⁴.
鞋鞓子淺了 — the *upper* of the shoe is too short.

(561)

西蜀方言

革 13-16 韋 10 韭 4

13 鞴	PE⁴.	
	把馬鞴起	*harness* the horse; *saddle* the horse.
鞺	PANG¹.	
	鞋鞺子	the *upper* of a shoe.
韂	CH'AN⁴.	
	鞍韂	a horse's *trappings*.
韁	CHIANG¹.	same as 繮.
鞑	TA⁵.	
	毛鞑兒	the Chinese *queue*.
	鞑子	a name for the *Mongols*.
	TS'IEN¹.	
	鞦韆架	a frame for a child's *swing*.
15 韤	UA⁵.	
	一雙韤子	a pair of *socks* or *stockings*.
16 韃	LONG².	
	馬韃頭	a horse's *halter*.

The 178th radical. **(韋)**

10 韜	T'AO¹.	
	胸有韜畧	he is well versed in *military tactics*.

The 179th radical. **(韭)**

4 韭	CHIU³.	
	韭菜	*leeks*.

注释

鞴 [pei⁴]
【把马鞴起】把鞍辔等套在马身上。
鞺 [paŋ¹]
韂 [tʂʰan⁴]
【鞍韂】马鞍子下面垫的东西，垂在马背两旁可以挡泥土。
韁(缰) [tɕiaŋ¹]
鞑(鞑) [ta⁵]
【毛鞑儿】辫子。
韆(千) [tɕʰien¹]
韤(袜) [ua⁵]
韃(笼) [loŋ²]
韜(韬) [tʰao¹]
韮(韭) [tɕiəu³]

注 释

音[in¹]
誩（哄）[xoŋ¹]
韻（韵）[yn⁴]
響（响）[ɕiaŋ³]

【打响器】打击手鼓等乐器。
【没得影响】没有踪迹，音信全无。
【响子花生】干花生。
【响锡】纯度高的锡。
【几响子就打开了】几响子：(打了)几下。

音 6-13

The 180th radical. (音)

音 6　　IN¹.

聲音	a *sound*.
這是那個的聲音	whose *voice* is it?
口音不同	his *accent* is different.
字音不同	the *pronunciation* is different.
八音琴	a *musical box*.
音信都沒得	there is no *news*.

誩 10　　HONG¹.

| 鬧誩誩的 | *clamorous; uproarious*. |

韻　　ÜIN⁴.

| 沒得韻脚 | it has no *rhyme*. |
| 押韻得好 | well *rhymed*. |

響 13　　SHIANG³.

聽倒一個響聲	I heard a *noise*.
是甚麼響一聲	what *made* that *noise*?
打響器	to beat *tomtoms* and all the *noisy* instruments of the priests.
有個響動沒得	is there any *trace* of him?
沒得影響	there is no trace of him; lit., neither shadow nor *sound*.
響鈴兒	*jingles*; small *bells*.
響子花生	well dried pea-nuts which *rattle* in the shell (not roasted).
響錫	good pewter, which emits a *ringing* sound [when struck.
響馬強盜	*notorious* highwaymen.
招牌做響了	his shop is *celebrated*.
幾響子就打開了	a few strokes of the large wooden *mallet* sufficed to split it.

(563)

西蜀方言

頁 2-3

The 181st radical. (頁)

IE⁶.

| 番夾了頁 | to turn two *leaves* of a book at a time. |

CH'ÜIN¹.

	in the first sentence same as 傾.
傾耳而聽	to *incline* the ear to hear.
頃刻之間	in an *instant*.

TIN³.

山頂頂	the *top* of a mountain.
冒頂兒	a *leader* in a seditious society.
戴頂子	to wear a *button* on the top of the hat.
打頂馬	to ride in an official's train.
頂好的飲食	the *best* food.
頂喜歡	*very* pleased.
頂在頭上	to *carry on the head*, as a baker carries his [board.
頂天立地的漢子	a very talented person.
把生意頂給人做	to *transfer*, or *sell* a business to another.
我來頂	I will *take it over*; I will *undertake* it.
要好多頂頭	how much money do you want for the business?
病頂了眞	the sickness has *become* serious.
他兩個頂起的	they are *at variance*.
頂倒	to *oppose*.
頂門杠	a large *cross-bar* for bolting a door.
一頂帽子	one hat. (*N. A.*)
一頂轎子	one sedan. (*N. A.*)

HANG⁴.

頸項	the *nape* of the neck.
項圈	a *neck*-ring of silver; a *neck* of pork.
別項事	another *kind* of affair.
各項貨物	each *class* of goods.
公項	public funds.

(564)

注　释

頁（页）[ie⁵]
【番夹了页】一次翻了两页书。

顷（顷）[tɕʰyn¹]

顶（顶）[tin³]
【山顶顶】山巅。
【冒顶儿】土匪头子。
【打顶马】侍卫长。
【病顶了真】病情加重了。
【他两个顶起的】他们两个人不和。
【顶倒】反对。

项（项）[xaŋ⁴]
【别项事】别的事情。
【公项】公共基金。

注释

顺(顺)[ʂuən⁴]
【横顺是好宽】长度和宽度是多少？
【横顺是一样】反正是一样。
【他的口不顺】他口齿不清。
【把东西检顺】把东西收拾好。
【顺子行】顺着走（轿夫喊话）

须(须)[sy¹]
颁(颁)[pan¹]
【颁指】弓箭手的拇指环。
颂(颂)[soŋ⁴]
顿(顿)[tən⁴]
【顿稳】放稳。

頁 3-4

順

SHUEN⁴.

順從	to *obey*.
順天者存逆天者亡	those who *obey* Heaven live, those who *disobey* perish.
事情順遂	the affair is *successful*.
順風	a *fair* wind.
橫順是好寬	how large is it crosswise and *lengthwise*?
橫順是一樣	it is the same in any case.
順手	*convenient* to one's hand.
他的口不順	he has difficulty in pronouncing his words [distinctly.
順口就說出來了	he spoke lightly and without thought.
順便幫我帶個信	take this letter with you at the *same* time, please.
走那個地方還是順路	the road to that place is the *same*, or, not much out of the way.
把東西檢順	*arrange* the things a bit. [shuen! shuen!).
順子行	chair-bearers (from their common cry,

須

sü¹. interchanged with 需.

我們須用的	what we *need* to use.
須要小心	you *must* be careful.

頒

PAN¹.

頒行天下	to *publish* throughout the empire, as a proclamation. [by the Emperor.
頒指	an archer's thumb-ring, anciently *conferred*
頭髮頒白	his hair is iron-gray (perhaps used for 斑).

頌

SONG⁴.

沒得人稱頌他	no one *praises* him.

頓

TEN⁴.

罵他一頓	he cursed him for a *spell*.
一頓就斷了	one *jerk* and the string broke.
安頓	to *set in order*.
頓穩	*set it up* firmly.
兩頓飯	two *meals* of rice. (*N. A.*)

(565)

頁 4-7

UAN².

頑梗不化的	*perverse; stubborn.*
愚頑	*stupid.*
頑疲	*slow; dilatory; impassive.*
搬個頑石打坐	fetch a stone and sit on it.

Ü⁴. same as 豫.

LIN³.

衣領	the *collar* of a garment.
領架子	a waist-coat, to which a *collar* is attached.
領他出去	*lead* him out.
統領做工的人	to *lead*, or *oversee* workmen.
領頭子	a *head* workman; a contractor.
我來領一本書	I have come to *receive* a book.
領敎	I have *received* your teaching; teach me.
領情	reckon that I have *received* your present; excuse me taking it.

P'O³.

頗倒氣力不上算	to *exert* one's strength is of no consequence—I'll do it.

CHIN³.

吊頸	to hang one's self by the *neck*.
手頸頸 and 脚頸頸	the *wrist* and the *ankle*.

P'IN².

久坐令人厭 頻來親也疏	if you sit long in a person's house, it makes him dislike you; if you are *incessantly* coming, even near relatives grow distant.

T'EO².

在頭上	on the *head*.
在上頭	on the *top*.
靠頭裏	moor the boat at the *upper* end of the landing.
頭人	a *headman*.

(566)

注釋

頑（頑）[uan²]
【頑疲】緩慢，拖拉。
預（預）[y⁴]
領（領）[lin³]
【領架子】帶領子的馬甲。
【領頭子】工頭；包工頭。
頗（頗）[pʰo³]
【頗倒氣力不上算】頗倒：使勁。
頸（頸）[tɕin³]
【吊頸】上吊自殺。
【手頸頸and脚頸頸】腕關節和踝關節。
頻（頻）[pʰin²]
頭（頭）[tʰəu²]
【靠頭里】使船停泊在碼頭的上游位置。
【頭人】首領。

注释

【三个头】三人抬的轿子。
【难得排头】万事开头难。
【打头子】训斥。
【在河头】在河里。
【说一头亲】说一门亲事。
颗（颗）[kʰo³]
额（额）[ŋe⁵]
【灶额子】防火门的过梁。
【额子】也作"横批"，门楣上的题字。
题（题）[tʰi²]
【题个头子】提示，题词。
颜（颜）[ien²]

頁 7-9

三個頭	a chair carried by three *men*.
頭一回	the *first* time.
難得排頭	it is difficult to make a *beginning*.
摸不倒頭腦	I cannot get into the *way* of it.
兩頭	the two *ends* of a thing; two *aspects of*, or *parties in*, a case.
打頭子	to reprimand.
在這頭	at this *end*.
裏頭 and 外頭	inside and outside.
一年到頭	from one year's *end* to the other.
前頭 and 後頭	before and behind.
在河頭	*in* the river.
說一頭親	to settle a marriage contract. (*N. A.*)
頭頭是道	every word is true. (*N. A.*)
木頭	wood (a particle added to certain nouns).

8 顆 K'O³.

| 一顆麥子 | a *grain* of wheat. (*N. A.*) |
| 一顆珠子 | one bead. (*N. A.*) |

9 額 NGE⁵.

額頭	the *forehead*; the *brow*.
額角	the *temples*.
竈額子	the *lintel* of a fire door.
額子	a four character *inscription* pasted *on the* [lintel.
數有定額	there is a fixed *number*.

題 T'I².

題目	a *theme*.
題個頭子	to *write* a copy line; to *prompt*.
不消題	you need not *mention* it.

顏 IEN².

容顏	the *expression* of the face.
這個顏色鮮得好	this *colour* is nice and fresh.
顏料	*paints* for painting pictures.

(567)

頁 10-14

10 類 LUE⁴.

| 一類的 | of the same *sort*. |

顛 TIEN¹.

樹子顛顛	the *top* of a tree.
打個顛倒	turn it *upside* down; reverse it.
顛兌兩斗米	be surety for two bushels of rice for me at the riceshop.

願 ÜEN⁴.

心甘情願	*willing*.
不願意	un*willing*; he does not *wish* it.
難遂心願	it is difficult to gratify one's heart's *desires*.
願你發財	I *wish* you wealth.

麻 MA².

| 密密麻麻的 | *indistinct* muttering; *incoherent* talk. |

12 顧 KU⁴.

顧臉	to *regard* one's reputation.
看顧朋友	*care for* your friends.
錢要顧惜倒用	you must use the money *economically*.
不隨顧得	I did not *notice* it.
照顧	to *patronize*.
主顧	a *customer*.

13 顫 CHAN⁴.

周身發顫	*trembling* all over the body.
冷得打顫	*shivering* with cold. [*quiver*.
花顫顫	*artificial* flowers, so called because they

蓋 KAI¹.

| 天靈蓋 | the *top of the skull*. |

顯 SHIEN³.

| 顯明出來 | to *manifest*. |
| 顯手段 | to *show off* one's skill. |

(568)

注 釋

類（类）[luei⁴]
顛（颠）[tien¹]
【树子颠颠】树梢。
【打个颠倒】把它倒过来。
【颠兑两斗米】颠兑：担保。
願（愿）[yen⁴]
麻（麻）[ma²]
顧（顾）[ku⁴]
【钱要顾惜倒用】钱要省着花。
【不随顾得】没注意到。
顫（颤）[tṣan⁴]
【花颤颤】人造花。
蓋（盖）[kai¹]
顯（显）[ɕien³]

注释

【字不显】字迹模糊。
顯(颅)[lu²],[ləu²]
　【额颅】额头。
風(风)[foŋ¹]
　【风篷】风帆。
　【风谷子】扬谷。
　【风快】飞快。
　【冒了风】感冒了。
　【事情通不得风】事情不能公开。
　【听倒一点风风】听到一点传闻。
　【门风要紧】门风：家庭声誉。
颰[ia¹]
　【还在颰气】颰气：喘气，吐气。
颯(飒)[sa⁵]
　颳(刮)[kua⁵]
　【刮地风】掠地大风。

頁 14-16　風 4-6

顯點功夫看	show us a little of your skill.
大顯其道	to *promulgate* a doctrine openly.
那個樹子顯了聖	that tree has *exhibited* divine power.
明明顯顯的	*clear*; *obvious*.
顏色不顯	the colour is not *bright*.
字不顯	the characters are not *distinct*.

16 顱　　LU², LEO².

| 額顱 | the *brow*; the *forehead*. |

The 182nd radical. (風)

風　　FONG¹.

吹風	the *wind* blows.
風水	the good and evil influences carried or [hindered by *wind* or water.
風篷	the sail of a boat.
風穀子	to *winnow* grain.
風快	*very* fast; like the *wind*.
冒了風	I have caught cold.
惹風波	to stir up *trouble*.
聽他的口風	listen to his *talk*.
事情通不得風	the matter must not be made public.
喫接風酒	to drink wine on arrival at a wedding feast.
聽倒一點風風	I heard a *rumour* of it.
不好的風聲	an evil *report*.
門風要緊	the *reputation* of the house is important.
風俗不好	the *customs* are bad.

4 颰　　IA¹.

| 還在颰氣 | he is still *gasping* for breath. |

5 颯　　SA⁵.

| 風颯颯的吹 | the wind blows in *gusts* (from the sound). |

6 颳　　KUA⁵.

| 颳地風 | a wind that *raises* the dust; a *blast*. |

(569)

颸 10-11 飛. 食 4

10 颸

SEO¹.

| 冷颸颸的 | cold. |
| 風吹得涼颸颸的 | the wind blows *chill*. |

11 飄

P'IAO¹.

飄落多少遠	*blown* to a great distance by the wind.
買一副飄帶	buy a pair of hat strings.
飄雨	a *driving* rain.
輕飄飄的	very *light*.

The 183rd radical. (飛)

FE¹.

飛在空中	to *fly* in mid-heaven.
飛鳥	*flying* birds.
飛雪	*snowing*.
下飛飛雨	*fine* rain.
飛跑	to run *swiftly*.
薄飛飛	very *thin*.
錢飛子	*cash tickets*.

The 184th radical. (食)

SHĬ⁵.

飲食	*food*.
伙食	*provisions*.
糧食	*cereals*.
糖食	*confectionery; sweetmeats*.

CH'Ĭ⁵.

| 大受申飭 | to be strictly *enjoined*. |

FAN⁴.

| 白米飯 | plain cooked *rice*. |
| 沒得飯喫 | I have no *food* to eat. |

(570)

注 釋

颸（飕）[səu¹]
飄（飘）[pʰiao¹]
【飄雨】大雨。
飛（飞）[fei¹]
【下飞飞雨】飞飞雨：细雨。
【薄飞飞】很薄。
【钱飞子】到钱号领钱的票据。
食 [ʂʅ⁵]
飭（饬）[tʂʰʅ⁵]
飯（饭）[fan⁴]

注释

飲(饮) [in³] [in⁴]
【吃饮食】分享食物。
【饮花】浇花。
飽(饱) [pao³]
【看都看不饱】羡慕。
【十里饱足】富足的景象。
飾(饰) [sï⁵]
餉(饷) [ɕiaŋ³]
【关饷】(军队)发饷,泛指发工资。
餃(饺) [tɕiao³]
餅(饼) [pin³]
【头发结了饼】头发乱而脏。
餂(舔) [tʰien³]
【用舌片儿餂】舌片儿:舌头。
【餂肥】奉承巴结富人。

食 4-6

飲

IN³.

一飲而盡　　he *drinks* it at one draught.
飲酒　　　　to *drink* wine.
喫飲食　　　to partake of *food*.

READ IN⁴.

5 飲花　　　　to *water* plants.

飽

PAO³.

喫飽了　　　*satisfied* with eating.
一飽百不思　when a man is *full* he desires nothing else.
看都看不飽　he cannot admire his child *enough*.
飽學秀才　　a *thoroughly* learned B.A.
十里飽足　　*full* ten Chinese miles.

飾

SHÏ⁵.

收飾得好好的　well *dressed*.
戴首飾　　　to wear *ornaments*.
替他遮飾　　to *palliate* another's shortcomings.

6 餉

SHIANG³.

關餉　　　　to pay soldiers' *rations*.

餃

CHIAO³.

水餃子　　　*dumplings*.

餅

PIN³.

糖餅子　　　*cakes* with a lump of sugar in them.
鍋巴餅　　　the *crust* of rice off the pan.
頭髮結了餅　his hair is matted into a *pad*.
黃蠟餅　　　a *cake*, or *block* of bees-wax.
橘餅　　　　preserved orange peel.
柿餅　　　　dried persimmons.

餂

T'IEN³.

用舌片兒餂　*lick* it with your tongue.
餂肥　　　　to *flatter* the rich.

(571)

西蜀方言

食 6-8

	IANG³.	[children.
養育恩		the grace of parents in *nourishing* their
養老田		fields set apart for the *maintenance* of parents. [valescence.
養病		to *nurse* or *take care of* one's self in con-
養神		to *take care of* one's health. [(meritorious).
養生池		a pool in a temple where fishes etc. are *fed*
養花水		water with which flowers are *watered*.
	READ IANG⁴.	
奉養父母		to *provide for* one's parents.
	O⁴.	
肚皮餓了		I am *hungry*.
看人看得餓		to stare incessantly at.
	TS'AN¹.	
兩餐茶飯		two *meals*. (*N. A.*)
	Ü².	[spare.
穿喫有餘		of food and clothing there is *enough and to surplus*; what is *left over*.
餘下的		
餘外的		besides; over and above.
	SHIAO².	
餚饌		meats; delicacies.
	CHÜEN³.	
春餰兒		minced meat rolled in wafers; *dumplings*.
	KO³.	
京餜		cakes; confectionery.
	KUAN³.	
		same as 舘.
	TSIEN⁴.	[journey.
餞行		to *entertain* a person before he starts on a

(572)

注 释

養（养）[iaŋ³] [iaŋ⁴]
餓（饿）[o⁴]
【看人看得饿】紧盯着看。
餐 [tsʰan¹]
餘（余）[y²]
餚（肴）[ɕiao²]
餰（卷）[tɕyen²]
餜（粿）[ko³]
【京餜】糕点糖果。
館（馆）[kuan³]
餞（饯）[tsien⁴]

注 释

餬（糊）[fu²]
【将够糊嘴】仅够吃饭。
餾（馏）[liəu⁴]
【馏个笼】放蒸笼里热一下。
餿（馊）[səu¹]
饈（馐）[siəu¹]
餗（素）[su⁴]
饅（馒）[man²]
饌（馔）[tʂuan⁴]
餳（噔）[tən⁴]
【扯膈噔儿】打嗝。
饒（饶）[zao²]
（RAO⁴当为RAO²，见803页勘误表）
饑（饥）[tɕi¹]

食 9-12

9 餬	FU².	
	餬口	to *get a living* by teaching.
	將够餬嘴	just sufficient to *feed* one.
10 餾	LIU⁴.	
	餾個籠	*warm* it *up again* in the steamer.
餿	SEO¹.	
	飯餿了	the rice is *sour*.
	汗餿氣氣	the *offensive* smell of perspiration.
饈	SIU¹.	
	珍饈美味	*delicacies*.
餗	SU⁴.	
	喫餗	to fast on *vegetable food*.
11 饅	MAN².	
	饅頭	*steamed bread*.
12 饌	CHUAN⁴.	for example of use see 餾.
餳	TEN⁴.	
	扯膈餳兒	to *hiccough*.
饒	RAO⁴.	
	家屋富饒	an *affluent* family.
	饒人不是癡漢 癡漢不會饒人	the man who *forgives* another is not a fool, a fool cannot *forgive*.
	得饒人處且饒人	*forgive* if it be at all possible.
	饒舌	to be *liberal* with the tongue, as a busy-body.
饑	CHI¹.	
	年歲饑荒	a year of *dearth*.
	肚中饑餓	*famished*.
	煮些野菜充饑	to cook weeds to appease *hunger*.

(573)

食 12-17 首 2 香

16 饊	SAN³.	
	饊子	wheat *cakes* fried in oil.
17 饝	MO².	
	饝饝	steamed bread.
饞	TS'AN².	
	嘴饞得很	very *gluttonous*.

The 185th radical. (首)

首	SHEO³.	
	首飾	female *head* ornaments.
	屍首	a corpse.
	首縣	the *chief* district in a prefecture.
	首事	a *head*man; a street official.
	一首詩	a poem. (*N. A.*)
	READ SHEO⁴.	
	首兒子	to *deliver up* a bad son to the magistrate [for punishment.
²馗	K'UE².	
	黑起臉像鍾馗	as black in the face as Chong-*k'ue* (an idol).

The 186th radical. (香)

香	SHIANG¹.	
	一股香氣	a *sweet smell*; *fragrance*.
	花香得好	the flowers are very *fragrant*.
	香油	sesame oil.
	燒香	to burn *incense*.
	書香人戶	a literary family.
	花香不及書香	adultery is not comparable to learning.
	松香膏藥	plasters containing pine *rosin*.
	香柏枝	cedar branches used in fumigating rooms or in making bacon.

(574)

注 释

饊（馓）[san³]
【馓子】油煎麦饼。
饝（馍）[mo²]
饞（馋）[tsʰan²]
首 [ʂəu³] [ʂəu⁴]
【首事】头面人物。
【首儿子】将犯事的儿子主动交官府法办。
馗 [kʰuei²]
香 [ɕiaŋ¹] [ɕiaŋ⁴]

注 释

【拿来香菜】拿来作调味。

䪞 [pʰoŋ]

【这个花䪞香】这个花很香。

馨 [ɕin¹]

馬(马) [ma³]

【骚马, 骟马 and 骒马】马、阉割的马和母马。

【野马连天的】狂猛, 不受约束。

【木马】木匠用于锯木的支架。

【马头】集市; 栈桥; 广场。

【马得很】不熟练; 笨拙。

【马货】劣质货。

【马不的】说不准, 不能确定。

【遇倒马子】马子: 土匪; 旗鼓相当的对手。

【马住】压抑, 压制住。

馱(驮) [tʰo²]

香 8-11 馬 3

8 䪞

READ SHIANG¹,⁴.

香料　　　　　spices.

READ SHIANG⁴.

拿來香菜　　　*season* the food with it.

P'ONG⁴.

這個花䪞香　　this flower is *very fragrant*.

11 馨

SHIN¹.

一時的馨香　　his *pleasantness* is only for the hour.

The 187th radical. (馬)

馬

MA³.

一匹馬　　　　one *horse*.
騷馬, 騙馬 and 騍馬　*horse, gelding,* and *mare*.
野馬連天的　　rude, boisterous, like a wild *horse*.
馬兵　　　　　*cavalry*.
記得當年騎竹馬 } I remember when he used to ride on a
看看又是白頭翁 } stick, and now, before one is aware
　　　　　　　of it, he is a gray-haired old man.
木馬　　　　　a *trestle* for sawing wood on.
馬頭　　　　　a country *market*; a *landing stage*; *place of concourse*. [slipping.
腳馬子　　　　*clamps* worn by coolies to keep them from
馬得很　　　　*unskilful*; *clumsy*.
馬貨　　　　　a *poor, badly made* article.
莊稼馬點兒　　farming is very *poor* or *bad*.
馬不的　　　　I cannot *say* for certain.
遇倒馬子　　　to meet with one's *match* at roguery.
馬住　　　　　to *oppress*; to *force*; to *retain by force*.

3 馱

T'O².

馱東西　　　　to *carry on the backs* of animals.
馱騾　　　　　*pack* mules.

(575)

馬 3-5

READ TO⁴.

一馱羊毛	a mule *load* of wool.
吆馱子	*muleteers*.

CH'I².

他一個人馳馳說	he talks *incessantly*.

PO⁵.

辯駁道理	to *argue*; to *criticise*.
駁載	to *tranship* goods.

CHU⁴.

在那裏駐脚	where do you *lodge*?

SĪ⁴.

一言旣出駟馬難追	when a word is once uttered a *team of four horses* could not overtake it.

FU⁴.

駙馬公	a *son-in-law* of the Emperor.

T'AI³.

平路駘人	a level road *wearies* one.
大駘駘的	*negligent* of guests; *uppish*.

CHIA⁴.

出駕	to *ride* out in state, as an idol.
尊駕	*Sir*.
駕船	to *sail* in a boat; to be a boatman.
說駕雲的話	to tell lies, lit., to speak of *riding* on the [clouds.

CHÜ¹.

駒駒	a *fool*.
千里駒	a good *horse*, and, metaphorically, a good [son.

T'O².

駱駝	a *camel*.

(576)

注 釋

【吆馱子】赶骡的人。
馳（驰）[tʂʰʅ²]
【他一个人驰驰说】驰驰：不停地。
駁（驳）[po⁵]
駐（驻）[tʂu⁴]
駟（驷）[sʅ⁴]
駙（驸）[fu⁴]
駘（骀）[tʰai³]
【平路駘人】駘：使人疲倦。
【大駘駘的】盛气凌人的，傲慢的。
駕（驾）[tɕia⁴]
【说驾云的话】说谎。
駒（驹）[tɕy¹]
【駒駒】傻瓜。
駝（驼）[tʰo²]

注 释

骆（骆）[lo⁵]
隲（骘）[tṣʅ⁵]
【阴骘文】劝人积阴德。
骑（骑）[tɕʰi²]
骒（骒）[kʰo⁴]
【骒马】母马。
鬃（鬃）[tsoŋ¹]
验（验）[ɳien⁴]
【验照】检查护照。
【效验】有效。
骗（骗）[pʰien⁴]
骝（骝）[liəu²]
骚（骚）[sao¹]
【骚马】种马。
騲（草）[tsʰao³]
【草猪】被阉割的母猪。
骟（骟）[ʂan⁴]
【骟马】阉割的马。

馬 6-10

6 駱	LO⁵.	for example of use see last.
7 隲	CHĪ⁵.	
陰隲文		tracts exhorting to *good deeds*.
8 騎	CH'I².	
騎馬		to *ride* on a horse.
騍	K'O⁴.	
騍馬		a *mare*.
騌	TSONG¹.	
馬騌		a horse's *mane*.
騌刷子		a brush made of hog's *bristles*.
驗	NIEN⁴.	
驗照		to *inspect* a passport.
驗屍		to *examine* a corpse; a post-mortem [examination.
應驗		to *verify*; to *fulfil*; to *come to pass*.
效驗		*efficacious*, as a medicine.
靈驗		*responsive*, as a god.
9 騙	P'IEN⁴.	
我沒有哄騙你		I have not *cheated* you.
騮	LIU².	
棗騮馬		a *bay* horse with a black mane and tail.
騷	SAO¹.	
騷馬		an *entire* horse; a stallion.
騷擾百姓		to *harass* the people as soldiers do.
騲	TS'AO³.	
騲猪		a *gelded* female pig.
10 騸	SHAN⁴.	
騸馬		a *gelding*.
騸牛		a *steer*.
騸猪		a *hog*.

(577)

馬 10-13

ME⁵.

	[relatives, lit., to overstep.
蕎買蕎賣	to buy and sell property unknown to one's

T'EN².

騰雲	to mount on the clouds, as the genii.
騰個盆	to empty a basin by turning the contents into another one.
騰房圈	to empty out a room.
車騰兩串錢	lend me two thousand cash.

LO².

騾子	a mule.

CH'Ü¹.

驅逐	to expel.
受人驅使	to be ordered about by another.

RAO², SHIAO¹.

驍勇	brave soldiers.

READ SHIAO¹.

生意做得驍勇	he does a brisk business.

CHIAO¹.

驕傲自大	proud; haughty.

CHIN¹.

把你們受驚	it frightened you.
不驚動他	don't disturb him, as one sleeping.
把馬驚跑了	it scared the horse.
驚瘋病	convulsions of young children.
冷水驚人	cold water makes one shiver.

I⁵.

驛棧	a government post house.
驛馬星	restive, as a post-horse.

(578)

注 釋

蕎（荞）[me⁵]
【蕎买蕎卖】瞒着家人买卖家产。
腾（腾）[tʰən²]
【腾房圈】腾空一个房间。
【车腾两串钱】借两串钱给我。
骡（骡）[lo²]
驱（驱）[tɕʰy¹]
骁（骁）[zɑo²][ɕiɑo¹]
【生意做得骁勇】骁勇：敏锐。
骄（骄）[tɕiɑo¹]
惊（惊）[tɕin¹]
【惊疯病】少儿抽搐。
【冷水惊人】水冷得使人哆嗦。
驿（驿）[i⁵]

578 西蜀方言

注释

骤（骤）[tsʰəu⁴]
【气骤】气喘，喘息。
驢（驴）[ly²]
【驴驴儿】小驴。
骨 [ku⁵]
【冷骨疯】风湿病。
【牙骨签子】象牙制作的牙签。
【桃子骨骨】桃子的内核。
骭 [kan³]
【手骭】前臂。
【脚骭骨】胫骨。
肮（肮）[ŋaŋ¹]
靶（把）[pa³]
【那个人做事没把柄】没把柄：没有原则。
骸 [ɕiai²]
髈（膀）[paŋ³] [pʰaŋ³]
【手髈】上臂。
【报髈子】给人支持、参谋。

馬 14-16 骨 3-10

14 骤 TS'EO⁴.
氣骤 panting for breath.

16 驢 LÜ².
驢驢兒 a donkey.

The 188th radical. (骨)

KU⁵.
骨頭 a bone.
骨格長得好 a fine figure, lit., bone frame.
冷骨瘋 rheumatism.
我們是骨肉親 we are relatives.
親骨肉 brothers and sisters.
牙骨籤子 an ivory tooth-pick.
菸骨頭 the leaf-stalk of dried tobacco.
扇骨子 the ribs of a fan.
桃子骨骨 peach stones.

3 骭 KAN³.
手骭 the forearm.
脚骭骨 the shinbone.

4 肮 NGANG¹.
肮髒 filthy.

靶 PA³.
那個人做事沒靶柄 that man acts without any fixed principle.

6 骸 SHIAI².
四肢百骸 the whole body, lit., four limbs and hundred bones.

10 髈 PANG³, P'ANG³.
肩髈 the shoulder.
手髈 the upper arm; the humerus.
報髈子 to stand behind and prompt; to aid another in any design.

骨 10-13 高

	PO⁵.	
13 髆	背髆子	the *shoulder-blade*; a *backer*.
髓	SUE³.	
	骨髓	*marrow*.
	木頭髓了	the wood has *dry-rot*.
體	T'I³.	
	身體軟弱	weak in *body*.
	體貼	to *consider* the feelings and circumstances [of others]
	一體的看待	to treat all *alike*.
	辦得體面	to do things in *grand* style.
	穿得體面	to wear *fine* clothes.
	體面話	*grandiloquent* words.
	莊稼體面	the harvest is *good*.
髒	TSANG¹.	
	髒得很	very *dirty*; *filthy*.
	說些髒話	to use *vile* language; *filthy* conversation.

The 189th radical. (高)

高	KAO¹.	
	不上高山不得曉平地	if you have not ascended *high* hills you do not know the benefits of the plain.
	高漢子	a *tall* fellow.
	高見些	be *magnanimous*; excuse me.
	這些貨高	these goods are of *superior* quality.
	高傲	*proud*; *haughty*.
	在高頭	on the *top* of.
	米價高	the price of rice is *high*; rice is *dear*.
	高姓	what is your *exalted* name?
	高名	*famous*.
	高手匠人	a *skilful* workman.
	高聲說	speak in a *loud* voice.
	高陞點	give a little more.

(580)

注 释

髆（膊）[po⁵]
【背髆子】肩胛骨；支持者。
髓 [suei³]
【木头髓了】木头干枯腐败了。
體（体）[tʰi³]
【庄稼体面】庄稼长势好。
髒（脏）[tsaŋ¹]
高 [kao¹]
【高汉子】高个子男人。
【高见些】有雅量。
【这些货高】这些货质量好。
【高名】有名。
【高升点】再给点。

注 释

髞 [sao⁴]
【亮髞】光亮。
髭 [tsɿ³]
髮（发）[fa⁵]
髼 [pʰoŋ²]
【髼头妇人】髼头：头发凌乱。
髶 [pʰoŋ¹]
【盖耳髶】让头发盖住耳朵的发型。
鬆（松）[soŋ¹]
【松个肩】休息一下。
【病松活了】松活：减轻。
【他的手松】手松：浪费，随意花钱。
鬍（胡）[fu²]
【落耳胡】络腮胡。
鬌 [tsiɑu¹]
鬚（须）[sy¹]

髟 13 髟 5-12

13 髞   SAO⁴.
亮髞   *light*, as a room.

The 190th radical. (髟)

5 髭   TSĪ³.
髭髭   the *mustache* or *beard* (general name).

髮   FA⁵.
頭髮   the *hair* on the head.

7 髼   P'ONG².
髼頭婦人   a woman with *dishevelled* hair.

8 髶   P'ONG¹.
盖耳髶   a style of dressing the hair over the ears.

鬆   SONG¹.
細鬆了   it is bound *loosely*.
放鬆   *slacken* it.
鬆個肩   to *ease* the shoulder; to rest.
病鬆活了   the sickness is *abated*.
他的手鬆   he is *extravagant*; *loose* with money.

9 鬍   FU².
八字鬍   the *mustache*.
滿臉鬍髭   a full *beard*.
落耳鬍   *whiskers*.   [or *mustache*.
只長了幾根鬍髭   I have only got a few *hairs* in my beard

鬌   TSIU¹.
    [the head.
頭髮挽個鬌鬌   to wind the queue in to a *coil* on the top of

12 鬚   SÜ¹.
鬍鬚   the *mustache* and *beard*.
花鬚   the *stamens* and *pistils* of flowers.

(581)

髟 12-19　鬥 10-17　鬯 19

13 鬟	御麥鬚	the silky *tassels* of maize.	
	耍鬚帽	a hat with a long red *tassel* behind, worn by [officials.	
	HUAN².		
14 鬟	丫鬟	a *slave girl* (from the *hair-tufts*).	
	PIN⁴.		
19 鬢	鬢腳	the *temples*.	
	TSAN⁴.		
	腦鬢	the *top of the head*.	
	READ TSUAN³.		
	挽鬢	to do the hair up in a *knot*, to become a [Taoist priest.	

The 191st radical. (鬥)

TEO⁴.

10 鬥	鬥罵	to *wrangle*.
	爭鬥	to *fight*.
	鬥櫺子	to *insert* a handle in anything.
	事情不鬥頭	the affair cannot be *arranged*.
	鬥事的人	a middleman; one who *adjusts* business.
	鬥點錢給他	*collect* a little money and give it him.
	來得鬥頭	to come *opportunely*; in the nick of time.
	他兩個不鬥頭	they are not *friendly*.
	鬥耳朵勁	to talk over business matters as middle-[men do.

CHIU¹, KEO¹.

|17 鬮| 鬮砣砣 | *lots* written on paper. |

The 192nd radical. (鬯)

IO⁵, ÜE⁵.

|19 鬱| 鬱結在心裏 | *brooding* over a sorrow; *desponding*. |

(582)

注　釋

鬚 [xuan²]
鬟(鬓) [pin⁴]
鬢 [tsan⁴] [tsuan³]
【脑鬢】头顶。
【挽鬢】头顶挽个像道士一样的发髻。
鬥(斗) [təu⁴]
【斗把子】安上把手。
【事情不斗头】不斗头：没有安排布置好。
【斗事的人】中间人。
【斗点钱给他】给他点小钱。
【来得斗头】来得正是时候。
【他两个不斗头】他们两个人不友好。
【斗耳朵劲】谈生意。
鬮(阄) [tɕiəu¹] [kəu¹]
【阄砣砣】写上字或画上记号用来抓阄的小纸团。
鬱(郁) [io⁵] [ye⁵]

注释

鬼 [kuei³]
【说鬼话】大声地自言自语。
【剥鬼皮】偷窃尸体上的衣服。
魂 [xuən²]
魁 [kʰuei¹]
【魁肥】十分肥胖。
魃 [pʰa⁴]
【旱魃儿】传说中引起旱灾的怪物。
魄 [pʰe⁵]
魅 [mei⁴]
魎（魍）[liaŋ³]
魍 [uaŋ³]

髟· 鬼 4-8

The 193rd radical. (髟)

The 194th radical. (鬼)

KUE³.
送鬼　to get rid of *demons* from a house. [*spirit*.
說鬼話　to talk aloud to one's self, as if talking to a
鬼蛋蛋　a *bewitched* egg.
剝鬼皮　to steal the clothes off a *corpse*.
酒醉鬼　a drunken *wretch*.

HUEN².
嚇掉魂　scared out of one's *wits*.
叫魂　to recall the *spirit* of a sick person.
引魂旛　a streamer carried before the coffin to lead the *soul*. [to worship them.
孤魂野鬼　solitary *spirits* who have no descendants
寃魂不散　the unrevenged *ghost* will not leave him.
還魂　to revive; to resuscitate.

K'UE¹.
罪魁　a *leader* of villains.
鍋魁　a *large scone*.
魁肥　very fat, as a pig.

P'A⁴.
旱魃兒　the *demon of drought*.

P'E⁵.
　　　　　　　　　　　　　　　　　　　　　　[man.
三魂七魄　the three spirits and the seven *souls* of a

ME⁴.
　　for example of use see 魅.

LIANG³.
　　for example of use see 魎.

UANG³.
　　for example of use see 魍.

(583)

鬼 11-14 魚 4-8

11 魑

LI².

魑魅魍魎　　evil spirits.

14 魘

MO².

四川是個邪魔地　SI-chu'an is a place of ·evil spirits or [demons.

IEN³.

魘夢　　nightmare.

The 195th radical. 〔魚〕

Ü².

跑了的魚兒大　the fish that escapes is always a big one.
油魚　　the squid.
打魚船　　a fishing boat.
魚鰾膠　　fish glue.

4 魯

LU³.

說得粗魯　　to speak vulgarly, or obscenely.
飲食粗魯　　the food is coarse.

5 鮓

CHA³.

鮓魚　　fish devilled in salt and pea flour.
鮓巴眼　　inflamed eye-lids.

6 鮮

SÜEN¹, SHÜEN¹, SIEN¹.

鮮魚　　fresh fish.
新鮮的　　new; in good spirits.

7 鯉

LI³.

鯉魚　　carp.

鯊

SHA¹.

鯊魚　　the shark.

8 鯨

CHIN¹.

鯨魚　　the whale.

(584)

注　釋

魑 [li²]
魔 [mo²]
魘（魇）[ien³]
【魇梦】恶梦。
魚（鱼）[y²]
【油鱼】鱿鱼；乌贼。
【鱼鳔膠】鱼胶；花胶。
魯（鲁）[lu³]
鮓（鲊）[tṣa³]
【鲊巴眼】眼睛发炎。
鮮（鲜）[syen¹] [ɕyen¹]
　[sien¹]
鯉（鲤）[li³]
鯊（鲨）[ṣa¹]
鯨（鲸）[tɕin¹]

注 释

蝦（虾）[ɕia¹]
鰉（鳇）[xuaŋ²]
【鳇刺骨】鲟鱼。
鰓（鳃）[sai¹]
【鱼鳃壳子】鱼鳃。
鯻 [la⁵]
【黄鯻钉儿】黄辣丁，一种小鱼。
鰍（鳅）[tsʰiəu¹]
【鳅鱼】泥鳅。
鯽（鲫）[tsi⁵] [tsie⁵]
鰥（鳏）[kuan¹]
鰢 [ma³]
【鰢蝦】水马，一种海虾。
鰱（鲢）[lien²]
鰲（鳌）[ŋao²]
【占鳌头】俗称科举时状元及第。英文释义应为：to attain the first place in the imperial examinations or to be best in doing sth.
鰾（鳔）[pʰiao⁴]
鱗（鳞）[lin²]
鱉（鳖）[pie⁵]

魚 9-12

9			
鰕		SHIA¹.	
	鰕子		shrimps.
鰉		HUANG².	
	鰉刺骨		sturgeon.
鰓		SAI¹.	
	魚鰓殼子		the *gills* of a fish.
鯻		LA⁵.	
	黄鯻釘兒		a small species of fish.
鰍		TS'IU¹.	
	鰍魚		a short species of *eel*.
		TSI⁵, TSIE⁵.	
鯽	鯽魚		*bream*.
10			
鰥		KUAN¹.	
	鰥夫		a *widower*.
鰢		MA³.	
	鰢蝦		*prawns*.
11			
鰱		LIEN².	
	鰱魚		*tench*.
鰲		NGAO².	
	占鰲頭		to stand on the *whale's* head, i. e., to become [senior wrangler.
	搬鰲頭		to make a *gargoyle like a fish*.
		P'IAO⁴.	
鰾	鰾膠		*isinglass*.
12			
鱗		LIN².	
	魚鱗甲		fish *scales*.
鱉		PIE⁵.	
	鱉甲		*turtle* shells.

(585)

魚 12-16　鳥 2-5

鱔 16	肥鱉 木鱉子	a bed *bug*; a rich person, lit., fat *turtle*. a name for the *Nux vomica bean*.
	SHAN⁴.	
	黃鱔 乾黃鱔	the yellow *eel*. a *snake*.
鰵	TS'AN¹.	
	鰵子	the *girdle-fish*.

The 196th radical. （鳥）

鳥 2	NIAO³.	
	雀鳥 鳥鎗	a *bird*. a *fowling*-piece.
鳩 3	CHIU¹.	
	斑鳩	the *turtle-dove*.
鳳	FONG⁴.	
	捨得金彈子 打得鳳凰鳥	} if you don't begrudge a golden bullet you may hit the *phœnix*, met., if you want a good thing you must pay good money.
	鳳冠	a cap presented to an *official's lady* by the Emperor.
鴉 4	IA¹, UA¹.	
	處處老鴉一般黑 老鴉船	[all alike). *crows* are everywhere black, (met., we are *cormorant* fishing boats.
	READ IA¹.	
	鴉片煙 鴉鵲子	[*black* colour). opium (so called perhaps because of the the *magpie*.
鴈 5	NGAN⁴.	same as 雁.
鴨	IA⁵.	
	鴨子· 鴨青 and 鴨婆	a *duck*, a Chinese *spoon*. a *drake* and a *duck*.

(586)

注　釋

鱔（鳝）[ṣan⁴]
【干黃鱔】蛇。
鰵 [tsʰan¹]
【鰵子】带鱼。
鳥（鸟）[ȵiao³]
鳩（鸠）[tɕiəu¹]
鳳（凤）[foŋ⁴]
鴉（鸦）[ia¹]，[ua¹]
【老鴉船】鸬鹚渔船。
【鴉鵲子】喜鹊。
鴈（雁）[ŋan⁴]
鴨（鸭）[ia5]
【鴨青and鴨婆】公鸭和母鸭。

注释

【鸭儿子】小鸭子。
鸽（鸽）[ko⁵]
鹅（鹅）[o²]
鹃（鹃）[tɕyen¹]
鹌（鹌）[ŋan¹]
鹑（鹑）[ʂuən²]
鹊（鹊）[tsʰio⁵]
鹛[mei²]
【鹈子】又叫"囮子"，"鹝子"，是一种用来引诱猎物的鸟。
【当鹈子】当诱饵。
鹤（鹤）[xo⁵]
鸡（鸡）[tɕi¹]
鸽[ko¹]
【鬼灯鹠】猫头鹰。
鹞（鹞）[iao⁴]
鹰[ma²]

鳥 5-10

	鴨兒子	ducklings.
	建昌鴨子	a kind of muscovy-*duck*; an empty brag-[gart.
6 鴿	KO⁵.	
	鴿子	a *dove*.
7 鵝	O².	
	餵鵝	to rear *geese*.
	鵝兒子	*goslings*.
	鵝子石	*cobble-stones*.
	CHÜEN¹.	for example of use see 杜.
鵑	NGAN¹.	
8 鶴	鵪鶉	a *quail*.
	SHUEN².	for example of use see last.
鶉	TS'IO⁵.	same as 雀.
鵲	ME².	
	鶨子	a *decoy* bird.
鶨	當鶨子	to act the *decoy* in any transaction.
10 鶴	HO⁵.	
	白鶴	the *crane*.
	CHI¹.	same as 雞.
雞	KO¹.	
鴿	綠鸚鵡	a green *parrot*.
	鬼燈鵡	the *owl*.
	IAO⁴.	
鷂	鷂子	a *kestrel*.
	MA².	
鷹	鷹雀	a *sparrow*.

（587）

鳥 12-17　鹵 9-13　鹿 2-8

12 鷥	SÏ¹.	for example of use see next.
13 鷺	LU⁴.	
鷺鷥		the white *egret heron*.
	IN¹.	
17 鸚	巖鷹	an *eagle*.
	放鷹	to fly a *falcon* or *kite*.
	IN¹, NGEN¹.	
	白鸚鵡	a *cockatoo*.
	鸚鵡綠的轎子	a *parrot*-green chair (used by high offi-[cials]).

The 197th radical. (鹵)

9 鹹	HAN².	
	放鹹了	you have made it too *salt*.
	水是鹹的	the water is *brackish*.
10 鹻	CHIEN³.	
	熬鹻	to boil *soda* ash.
13 鹽	IEN².	
	鹽井	*salt* wells.
	鹽巴	*salt*.
	鹽蛋	*salted* eggs.

The 198th radical. (鹿)

鹿	LU⁵.	
	鹿子	a *deer*.
2 麂	CHI³.	
	麂子皮	the skin of a small kind of *deer*.
8 麒	CH'I².	
	麒麟	the Chinese *unicorn*; a fabulous animal.

(588)

注 釋

鷥（鸶）[sɿ¹]
鷺（鹭）[lu⁴]
鷹（鹰）[in¹]
鸚（鹦）[in¹] [ŋən¹]
鹹（咸）[xan²]
鹻（硷）[tɕien³]
【熬硷】煮苏打粉。
鹽（盐）[ien²]
【盐蛋】咸蛋。
鹿 [lu⁵]
麂 [tɕi³]
麒 [tɕʰi²]

| 注 释 |

麗（丽）[li⁴]
麝[ʂei⁴]
麞（獐）[tʂaŋ¹]
　【獐子】麝香鹿。
麟[lin²]
麥（麦）[me⁵]
　【油麦】燕麦。
　【御麦】玉米。
麩（麸）[fu¹]
　【麦麸子】麸皮，糠。
麨（坨）[tʰo²]
麯[tɕʰy⁵] [tɕʰio⁵]
麵（面）[mien⁴]
　【灰面】面粉。
　【药面子】药粉。
　【炭面面】煤渣。

鹿 8-12　麥 4-9

麗	LI⁴.	
10	穿得華麗	elegantly dressed.
麝	SHE⁴.	
11	麝香	musk.
	一個麝	one bag of musk.
麞	CHANG¹.	
12	麞子	the musk-deer.
麟	LIN².	for example of use see 麒.

The 199th radical. (麥)

麥	ME⁵.	
	小麥	wheat.
	大麥	barley.
	油麥	oats.
	御麥	maize.
麩	FU¹.	
5	麥麩子	bran.
麨	T'O².	
	一麨泥巴	a lump of earth.
6	糯米麨	a glutinous rice cake.
麯	CH'Ü⁵, CH'IO⁵.	
	麯子	leaven, used for fermenting liquors only.
9	爛精的麯子	a busy-body.
麵	MIEN⁴.	
	灰麵	flour.
	一盌麵	a basin of vermicelli.
	喫麵食	to eat wheaten food as a staple.
	擂成麵麵	grind it into powder.
	藥麵子	medicine in powder.
	炭麵麵	coal dross.

(589)

麻 3 黃 13

The 200th radical. (麻)

MA².

火麻	hemp.
麻布	hempen cloth; grass-cloth.
竹麻	fibre of young bamboos used for making [sandals.
草麻子	the castor-oil plant.
芝麻油	sesame oil.

MO¹.

甚麼事	what's the matter?
你曉得麼	do you know?
是這麼的	it is *this* way.

The 201st radical. (黃)

HUANG².

黃顏色	*yellow*.
蛋黃	the *yolk* of an egg.
大黃	*rhubarb*.
青黃不接的時候	between spring and *harvest*.
牛黃	cow's *bezoar*.
黃牛	the common cow.
流黃水	to exude watery matter from a sore.
黃昏時候	at *dusk*.
那纔是個黃昏子	he is an *ignorant* fellow.
事情黃了	the affair has *miscarried*.
雨落黃了	the rain has not come, though it looked [like it.
黃虫	*ticks* on dogs.
黃腫病	*jaundice*.
黃花	the day-lily, Hemerocallis flava.

HONG³.

| 黌牆 | the *wall of a literary temple*. |

(590)

注 释

麻 [ma²]
【火麻】大麻。
麼(么) [mo¹]
黃 [xuaŋ²]
【那才是个黄昏子】黄昏子：无知、愚昧的人。
【雨落黄了】雨并没下（看起来要下雨的样子）。
【黄肿病】黄疸。
黌(黉) [xoŋ³]
【黌墙】学校或庙宇的墙。

注 释

黍 [ʂu³] [ʂuei³]
黎 [li²]
(LI⁴当为LI², 见803页勘误表。)
黏 [nien⁴]
黑 [xe⁵]
【走黑路】夜里去偷窃。
【这件事我在黑处】这件事我并不知情。
【挨黑打】遭暗算。
【他红黑不拿给我】红黑:无论如何。
【买黑货】买偷窃来的物品。
黚 [kan⁴]
默 [me⁵]
【你默倒我不晓得】默倒:以为。

黍 3-5　黑 3-4

The 202nd radical. (黍)

SHU³, SHUE³.

黍子　　　　　panicled millet.

LI⁴.

黎民百姓　　　the Chinese, lit., the *black*-haired people.
黎明的時候　　at *gray* dawn.

NIEN⁴.

米湯黏　　　　the rice-water is *thick;* (*viscid, glutinous, [sticky]*).

The 203rd radical (黑)

HE⁵.

一定墨黑　　　as *black* or *dark* as a stick of ink.
天要黑了　　　it will soon be *dark*.
走黑路　　　　to go thieving at *night*.
走黑了　　　　walking in the *dark*.
作黑了　　　　yesterday *evening*.
天黑得很　　　the day is very *dull*.
黑臉　　　　　a *frowning* face.
黑良心　　　　an *evil* conscience.
這件事我在黑處　I was kept in *ignorance* of this matter.
捱黑打　　　　to receive a blow in the *dark*; *secretly wounded*.
他紅黑不拿給我　he would on no account give it to me, lit., [by red or *black*.
買黑貨　　　　to purchase *stolen* property.

KAN⁴.

盆起黑黚黚　　the basin has a *dirty streak* round it, showing high water mark.

ME⁵.

默念　　　　　to *reflect* on.
你默倒我不曉得　you thought I did not know.

(591)

黑 5-15

5 黜 CH'O⁵.
| 你要黜拐 | you will be *reprimanded*. |
| 亂黜 | to recklessly *push at* one with a stick. |

點 TIEN³.
一點	a *dot*; a *drop*; a *little*.
雨點子	rain-*drops*.
慢點	a *little* slower; slowly.
斑點	*spots*; *specks*.
幾點鐘	what o'clock is it? (*point*).
點書	to *punctuate*.
點數	*count* the number.
點團	to call over and *tick off* the names of the heads of the families in a parish.
點工活路	work paid *by* the day.
點狀元	to *attain* to the highest literary honours.
求你指點	please *instruct* me; *point out* to me.
好生打點	*beware*. [nearly got into a scrape.]
顯點兒	beware! you are a *marked* man; you
點腦殼	to *nod* the head.
遞個點子	to give one a *hint*.
點豌荳	to *sow* beans in patches; to *dibble*.
點燈	to *light* a lamp. [cending a hill.]
打個點子	to *swing* a chair up and down when as-
點水	to *inform on* a thief.
點心	*confectionery*.

8 黨 TANG³.
那一黨子人	that *class* of people.
我們黨家子	our *kindred*.
黨子行	the people of a *parish* or *ward*.

9 黯 NGAN³.
| 天色黯得很 | the sky is very *dark*; a *dull* day. |

15 黶 T'EN³.
| 黑黶黶的 | very *dark* or *sombre*. |

(592)

注 釋

黜 [tʂʰo⁵]
【你要黜拐】你要遭谴责。
【乱黜】鲁莽地用棍子或手杖推人。

點（点）[tien³]
【点书】给书加标点。
【点团】点名并给教区内家长的名字标上记号。
【好生打点】好好注意。
【显点儿】当心点儿。
【递个点子】暗示一下。
【点豌豆】播种豌豆。
【打个点子】上坡时轿子上下晃动（轿夫语）。
【点水】检举小偷。

黨（党）[taŋ³]
【那一党子人】那帮子人。
【我们党家子】党家子：同一家族的人。
【党子行】某一教区的人。

黯 [ŋan³]

黶 [tʰən³]

注释

黹 [tsɿ⁵]
黿(鼋) [yen²]
【癞头黿】癞蛤蟆。
鼎 [tin³]
鼓 [ku³]
鼕(冬) [toŋ¹] [toŋ²]
鼠 [su³] [suei³]
【地老鼠】鼹鼠；烟火。
【檐老鼠】蝙蝠。
【银鼠】貂。

黹 黿 4 鼎. 鼓 5 鼠.

The 204th radical. (黹)

CHĪ⁵.

鍼黹 — *needlework*.

The 205th radical. (黿)

ÜEN².

癩頭黿 — a *toad*.

The 206th radical. (鼎)

TIN³.

鼎鍋 — a pot with three ears made to stand on a [*tripod*.

The 207th radical. (鼓)

KU³.

堂鼓 — a *court-house* drum.
鼓起的 — *swollen*, as a limb; *risen*, as bread.
鼓劢 — *exert* yourself; make an effort.

TONG¹ ².

鼕鼕的響 — the *rolling sound* of a drum.

The 208th radical. (鼠)

SHU³, SHUE³.

老鼠 — a *rat*.
地老鼠 — a *mole*; catharine-wheel fireworks.
簷老鼠 — a *bat*.
銀鼠 — an *ermine*.

(593)

鼻 1-5 齊

The 209th radical. (鼻)

PI⁵.

鼻子	the *nose*.
草鞋鼻鼻	the *front strap* on a sandal.
針鼻子	the *eye* of a needle.

CH'IAO⁴.

鼽鼻子	a *turned-up* nose.
鼽起嘴	to *pout* the lips.

HAN⁴.

扯 p'u⁵ 鼾	to *snore*.

HEO¹.

儠得七齁八齁	*panting* with exhaustion.
齁喘	*asthma*.

ONG⁴.

說話齆聲齆氣的	to speak in a *nasal* tone; to speak through [the nose.
齆鼻子	a *stoppage* of the nose.
齆雷	*muffled* thunder.

The 210th radical. (齊)

TS'I².

一齊起身	start all *together*.
大家要齊心	we must be all of *one* mind.
人還沒有來齊	the people have not *all* come yet.
長齊了	to grow *of equal length*; *full*-grown.
場齊了	the market-place is *full*; the market is *at its height*.
他屋頭的人還齊全	his family is still *complete*, no members are lost.

(594)

注 释

鼻 [pi⁵]

鼽 [tɕʰiao⁴]
【鼽鼻子】朝天鼻。
【鼽起嘴】撅嘴，生气的样子。

鼾 [xan⁴]
【扯pʰu⁵鼾】打呼噜。

齁 [xəu¹]
【累得七齁八齁】因疲惫而喘息。
【齁喘】哮喘，气喘。

齆 [oŋ⁴]
【说话齆声齆气的】齆声齆气：鼻音重。
【齆鼻子】鼻孔堵塞而发音不清。
【齆雷】闷雷。

齊（齐）[tsʰi²]
【长齐了】生长完全。
【场齐了】市场客满了。

注释

【年事齐备了】过年的东西都准备好了。
齎（斋）[tṣaiˈ]
【斋公】素食者。
齒（齿）[tṣʰʅ³]
【没口齿的人】不诚实的人。
齩 [kʰo⁴]
齙（龅）[pao⁴]
齦（龈）[kən³] [kən⁴]
【龈骨头】啃骨头。
齼（龊）[tṣʰo⁵]
齷（龌）[o⁵]
齶（腭）[ŋo⁵]

齊 3　齒 5-9

3 齎	擺得整整齊齊的	all arranged in *good order*.
	年事齊備了	you are *prepared* for the New Year.
	CHAIˈ.	
	喫齎	to *fast* from meat.
	齎公	a *vegetarian*.
	書齎	a student's *room*; a *study*.

The 211th radical. (齒)

齒	CHʻĪ³.	
	取牙齒	to extract *teeth*.
	不好啟齒	I am ashamed to speak.
	沒口齒的人	a person with no sincerity.
	我們今天序齒	we will go by *age* to-day (polite).
	鋸子齒	the *teeth* of a saw.
5 齩	KʻO⁴.	
	齩瓜子	to *crack* melon seeds *with the teeth*.
齙	PAO⁴.	
6	齙牙齒	*protruding* teeth.
齦	KEN³.	
	齦骨頭	to *pick* or *gnaw* a bone.
	READ KEN⁴	
	牙齦	the *gums*; *tartar* on the teeth.
7 齼	CHʻO⁵.	for example of use see next.
9 齷	O⁵.	
	齷齼	*filthy*.
齶	NGO⁵.	
	舌抵上齶	put the tongue in the *roof of the mouth*.

(595)

西蜀方言

龍 6. 龜. 龠.

The 212th radical. (龍)

LONG².

龍王	King *Dragon*; Neptune.
尋龍脈	to seek for the *dragon's* pulse, as geo-mancers do.
耍龍燈	to parade with *dragon* lanterns.
過江龍	a *syphon*.
水龍	a *hose-pipe*.

K'AN¹.

神龕子	an idol *shrine*, either in a house or a temple.

The 213th radical. (龜)

KUE¹.

爲人學得烏龜法 得縮頭來且縮頭	in your life as a man try the *tortoise's* plan, pull your head safely in whenever you can.
龜頭	the *glans-penis*; a *cuckold*.
龜兒子	a *bastard*.

The 214th radical. (龠)

YO.

注 釋

龍（龙）[loŋ²]
【寻龙脉】龙脉：风水学称绵延的山脉为龙脉。
龕（龛）[kʰan¹]
龜（龟）[kuei¹]
龠 [yo]

注释

昭[tṣao³] 现多写作"遭"。

【我丨了】我被骗了，或我遭受了某件事。

【丨了几百钱】被骗了几百块钱，或花了几百块自己并不想花的钱。

【丨打】被打。

【风把我吹丨了】风把我吹生病了。

【我丨几口水】（游泳时）我呛了几口水。

唽[tṣe⁵]

【床笆丨】平放在床底部的竹架子。

啁[tṣəu¹]

吃[tṣʅ¹]

嗤[tṣʰʅ¹]

【药铺里莫乱动口，铁铺里莫乱丨手】嗤：伸。在药铺里不要随便吃东西，在铁铺里不要随便伸手。

咔[tɕʰia¹]

【瘦丨丨的】很瘦，"咔咔"为叠音后缀。

WORDS WITHOUT CHARACTERS.

NOTE.—With most of the words a character of the same sound, with the 30th radical added, has been given for the convenience of Chinese teachers. In some cases where the tones differ, a tone-mark has also been added.

啁	CHAO³.	sign of the *passive*. Ch.
我丨了		I am *taken in*; I have been *cheated* or *wronged*.
丨了幾百錢		*cheated* to the extent of a few hundred [cash.
丨打		to *receive* a beating.
風把我吹丨了		I have been *affected* by the wind; caught [cold.
丨一場病		I have *contracted* an illness.
我丨幾口水		I swallowed a few mouthfuls of water when in the river.
唽	CHE⁵.	
床笆丨		a bamboo *frame*, laid on the bottom of a [bed to retain the straw.
啁	CHEO¹.	
丨兒		*dung*.
吃	CHĪ¹.	
一丨子油		a basketful of oil (the baskets are papered [and varnished).
嗤	CH'Ī¹.	
藥鋪裏莫亂動口 鐵鋪裏莫亂丨手		you must not recklessly taste things in a medicine shop, nor carelessly *thrust forth* your hand in a smithy.
咔	CH'IA¹.	
瘦丨丨的		very lean.

CHIN-CHUAI.

Ch. 哜

CHIN⁴.
湯 | 了   the gravy has *congealed*.

CHIN⁴.
| 牙齒   to *set* the teeth *on edge*.

CHIN⁴.
| 翡翠   to *grow* mustachios or beard.

CH'IU¹.
當 | 二   domestic *servants*.

CH'ONG⁴.
| 鼻子   it has a strong smell, lit., *strongly affects* [the nose.

CH'Ü¹.
| 燈兒   pine splints dipped in sulphur and used [as *matches*.

CHUA³.
| 手兒   a man with a *palsied* hand.

CHUA⁵.
| 毽子   to *kick* the shuttlecock.
| 蹶子   to *kick*, or *fling*, like a horse.

CH'UA¹.
| 一 | 一的   in *strings* or *bunches* like beans.
筋筋 | | 的   *sinewy*, as meat; *stringy*, as vegetables.
爛 | | 的   *broken*; *fragmentary*.

CHUAI³.
細搖細 | 的   to *waddle* like a woman walking with bound feet.
你莫 | don't *shake* your head and refuse in that [way.

CHUAI⁴.
li⁴ 揎 | to *pommel* with the knuckles.

(598)

注 释

哜[tɕin⁴]
哜[tɕin⁴]
【| 牙齿】吃生冷刺激的食物时牙齿不舒服的感觉。
哜[tɕin⁴]
䞭[tɕʰiəu¹]
㨯[tʂʰoŋ⁴]
【| 鼻子】刺鼻。
嘔(呕)[tɕʰy¹]
唰[tʂua³]
【| 手儿】拿不稳东西的人。
啄[tʂua⁵]
【| 毽子】踢毽子。
[tʂʰua¹]
【| 一 | 一的】成束的。
【筋筋 | | 的】(食物)多筋的。
【烂 | | 的】有点损坏的,不太新鲜的。
[tʂuai³]现多写作"拽"。
【细摇细 | 的】走路很慢,脚步很小。
【你莫 | 】你不要太嚣张。
[tʂuai⁴]

注释

觉[tɕye⁵]
【｜人】骂人。

卷[tɕyen³]
【｜人】骂人。

㪚唹[fan⁴y²]
【何｜｜】犯得着吗?
【我才不｜｜】我才犯不着。

痱[fei⁴]现多写作"费"。
【娃娃｜】孩子很淘气。
【｜头子】淘气的、不听话的孩子。

䵝[fu³]
【墨｜｜的】像有一层雾气一样很模糊。

𪘧𪘲[fu⁵la⁵]
【结结｜｜的】结结巴巴的。

嗄[xa³]
【干｜事】做蠢事。
【你才是个｜保】你就是个傻子。

嗄[xa⁴]现多写作"哈"。
【等一｜】等一下。
【一｜买】全部一起买。
【定个｜数】（在心里）定个标准。

嚆[xao²]

㘥[xao⁴]

CHÜE-HAO.

CHÜE⁵.　　　　　　　　　　　　　　　Ch.
｜人　　　to *curse* people.　　　　　F.
　　　　　　　　　　　　　　　　　　H.
CHÜEN³.
｜人　　　to *curse* people.

FAN⁴-Ü².
何｜｜　　　what *right* had I to do it?
我纔不｜｜　then I am not *right*.

FE⁴.
娃娃｜　　　the child is *mischievous*, or *naughty*.
｜頭子　　　a *blackguard*.

FU³.
墨｜｜的　　*dusk*.

FU⁵-LA⁵.　　　　　　　　　　　　[speech.
結結｜｜　　*unintelligible*, as a book, or a person's

HA³.
幹｜事　　　to do *evil* deeds.
你纔｜　　　you are *reckless*, or *stupid*.
你纔是個｜保　you are a great *blockhead*.

HA⁴.　　　　may be a corruption of 下.
等一｜　　　wait a *little*.
一｜買　　　buy them *all*; buy the *whole lot*.
定個｜數　　fix a *number*; decide the *portions* or *lots*.

HAO².
安｜子　　　to set a fish, or eel *trap*.

HAO⁴.
把船｜倒　　*tie up* the boat to the bank.

(599)

HO-K'A.

H. I. K.

呵 吶 㓦 嗯 㖇 㗒 哟

	HO¹.	
	｜嘴皮	a *hare-lip*.
	HO¹.	
	｜皮	the outer board on timber, which has a [rounded side.
	HUA².	
	我不會｜算	I cannot *calculate*.
	打｜	to *reckon*; to *consider*.
	｜不來	I cannot *afford* it.
	｜拳	*guessing* fingers, a game played when [drinking.
	IEN⁴.	
	到處｜起	*scattered* everywhere.
	瘡上｜點藥	*sprinkle* a little medicine on the sore.
	IN¹.	
	蘿蔔｜｜	turnip and carrot *tops*.
	IO.	
		an exclamation, in any tone as occasion may require.
	KA³.	
	喫｜｜	to eat *meat*.
	他一身的好｜	he is a fat fellow; *full-fleshed*.
	K'A¹, CH'IA¹.	
	黑｜｜頭	a dark *hole* or corner.
	找那些背｜｜頭	search in the *spaces* behind cupboards, etc.
	門｜｜頭	the *space* behind the door.
	｜倒人	to *oppress* people; to *force* one.
	｜在壁縫子上	squeeze it into the crack in the wall.
	把衣裳｜起	*tuck* up your gown.
	豆芽｜牙齒	bean-sprouts *stick* in one's teeth.
	K'A¹³.	
	眼睛｜	my eyes *smart*, as when some foreign sub- [stance gets into them.

(600)

注 釋

呵[xo¹]
【｜嘴皮】兔唇。

呵[xo¹]

㓦 [xua²]现多写作"划"。
【我不会｜算】我不会精打细算，我不会计算。
【｜不来】不划算。

嗯[ien⁴]
【到处｜起】(一般指污渍)搞得到处都是。
【疮上｜点药】给伤口上点药。

㖇[in¹]
【萝卜｜｜】萝卜上端绿色的梗。

哟[io]语气词,表惊叹。

[ka³]
【喫｜｜】吃肉。
【他一身的好｜｜】他长了一身的肉。

[kʰa¹] [tɕʰia¹]
【黑｜｜头】光线很暗的角落里。
【门｜｜头】门背后。
【｜倒人】(门等)夹到人。
【豆芽｜牙齿】豆芽很容易塞牙。

[kʰa¹][kʰa³]
【眼睛｜】眼贼,眼睛好使。

注释

唧[kaŋ³]

吭[kʰaŋ²]
【｜背背】驼背。

吭[kʰaŋ³]
【把水缸｜倒】把水缸的盖子盖上。
【安｜｜】安装个盖子。
【隔墙尥簸箕晓得｜不｜得倒】隔着墙扔簸箕，不知道能不能盖住什么东西。
【｜帽子】戴帽子，形容把罪名或赞扬之词按在某人的头上。

喀[kei⁴]
【蛮｜｜的】形容人外表或行为很鲁莽。

呿[kʰe⁵]
【｜膝子】膝盖。

[kən²lən²koŋ²loŋ²]
【｜｜｜｜】小声地嘟哝或抱怨。

哏[kən⁴]
【垒个｜子】用草或泥垒个低埂。
【织的一｜一｜的】织的一顿一顿的，因为不娴熟而织得不顺畅。

吭[kʰən¹]

㧼[kʰəu²]
【拿碗｜倒】拿碗反过来盖住。

KANG-K'EO.   K.

KANG³.
｜結子   a *cross-grained* fellow.

K'ANG².
｜背背   a *humpback*.   [shouldered.
他的背有些｜   his back is a little *humped*; he is round-

K'ANG³.
把水缸｜倒   *cover* the water tank.
安｜｜   to set a *bird-trap*.
隔墙尥簸箕曉   } like throwing a winnowing-basket over a
得｜不｜得倒 } wall, who knows if it will *entrap* any-
              } thing or not.
｜帽子   to secretly *add* to the price of a thing.
你拿大帽子   } do you think to *overshadow*, or *overawe*
我嗎   } me with a pretence of power?

KE⁴.
蠻｜｜的   *big and coarse* in person.

K'E⁵.
｜膝子   the *knee*.

KEN²-LEN²-KONG²-LONG².
｜｜｜｜   indistinct *muttering*.

KEN⁴.
壘個｜子   throw up a low mud *wall*.
身上起了一｜   it raised a *wale* on my body.
織的一｜一｜的 *unevenly* woven.
一個高｜子   a high *bank*.

K'EN¹.
｜客   stingy.

K'EO².
拿盆｜倒   *cover* it with a basin.

(601)

KO-KUANG.

K. 哿　　KO⁵.

| 丨線 | to *twist* two threads *together*. |
| 兩個丨不得 | they are *unfriendly*. |

咕嚕　KU¹-LU¹.

| 二丨丨的轎子 | a two-*bearer* chair. |

咶　KUA³ ⁵.

| 左丨丨 | a left-handed person. |

啩　KUA⁴.

| 丨子船 | a house-boat. |

咶　KUA⁵.

| 丨苦 | very bitter. |

胯　K'UA³.

| 了丨 | the *fork* of a tree. |

胯　K'UA³.

丨衣裳	to *strip* off a person's clothes, as for debt.
牆丨了	the wall has *fallen*.
米價丨下來了	the price of rice has *fallen greatly*.
堰丨了	the dam has *burst*.

胯　K'UA⁵.

| 丨丨兒 | a bamboo *rake*. |

嚝　KUAŊ³.

| 丨忙些 | quickly ; quicker. |

嚝　KUAŊ³.

| 你纔是個丨丨 | you are a great *dolt*, or *blockhead*. |
| 打丨子 | to act the *rogue* ; to play the *knave*. |

䞈　KUAŊ⁴.

| 我丨你兩耳巴子 | I will *hit* you two slaps on the ear ; I will [*box* your ears. |

(602)

注　释

哿[ko⁵]

【兩个丨不得】两个人相处不好。

咕嚕[ku¹lu¹]

咶[kua³][kua⁵]

【左丨丨】左撇子。

啩[kua⁴]

咶[kua⁵]

【丨苦】很苦。

胯[kʰua³]

【了丨】("了"当作"丫"，见803页勘误表。) 丫胯：树丫，树杈。

胯[kʰua³]

【丨衣裳】脱（并不完全脱下）衣服。

【牆丨了】墙塌了。

【米价丨下来了】米价降下来了。

胯[kʰua⁵]

嚝[kuaŋ³]

【丨忙些】搞快点儿。

嚝[kuaŋ³]

【你才是个丨丨】你就是个不务正业的人，也有不仔细、马虎之意。

【打丨子】找借口掩饰。

䞈[kuaŋ⁴]

【我丨你两耳巴子】我扇你两耳光。

注释

哐[kuaŋ⁴]

唻[lai⁴]

啷[laŋ³]

【革丨他几句】责骂或讽刺他几句。

啷[laŋ³] [noŋ³]现常写作"啷"。

【丨个】干嘛? 怎么样?

唠[lao¹]

【松松丨丨的】(草或粮食等)长得很稀疏,密度很小。

【这点活路稀丨松】这点儿工作很轻松。

唠[lao¹]现多写作"捞"。

【丨一点泡菜吃】(从泡菜坛里)夹点儿泡菜出来。

佬[lao³]

【丨火】困难的;不舒服的;看着让人着急的。

啦[lən⁴]

【丨冰】整块的冰。

哩[li¹]

【花丨丨的】颜色太多的。

【花丨ku³ tang³的】花里胡哨的。

哩[li⁴]

【丨巴儿来的】专程来的。

KUANG-LI.

KUANG⁴.

| 油　　a kind of *varnish* made by boiling the oil [of Aleurites, or t'ong-in.
| 過兩道　it has been *varnished* twice (two coats).
顏色放 |　the paint is *brilliant*.

LAI⁴.

水 |　the water is *scalding hot*.

LANG³.

革 | 他幾句　*reprove* him.

LANG³ or NANG³.

| 個　*how?*

LAO¹.

鬆鬆 | | 的　*loosely* piled up, as grass, etc.
這點活路稀 | 鬆　this little job is very *easy*.
稀稀 | | 生了點　the seed has come up very *thinly*.

LAO¹.

| 一點泡菜喫　*take* some pickle out of the jar for dinner.
| 黃鱔　to *catch* eels.

LAO³.

| 布細子　to *carry* rolls of cloth *on the shoulder* like [a peddler.
| 火　*grievous; dreadful.*
望你 | 大鎚　I look to you to help me greatly.

LEN⁴.

| 冰　*ice.*

LI¹.

花 | | 的　*variegated; gaily coloured.*
花 | ku³ tang³ 的　*daubed; mottled; besmirched.*

LI⁴.

| 巴兒來的　I came *on purpose.*

LI-MI.

L.
M.

哽　　　LI⁴.
｜揣　chuai⁴　　to *pommel* with the knuckles.

　　　　LIA³.
｜起的　　　*slanting; sloping; askew.*

唥　　　LIN².
抖｜｜戰　　　to *tremble*.

嚠　　　LIU¹.
紅｜｜的　　　*bright* red.
｜尖的　　　*very* sharp-pointed.
一｜地方　　　a *narrow strip* of land.
一｜布　　　a *narrow strip* of cloth.

柳　　　LIU³.
猪背｜　　　*chine* of pork.

嚅　　　LO³.
｜連　　　*slow; dilatory.*
一天｜一天　　　to *delay* from day to day.
｜子果子的話　　　*mumbled* words; *vague, uncertain, indefi-*[nite talk.

嗎　　　MA².
你｜不倒我　　　you cannot *hoodwink* me.

嗎　　　MA².
喫｜娃兒了　　　*drunk.*

𠳕　　　MANG¹.
｜娃娃的飯　　　to *chew* food for an infant.
喫｜｜　　　to *eat* food so chewed.

眯　　　MI¹.
笑｜｜的　　　*smilingly; laughingly.*

(604)

注　釋

哽[tṣuai⁴]
　[lia³]
【｜起的】斜着的，没对齐的。
唥[lin²]
【抖｜｜战】发抖，打颤。
嚠[liəu¹]
【红｜｜的】红得发亮的。
【｜尖的】非常尖。
【一｜地方】一段比较狭长的地方。
柳[liəu³]
【猪背｜】猪背部的肉。
嚅[lo³]
【｜连】拖沓，动作慢。
【一天｜一天】（事情）一天一天地往后拖。
嗎[ma²]现多写作"麻"。
【你｜不到我】你骗不了我。
嗎[ma²]
【吃｜娃儿了】喝多了，喝醉了。
𠳕[maŋ¹]
【｜娃娃的饭】喂孩子吃饭。
【吃｜｜】吃饭。
眯[mi¹]现多写作"眯"。
【笑｜｜的】即笑眯眯的。

注释

咪[mi⁴]
【打个｜头】扎个猛子。
【水｜子】水性很好的人。

呡[min¹]
【｜甜】非常甜。呡：表示程度很深。

呡[min³]现多写作"抿"。
【打个｜笑】微微一笑。
【拿在口头｜】放在嘴里抿，不咬碎。

哞[mo³]
【那个路是｜斜｜斜的】那个路是有点儿斜斜的。

幪[moŋ²]
【蛋｜｜】鸡蛋上的白膜。

嗼[mu²] [ŋa1kʰa¹]
【｜｜人】强迫人，折磨人。

啌[ŋaŋ¹]
【耳朵｜】耳朵老是听到响声。

噁[ŋo⁵]
【草｜坏了】因为潮湿导致草腐烂。
【衣服｜齨了】衣服因潮湿而长霉或有气味。

[n.ia¹]
【放｜】撒娇。
【｜声｜气的说话】嗲声嗲气地说话。

MI-NIA.

M.
N.

MI⁴.

打個｜頭 — to *dive*.
水｜子 — a *diver*.

MIN¹. probably a corruption of 蜜.

｜甜 — *very sweet*.

MIN³.

打個｜笑 — to *smile*.
｜笑｜笑的 — *smilingly*; *smirkingly*.
拿在口頭｜ — *suck* it in your mouth, as a medicine.

MO³.

那個路是｜斜｜斜的 } that road is an *easy* incline.
｜斜坡 — a *gentle* slope.

MONG².

蛋｜｜ — the *pellicle* of an egg.

MU².

｜子 — thick *woolen cloth* about 6 inches wide.

NGA¹-K'A¹. [ingly.

｜｜人 — to *force* people; to treat people *overbear-*

NGANG¹.

耳朵｜ — a *ringing sound* in the ears.

NGO⁵.

草｜壞了 — the grass is *musty*.
衣服｜齨了 — the clothes are *rotted with damp*.

NIA¹.

放｜ — *wheedling*.
娃娃放｜ — a child *whining* for something. [voice.
｜聲｜氣的說話 — to talk in a *drawling*, or *affected*, tone of

西蜀方言

NIANG-P'A.

N. O. P.

嚷 NIANG¹.
你做丨個兒　what are you doing?

妞 NIU⁴.
丨都丨不得　I cannot *move* it, as a painful limb.
丨不動　you *walk* very slowly.
丨起點　hurry up?

嗡 ONG⁴.
丨起丨起的熱　very *close* and hot, as on a dull day in [summer.

呢 P'A¹.
床鋪丨和得好　the bed is *nice* and *soft*.
煮的稀流丨　boiled very *soft*; *sloppy*.
路稀丨爛　the road is very *muddy*.
衣裳稀丨爛　the clothes are very *ragged*.
打得稀丨爛　broken into *fragments*.
我人丨得很　I am very *weak*.
我要丨些嗎　am I going to be the *softy*?
你繞丨疲　you are really *cowardly*.
丨耳朵　a hen-pecked husband, lit., *soft ears*.
他的功名是丨的　his degree is a bought one.

呢啦 P'A¹-LA¹.
說了一丨丨　he uttered a *torrent of words*.

呢 P'A².
下丨　the lower *jaw*.

呢薩 P'A²-SA¹.
嘆氣丨丨　*sighing* and *whining*.

呢 P'A².
丨頭　a large *lever* used for straightening leaning [houses.

(606)

注　釋

嚷[ȵiaŋ¹]
【你做丨个儿】你在干嘛?
妞[ȵiəu⁴]
【丨都丨不得】因为身体原因而动不了。
【丨起点】赶紧行动起来。
嗡[oŋ⁴]
【丨起丨起的热】很闷热。
呢[pʰa¹]现多写作"耙"。
【煮得稀流丨】（食物）因煮的时间长而很软。
【路稀丨烂】稀呢: 表示程度深。路特别不平或泥泞。
【我人丨得很】我（因为生病）而没有力气。
【我要丨些吗】我是好欺负的吗?
【你才丨疲】你真是太懦弱了。
【丨耳朵】指怕老婆的男子。
【他的功名是丨的】他的功名是不正当途径得来的。
呢啦[pʰa¹la¹]
【说了一丨丨】说了一大堆。
呢[pʰa²]
【下丨】即下巴。
呢薩[pʰa²sa¹]
【叹气丨丨】不停地叹气。
呢[pʰa²]

注释

唻[pai¹]
【｜子】即瘸子。
【跳｜｜脚】只用一只脚跳着走。

啡[pʰai¹]
【拿手一｜】用手轻轻一掸。

啡[pʰai³]

斑[pan¹]
【｜干柴】将干的柴火折断备用。
【｜舵】搬动船舵，即掌舵。
【｜包谷】掰玉米。

哞[pʰan⁴]现多写作"绊"。
【｜倒】即绊倒。

𢶍[pʰan¹]

𢶍[pʰan²]
【舌头有些｜】说话有点儿结巴。

啉[pʰan⁴]

嘣[paŋ¹]
【｜硬】嘣：表示程度很深。非常硬。
【人到硬｜】人身体强壮。
【｜臭】特别臭。

嘭[pʰaŋ³]
【｜坏了】碰坏了。

PAI-P'ANG.

P.

PAI¹.

| 子 — a *lame* man.
跳 | | 脚 — to *hop* on one foot.

P'AI¹.

拿手一 | — give it a *flick* with your hand.

P'AI³.

一 | 長 — a *fathom* long; 5 feet or ½ a chang, measured with the arms.

PAN¹.

| 乾柴 — to *break off* dry branches for fuel.
| 舵 — to *work* the helm of a boat.
| 包穀 — to *gather* maize.

P'AN⁴.

| 倒 — to *fall down*.

P'AN¹.

| 胸 — the breast-band on a horse's harness.

P'AN².

舌頭有些 | — he has an *impediment* in his speech.

P'AN⁴.

| 蠟樹 — to *rent* white wax trees.

PANG¹.

| 硬 — very *hard*.
人到硬 | — I am *strong* in body.
| 臭 — very *stinking*.

P'ANG³.

| 壞了 — spoiled through being *knocked*.
| 拐子 — to *nudge* with the elbow.
他兩個有一 | — they are *equals* at anything; well *matched*.

(607)

P'AO-P'IA.

P. 拋

P'AO¹.

穀子嘟｜	the grain is *filling*.
桑｜兒	*mul*berries.
茨｜兒	bramble *berries*.
蛇｜兒	*straw*berries, or the fruit of Fragaria [japonica.

啃

PE³.

| 把火｜倒 | *bank* the fire. |
| 把事情｜倒 | to *smother* up a quarrel. |

呲

P'E¹.

| ｜手 | to *harden* or *season* the hands for boxing. |

喯

PEN⁴.

一些｜	to *mix* up; to *tumble* things about.
稽巴饟｜糖	to *roll* the glutinous rice balls among treacle when eating them.
｜胙脺	to *devil* meat.

嘭

P'EN¹.

｜在門方上	to *lean* against the door-post.
｜六扇門	to be a runner in a yamên.
｜椅	a *resting*-chair; an arm-chair.
嘴都｜了	his lips are *sunken*, from the loss of teeth.
不要來｜倒我	don't *rely on*, or *toady on*, me.
喫｜｜飯	to *sponge on* another for food.

PIA³.

| 缸子是個｜的 | the water-pot is a *distorted* one. |

P'IA³. [cracked pot.

敲得｜｜的響	to emit a *dull* sound when struck, like a
黃｜｜的	*yellow*.
淡｜｜的	*insipid*; *tasteless*.
餓｜｜的	*hungry*.
鞋子穿｜了	his shoes are worn down at one side.

(608)

注 释

拋[pʰao¹]
【桑｜兒】即桑葚。
【茨｜兒】茨菰。
【蛇｜兒】草莓。

啃[pei³]
【把火｜倒】把火扑灭。
【把事情｜倒】解决棘手的事情, 平息争端。

呲[pʰei¹]

喯[pən⁴]

嘭[pʰən¹]
【｜在门方上】靠在门上。
【｜六扇门】在衙门里当差。
【｜椅】有扶手的椅子。
【不要来｜倒我】不要靠着我。
【喫｜｜饭】依靠别人生活。

[pia³]
【缸子是个｜的】缸子是畸形的, 有点儿往里面凹的。

[pʰia³]
【敲得｜｜的响】敲得啪啪的响。
【黃｜｜的】颜色黄黄的, 也有水果、蔬菜黄了不新鲜的意思。
【淡｜｜的】味道很淡的。
【饿｜｜的】有点儿饿了。
【鞋子穿｜了】鞋子因为穿久了鞋帮往一个方向歪。

注释

[piaŋ²]
【买个老丨丨牛】买头很老的牛。

嘌[piao¹]

咧[pie⁴]
【看火砲丨倒你】小心火炮蹦到你。

唠[pʰie⁵]现多写作"别"。
【把门丨到】把门的插销插上,把门反锁上。
【门丨子】锁门用的插销。

[pʰien³] [pien³]
【在那山丨丨上】在山边上。

哖哖唪唪[pin¹pin¹poŋ¹poŋ¹]
【丨丨丨丨】象声词,同"噼里啪啦",形容声音很大。

啵[po¹]

嘴[po⁴]现多写作"啵"。
【打个丨】亲嘴。

哱[po⁵]

PIANG-PO.

P.

PIANG².

買個老丨丨牛　　buy an *old* cow.

PIAO¹.

按丨了　　it *spurted* from my grasp; he *escaped* my [clutches.

PIE⁴.　　same meaning as 爆.

丨穀花　　to *pop* rice for making sweetmeats.
沙胡荳丨得好　　the beans *crackle* well in the pan.
看火砲丨倒你　　take care lest the crackers *shoot* against [you.
丨芽子　　to *sprout*.
把他激得丨丨跳　　it made him *hop* about with anger.
丨呱呱　　to *cry* like a child.
丨了　　*cracked*, as glass.
桶箍丨了　　the hoops of the bucket have *burst*.

Pʼ IE⁵.

把針丨在罩子上　　*stick* the needle into the bed-curtains.
把門丨倒　　*bar* the door.
門丨子　　a door *bar* (small).

Pʼ IEN³, PIEN³.

在那山丨丨上　　on the *side* of that hill.

PIN¹-PIN¹-PONG¹-PONG¹.

丨丨丨丨　　a *banging* sound.

PO¹.

丨絲網　　a *spider's* web.

PO⁴.

打個丨　　to give a *kiss*.

PO⁵.

犁丨子　　the *stock* of a plough.

(609)

P'O-RAN.

P. R. 嚩 P'O³.

| 倒錢不上算 | to *lose* money is of no consequence in this [matter. |
| 一 \| 人 \| 死十人難當 | if one man will *risk* his life ten men will hardly withstand him. |

嚩 P'O⁵.

| 一 \| 人 | a *company* of men. |
| 一 \| 斑子 | a *troupe* of players. |

嘣 PONG⁴.

| 在牆邊	*prop* it against the wall.
| 倒山邊走	go *along* the side of the hill.
魯班雖巧 | 墨而行	although Lu-pan was clever he worked *according* to the marking line—met., though clever you must act *according* to rectitude.

嘣 PONG⁴.

| 打個 \| | to *kiss*. |

**** P'ONG³, PONG³.

| \| 的一聲 | a *bang*, like the sound of a gun. |

哺 PU¹.

| 沒得牙齒嘴都 \| 進去了 | I have no teeth, and now my lips are *sunken*. |

嘈 P'U³.

| 墨 \| \| 的 | *dusk*; dark. |

咐 P'U³.

| 扯 \| 鼾 | to *snore*. |

咐 P'U⁵.

| 放 \| 鴿兒 | to fly a *decoy* pigeon; husband and wife [scheming to trap a rich man. |

嘫呱呱 RAN²-UA³-UA³.

| \| \| \| 的 | *dilatory*; difficult to swallow, as half [cooked food. |

(610)

注 释

嚩[pʰo³]
嚩[pʰo⁵]
【一丨人】一大批人。
【一丨斑子】一个（演艺或政治上的）班子。
[poŋ⁴]
【丨在墙边】靠在墙边。
【丨倒山边走】沿着山边走。
【鲁班虽巧丨墨而行】鲁班的手艺虽然巧妙，但也必须得沿着画好的墨迹来做。比喻人即使再聪明，也必须要依照规矩做事。
嘣[poŋ⁴] [pʰoŋ³] [poŋ³]
【丨的一声】即砰的一声，形容声音很大。
哺[pu¹]
【没得牙齿嘴都丨进去了】因为没有牙齿，导致嘴唇往里凹陷。
嘈[pʰu³]
【墨丨丨的】感觉像蒙着一层雾气而很模糊。
咐[pʰu³]
【扯丨鼾】打鼾。
咐[pʰu⁵]
嘫呱呱 [zan²ua³ua³]
【丨丨丨的】办事拖拉的；（因食物半生不熟）难以下咽的。

注释

嚷[zaŋ⁴]
【水丨进屋来了】水淹到屋子里来了。

哰 [zɿ³]
[zɿ⁵]动物的交配行为,也是用来骂人的脏话。
[zua²]
【丨面】揉面。
【这个活路丨人】这个工作比较麻烦,很磨人。
【丨泥巴饼饼】揉泥巴,代指干农活。
【丨了一百钱下来】硬是扣了一百块钱下来。

撒[sa⁵]
【炒的干丨丨的】(食物)吵得很干,没有水分。

嗓[saŋ³]
【丨性点】麻利点。
【走人户离丨】走亲戚很洒脱麻利(含不被家务牵绊之意)。
【房子亮丨】即房子亮堂。

嗮[sao⁴]现多写作"潲"。
【肉丨子】即肉沫做的浇头。
【丨水】即潲水,喂牲口的剩菜。

嵕[sən³]

嗖[səu¹]
【娄丨得很】形容人身上很脏,不修边幅的样子。

RANG-SEO.

R. S.

嚷 RANG⁴.
丨棉袄 to *stuff* a gown with cotton wool.
丨肠 the intestines of an animal *stuffed* with minced meat; sausages.
水丨進屋來了 the water has *inundated* the house.

哰 RĬ³.
丨在水裏頭 throw it into the water.
RĬ⁵. *copulate*; a word indiscriminately used in cursing.
RUA².
丨麵 to *knead* dough.
你莫丨我 don't *knock* me about.
這個活路丨人 this job is very *tiresome*.
丨泥巴 to *mix* mud for plastering.
丨泥巴餅餅 *farming*.
好生莫丨爛了 take care and not *rub* it to bits.
丨了一百錢下來 I beat him *down* a hundred cash.

撒 SA⁵.
炒的乾丨丨的 the food is fried too *dry*.

嗓 SANG³.
丨性點 be *quick*. [duties.
走人戶離丨 *free* to go visiting; not tied by household
房子亮丨 the room is light and *bright*.

嗮 SAO⁴. [celli.
肉丨子 minced meat and *gravy* eaten with vermi-
丨水 kitchen *slops*.

嵕 SEN³.
酒丨丨 a wine *jar*.
長得丨莊 a *stout* person.

嗖 SEO¹.
䯓丨得很 very *troublesome*, *dirty* or *mischievous*.

(611)

SĬ-SHAO.

S. Sh.	嘶	SĬ¹.	
	｜臭		stinking, as spoiled food or damp clothes.
	嗩	SIAO¹.	
	打兩個｜		fix the boards together with two cross-bars mortised across the back of them.
	｜楔兒		the catch of a rat-trap; the snib of a door; the string of a puppet.
	哓	SIE¹.	
	盆子曬｜了		the tub is cracked with the drought.
	｜起口哭		crying there with your mouth open.
	｜牙露齒		to show the teeth, like a dog; protruding [teeth.
	呦	SIU².	
	｜皮		slow; dilatory.
	｜臉		brazen; with no sense of shame.
	娃娃｜得很		the child is very mischievous.
	䯳	SONG².	
	餓｜		gluttonous; greedy.
	㳘	SÜEN⁴.	
	兩｜後		the wives of brothers.
	䚎	SÜIN⁴.	
	｜白		pure white.
	吵	SHA⁴.	
	｜帕		a straining cloth.
	吵	SHA⁴.	
			same as 甚麼.
	你做｜子		what are you doing?
	爲｜子		why?
	沒得｜子東西		there is not anything.
	是｜人都有		there are all sorts of men.
	哨	SHAO¹.	
	花兒烏｜		daubed; mottled.

(612)

注释

嘶[sɿ¹]
【｜臭】腐烂的臭味。

嗩[siao¹]

哓[sie¹]
【盆子晒｜了】盆子因为晒久了而变得很脆，易折。
【｜起口哭】张着嘴露出牙来哭。
【｜牙露齿】露出牙齿，指嬉皮笑脸。

呦[siəu²]
【｜皮】缓慢的，拖拉的。
【｜脸】脸皮厚的，不知羞耻的。
【娃娃｜得很】小孩子很不听话，骂了也不听。

䯳[soŋ²]
【饿｜】形容吃东西狼吞虎咽的样子，或特别贪吃的样子。

㳘[syen⁴]

䚎[syn⁴]
【｜白】纯白。

吵[ʂa⁴]
吵[ʂa⁴]现多写作"啥子"。
【你做｜子】你在干什么?
【为｜子】为什么?
【是｜人都有】真是什么人都有。

哨[ʂao¹]
【花儿乌｜】颜色很杂的，花里胡哨的。

注释

唏咙[ɕi1xua1zˌ]

呲呀[sˌ4tɕiai4]

嘏[ɕia¹][xa¹]

【拿|耙儿|谷子】用耙把稻谷抓得分散开。

【不要鸡去|】不要乱动某物,或不要随便去把某物抓散。

【账多了|不开】外债太多理不清楚或无法承受。

㗛[ɕiao¹]

【|铺盖】踢被子。

听[ɕin³]

【|了耍】无聊,爱恶作剧。

【你莫|】你不要犹豫了。

听[ɕin²]

【布|】布变得松松垮垮的。

嘘[ɕy¹]

【||眼】眼睛半睁半闭的。

哒[tai³][tai²]现多写作"逮"。

【|倒】抓住,逮住。

嚏[tʰai¹]

【|点棉花】往某物里塞点儿棉花。

嚪[tan³]

噹[taŋ¹]

【茶||】一种竹制有长柄的舀水用的器具。

SHI -TANG

		Sh. T.

SHÏ¹-HUA¹-RĬ.

| | 兒 跌 倒 | I *nearly* fell. |
| | 兒 走 不 攏 | I was *almost* unable to reach the place. |

SHÏ⁴-CHIAI⁴.

| 銅 | | | brass *hinges*. |

SHIA¹ HA¹. [the mats.

拿	耙 兒	穀 子	bring the *grain-rake* and *rake* the grain on
不 要 雞 去		don't let the hens go and *scrape* it. [up.
賬 多 了	不 開	my debts are so many I cannot *clear them*

SHIAO¹.

給 他 一		give him a *push*.
	鋪 蓋	*throw off* the bed quilt.
	在 河 裏 頭	*push* it into the river.

SHIN³.

| | 了 耍 | *horse-play*; practical joking. |
| 你 莫 | | don't be *boisterous*. |

SHIN².

| 布 | | the cloth is *loosely woven*. |

SHÜ¹. [sighted.

| | | 眼 | *bleared* eyes; *peering* closely at, as if short- |

TAI³ ².

| | 倒 | to *catch*; *catch* him. |
| | 倒 人 沒 有 | have you *caught* him or not ? |

T'AI¹. [a collar.

| | 點 棉 花 | *pad* or *stuff* it with a little cotton wool, as |

TAN³.

| | 巴 | a residuum from salt. |

TANG¹.

| 茶 | | | a water-*ladle* made of bamboo. |

TANG-TO.

T.

噇 噔 噔 嵉 唗

叮 叮 嚉

	T'ANG⁴.	
斗丨子		a *striker* for leveling grain in the measure.
	TEN¹.	
馬丨子		a riding *jacket*.
	TEN¹.	
臉丨兒紅紅的		his *cheeks* are rosy.
	T'EN³.	
慢丨丨的		*slow*; *dawdling*.
	TEO¹.	
丨狗兒咬人 丨娃娃罵人		to *tease* a dog till it bites, or child till he curses.
丨鷄要一把米 丨羊子要一把草		to *entice* a chicken you need a handful of rice, to *entice* a sheep you need a handful of grass.
要丨人愛莫討 八嫌		you should *induce* people to love you, not to dislike you.
丨病痛		*constantly* ailing.
丨唎唎		*incessantly* fretful.
	TIA¹.	
丨起來		*lift* it up.
給我丨回去		*carry* it back home for me.
	T'IA³.	
粧丨眼皮		to pretend not to have seen; lit., pretend [to *drop* the eyelids.
	TIN¹.	
掉丨		to lose *money* in business.
	TIN¹.	
一丨丨兒		a *very little*.
	TO⁵.	
碗丨丨		the *bottom* of a basin.

(614)

注　释

噇[tʰaŋ⁴]
噔[tən¹]
噔[tən¹]
嵉[tən³]
【慢丨丨的】慢悠悠的。
唗[təu¹]现多写作"逗"。
【丨狗儿咬人,丨娃娃骂人】把狗逗得要咬人,把小孩儿逗得要骂人。
[tia¹]
【丨起来】提起来。
【给我丨回去】把这个替我提回去。
[tʰia³]
叮[tin¹]
叮[tin¹]
【一丨丨儿】同"一丢丢",一点儿,很少。
嚉TO⁵[to⁵]
【碗丨丨】碗底部的凸出来的一圈。

注 释

嚲[to⁵]
【｜窗子】把纸窗户戳破。
【把阴沟｜通】把堵上的阴沟疏通。
【｜个橙子下来】用竹竿儿把树上的橙子戳下来。
【十个说客敌不住一个｜客】十个支持的人抵不过一个说坏话的人。

㦂[toŋ³]
【打光｜｜】不穿衣服。

㦂[toŋ³]
【黑脸｜嘴】黑着脸嘟着嘴，形容人脸色不好看。

嘟[tu⁵]
【｜杵杵的】形容人的身材矮胖粗短的。

嘶[tsʰan²]

囃[tsaŋ²][tsaŋ³]
【｜核桃】把核桃壳敲碎。

唣[tsao⁴]
【虫把树子｜空子】虫把树里面啃噬空了。

嗾[tsəu⁴]
【｜｜】瓶子等的塞子。
【好生｜倒】好好儿塞住。

唧[tsi¹]
【酸｜｜的】酸酸的。

TO-TSI.

嚲	TO⁵.	T. Ts. [finger.
｜窗子		to *perforate* a paper window with the
把陰溝｜通		*push* a rod through the drain to clean it.
｜個橙子下來		*knock* a pumelo *down with a pole*.
｜草上來		*fork* up the straw.
｜肋巴骨		to *tickle* one's ribs; to *poke* fun at.
十個說客敢不住一個｜客		ten peace makers cannot withstand one *mischief maker*.

㦂 TONG³.
打光｜｜　　to go with the *body* naked.
山｜｜　　a bare *peak*.

㦂 TONG³.
黑臉｜嘴　　black looks and *pouting* lips.

嘟 TU⁵.
｜杵杵的　　*stumpy*, as a pencil.
｜尾子狗　　a dog with a *stumped* tail.

嘶 TS'AN².　　same as 別.
我們不說｜的　　we will not speak about any *other* subject.
是｜的人　　it is *another* person.

囃 TSANG², ³.
｜核桃　　to *break* or *crack* walnuts.
你莫｜　　don't *shame* me in that way.
｜房　　a wedding custom.

唣 TSAO⁴.
虫把樹子｜空子　　worms have *bored* the tree hollow.

嗾 TSEO⁴.
｜｜¹　　a *cork*; a *stopper* for a bottle, or a jar.
好生｜倒　　*cork* it carefully.

唧 TSI¹.
酸｜｜的　　*sour*.

(615)

西蜀方言

TSI-Ü.

Ts. Ü.

TSI⁵-LI³-KU³-LU³.

噦 ｜｜｜｜ gabbling, like the language of foreigners.

TS'Ï¹.

膩 ｜｜的 grudging.

TS'Ï²-PU⁵-LONG³-TONG³.

｜不｜｜ naked.

TS'IANG¹.

嗆 給你｜點錢 I want to *borrow* some money from you [(without interest).

沒得錢｜給你 I have no money to *lend* you.

TS'IAO⁴.

哨 這兩天的肉｜ butcher's meat is *scarce* just now.

人｜ workmen are *scarce*, as in harvest time.

TSIU¹.

揪 圓｜｜的 globular.

TSONG³.

㧡 我｜成你買房子 I will *assist* you to buy a house; I will [*recommend* you.

TS'UAN¹.

嚃 你亂｜嗎 you are *intruding* here.

跌跌｜｜的 to *stagger* like a little child or a drunk [person.

｜瞌睡 to *nod* with sleep.

TS'UE¹.

啐 ｜壺 a large kettle.

Ü².

吤 弄｜帖了 prepared; ready.

Ü⁴.

嘀 用｜了 worn with use.

嘴巴皮說｜了 my lips are *worn* away with speaking.

Ü⁴.

嘀 把蠶子｜了 the silk-worms have been killed by a [*stench*.

小｜ urine.

(616)

注 释

[tsi⁵li³ku³lu³]
【｜｜｜｜】说话含含糊糊的，让人完全听不懂。

噦[tsʰꞮ¹]
【膩｜｜的】因为有油而很滑腻的状态。

[tsʰꞮ²pu⁵loŋ³toŋ³]

嗆[tsʰiaŋ¹]
【给你｜点钱】向你借点儿钱。

哨[tsʰiao⁴]
【这两天的肉｜】这两天的肉供不应求。
【人｜】人手紧缺。

揪[tsiəu¹]
【圆｜｜的】即圆滚滚的。

㧡[tsoŋ³]

嚃[tsʰuan¹]
【跌跌｜｜的】即跌跌撞撞的。
【｜瞌睡】打瞌睡。

啐[tsʰuei¹]
【｜壺】壶嘴很长的壶。

吤[y²]
【弄｜贴了】弄妥帖了，准备好了。

嘀[y⁴]
【用｜了】使用太久而损坏了。
【嘴巴皮说｜了】嘴皮都快说破了。

嘀[y⁴]

TABLE OF RELATIONSHIPS.

1. Father's Family.

Father.

Father	父親
Father (direct address)	{ 爹 / 爺 / 爸 }
Father (vulgar)	{ 老漢兒 / 老人家 }

Father's Brother.

Father's elder brother	{ 伯父 / 胞伯 / 伯伯 }
Father's elder brother (according to rank) ...	{ 大爺 / 二爺 / 三爸 }
Father's elder brother (according to rank) ...	{ 大滿 / 二滿 / 三滿 }
Father's elder brother's wife	{ 伯娘 / 大嬸 / 大媽 / 大娘 }
Father's younger brother	{ 胞叔父 / 叔叔 / 叔叔 }
Father's youngest brother	幺叔
Father's younger brother's wife	{ 叔娘 / 嬸娘 }
Father's brother's sons	叔伯弟兄
Father's brother's son (elder)	哥哥

(617)

FATHER'S BROTHER.

Wife of the last ...	大嫂嫂 / 嫂嫂
Father's brother's son (younger)	兄弟
Wife of the last	弟媳
Father's brother's daughters	叔伯姊妹
Father's brother's daughter (elder)	姐姐
Husband of last ...	姐夫 / 姐丈
Father's brother's daughter (younger)	妹妹
Husband of last ...	妹夫 / 妹弟
Father's brother's grandson	姪兒子 / 姪男 / 姪

Father's Sister.

Father's sister ...	姑娘 / 姑母
Father's sister's husband ...	姑爺 / 姑父
Father's sister's son	老表
Father's sister's son (elder)	表兄
Father's sister's son (younger)	表弟
Father's sister's son's wife	表嫂
Father's sister's daughter ...	表姊妹
Father's sister's daughter (elder)	表姐
Father's sister's daughter (younger)	表妹
Father's sister's grandson	表姪
Father's sister's granddaughter ...	表姪女

Grandfather.

Grandfather ...	祖爺公 / 父爺公

(618)

GRANDFATHER.　　　　　　　　　　　　BROTHER.

Grandmother	{ 祖母 奶奶 婆婆
Grandfather's brother	叔祖
Grandfather's brother (eldest)	大祖
Grandfather's brother (second)	二祖
Grandfather's brother (youngest)	幺祖
Grandfather's brother's son (elder)	伯父
Grandfather's brother's son (younger)	叔父
Grandfather's brother's son (youngest)	幺叔
Grandfather's brother's grandsons	同堂弟兄
Grandfather's sister	姑婆
Grandfather's sister's husband	姑公
Grandfather's sister's son	表叔

Great-grandfather.

Great-grandfather	{ 曾祖 太公
Great-grandmother	{ 曾祖母 太婆

Great-great-grandfather.

Great-great-grandfather	高祖
Great-great-grandmother	高祖母

Brother.

Elder brother	{ 兄哥 胞哥
Elder brother's wife	嫂嫂
Eldest brother	大哥
Eldest brother's wife	大嫂
Second brother (older)	二哥

BROTHER.		SISTER.
Second brother's wife	... ...	二嫂
Younger brother	... ...	{胞弟 / 兄弟}
Fourth brother (younger)	... ...	四弟
Youngest brother	... ...	{幺弟兒 / 弟娃}
Younger brother's wife	... ...	弟媳
Brother's son	... ...	{姪兒 / 姪子 / 姪男}
Brother's son's wife	... ...	姪媳
Brother's daughter	... ...	姪女
Brother's daughter's husband	... ...	姪女婿
Brother's grandson	... ...	姪孫
Brother's granddaughter	... ...	姪孫女

Sister.

Elder sister	... ...	{胞姐 / 姐姐}
Eldest sister	... ...	大姐
Second sister (elder)	... ...	二姐
Third sister (elder)	... ...	三姐
Elder sister's husband	... ...	{姐丈 / 姐夫}
Younger sister	... ...	{胞妹 / 妹妹}
Third sister (younger)	... ...	三妹
Youngest sister	... ...	幺妹
Husband of younger sister	... ...	{妹丈 / 妹夫}
Sister's son	... ...	{外姪子 / 外姪}
Sister's daughter	... ...	外姪女

(620)

Son.

Son	兒子
Son (polite)	少爺
Son (eldest)	{ 大公子 老大
Son (second)	{ 二公子 二老
Son (youngest)	{ 幺兒子 老幺
Son's wife	媳婦
Son's wife (direct address)	{ 姑兒 女兒

Daughter.

Daughter	{ 女兒子 女女娘 姑
Daughter (polite)	{ 小姐 千金
Daughter's husband	{ 女婿 乾兒
Daughter's son	外孫
Daughter's daughter	外孫女

Grandson.

Grandson	{ 孫子 孫頭兒
Grandson's wife	孫媳婦
Grandson's daughter	孫女
Grandson's daughter's husband	孫女婿

Great-grandson.

Great-grandson	{ 曾孫 蠱蠱
Great-grandson's daughter	曾孫女

(621)

Great-great-grandson.

Great-great-grandson	{ 玄孫 末末 }

2. Mother's Family.

Mother.

Mother	{ 母親 媽娘 }

Mother's Brother.

Mother's brother	{ 舅父 舅舅母 }
Mother's brother's wife	{ 舅母 舅舅娘 }
Mother's eldest brother	大舅
Wife of the last	大舅母
Mother's second brother	二舅
Wife of the last	二舅母
Mother's youngest brother	么舅舅
Wife of the last	么舅母
Mother's brother's son	老表
Wife of the last	表嫂
Mother's brother's son (elder)	表兄
Mother's brother's son (younger)	表弟
Mother's brother's daughter	表姊妹
Mother's brother's daughter (elder)	表姐
Mother's brother's daughter (younger)	表妹
Mother's brother's grandson	表姪

Mother's Sister.

Mother's sister	{ 姨母 姨娘 }

MOTHER'S SISTER.　　　　　　　WIFE'S FATHER.

Mother's sister's husband	姨父
Mother's sister's son	姨表
Mother's sister's daughters	姨娘姊妹

Mother's Father.

Mother's father	{ 家公 / 外公
Mother's mother	{ 家婆 / 外婆
Mother's father's brother (eldest)	大家公
Wife of the last	大家婆
Mother's father's brother (second)	二家公
Wife of the last	二家婆

---

3. Wife's Family.

Wife.

Wife	妻子
Wife (vulgar)	{ 婆娘 / 媳婦人
Wife (used by the husband when speaking of the wife)	{ 家裏人 / 屋裏頭 / 屋裏人 / 內人 / 室拙荊

Wife's Father.

Wife's father	{ 岳父 / 親爺 / 老丈人

(623)

WIFE'S FATHER.

Wife's mother	岳母 / 親娘 / 老丈母
Wife's father's brother	叔岳父
Wife of the last	叔岳母
Wife's father's brother's son (elder)	內兄
Wife's father's brother's son (younger) ...	內弟
Wife's father's brother's daughters	姨姊妹
Wife's father's sister	妻姑娘
Husband of the last	妻姑爺

Wife's Grandfather.

Wife's grandfather	親公
Wife's grandmother	親婆

Wife's Brother.

Wife's brother	舅子
Wife of the last	嫂嫂 / 舅母子
Wife's brother (elder)	內兄
Wife's brother (younger)	內弟
Wife's brother's son	內姪兒
Wife's brother's daughter	內姪女

WIFE'S SISTER.

Wife's Sister.

Wife's eldest sister	大姨姐
Wife's second sister (elder)	二姨姐
Wife's fourth sister (younger)	四姨妹
Wife's youngest sister	幺姨妹
Wife's sister's husband	姨夫
Wife's sister's son	姨姪兒
Wife's sister's daughter	姨姪女

4. Son-in-law's Family.

Son-in-law's father	親家
Son-in-law's mother	親家母
Son-in-law's father's eldest brother	大親家
Son-in-law's father's second brother	二親家
Son-in-law's father's youngest brother	么親家
Son-in-law's grandfather	親翁
Son-in-law's grandmother	親母
Son-in-law's brother	兄弟
Son-in-law's sister	姊妹

5. Daughter-in-law's Family.

(The same as Son-in-law's Family).

6. Husband's Family.

Husband.

Husband	丈夫
Husband (vulgar)	{ 老公 / 男人 }
Husband (used by the wife when speaking of husband)	{ 外前人 / 娃娃的爹 }

Husband's Father.

Husband's father	{ 老人公 / 公公婆 }
Husband's mother	{ 老人婆 / 婆婆 }

Husband's Brother.

Husband's elder brother	{ 伯子 / 大哥哥
Wife of the last	{ 嫂嫂 / 大嫂
Husband's younger brother	{ 叔子 / 小兄弟弟
Wife of the last	弟媳
Husband's brother's son	姪兒
Husband's brother's daughter	姪女

Husband's Sister.

Husband's elder sister	姐姐
Husband's eldest sister	大姐
Husband's second sister (elder)	二姐
Husband's elder sister's husband	{ 姐丈 / 姐夫
Husband's younger sister	妹妹
Husband's fourth sister (younger)	四妹
Husband's youngest sister	幺妹
Husband's younger sister's husband	{ 妹弟 / 妹夫
Husband's unmarried sister	小姑子
Husband's sister's son	外姪
Husband's sister's daughter	外姪女

7. Miscellaneous.

Distant relatives	瓜葛親
Step-father	{ 繼父 / 皮老漢

MISCELLANEOUS.

Step-mother	{ 繼母 / 後娘 / 晚母 }
Step-son	{ 繼子 / 皮兒子 }
Step-daughter	皮女
Principal wife	正妻
Concubine	{ 側室 / 小婆子 / 妾 }
Father's principal wife	庶母
Father's concubine	嫡母
Mother (said by the son of a concubine)	{ 生母 / 乃媽媽 / 親親媽 }
Wet-nurse	{ 奶媽 / 乳母 }
A kind of God-father	{ 乾父 / 寄父 / 保爺 }
God-mother	{ 乾母 / 寄母 / 保娘 }
God-son	{ 乾兒子 / 寄兒子 / 乾殿下 }
God-daughter	乾女
Girl living in the house of her future husband's parents	{ 乾女子 / 開房媳婦 }
Adopted son	抱的兒子
Foundling, or Foster, son	{ 收的兒子 / 義子 }
Foundling, or Foster, daughter	義女
Foster parents	義父母
Sworn sisters	仁義姊妹
Covenant brothers	{ 盟兄弟 / 盟 }

MISCELLANEOUS.

Father's covenant brother	盟叔
Covenant brother's son	盟姪
Man born in the same year	{ 老庚 庚兄
Elder and younger brothers of the last	{ 同年哥 同年弟
Son of a man born in the same year	同年姪
Man who obtained his degree in the same year	{ 年兄 年弟
Son of last	年姪
Man who obtained his degree in the same year as my father	年伯

SYLLABIC INDEX.

[a]	**A.**	阿[1] oh! 548					
[ai]	**Ai.**	哎[4] ! 84					
[tṣa]	**Cha.**	渣[1] dregs. 308	奓 stretch. 121	鲊[3] salted. 584	蚱 locust. 460	栅[4] gate. 268	楂 haw. 277	榨 press. 278
		炸 sudden. 319	炸 crack. 320	詐 guile. 479	閘 gate. 545	乍 sudden. 7	扎[5] sew. 202	炸 fry. 320
		紮 bind. 403	鍘 chop. 540	劄 lodge. 390	劄 strong. 58			
[tṣʰa]	**Ch'a.**	叉[1] fork. 68	差 err. 158	揸 pinch. 223	蹅 step. 503	扠 fork. 203	查[2] patrol. 267	茶 tea. 446	扠[3] erect. 214
		衩 pants. 468	岔[4] diverge. 155	杈 branch. 263	汊 stream. 296	刹 temple. 47	詫 strange. 480		
		察[5] examine. 142	插 plant. 223	搽 smear. 226					
[tṣai]	**Chai.**	齋[1] fast. 595	債[4] debt. 27	寨 fort. 143	砦 fort. 369				

(629)

CH'AI-CH'ANG.

| Ch'ai. | 差¹ send. 158 | 釵 pin. 531 | 豺² wolf. 490 | 柴 wood. 268 | 踹³ tread. 504 | | | [tʂʰai] |

Chan.	占¹ divine. 64	氈 rug. 293	氊 rug. 294	沾 receive. 298	瞻 grand. 367	苫 mattress. 446	粘 paste. 397	[tʂan]
	展³ open. 153	斬 behead. 248	搌 wipe. 227	盞 lamp. 359	輾 revolve. 509	佔⁴ usurp. 15	戰 war. 199	
	暫 brief. 257	棧 inn. 275	站 stand. 385	顫 shake. 568				

| Ch'an. | 孱¹ weak. 134 | 纏² bind. 414 | 搀³ beat. 226 | 產 bear. 343 | 諂 flatter. 483 | 闡 open. 547 | 懺¹ regret. 197 | [tʂʰan] |
| | 韂 saddle. 562 | 綻 torn. 407 | | | | | | |

Chang.	豇¹ bean. 489	張 open. 172	彰 exhibit. 175	樟 camphor. 279	章 chapter. 386	獐 deer. 337		[tʂaŋ]
	麞 musk. 589	璋 jade. 340	掌³ control. 219	漲 rise. 312	長 grow. 542	韔 patch. 561	丈⁴ yard. 2	
	仗 battle. 12	帳 screen. 161	杖 staff. 263	脹 swell. 364	脹 swell. 431	賬 debt. 495		

| Ch'ang. | 娼¹ whore. 128 | 昌 prosperity. 252 | 菖 flag. 448 | 猖 mad. 335 | 場² market. 107 | 腸 bowels. 432 | | [tʂʰaŋ] |

(630)

CH'ANG-CHEN.

		長 long. 541	廠[3] shed. 67	廠 shed. 168	敞 open. 244	倡[4] lead. 22	唱 sing. 87	暢 joyous. 257
[tʂao]	Chao.	招[1] call. 208	朝 early. 261	找[3] seek. 204	爪 claws. 329	兆[4] omen. 32	照 shine. 323	罩 cover. 416	召 summon. 73
[tʂʰao]	Ch'ao.	抄[1] copy. 205	吵 annoy. 478	超 surpass. 499	鈔 money. 532	秒 plough. 422	吵 plough. 346	嘲[2] ridicule. 94
		朝 court. 261	潮 damp. 315	綽 wide. 407	吵[3] clamour. 79	炒 fry. 320	秒[4] plough. 422	吵 plough. 346
[tʂe] [tʂei[1]]	Che.	遮[1] screen. 522	者[3] who. 420	柘[4] tree. 268	蔗 cane. 453	這 this. 514	折[5] break. 205	摺 fold. 229	褶 fold. 473
[tʂʰe] [tʂʰei[1]]	Ch'e.	車[1] cart. 507	扯[3] haul. 205	徹[5] through. 178	撤 remove. 232
[tʂən]	Chen.	正[1] first. 287	征 war. 175	徵 levy. 178	斟 pour. 248	蒸 steam. 321	珍 pearl. 338	眞 true. 363	砧 anvil. 369
		蒸 sacrifice. 452	貞 chaste. 490	針 needle. 531	拯[3] save. 315	整 arrange. 246	枕 pillow. 265
		疹 rash. 349	賑 give. 494	正[4] upright. 287	症 malady. 349	証 evidence. 479	鎭 guard. 537
		陣 battle. 549	震 shake. 557	證 evidence. 486	振 floor. 217	澄 purify. 315	鄭 prudent. 526

(631)

CH'EN-CHI.

Ch'en.	伸[1] stretch. 17	稱 style. 380	呻 groan. 83	呈[2] state. 79	城 wall. 103	懲 punish. 196	塵 dust. 110	[tʂʰən]
	成 become. 198	承 receive. 205	沉 sink. 297	沈 sink. 297	程 road. 379	乘 N. A. 7	臣 noble. 437	
	誠 sincere. 481	陳 old. 550	辰 time. 511	澄 purify. 315	懲[3] punish. 196	慎[4] careful. 192	秤 weigh. 378	
	稱 suit. 380	趁 seize. 499						

Cheo.	周[1] around. 81	州 district. 157	賙 aid. 495	週 revolve. 517	箒[3] broom. 390	杻 manacle. 265		[tʂəu]
	肘 cubit. 426	紂[4] king. 401	晝 day. 255	冑 armour. 38	咒 curse. 41			

Ch'eo.	抽[1] draw. 209	仇[2] enemy. 12	稠 close. 380	綢 silk. 407	酬 entertain. 527	醻 entertain. 527		[tʂʰəu]
	籌 reckon. 395	躊 waver. 505	瞅[3] look. 367	醜 ugly. 528	臭[4] stinking. 437			

Chi.	乩[1] divine. 8	几 table. 42	基 site. 105	幾 almost. 165	機 loom. 282	稽 examine. 381	箕 basket. 390	[tɕi]
	譏 ridicule. 486	雞 fowl. 554	饑 hungry. 573	鷄 chicken. 587	肌 flesh. 426	笄 girl. 389	羇 halter. 417	

CHI-CHI.

[tɕʰi] **Ch'i.**

己³ self. 158	幾 few. 165	紀 age. 401	蟣 nit. 464	麂 deer. 588	杞 tree. 263	妓⁴ whore. 125	季 season. 133
寄 lodge. 140	忌 shun. 180	旣 since. 251	穊 succeed. 413	計 plan. 477	記 record. 478	技 skill. 207	
媢 envy. 128							

期¹ time. 262	欺 cheat. 286	溪 stream. 311	奇² strange. 121	旗 flag. 251	棋 chess. 275	基 chess. 275
祈 pray. 374	奇 strange. 385	耆 old. 420	蝦 frog. 462	騎 ride. 577	碁 chess. 371	麒 unicorn. 588
崎 rough. 156	其 its. 37	啓³ open. 243	豈 how? 489	起 rise. 498	器⁴ dish. 95	契 deed. 121	憇 rest. 193
棄 reject. 275	氣 breath. 294						

[tʂʅ] **Chi.**

梔¹ gardenia. 273	枝 branch. 265	支 tribe. 241	知 know. 367	肢 limb. 427	脂 fat. 429	芝 sesamum. 443
蜘 spider. 462	隻 N. A. 553	之 particle. 7	只³ only. 73	址 site. 102	指 point. 214	止 stop. 287
紙 paper. 401	旨 will. 252	誌⁴ honour. 482	制 govern. 47	志 bent. 180	治 heal. 298	智 wisdom. 256

(633)

CHÏ-CHIA.

挈 grasp. 219	致 cause. 243	滯 obstruct. 312	痣 mole. 350	痔 piles. 350	緻 fine. 410	翅 wing. 419
至 arrive. 438	製 make. 471	執[5] grasp. 105	姪 nephew. 127	擲 throw. 237	植 plant. 275	汁 juice. 296
直 straight. 361	值 cost. 22	織 weave. 412	置 appoint. 416	職 duty. 425	質 body. 495	贄 present. 497
隲 conceal. 577	黹 sew. 593					

Chʻï. [tṣʰɿ]

痴[1] stupid. 351	癡 stupid. 353	脀 crop. 429	池[2] tank. 296	馳 constant. 576	遲 slow. 522	持 support. 214
剭 slow. 52	侈[3] waste. 18	恥 shame. 184	耻 shame. 423	齒 teeth. 595	侈[4] waste. 18	恃 trust. 185
滯 obstruct. 312	喫[5] eat. 90	尺 foot. 151	敕 order. 243	赤 naked. 497	飭 enjoin. 570
吃 stammer. 77						

Chia. [tɕia]

稼[1] farm. 381	家 home. 139	佳 good. 18	傢 tool. 25	加 add. 53	嘉 good. 94	枷 cangue. 269
袈 gown. 469	耞 flail. 423	假[3] false. 24	價[4] price. 29	嫁 marry. 130	假 absence. 24	架 frame. 269

(634)

CHIA-CHIAO.

		稼	耞	駕	夾⁵	挾	梜	甲
		farm.	flail.	ride.	press.	clasp.	squeeze.	scale.
		381	423	576	120	217	273	344
		篋	鋏					
		case.	tongs.					
		392	534					
[tɕʰia]	Ch'ia.	跒²	卡³	恰⁵	㤖	掐		
		stride.	guard.	timely.	heartless.	pinch.		
		502	64	184	184	220		
[tɕiai]	Chiai.	皆¹	解³	戒⁴	界	疥	芥	械
		all.	open.	warn.	boundary.	itch.	mustard.	arms.
		356	476	198	345	349	444	274
		解						
		transmit.						
		477						
[tɕiaŋ]	Chiang.	韁¹	僵	江	疆	繮	薑	豇
		reins.	numb.	river.	boundary.	reins.	ginger.	bean.
		562	29	296	348	413	454	489
		講³	悻⁴	降				
		preach.	perverse.	descend.				
		486	184	548				
[tɕʰiaŋ]	Ch'iang.	匡¹	框	筐	腔	閶	強²	強³
		assist.	frame.	basket.	speech.	frame.	strong.	force.
		60	270	388	432	545	173	173
[tɕiao]	Chiao.	交¹	嬌	敎	澆	膠	蛟	驕	憍
		join.	pet.	teach.	pour.	glue.	dragon.	proud.	spoil.
		10	131	243	315	434	461	578	195
		攪³	痂	狡	矯	繳	鉸	絞	
		stir.	colic.	crafty.	obstinate.	deliver.	shear.	twist.	
		240	348	335	368	413	533	405	

(635)

CHIAO-CHIEN.

	餃	敎[4]	校	叫	覺	較		
	dumpling.	teach.	strive.	call.	sleep.	compare.		
	571	243	271	73	476	508		
	轎	酵	呌					
	chair.	leaven.	call.					
	510	527	70					
Ch'iao.	撬[1]	蹺	橋[2]	蕎	巧[3]	竅[4]	𠑽	[tɕʰiao]
	pry.	cross.	bridge.	grain.	clever.	cavity.	tilt.	
	233	504	282	454	157	385	594	
	撬	蹺						
	rack.	tilt.						
	233	504						
Chie.	給[5]	傑	劫	及	吉	吸		[tɕie]
	provision.	hero.	plunder.	reach.	lucky.	smoke.		
	405	26	54	69	77	80		
	急	揭	極	棘	潔	激	竭	級
	hasty.	lift.	very.	bush.	clean.	excite.	exert.	step.
	182	224	276	275	316	316	386	402
	結	茇	偈					
	knot.	orchid.	rhyme.					
	404	444	25					
Ch'ie.	茄[2]	蝦	趄[4]	乞[5]	怯			[tɕʰie]
	brinjal.	frog.	limp.	beg.	fear.			
	445	462.	499	8	182			
Chien.	兼[1]	堅	奸	悭	監	肩	艱	[tɕien]
	both.	firm.	crafty.	stingy.	prison.	shoulder.	hard.	
	37	105	124	193	359	427	502	
	姦	間	減[3]	儉	柬	謇		
	adultery.	between.	reduce.	careful.	card.	stutter.		
	127	545	42	30	269	485		

(636)

CHIEN-CHIN.

檢	筧	简	繭	趼	鐧	鹻
examine.	gutter.	curt.	cocoon.	corns.	rapier.	soda.
283	389	394	413	502	539	588

揀	健⁴	儉	劍	建	毽	監
pick.	strong.	careful.	sword.	build.	toy.	inspect.
224	24	30	52	169	294	360

見	諫	間	件
see.	rebuke.	separate.	N. A.
474	484	545	15

[tɕʰien] **Ch'ien.**

牽¹	縴	謙	乾²	虔	鉗	遣³
lead.	rope.	humble.	Heaven.	devout.	tongs.	send.
333	411	486	8	457	533	521

膁	歉⁴	欠	芡	縴	椽
fur.	dearth.	owe.	flour.	traces.	rafter.
435	286	285	444	411	283

[tɕin] **Chin.**

今¹	巾	斤	京	兢	矜
now.	kerchief.	pound.	capital.	tremble.	pity.
12	159	248	11	34	367

筋	經	驚	荆	襟	金	鯨
sinew.	classic.	scare.	bush.	lapel.	metal.	whale.
388	406	578	447	473	530	584

境³	儆	景	槿	緊	頸
boundary.	notice.	view.	Hibiscus.	tight.	neck.
110	195	256	280	407	566

警	錦	謹	勁⁴	禁	敬	禁
warn.	silk.	careful.	congenial.	sick.	respect.	forbid.
487	535	486	55	96	245	376

竟	脛	劤	濮	近	鏡
finally.	shin.	strength.	shiver.	near.	glass.
386	430	54	42	512	539

(637)

CH'IN-CHIU.

Ch'in. 卿[1] noble. 66 — 欽 royal. 286 — 輕 light. 508 — 勤[2] diligent. 57 — 擒 hold. 95 — 懃 diligent. 195 — 擔 seize. 235   [tɕʰin]

擎 uphold. 235 — 檎 apple. 283 — 檠 bench. 284 — 琴 lute. 340 — 禽 bird. 377 — 芹 celery. 444 — 衾 coverlet. 468

慶[4] happy. 193 — 磬 bell. 373 — 罄 exhaust. 415

Chio. 卒[5] lictor. 63 — 脚 foot. 430 — 覺 perceive. 476.   [tɕio]

Ch'io. 却[5] still. 65 — 屈 wrong. 152 — 曲 bent. 258 — 確 certain. 372 — 蛐 worm. 461 — 麯 leaven. 589   [tɕʰio]

Chiong. 弓[1] bow. 171   [tɕioŋ]

Ch'iong. 窮[2] poor. 384   [tɕʰioŋ]

Chiu. 鳩[1] turtle. 586 — 赳 martial. 498 — 鬮 lot. 582 — 糾 twist. 400 — 韭[3] leek. 562 — 久 long. 6 — 九 nine. 7   [tɕieu]

舅[4] uncle. 438 — 舊 old. 439 — 柩 corpse. 269 — 究 explain. 382 — 救 save. 244 — 咎 fault. 81

(638)

CH'IU-CHU.

[tɕʰiəu] **Ch'iu.**

毬²	求	屎
ball.	beseech.	penis.
293	296	153

[tʂo] **Cho.**

嘱⁵	捉	桌	濁	綽	著	觸
enjoin.	seize.	table.	turbid.	name.	fix.	butt.
97	217	275	316	407	418	477

逐	竹	妯
expel.	bamboo.	sister.
514	387	126

[tʂʰo] **Ch'o.**

戳⁵	濁	矬	綽	黜	脞
stamp.	foul.	short.	name.	degrade.	mean.
200	316	368	407	592	595

[tsoŋ] **Chong.**

中¹	忠	終	舂	鐘	鐘	塚³
middle.	faithful.	end.	pound.	cup.	bell.	grave.
5	180	403	438	537	539	108

種	腫	眾⁴	眾	重	種	中
sow.	swell.	all.	all.	heavy.	seed.	hit.
380	432	363	465	529	380	5

[tsʰoŋ] **Ch'ong.**

充¹	冲	舂	囱	虫²	蟲	重
fill.	strike.	pound.	flue.	insect.	insect.	again.
32	39	438	98	459	464	529

寵³	揰⁴	銃
love.	burst.	petard.
144	224	533

[tʂu] **Chu.**

朱¹	猪	珠	硃	蛛	誅	銖	株
red.	pig.	pearl.	red.	spider.	kill.	money.	trunk.
263	336	339	370	461	480	534	270

主³	煮	柱⁴	注	炷	住	箸
lord.	boil.	post.	look.	N. A.	dwell.	chopstick.
6	323	268	298	320	16	391

(639)

CHU-CHUA.

	苧 hemp. 444	蛀 eat. 460	註 comment. 480	貯 retain. 492	駐 lodge. 576	囑[5] enjoin. 97	烄 candle. 321	
	燭 candle. 327	祝 bless. 375	竹 bamboo. 387	築 ram. 391	妯 sister. 126			
Ch'u.	儲[2] amass. 31	厨 cook. 67	躇 waver. 505	鋤 hoe. 534	除 without. 549	杵[3] pestle. 265	處 chastise. 457	[tṣʰu]
	處[4] place. 458	出[5] out. 43						
Chü.	車[1] pipe. 507	俱 all. 22	居 dwell. 152	駒 foal. 576	拘 adhere. 209	矩[3] rule. 367	舉 raise. 439	具[4] utensil. 36	[tɕy]
	剑 execute. 53	句 phrase. 74	懼 fear. 198	據 evidence. 235	鋸 saw. 535	拒 reject. 213	巨 great. 157	
	局[5] office. 151	橘 orange. 282	菊 aster. 449	足 full. 500				
Ch'ü.	區[1] plan. 61	嶇 rough. 156	軀 person. 507	驅 expel. 578	劬[2] toil. 54	去[4] go. 68	砌 lay. 369	屈[5] wrong. 152	[tɕʰy]
	曲 bent. 258	蛐 worm. 461	麯 leaven. 589					
Chua.	哑[1] cry. 83	抓 clutch. 204	啄[5] peck. 87	拙 stupid. 209				[tṣua]

(640)

CHUAI-CH'UANG.

[tṣuai] **Chuai.** 栽¹ tumble. 272

[tṣʰuai] **Ch'uai.** 搋¹ pocket. 227 | 喘³ asthma. 88 | 揣 examine. 223 | 蠆⁴ bully. 464

[tṣuan] **Chuan.** 耑¹ only. 421 | 專 singly. 146 | 甎 brick. 342 | 磚 brick. 373 | 轉 turn. 510 | 饌 meat. 573 | 傳 annals. 27
篆 seal. 392 | 賺 gain. 496 | 轉 turn. 510

[tṣʰuan] **Ch'uan.** 川¹ stream. 156 | 穿 wear. 382 | 釧 bracelet. 531 | 傳² tell. 27 | 椽 rafter. 278 | 船 boat. 441 | 鏟³ shovel. 538
喘 asthma. 88 | 串⁴ string. 5

[tṣuaŋ] **Chuang.** 庄¹ farm. 166 | 椿 post. 280 | 粧 adorn. 398 | 莊 sedate. 447 | 裝 fill. 470 | 奘³ large. 122 | 裝 fill. 470 | 壯⁴ robust. 114
撞 strike. 232 | 狀 form. 334

[tṣʰuaŋ] **Ch'uang.** 瘡¹ sore. 352 | 窗 window. 383 | 窻 window. 383 | 床² bed. 166 | 牀 bed. 331 | 撞³ knock. 232 | 闖 rush. 564
創⁴ create. 51 | 撞 meet. 232

CHUE-CH'ÜEN.

Chue.	墜⁴ fall. 111	縋 suspend. 410	贅 toady. 497				[tʂue] [tʂuei]

Ch'ue.	吹¹ blow. 79	垂² drop. 103	捶 beat. 226	槌 mallet. 278	鎚 hammer. 538		[tʂʰue] [tʂʰuei]

Chüe.	决⁵ decide. 40	拙 stupid. 209	訣 mystery. 479	蹶 kick. 505	決 decide. 297	[tɕye]

Ch'üe.	𣂪⁵ piece. 282	缺 vacancy. 415	闕 court. 547	[tɕʰye]

Chuen.	准⁵ permit. 41	準 permit. 310	[tʂuən]

Ch'uen.	春¹ spring. 253	椿 Cedrela. 277	蠢³ stupid. 464	[tʂʰuən]

Chüen.	捐¹ give. 217	鵑 azalea. 587	踡 double. 503	捲³ roll. 220	錈 turn. 536	錈 dumpling. 572	倦⁴ weary. 23	[tɕyen]
	卷 book. 65	圈 fold. 98	眷 love. 363	絹 silk. 406			

Ch'üen.	圈¹ circle. 98	拳² fist. 215	權 power. 285	犬³ dog. 334	勸⁴ exhort. 58	[tɕʰyen]

CHÜIN-FE.

[tɕyn]	Chüin.	君¹ prince. 80	均 even. 102	軍 army. 507	迥² very. 513	俊⁴ handsome. 22	竣 end. 386	菌 agaric. 448
		腌 crop. 426						
[tɕʰyn]	Ch'üin.	傾¹ pour. 27	頃 incline. 564	羣³ flock. 418	群 flock. 418	裙 skirt. 470	瓊 good. 341	
[fa]	Fa.	乏⁵ weary. 7	伐 fell. 14	法 plan. 298	發 issue. 355	罰 punish. 416	髮 hair. 581	
[fan]	Fan.	旛¹ flag. 251	番 foreign. 346	翻 turn. 420	繙 translate. 412	凡² all. 42	煩 trouble. 323	礬 alum. 374
		繁 many. 411	藩 fence. 456	帆 sail. 160	反³ turn. 69	返 turn. 512	泛⁴ float. 299	犯 sin. 334	販 barter. 491
		飯 rice. 570	範 pattern. 392					
[faŋ]	Fang.	坊¹ arch. 102	方 square. 249	枋 plank. 267	芳 scent. 443	妨 oppose. 125	坊² shop. 102	妨 oppose. 125
		房 house. 200	防 guard. 547	仿³ like. 14	彷 like. 175	紡 spin. 401	訪 ask. 478	放⁴ loose. 242
[fe] [fei]	Fe.	緋¹ very. 407	飛 fly. 570	非 not. 559	肥² fat. 427	匪³ villain. 61	翡 blue. 419	菲 mean. 448	廢⁴ exhaust. 168

(643)

西蜀方言

FE-FU.

	痱	肺	費				
	rash.	lungs.	spend.				
	349	427	492				

Fen.
分¹	吩	紛	芬	墳²	焚	粉³	[fən]
divide.	order.	confused.	scent.	grave.	burn.	flour.	
44	79	401	443	111	322	397	

噴⁴	奮	忿	憤	糞	分
sneeze.	earnest.	angry.	zeal.	dung.	part.
96	123	181	194	399	44

Fong.
封¹	楓	瘋	蜂	豐	鋒	風	縫²	[foŋ]
seal.	plane.	mad.	bee.	plenty.	spear.	wind.	seam.	
145	278	352	461	489	534	569	411	

逢	俸⁴	奉	脧	縫	鳳
meet.	stipend.	receive.	close.	seam.	phœnix.
515	24	121	364	411	586

Fu.
呼¹	夫	敷	桴	烰	沸	膚	[fu]
breathe.	man.	apply.	pip.	charcoal.	boil.	skin.	
81	118	246	270	273	300	434	

麩	扶²	浮	湖	狐	瑚	壺	煳
bran.	uphold.	float.	lake.	fox.	coral.	pot.	charred.
589	206	302	308	334	340	115	323

符	糊	胡	芙	葫	蝴
match.	paste.	reckless.	Hibiscus.	gourd.	moth.
387	398	428	443	450	462

衚	餬	鬍	蚨	俯³	哺	府
street.	living.	beard.	cash.	fall.	feed.	prefect.
467	573	581	460	22	86	166

撫	斧	琥	甫	腐	腑	虎
cherish.	axe.	amber.	style.	rotten.	belly.	tiger.
233	248	340	344	431	431	457

(644)

FU-HAN.

諕	輔⁴	付⁴	傅	副	附	婦
call.	help.	give.	teach.	second.	order.	woman.
483	509	13	26	50	81	129

富	洰	父	戶	護	負	賦
rich.	bade.	father.	house.	protect.	slight.	pay.
142	304	330	200	487	490	495

附	駙	袝	赴	互	冱
adjacent.	near.	pad.	attend.	mutual.	congeal.
548	576	469	498	10	40

伏⁵	佛	幅	彿	復	服	福
fall.	Buddha.	width.	like.	again.	clothes.	happiness.
14	16	163	175	178	260	376

腹	蝠	蝮	袱	覆	拂	複
belly.	bat.	viper.	cloth.	turn.	duster.	repeat.
433	462	462	469	474	211	472

[xa] Ha.

哈¹	嗄	犽²
laugh.	hoarse.	wild.
84	92	485

[xai] Hai.

偕²	鞋	孩	海³	盇	蟹	薤⁴	嗐
harmony.	shoe.	child.	sea.	jar.	crab.	onion.	alas.
24	561	134	302	358	464	454	93

害	蟹
hurt.	crab.
139	464

[xan] Han.

憨¹	含²	唅	寒	涵	銜
stupid.	patient.	hold.	cold.	patient.	official.
194	79	89	142	304	533

閒	鹹	喊³	罕	漢⁴	旱	翰
idle.	salt.	call.	few.	Chinese.	dry.	pencil.
543	588	88	415	312	252	419

(645)

HAN-HO.

	蓻 plant. 447	釬 solder. 532	限 limit. 548	陷 sink. 550	鼾 snore. 594	汗 sweat. 296	
Hang.	硋[1] ram. 370	唧[2] hold. 89	行 space. 466	巷[4] alley. 159	項 neck. 564		[xaŋ]
Hao.	蒿[1] weed. 452	薅 weed. 454	壕[2] moat. 113	毫 atom. 293	濠 ditch. 317	號 weep. 459	篙 pole. 393	[xao]
	豪 hero. 489	好[3] good. 123	號[4] mark. 458	浩 great. 303	耗 waste. 422	好 like. 124	壕 pool. 113	
He.	劾[5] inform. 55	嚇 startle. 96	核 kernel. 270	黑 black. 591				[xe] [xei]
Hen.	亨[1] succeed. 11	哼 ! 85	恒[2] constant. 184	痕 scar. 350	很[3] very. 176	悻 huff. 188	狠 very. 335	[xən]
	恨[4] hate. 184	杏 apricot. 264						
Heo.	後[1] within. 176	齁 pant. 594	侯[2] noble. 20	喉 throat. 88	猴 monkey. 336	吼[3] call. 80	候[4] wait. 22	[xəu]
	厚 think. 66	后 queen. 76	後 after. 176					
Ho.	喝[1] drink. 89	呵 yawn. 81	蠚 sting. 465	何[2] how. 16	和 harmony. 82	河 river. 299	禾 grain. 377	[xo]

(646)

		荷	蠚	伙³	火	夥	和⁴	祸	货
		lotus.	sting.	mate.	fire.	mate.	accord.	evil.	goods.
		448	465	14	318	117	82	376	491
		贺	合⁵	喝	忽	惚	活	获	癨
		rejoice.	join.	drink.	sudden.	dull.	alive.	get.	cholera.
		492	76	89	181	188	301	337	354
		盒	豁	阖	鹤	嗑	霍	藿	
		box.	liberal.	all.	egret.	hubbub.	quick.	betony.	
		358	489	547	587	92	557	456	

[xoŋ] Hong.

	哄¹	烘	轰	䛽	宏	洪	红
	noisy.	dry.	noise.	clamour.	vast.	vast.	red.
	84	321	510	563	136	301	400
	䜌	哄³					
	wall.	cheat.					
	590	84					

[xu] Hu. 核¹ For words sometimes pronounced *hu* see under *fu*.
pip.
270

[xua] Hua.

	劃¹	花	哗²	划	华	铧	划⁴
	split.	flower.	clamour.	row.	glorious.	share.	cut.
	52	443	95	45	448	539	52
	化	桦	画	话	滑⁵	猾	幔
	change.	birch.	draw.	word.	slippery.	crafty.	rip.
	60	282	347	480	310	336	162
	或	画					
	whether.	stroke.					
	199	347					

[xuai] Huai.

怀²	槐	坏⁴
breast.	locust.	spoil.
197	279	113

HUAN-HUE.

Huan. 歡¹ 橫² 環 還 鐶 奐 桓　　[xuan]
pleased. cross. ring. still. ring. slave. wander.
287　281　341　523　540　582　270

綏³ 喚⁴ 宦 患 換 槵 幻 橌
delay. call. eunuch. evil. change. soap. magic. bar.
409　89　138　186　224　280　165　284

Huang. 怳¹ 荒 煌² 皇 鰉 癀　　[xuaŋ]
fearful. desert. lustre. king. sturgeon. jaundice.
192　446　323　356　585　353

凰 黃 磺 蝗 蟥 隍
phœnix. yellow. sulphur. locust. leech. moat.
42　590　373　462　464　551

怳³ 謊 晃⁴ 熀 橌
confused. lies. glitter. bright. bar.
184　485　254　325　284

Hue. 徽¹ 恢 灰 輝 揮 隳 回²　　[xue] [xuei]
town. more. ashes. lustre. shake. destroy. return.
179　185　319　323　226　196　37

茴 蛔 洄 悔³ 毀 賄 卉⁴
fennel. worm. pool. repent. destroy. promise. herbs.
446　461　301　186　291　493　63

彗 惠 慧 晦 會 滙
broom. grace. wisdom. dark. meet. transmit.
174　188　192　256　259　310

穢 膾 繪 諱 賄 誨 惑⁵
foul. meat. draw. avoid. bribes. teach. doubt.
381　435　413　484　493　482　188

或
whether.
199

(648)

HUEN-IANG.

[xuən] **Huen.**

婚[1]	惛	昏	渾	閽	葷	橫[2]
marry.	stupid.	dark.	turbid.	gate.	gross.	cross.
129	188	252	309	546	450	281

魂	渾	混[4]
soul.	whole.	chaos.
583	309	304

[i] **I.**

依[1]	衣	醫	咿	夷[2]	姨	逸	移
trust.	clothes.	heal.	!	wild.	sister.	ease.	move.
18	467	528	79	120	127	518	379

胰	遺	以[3]	椅	苡	巳	尾	裏
soap.	leave.	do.	chair.	coix.	already.	tail.	within.
429	522	13	275	444	158	152	520

噫[4]	意	易	異	翳	翼	裔
!	mind.	easy.	strange.	screen.	wings.	posterity.
95	190	253	346	420	420	470

肄	揖[5]	益	驛	一	佾
study.	bow.	benefit.	station.	one.	student.
425	226	358	578	1	20

[ia] **Ia.**

丫[1]	椏	鴉	颬	閜	呀	涯[2]	牙	芽
fork.	fork.	crow.	gasp.	ajar.	!	end.	tooth.	shoot.
5	277	586	569	544	81	308	331	444

衙	啞[3]	雅	壓[4]	呀	押[5]	鴨
office.	dumb.	good.	press.	!	sign.	duck.
467	88	554	113	81	213	586

[iaŋ] **Iang.**

殃[1]	秧	佯[2]	楊	揚	洋	瘍	羊
calamity.	rice.	false.	willow.	publish.	sea.	sore.	sheep.
290	378	20	278	226	302	352	417

陽	痒[3]	仰[3]	養	懩	恙[4]	樣[4]	養
sun.	itch.	look.	nourish.	itch.	disease.	kind.	provide.
551	353	15	572	197	186	281	572

(649)

IAO-IEN.

Iao.

幺¹	吆	夭	妖	殀	腰	褾	[iao]
small.	cry.	wanton.	sprite.	untimely.	waist.	plait.	
67	79	119	125	289	433	472	

邀	搖²	窰	謠	遙	罾³	耀⁴
invite.	shake.	kiln.	rumour.	distant.	bale.	glory.
524	229	384	486	521	438	420

鷂	靿	要	躍
kite.	boot.	want.	spry.
587	469	474	505

Ie.

爺²	也³	野	夜⁴	液	腋	穧⁵	腌	[ie]
size.	also.	wild.	night.	fluid.	wing.	poor.	fish.	
330	8	530	117	308	432	381	432	

葉	頁	閱
leaf.	page.	porter.
452	564	564

Ien.

咽¹	烟	淹	湮	煙	胭	菸	[ien]
throat.	smoke.	drown.	lost.	opium.	throat.	tobacco.	
85	321	308	310	324	430	450	

蔫	醃	炎	延²	淹	筵	簷
droop.	pickle.	flame.	protract.	long.	feast.	eaves.
453	528	320	169	308	390	395

言	顏	盬	鹽	演³	眼	掩	揜
words.	colour.	salt.	salt.	drill.	eye.	screen.	cover.
477	567	359	588	315	364	223	106

奄	魘	衍	厭⁴	堰	宴	焰
stop.	dream.	plenty.	loathe.	dam.	feast.	flame.
121	584	467	67	108	140	323

燕	艷	咽
swallow.	wanton.	swallow.
327	442	85

IN-IONG.

[in] **In.**

因¹	姻	嬰	慇	應	櫻
because.	wedding.	child.	careful.	ought.	cherry.
98	128	132	192	196	285

殷	纓	罌	英	陰	音	鷹
full.	tassel.	jar.	brave.	female.	sound.	eagle.
291	414	415	446	550	563	588

鸚	淫²	營	蠅	贏	迎	銀
parrot.	adultery.	camp.	fly.	win.	meet.	silver.
588	308	328	464	497	512	534

盈	吟	飲³	引	影	癮	隱
full.	hum.	drink.	lead.	shadow.	craving.	retired.
358	81	571	171	175	354	552

飲⁴	應	蔭	窨	印	揞
water.	answer.	shady.	cellar.	print.	measure.
571	196	454	383	64	230

[io] **Io.**

岳⁵	嶽	役	樂	欲	獄	疫
relative.	hill.	lictor.	music.	desire.	hell.	plague.
155	156	175	280	286	336	349

約	育	藥	鑰	閱	鬱
agree.	nourish.	medicine.	key.	know.	despond.
401	427	456	541	546	582

浴	慾
wash.	desire.
304	194

[ioŋ] **Iong.**

癰¹	傭²	容	庸	氄	蓉	融
boil.	hire.	bear.	service.	down.	Hibiscus.	combine.
354	28	140	168	294	453	463

鎔	勇³	壅	擁	氄	湧	蛹	用⁴
melt.	brave.	screen.	crowd.	down.	bubble.	pupa.	use.
538	55	113	236	294	310	461	344

(651)

IU-KAN.

Iu. [iəu]

優¹	悠	憂	幽	油²	猶	由	尤
excel.	far.	grieve.	dark.	oil.	still.	from.	grumble.
30	187	194	165	300	336	345	150

游	逰	友³	有	誘	佑⁴	右
travel.	travel.	friend.	have.	beguile.	protect.	right.
310	520	70	260	482	18	76

又	宥	幼	柚	泑	侑
again.	forgive.	young.	pumelo.	glaze.	attend.
68	138	165	270	299	19

Ka. [ka]

鋏⁵
tongs.
534

K'a. [kʰa]

跒²
stride.
502.

Kai. [kai]

堦¹	皆	街	該	階	改³	解
steps.	all.	street.	ought.	steps.	change.	loose.
107	356	467	480	551	241	476

蓋⁴	戒	蓋	解	頶	械
cover.	warn.	cover.	transport.	head.	flail.
452	198	358	477	568	274

K'ai. [kʰai]

揩¹	開	鎧³	劀	凱	楷	槩⁴
wipe.	open.	armour.	fully.	victory.	writing.	all.
224	544	538	52	42	278	280

慨
liberal.
193

Kan. [kan]

乾¹	干	杆	柑	甘	疳	竿
dry.	war.	pole.	orange.	willing.	disease.	pole.
8	163	264	268	342	349	387

(652)

KAN-KAO.

肝	間	泔	骭³	擀	感	觡	稈
liver.	N. A.	slops.	shin.	roll.	move.	shaft.	straw.
426	545	300	579	235	191	394	379

趕	桿	敢	橄	幹⁴	榦	骭
drive.	N. A.	dare.	olive.	do.	stem.	wall.
499	273	244	282	165	279	104

旰	悍
mark.	brawl.
591	186

[kʰan] K'an.

看¹	勘	堪	嵌	杠	龕	刊
see.	inquire.	bear.	glaze.	charcoal.	shrine.	engrave.
362	55	107	156	292	596	45

坎³	砍	闞	墈	看⁴
crisis.	chop.	sill.	dike.	see.
102	369	545	111	361

[kaŋ] Kang.

剛¹	扛	杠	肛	綱	缸	豇
hard.	help.	tree.	anus.	principle.	jar.	bean.
50	204	264	426	407	414	489

鋼	扛⁴	杠	蜂	逛
steel.	carry.	basket.	rainbow.	ramble.
535	203	264	461	515

[kʰaŋ] K'ang.

㾖¹	康	慷	糠	匟⁴	抗
cough.	peace.	generous.	chaff.	divan.	rebel.
94	168	193	399	60	206

炕	伉
dry.	match.
320	15

[kao] Kao.

糕¹	羔	膏	高	藁	攪	槁	稿
pastry.	lamb.	oil.	high.	straw.	do.	dry.	straw.
399	417	434	580	455	240	279	380

(653)

KAO-KEO.

	告⁴	窖	窖	覺	較			
	tell.	pit.	pit.	sleep.	adjust.			
	80	383	383	476	508			

K'ao.	敲¹	拷³	烤	考	犒⁴	靠	[kʰao]
	rap.	examine.	toast.	examine.	bounty.	trust.	
	246	215	321	421	333	558	

Ke.	給¹	膈³	隔⁵	格	革	疙	[ke] [kei]
	give.	belch.	partition.	rule.	degrade.	pimple.	
	404	434	552	271	560	349	
	節	紇	膈	虼	瘑		
	knot.	knot.	midriff.	flea.	itch.		
	392	400	434	459	352		

K'e.	蝦²	克⁵	刻	欬	客	尅	欯	[kʰe] [kʰei]
	frog.	able.	carve.	cough.	guest.	repress.	cough.	
	462	33	47	84	138	146	286	

Ken.	庚¹	更	根	羹	耕	跟	齦³	哽	[kən]
	age.	change.	root.	soup.	till.	heel.	gums.	choke.	
	166	258	270	418	422	502	595	85	
	梗	更	齦						
	stem.	more.	gums.						
	273	258	595						

K'en.	坑¹	啃³	墾	懇	肯	掯⁴	[kʰən]
	pit.	bite.	till.	urgent.	willing.	extort.	
	102	87	112	195	427	220	

Keo.	勾¹	拘	溝	鈎	鬮	狗³	苟	[kəu]
	entice.	hook.	drain.	hook.	lot.	dog.	careless.	
	57	206	311	532	582	334	445	
	枸	垢⁴	够	姤	彀	搆		
	tree.	filth.	enough.	pair.	notch.	reach.		
	268	104	117	127	173	227		

K'EO-KONG.

[kʰəu] **K'eo.**

扣¹	摳	釦	口³	犼	叩⁴	寇
knot.	lift.	link.	mouth.	animal.	rap.	rob.
204	230	532	71	332	73	141

扣	蔻	蔻	釦
button.	reed.	nutmeg.	button.
204	393	453	532

[ko] **Ko.**

歌¹	哥	戈	鍋	鸽	餜³	果
song.	brother.	spear.	pot.	parrot.	cake.	fruit.
286	85	198	537	587	398	265

菓	裹	餜	個⁴	過	箇	割⁵	各
fruit.	wrap.	cake.	N.A.	pass.	N.A.	cut.	each.
449	471	572	22	518	390	52	77

擱	桷	搁	葱	葛	角	閣	鴿
delay.	rafter.	box.	onion.	plant.	horn.	room.	dove.
237	273	214	447	450	476	545	587

[kʰo] **K'o.**

奇¹	珂	科	稞	哿	可³	顆
annoy.	trouble.	series.	wheat.	rap.	may.	grain.
445	103	378	380	243	74	567

擱⁴	課	蚵	騍	壳⁵	涸	渴
place.	work.	crack.	mare.	husk.	dry.	thirsty.
237	483	595	577	114	304	309

揢	瞌	磕
rap.	sleep.	knock.
288	366	372

[koŋ] **Kong.**

供¹	公	功	宮	工	弓
evidence.	public.	merit.	palace.	work.	bow.
19	36	54	140	157	170

恭	攻	蚣	躬	拱³	礦
respect.	attack.	centipede.	body.	arch.	ore.
185	241	460	506	215	374

(655)

KONG-KUA.

	頓	貢⁴	共	矼	供		
	snout.	tribute.	total.	rush.	offer.		
	463	491	36	419	19		
K'ong.	空¹	孔³	恐	焢	控⁴	空	悾	[kʰoŋ]
	empty.	hole.	fear.	steam.	accuse.	idle.	rustic.	
	382	132	185	322	220	382	188	
Ku.	啯¹	跍	姑	孤	沽	菇	辜	[ku]
	robber.	squat.	girl.	orphan.	buy.	plant.	guilt.	
	94	501	125	133	299	448	511	
	蛄	估³	古	牯	鹽	股	臌	
	insect.	guess.	old.	bull.	pot.	stream.	dropsy.	
	460	16	74	333	360	427	435	
	蠱	鼓	僱⁴	固	故	痼	顧	
	poison.	drum.	hire.	stable.	cause.	disease.	care.	
	465	593	28	98	242	351	568	
	榖⁵	骨	酷					
	grain.	bone.	oppress.					
	381	579	527					
K'u.	枯¹	箍	葫²	苦³	庫⁴	褲	哭⁵	[kʰu]
	dry.	hoop.	gourd.	bitter.	safe.	pants.	cry.	
	269	390	450	445	167	472	86	
	脞	窟						
	squat.	hole.						
	431	383						
Kua.	瓜¹	劀³	寡	卦⁴	挂	掛	詿	[kua]
	melon.	flay.	widow.	sign.	hang.	hang.	think.	
	341	51	143	64	215	220	416	
	褂	括⁵	聒	颳	刮			
	jacket.	ladle.	croak.	blast.	scrape.			
	471	215	423	569	47			

(656)

K'UA-KUE.

[kʰua] **K'ua.**

誇¹	胯³
boast.	thigh.
481	429

[kuai] **Kuai.**

乖¹	拐³	枴	怪⁴
perverse.	corner.	staff.	strange.
7	210	269	182

[kʰuai] **K'uai.**

塊³	快⁴
piece.	quick.
108	181

[kuan] **Kuan.**

鰥¹	冠	官	棺	觀	關	管³	館
alone.	cap.	official.	coffin.	see.	shut.	rule.	inn.
585	39	137	276	476	547	391	572

舘	慣⁴	灌	罐	貫	冠	觀
hall.	habit.	pour.	jug.	string.	cap.	temple.
440	194	318	415	491	39	476

[kʰuan] **K'uan.**

寬¹	欵³	撯
broad.	article.	stick.
143	286	233

[kuaŋ] **Kuang.**

光¹	廣³	礦	逛	逛⁴
light.	wide.	lime.	wander.	stroll.
33	168	374	515	515

[kʰuaŋ] **K'uang.**

匡¹	眶	筐	誆	狂²	壙⁴	曠	況
assist.	socket.	basket.	cajole.	mad.	tomb.	wild.	more.
60	364	388	481	334	113	258	41

[kue] [kuei] **Kue.**

晷¹	歸	規	閨	龜	傀³
dial.	return.	custom.	room.	tortoise.	puppet.
256	289	475	546	596	26

KUE-LAI.

	鬼	宄	曘	詭	桂[4]	櫃	瑰		
	demon.	traitor.	dial.	guile.	cassia.	counter.	rose.		
	583	135	256	481	271	284	340		
	貴	跪	國[5]	梛					
	dear.	kneel.	state.	coffin.					
	492	502	99	280					
K'ue.	盔[1]	魁	窺	虧	奎[2]	揆	葵	尷	[kʰue] [kʰuei]
	cap.	leader.	spy.	wrong.	star.	cousider.	plant.	idol.	
	359	583	384	459	121	225	450	574	
	愧[4]	潰	殨	跪	瞶	闊[5]	濶		
	shame.	disperse.	burst.	kneel.	dim.	wide.	wide.		
	192	315	290	502	366	546	317		
Kuen.	滾[3]	肱	袞	輥	棍[4]				[kuən]
	boil.	arm.	trim.	roller.	club.				
	312	427	468	509	276				
K'uen.	坤[1]	昆	渾[2]	細[3]	閫[4]	困[4]	睏		[kʰuən]
	earth.	brother.	whole.	bind.	room.	poor.	sleep.		
	103	253	309	406	546	98	364		
La.	拉[1]	拏[2]	拿	拿	喇[3]	那	那[4]	辣[5]	[la]
	pull.	take.	take.	take.	trump.	who.	that.	pungent.	
	210	215	210	215	90	524	525	511	
	瓕	撒	衲	納	臘	蠟	邋		
	splash.	bind.	patch.	pay.	cure.	wax.	filthy.		
	557	237	468	402	436	465	524		
	訥	縭	蜊	鱲					
	shout.	rope.	grub.	fish.					
	479	393	462	585					
Lai.	嬭[1]	來[2]	嬭[3]	崽	奈[4]	癩	耐	賴	[lai]
	breast.	come.	milk.	son.	but.	leprosy.	endure.	rely.	
	131	19	131	135	121	354	421	496	

LAN-LE.

[lan] **Lan.**

婪²	欄	攔	嵐	南	男	楠
covet.	railing.	hinder.	coke.	south.	male.	tree.
129	284	239	156	64	345	278

籃	腩	藍	蘭	襴	難	欖³
basket.	salt.	indigo.	orchid.	trim.	hard.	olive.
395	432	455	457	473	555	285

懶	攬	淥	濫⁴	爛	難
lazy.	contract.	cure.	waste.	rot.	difficulty.
197	240	312	317	328	555

襤
filthy.
473

[laŋ] **Lang.**

哴¹	囊²	榔	狼	郎	攮³	朗³	眼⁴
tall.	bag.	betel.	wolf.	Mr.	push.	distinct.	dry.
506	97	279	335	525	241	261	256

浪	閬
wave.	spacious.
303	546

[lao] **Lao.**

撩¹	牢²	撈	撩	癆	砲	勞
hold.	secure.	drag.	hold.	wasting.	chemical.	toil.
233	332	233	233	253	370	56

哰	醪	惱³	璐	老	腦	狫
gabble.	wine.	angry.	agate.	old.	brain.	itch.
85	528	191	340	420	433	350

鬧⁴	癆
noisy.	poison.
545	353

[le] [lei] **Le.**

捋⁵	勒	肋	擸
strip.	rein.	rib.	bind.
217	55	426	237

(659)

LEN-LI.

Len. [lən]

綸¹	掄²	淪	稜	倫	綸	能
twist.	strike.	sink.	edge.	relation.	twist.	able.
407	219	305	380	23	407	429

輪	睖	冷³	論⁴	嫩		
wheel.	glare.	cold.	discuss.	tender.		
509	365	40	483	131		

Leo. [ləu]

樓²	嘍	羺	顱	僂	摟³	撈
loft.	troops.	lazy.	brow.	robber.	lift.	kidnap.
280	94	128	569	26	230	235

簍	褸	漏⁴	瘺	鏤	陋	
basket.	filthy.	leak.	piles.	bore.	vile.	
393	472	313	353	537	548	

Li. [li]

唎¹	厘²	梨	璃	籬	釐	離
fret.	fraction.	pear.	glass.	fence.	fraction.	leave.
86	66	273	341	396	530	555

黎	犁	魖	娌³	李	狸	理	禮
black.	plough.	spirit.	sisters.	plum.	fox.	right.	rite.
591	333	584	128	264	335	339	376

礼	裏	里	鯉	例⁴	俐	唎	儷
rite.	lining.	mile.	carp.	law.	clever.	talk.	pair.
374	470	529	584	20	20	86	31

利	勵	厲	吏	濾	痢	篱	
profit.	incite.	evil.	official.	strain.	dysentery.	ladle.	
46	58	67	77	318	350	393	

莉	隸	離	麗	茘	曆⁵	栗	
plant.	lictor.	off.	elegant.	lichee.	calendar.	chestnut.	
448	553	555	589	447	258	271	

歷	立	笠	粒	力	劣	靈	
pass.	erect.	hat.	grain.	strength.	bad.	thunder.	
288	385	388	397	53	54	558	

LIANG-LIEN.

[liaŋ] **Liang.**

凉²	涼	梁	糧	樑	良	量
cool.	cool.	millet.	cereals.	beam.	good.	discuss.
41	305	398	399	273	441	530

兩³	两	魎	亮⁴	晾	諒	量
two.	two.	spirit.	light.	air.	guess.	consider.
35	4	583	11	256	483	530

[liao] **Liao.**

撩¹	撩²	嘹	療	聊	簝	佬
hem.	hem.	clear.	cure.	depend.	bamboo.	fellow.
233	233	95	353	423	523	18

僚	鐐	寮	繚	了³	蓼	瞭
mate.	fetters.	mate.	confused.	end.	weed.	know.
29	540	144	412	9	453	366

尥⁴	料
kick.	material.
150	248

[lie] **Lie.**

曆⁵	歷	瀝⁵	烈	獵	立	笠
calendar.	pass.	strain.	fiery.	hunt.	erect.	hat.
258	288	317	317	337	385	388

裂	靂⁵	列	力	劣		
crack.	thunder.	rank.	strength.	bad.		
469	558	45	53	54		

[lien] **Lien.**

奩²	鐮	鰱	廉	憐	簾	聯
outfit.	sickle.	tench.	shame.	pity.	screen.	join.
122	540	485	168	195	394	424

臁	蓮	連	褳	臉³	戀⁴	歛
calf.	lotus.	unite.	purse.	face.	lust.	amass.
435	453	515	472	436	198	247

殮	煉	練	鍊	蹥		
wrap.	try.	drill.	chain.	tread.		
290	324	409	537	504		

(661)

LIN-LO.

Lin. [lin]

伶²	凌	宁	林	淋	玲	痳
clever.	insult.	peace.	wood.	drip.	fine.	gravel.
19	41	141	266	305	338	351

綾	翎	臨	菱	鄰	鈴	零
damask.	plume.	descend.	plant.	near.	bell.	surplus.
408	419	437	449	526	533	556

靈	灵	鱗	麟	哼	廩³	嶺
soul.	soul.	scale.	unicorn.	enjoin.	stipend.	range.
558	319	585	589	96	169	156

檁	領	令⁴	另	賃	凝	吝
beam.	lead.	order.	besides.	hire.	freeze.	stingy.
284	566	13	75	494	42	80

Lio. [lio]

掠⁵	略	畧
plunder.	careless.	careless.
221	346	346

Liu. [liəu]

溜¹	旒²	榴	流	琉	留	硫
slippery.	tassel.	tree.	flow.	glass.	detain.	sulphur.
311	251	279	303	340	346	370

遛	駠	柳³	綹	扭	溜	餾	搊
loiter.	bay.	willow.	purse.	cling.	slide.	warm.	poke.
521	577	270	408	213	311	573	226

Lo. [lo]

邏¹	囉²	挪	摞	籮	羅	膈
brisk.	robber.	move.	sort.	basket.	net.	striæ.
524	97	217	230	396	417	433

蘿	螺	騾	鑼	儸	懦⁴	糯
turnip.	spiral.	mule.	gong.	robber.	timid.	sticky.
457	463	578	541	31	196	400

諾	摞	咯⁵	樂	駱	烙	絡	落
respond.	pile.	!	joy.	camel.	singe.	reel.	fall.
485	230	84	281	577	321	405	450

LONG-LUE.

[loŋ] **Long.**

聾[1]	弄	龍[2]	嚨	噥	欕	瓏
deaf.	do.	dragon.	throat.	mutter.	cage.	fine.
425	169	596	96	96	234	341
濃	籠	農	隆	韃	窿	聾
rich.	basket.	farmer.	prosper.	halter.	hole.	deaf.
316	395	512	551	562	385	425
膿	攏[3]	籠	檁			
pus.	reach.	basket.	basket.			
436	238	396	279			

[lu] **Lu.**

盧[2]	奴	爐	炉	蘆	鑪	顱
hut.	slave.	stove.	stove.	reed.	censer.	brow.
169	123	328	320	456	541	569
魯[3]	滷	努	𤷆	怒[4]	賂	路
coarse.	brine.	exert.	sore.	anger.	bribe.	road.
584	313	54	428	182	494	502
露	鷺	鹿[5]	陸	律	碌	祿
dew.	egret.	deer.	constant.	law.	toil.	pay.
558	588	588	550	176	371	376
綠	蔍	六				
green.	lentils.	six.				
408	449	36				

[ly] **Lü.**

驢[2]	旅[3]	履	慮[4]
donkey.	guest.	shoe.	think.
579	250	154	193

[luan] **Luan.**

㝈[2]	卵	暖	煖	亂[4]
full.	testicle.	mild.	warm.	confused.
100	65	257	324	8

[lue] [luei] **Lue.**

擂[1]	擂[2]	羸	雷	儡	壘
tumble.	grind.	weak.	thunder.	puppet.	heap.
284	235	418	556	30	113

LUE-MANG.

屢	累	彙[4]	擂	擂	淚	內
often.	involve.	book.	beat.	hurl.	tears.	within.
154	403	174	237	283	305	35

累	儽	類
involve.	tire.	sort.
403	31	568

Ma. [ma]

嗎[1]	媽	痲[2]	瘖	蔴	蟇	顢
?	mother.	measles.	blur.	hemp.	fly.	dull.
92	130	351	366	453	462	568

麻	鷹	嗎[3]	瑪	蔆	碼	螞
hemp.	sparrow.	!	agate.	plant.	weight.	leech.
590	587	92	340	454	372	462

蟆[3]	馬	鰢	榪	禡	罵[4]	抹[5]
frog.	horse.	prawn.	pail.	pile.	curse.	wipe.
463	575	585	279	551	416	209

Mai. [mai]

埋[2]	買[3]	蕒	賣[4]	邁
bury.	buy.	plant.	sell.	old.
105	493	454	495	523

Man. [man]

瞞[2]	蠻	饅	褸	輓	滿[3]	慢[4]
conceal.	rude.	bread.	close.	cover.	full.	slow.
366	465	573	472	561	313	193

漫	墁	鏝
flood.	pave.	obverse.
313	110	539

Mang. [maŋ]

悗[1]	忙[2]	盲	茫	莽[3]	蟒
stupid.	busy.	blind.	vague.	rude.	snake.
187	180	361	447	449	463

鯍
bass.
85

(664)

MAO-MIAO.

	Mao.	猫¹	旄²	毛	矛	貓	茅	錨
[mao]		cat.	yak.	hair.	spear.	cat.	grass.	anchor.
		336	250	293	367	336	445	536
		冒⁴	帽	冐	瑁	貌		
		assume.	hat.	spurt.	shell.	figure.		
		38	162	310	340	490		

	Me.	媒²	枚	梅	煤	玫	脢	霉
[me] [mei]		medium.	N. A.	plum.	coal.	rose.	brisket.	mould.
		130	266	274	324	338	430	557
		媒	嵋	美³	每	妹⁴	媚	寐
		decoy.	hill.	good.	each.	sister.	flatter.	asleep.
		587	156	417	292	126	130	142
		昧	眛	魅	脈⁵	脉	麥	默
		foolish.	blind.	spirit.	pulse.	pulse.	wheat.	reflect.
		253	363	583	428	429	589	591
		墨	驀					
		ink.	overstep.					
		112.	578					

	Men.	們¹	們²	門	悶⁴	漫		
[mən]		plural.	plural.	door.	sad.	flood.		
		23	23	542	188	313		

	Mi.	咩¹	蜜	眯	嵋²	彌	糜	迷
[mi]		lamb.	honey.	blink.	hill.	conceal.	millet.	delude.
		84	462	364	156	173	381	513
		米³	謎⁴	密⁵	眉	蜜	篾	
		rice.	riddle.	close.	eyebrow.	honey.	bamboo.	
		397	486	141	362	462	393	

	Miao.	猫¹	描²	眇	矛	苗	猫	渺³
[miao]		cat.	sketch.	look.	lance.	shoot.	cat.	vague.
		336	225	362	367	445	336	309

MIAO-MO.

	藐 disdain. 455	杳 dim. 267	妙⁴ clever. 125	廟 temple. 169			
Mie.	搣³ break. 228	弭⁵ quash. 172	滅 destroy. 311	篾 bamboo. 393	衊 small. 414		[mie]
Mien.	棉² cotton. 276	眠 sleep. 363	綿 soft. 408	免³ escape. 33	冕 crown. 38	勉 exert. 55	挽³ bear. 134	[mien]
	緬⁴ Burmah. 409	面 face. 559	麵 flour. 589				
Min.	冥² dark. 39	民 people. 294	名 name. 77	明 dawn. 253	盟 covenant. 359	銘 carve. 534	[min]
	鳴 sound. 93	瞑 close. 366	酩 drunk. 527	憫³ pity. 195	刡 brnsh. 46	抿 brush. 210	敏 clever. 244
	皿 dish. 357	命⁴ life. 82					
Mo.	摸¹ touch. 230	摹 copy. 231	麽 ? 590	摩² consider. 230	磨 polish. 373	茉 flower. 445	蘑 agaric. 456	[mo]
	饃 bread. 574	魔 demon. 584	抹³ rub. 209	募⁴ enlist. 57	墓 grave. 110	漠 rude. 313	磨 mill. 373
	幕 tent. 162	慕 love. 193	末⁵ last. 262	歿 death. 289	沐 wash. 297	沒 not. 297	莫 don't. 448	寞 lonely. 143	漠 sand. 313

MONG-NIEN.

[moŋ] **Mong.**

朦²	濛	蒙	虻	謀	醾	懵³
impose.	drizzle.	dark.	cleg.	plan.	scum.	blindly.
262	317	452	460	485	529	197

某	猛	畝	蜢	夢⁴	孟	茂	貿
certain.	cruel.	acre.	locust.	dream.	sage.	rank.	barter.
270	355	346	462	117	133	445	493

[mu] **Mu.**

模²	母³	牡	拇	慕⁴	瞀	暮
model.	mother.	peony.	finger.	love.	dull.	close.
281	291	338	211	193	365	257

木⁵	沒	睦	目	苜	牧
wood.	not.	peace.	eye.	clover.	herd.
262	297	365	361	444	332

[n̦i] **Ni.**

呢²	坭	尼	泥	你³	膩⁴
?	mud.	nun.	mud.	you.	oily.
83	103	151	299	17	435

[n̦iaŋ] **Niang.**

娘¹	娘²	釀	仰³	釀⁴
wife.	mother.	wine.	look.	ferment.
128	128	529	15	529

[n̦iao] **Niao.**

咬³	鳥	尿⁴
bite.	bird.	urine.
85	586	151

[n̦ie] **Nie.**

匿⁵	孽	捏	業	搦	捻	梟
conceal.	sin.	mould.	calling.	fight.	pinch.	baton.
61	135	225	278	228	221	437

迷	鑷	溺
disobey.	nippers.	drown.
513	541	311

[n̦ien] **Nien.**

拈¹	嚴²	年	研	閫	撚³	儼	撵
take.	strict.	year.	rub.	judge.	roll.	exactly.	expel.
211	97	164	370	546	234	31	238

NIEN-NGANG.

	碾	趂	念⁴	駼	黏	醲	硯
	crush.	pursue.	think.	inspect.	thick.	strong.	inkslab.
	372	500	181	577	591	529	370

Nin. 㧥² 宁 吝⁴   [ȵin]
sprain. silk. stingy.
237   141   80

Nio. 瘧⁵ 虐   [ȵio]
ague. oppress.
352   457

Niu. 牛² 扭³ 狃 鈕   [ȵieu]
ox. twist. set. button.
332   206   334   532

Nü. 女³   [ȵy]
woman.
123

Ngai. 挨¹ 哀 埃² 巖 研 捱 矮³ 躧   [ŋai]
trust. pity. dead. cliff. rub. be. short. short.
217   84   105   156   370   223   368   506

   愛⁴ 礙 艾 隘 硋
   love. hinder. mugwort. pass. hinder.
   191   374   442   551   371

Ngan. 安¹ 淹 菴 鞍 鵪 研 䴼² 暗³   [ŋan]
peace. drown. hut. saddle. quail. rub. fit. dark.
135   308   449   561   587   370   485   592

   揞 岸⁴ 按 晏 暗 桉 雁 鴈
   hide. bank. place. late. dark. table. goose. goose.
   226   155   215   255   257   271   554   586

Ngang. 肮¹ 昂² 揞³   [ŋaŋ]
filthy. dear. hide.
579   252   226

NGAO-O.

[ŋao] Ngao.
燻¹	熬	鰲²	熬	襖³	咬	傲⁴	坳
stew.	bear.	whale.	boil.	gown.	bite.	proud.	pass.
328	326	585	326	473	85	28	103

奥	懊	拗	鏊
deep.	pity.	lever.	oven.
122	195	214	539

[ŋe] [ŋei] Nge.
額⁵	搤
brow.	grasp.
567	207

[ŋən] Ngen.
恩¹	櫻	鸚³	硬³	硬⁴
grace.	cherry.	parrot.	bruise.	hard.
185	285	588	371	370

[ŋəu] Ngeo.
嘔³	偶	殴	藕	慝⁴	漚	怄
vomit.	idol.	fight.	lotus.	grieve.	damp.	grieve.
94	25	291	456	190	313	193

熅
warm.
325

[ŋi] Ngi.
宜²	儀	疑	擬³	議⁴	義
ought.	etiquette.	doubt.	decide.	discuss.	right.
136	29	348	237	487	418

藝	蟻
trade.	ant.
456	464

[ŋo] Ngo.
娥²	我³	惡⁵	齶
lady.	I.	evil.	mouth.
128	199	189	595

[o] O.
屙¹	窝	萵	阿	倭	渦	鵝²	峩
pass.	nest.	lettuce.	oh.	Japanese.	pool.	goose.	hill.
153	383	452	548	24	305	587	155

(669)

O-PAI.

	蛾 moth. 461	訛 alter. 478	餓⁴ hungry. 572	臥 lie. 437	杌⁵ stool. 265	屋 house. 153	腥 filthy. 595
Ong.	壅¹ cover. 113	翁 old. 419	甕⁴ boiler. 342	甕 boiler. 415	塕 bastion. 109	腌 stink. 434	齆 upper. 561	[oŋ]
	齆 nasal. 594						
Pa.	吧¹ dumb. 80	巴 stick. 158	杷 loquat. 266	琶 guitar. 340	疤 scar. 349	芭 mat. 387	芭 banana. 444	[pa]
	爸 father. 330	爸² father. 330	把³ take. 206	靶 handle. 579	靶 target. 561	壩⁴ plain. 114	播 spread. 241	
	欛 handle. 285	罷 desist. 416	耙 harrow. 422	鈀 harrow. 532	霸 usurp. 558	八⁵ eight. 35		
	叭 trumpet. 75	拔 pull. 211	跋 cross. 501	叭 bird. 85				
P'a.	鈀² harrow. 532	爬 rake. 329	筏 raft. 388	耙 harrow. 422	蚆 cowry. 460	筢 rake. 390	趴³ sprawl. 500	[pʰa]
	帕⁴ kerchief. 160	怕 fear. 182	魄 demon. 583	拍⁵ pat. 212	扳 pull. 211			
Pai.	擺³ spread. 238	拜⁴ worship. 211	敗 defeat. 244	稗 tares. 380				[pai]

P'AI-PAO.

[pʰai]	P'ai.	排² row. 221	牌 shield. 331	派⁴ lot. 301				
[pan]	Pan.	搬¹ flit. 227	斑 spot. 247	瘢 rash. 353	般 sort. 441	螌 fly. 463	頒 publish. 565	班 class. 339	版³ board. 331
		板 board. 266	伴⁴ mate. 17	半 half. 63	扮 dress. 207	拌 mix. 211	瓣 petal. 341	辦 manage. 511	
		蚌 clam. 460							
[pʰan]	P'an.	攀¹ drag. 238	跁² cross. 504	盤 plate. 360	搬 remove. 227	槃 tray. 279	蟠 coil. 464	判⁴ judge. 46	叛 rebel. 71
		泮 pool. 299	盼 care. 362	絆 trip. 403	襻 loop. 473				
[paŋ]	Pang.	幫¹ help. 161	梆 rattle. 274	邦 country. 525	鞤 upper. 562	榜³ list. 279	綁 bind. 406	膀 shoulder. 579	
		傍⁴ near. 26	謗 vilify. 486	棒 stick. 276	蚌 clam. 460	胖 swell. 426			
[pʰaŋ]	P'ang.	旁² side. 250	滂 rain. 311	螃 crab. 463	膀³ ham. 434	膀 shoulder. 579	胖⁴ fat. 428		
[pao]	Pao.	襃¹ praise. 471	包 wrap. 59	脬 bladder. 430	苞 bud. 445	胞 placenta. 428	保³ protect. 20		

PAO-P'E.

	寶 precious. 144	飽 fall. 571	抱[4] carry. 211	報 reward. 108	刨 plane. 46	暴 fierce. 257	爆 burst. 328
	菢 hatch. 449	豹 leopard. 490	鮑 jut. 595				
P'ao.	拋[1] fling. 207	脬 bladder. 430	抱[2] dig. 217	袍 gown. 468	炮 roast. 320	跑[3] run. 501	橀[4] ten. 277	[pʰao]
	泡 froth. 299	疱 blister. 349	砲 gun. 369	礟 gun. 374			
Pe.	背[1] carry. 428	卑 low. 63	杯 cup. 266	盃 cup. 358	碑 tablet. 371	悲 pity. 188	稍[4] card. 471	倍 fold. 23	[pe] [pei]
	偝 carry. 20	婢 slave. 129	悖 rebel. 187	焙 dry. 322	背 back. 428	貝 precious. 490	輩 life. 509
	陛 audience. 548	鞴 harness. 562	伯[5] uncle. 17	北 North. 60	柏 cedar. 270	百 100. 356
	白 white. 355	栢 cedar. 271	帛 silk. 160	泊 poor. 300			
P'e.	坯[1] rough. 103	批 offer. 207	披 throw. 212	砒 arsenic. 369	胚 body. 429	岥 cape. 160	[pʰe] [pʰei]
	培[2] improve. 106	賠 repay. 495	陪 entertain. 550	呸[3] spit. 83	庀 repair. 165	臂[4] back. 435

(672)

P'E-P'I.

譬	轡	配	拍⁵	珀	魄
illustrate.	bridle.	match.	pat.	amber.	soul.
487	510	526	212	338	583

砒	迫
hurry.	urge.
169	513

[pən] **Pen.**

錛¹	奔	崩	綳	挷	本³
adze.	rout.	fall.	pinafore.	stretch.	origin.
536	121	156	408	172	262

笨⁴	逩
stupid.	run.
388	517

[pʰən] **P'en.**

膨¹	盆²
distend.	tub.
435	358

[pʰəu] **P'eo.**

剖³	剖⁴
tell.	split.
50	50

[pi] **Pi.**

荸¹	比³	彼	俻⁴	弊	敝	斃
oil.	equal.	that.	ready.	mischief.	mean.	dead.
449	292	175	26	170	245	247

篦	被	避	比	閉	壁⁵	必	畢
comb.	sheet.	flee.	equal.	close.	wall.	must.	finish.
393	469	524	292	543	112	179	346

煏	筆	逼	鼻	潷
roast.	pencil.	annoy.	nose.	skim.
324	389	519	594	315

[pʰi] **P'i.**

屄¹	皮²	疲	脾	枇	琵	秕³
vagina.	skin.	tired.	spleen.	loquat.	gnitar.	empty.
153	356	349	432	266	340	378

(673)

P'I-PIEN.

	鄙 vulgar. 526	匹 mate. 61	否 bad. 80	痞 beg. 351	屁⁴ wind. 151	痞 sponge. 351	匹⁵ mate. 61	
	疋 piece. 348	霹 thunder. 558						
Piao.	僄¹ quickly. 31	漂 spurt. 314	標 ticket. 281	膘 fat. 436	標 azure. 411	表³ outside. 468	婊 whore. 129	[piao]
	裱 mount. 471							
P'iao.	漂¹ float. 314	薸 weed. 455	飄 blow. 570	瓢² ladle. 341	嫖 cohabit. 131	薸 weed. 455	瞟³ squint. 366	[pʰiao]
	熛 blaze. 325	漂⁴ bleach. 314	票 draft. 375	鰾 glue. 585	膘 white. 356			
Pie.	逼¹ annoy. 519	爊⁵ roast. 324	潎 skim. 315	別 other. 46	逼 annoy. 519	鱉 turtle. 585		[pie]
P'ie.	擘³ break. 236	撇 snap. 244	孬⁴ bad. 134	僻⁵ mean. 30	劈 break. 53	撇 skim. 234	開 open. 547	[pʰie]
	憋 quick. 195	霹 thunder. 558						
Pien.	編¹ braid. 409	鞭 whip. 561	邊 side. 524	匾³ board. 61	扁 flat. 201	楄 flat. 380	緶 hem. 409	旛 flag. 450	[pien]

(674)

PIEN-P'IN.

褊	貶	蝙	便⁴	辮	變	辨
small.	degrade.	bat.	handy.	braid.	change.	differ.
471	493	462	20	413	488	511

辯
state.
511

[pʰien] P'ien.

偏¹	楄	篇	便²	副	片	片⁴	徧
oblique.	cross.	leaf.	cheap.	cnt.	slice.	card.	all.
25	333	392	21	51	331	331	178

遍	騙	副
all.	cheat.	slice.
519	577	51

[pin] Pin.

兵¹	冰	氷	檳	賓	賓	迸	鑌
soldier.	ice.	ice.	tree.	guest.	guest.	crack.	tin.
36	40	296	284	494	494	513	540

柄³	稟	秉	餅	病⁴	殯	並
right.	state.	hold.	cake.	disease.	coffin.	abreast.
270	376	377	571	349	290	5

竝	鬢
abreast.	temple.
386	582

[pʰin] P'in.

奵	拚	汾	平²	憑	蘋²	瓶
share.	divide.	share.	level.	proof.	apple.	vase.
45	211	242	164	195	285	342

缾	萍	評	貧	頻	屛	品³
bottle.	weed.	discuss.	poor.	often.	screen.	rank.
415	449	480	491	566	154	84

聘⁴
betroth.
423

(675)

PO-PU.

Po.	波¹ wave. 300	玻 glass. 338	菠 spinach. 449	簸³ winnow. 394	跛 lame. 501	播⁴ sow. 234	膊⁵ shoulder. 580	[po]
	剝 skin. 50	博 gamble. 64	撥 set. 234	潑 lively. 316	脖 surety. 431	薄 thin. 455	鉑 tinsel. 533	
	鉢 basin. 533	鈸 cymbals. 533	駁 argue. 576	不 not. 4	泊 poor. 300			
P'o.	坡¹ slope. 104	婆² woman. 129	剖³ tell. 50	頗 exert. 566	破⁴ break. 369	勃⁵ sudden. 55		[pʰo]
	潑 sprinkle. 316	瀑 fall. 318	剖 split. 50					
Pong.	弸¹ stretch. 172	嗙³ crisp. 87						[poŋ]
P'ong.	揰¹ fly. 111	烹 cook. 321	鬅 hair. 581	髼² untidy. 581	蓬 mat. 393	棚 tent. 276	朋 friend. 261	[pʰoŋ]
	硼 borax. 371	捧³ scoop. 219	撞⁴ knock. 225	馞 fragrant. 575	碰 knock. 372			
Pu.	補³ patch. 470	拊⁴ appoint. 210	布 calico. 159	捕 catch. 218	步 step. 288	簿 book. 394	蔔 turnip. 453	[pu]
	部 book. 525	不⁵ not. 4						

(676)

	P'u.	鋪[1] spread. 534	葡[2] vine. 450	蒲 rush. 453	菩 idol. 449	譜[3] register. 487	普 large. 256	瞨 dim. 366
[pʰu]		補 patch. 471	舖[4] shop. 440	仆[5] fall. 12	卜 divine. 64	扑 sprawl. 202	撲 flap. 234	僕 slave. 29
		𠬧 card. 477	樸 plain. 283	沸 boil. 300				
[zạn]	Ran.	燃[2] light. 326	然 natural. 322	染[3] dye. 268				
[zạŋ]	Rang.	瓤[2] pulp. 341	禳 pray. 377	嚷[3] wrangle. 96	讓 reprove. 488	壤 matter. 114	讓[4] yield. 488	
[zạo]	Rao.	橈[2] oar. 282	鐃 cymbals. 540	饒 forgive. 573	驍 brave. 578	擾[3] disturb. 237	繞 surround. 412	
		遶 surround. 523						
[zẹ] [zẹi]	Re.	惹[3] provoke. 190	熱[5] warm. 325					
[zẹn]	Ren.	人[2] man. 11	仍 still. 12	仁 good. 12	忍[3] endure. 180	認 confess. 482	任[4] office. 14	
[zẹu]	Reo.	揉[2] rub. 224	柔 gentle. 268	膄[4] meat. 433				

(677)

Rĭ.	兒² son. 34	而 and. 421	耳³ ear. 423	二⁴ two. 9	貳 two. 492	日⁵ sun. 251	[zɿ]
Ro.	弱⁵ weak. 172	若 if. 444					[zo]
Rong.	絨² velvet. 404	茸 antler. 446	毧 down. 294	毧³ down. 294			[zoŋ]
Ru.	褥² rug. 472	如 like. 124	儒 literary. 30	臑 weak. 436	乳³ milk. 8	孺 child. 135	孺⁴ wife. 135	[zu]
	辱⁵ insult. 512	入 enter. 34	肉 flesh. 425				
Ruan.	軟³ weak. 508						[zuan]
Rue.	銳⁴ valiant. 534						[zue] [zuei]
Ruen.	孕⁴ pregnant. 132	潤 moist. 315	閏 extra. 544				[zuən]
Sa.	薩¹ idol. 455	灑³ sprinkle. 318	撒 sow. 234	洒 sprinkle. 301	颯⁵ gust. 569	撒 sow. 234	霎 shower. 557	[sa]
	鋸 saw. 532	跴 tread. 501					

SAI-SI.

[sai] **Sai.**
㩙¹	腮	鰓	賽⁴
wedge.	cheek.	gills.	rival.
235	433	585	496

[san] **San.**
三¹	傘³	饊	散	散⁴
three.	umbrella.	cake.	loose.	scatter.
3	27	574	245	245

[saŋ] **Sang.**
喪¹	桑	嗓³	㩙	磉	喪⁴
mourn.	mulberry.	throat.	wedge.	plinth.	lose.
90	271	92	226	373	91

[sao] **Sao.**
臊¹	騷	掃³	嫂	掃⁴	瘙	㷮
stink.	entire.	sweep.	wife.	broom.	itch.	light.
436	577	221	130	221	352	581

燥
friable.
328

[se] [sei] **Se.**
虱⁵	嗇	塞	澀	色	濇
louse.	stingy.	stop.	rough.	colour.	rough.
459	92	109	316	442	317

[sən] **Sen.**
僧¹	孫	生	森	牲	甥
priest.	grandson.	bear.	severe.	animal.	nephew.
29	134	343	276	333	343

參	損³	榫	省	笋	筍	濻⁴
Orion.	injure.	tenon.	province.	sprout.	sprout.	soak.
68	228	279	362	387	389	314

[səu] **Seo.**
搜¹	鎪¹	餿	颼¹	撒³	叟	㖤⁴	瘦
search.	mortise.	sour.	cold.	arouse.	sir.	spit.	lean.
227	538	573	573	238	71	94	352

[si] **Si.**
西¹	洗³	細	婿⁵	媳	息	惜	熄
west.	wash.	fine.	son.	bride.	breath.	pity.	extinguish.
473	301	404	130	131	185	188	325

(679)

SI-SIAO.

	習	膝	席	蓆	蟋	錫	聲	
	habit.	knee.	feast.	mat.	cricket.	pewter.	sound	
	419	435	161	453	464	536	384	
	夕	昔						
	evening.	former.						
	116	253						
SI.	厮¹	司	師	思	斯	撕	獅	[sɿ]
	privy.	manage.	sir.	think.	genteel.	tare.	lion.	
	67	75	161	183	249	235	336	
	私	絲	螄	鷥	死³	四⁴	事	似
	private.	silk.	spiral.	egret.	die.	four.	affair.	like.
	377	405	463	588	289	97	9	17
	士	肆	寺	祀	伺	思		
	scholar.	loose.	mosque.	sacrifice.	attend.	think.		
	114	425	145	374	17	183		
	駟	泗						
	team.	paper.						
	576	300						
Siang.	廂¹	橡	相	箱	鑲²	祥²	詳	[siaŋ]
	room.	oak.	mutual.	box.	piece.	lucky.	detail.	
	168	283	362	392	541	375	481	
	庠	想³	像⁴	象	相			
	school.	think.	image.	elephant.	face.			
	167	191	29	489	362			
Siao.	宵¹	消	硝	簫	霄	銷	逍	[siao]
	night.	melt.	tan.	whistle.	cloud.	cast.	ramble.	
	140	303	370	394	557	535	514	
	小³	笑⁴	肖	鞘				
	small.	laugh.	like.	sheath.				
	148	387	426	561				

(680)

[sie]	Sie.	些¹ little. 10	斜² slant. 248	邪 heresy. 525	寫³ write. 144	卸⁴ doff. 65	瀉 purge. 318	謝 thanks. 486
		楔⁵ wedge. 277	褻 profane. 472					
[sien]	Sien.	仙¹ god. 13	先 first. 33	籼 rice. 378	鮮 fresh. 584	絃² string. 403	線⁴ thread. 409	
[sin]	Sin.	心¹ heart. 179	新 new. 249	星 star. 254	煋¹ spark. 324	猩 monkey. 336	腥 rank. 433	薪 fuel. 455
		辛 bitter. 510	搱³ blow. 236	醒 awake. 528	信⁴ believe. 21	性 nature. 182	姓 name. 127	鋝 rust. 537
[sio]	Sio.	削⁵ pare. 49	宿 lodge. 141	屑 dust. 153	俗 common. 21	粟 grass. 398	窣 sound. 383	續 join. 413
		速 haste. 516						
[siəu]	Siu.	羞¹ shame. 418	脩 fees. 431	鑐¹ meats. 573	修 build. 23	囚² prison. 97	秀⁴ elegant. 377	繡 sew. 407
		繡 sew. 412	袖 sleeve. 469	銹 rust. 535	岫 hills. 155			
[so]	So.	唆¹ incite. 86	娑 trouble. 128	梭 shuttle. 274	蓑 coir. 453	趖 glide. 499	瑣² spy. 364	所³ place. 201

SO-SUAN.

	鎖 lock. 538	窣[5] sound. 383	朔 first. 261	率 lead. 337	索 rope. 402	縮 shrink. 411	蟀 cricket. 464	
	鎨 rod. 538							
Song.	松[1] pine. 267	鬆 loose. 581	㧲[3] shake. 239	竦 excite. 386	聳 high. 420	訟[4] law. 479	送 present. 513	[soŋ]
	頌 praise. 565	誦 chant. 482						
Su.	搔[1] tickle. 239	梳 comb. 274	甦 revive. 344	疏 thin. 348	蔬 greens. 454	疎 thin. 348	蘇 proper. 456	[su]
	酥 butter. 527	數[3] count. 246	嗾[4] crop. 93	塑 model. 109	漱 rinse. 314	數 sum. 246	素 plain. 402	
	訴 state. 480	鎨 greens. 573	束[5] bind. 264	俗 common. 21				
Sü.	繻[1] fray. 413	雖 though. 554	需 need. 557	𤲞 wards. 540	鬚 beard. 581	須 need. 565	荽 seed. 448	[sy]
	敘[4] talk. 244	序 preface. 166	敍 chat. 71	絮 cotton. 405	緒 clew. 410	遂 smooth. 519	堅 add. 106	
Suan.	酸[1] sour. 527	痠 ache. 350	蒜[4] garlic. 453	算 reckon. 390	算 reckon. 391			[suan]

(682)

SUE-SHAN.

[sue] [suei]	Sue.	痠¹ feeble. 353	隨² follow. 552	髓³ marrow. 580	歲⁴ age. 288	碎 small. 371	祟 evil. 375	絮 cotton. 405

錐
bobbin.
411

[sye] Süe.   雪⁵
              snow.
              556

[syen]	Süen.	宣¹ preach. 138	鮮 fresh. 584	旋² whirl. 250	涎 spittle. 307	燒 scald. 326	癬 ringworm. 354
		選 select. 523	漩⁴ swirl. 314	剬 cut. 47	選 select. 523	旋 whirl. 250	鏇 whorl. 539

[syn]	Süin.	巡² patrol. 157	循 follow. 178	巡 patrol. 512	汛⁴ guard. 297	遜 meek. 521	訊 try. 478

[ṣa]	Sha.	杉¹ pine. 264	沙 sand. 297	牸 cow. 333	莎 cholera. 350	砂 cinnabar. 369	糖 sugar. 397	紗 crape. 402
		裟 coarse. 470	鯊 shark. 584	殺 kill. 291	煞 evil. 324			

[ṣai]	Shai.	篩¹ sieve. 393	曬⁴ dry. 258	晒 dry. 255

[ṣan]	Shan.	山¹ hill. 155	揚 fan. 227	煽 excite. 325	珊 coral. 338	羶 rank. 418	衫 gown. 468	蟬³ cicada. 464

(683)

西蜀方言

SHAN-SHEN.

	蟾	禪	閃³	陝	善⁴	騸	磉	
	toad.	meditate.	slip.	place.	good.	geld.	clay.	
	464	376	543	549	91	577	373	
	鱔	膳	扇	蟮	剼			
	eel.	food.	fan.	worm.	geld.			
	586	435	201	464	52			
Shang.	傷¹	商	嘗²	嫦	常	裳	償³	[ʂaŋ]
	hurt.	consult.	taste.	lady.	usual.	clothes.	restore.	
	28	87	93	131	162	471	30	
	晌	賞	上⁴	尙				
	noon.	reward.	top.	like.				
	255	496	3	149				
Shao.	捎¹	梢	燒	稍	筲	茗²	少³	紹⁴	[ʂao]
	tie.	twig.	burn.	little.	basket.	vetch.	few.	meet.	
	218	274	326	379	390	446	148	404	
	哨	少	捎					
	spy.	young.	carry.					
	86	149	218					
She.	奢¹	賒	蛇²	捨³	舍⁴	社	射	[ʂe] [ʂei]
	waste.	give.	snake.	give.	hut.	earth.	shoot.	
	122	494	460	221	440	374	146	
	赦	麝	舌⁵	設	賒	涉		
	forgive.	musk.	tongue.	spread.	lose.	ford.		
	497	589	440	479	494	303		
Shen.	伸¹	升	斟	深	申	紳	聲	[ʂən]
	redress.	peck.	pour.	deep.	state.	gentry.	sound.	
	17	62	248	305	345	403	424	
	身	賸²	陞	乘²	唇	晨	神	辰
	body.	fill.	rise.	ride.	lip.	morning.	gods.	hour.
	505	57	549	7	86	255	575	511

(684)

SHEN-SHI.

嬸[3]	審	剩[4]	勝	甚	盛	聖
aunt.	try.	over.	conquer.	very.	full.	sacred.
132	144	51	57	342	359	424

賢
testicle.
432

[ʂəu] Sheo.

收[1]	收	手[3]	守	首	壽[4]	授
receive.	receive.	hand.	guard.	head.	age.	give.
69	241	201	136	574	115	221

獸	受	首
beast.	receive.	deliver.
337	70	574

[ɕi] Shi.

嘻[1]	希	攜	犧	稀	喜[3]	係[4]
laugh.	few.	lead.	animal.	sparse.	joy.	really.
94	160	227	333	379	88	20

系	戲	繫
join.	play.	handle.
400	199	413

[ʂʅ] Shï.

匙[1]	尸	屍	施	獅	詩	豉
key.	corpse.	corpse.	give.	lion.	poem.	beans.
60	151	153	250	336	481	489

時[2]	始[3]	史	使	匙	屎	世[4]
time.	first.	history.	use.	key.	dung.	world.
255	126	75	20	60	153	4

勢	市	弒	是	柿	氏	示	視
power.	market.	kill.	yes.	tree.	née.	sign.	see.
57	160	170	254	267	294	374	475

試	誓	式	失[5]	室	拾	涉
try.	oath.	form.	lose.	house.	gather.	ford.
481	481	170	120	138	215	303

(685)

SHI-SHIAO.

十	濕	蝕	識	釋	食	飾
ten.	wet.	eclipse.	know.	loose.	food.	dress.
61	317	462	487	529	570	571
適	實	石				
happen.	real.	stone.				
522	143	368				

Shia. [ɕia]

鰕¹	瑕²	諕	霞	下⁴	嚇	夏
shrimp.	flaw.	reckless.	red.	under.	scare.	summer.
585	340	485	557	2	96	115
暇	俠⁵	匣	峽	挾⁵	狹⁵	瞎
leisure.	zeal.	box.	gorge.	cherish.	narrow.	blind.
257	20	61	155	217	335	366
轄	狎					
govern.	dote.					
509	334					

Shiai. [ɕiai]

偕²	骸	孩	蟹³	懈⁴	蟹
harmony.	bone.	child.	crab.	lazy.	crab.
24	579	134	464	195	464

Shiang. [ɕiaŋ]

香¹	鄉	降²	享³	響	餉
scent.	country.	submit.	enjoy.	noise.	rations.
574	525	548	11	563	571
向⁴	香				
face.	spice.				
76	575				

Shiao. [ɕiao]

僥¹	梟	磽	驍	餚²	餚
lucky.	expose.	barren.	brave.	viands.	meat.
30	274	373	578	291	572
曉³	孝⁴	效	効		
know.	respect.	imitate.	toil.		
258	133	243	55		

SHIE-SHO.

[ɕie] **Shie.**

協⁵	吸	恤	歇	泣	燋	胁
unity.	breathe.	pity.	rest.	weep.	scorch.	loins.
63	80	186	286	299	325	429

血	隙	蠍	穴
blood.	crack.	scorpion.	den.
465	552	464	382

[ɕien] **Shien.**

嫌²	銜	賢	閒	憲³	險	顯
dislike.	rank.	virtue.	leisure.	officer.	danger.	show.
130	533	495	543	194	552	568

獻⁴	献	現	縣	憲	限
offer.	offer.	show.	county.	official.	set.
337	336	339	410	194	548

[ɕin] **Shin.**

興¹	馨	行²	刑	尋	形
prosper.	pleasant.	walk.	punishment.	seek.	form.
439	575	466	45	147	174

倖⁴	幸	興	行	釁	烌
lucky.	lucky.	elation.	temper.	fault.	warm.
22	165	439	466	529	322

[ɕio] **Shio.**

學⁵	畜	續	蓄	速
study.	animal.	mend.	gather.	quick.
134	346	414	452	516

[ɕioŋ] **Shiong.**

兄¹	兇	凶	胸	芎	熊²	雄
brother.	cruel.	bad.	breast.	angelica.	bear.	male.
32	32	43	429	442	325	553

[ɕiəu] **Shiu.**

休¹	朽³
cease.	rot.
14	263

[ṣo] **Sho.**

㺺³	屬⁵	芍	說	囑
hound.	belong.	peony.	speak.	will.
94	154	442	482	97

(687)

SHU-SHUE.

Shu.	書¹ book. 258	殊 really. 290	舒 easy. 440	輸 lose. 509	暑³ hot. 257	黍 millet. 591	鼠 rat. 593	術⁴ craft. 467	[ṣu]
	恕 forgive. 185	樹 tree. 283	庶 common. 168		署 oversee. 416	叔⁵ uncle. 70	塾 school. 110		
	孰 which. 134	屬 belong. 154	束 bind. 264	淑 virtue. 305	熟 ripe. 326	嘱 will. 97	蜀 Sĭ-ch'nan. 461		
	術 craft. 467	贖 atone. 497							

| Shü. | 噓¹ blow. 93 | 虛 empty. 458 | 許³ allow. 479 | | | | | | [çy] |

| Shua. | 耍³ play. 421 | 廈 room. 67 | 刷⁵ brush. 48 | | | | | | [ṣua] |

| Shuai. | 衰¹ feeble. 468 | 摔³ flap. 231 | 甩 throw. 344 | 帥⁴ general. 161 | | | | | [ṣuai] |

| Shuan. | 拴¹ bind. 216 | 珊 coral. 338 | 閂 bar. 543 | 涮⁴ rinse. 306 | 疝 hernia. 349 | 閂 bar. 543 | 訕 bandy. 478 | | [ṣuan] |

| Shuang. | 孀¹ widow. 132 | 艭 boat. 441 | 雙 pair. 554 | 霜 frost. 557 | 爽³ easy. 330 | | | | [ṣuaŋ] |

| Shue. | 誰² who. 483 | 隨 follow. 552 | 水³ water. 295 | 鼠 rat. 593 | 黍 millet. 591 | 瑞⁴ lucky. 340 | 睡 sleep. 365 | 稅 duty. 379 | [ṣue] [ṣuei] |

(688)

SHÜE-T'A.

[ɕye]	Shüe.	靴¹ boot. 560	屑⁵ dust. 153					
[ʂuən]	Shuen.	淳² good. 306	湻 good. 309	純 loyal. 402	繩 string. 413	醇 rich. 527	鶉 quail. 587	順⁴ obey. 565
[ɕyen]	Shüen.	喧¹ wrangle. 89	掀 shake. 219	萱 lily. 450	軒 shop. 508	鮮 fresh. 584	弦² string. 171	懸 hang. 197
		玄 dark. 337	絃 string. 403	癬³ ringworm. 354	楦⁴ last. 278	眩 giddy. 363		
[ɕyn]	Shüin.	熏¹ smoke. 325	醺 drunk. 528	勳 loyal. 58	尋² seek. 147	訓⁴ teach. 477		
[ta]	Ta.	打³ beat. 202	大⁴ great. 117	嗒⁵ smack. 93	搭 carry. 228	撻 thrash. 235	溚 wet. 311	答 reply. 389
		縺 knot. 412	榻 smack. 440	墥 crash. 105	躂 fall. 505	褡 purse. 472	達 know. 519	韃 queue. 562
		瘩 wen. 353	沓 place. 297	畲 wrinkle. 357	砘 smash. 369			
[tʰa]	T'a.	他¹ he. 13	塔⁵ pagoda. 109	獺 otter. 337	踏 tread. 503	遢 filthy. 521	榻 bed. 278	㥪 despair. 192
		塌 fall. 109	沓 place. 297	褟 shirt. 472				

(689)

TAI-T'AN.

Tai.	懛¹ pedant. 196	獃 stupid. 336	呆 stupid. 264	歹³ evil. 289	代⁴ year. 13	帶 belt. 162	大 chief. 118	[tai]
	待 wait. 177	怠 rude. 183	戴 wear. 200	玳 shell. 338	袋 sack. 469	貸 borrow. 493		
T'ai.	擡¹ lift. 237	抬 lift. 212	胎 fœtus. 429	台² sir. 75	抬 carry. 212	擡 carry. 237	檯 table. 284	臺 stage. 438	[tʰai]
	苔 moss. 446	薹 stalk. 455	駘³ weary. 576	太⁴ too. 118	泰 peace. 300	態 way. 192		
Tan.	丹¹ red. 6	單 single. 91	擔 carry. 236	簞 basket. 394	襌 sheet. 472	貤 delay. 506	担³ duster. 213	[tan]
	胆 gall. 429	膽 gall. 436	但⁴ but. 17	石 picul. 368	擔 load. 236	淡 insipid. 306	蛋 egg. 460	誕 natal. 482
	談 chat. 484	彈 ball. 173	旦 morning. 252				
T'an.	探¹ try. 222	攤 spread. 239	灘 rapid. 318	癱 palsy. 354	貪 covet. 492	壇² altar. 113	彈 thrum. 173	[tʰan]
	檀 tree. 284	鐔 jar. 415	談 chat. 484	痰 phlegm. 352	坦³ level. 104	毯 rug. 294	嘆⁴ sigh. 94	炭 coal. 320
	歎 sigh. 287	探 spy. 222					

(690)

TANG-T'E.

[taŋ]	Tang.	當¹ ought. 347	禧 seat. 473	鐺 gong. 540	攩³ stop. 240	黨 class. 592	宕⁴ pool. 138	攩 hinder. 240	檔 end. 284
		當 pawn. 347	蕩 wild. 454	擋 stop. 235	鐺 gong. 540				
[tʰaŋ]	T'ang.	湯¹ broth. 309	堂² hall. 106	塘 tank. 109	棠 Pyrus. 277	糖 sugar. 399	膛 chest. 435	搪 stop. 228	倘³ if. 23
		躺 lie. 506	淌 gush. 305	燙⁴ scald. 327	趟 run. 519				
[tao]	Tao.	刀¹ knife. 43	倒³ fall. 23	島 island. 155	禱 pray. 377	到⁴ arrive. 48	導 lead. 148	盜 robber. 359	
		盜 robber. 359	道 road. 519	蹈 tread. 505	倒 turn. 23				
[tʰao]	T'ao.	叨¹ favour. 75	掏 pick. 228	滔 reach. 311	縚 cord. 410	韜 strategy. 562	桃² peach. 272	淘 wash. 306	
		萄 vine. 450	逃 escape. 514	濤 wave. 317	討³ beg. 478	套⁴ cover. 122			
[te] [tei]	Te.	德⁵ virtue. 178	得 get. 177						
[tʰe] [tʰei]	T'e.	特⁵ special. 333							

(691)

TEN-TI.

Ten.	墩¹	敦	燈	灯	登	蹬	戥³	[tən]
	block.	stout.	lamp.	lamp.	ascend.	stamp.	scale.	
	112	245	324	319	354	505	199	
	等	凳⁴	囤	橙	沌	燉	盹	遁
	sort.	stool.	bin.	stool.	chaos.	steam.	nod.	vanish.
	389	43	98	284	298	327	363	520
	鈍	鐙	頓	噔				
	blunt.	stirrup.	jerk.	hiccough.				
	532	540	565	573				

Ten.	吞¹	屯²	疼	藤	謄	騰	撐³	[tʰən]
	swallow.	store.	ache.	creeper.	copy.	mount.	jolt.	
	81	154	350	395	486	578	232	
	腯	黱	唚⁴	掭				
	fat.	dark.	hesitate.	delay.				
	433	592	79	208				

Teo.	抙¹	樖	兜	篼	陡³	斗	鬪⁴	[təu]
	lift.	root.	lap.	basket.	steep.	bushel.	wrangle.	
	231	280	34	393	549	247	582	
	荳	痘	逗	讀				
	bean.	pox.	delay.	phrase.				
	448	551	516	488				

Tʻeo.	偸¹	投²	頭	抖³	透⁴			[tʰəu]
	steal.	yield.	head.	shake.	through.			
	25	208	566	207	516			

Ti.	爹¹	低	地	底³	抵	牴	地⁴	[ti]
	father.	low.	little.	bottom.	resist.	gore.	earth.	
	330	17	101	166	212	333	101	
	弟	棣	帝	第	蒂	遞	遞	
	brother.	Kerria.	ruler.	order.	calyx.	hand.	hand.	
	171	277	161	388	450	516	521	

(692)

TI-T'IAO.

		敵⁵ enemy. 246	滴 drop. 314	的 certain. 356	笛 flute. 388			
[tʰi]	T'i.	剔¹ trim. 50	梯 ladder. 274	啼² weep. 92	堤 dike. 108	提 carry. 225	蹄 hoof. 504	隄 dike. 551
		題 theme. 567	體³ body. 580	剃⁴ shave. 49	屉 drawer. 153	替 for. 259	嚔 sneeze. 96	剔⁵ trim. 50
		踢 kick. 503						
[tia]	Tia.	爹¹ father. 330						
[tiao]	Tiao.	叼¹ seize. 75	凋 fall. 41	刁 stir up. 44	剫 pry. 47	貂 sable. 490	雕 carve. 554	碉 stone. 372	屌³ penis. 153
		吊⁴ hang. 78	弔 hang. 171	扚 carry. 208	掉 fall. 222	钓 ear. 378	鸢 project. 384	绸 tie. 402	銚 tall. 506
		釣 angle. 532	調 tune. 484					
[tʰiao]	Tiao.	挑¹ carry. 216	條² rod. 272	調 mix. 484	笤 broom. 388	掉³ change. 222	糶⁴ plank. 441	跳 leap. 503
		祧 inherit. 375	銚 pot. 415					

TIE-TIN.

Tie.	爹¹	疊⁵	帖	褶	滴	碟	笛	[tie]
	father.	serried.	card.	fold.	drop.	plate.	flute.	
	330	71	160	241	314	372	388	
	蝶	跌	蹀	疊				
	moth.	fall.	stamp.	serried.				
	462	502	504	348				
T'ie.	刵¹	刵⁵	睇	貼	踢	鉄	鐵	帖	[tʰie]
	trim.	trim.	spleen.	paste.	kick.	iron.	iron.	card.	
	50	50	432	493	503	533	540	160	
Tien.	癲¹	顛	典³	點	点	佃⁴	墊		[tien]
	mad.	top.	record.	dot.	dot.	till.	deposit.		
	354	568	37	592	321	18	111		
	奠	店	殿	墊	電	靛			
	pour.	inn.	hall.	wedge.	electric.	indigo.			
	122	167	291	342	556	559			
	玷	簟							
	dishonour.	mat.							
	338	394							
T'i'en.	天¹	添	塡²	田	甜	恬	忝³		[tʰien]
	sky.	add.	fill.	field.	sweet.	content.	unworthy.		
	119	306	109	344	342	186	181		
	殄	舔	捵⁴						
	waste.	lick.	raise.						
	289	571	220						
Tin.	丁¹	疔	叮	酊	釘	釘	虰	瞪²	[tin]
	person.	boil.	enjoin.	drunk.	nail.	fill.	fly.	look.	
	2	349	75	526	531	560	459	365	
	頂³	鼎	定⁴	碇	釘	錠	訂		
	top.	tripod.	fix.	anchor.	nail.	ingot.	fix.		
	564	593	137	372	531	536	477		

(694)

T'IN-TONG.

[tʰin] T'in.

聽¹	廳	停²	庭	廷	疼	錠
hear.	hall.	adjust.	home.	court.	sore.	spindle.
425	169	25	168	169	424	534

霆	亭	挺³	聽⁴
thunder.	arbour.	drive.	hear.
557	11	218	425

[tiəu] Tiu.

丟¹
reject.
4

[to] To.

多¹	朵	朵³	垛	躲	剁⁴	墮	惰
many.	ear.	N.A.	target.	hide.	mince.	fall.	lazy.
116	263	263	104	506	49	112	191

舵	馱	奪⁵	度	橐
helm.	load.	snatch.	consider.	bag.
441	576	122	167	283

[tʰo] T'o.

拖¹	沱²	砣	砣	馱	駝	毻
drag.	pool.	hump.	weight.	carry.	camel.	lump.
213	300	350	370	575	576	589

陀	妥³	庹	嚲	托⁵	挩	脫
place.	secure.	fathom.	dangle.	decline.	rude.	undress.
548	125	168	507	204	225	431

痞	禿	託
scall.	bald.	entrust.
351	377	478

[toŋ] Tong.

鼕¹	冬	東	烔	鼕²	棟³	懂
sound.	winter.	east.	flame.	sound.	stupid.	know.
593	39	267	321	593	189	196

涷	硧	朣	董	動⁴	凍	棟	洞
turbid.	sound.	large.	antique.	move.	cold.	pillar.	cave.
309	369	435	450	56	41	277	302

(695)

T'ONG-TUAN.

T'ong.	通¹ pervade. 516	蓪 Fatsia. 454	同² with. 78	桐 tree. 272	瓵 tile. 342	瞳 pupil. 366	銅 brass. 534	[tʰoŋ]
	幢 streamer. 163	童 boy. 386	筒 tube. 389	蓎 plant. 447	衕 alley. 467	桶³ pail. 274	箌 quiver. 390	
	統 lead. 405	痛⁴ ache. 351						
Tu.	都¹ all. 525	堵³ stop. 108	睹 look. 365	肚 bladder. 426	覩 look. 475	賭 gamble. 496	妒⁴ envy. 125	[tu]
	度 laws. 167	杜 stop. 264	渡 ferry. 309	肚 belly. 426	鍍 plate. 537	瀆⁵ insult. 42	毒 poison. 292	
	獨 only. 337	督 lead. 365	纛 flag. 414	讀 study. 488	贖 atone. 497			
Tu.	圖² map. 100	塗 mud. 110	屠 kill. 154	徒 pupil. 177	途 way. 516	土³ earth. 100	吐 spit. 78	兔⁴ rabbit. 34	[tʰu]
	疣⁵ scall. 351	禿 bald. 377						
Tuan.	端¹ straight. 386	短³ short. 367	斷⁴ break. 249	段 lot. 290	緞 satin. 410			[tuan]
T'uan.	團² lump. 100	摶 gather. 231	糰 ball. 400					[tʰuan]

(696)

TUE-TSAN.

[tue] [tuei]	Tue.	堆¹ pile. 107	堆³ wholesale. 115	兌⁴ change. 34	對 match. 147	碓 mortar. 372	隊 ranks. 551
[tʰue] [tʰuei]	T'ue.	推¹ push. 222	腿³ leg. 434	退⁴ recede. 514			
[tsa]	Tsa.	嚌¹ noise. 94	雜⁵ mix. 555	咂 bite. 83	嘖 noise. 94	眨 wink. 363	砸 crush. 370	喳 noisy. 97
		摘 pick. 231	怎 how. 183				
[tsʰa]	Ts'a.	擦⁵ rub. 238	側 nearly. 26				
[tsai]	Tsai.	哉¹ ! 85	栽 plant. 272	災 calamity. 319	灾 calamity. 320	宰³ ruler. 140	載 year. 508	崽 pup. 156
		在⁴ in. 101	再 again. 38	載 load. 508			
[tsʰai]	Ts'ai.	猜¹ guess. 335	才² ability. 202	裁 cut. 469	財 money. 491	纔 just. 414	材 stuff. 264	睬³ notice. 365
		彩 luck. 174	採 sip. 222	綵 luck. 408	菜⁴ meat. 450			
[tsan]	Tsan.	簪¹ clasp. 394	拶³ torture. 216	㯏 torture. 275	儹 amass. 31	藏 meal. 456	趲 move. 500	昝 time. 254

(697)

TS'AN-TS'AO.

	湛[4]	濺	蘸	讚	鏨	顙	綻	
	glitter.	splash.	dip.	praise.	chisel.	skull.	unrip.	
	308	318	457	488	539	582	407	
Ts'an.	參[1]	摻	攙	餐	鰺	慚[2]	殘	[tsʰan]
	visit.	add.	support.	meal.	fish.	shame.	cruel.	
	68	231	239	572	586	193	290	
	蠶	譏	饞	慘[3]	產	儳[4]		
	grub.	change.	greedy.	bad.	bear.	villain.		
	465	488	574	194	343	31		
Tsang.	髒[1]	賍	賺	藏[3]	藏[4]	塟	臟	葬	[tsaŋ]
	filthy.	booty.	booty.	meal.	Tibet.	bury.	entrails.	bury.
	580	494	497	456	456	110	436	450
Ts'ang.	倉[1]	窓	窗	艙	蜣	藏[2]		[tsʰaŋ]
	granary.	window.	window.	hold.	fly.	conceal.		
	24	383	383	441	463	455		
Tsao.	慒[1]	糟	遭	醋	早[3]	澡	蚤	[tsao]
	crisp.	draff.	incur.	wine.	early.	bathe.	flea.	
	326	399	522	528	252	317	460	
	棗	懆[4]	皂	竈	灶	造		
	jujube.	dull.	black.	stove.	stove.	rebel.		
	277	196	·356	385	320	517		
Ts'ao.	操[1]	噪[2]	嘈	敞	懆	曹	槽	[tsʰao]
	drill.	chirp.	noisy.	worn.	confused.	Hades.	trough.	
	236	96	94	150	194	259	281	
	漕	糟	膉	蠅[2]	草[3]	譟		
	channel.	distillery.	weak.	worm.	grass.	trouble.		
	314	399	435	463	447	487		
	騲	燥[4]	糙	躁	造			
	geld.	hot.	coarse.	hasty.	create.			
	577	328	399	505	516			

TSE-TS'EO.

[tse] [tsei]	Tse	仄⁵ slant. 12	則 rule. 49	摘 pick. 231	窄 narrow. 383	賊 thief. 494	責 reprove. 492	側 side. 26
[tsʰe] [tsʰei]	Ts'e.	側⁵ side. 26	册 list. 38	宅 house. 136	拆 break. 213	擇 select. 236	測 know. 310	澤 grace. 317
		皵 wrinkle. 357	策 plan. 389					
[tsən]	Tsen.	增¹ add. 112	尊 noble. 147	曾 past. 259	爭 exert. 329	睜 open. 365	箏 kite. 390	罾 net. 417	遵 obey. 523
		酇³ rotten. 52	怎 how. 183	挣⁴ exert. 219	甑 steamer. 342			
[tsʰən]	Ts'en.	撐¹ prop. 232	村 village. 265	樘 bracket. 281	邨 village. 525	存² retain. 132	層 layer. 154
		曾 past. 259	橙 orange. 283	忖³ reflect. 180	逞 presume. 514	磣 gritty. 373	寸⁴ inch. 145	櫬 assist. 473
		蹭 ache. 505	撐 prop. 232					
[tsəu]	Tseo.	走³ walk. 498	奏⁴ report. 122					
[tsʰəu]	Ts'eo.	掬¹ lift. 229	愁² grief. 191	凑⁴ amass. 42	瘶 pant. 579	湊 amass. 310		

(699)

TSI-TS'Ĭ.

Tsi.

唧¹	擠²	擠³	濟	祭⁴	劑	濟	[tsi]
noise.	crowd.	crowd.	array.	sacrifice.	course.	aid.	
92	237	237	317	375	53	317	

嫉⁵	疾	稷	積	集	喞	鯽
envy.	haste.	earth.	pile.	meet.	squeak.	bream.
131	350	381	381	553	96	585

脊	卽
spine.	instant.
430	65

Ts'i.

凄¹	凄	妻	悽	棲	臍²	齊	砌⁴	[tsʰi]
cold.	cold.	wife.	grieve.	rest.	navel.	all.	pave.	
307	41	126	189	276	436	594	369	

七⁵	戚	漆
seven.	kin.	lacquer.
2	199	315

Tsĭ.

錙¹	姿	孳	恣	滋	疵	貲	[tsɿ]
cash.	beauty.	gain.	vicious.	moist.	flaw.	money.	
536	127	134	186	312	350	493	

姊³	子	梓	滓	紫	髭	仔
sister.	son.	tree.	refuse.	purple.	beard.	careful.
126	132	273	312	404	581	14

自⁴	字	牸
from.	letter.	cow.
437	133	333

Ts'ĭ.

玼¹	辞²	辭	慈	雌	磁	祠	[tsʰɿ]
wipe.	refuse.	refuse.	love.	female.	china.	ancestral.	
501	311	511	192	554	373	375	

楮	詞	嗣	此³	刺⁴	次	朿	賜
sticky.	accuse.	heir.	this.	thorn.	next.	prick.	bestow.
398	480	93	287	48	285	447	496

TSIANG-TS'IE.

[tsiaŋ] **Tsiang.**

將¹	漿	獎³	槳	匠⁴	醬	將
future.	starch.	boast.	oar.	mechanic.	soy.	leader.
146	314	123	280	61	528	146

糨
paste.
399

[tsʰiaŋ] **Ts'iang.**

搶¹	鎗	墻²	牆	搶³	嗆⁴	像
resist.	rifle.	wall.	wall.	plunder.	choke.	like.
229	538	113	331	229	93	29

[tsiao] **Tsiao.**

椒¹	焦	蕉	僬²	勦³	噍⁴
pepper.	scorch.	banana.	wanton.	suppress.	chew.
277	322	454	29	52	97

醮	燋
thank.	sting.
528	327

[tsʰiao] **Ts'iao.**

悄¹	鍫	樵²	瞧	憔	誚⁴	俏
still.	scoop.	chop.	look.	haggard.	ridicule.	handsome.
187	537	283	366	195	482	22

[tsie] **Tsie.**

姐³	借⁴	妾⁵	嫉	寂	接	漬
sister.	lend.	concubine.	envy.	still.	receive.	stain.
126	24	126	131	141	222	315

疾	瘠	積	節	籍	績	跡
haste.	sore.	pile.	joint.	book.	splice.	trace.
350	353	381	392	395	411	503

鯽	卽
bream.	instant.
585	65

[tsʰie] **Ts'ie.**

且³	緝⁵	切	截	捷	窃	竊	七
careless.	splice.	cut.	cut.	near.	steal.	steal.	seven.
4	411	44	199	223	383	385	2

(701)

TSIEN-TSIO.

Tsien.	尖¹ point. 149	煎 fry. 324	箋 paper. 391	剪³ clip. 51	搀 prop. 231	翦 clip. 419	踐 tread. 503	僭⁴ pass. 31	[tsien]
	漸 little. 315	搴 prop. 333	箭 arrow. 392	薦 introduce. 455		賤 cheap. 496		餞 entertain. 572	
	煎 melt. 324								

Ts'ien.	千¹ 1000. 62	釗 stick. 53	韆 swing. 562	殲 destroy. 290	簽 sign. 395	籤 tally. 396	遷 remove. 523	[tsʰien]
	籤 pole. 541	懺 slip. 163	錢² cash. 536	前 front. 49	淺³ shallow. 307	籤⁴ splinter. 395		

Tsin.	旌¹ flag. 251	津 ford. 302	睛 eye. 365	精 fine. 398	睛 lean. 432	晶 crystal. 256	井³ well. 10	儘 let. 30	[tsin]
	窆 grave. 383	晉⁴ rise. 255	淨 clean. 307	盡 end. 360	進 enter. 517	靜 quiet. 559	凊 cold. 41		

Ts'in.	清¹ clear. 307	親 kin. 475	青 green. 558	情² feeling. 189	晴 clear. 256	寢³ sleep. 143	請 invite. 484	[tsʰin]
	侵⁴ usurp. 21	浸 soak. 304	凊 cold. 41					

Tsio.	足⁵ full. 500	嚼 bit. 97	[tsio]

(702)

TS'IO-TSONG.

[tsʰio] **Ts'io.**
雀⁵	鵲	攫
bird.	bird.	seize.
553	587	240

[tsiəu] **Tsiu.**
啾¹	揪	鬏	揪³	酒	揫⁴	就
whine.	pinch.	coil.	wring.	wine.	contort.	just.
92	225	581	225	526	352	150

揪
sprain.
226

[tsʰiəu] **Ts'iu.**
秋¹	鞦	楸	煍	偢	鰍
autumn.	swing.	tree.	smoke.	notice.	eel.
378	561	278	324	25	585

[tso] **Tso.**
左³	坐⁴	佐	座	挫	昨⁵	作	𥿄
left.	sit.	vice.	throne.	bent.	last.	make.	patch.
157	102	18	168	150	254	15	294

撮	縋
pinch.	firm.
235	412

[tsʰo] **Ts'o.**
磋¹	搓	挫⁴	銼	錯	促⁵	撮
grind.	twist.	sprain.	file.	wrong.	urge.	gather.
373	229	218	535	536	21	235

攫	鑿	猝	卒
seize.	chisel.	abrupt.	hurry.
240	541	335	64

[tsoŋ] **Tsong.**
棕¹	宗	踪	騌	總³	縱⁴	皺
palm.	ancestor.	trace.	mane.	sum.	follow.	wrinkle.
277	137	503	577	412	411	357

粽	縐	從
dumpling.	wrinkle.	second.
398	410	177

TS'ONG-TSUE.

Ts'ong.	從¹ follow. 177	聰 clever. 425	葱 onion. 450	從² follow. 177	叢 grove. 71			[tsʰoŋ]
Tsu.	租¹ rent. 378	祖³ ancestor. 375	阻 impede. 547	煮 boil. 323	做⁴ do. 26	助 help. 54	足⁵ full. 500	[tsu]
	卒 lictor. 63							
Ts'u.	初¹ begin. 45	粗 coarse. 397	鋤² hoe. 534	楚³ distress. 277	醋⁴ vinegar. 527	族⁵ clan. 251		[tsʰu]
	猝 abrupt. 335	卒 hurry. 64						
Tsü.	咀¹ suck. 83	疽 abscess. 350	錐 prick. 535	娶⁴ marry. 129	聚 meet. 424	最 very. 259		[tsy]
Ts'ü.	淬¹ fizz. 306	蛆 maggot. 461	取³ take. 71	堅⁴ pile. 106	趣 fun. 500			[tsʰy]
Tsuan.	鑽¹ push. 541	纂³ concoct. 413	賛³ knot. 582	鑽⁴ awl. 541				[tsuan]
Ts'uan.	攢² gather. 239	籹⁴ hull. 247	爨 board. 328	竄 hide. 385	篡 usurp. 393			[tsʰuan]
Tsue.	追¹ press. 513	錐 awl. 535	賊² thief. 494	嘴³ lip. 95	最⁴ very. 259	罪 sin. 416	醉 drunk. 527	[tsue] [tsuei]

TS'UE-Ü.

[tsʰue] [tsʰuei]	**Ts'ue.**	摧[1] drive. 232	催 urge. 28	悴[4] haggard. 189	翠 bird. 419	脆 crisp. 430	
[tsye]	**Tsüe.**	絕[5] reject. 405					
[tsʰuən]	**Ts'uen.**	邨[1] village. 525	村 village. 265	寸[1] inch. 145			
[tsʰyen] (Tsüen当作Ts'üen，见803页勘误表。)	**Tsüen.**	全[2] entire. 35	泉 spring. 300	痊 heal. 350			
[u]	**U.**	嗚[1] alas. 93	巫 wizard. 158	污 dirt. 297	烏 black. 321	誣 blame. 482	吾[2] me. 80	梧 tree. 275	毋 don't. 291

	無 without. 322	蝥 insect. 461	唔 gabble. 86	五[3] five. 10	侮 insult. 22	伍 rank. 15	午 noon. 62
	忤 unruly. 182	武 army. 288	舞 dance. 440	摀 cover. 228	仵 coroner. 15	務[4] must. 55	悟 arouse. 187
	悮 mistake. 187	惡 hate. 189	誤 mistake. 482	霧 fog. 558	物[5] thing. 332	屋 house. 153	搗 cover. 228
	杌 stool. 265						

[y]	**Ü.**	紆[1] bend. 401	迂 perverse. 512	愚[2] stupid. 192	於 at. 250	盂 basin. 358	紓 bend. 401	虞 careful. 459

(705)

Ü-UAN.

譽	輿	逾	餘	魚	漁	羽³
flatter.	earth.	pass.	surplus.	fish.	fish.	feather.
488	510	518	572	584	312	419
與	雨	語	喻⁴	女	寓	御
with.	rain.	word.	explain.	betroth.	lodging.	royal.
438	556	483	92	123	142	178
慰	玉	芋	諭	瘀	豫	遇
comfort.	gem.	taro.	edict.	clot.	ready.	meet.
194	337	442	485	352	490	520
愈	裕	籰	預			
heal.	plenty.	bobbin.	prepare.			
190	470	396	566			

Ua. [ua]

鴉¹	娃	剮	哇	挖	漥	娃²	瓦³
crow.	baby.	gore.	cry.	dig.	wet.	baby.	tile.
586	127	50	83	216	312	127	342
抓	韈⁵						
scoop.	sock.						
229	562						

Uai. [uai]

歪¹	歪³	外⁴
awry.	sprain.	outer.
288	288	116

Uan. [uan]

彎¹	灣	剜	豌	丸²	完	玩	頑
bent.	bend.	gore.	pea.	pill.	done.	amuse.	perverse.
174	318	50	489	6	136	338	566
挽³	晚	腕	碗	盌	婉	萬⁴	院
tie.	late.	elbow.	basin.	basin.	nice.	all.	yard.
218	256	432	372	358	129	452	550
卍	玩						
sign.	enjoy.						
63	338						

UANG-UEN.

[uaŋ] **Uang.**

汪¹	尫	亡²	忘	王	往³	柱	網
vast.	weak.	death.	forget.	king.	go.	wrong.	net.
298	150	10	180	338	175	267	408

魍	旺⁴	妄	望
spirit.	vigour.	silly.	hope.
583	253	124	261

[ue] [uei] **Ue.**

威¹	煨	痿	矮	萎	圍²	幃
majestic.	roast.	weak.	tassel.	droop.	round.	apron.
128	324	351	407	450	99	162

微	惟	桅	為	衛	違	闈	維
little.	only.	mast.	be.	guard.	oppose.	hall.	uphold.
178	189	273	329	467	520	546	407

危	委³	尾	諉	喂⁴	位	味
peril.	deputy.	tail.	excuse.	feed.	seat.	flavour.
65	126	152	483	92	18	83

慰	未	為	畏	緯	胃	偽
comfort.	not.	reason.	dread.	woof.	stomach.	false.
194	263	329	346	410	429	29

穢	衛
filth.	defend.
381	467

[ye] **Üe.**

拐¹	鬱⁵	悅	月	粵	越	抈	閱
bend.	brood.	glad.	moon.	Canton.	pass.	dent.	know.
208	582	187	260	398	499	208	546

[uən] **Uen.**

溫¹	瘟	文²	聞	紋	蚊	媼³
mild.	plague.	civil.	hear.	line.	gnat.	mid-wife.
310	353	247	424	403	460	131

穩	刎	問⁴	紊
steady.	cut.	ask.	confused.
381	45	88	402

ÜEN-ÜIN.

Üen.

冤¹	彎	淵	丸²	元	原	員	[yen]
wrong.	bent.	deep.	ball.	first.	level.	officer.	
142	172	308	6	31	66	86	

圓	援	垣	櫞²	沿	源	緣	芫
round.	save.	wall.	citron.	by.	source.	fate.	seed.
99	226	104	284	300	312	410	444

轅	鉛	黿	園	遠³	怨⁴	願	
door.	lead.	toad.	garden.	distant.	hate.	vow.	
510	533	593	99	521	183	192	

遼	院	願	緣
far.	yard.	wish.	trim.
522	550	568	410

Üin.

暈¹	螢²	勻	塋	榮	營	耘	雲	[yn]
giddy.	fly.	divide.	tomb.	glory.	camp.	thin.	cloud.	
257	463	59	110	279	328	423	556	

允³	永	熨⁴	暈	運	韻
grant.	ever.	iron.	giddy.	move.	rhyme.
32	296	325	257	520	563

(708)

ENGLISH INDEX.

A.

A, 1.
Abacus, 7, 360, 391.
Abandon, 4, 168, 180, 207, 275 438.
Abate, 42, 368, 368, 488, 514, 581.
Abatement, 377.
Abbreviate, 42.
Abdomen, 433.
Abide, 152.
Ability, 18, 43, 53, 149, 165, 189, 202, 245, 263, 429, 467, 484, 530.
Able, 117, 165, 173, 177, 259, 430.
Abode, 110, 152, 440.
Aboriginal, 101.
Aborigines, 445.
Abortion, 260, 343, 451.
About, 98, 159, 176, 203, 206, 260, 474, 487.
Above, 439.
Abreast, 5.
Abroad, 116.
Abrupt, 335.
Abruptly, 228, 549.
Abscess, 156, 350, 352, 353, 354.
Abscond, 10, 25, 61, 231, 242. 514.
Absence, 24, 80.
Absorbed, 443.

Abstain, 73, 198, 222.
Abstract, 458.
Abstruse, 122, 305, 337.
Abundance, 500.
Abundant, 470, 489.
Abuse, 491.
Abusive, 73.
Acacia, 76.
Academy, 167, 419, 550.
Accent, 72, 563.
Accident, 28.
Accidentally, 120.
Accommodate, 146.
Accommodating, 99, 150.
Accompany, 17, 513.
Accomplice, 420.
Accomplish, 150, 198.
Accomplishment, 179, 207, 456.
Accord, 82.
According, 18, 146, 215, 235, 323, 502, 610.
Account, 91, 391, 495.
Account-book, 229, 394.
Accumulate, 31, 31, 42, 381, 452.
Accusation, 281, 480.
Accuse, 37, 80, 220, 496.
Accuser, 67.
Accustomed, 194, 260, 537.
Ache, 350, 350, 351, 505.
Acknowledge, 482.

(709)

AC-AH.

Acknowledgment, 334.
Acorn, 283.
Acquaintance, 326, 487.
Acquainted, 194, 326, 519.
Acquiesce, 523.
Acre, 346.
Across, 518.
Act, 6, 15, 26, 32, 87, 240, 347, 466.
Active, 123, 181, 301, 505, 508, 517, 551.
Actor, 200, 273, 339.
Actual, 143.
Add; 53, 58, 106, 112, 231, 306, 601.
Addicted, 124, 194.
Addled, 143, 323.
Address, 82, 380.
Adequate, 57.
Adhere, 209.
Adjacent, 526, 548.
Adjectival, 356.
Adjoining, 362.
Adjust, 25, 164, 508, 582.
Admit, 223, 474.
Admonish, 58, 482.
Admonition, 58.
Adopt, 8, 212, 233, 385, 518.
Adorn, 23.
Adroitness, 488.
Adulterate, 231.
Adulterer, 127.
Adultery, 25, 127, 308, 327.
Advance, 111, 517, 519, 542.
Advantage, 7, 15, 21, 46, 123, 286, 358, 458, 499.

Adventure, 313.
Adventurer, 313.
Adversity, 555.
Advertisement, 108.
Advocate, 20, 431.
Adze, 536.
Affair, 9, 189, 286.
Affect, 38, 70, 597.
Affected, 605.
Affection, 185, 432.
Affinity, 128.
Afflicted, 186, 205.
Affliction, 445.
Affluent, 489, 573.
Afford, 499, 600.
Affront, 28, 265, 527.
Afraid, 139, 182, 198.
After, 2, 13, 18, 159, 176, 223, 502.
After all, 48, 167, 346, 382, 386.
Afternoon, 2.
Afterwards, 552.
Again, 38, 68, 178, 420.
Agate, 340.
Age, 2, 4, 115, 164, 166, 288, 401, 421, 595.
Aged, 523.
Aggravate, 53.
Agitated, 192.
Agnail, 395.
Ago, 50.
Agree, 76, 82, 177, 279, 387, 389, 401.
Agreeable, 89, 330.
Agreement, 78, 334, 401, 401.
Ague, 238, 352, 432.
Ah!, 93.

(710)

Ahead, 33.
Aid, 54, 161, 229, 317, 509, 579.
Aim, 296.
Air, 256, 256.
Ajar, 544.
A-kimbo, 269.
A la Grecque, 63.
Alarmed, 208.
Alas, 74, 81, 93, 93, 188.
Aleurites, 272.
Alias, 105.
Alight, 326.
Alike, 59, 281, 580.
Alive, 101, 133, 301.
All, 1, 5, 8, 22, 42, 45, 62, 77, 98, 118, 139, 254, 280, 356, 360, 363, 452, 466, 525, 594, 599, 612.
Allay, 287, 304, 476.
Alley, 159.
Allot, 301.
Allow, 41, 207, 389, 411, 479.
Alloy, 7, 379.
Allumette, 11.
Alluvium, 315.
Almond, 264.
Almost, 165, 329, 613.
Alms, 495.
Alone, 1.
Along, 300, 610.
Alphabet, 292.
Already, 158, 278.
Also, 8, 68, 525.
Altar, 113.
Alter, 241, 379, 478, 488.
Altercation, 72.

Alternately, 520.
Although, 412, 554.
Altogether, 35, 37.
Alum, 374.
Always, 30, 162, 176, 360.
Am, 254.
Amaranthus, 447.
Amass, 247.
Amaurosis, 361, 365.
Amazing, 480.
Ambassador, 158.
Amber, 338, 340.
Ambush, 14, 105.
Ammonia, 370.
Among, 5.
Amuse, 338.
Amusement, 421.
Ancestor, 375.
Ancestral, 138, 375, 375.
Anchor, 372, 536.
Ancient, 74.
And, 8, 37, 68, 82, 162, 421, 515, 556.
Angelica, 442.
Anger, 182, 295.
Angle, 532.
Angry, 20, 43, 182, 191, 294, 310, 319, 328.
Animal, 332, 333, 333, 337, 346.
Animate, 58.
Anise, 446.
Ankle, 210, 463, 566.
Annals, 27.
Announcement, 108.
Annoy, 56, 86, 322, 445, 478, 519.

AN-AR.

Anonymous, 77.
Another, 10, 46, 63, 68, 175, 176, 241, 615.
Answer, 37, 196, 207, 294, 389.
Ant, 461, 462, 464.
Ant-lion, 332.
Antecedent, 105, 154, 270, 288, 345.
Antidote, 476.
Antimacassar, 160.
Antique, 74, 338, 451.
Antler, 446.
Anus, 426.
Anvil, 379.
Anxiety, 193.
Anxious, 116, 194, 220, 236.
Anxiously, 94, 197.
Anything, 254, 612.
Apart, 245, 552, 555.
Apartment, 545, 546, 546.
Apostatize, 69.
Aphonia, 88.
Apoplexy, 352.
Appeal, 379, 546.
Appear, 310.
Appearance, 29, 151, 174, 202, 334, 490.
Appease, 32, 457.
Appetite, 72, 83, 191, 429, 432, 530.
Appetizing, 73.
Apple, 285, 401.
Apply, 136, 241, 246.
Appoint, 145, 210, 301, 416, 548
Appointment, 243, 523.
Apprehend, 211.

Apprehensive, 194, 458.
Apprentice, 171, 177.
Approach, 238.
Appropriate, 21, 81, 90, 558.
Approximately, 487.
Apricot, 264.
Apron, 162, 434, 472.
Aquilaria, 297.
Arable, 326.
Arbour, 11.
Arch, 171, 215, 302, 463.
Archer, 392.
Archery, 170.
Archway, 102.
Are, 124, 154, 254.
Areola, 323.
Ardent, 327.
Argue, 508, 511, 576.
Arithmetic, 391.
Arm, 579.
Armful, 212.
Armour, 345, 538.
Armpit, 384, 429.
Arms, 36, 95, 198, 274.
Army, 15, 288, 466, 507, 551.
Around, 510.
Arouse, 187, 238, 528.
Arrange, 45, 135, 152, 161, 241, 289, 409, 565, 582.
Arrangement, 262.
Array, 317.
Arrest, 209, 213, 217, 233, 286, 337.
Arrive, 48.
Arrogantly, 31.
Arrow, 392.

Arrow-head, 44, 448.
Arrowroot, 456.
Arsenal, 96.
Arsenic, 369.
Arson, 242.
Art, 207.
Article, 15, 95, 286, 332, 491.
Artifice, 282.
Artimisia, 452.
Artisan, 157.
As, 15, 17, 323, 345, 552.
As before, 12.
As for, 438.
As soon as, 1.
As though, 336.
Ascend, 62, 354.
Ascendency, 57.
Ashamed, 79, 139, 183, 190, 192, 193, 518.
Ashen, 319.
Ashes, 319.
Aside, 250.
Ask, 22, 73, 80, 88, 296.
Askew, 288, 604.
Asleep, 365, 418.
Asparagus, 39.
Aspect, 58, 76, 567.
Aspen, 278.
Assassin, 48.
Assault, 241.
Assemble, 100, 259, 424, 553.
Assist, 60, 161, 227, 473, 509, 616.
Assistant, 18.
Assizes, 144.
Associate, 29, 70, 82, 292.

Assume, 38, 146, 173.
Aster, 449.
Asthma, 88, 594.
Astringent, 120, 316.
Astronomy, 119.
At, 101, 250, 552.
At once, 408.
Atlas, 235.
Atom, 110.
Atone, 30, 497.
Attached, 180, 475, 493.
Attain, 592.
Attempt, 170.
Attend, 17, 22, 121, 339, 365, 406, 499, 502, 513.
Attendant, 118.
Attention, 55, 101, 344, 346, 418, 423.
Attentive, 192.
Attract, 205.
Attractive, 191, 364.
Audience, 548.
Aunt, 127, 132.
Auspicious, 77, 340.
Authority, 65, 270, 270, 285.
Autograph, 259.
Autumn, 378.
Avaricious, 492.
Avenge, 108.
Avoid, 34, 180, 198, 264, 484, 506.
Await, 22.
Awake, 528.
Aware, 476.
Away, 68.
Awkward, 388.

Awl, 535, 541.
Awning, 119, 220, 393.
Awry, 288.
Axe, 51, 248.
Axle, 179.
Azalea, 264.
Azure, 411, 558.

B.

B. A., 271, 377.
Baby, 117, 127, 148.
Bachelor, 91.
Back, 176, 426, 428.
Backbite, 97, 146.
Backbone, 430.
Backer, 580.
Backward, 69, 486, 514.
Bad, 43, 54, 80, 114, 134, 194, 293, 431, 437, 474, 528, 575.
Badly, 423.
Bag, 73, 97, 218, 283, 472.
Baggage, 97, 466.
Bailbond, 20.
Bait, 532.
Bake, 321, 321.
Baker, 271.
Balance, 208.
Bald, 377.
Bale, 304.
Ball, 6, 173, 400.
Balsam, 382.
Balustrade, 264.
Bamboo, 192, 387, 393, 523.
Banana, 444, 454.
Band, 117, 162, 243, 274, 400.
Banditti, 26, 97.

Bandy, 478.
Bang, 609, 610.
Banish, 32.
Banishment, 507, 521.
Bank, 111, 155, 318, 375, 438, 601, 608.
Bankrupt, 23, 205.
Banner, 251.
Bannerman, 251.
Bar, 203, 282, 396, 543, 564, 609.
Barbarian, 120, 139, 347, 465.
Barber, 67, 73.
Bare, 33.
Barebacked, 244.
Barefoot, 33, 497.
Bargain, 221, 235, 486, 487.
Bark, 357.
Bark, to, 85, 89.
Barley, 589.
Barm, 527.
Barrack, 143, 328.
Barren, 134, 373, 427.
Barrier, 547.
Barter, 10, 253, 493.
Base, 18, 167, 430.
Basin, 358, 358, 358, 359, 414, 533.
Bask, 258.
Basket, 59, 172, 225, 235, 264, 279, 357, 388, 390, 390, 393, 393, 394, 395, 396, 396, 429, 597.
Bas-relief, 537.
Bass, 85.
Bastard, 127, 555, 596.

Baste, 466.
Bastion, 109.
Bat, 395, 462, 593.
Bath, 317.
Bathe, 302, 317.
Baton, 45.
Battle, 12, 199, 549.
Bawl, 79.
Bay, 577.
Be, 16, 26, 32, 70, 121, 152, 223, 242, 329, 347.
Bead, 339.
Beak, 95.
Beam, 265, 267, 273, 284.
Bean, 380, 448, 489, 489.
Bean-curd, 319, 431.
Bear, a, 325.
Bear, to, 7, 79, 90, 134, 162, 326, 343, 343, 404, 517.
Beard, 73, 581, 581, 581.
Beast, 337.
Beastly, 337.
Best, 151, 202, 207, 226, 226, 232, 237, 263, 278, 291, 298, 497, 611.
Beautiful, 417.
Beautify, 23.
Beauty, 137, 442.
Because, 98, 329.
Beckon, 208.
Becloud, 558.
Become, 38, 198, 240, 355, 564.
Bed, 60, 278, 311, 318, 320, 440, 541, 550.
Bed-cover, 472.
Bedding, 535, 550.

Bed-quilt, 535.
Bed-room, 144.
Bed-stead, 166.
Bee, 461.
Beef, 332, 425, 450.
Bee-hive, 275.
Beetle, 152.
Before, 13, 33, 49, 263, 439, 560, 567.
Beforehand, 33, 490.
Beg, 60, 296, 351, 478, 524.
Beggar, 8, 60, 351, 453, 478.
Beggary, 495.
Begin, 4, 35, 56, 498, 544.
Beginning, 45, 126, 498, 544, 567.
Begone, 312.
Begrudge, 80, 189, 221.
Behaviour, 192.
Behead, 51, 248, 402.
Behind, 176, 567.
Belch, 434.
Believe, 21.
Bell, 373, 533, 539, 563.
Bellows, 392.
Belly, 426, 433.
Belong, 289.
Below, 167, 223.
Belt, 162.
Bench, 271, 284.
Bend, 95, 152, 174, 208, 227, 318.
Benefactor, 185.
Beneficial, 21.
Benefit, 33, 123, 250, 358, 427, 458.
Benevolent, 91, 531.
Bent, 180, 401.

(715)

Benumb, 29, 262, 351.
Bequeath, 522.
Bereave, 91.
Beseech, 195, 296, 374, 377, 524.
Beside, 524.
Besides, 13, 75, 116, 271, 549, 572.
Besiege, 99.
Besmirch, 603.
Bespeak, 482.
Best, 3, 123, 564.
Bestir, 56.
Bestow, 250, 495, 496.
Betel-nut, 279.
Betimes, 252.
Betony, 456.
Betray, 495.
Betroth, 123, 242, 423, 479.
Better, 57, 123, 124, 173.
Between, 5, 545.
Beware, 225, 283, 362, 486, 547, 592.
Bewitch, 583.
Beyond, 116.
Bezoar, 144, 590.
Bib, 162.
Bicker, 388.
Bifurcated, 296.
Big, 31, 117, 298, 601.
Bilge-water, 315.
Bill-hook, 44.
Bin, 98.
Bind, 59, 216, 237, 264, 403, 406, 406, 414, 508, 531.
Birch, 282.
Bird, 377, 553, 586.

Birth, to give, 3.
Birthday, 115, 343, 482, 555.
Bit, 97, 405, 533.
Bitch, 292, 335.
Bite, 73, 75, 83, 85.
Bitter, 445.
Bitterly, 41, 84, 351.
Bitterness, 510.
Black, 112, 321, 322, 356, 558, 591, 591.
Blackguard, 33, 494, 599.
Black-head, 350, 353.
Blacksmith, 540.
Bladder, 299, 426, 430.
Blade, 95, 348.
Blame, 182, 457, 482.
Blanc-mange, 41, 399.
Blast, 569.
Blaze, 325.
Bleach, 314.
Blear, 613.
Bleat, 89.
Bleed, 303.
Blind, 289, 363, 366, 394.
Blindly, 197.
Blind-man's-buff, 366.
Blindness, 361.
Blink, 364.
Blister, 299, 349.
Block, 112, 266, 271, 369, 571.
Blockhead, 599, 602.
Blood, 253, 400, 428, 465.
Bloodstone, 340.
Blood-vessel, 405.
Bloom, 544.
Blot, 110, 297.

Blow, 40, 79, 93, 205, 236, 570.
Blue, 337, 411, 455.
Blunt, 203, 361, 532.
Blur, 366, 366, 443.
Blush, 401.
Bluster, 172.
Boar, 336.
Board, 14, 115, 228, 266, 271, 279, 331, 600.
Boast, 123, 481.
Boastful, 172, 467.
Boat, 63, 441, 441.
Boat-load, 508.
Boatman, 202, 576.
Boat-pole, 393.
Bob, 354.
Bobbin, 396, 411.
Body, 151, 153, 425, 429, 505, 579, 580, 615.
Body-guard, 467.
Boil, a, 349.
Boil, to, 300, 312, 323, 326, 327, 545.
Boiler, 342.
Boisterous, 172, 575, 613.
Bold, 549.
Boldness, 489.
Bolt, 519.
Bolter, 417.
Bond-servant, 129.
Bone, 579, 579.
Bonus, 527.
Book, 38, 65, 258, 395, 525.
Bookcase, 269, 284.
Boot, 469, 560, 561.

Booth, 276.
Booty, 497.
Borax, 371.
Border, 515, 524.
Bore, 535, 537, 541, 615.
Born, 43.
Borrow, 24, 218, 227, 234, 493, 616.
Both, 8, 35, 37, 68.
Bother, 240, 309.
Bottle, 342.
Bottle-gourd, 450.
Bottom, 166, 614.
Boulder, 9.
Bounce, 84.
Bound, 313.
Boundary, 10, 110, 345, 348.
Boundary-stone, 331, 345.
Boundless, 168, 348, 548.
Bounds, 167.
Bow, a, 170.
Bow, to, 18, 62, 62, 105, 215, 226, 506.
Bowl, 247, 358, 414.
Bow-string, 171.
Box, a, 61, 239, 358, 392.
Box, to, 159, 215, 231, 602.
Boxing, 243.
Box-tree, 278.
Boy, 363, 386.
Brace-bit, 541.
Bracelet, 98, 341, 395, 531.
Bracket, 281, 332.
Brackish, 588.
Bradawl, 541.
Brae, 104.

(717)

BRA-BRO.

Brag, 367, 481.
Braggart, 587.
Braid, 409, 413.
Brain, 433.
Braird, 95, 377.
Bramble, 608.
Bran, 589.
Branch, 201, 263, 265, 301.
Brand, 65.
Brasier, 358.
Brass, 534.
Brave, 38, 55, 457, 553, 578.
Brawl, 79, 186.
Brawn, 42.
Bray, 74.
Brazen, 612.
Bread, 59, 573, 574.
Breach, 72.
Break, 9, 53, 120, 205, 236, 244, 249, 328, 355, 415, 615.
Break loose, 311.
Break off, 198, 213, 220, 228, 234, 405, 607.
Break open, 47, 213, 369.
Break out, 16, 38, 355, 382.
Break up, 112, 395.
Breakfast, 252.
Bream, 585.
Breast, 131, 197, 250, 429, 432.
Breast-band, 607.
Breast-plate, 539.
Breath, 43, 73, 185, 294.
Breathe, 81, 92.
Breed, 542.
Bribe, 167, 235, 296, 493, 493, 494, 495, 497.

Bribery, 165.
Bric-a-brac, 286.
Brick, 342.
Bridal, 130.
Bride, 126, 129, 131, 249.
Bridegroom, 249, 492, 525.
Bridge, 280, 282, 311.
Bridge of nose, 270, 274.
Bridle, 510.
Brief, 257.
Brigadier-general, 537.
Bright, 11, 33, 112, 276, 356, 407, 569, 604, 611.
Brighten, 323.
Brilliant, 254, 448, 603.
Brimstone, 370, 373.
Brine, 313.
Bring, 19, 162, 203, 210, 212, 306, 339, 386.
Brinjal, 445.
Brisk, 181, 524, 578.
Brisket, 430.
Bristle, 577.
Brittle, 326, 430.
Broad, 143.
Broadcloth, 83.
Brocade, 535.
Broken, 263, 328, 598.
Brood, 582.
Broom, 221, 388, 390.
Broth, 309.
Brothel, 106, 159, 384, 384, 443, 550.
Brother, 32, 85, 118, 137, 171, 202, 253, 428, 440, 525, 579.
Brotherly, 70.

(718)

Brow, 567, 569.
Brown, 100.
Bruise, 59, 225, 371, 412.
Brush, 48, 210, 210, 226, 238.
Brushwood, 268.
Bubble, 310.
Bubo, 274.
Bucket, 274.
Bucketful, 275.
Buckle, 204.
Buckwheat, 454.
Bud, 444, 445.
Buddha, 16, 173.
Buddhist, 16, 29, 114.
Buffalo, 332.
Bug, 437, 459, 586.
Build, 23, 26, 169, 241, 369, 498, 517.
Building, 153.
Bulge, 171.
Bull, 332, 333.
Bullet, 173.
Bully, 464, 490.
Bulrush, 327.
Bunch, 132, 598.
Bundle, 59, 206, 403, 406, 469.
Burglar, 173, 494.
Burial-ground, 108, 110, 112, 155, 550.
Burmah, 409.
Burn, 322, 322, 323, 326.
Burning-glass, 539.
Burst, 224, 290, 310, 320, 328, 602, 609.
Bury, 105, 110, 155.
Bush, 275.

Bushel, 247.
Business, 9, 44, 55, 72, 151, 158, 190, 253, 278, 377, 458, 466, 493.
Bustle, 121.
Busy, 133, 169, 180, 545.
Busybody, 589.
But, 17, 33, 65, 73, 121, 143.
Butcher, 140, 154, 433.
Butter, 301, 527.
Butterfly, 397, 461, 462.
Buttock, 427.
Button, 204, 532, 532, 564.
Button-hole, 543.
Button-loop, 204.
Buy, 52, 71, 203, 205, 217, 224, 230, 241, 299, 493.
Buyer, 493.
By, 1, 70, 215, 300, 469, 515, 592.
By-stander, 250.
By-way, 148, 223.

C.

Cabbage, 59, 453.
Cabin, 137.
Cable, 402.
Cackle, 73, 87.
Cactus, 13.
Cadaverous, 269.
Cage, 284, 395, 396.
Cajole, 481.
Cake, 398, 399, 571, 572, 574, 589.
Calabash, 341.
Calamitous, 43.
Calamity, 54, 290, 319, 375, 555.

(719)

CAL-CAS.

Calamus, 448.
Calculate, 600.
Calendar, 258.
Calf, 34, 132, 332, 426, 435.
Calico, 159, 204, 447.
Calk, 312, 403.
Call, 73, 82, 88, 89, 380.
Calling, 278.
Calomel, 509.
Caltrops, 449.
Calve, 514.
Calyx, 451.
Camel, 576.
Camellia, 446.
Camlet, 410, 419.
Camp, 328.
Campaign, 507.
Camphor, 433.
Can, 19, 33, 74, 165, 177, 418, 430.
Cancel, 58, 110, 535.
Candle, 327, 465.
Candle-stick, 323.
Candy, 399.
Cane, 395.
Cangue, 269.
Canister, 389.
Cannon, 369.
Canopy, 27.
Cantharides, 463.
Cantonese, 168, 398.
Cap, 39, 163, 293, 341, 359, 482, 586.
Capable, 53, 96.
Capacity, 530.
Cape, 160.

Capital, 11, 104, 157, 263, 362, 379, 536, 551.
Capitalist, 267.
Capon, 47, 554.
Capsicum, 277, 511.
Captain, 27, 36, 86, 266, 546.
Capture, 235.
Carapace, 115.
Caravan, 161.
Carbuncle, 59.
Card, 160, 263, 331, 331, 452.
Care, 20, 362, 363, 568, 572.
Careful, 14, 30, 148, 188, 191, 192, 192, 283, 404, 459, 486.
Carefully, 124, 206, 343, 485.
Careless, 63, 118, 181, 190, 346, 348.
Carelessly, 4, 80, 91, 337, 398.
Careworn, 189.
Carp, 584.
Carpenter, 112, 262.
Carriage, 430.
Carrot, 453, 457.
Carry, 27, 162, 202, 203, 203, 210, 211, 212, 214, 216, 218, 225, 228, 230, 231, 236, 428, 501, 520, 564, 575, 603, 614.
Carrying-pole, 27, 201, 541.
Carve, 56, 554.
Carver, 554.
Case, 61, 120, 122, 201, 223, 271, 358, 392, 488, 561.
Cash, 132, 460, 536.
Cast, 4, 24, 170, 224, 234, 344, 431, 451, 535.
Castor-oil, 449, 590.

(720)

Castrate, 47.
Casual, 299.
Casually, 25, 306.
Cat, 336, 337.
Catalogue, 91.
Catamite, 36, 127.
Catch, 28, 38, 187, 202, 217, 218, 222, 230, 409, 416, 603, 612, 613.
Caterpillar, 462, 465.
Cat's-eye, 364.
Cattle, 332.
Cause, 13, 19, 189, 243, 345, 355, 410.
Caustic, 328.
Cautious, 408.
Cavalry, 36, 575.
Cave, 302.
Cavity, 24.
Caw, 89.
Cease, 14, 16, 26, 249, 287.
Cedar, 270, 574.
Cedrela, 277.
Ceiling, 261.
Celebrated, 78, 563.
Celery, 444.
Celestial, 119.
Cellar, 383, 383.
Cement, 77.
Censer, 541.
Cent, 44.
Centipede, 62, 461, 556.
Centre, 5, 72, 179.
Centurion, 206, 356, 412.
Cercis, 447.
Cereals, 399, 570.

Ceremony, 6, 138.
Certain, 1, 262, 270, 356, 372.
Certainly, 5, 25, 38, 40, 45, 101, 137, 179, 249, 263, 406, 412, 452.
Certainty, 54.
Cesspool, 102.
Chaff, 399.
Chain, 537.
Chair, 269, 275, 394, 510, 602.
Chair-bearer, 339, 556, 565.
Chamaerops, 277.
Chamber, 201.
Chance, 25, 262.
Chancellor, 138.
Changeable, 7, 178.
Change, 34, 69, 155, 157, 186, 222, 224, 241, 258, 379, 420, 488, 500, 523, 560.
Channel, 311, 314.
Chant, 87, 181, 286, 482.
Chaos, 298, 304.
Chaotic, 316.
Chapel, 106.
Chapped, 357, 513, 535.
Chapter, 386.
Char, 323.
Character, 133, 182.
Charcoal, 264, 273.
Charge, 54, 108.
Charity, 195, 418.
Charm, 388.
Chaste, 321, 490.
Chastise, 289, 416, 457.
Chat, 71, 94, 238, 484.
Chatter, 74, 79, 89, 92, 94.

CHE-CLA.

Cheap, 21, 253, 362, 496.
Cheaply, 21, 277, 286, 362.
Cheat, 84, 89, 122, 286, 396, 422, 524, 577, 579.
Check, 109.
Checkered, 275.
Cheek, 59, 433, 560, 614.
Cheerful, 153, 330.
Cherish, 197, 217.
Cherry, 272, 285.
Cherry-apple, 283.
Chess, 275.
Chest, 72, 429, 435.
Chestnut, 266, 271.
Cheval-de-frise, 143.
Chew, 85, 97, 604.
Chicken, 554.
Chief, 31, 75, 118, 574.
Chilblain, 42.
Child, 127, 134, 135, 156.
Childless, 337.
Children, 34, 109, 148.
Chiliarch, 62, 412.
Chill, 41, 570.
Chimney, 98, 416.
China, 99, 117, 448.
China-grass, 444.
China-ware, 373.
Chine, 604.
Chinese, 312, 591.
Chipped, 415.
Chips, 262, 308.
Chiropodist, 23.
Chirp, 89, 96.
Chisel, 539, 541.
Chloranthus, 457.

Choke, 85, 93.
Cholera, 78, 350, 354.
Choose, 236.
Chop, 140, 369, 540.
Chopper, 44.
Chopstick, 181, 391.
Chronicle, 27.
Chrysalis, 115.
Chrysanthemum, 447, 449.
Church, 243.
Cicada, 464.
Cinder, 320.
Cinnabar, 369.
Cinnamon, 271.
Circle, 98, 390.
Circuit, 519.
Circuitous, 510.
Circulate, 27.
Circumference, 99, 218.
Circumspect, 526.
Circumstance, 41, 110, 256, 285.
Cistern, 296.
Citron, 16, 201, 268, 284.
City, 103.
Civil, 77, 243, 247.
Clam, 460.
Clamorous, 563.
Clamour, 95.
Clamp, 575.
Clan, 138, 241, 251, 330.
Clap, 212.
Clapper, 433.
Clarify, 315.
Clasp, 217, 394, 532.
Class, 339, 499, 564, 592.
Classic, 30, 406.

(722)

Classical, 247, 339.
Claw, 120, 329, 534.
Clay, 104, 373.
Clean, 8, 71, 112, 228, 306, 307, 316, 365.
Cleanliness, 316.
Cleanly, 32.
Cleanse, 302.
Clear, 11, 95, 221, 232, 254, 256, 277, 298, 307, 348, 356, 468, 549, 558, 569, 613.
Clearly, 52, 165, 253, 257, 277, 307.
Cleg, 332, 460.
Clerk, 37.
Clever, 19, 20, 157, 244, 398, 425, 558.
Cleverly, 125.
Clew, 410.
Cliff, 111, 156.
Climate, 101, 295.
Climb, 158, 420.
Cling, 213.
Clip, 51, 533.
Clique, 360.
Cloak, 468.
Clock, 468, 512, 539.
Clod, 109, 159, 370.
Clog, 266, 561.
Close, 141, 152, 257, 325, 543, 606.
Close, to, 145, 364, 364, 366.
Close-fisted, 120, 313, 407.
Clot, 352.
Cloth, 159, 160, 294, 404, 419, 450, 605.

Clothes, 260, 467, 471.
Clothes-horse, 269.
Clothing, 203.
Cloud, 556, 557.
Clover, 446.
Cloves, 2.
Club, 276.
Clump, 266.
Clumsily, 388, 399.
Clumsy, 575.
Cluster, 370.
Clutch, 204, 218, 225.
Coal, 320, 324.
Coarse, 265, 293, 397, 470, 584, 601.
Coarsely, 293, 399.
Cobble-stones, 9, 587.
Cobweb, 110.
Cock, 36, 553, 554.
Cockatoo, 588.
Cockroach, 25, 436.
Cock's-comb, 554.
Cocoon, 413.
Coffin, 61, 77, 90, 115, 262, 266, 267, 269, 276, 280, 290, 290, 420, 558.
Cohabit, 131.
Coil, 464, 581.
Coin, 536.
Coir, 277.
Coix, 444.
Coke, 156.
Colander, 313.
Cold, 40, 41, 41, 41, 142, 306, 569, 570, 597.
Colic, 348, 349.

COL-CON.

Collide, 39.
Collapse, 431.
Collar, 533, 566.
Collect, 60, 69, 100, 239, 400, 582.
Colonel, 63.
Colonist, 154.
Colour, 442, 465, 567.
Coloured, 174, 461, 603.
Comb, 39, 274, 393.
Combine, 463.
Come, 19, 48, 62, 150, 437, 438, 512.
Comet, 174, 221, 254.
Comfort, 135, 194.
Comfortable, 181, 330, 440.
Command, 81, 337, 391, 458.
Commander, 405.
Commence, 3, 35, 56, 355, 439, 439, 498.
Commend, 380.
Comment, 480.
Commentary, 477, 480, 529.
Commiserate, 84.
Commission, 13, 97, 479, 521, 556.
Commissioner, 75, 158, 550.
Commit, 70, 334.
Commode, 279.
Common, 21, 36, 37, 42, 164, 356, 487, 496.
Communication, 516.
Communion, 10.
Companion, 17.
Company, 86, 117, 161, 241, 259, 499, 512, 524, 610.
Comparative, 10, 292, 499.

Compare, 147, 292, 508.
Comparison, 292, 439.
Compartment, 441, 551.
Compass, 64, 417.
Compassion, 188.
Compassionate, 12, 191, 192, 367.
Compel, 173, 214, 518.
Compensation, 46.
Competent, 430.
Complaisant, 488.
Completion, 442.
Complete, 35, 81, 99, 136, 150, 198, 289, 309, 313, 383, 451, 535, 594.
Completely, 8.
Completion, 386.
Compliant, 488.
Comply, 177.
Composition, 112, 389.
Comprehend, 187, 191, 259, 339, 477, 516.
Comrade, 17.
Concave, 384.
Conceal, 61, 173, 359, 366, 455, 552.
Conceive, 191.
Concern, 163, 303, 323, 362, 547.
Conch, 302, 463.
Conciliate, 82.
Conciliatory, 127.
Concisely, 45.
Conclusion, 392.
Concoct, 191, 413.
Concrete, 143.
Concubine, 126, 138, 144, 148, 168, 176, 201.

(724)

CON-CON.

Condescend, 153.
Condiment, 313.
Condition, 18, 57, 101, 288.
Condole, 78.
Conduct, 56, 85, 170, 329, 466, 559.
Confectionery, 179, 266, 398, 446, 570, 572, 592.
Confederate, 420.
Confess, 209, 260, 482, 484, 495.
Confidence, 21.
Confident, 514.
Confidently, 301.
Confine, 209.
Confinement, 102, 260.
Confirm, 334.
Confiscate, 32, 205.
Conform, 18, 146.
Confront, 147, 495.
Confucian, 30, 424.
Confucius, 132.
Confuse, 184, 188, 194, 252, 316, 399, 402, 412, 471.
Confusedly, 196, 304, 401.
Congeal, 40, 42, 42, 598.
Congee, 379.
Congenial, 55.
Congratulate, 89, 193, 492.
Congratulatory, 492.
Conjunction, 421.
Connect, 405.
Connive, 411.
Conquer, 57.
Conscience, 119, 179, 441.
Conscription, 209.
Consequence, 19, 20, 163, 547.

Consequently, 201.
Consider, 180, 183, 223, 225, 248, 329, 530, 580, 600.
Considerate, 346, 493.
Considerately, 185.
Consist, 101.
Constant, 98, 184, 542, 550.
Constantly, 47, 154, 162, 255, 292, 333, 614.
Constipated, 404, 516.
Constitution, 32.
Constrain, 55.
Constraint, 209.
Consult, 87, 530.
Consumption, 172, 349, 353.
Contact, 222.
Contagious, 190.
Contemptible, 63.
Contented, 186.
Contents, 361.
Continent, 392.
Continually, 414.
Continuous, 515.
Contract, 10, 59, 139, 177, 343, 404, 597.
Contractor, 240, 566.
Contradict, 39, 511.
Contrary, 69, 322, 510, 513.
Contribute, 19, 43, 217.
Contributor, 250.
Control, 47, 391, 401.
Convenient, 20, 249, 253, 563.
Conventional, 170, 382.
Conversation, 483.
Converse, 480, 484.
Convert, 60, 121.

(725)

CON-COW.

Convex, 215.
Convey, 170.
Convince, 516.
Convulsions, 205, 352, 578.
Coo, 89.
Cook, a, 67, 201, 319.
Cook, to, 67, 170, 321, 326.
Cooking-range, 385.
Cool, 40, 41, 41, 165.
Coolie, 118, 201, 203, 216, 231, 339, 430.
Cooling, 165.
Coop, 99, 395, 416.
Cooper, 274.
Coping, 163.
Copiously, 335.
Copper, 440, 534, 536.
Copy, 138, 161, 205, 231, 271, 431, 486.
Copyist, 14.
Coral, 338.
Cord, 402, 410, 413.
Coriander, 444.
Cork, 615.
Cormorant, 586.
Corns, 502, 554.
Corner, 95, 174, 210, 476, 600.
Coroner, 15.
Corpse, 90, 151, 153, 269, 574, 583.
Correct, 147, 401.
Correction, 196.
Correctly, 307.
Correspond, 76.
Cotton, 276, 405, 443.
Couch, 166.

Cough, 84, 94.
Could, 418.
Connt, 246, 592.
Countenance, 85, 140, 436, 542.
Counter, 39, 284.
Countrified, 265.
Country, 99, 140, 265, 525, 525, 526.
Country-man, 526.
County, 410.
Couple, 147.
Couplet, 424.
Courage, 90, 180, 436, 530.
Courageous, 55, 553.
Courier, 98.
Conrse, 53, 225, 437.
Course, of, 322.
Court, 261.
Conrteous, 286.
Court-house, 467.
Court-room, 106.
Courtyard, 114, 550.
Cousin, 32, 86, 127, 153, 171, 465, 468.
Covenant, 359.
Cover, a, 122, 358, 468, 535.
Cover, to, 106, 113, 145, 223, 288, 359, 522, 543, 561, 601, 601.
Covered, 551.
Covering, 416.
Coverlit, 359, 468, 469.
Covet, 160, 492.
Covetous, 129, 153, 290, 530.
Cow, 292, 332, 333, 333, 590.
Cowardly, 606.
Cow-herd, 332.

(726)

Cowry, 460.
Cozen, 84.
Crab, 463.
Crab-apple, 401.
Crack, 121, 320, 328, 357, 370, 406, 411, 469, 513, 595, 609, 612, 615.
Cracker, 369.
Crackle, 609.
Cradle, 395.
Craft, 467, 519.
Crafty, 124, 158, 335, 336.
Cramp, 335, 388.
Crane, 507, 587.
Crape, 402.
Crash, 105, 163.
Craving, 354.
Crawl, 329.
Crazy, 125, 194, 352, 354.
Create, 51, 60, 517.
Creation, 547.
Creator, 517.
Credentials, 195.
Credit, 19, 210, 494.
Creel, 396.
Creeper, 395, 450.
Crevice, 411.
Cricket, 464, 554.
Criminal, 334, 416.
Cripple, 501.
Crisis, 102.
Crisp, 87, 326, 430, 527.
Criticise, 368, 480, 483, 484, 576.
Croak, 423.
Crockery, 359.

Crooked, 7, 25, 174, 210, 258, 288.
Crop, 253, 343, 380.
Crop, a chicken's, 93, 426, 429.
Cross, 25, 62, 248, 420, 501, 518.
Cross-bar, 284, 564, 612.
Cross-breed, 333.
Cross-eyed, 366.
Cross-grained, 172, 601.
Cross-legged, 504, 504.
Cross-purposes, 214.
Cross-roads, 62, 64.
Crosswise, 281.
Croton, 159.
Crouch, 431.
Crow, 73, 321, 586.
Crow-bar, 214, 248.
Crowd, 98, 107, 220, 236, 237, 418, 548.
Crown, 38, 39, 39, 250.
Crown-prince, 118.
Crucify, 542.
Cruel, 32, 290, 292, 335, 355.
Crumby, 328.
Crupper, 561.
Crush, 113, 278, 370, 372, 501.
Crust, 159, 323, 571.
Cry, 73, 83, 86, 88, 89, 299, 609.
Crystal, 256.
Crystallize, 40.
Cube, 249.
Cubit, 151.
Cuckold, 596.
Cucumber, 341.
Cuff, 204.
Cul-de-sac, 289.

(727)

Cultivate, 106, 275, 422, 544.
Cunning, 7.
Cup, 247, 266, 358, 537.
Cupboard, 284, 358.
Cupping, 83, 415.
Cure, 312, 353, 368, 432, 436, 436.
Curiosity, 451.
Current, 466.
Currier, 357.
Curry-comb, 393.
Curry favour, 404.
Curse, 81, 416, 599, 599, 611.
Curtain, 161, 162, 416.
Curtly, 394.
Curve, 171, 174.
Cushion, 111.
Custom, 20, 21, 60, 271, 295, 367, 475, 526, 531, 569, 615.
Customer, 138, 568.
Cut, 14, 44, 45, 45, 47, 49, 51, 51, 51, 52, 52, 202, 209, 369, 469, 499, 539.
Cute, 149.
Cuttle-fish, 112.
Cycad, 269.
Cycle, 344.
Cylinder, 115.
Cymbals, 533, 540.
Cypress, 270.

D.

Daft, 194, 334, 354.
Dagger, 64.
Dahlia, 442, 449.
Dainty, 75.
Dam, 108, 547.
Damage, 228, 317.
Damask, 408.
Damp, 294, 313, 315, 315, 317, 557.
Damsel, 125.
Dance, 440.
Dandelion, 454.
Dandy, 221.
Dangerous, 65, 156, 197, 552.
Dangle, 507.
Dare, 244.
Daring, 55, 176, 464.
Dark, 39, 257, 302, 305, 558, 591, 592, 592, 610.
Darken, 452.
Dart, 392.
Date, 251, 262, 277.
Daub, 603, 612.
Daughter, 62, 123, 125, 128, 191, 531, 544.
Daughter-in-law, 131, 544.
Dawdle, 125, 213, 614.
Dawn, 178, 252, 253, 258, 261.
Day, 119, 251, 255, 255, 355, 401.
Day-book, 303.
Day-break, 11.
Day-lily, 431, 590.
Dazed, 194, 513.
Dazzle, 254, 325.
Dead, 68, 73, 74, 102, 105, 114, 221, 243, 247, 249, 289, 518.
Dead-lock, 233.
Deaf, 232, 425, 429.
Dealer, 491.

(728)

DEA-DEN.

Dealing, 217.
Dear, 105, 252, 493, 580.
Dearth, 446, 573.
Death, 10, 194, 289.
Death-warrant, 531.
Debase, 114.
Debate, 487.
Debilitate, 459.
Debt, 27, 152, 285, 328, 428, 495.
Début, 43.
Decapitate, 140, 248.
Deceased, 33.
Deceitful, 174, 481.
Deceitfulness, 210.
Deceive, 84, 187, 286, 304, 405, 552.
Deception, 38.
Deceptive, 479.
Decide, 46, 237, 416.
Decided, 310, 371.
Decidedly, 25.
Decision, 6, 32, 40, 190, 539.
Decisively, 48, 52.
Decline, 204, 222, 248, 468.
Declivity, 104, 248.
Decoct, 326.
Decoration, 174.
Decorous, 381.
Decoy, 210, 587, 610.
Decree, 83, 410, 480.
Deduct, 204.
Deed, 9, 121.
Deem, 329.
Deep, 66, 305.
Deepen, 306.
Deep-seated, 124, 305.

Deer, 588.
Defeat, 244.
Defect, 349.
Defence, 480.
Defend, 467.
Defer, 187.
Deficiency, 167.
Deficient, 149, 184, 285, 415.
Deficit, 459.
Defile, 156.
Defilement, 297.
Definite, 125, 418, 451.
Deformed, 270.
Defraud, 491.
Defy, 496.
Degenerate, 426.
Degrade, 68, 402, 493, 548, 560.
Degree, 360, 370, 379.
Deify, 145.
Delay, 208, 213, 237, 403, 409, 506, 516, 550, 604.
Deliberate, 237, 395.
Deliberately, 190.
Delicacy, 83, 252, 338, 572, 573.
Delicate, 172, 410.
Delicious, 417.
Delighted, 342.
Delirious, 110, 334.
Deliver, 11, 226, 413, 513, 574.
Delude, 286, 465, 513.
Deluge, 301.
Demand, 88, 88, 204, 474.
Demon, 583, 583, 584.
Demoralize, 28, 244.
Den, 382.
Densely, 380.

(729)

Dent, 208.
Deny, 69.
Department, 157.
Depend, 101, 345, 478, 559.
Dependent, 154.
Deportment, 29.
Deposit, 18, 111, 140, 213, 378.
Depôt, 166.
Depraved, 30, 76, 289.
Depreciate, 496.
Depressed, 98, 196.
Deprive, 560.
Depute, 127, 521.
Deputy, 50, 126, 169.
Derange, 213.
Descend, 437, 451, 548.
Descendants, 93, 176, 445.
Describe, 174.
Desert, 297, 514.
Deserted, 559.
Deserter, 514.
Deserve, 22.
Design, 282.
Desire, 191, 286, 325, 568.
Desirous, 189.
Desist, 416.
Desolate, 142.
Despair, 192.
Desperate, 534.
Despicable, 67.
Despise, 130, 180, 193.
Despond, 582.
Despondent, 196.
Destitute, 384, 445, 491.
Destroy, 91; 109, 291.
Destruction, 297.

Detail, 404, 481.
Detain, 213, 233, 286, 346, 381, 417.
Detective, 157.
Determination, 206, 498.
Determine, 385.
Determined, 40, 98, 105, 105, 152, 190, 371.
Detest, 184.
Detestable, 67, 189.
Devil, 584, 608.
Develop, 355.
Device, 409.
Devise, 479.
Devoted, 55, 146, 181.
Devotee, 114, 152.
Devout, 457.
Dew, 295, 558.
Dexterous, 157.
Diagram, 64.
Dial, 256.
Dialect, 432, 484.
Diameter, 179, 518.
Diamond, 535.
Diamond-shaped, 275.
Diarrhœa, 153, 318, 498, 518.
Dibble, 592.
Dicé, 442.
Dictionary, 37, 174.
Die, 70, 156, 275, 289, 294, 403, 406.
Differ, 214.
Difference, 46.
Different, 346, 552.
Difficult, 555.
Difficulty, 10, 102, 186, 555.

Dig, 216, 216, 217, 220, 228.
Digest, 60, 303.
Digit, 62.
Dignified, 97, 177, 493.
Dike, 108, 111.
Dilatory, 169, 408, 522, 566, 604, 610, 612.
Diligence, 57.
Diligent, 57, 181, 192.
Dill, 446.
Dim, 184, 252, 302, 366, 366, 424, 558.
Diminish, 494.
Dinner, 5, 149, 255.
Dip, 229, 315, 434, 457.
Dipper, 215.
Diphtheria, 461.
Direct, 214, 214, 365.
Direction, 249.
Dirt, 104.
Dirty, 580, 591, 611.
Disagree, 39.
Disavow, 69.
Disband, 245.
Discard, 168, 469.
Disciple, 177, 343, 542.
Disclose, 313.
Disconnected, 372, 400, 491.
Discount, 205.
Discouraged, 196.
Discourse, 483.
Discriminate, 144.
Discuss, 46, 480, 483, 486, 487, 530.
Disdain, 130, 231, 455.
Disease, 186, 293, 548.
Disembark, 498.

Disesteem, 496, 509.
Disgrace, 244, 512, 528.
Disgraceful, 474.
Disguise, 436.
Disgust, 67.
Dish, 95, 360, 450, 457.
Dishcloth, 160, 227, 552.
Dishevelled, 8, 212, 581.
Dishonest, 8, 304.
Dishonour, 338.
Dislike, 28, 67, 130, 184, 191.
Dislocate, 218.
Dismemberment, 52.
Dismiss, 24, 231, 391, 535.
Dismount, 2.
Disobedient, 182, 513.
Disorder, 350.
Disorderly, 9, 124, 399, 517.
Disown, 514.
Dispatch, 247, 258.
Dispel, 245, 311, 521.
Dispensary, 440, 528.
Dispense, 160, 355.
Disperse, 44, 234, 245, 315, 544.
Display, 172, 256, 339.
Displeased, 89, 102, 287, 474.
Displeasure, 67, 130.
Dispose, 304.
Disposition, 84, 182, 189, 432, 466.
Dispute, 79, 511.
Disregard, 490.
Disrespectful, 42.
Dissatisfied, 184.
Dissipate, 477.
Dissipated, 303, 454.

DIS-DOW.

Dissolute, 425.
Distance, 384, 512, 522.
Distant, 40, 177, 187, 348, 521.
Distend, 431, 435.
Distillery, 327, 399.
Distinct, 339, 569.
Distinction, 46.
Distinctly, 261.
Distinguish, 44, 46, 487, 511.
Distort, 210, 354, 608.
Distrain, 52.
Distress, 56, 84, 98, 277, 441, 445, 555.
Distribute, 245.
District, 44, 157, 410.
Disturb, 56, 96, 237, 578.
Divan, 60, 166.
Dive, 605.
Diver, 605.
Diverge, 44.
Divergent, 155, 296.
Diversion, 338.
Divide, 35, 44, 59, 211, 239, 341.
Divine, 8, 64, 64, 336.
Divining-cone, 64.
Divinity, 375.
Division, 44, 154, 157, 271, 341, 517.
Divorce, 14, 555.
Divulge, 207.
Dizzy, 363.
Do, 13, 26, 136, 148, 165, 170, 202, 214, 240, 246, 250, 329, 438, 439, 466, 499.
Doctor, 99, 528.
Doctrine, 339, 519.

Doff, 65.
Dog, 334, 334.
Dog-days, 14.
Dog-flesh, 417.
Doll, 25.
Dollar, 302.
Dolt, 187, 602.
Dome, 215.
Domestic, 139.
Domesticate, 140.
Domino, 331.
Done, 136, 158.
Donkey, 579.
Don't, 14, 34, 291, 448, 474.
Door, 510, 542.
Door-frame, 545.
Door-keeper, 2, 361, 362, 546.
Door-post, 267.
Door-screen, 154.
Door-sill, 545.
Doorway, 519.
Dose, 520.
Dot, 592.
Dotage, 184.
Dote, 25, 191, 311, 334.
Double, 23, 53, 147, 230, 493, 503, 554.
Doubt, 348.
Doubtful, 179.
Doubtless, 559.
Dove, 247, 587.
Dovetail, 279.
Dowry, 491.
Down, 2, 294.
Downward, 12.
Downy, 293.

(732)

Draff, 399.
Draft, 310, 375, 380.
Drag, 213, 233, 238.
Dragon, 461, 492, 596.
Dragon-fly, 459.
Drain, 311, 315.
Drake, 586.
Drastic, 216.
Draw, 71, 88, 144, 203, 211, 217, 347, 411, 413, 503.
Drawer, 153, 209.
Drawl, 605.
Dread, 180, 182, 346.
Dreadful, 67, 603.
Dreadfully, 176.
Dream, 117.
Dregs, 308, 312, 430.
Dress, 207, 216, 398, 571.
Drift, 303, 501.
Driftwood, 233.
Drill, 234, 315, 409.
Drink, 89, 90, 526, 571.
Drip, 305.
Drive, 28, 79, 212, 218, 224, 232, 246, 499, 501, 519, 524, 570.
Drizzle, 141, 178, 293, 317.
Droll, 500.
Droop, 450, 453.
Drop, 120, 305, 314, 451, 592.
Dropsy, 431, 435.
Dross, 589.
Drought, 8, 252.
Drown, 308, 311.
Drum, 593.
Drummer, 202.
Drumstick, 278.

Drunk, 159, 328, 515, 527, 527, 604.
Dry, 8, 252, 256, 258, 269, 304, 320, 321, 321, 322, 328; 611.
Dry-rot, 580.
Duck, 266, 302, 586.
Duckling, 587.
Duckweed, 449, 455.
Due, 481.
Dues, 379.
Dull, 40, 124, 188, 196, 269, 306, 357, 365, 391, 522, 550, 552, 591, 592, 608.
Dulness, 109.
Dumb, 80, 88.
Dumpling, 205, 398, 571, 572.
Dumpy, 368, 431.
Dun, 28, 169, 296, 478, 513.
Dung, 399, 597.
Duplicity, 10.
Durable, 58, 105, 404, 406, 426, 537.
During, 545.
Dusk, 238, 249, 252, 366, 590, 599, 610.
Dust, 110, 308, 319.
Duster, 211, 213, 221.
Dutiful, 133.
Duty, 44, 287, 379, 425.
Dwarf, 329, 368.
Dwarfish, 368.
Dwell, 16, 152, 431.
Dwelling, 103, 139, 152.
Dye, 268.
Dyer, 268.
Dynasty, 261.
Dysentery, 153, 318, 350.

E.

Each, 15, 77, 292, 515.
Eagerly, 194.
Eagle, 156; 588.
Ear, 263, 378, 423.
Early, 1, 252, 307.
Earnest, 363, 465, 482, 497.
Earnest money, 11, 137.
Earnestly, 195.
Ear-ring, 111, 341.
Earth, 100, 101, 103, 113, 374, 381.
Earthenware, 95, 100, 298.
Earthquake, 56.
Ease, 21, 135, 308, 409, 437, 476, 518, 581.
Easily, 30, 253.
East, 267.
Easy, 123, 140, 144, 440, 509, 603, 605.
Eat, 73, 90, 197, 344, 460.
Eatables, 90.
Eau-de-cologne, 558.
Eaves, 314, 395.
Eaves-dropping, 149.
Echo, 424.
Eclipse, 335, 462.
Economical, 30, 392, 401.
Economically, 184, 568.
Economize, 31.
Edge, 72, 380.
Edict, 485.
Eel, 585, 586.
Eel-trap, 396, 413.
Efficacious, 196, 243, 425, 558, 577.
Efficacy, 54, 310.
Effigy, 12, 293.
Effort, 593.
Effusion, 38.
Egg, 460.
Egg-plant, 445.
Egret, 588.
Eight, 35.
Eighth, 35.
Either, 199.
Eject, 498, 514.
Elatedly, 439.
Elbow, 174, 210, 432.
Elder, 542.
Eldest, 542.
Electricity, 556.
Elegant, 535.
Elegantly, 554, 589.
Element, 466.
Elephant, 489.
Elevate, 229.
Elf, 125.
Elope, 242, 498.
Emaciated, 174, 357.
Embarrass, 213, 219, 400, 412.
Embezzle, 138, 232.
Embezzler, 138.
Emboss, 539.
Embrasure, 104.
Embroider, 48, 216, 269, 412.
Embroidery, 412.
Eminent, 26.
Emission, 523.
Emperor, 161, 356, 452.
Empire, 3, 296, 381.
Employ, 344.

Employment, 278.
Empress, 76, 292.
Empty, 24, 27, 382, 402, 458, 485, 578.
Empty-handed, 150.
Emulate, 496.
Encase, 59.
Enceinte, 89, 344, 382, 506.
Encircle, 59, 212, 341.
Enclosure, 67, 109.
Encourage, 58.
Encroach, 15.
Encumbrance, 403, 497.
End, 3, 8, 9, 14, 152, 167, 186, 190, 274, 284, 287, 290, 308, 347, 360, 403, 567.
Endless, 360.
Endure, 6, 7, 70, 180, 406, 421, 428.
Enemy, 12, 139, 141, 142, 147, 246.
Energetic, 50, 523.
Energy, 294.
Enervating, 442.
Enfeebled, 172.
Engage, 10, 484, 547.
Engaged, 137.
Engrave, 45, 47, 554.
Engross, 240.
Enjoin, 75, 96, 97, 570.
Enjoy, 11, 338, 402, 496.
Enlarge, 547.
Enlighten, 148, 225.
Enlist, 57, 208.
Enmity, 12, 227.
Enough, 117, 260, 416, 500, 571, 572.

Enroll, 220.
Enshroud, 290.
Enter, 4, 34, 43, 220, 354, 517.
Enteritis, 348.
Entertain, 19, 169, 196, 365, 513, 527, 550, 572.
Entice, 58, 171, 409, 482, 614.
Entire, 35, 273, 309, 577.
Entirely, 415.
Entrails, 555.
Entrance, 72.
Entrap, 601.
Entwine, 414.
Envelope, 115, 389, 390.
Envious, 125.
Environ, 412.
Envy, 128, 131, 325.
Epidemic, 347.
Epilepsy, 352.
Equal, 69, 102, 117, 124, 147, 292, 499, 526, 594, 607.
Equalize, 59.
Equally, 164.
Eradicate, 211, 549.
Erase, 216.
Erect, 214, 228.
Erianthus, 445.
Ermine, 593.
Error, 158.
Escape, 33, 313, 431, 501, 514, 609.
Escort, 213, 487.
Essay, 247, 386.
Essay paper, 65.
Essence, 296.
Establish, 169, 385, 479.

EST-EXP.

Estate, 105, 167, 278, 343.
Esteem, 149, 338, 362, 475.
Estimate, 16, 29, 53, 310, 362, 530.
Estrange, 346.
Eternal, 296.
Eternally, 522.
Etiquette, 29, 271, 286, 376.
Eunuch, 137, 138, 360.
Evacuate, 153.
Evaporate, 494.
Even, 164, 515.
Evening, 116, 140, 256, 591.
Evenly, 59.
Ever, 296, 522.
Everlasting, 496.
Every, 15.
Everybody, 12, 98.
Everything, 98, 545.
Everywhere, 48, 77, 97, 256, 313, 510, 516, 519.
Evidence, 49, 195, 206, 235, 479.
Evil, 67, 134, 135, 186, 189, 292, 316, 324, 376, 525, 591, 599.
Ewe, 417.
Exact, 220.
Exactly, 31, 184, 287.
Exalted, 580.
Examination, 378, 421, 481, 577.
Examination halls, 107, 546.
Examine, 142, 267, 283, 361, 362, 381, 421, 479, 577.
Example, 279, 292.
Exceedingly, 124, 176, 407.
Excel, 496, 542.

Excellency, 84, 118, 176.
Excellent, 30, 341.
Excessive, 30.
Excessively, 25.
Exchange, 34, 224, 523.
Excite, 56, 316, 325, 386.
Exclamation, 81, 84, 85, 93, 95.
Excuse, 67, 138, 204, 483, 483 566, 580.
Execute, 40.
Executioner, 53.
Execution ground; 107.
Exercise, 56, 113, 219, 236, 311, 520.
Exert, 55, 90, 173, 176, 219, 329, 355, 386, 402, 566, 593.
Exhausted, 98, 382.
Exhibit, 256, 569.
Exhort, 55, 58, 528.
Exhortation, 58, 60.
Exile, 507.
Existence, 102.
Exit, 43.
Exorcise, 548.
Expect, 248, 261, 485.
Expectation, 190, 261.
Expectorate, 94.
Expediency, 285.
Expedient, 272.
Expel, 170, 238, 499, 500, 514, 578.
Expend, 422, 492.
Expenditure, 13, 240, 414, 422.
Expense, 20, 118, 248, 344, 360, 443, 492.
Experience, 367, 475, 487, 546.

(736)

Experienced, 198, 421.
Experiment, 481.
Expert, 91.
Explain, 374, 477, 486, 511, 547.
Expose, 76, 197, 244, 274, 474, 558.
Expound, 477.
Express, 174, 520.
Expression, 295, 567.
Extenuate, 144.
Exterior, 116.
Exterminate, 175, 311, 406.
External, 116.
Extinct, 549.
Extinguish, 244, 311, 325.
Extirpate, 52.
Extort, 56, 90, 228, 246, 378, 402.
Extra, 148.
Extract, 71, 211.
Extraordinary, 9, 121.
Extravagant, 18, 122, 458, 581.
Extravagantly, 303.
Extravasated, 352.
Extreme, 9, 360.
Extremely, 118, 276, 351, 406, 438, 551.
Extremity, 182, 406.
Eye, 361, 364, 594.
Eye-ball, 365.
Eye-brow, 362.
Eye disease, 420.
Eye-lash, 293.
Eye-lid, 357.
Eye-shade, 27.

F.

Fabricate, 517.
Face, 76, 140, 147, 360, 436, 495, 559.
Fact, 143, 189.
Factory, 15, 151.
Fade, 66, 244, 355, 439, 514.
Fail, 23, 244.
Failing, 350, 368.
Faint, 192, 252.
Fair, 36, 256, 259, 565.
Fairy, 148, 375.
Faith, 21.
Faithful, 21, 181.
Falcon, 588.
Fall, 3, 12, 14, 18, 22, 23, 41, 103, 109, 148, 156, 222, 369, 451, 502, 505, 602, 607.
False, 24, 29, 458.
Falsetto, 131.
Fame, 77.
Familiar, 72, 159, 316, 326.
Family, 138, 139, 200, 241, 322, 363, 505, 543.
Famished, 573.
Famous, 510, 540, 580.
Fan, 201, 227.
Fanners, 507.
Far, 118, 521.
Farm, 166.
Farmer, 166.
Farming, 103, 381, 611.
Fashion, 439.
Fast, 402, 595.

(737)

FAS-FIN.

Fasten, 216.
Fat, 142, 300, 427, 428, 433, 435, 436, 600.
Fate, 410.
Father, 2, 97, 119, 147, 312, 330, 330, 330, 330.
Father-in-law, 330.
Fathom, 168, 607.
Fatigue, 31.
Fatsia, 454.
Fatten, 500.
Fault, 81, 120, 349, 411, 416, 518, 529.
Favour, 37, 75, 185, 317, 362, 476.
Favourite, 437.
Fear, 139, 182, 182, 183, 198, 236.
Fearful, 208.
Fearlessly, 55.
Feast, 90, 93, 140, 161, 390, 456, 526, 527.
Feather, 293, 419, 419, 420.
Fee, 376, 428, 431, 483, 486, 493, 536.
Feeble, 268, 353, 468, 508, 523.
Feed, 86, 90, 92, 572, 573.
Feel, 45, 84, 212, 230, 361, 476.
Feeling, 189.
Feign, 24, 38, 107, 504.
Feint, 281, 518.
Fell, to, 216.
Fellow, 14, 18, 25, 117, 312, 442.
Felt, 293.
Female, 123, 129, 333, 333, 531, 546, 551, 554.

Fence, 264, 285, 387, 396, 422, 440, 475, 522.
Fennel, 446.
Ferment, 355, 528, 529.
Ferry, 72, 302, 309.
Fertile, 114, 427.
Festival, 31, 62, 259, 374, 392, 512, 528.
Fetter, 540.
Fever, 325.
Feverish, 327.
Few, 10, 35, 143, 148, 165, 246, 509.
Fibre, 159, 341, 590.
Fiddle, 340.
Field, 101, 114, 344.
Fiend, 125.
Fierce, 32, 190, 257, 291, 321, 335, 511.
Fiery, 319, 321.
Fifth, 10.
Fight, 199, 202, 214, 226, 228, 246, 269, 291, 329, 582.
Fighter, 291.
Figure, 140, 174, 332, 372, 443, 468, 490, 493, 579.
File, 5, 535.
Filial, 133.
Fill, 32, 109, 152, 318, 470, 608.
Filler, 244.
Filter, 298.
Filth, 104, 381.
Filthy, 472, 473, 521, 524, 579, 580, 595.
Fin, 419.
Finally, 386.

(738)

Find, 147, 204, 225, 283.
Fine, 141, 281, 293, 398, 405, 416, 492, 570, 580.
Finely, 38, 141, 338, 410.
Finger, 211, 214.
Finger-breadth, 214.
Finger-nail, 329, 345.
Finger-post, 371.
Finger-ring, 198.
Finish, 1, 99, 136, 152, 161, 221, 289, 323, 346.
Fire, a, 132, 318, 319, 320.
Fire, on, 326.
Fire, to, 93, 203, 242, 319, 327, 549.
Firearms, 319.
Fire-basket, 396.
Fire-fly, 11, 463.
Fire-pan, 358.
Fire-wall, 145.
Firewood, 149, 268, 443.
Fireworks, 389, 593.
Firing, 319.
Firm, 50, 105, 280, 426, 540.
Firmly, 16, 105, 381, 412.
First, 1, 31, 33, 45, 126, 261, 287, 344, 567.
First-rate, 3.
Fish, 299, 312, 532, 584.
Fissure, 415.
Fist, 215.
Fisticuffs, 215.
Fit, 5, 170, 307, 470, 485, 526, 541.
Five, 10.
Fix, 9, 10, 103, 121, 136, 137, 159, 216, 418, 438, 477, 500.

Fixture, 262.
Fizz, 306.
Flag, 251, 448, 450, 451, 453, 453.
Flagstaff, 273.
Flag-stone, 266.
Flail, 274, 423.
Flake, 331.
Flame, 152.
Flaming, 321.
Flank, 435.
Flap, 231, 234, 357, 419, 423, 473.
Flash, 226, 254, 556.
Flat, 201, 365.
Flatter, 123, 130, 205, 212, 229, 443, 471, 483, 488, 571.
Flattery, 483, 497.
Flavour, 72, 83, 312.
Flaw; 340, 350.
Flay, 51, 357.
Flea, 459, 460.
Flee, 514, 517, 524.
Flesh, 425, 433.
Fleshless, 426.
Flick, 173, 607.
Fling, 150, 207, 598.
Flint, 368.
Flirt, 200.
Flit, 227, 500.
Float, 302, 303, 314.
Flock, 418.
Flog, 202.
Flood, 301, 319.
Flooding, 156.
Floor, 217, 280.

(739)

Flotilla, 161.
Flour, 319, 397, 589.
Flourish, 439, 445.
Flow, 303.
Flower, 443, 447, 568.
Flower-stalk, 455.
Flue, 98.
Flurried, 24, 180.
Flushed, 401.
Flute, 388.
Fly, 111, 234, 242, 463, 501, 570.
Foal, 576.
Fob, 69.
Fodder, 92.
Fog, 322, 416, 558.
Fold, 23, 76, 229, 241.
Folk, 166.
Follow, 138, 177, 178, 303, 425, 502, 513, 520, 552.
Follower, 177, 343, 542.
Fond, 124, 191, 193, 316, 492.
Fondly, 334.
Fontanel, 179.
Food, 14, 72, 450, 570, 570, 571, 604.
Fool, 341.
Foolish, 125, 192, 194, 209, 252, 253, 353, 464.
Foot, 151, 167, 288, 430, 504.
Foot-print, 65, 503.
Foot-rule, 151.
Foot-stool, 43, 503.
For, 14, 259, 329, 404.
Forbear, 144.
Forbearance, 79, 140, 180.
Forbearing, 304.

Forbid, 376.
Force, 16, 55, 173, 219, 272, 370, 575, 600, 605.
Ford, 302, 303.
Forearm, 202, 579.
Forefathers, 33, 137, 509.
Forehead, 567, 569.
Foreign, 116, 302, 346, 428, 474.
Forenoon, 3.
Forest, 266.
Foretell, 322.
Forfeit, 212.
Forget, 65, 180, 197, 240, 478.
Forgetfulness, 180, 523.
Forgive, 34, 138, 184, 497, 573.
Fork, 68, 203, 277, 602, 615.
Form, 43, 170, 174, 228.
Formality, 286.
Former, 33, 50, 74, 175, 253, 254. 289.
Formerly, 49, 243.
Fornication, 127, 445.
Fornicator, 131.
Fort, 143.
Forth, 43, 474.
Forthwith, 322.
Fortunate, 22, 165, 184.
Fortune, 103, 376, 517, 521.
Fortune-teller, 64, 83.
Forward, 477.
Foster-father, 330.
Foul, 316.
Found, to, 51.
Foundation, 102, 105, 167, 270, 430.
Four, 97.
Fourth, 97.

Fowling-piece, 538, 586.
Fox, 293, 334, 335.
Fraction, 66, 293.
Fracture, 236.
Fragaria, 460.
Fragment, 371, 397, 606.
Fragmentary, 598.
Fragrance, 574.
Fragrant, 574, 575.
Frame, 269, 270, 387, 392, 416, 545, 597.
Fray, 413.
Freckles, 350.
Free, 58, 301, 611.
Freeze, 40, 41, 42.
Freightage, 295.
Frequently, 57, 154.
Fresh, 131, 249, 315, 317, 584.
Fret, 190.
Fretful, 86.
Fret-saw, 536.
Friable, 299, 328.
Friend, 70, 261, 512.
Friendless, 133.
Friendly, 124, 582.
Frighten, 96, 578.
Frisky, 334.
Frog, 462, 554.
Frolicsome, 334.
From, 76, 177, 178, 203, 345, 437, 439.
Front, 49, 560.
Frontier, 72, 345.
Frost, 42, 557.
Froth, 299.
Frown, 50, 365, 591.

Frozen, 40.
Fruit, 265, 449.
Fry, 320, 320, 324.
Fuel, 455.
Fulfil, 196, 313, 503, 577.
Full, 57, 99, 100, 100, 143, 173, 273, 313, 358, 500, 571, 594.
Fuller's-earth, 397.
Full-fleshed, 600.
Full-grown, 96, 354.
Fully, 98, 302.
Fulsomely, 72.
Fumigate, 324.
Fun, 170, 421, 500.
Fund, 564.
Funeral, 90, 171.
Funnel, 244.
Fur, 93, 357, 435.
Furious, 181.
Furnace, 319, 328.
Furnish, 43.
Furniture, 14, 25.
Fuse, 409.
Futile, 391.
Future, 19, 146.

G.

Gab, 533.
Gabble, 423, 616.
Gable, 284.
Gad-fly, 332, 460.
Gain, 46, 134, 219, 491, 496, 542.
Gall, 436.
Gallop, 501.
Gamble, 64, 422, 496.
Gape, 121.

GAR-GLO.

Garden, 99.
Gardenia, 273.
Gargoyle, 585.
Garlic, 453.
Garment, 467.
Garrulous, 301.
Gash, 72.
Gasp, 569.
Gate, 72, 268, 281, 284, 542.
Gather, 209, 215, 225, 231, 235, 239, 283, 289, 607.
Gathering, 100.
Gaudily, 442.
Gauge, 120, 151.
Gauze, 402.
Gazette, 108.
Geld, 577.
Gelding, 575, 577.
Gem, 144, 337.
General, 161, 225, 280, 346, 487.
General, a, 31, 146.
General, in, 42.
Generally, 118, 280, 401.
Generation, 4, 14, 339, 509.
Generous, 185.
Genial, 81, 82, 303.
Genii, 13.
Genitals, 551.
Genteel, 247, 249.
Gentian, 436.
Gentle, 268, 306, 310, 441, 605.
Gentleman, 36, 45, 87, 310, 330, 343.
Gentry, 114, 403.
Genuine, 101, 363.
Geography, 101.

Geomancer, 107, 551.
Germinate, 95, 444.
Get, 7, 177, 343, 355.
Get on, 240.
Get up, 498.
Ghastly, 189.
Ghost, 583.
Giddy, 250, 257, 302, 334, 363, 508.
Gift, 202.
Gill, 585.
Gild, 225.
Gin, 173.
Ginger, 132, 454.
Ginseng, 12, 68.
Girder, 273.
Girdle, 162, 433.
Girdle-fish, 586.
Girl, 123, 126.
Girth, 162.
Give, 65, 207, 211, 221, 228, 230, 250, 404, 517.
Give up, 70, 275, 514.
Gladly, 187.
Glance, 366.
Glans-penis, 596.
Glare, 365.
Glass, 248, 338, 340.
Glaze, 156, 299.
Gleam, 254.
Glide, 499.
Glittering, 308.
Gloaming, 252.
Globular, 99, 293, 616.
Glorious, 448.
Glory, 57, 279, 420, 448.

(742)

Glue, 397, 434.
Glutinous, 398, 400, 591.
Gluttonous, 94, 574, 612.
Gnash, 45.
Gnat, 262, 460.
Gnaw, 83, 87, 595.
Go, 3, 68, 175, 417, 498, 498, 501.
Goat, 417.
Gobble, 229.
Go-between, 14, 130, 400, 531.
God, 119, 140, 374, 375, 381.
Goddess of Mercy, 476.
Goiter, 336.
Gold, 530.
Gong, 540, 541.
Good, 7, 8, 19, 47, 58, 74, 85, 91, 118, 123, 124, 125, 144, 173, 178, 306, 375, 404, 417, 441, 577, 580.
Good at, 15.
Good-bye, 511.
Good-for-nothing, 198, 255, 467.
Good-natured, 183, 473.
Goodness, 123.
Good-tempered, 167.
Goods, 491.
Goose, 554, 587.
Gore, 50.
Gorge, 155.
Gorgeously, 448.
Goslings, 587.
Gossip, 54, 95, 211, 238, 254, 484, 515, 544.
Gouge, 216.
Gourd, 341.
Govern, 339, 391, 509.

Governor, 47, 157, 233.
Government, 169.
Gown, 468, 468, 469, 473.
Grab, 204, 206, 230.
Grace, 37, 144, 185, 317.
Gracious, 188.
Gradation, 154.
Gradually, 315.
Graduate, 35, 134, 167, 202, 377, 477, 491.
Graft, 222, 559.
Grain, 381, 397, 567.
Grand, 39, 560, 580.
Grand-children, 116.
Grand-father, 36, 330, 330, 375.
Grandiloquent, 580.
Grandly, 38, 325, 560.
Grand-mother, 129.
Grand-son, 134.
Grand-uncle, 70.
Granary, 24.
Grant, 32, 41, 196, 250, 544.
Grapes, 450, 451.
Grapple, 233.
Grasp, 207.
Grasping, 66, 176, 305.
Grass, 398, 445, 447.
Grass-cloth, 159, 590.
Grasshopper, 460.
Grater, 238.
Gratuity, 11.
Grave, 110, 136, 300, 383.
Grave-clothes, 468.
Gravel, 351.
Grave-stone, 371.
Grave-yard, 100, 110, 155.

GRA-HAI.

Gravy, 611.
Gray, 319, 351, 391.
Greasy, 435.
Great, 31, 117, 122, 168, 298, 303, 305, 530.
Great-grandfather, 259.
Great-grandson, 259.
Greatly, 302.
Greedy, 66, 290, 335, 612.
Green, 337, 408, 558.
Greenhorn, 466.
Greet, 211.
Griddle, 529.
Grief, 56, 192.
Grievance, 142.
Grieve, 9, 28, 142, 189, 190.
Grievous, 190, 603.
Grind, 222, 235, 373, 501.
Grip, 233, 400.
Gripe, 217.
Grit, 341.
Gritty, 373.
Groan, 83, 90.
Grocery, 8.
Groom, 459.
Groove, 281.
Grope, 230.
Ground, 101, 167, 237, 357.
Grove, 71, 266.
Grow, 343, 542, 598.
Grown, 118, 385.
Grub, 465.
Grudge, 435, 616.
Gruel, 397.
Gruff, 92.
Grumble, 150.

Guarantee, 6, 60.
Guard, 26, 108, 136; 206, 297, 361, 537, 547.
Guard-house, 64, 107.
Guardian, 20.
Guerilla, 94.
Guess, 16, 54, 335, 483, 485, 600.
Guest, 138, 494.
Guide, 162, 171, 409.
Guild-hall, 440.
Guileless, 263.
Guiltless, 511.
Guilty, 71.
Guitar, 340.
Gullet, 88.
Gumption, 341.
Gums, 595.
Gun, 528.
Gun-boat, 36, 369.
Gunpowder, 456.
Gush, 305.
Gust, 569.
Gutter, 389.
Gypsum, 319, 368, 434.

H.

Ha, 85, 93.
Habit, 419.
Habitually, 194.
Hack, 415.
Had, 254.
Hades, 39, 165, 259, 551.
Haggard, 195.
Haggle, 455, 486.
Hail, 41, 173.
Hair, 293, 294, 581.

HAI-HEA.

Hair-brush, 46.
Hair-oil, 300.
Hair-pin, 216, 531.
Hairy, 293.
Hale, 24, 168, 371.
Half, 63, 147, 524.
Half-cooked, 120, 343, 518.
Half-way, 434.
Hall, 106, 169, 169, 291.
Halter, 413, 562.
Ham, 434.
Hammer, 538.
Hand, 201, 215, 329.
Hand in, 27, 79, 521.
Hand down, 27, 522.
Handful, 206.
Handicraft, 202, 456.
Hand-cuff, 231.
Hand over, 11, 13, 66, 379.
Handkerchief, 159, 469.
Handle, 210, 273, 285, 413, 423, 540.
Hand in hand, 218.
Hand-rail, 206.
Handsome, 22, 131, 307, 377, 410, 468, 554, 560.
Handy, 53.
Hank, 204, 388, 405.
Hang, 78, 197, 213, 220, 269.
Happen, 22, 520, 522, 522.
Happiness, 295, 376.
Happy, 168, 181.
Harass, 169, 519, 577.
Harbour, 105, 208, 384, 533.
Hard, 50, 58, 105, 289, 304, 370, 371, 421, 555, 607.

Hard np, 406.
Harden, 608.
Hard-headed, 87.
Hard-hearted, 540.
Hardship, 220.
Hare, 34.
Hare-lip, 415, 600.
Hark, 361.
Harmonious, 82, 295.
Harmoniously, 554.
Harmony, 136, 295, 365.
Harness, 562.
Harrow, 422.
Harsh, 180.
Harshly, 505.
Harvest, 69, 164, 198, 288, 378, 590.
Hassock, 453.
Haste, 516.
Hastily, 350.
Hasty, 182, 505, 549.
Hat, 39, 163, 200, 388, 582.
Hat strings, 570.
Hatch, 449.
Hatchet, 51, 248, 544.
Hate, 130, 180, 181, 183, 184, 189, 292.
Hateful, 74, 478.
Haughty, 170, 578, 580.
Haul, 205, 210, 233, 409.
Haunted, 148.
Have, 177, 260.
Haw, 277.
He, 13.
Head, 115, 154, 196, 330, 347, 361, 394, 405, 433, 542, 566, 574, 582.

HEA-HOA.

Head-workman, 566.
Headache, 352.
Head-man, 200, 344, 469, 542, 566, 574.
Heal, 145, 190, 298, 383, 528.
Healthy, 24, 114, 181.
Heap, a, 107.
Heap, to, 38, 107, 113, 381.
Hear, 424, 425, 475.
Heart, 145, 179, 197, 344.
Heartily, 189, 193.
Heartless, 184.
Hearty, 24.
Heat, 257, 319, 327, 327, 519.
Heaven, 8, 107, 119, 139.
Heavy, 364, 529.
Heedful, 486.
Heedlessly, 91, 398.
Heel, 502, 504.
Heigh, 93.
Heir, 93.
Hell, 336.
Helm, 441.
Helmet, 38, 359.
Help, 16, 54, 118, 161, 204, 206, 224, 224, 229, 244, 299, 463, 603.
Helper, 161, 202.
Hem, 409, 410.
Hemp, 590.
Hen, 129, 292, 554.
Hen-pecked, 506.
Hen-roost, 99.
Herd, 242, 418.
Here, 50, 102, 470, 502.
Hereafter, 158.

Heresy, 525.
Heretofore, 402.
Hernia, 349, 430.
Hero, 553.
Heron, 588.
Hesitate, 76.
Hibiscus, 280, 443.
Hiccough, 434, 573.
Hidden, 141.
Hide, an ox, 357.
Hide, to, 105, 145, 223, 226, 385, 506.
Higgledy-piggledy, 440.
High, 424, 580.
Highwayman, 141, 173.
Hill, 104, 155, 155.
Hillside, 107.
Hill-top, 59.
Hilt, 285.
Him, 37.
Hinder, 125, 187, 233, 239, 286, 547.
Hindrance, 125, 240, 374, 403.
Hinge, 282, 613.
Hint, 175, 270, 592.
Hip, 285.
Hire, 28, 28, 60, 144, 242, 311, 378, 494.
His, 13.
Historiographer, 75.
History, 75, 258.
Hit, 5, 87, 438, 602.
Hitch, 220, 282.
Hitherto, 76.
Hive, 209, 275, 390.
Hoarse, 92.

Hobbledehoy, 280.
Hodge-podge, 435.
Hoe, 217, 534, 538.
Hog, 331, 577.
Hold, 16, 89, 90, 152, 211, 212, 218, 219, 232, 233, 492.
Hole, 72, 102, 132, 302, 364, 383, 585, 600.
Hollow, 216, 384.
Home, 139, 152, 168, 239.
Hone, 454.
Honest, 8; 143, 181, 306, 307.
Honestly, 164, 421.
Honesty, 66.
Honey; 399, 462.
Honey-comb, 45, 201.
Honey-suckle, 531.
Honour, an, 54.
Honour, His, 118, 421.
Honour, to, 133, 147, 245.
Honourable, 13, 144, 147, 492.
Hood, 163.
Hood-wink, 604.
Hoof, 504.
Hook, 204, 532, 540.
Hoop, 390.
Hop, 607, 609.
Hope, 261.
Horn, 476.
Hornet, 461.
Horoscope, 83, 166.
Horrified, 386.
Horse, 575, 576.
Horse-play, 613.
Horse-tail, 494.
Hose-pipe, 596.

Hospitable, 66, 356.
Host, 6.
Hot, 257, 320, 325, 511.
Hotel, 167.
Hound, 94.
Hour, 255, 511.
House, 136, 152, 153, 166, 200.
House-boat, 602.
Household, 139.
House-warming, 545.
How, 16, 124, 124, 136, 165, 183, 281, 489, 525, 603.
How many, 149; 165.
However, 38.
Hubbub, 92.
Hue, 442.
Huff, 188.
Hug, 211, 230.
Hull, 237, 247, 372.
Human, 12.
Humble, 14, 63, 192, 458, 488, 521.
Humerus, 579.
Humpback, 215, 350, 601.
Hundred, 356.
Hunger, 573.
Hungry, 572, 608.
Hunt, 227, 337, 500.
Hurriedly, 64, 286, 423.
Hurry, 169, 180, 181, 182, 192, 208, 229, 418, 499, 606.
Hurt, 28, 139, 371, 459.
Husband, 2, 116, 118, 139, 345, 543.
Husbandman, 512.
Husband's sister, 126.

(747)

Husk, 114, 378.
Hustle, 84, 220.
Hut, 169, 449.
Hydrangea, 293.
Hydrocele, 349.
Hydrophobia, 229, 292.
Hypocritical, 24, 38, 77, 174, 179, 359.

I.

I, 11, 192, 199, 262.
Ice, 40, 42, 603.
Icy, 40.
Idea, 183, 190, 243.
Idle, 197, 382, 421, 423, 520.
Idleness, 305, 422, 544.
Idler, 86, 544, 555.
Idol, 25, 29, 104, 449.
If, 23, 444.
Ignoble, 496.
Ignominious, 41.
Ignoramus, 188.
Ignorant, 9, 142, 192, 197, 343, 367, 452, 590.
Ignorance, 591.
Ill-bred, 382.
Illegitimate, 377.
Illtreat, 33, 522.
Illustrate, 292, 487.
Illustration, 92, 249.
Ill-will, 184.
Image, 29, 175.
Imagine, 483.
Imitate, 134, 243, 299, 556.
Immaculate, 337.
Immature, 509.

Immediately, 47, 65, 111, 146, 150, 255, 385, 502.
Imminent, 212.
Immortal, 13.
Immovable, 105.
Imp, 182.
Impartial, 102.
Impassable, 518.
Impassive, 566.
Impeach, 55.
Impede, 547.
Impediment, 607.
Imperata, 445.
Imperial, 3, 178, 286, 356, 424.
Imperious, 519.
Impetuous, 335, 534.
Implement, 36, 537.
Implicate, 69, 85, 333, 482, 515, 550.
Important, 322, 408, 474, 474, 530.
Importunate, 296, 351.
Importune, 136, 464.
Importunity, 414.
Impose, 239, 479.
Imposing, 553.
Impoverish, 27, 41, 495.
Impression, 65.
Improper, 456, 559.
Improperly, 147.
Improve, 106, 542.
Impure, 316, 525.
In, 5, 101, 250, 470, 545, 567.
Inattentive, 195, 423.
Inauspicious, 43.
Incantation, 81.

Incapable, 205, 317.
Incense, 574.
Incessantly, 16, 30, 566, 576, 614.
Inch, 145.
Incite, 58, 86.
Inclination, 180.
Incline, 12, 25, 26, 564.
Inclose, 59, 99.
Include, 35, 59.
Incoherent, 568.
Income, 35, 376.
Incompetent, 430.
Incomprehensible, 310.
Inconstant, 178.
Inconvenience, 237, 240, 555.
Incorrigible, 60.
Increase, 53, 112, 116, 306, 545.
Incubator, 449.
Incur, 522.
Incurable, 351.
Indecision, 10.
Indefinite, 604.
Indefinitely, 30.
Independent, 345.
Index, 361.
India-rubber, 489.
Indictment, 79, 334.
Indifferent, 306, 313.
Indigestion, 26.
Indignant, 181.
Indigo, 455, 559.
Indispensable, 149, 555.
Indisposed, 453.
Indistinct, 568.
Indite, 23.

Induce, 478, 482, 614.
Indulge, 126, 411.
Indulgent, 304, 346.
Inert, 266.
Inevitable, 57, 149, 158.
Inexhaustible, 9, 360, 384.
Inexperienced, 297.
Infant, 8, 132, 134.
Infantry, 36.
Infectious, 268.
Inferior, 2, 17, 285, 368, 467.
Infinite, 9.
Infirm, 290, 523.
Infirmity, 290.
Inflamed, 327, 584.
Inflict, 54.
Influence, 53, 56, 57, 60.
Influential, 485.
Inform, 80, 208, 592.
Infuse, 299.
Ingeniously, 158.
Ingot, 5, 144, 536.
Inherit, 70, 375, 522.
Inimical, 146.
Injure, 28, 30, 139, 228, 290.
Injurious, 45, 139.
Injury, 52.
Ink, 112, 295.
Ink-slab, 344, 370.
Ink-well, 296.
Inn, 141, 167, 200, 386.
Inner, 35.
Inoculate, 242.
Inoffensive, 309.
Inopportunely, 520.
Inordinately, 303.

Inquest, 283.
Inquire, 88, 203, 425, 478.
Inscription, 61, 597.
Insect, 459.
Insensible, 381.
Insert, 582.
Inside, 35, 470, 567.
Insignia, 471.
Insignificant, 63, 178.
Insipid, 83, 306, 608.
Inspect, 360, 546, 577.
Inspiration, 80.
Inspire, 114.
Instance, 124, 292.
Instant, 47, 564.
Instantly, 65, 286, 510.
Instead, 259.
Instigate, 86, 241.
Instruct, 60, 106, 243, 477, 534, 592.
Instruction, 243, 477.
Instrument, 95.
Insufficient, 317, 368.
Insult, 22, 41, 83, 297, 316, 512.
Insurrection, 212.
Intelligence, 44.
Intelligent, 19.
Intention, 183, 190, 427.
Intentionally, 242.
Intercalary, 544.
Intercede, 99, 250, 303.
Intercept, 45, 51, 199, 240, 368.
Intercourse, 10, 19, 175, 516.
Interest, 46, 83, 186, 536.
Intermarry, 224.

Intermission, 545.
Internal, 35, 257.
Interpret, 99, 369, 477.
Interpreter, 516.
Interrogate, 360.
Interrogative, 83.
Interrupt, 405.
Intestine, 295, 431, 432.
Intimate, 66, 121, 141, 159, 316, 367, 433, 463, 475, 516.
Intimation, 477.
Intimidate, 483.
Intimidation, 16.
Into, 198.
Intoxicate, 527, 528.
Introduce, 171.
Introduction, 166, 455.
Intrude, 223, 419, 616.
Intrust, 13, 70, 483.
Inundate, 308, 611.
Invariably, 84.
Inveigle, 484.
Invent, 51, 269.
Invention, 409.
Inventory, 451.
Invert, 12, 23.
Investigate, 55, 88, 142, 144, 382, 421.
Invitation, 269.
Invite, 208, 423, 482, 484, 524.
Invoke, 73.
Involve, 210, 213, 238, 403, 515, 547.
I. O. U., 285.
Irascible, 471.
Iron, 247, 325, 540.

Iron-gray, 565.
Irreclaimable, 218.
Irrelevant, 63, 248, 550.
Irresolute, 3, 179, 199.
Irrigate, 318.
Irritate, 190, 319, 477.
Is, 254, 347, 474.
Isinglass, 585.
Islam, 37.
Island, 155.
Issue, 27, 43.
It, 37.
Italian cloth, 410.
Itch, 8, 197, 349, 350, 352, 353.
Ivory, 332, 489, 579.

J.

Jacket, 147, 296, 437, 468, 471, 472, 614.
Jade, 337, 340, 419.
Jail, 64, 339.
Jailor, 376.
Japanese, 24.
Jar, 358, 414, 415, 415, 611.
Jaundice, 353, 590.
Jaw, 332, 606.
Jimmy, 214.
Jerk, 219, 224, 517, 565.
Jessamine, 445.
Jest, 199, 387, 500.
Jewel, 144.
Jingles, 533, 563.
Job, 106.
Job's tears, 444.
Jocular, 500.
Jog, 224.

Joggle, 239.
Join, 76, 208, 222, 243, 414, 517.
Joint, 392.
Joke, 199, 500, 613.
Jolt, 232.
Journey, 386, 502.
Joy, 88, 281, 287.
Joyful, 193.
Joyfully, 88, 287.
Joyous, 257.
Judas-tree, 447.
Judge, 46, 144, 215, 437.
Judgment, 319, 376, 480.
Judgment-hall, 144, 249.
Jug, 415.
Juggler, 129.
Juggling, 200, 206.
Juice, 296, 301, 314.
Juicy, 295.
Jujube, 277.
Jump, 412, 503.
Just (adj.), 36, 102, 164.
Just (adv.), 45, 50, 73, 146, 150, 184, 250, 287, 414.
Justice, 412, 526.
Justly, 36, 164.
Jut, 384.

K.

Kalpa, 54.
Keep, 92, 136, 246, 326.
Keepsake, 191.
Kerchief, 160.
Kernel, 12, 270, 425.
Kerosene, 301, 319.

Kerria, 277.
Kestrel, 587.
Kettle, 115, 616.
Key, 60. 385, 541.
Kick, 150, 503, 504, 505, 598.
Kid, 417.
Kidnap, 210, 235, 336.
Kidney, 433.
Kill, 289, 291.
Kiln, 384.
Kin, 475.
Kind, 268, 281, 310.
Kind, a, 138, 170, 380, 441, 459, 543, 564.
Kindling, 171.
Kindly, 66.
Kindness, 185, 188.
Kindred, 475, 592.
King, 80, 143, 338.
Kingdom, 99.
Kingfisher, 419.
Kiss, 609, 610.
Kitchen, 67, 385.
Kitchen-god, 75.
Kite, 390, 588.
Kleptomania, 230.
Knave, 602.
Knead, 227, 611.
Knee, 174, 435, 601.
Kneel, 502.
Knee-pad, 469.
Knife, 43, 52.
Knit, 409, 424.
Knock, 73, 212, 218, 225, 232, 246, 372, 546, 607, 611, 615.
Knot, 122, 204, 392, 400, 404, 412, 582.
Know, 230, 258, 367, 487, 520.
Knowingly, 367.
Knowledge, 367.

L.

Laborious, 56, 77.
Laboriously, 371.
Labour, 53, 157, 495.
Labourer, 104, 157.
Labouring, 168.
Lackadaisical, 306.
Lacquer, 315, 514.
Ladder, 274.
Ladle, 341, 393, 438, 504, 613.
Lady, 118, 123, 135.
Lake, 302, 308.
Lama, 90.
Lamb, 417, 417.
Lame, 607.
Lamentable, 74.
Lamp, 115, 327, 383.
Lamp-stand, 438.
Lamp-wick, 447.
Lance, 367.
Land, 99.
Landing-stage, 575.
Landlord, 6.
Land-mark, 345.
Lane, 159.
Language, 480.
Languid, 188.
Lantern, 119, 323, 327, 396.
Lap, 34.
Lapel, 473.

Lard, 300.
Large, 85, 117, 136, 303, 435, 525, 583.
Larvae, 298.
Last, 138, 176, 208, 254, 262, 324, 391, 439.
Last, a, 278.
Latch, 204.
Late, 28, 256, 305, 522.
Lathe, 507.
Laugh, 84, 94, 387, 604.
Laughable, 387.
Lave, 219, 304.
Law, 20, 75, 167, 177, 298, 314.
Law-suit, 137.
Lay, to, 3, 238, 343, 363, 369, 506.
Lay by, 133, 242, 346, 549.
Lay on, 4, 359.
Lay out, 26, 228, 239.
Lay up, 23.
Layer, 154.
Layman, 21.
Lazy, 56, 128, 183, 195, 197.
Lead, 533.
Lead, to, 22, 148, 162, 171, 218, 234, 333, 337, 365, 566.
Leader, 26, 146, 446, 489, 553, 564, 583.
Leaf, 392, 452, 564.
Leaf-mould, 399.
Leaf-stalk, 579.
League, 491.
Leak, 16, 304, 313, 498.
Lean, 352, 426, 432.
Lean, to, 25, 608.

Leaning-board, 206.
Leap, 503.
Learn, 134, 236.
Learned, 253.
Learning, 134, 202, 574.
Least, 66, 293.
Leather, 357.
Leave, 4, 24, 43, 46, 133, 140, 207, 242, 511, 544, 555.
Leaven, 355, 527, 589.
Leavings, 290.
Leech, 462.
Leek, 562.
Left, 51, 157, 550, 572.
Left-handed, 602.
Leg, 275, 426, 430, 434, 434, 534.
Legal, 47.
Leggings, 122, 406, 472.
Leisure, 135, 257, 308, 382, 543.
Lend, 24, 218, 224, 242, 578, 616.
Length, 264, 389.
Lengthwise, 541, 565.
Leniency, 304.
Lenient, 140.
Lens, 33.
Lentil, 449.
Leopard, 490.
Leprosy, 351, 354.
Less, 149, 544.
Lest, 34, 185.
Let, 21, 30, 242, 345.
Let go, 4, 242.
Let off, 493.
Letter, 21, 97, 133, 258, 419.

Lettuce, 452.
Leucorrhoea, 162.
Level, 66, 104, 164.
Lever, 214, 606.
Levy, 178, 239.
Liar, 115, 150, 224, 485.
Libation, 122.
Liberal, 118, 185, 193, 301, 573.
Liberally, 66, 489.
Liberate, 242, 431, 529.
Licentions, 308, 425.
Lichee, 447.
Lichen, 270, 423, 443.
Lick, 571.
Lictor, 4, 356, 553.
Lid, 358.
Lie, a, 95, 114, 355, 437, 485, 506.
Lie, to, 111, 205, 365, 506, 576.
Life, 4, 82, 183, 343.
Life-boat, 244, 400.
Life-long, 505.
Life-time, 343, 509.
Lift, 212, 219, 224, 229, 230, 231, 261, 549, 614.
Light, 33, 112, 131, 158, 207, 299, 302, 306, 314, 334, 422, 508, 570, 581.
Light, a, 11, 318.
Light, to, 4, 83, 190, 326, 592.
Lighten, 205.
Lighter, a, 240.
Light-fingered, 307.
Lightly, 91.
Lightning, 543, 556, 557.

Like; 14, 17, 29, 78, 124, 149, 191, 388, 427.
Likely, 260.
Lily, 394.
Limb, 427.
Lime, 319, 374.
Limit, 271, 348, 384, 548.
Limited, 167, 368, 383.
Limitless, 322, 548.
Limp, 111, 344, 499, 500.
Line, 5, 403, 409, 502.
Lined, 120.
Linen, 159.
Lining; 470.
Link, 532.
Lintel, 567.
Lion, 336.
Lip, 86, 95, 159, 357.
Liquid, 295, 314.
Liquor, 529.
Liquorice, 342.
List, 38, 91, 279, 307.
Listen, 423, 425.
Listless, 188.
Literary, 30, 66, 134, 247, 345, 574.
Literati, 258, 424, 473, 488.
Literature, god of, 121.
Litter, 383, 449.
Litigation, 479.
Little, 10, 101, 143, 145, 148, 148, 178, 254, 259, 307, 315, 371, 379, 404, 457, 592, 599, 614.
Liturgy, 406.
Live, 103, 152, 301, 343, 451.

Lively, 316.
Liver, 426.
Living, 301, 328, 468, 573.
Livelihood, 343, 543.
Lizard, 460.
Load, 216, 236, 428, 508, 576.
Loadstone, 80, 373.
Loafer, 86.
Loafing, 307.
Loam, 103.
Lobe, 341, 452.
Local, 100, 101.
Lock, 538.
Locust, 460, 462, 462.
Lodge, 140, 141, 286, 386, 390, 576.
Lodging, 72, 142, 278.
Loft, 280.
Lofty, 508.
Loins, 429, 433.
Loiter, 78, 223, 516, 521.
Lonely, 133, 143, 337.
Lonesome, 40.
Long, 305, 308, 406, 408, 521, 541, 542.
Long, to, 285, 309.
Long ago, 6.
Long time, 6, 30, 74, 187, 439.
Longan, 271.
Longer, 38.
Long-standing, 141.
Look, to, 76, 261, 323, 361, 362, 365, 365, 366, 475, 476.
Look after, 19, 105, 136, 323, 361, 406.
Look for, 204, 361, 478.

Look out, 86, 365, 367.
Look to, 13, 261.
Look up, 15.
Loom, a, 282.
Loop, 423, 473.
Loose, 242, 245, 581, 603, 613.
Loosely, 379, 581.
Loquacious, 75.
Loquaciously, 85.
Loquat, 266.
Lord, 6.
Lose, 91, 120, 142, 187, 222, 234, 451, 494, 495, 509, 610.
Loss of appetite, 96.
Lost, 43, 68, 102, 474.
Lot, 83, 287, 290, 303, 582, 599.
Lottery, 175.
Lotus, 448, 453, 456.
Loud, 117, 580.
Loud-voiced, 85.
Lounge, 166, 217.
Louse, 459.
Love, 124, 144, 191, 192, 193.
Low, 17, 63, 148, 305, 368.
Low, to, 89.
Lower, 2, 103.
Loyal, 6, 58, 180, 402, 441.
Luck, 83, 175, 255, 295, 429, 521.
Lucky, 30, 77, 262, 281.
Luggage, 102, 264.
Luke-warm, 310.
Lump, 100, 109, 159, 370, 589.
Lunatic, 120, 352.
Lunch, 62, 149, 446, 518.
Lungs, 427.

(755)

Lust, 189, 198, 286.
Lusty, 465.
Lute, 340.
Luxuriant, 145, 445.
Luxuriantly, 359, 443.
Lycium, 268.

M.

M.A., 439.
Machilus, 278.
Machinations, 282.
Machine, 282.
Mad, 334, 352, 354.
Maggot, 459, 461.
Magic, 125, 165.
Magistrate, 75, 137, 292, 330.
Magnanimity, 143, 530.
Magnanimous, 181, 193, 249, 301, 489, 580.
Magnolia, 457.
Magpie, 89, 586.
Maid, 126.
Main, 117, 137.
Maintain, 105, 132, 377.
Maintenance, 572.
Maize, 59, 381, 589.
Majestic, 128, 276.
Major, 68, 75.
Make, 15, 26, 47, 55, 74, 170, 173, 203, 205, 241, 246, 411, 424, 466, 461, 504, 516.
Make up, 42, 137, 204, 246, 310, 470, 470, 493.
Male, 333, 345, 551, 553.
Malicious, 190.
Mallet, 278, 563.
Malva, 447.
Mammary, 131.
Man, 2, 11, 25, 114, 312, 345, 567.
Manacle, 265.
Manage, 6, 49, 75, 105, 121, 214, 236, 240, 248, 339, 370, 391, 511.
Management, 65.
Manager, 219, 391.
Manchu, 313.
Mandarin, 137.
Mane, 577.
Mange, 354.
Manger, 281.
Mangle, 504.
Manifest, 175, 568.
Manikin, 12.
Manipulate, 206.
Mankind, 42.
Manner, 281.
Manners, 376, 475.
Mansion, 138, 440.
Manslaughter, 291.
Manure, 399.
Manuscript, 144.
Many, 116, 149, 163, 356, 479, 521.
Map, 100.
Mare, 575, 577.
Margin, 524.
Mark, 49, 98, 403, 458, 478.
Market, 72, 107, 155, 160, 166, 515, 575.
Marking-line, 112.
Marquis, 20.

Marriage, 15, 128.
Marriageable, 389.
Marrow, 580.
Marry, 39, 43, 70, 88, 110, 129, 129, 130, 133, 222, 226, 241, 355, 402, 414, 526, 527, 528.
Marsh, 113.
Martial, 498.
Marvel, 182.
Mask, 115.
Mason, 61, 104.
Massage, 360.
Mast, 264, 273.
Master, 219, 266.
Mastiff, 334.
Masturbation, 224.
Mat, 276, 387, 393, 394, 453.
Match, 2, 147, 246, 409, 491, 526, 575, 607.
Matches, 319, 598.
Match-maker, 400, 531.
Mate, 61, 70, 117.
Material, 248, 264.
Matter, 114, 125, 183, 209, 391, 483.
Mattock, 534.
Mattress, 394, 446, 455, 472.
Maturity, 117.
May, 24, 74, 177, 260, 484.
Maze, 196.
Me, 80, 199.
Meal, 303, 456, 565, 572.
Mean, 7, 61, 148, 245, 448, 455, 496.
Meaning, 106, 183, 190.
Meanly, 47, 148, 455.

Means, 530, 536.
Measles, 351.
Measure, a, 49, 151, 372, 469, 530.
Measure, to, 2, 230, 292.
Measurement, 2, 145, 151.
Meat, 425, 433, 450, 450, 453, 572, 600.
Mechanic, 61.
Meddle, 268, 298.
Meddler, 105.
Meddlesome, 116.
Medical, 35.
Medicine, 6, 83, 171, 264, 456.
Meditate, 68, 191.
Medium, 5.
Meek, 268, 486, 521.
Meet, 225, 232, 259, 404, 474, 515, 520, 559.
Melancholy, 188.
Melodeon, 340.
Melon, 341.
Melt, 60, 303, 324, 538.
Member, 34, 70.
Memorial, 534.
Memory, 183, 478.
Menace, 281.
Mencius, 133.
Mend, 69, 246, 414, 470.
Menses, 406.
Menstruation, 260.
Mention, 567.
Merchandise, 491.
Merchant, 87.
Mercury, 534.
Mercy, 185.

MER-MON.

Merely, 33.
Merit, 54, 56, 179, 265, 542.
Mesh, 408.
Mess, 276.
Messenger, 158.
Metamorphosis, 488.
Meteor, 254, 518.
Method, 298.
Mice, 422.
Microscope, 539.
Mid-day, 255.
Middle, 5, 63, 179, 347, 434, 545.
Middleman, 5, 20, 40, 104, 130, 171, 200, 401, 582.
Midge, 262.
Midnight, 63.
Midrib, 161.
Midriff, 434.
Mid-wife, 129, 131.
Mild, 82, 257, 268, 310, 508.
Mildew, 557.
Mile, 529.
Military, 288, 507.
Milk, 8, 131, 237.
Mill, 200, 372, 373.
Miller, 397.
Millet, 381, 398, 591.
Millepede, 430.
Millstone, 509.
Mince, 49.
Mind, 135, 179, 190.
Mind, 67, 77, 101, 199, 320.
Minister, 362.
Mint, 24, 151.
Minutely, 404.

Mire, 104, 110, 314, 379.
Mirror, 539.
Miscarriage, 112.
Miscarry, 590.
Mischief, 170, 227, 351, 615.
Mischievous, 411, 599, 611, 612.
Miser, 92.
Misery, 376.
Misfortune, 139, 186, 290.
Mispronounce, 478.
Miss, 537.
Mist, 416, 558.
Mistake, 158, 187, 271, 330, 537.
Misuse, 522.
Mittens, 396.
Mix, 59, 82, 82, 211, 231, 435, 484, 555, 608, 611.
Moan, 92.
Moat, 113, 296, 311, 551.
Mock, 135.
Model, 109.
Moderate, 508.
Modest, 486.
Modesty, 184.
Mohammedan, 37, 117, 560.
Moist, 295, 312, 315.
Molar, 331.
Mole, 350, 593.
Moment, 255.
Momento, 191.
Monarch, 178.
Monastery, 47, 71, 145.
Money, 26, 89, 465, 491, 493, 532, 536, 614.
Mongol, 562.
Mongolia, 452.

MON-MUS.

Monkey, 336, 336.
Monopolize, 214, 240.
Month, 147, 260.
Monthly, 260.
Moon, 260.
Moor, 318, 559.
Moral, 179, 287.
More, 38, 68, 112, 116, 185, 258, 523, 580.
More than, 4, 116, 162, 518.
Moreover, 37, 41.
Morning, 252, 252.
Mortal, 42.
Mortar, 359, 372, 384, 545.
Mortgage, 347.
Mortise, 208, 279, 538.
Mosque, 145.
Mosquito, 298, 460.
Moss, 446.
Most, 1, 3, 259.
Mote, 48.
Moth, 461.
Mother, 106, 128, 129, 130, 291, 292.
Mother-in-law, 128.
Motherless, 84.
Mother's sister, 127.
Motion, 56.
Mottled, 247, 354, 603, 612.
Mould, 225, 281, 384, 557.
Mouldy, 307, 313.
Moult, 224.
Mound, 107, 108.
Mount, 471, 578.
Mountain, 155.
Mountainous, 299.

Mountebank, 308.
Mourn, 133, 188.
Mournful, 41.
Mourning, 2, 47, 90, 133, 260.
Mouth, 71, 432.
Mouthful, 73.
Mouth-piece, 95.
Movable, 301.
Move, 56, 191, 217, 379, 484, 500, 516, 520, 606.
Movement, 56.
Moxa, 327.
Mr., 161, 420, 525.
Mrs., 128.
Much, 30, 116, 258, 350.
Much more, 41.
Mud, 100, 103, 110, 159.
Muddled, 188, 399.
Muddy, 104, 109, 312, 328, 379, 606.
Muffled, 594.
Mugwort, 442.
Mulberry, 271, 608.
Mule, 578.
Muleteer, 576.
Multiply, 116.
Multitudinous, 303.
Mumble, 604.
Murder, 32, 291.
Murderer, 32.
Mushroom, 448, 448, 456.
Music, 280.
Musical, 280.
Musical-box, 563.
Musk, 437, 589.
Musk-deer, 589.

(759)

Musket, 538.
Muslin, 403, 417.
Must, 55, 62, 137, 157, 179, 565.
Mustache, 581, 581, 581.
Mustard, 444.
Musty, 605.
Mutiny, 488.
Mutter, 96, 601.
Mutton, 417, 425.
Mutually, 10, 362.
Muzzle, 95, 396.
My, 80, 199.
Myriad, 452.
Myself, 158, 192, 199.
Mysterious, 122, 125.
Mystery, 520.

N.

Nail, 531.
Naked, 33, 497, 616.
Name, 77, 127, 133, 443, 458.
Nap, 197.
Nape, 564.
Napkin, 331.
Narrow, 383.
Narrow-minded, 335.
Nasal, 594.
Native, 139, 243, 395.
Natural, 322, 437.
Naturally, 322, 425, 437.
Nature, 183.
Naughty, 599.
Navel, 436.
Near, 26, 26, 146, 159, 217, 223, 512.
Nearly, 26, 158, 329, 552, 613.
Necessary; 322.
Neck, 564, 566.
Necromancy, 467.
Nectar, 341.
Nectarine, 272.
Née, 294.
Need, 179, 304, 474, 481, 565.
Needful, 557.
Needle, 531.
Needless, 267.
Needlessly, 142.
Needlework, 409, 531, 593.
Negative, 263, 489.
Neglect, 120, 446.
Negligent, 193, 195; 197, 394, 576.
Negotiate, 382, 406.
Neigh, 89.
Neighbour, 102, 112, 152, 467, 512, 526, 552.
Neither, 8.
Nephew, 127, 127, 343, 345.
Neptune, 596.
Nervous, 192.
Nest, 383.
Net, 59, 357, 408, 417, 417.
Nether-world, 259.
Nettle, 465.
Never, 38, 71, 296.
Nevertheless, 65, 74, 290.
New, 249, 584.
News, 21, 108, 304, 424, 563.
Newspaper, 108.
Next, 2, 253, 285.
Nice, 19.
Nickname, 77, 304, 407.

Niece, 127.
Niggardly, 80, 92, 206.
Night, 117, 140, 256, 591.
Nightmare, 584.
Night-watch, 258.
Nine, 7.
Ninth, 7.
Nippers, 541.
Nipple, 131.
Nit, 464.
No, 4, 297, 322.
Noble, 66, 147.
Nod, 87, 203, 272, 363, 592; 616.
Nodule, 339.
Noise, 80, 424, 563.
Noisy, 84, 94, 545, 545.
Nondescript, 555.
Nonsense, 2, 9, 487.
Noon, 62, 255.
Nor, 8.
North, 60.
Northern, 60.
Nose, 95, 594.
Nostril, 132.
Not, 4, 263, 297, 322, 559.
Notable, 442.
Notch, 89, 173.
Note, 133, 451, 478.
Nothing, 297, 321, 322.
Noticeable, 364.
Notice, 25, 80, 172, 195, 355, 365, 367, 476, 568.
Notify, 485, 516.
Notorious, 563.
Nourish, 572.

Now, 101, 124, 339.
Now-a-days, 12.
Noxious, 292.
Nudge, 607.
Number, 246, 361, 372, 567, 599.

NUMERARY ADJUNCT for:—

Account, 389.
Affair, 107, 280.
Arrow, 265.
Basin, 51.
Bead, 567.
Bedquilt, 166.
Bite, 73.
Boat, 523.
Book, 525.
Box, 73.
Bridge, 520.
Cabbage, 394.
Cannon, 147, 543.
Cash, 108.
Chair, 7.
Chicken, 553.
Cloud, 263.
Coffin, 51.
Coolie, 78.
Cow-house, 364.
Cut, 44.
Dog, 272.
Door, 201.
Dress, 15.
Eye, 553.
Face, 51.
Feather, 348.
Field, 108.
Fish, 152.
Flame, 263.
Flower, 263.
Friend, 18.
Grab, 207.
Granary, 364.
Grave, 201.
Ground, 382.

Hand, 553.
Hat, 564.
Hill, 168.
Horse, 61.
Illness, 107.
Journey, 386.
Land, 108.
Letter, 146.
Life, 272.
Lock, 206.
Look, 364.
Man, 22, 207.
Map, 163.
Marriage, 567.
Medicine, 53, 91.
Odds and evens, 266.
Official, 87.
Paper, 44.
Paragraph, 290.
Pencil, 265.
Person, 22, 78.
Phrase, 74.
Picture, 163.
Plant, 383.
Poem, 574.
Pot, 73.
Push, 219.
Raft, 269.
River, 272.
Room, 545.
Rope, 270.
Scroll, 51.
Sedan, 564.
Sentence, 74.
Set, 51.
Sheep, 553.
Shoe, 553.
Sickness, 107.
Silver, 146.
Slap, 159.
Sleep, 476.
Smell, 427.
Snake, 272.
Steelyard, 273.
Street, 272.

Table, 172.
Tablet, 405.
Thought, 347.
Tree, 270, 271.
Wall, 108.
Wheelbarrow, 269.
Wife, 543.
Word, 567.

Numerous, 467.
Nun, 29, 126, 139, 151, 386.
Nunnery, 151, 449.
Nurse, 19, 171, 197, 484, 572.
Nurture, 427.
Nutmeg, 453.
Nux, 50, 586.

O.

O, 93.
Oak, 283.
Oar, 280, 282.
Oath, 81, 481.
Oats, 589.
Obdurate, 370.
Obey, 177, 425, 466, 523, 565.
Objection, 374.
Oblige, 298.
Obliging, 99.
Oblique, 25.
Oblong, 201.
Obscene, 8, 285, 308, 381, 437, 584.
Obscure, 39.
Obstacle, 372.
Obstinate, 28, 98, 105, 214, 266, 273, 512.
Obstinately, 368.
Obstruct, 85, 108, 109, 208, 233, 273, 312, 391, 547.

Obstruction, 543.
Obtain, 5, 177.
Obverse, 539.
Obvious, 569.
Occasion, 286.
Occasionally, 232.
Occupation, 9, 283, 301, 543.
Ocean, 302.
O'clock, 539.
Occupy, 15.
Ochre, 400.
Odd, 91, 371, 555, 556.
Odds and ends, 371, 556.
Odour, 294.
Off, 43, 555.
Off and on, 474.
Offend, 28, 182, 334, 416.
Offensive, 573.
Offer, 19, 121, 207, 337; 496, 517, 523.
Off-hand, 195, 394.
Office, 14, 44, 151; 201, 201, 425.
Officer, 75, 194, 427.
Official, 18, 77, 86, 118, 137, 138, 194, 466.
Offspring, 186, 384.
Oh, 95, 548.
Oil, 272, 300, 307, 434.
Oil-cake, 390.
Oil-cup, 359.
Oily, 435.
Old, 74, 118, 243, 383, 420, 439, 468, 523, 550, 609.
Old man, 13, 36, 330, 419, 420, 421.
Older, 117.

Old-fashioned, 74, 541.
Olive, 282, 558.
Omen, 32, 175.
On, 4, 101, 552.
Once, 1, 408.
One 1, 76, 78, 594.
One another, 287.
One by one, 22, 217.
Onion, 447, 451, 454.
Only, 17, 33, 73, 92, 189, 337.
Onward, 176.
Open, 121, 153, 203, 243, 244, 253, 333, 335, 365, 504, 516, 543, 544, 551, 612.
Opening, 10.
Openly, 253.
Ophiopogon, 39.
Opinion, 431, 475.
Opium, 104, 324, 586.
Opportune, 42, 255.
Opportunely, 158, 184, 582.
Opportunity, 259, 282.
Oppose, 16, 18, 69, 150, 187, 333, 477, 520, 547, 564.
Opposite, 147.
Oppress, 113, 370, 373, 445, 457; 503, 527, 575, 600.
Oppression, 217.
Or, 199.
Orange, 268, 282, 283.
Orchid, 444, 457.
Order, 13, 27, 79, 82, 137, 208, 286, 374, 388, 393, 480, 535, 565, 578, 595.
Orderly, 10, 166, 475.
Ordinal, 388.

(763)

Ordinary, 147, 162, 164, 310, 389.
Ore, 374.
Organ, 340.
Organize, 246.
Origin, 167, 189, 262, 270, 312, 345.
Original, 67.
Originally, 67.
Originator, 58.
Orion, 68.
Ornament, 531, 571.
Ornamented, 174, 316, 443.
Orphan, 84, 133.
Orphanage, 427.
Osmanthus, 271.
Ostentatiously, 325.
Other, 46, 615.
Other people, 13.
Otter, 336, 337.
Ought, 136, 196, 281, 347, 474, 481.
Ounce, 35.
Out, 43.
Outcome, 151.
Outer, 116.
Outlet, 43.
Outline, 175.
Out of sorts, 285.
Out-of-the-way, 25.
Outrunner, 80, 553.
Outside, 116, 468, 560, 567.
Outsider, 116.
Outward, 551.
Our, 199.
Oval, 99.
Oven, 539.

Over, 51, 518.
Over all, 37.
Overawe, 601.
Overbearing, 173, 465, 605.
Overcoat, 122.
Overcome, 56.
Overflow, 300, 313, 313.
Overland, 252.
Overreach, 360, 459.
Oversee, 360, 365, 391, 566.
Overseer, 391.
Overshadow, 601.
Overshoe, 396.
Overstep, 31, 499, 518, 518, 578.
Overstrain, 28.
Overtake, 497, 499, 500, 513.
Overturn, 23.
Owe, 149, 285, 480, 491.
Owl, 587.
Own, 35, 139, 158, 262, 437, 475, 587.
Owner, 6.
Oxen, 332.

P.

Pace, 288.
Pacify, 173.
Pack, 69, 406, 575.
Packet, 145, 469.
Pad, 571, 613.
Paddle, 282.
Page, 63.
Pagoda, 109.
Pail, 274.
Painful, 350.
Paint, 209, 301, 315, 347, 567.

Painter, 315, 347.
Pair, 76, 147, 554.
Palace, 140, 291, 547.
Pale, 307.
Pall, 416.
Palliate, 571.
Palm, 179, 219, 266, 277.
Palpitation, 503.
Palsy, 354, 598.
Pander, 548.
Pangolin, 345.
Panorama, 302.
Pant, 81, 88, 185, 497, 579, 594.
Pants, 148, 364, 468, 472.
Paper, 300, 374, 391, 397, 398, 401, 447.
Parade, 422, 520.
Parade-ground, 107.
Paradise, 119.
Paragraph, 290.
Paralysis, 352, 354.
Paralyzed, 12.
Parapet, 104, 264, 284.
Paraphernalia, 51, 105.
Parasite, 141.
Parcel, 59, 146.
Parched, 302.
Pardon, 81, 245, 416, 497.
Pare, 23, 49, 499.
Parent, 117, 119, 128, 262, 420, 425, 450, 475.
Parer, 498.
Parish, 592.
Parricide, 170.
Parrot, 587, 588.

Part, 26, 35, 44, 63, 221, 555.
Partial, 63.
Partiality, 25.
Particle, 458.
Particular, 481.
Partition, 45, 221, 552.
Partner, 9, 117.
Partnership, 117.
Parturition, 358.
Party, 517, 567.
Pass, a, 5, 88, 156, 551.
Pass, to, 153, 167, 250, 254, 288, 406, 495, 518, 537.
Passage, 228, 295, 499.
Passenger, 137.
Passer-by, 518.
Passive, sign of, 26, 223, 597.
Passport, 323.
Past, 68, 175, 259, 417.
Paste, 397, 398, 399, 493.
Pasteboard, 115, 471.
Pasture, 447.
Pat, 212.
Patch, 159, 294, 468, 470, 561.
Patience, 60, 79, 180, 421, 426.
Patient, 140, 304, 421.
Patrol, 157, 267.
Patronize, 323, 547, 568.
Pattern, 49, 271, 281, 281, 392.
Pause, 488.
Pave, 110, 369.
Pavement, 107.
Paw, 219.
Pawn, 347.
Pawn-shop, 37, 214, 347, 458.
Pay, 24, 376.

PAY-PEW.

Pay, to, 13, 43, 136, 204, 241, 259, 283, 304, 354, 355, 402, 495, 517, 518, 544.
Pay back, 30.
Pea, 397, 448, 489.
Peace, 82, 118, 141, 164, 300.
Peacefully, 135.
Peach, 272.
Peacock, 132.
Peak, 156, 615.
Peanut, 443.
Pear, 273.
Pearl, 144, 338, 339.
Peck, 62, 87.
Pedant, 196.
Peddler, 297.
Peel, 49, 50, 357, 357, 571.
Peep-show, 302.
Peer, 613.
Peevish, 90.
Peg, 531.
Pekin, 11.
Pellet, 132, 298.
Pellicle, 605.
Pen, 44, 284, 389.
Pencil, 389, 419.
Pencil-rest, 166.
Pendant, 78, 111, 331.
Penetrating, 385.
Penis, 153, 153, 426, 551.
Peony, 332, 442.
People, 11, 71, 127, 168, 294, 356, 363.
Pepper, 277.
Peppermint, 455.
Perceive, 195, 475.

Perceptible, 475.
Perception, 187.
Perfect, 35, 44, 136, 194.
Perfectly, 62.
Perforate, 615.
Perform, 122, 503.
Perhaps, 139, 182, 185, 199.
Peril, 65.
Perilla, 456.
Perilous, 552.
Period, 22, 295, 392.
Permit, 41.
Persecute, 169.
Persevering, 408.
Persimmon, 267, 295, 571.
Person, 2, 11, 18, 64, 138, 264, 506, 507.
Perspicuous, 356.
Perspiration, 295.
Perspire, 296, 306.
Pertain, 154.
Pertinent, 248.
Pervade, 516, 528.
Perverse, 7, 157, 172, 184, 281, 370, 512, 566.
Pestilence, 349.
Pestle, 265.
Pet, 131, 186, 191.
Petal, 341.
Petard, 533.
Petition, 79, 160, 376.
Pettifogger, 328, 387, 403, 479.
Pettifogging, 351.
Pettish, 188, 375.
Petty, 544.
Pewter, 536, 563.

(766)

Pheasant, 554.
Phlegm, 352.
Phœnix, 586.
Photograph, 29, 323.
Phrase, 74.
Physiognomist, 363.
Pick, 50, 75, 120, 211, 213, 216, 216, 224, 228, 231, 283, 306, 523, 534, 595.
Pickle, 295, 299, 312, 357, 450, 527, 528.
Pick-pocket, 3, 408.
Picnic, 501.
Picture, 174, 347.
Picul, 368.
Piebald, 443.
Piece, 15, 108, 282, 331, 348, 371, 392, 541.
Pierce, 48, 535.
Pig, 336, 463.
Pig-pen, 99.
Pile, a, 107, 230.
Pile, to, 106, 107, 230, 381, 529, 551.
Piles, 350, 353.
Piles, row of, 99.
Pilfer, 231.
Pill, 6.
Pillar, 268, 277.
Pillow, 265.
Pimple, 299, 353.
Pin, 172.
Pinafore, 408.
Pinch, 221, 223, 225, 235, 391.
Pine, 264, 267.
Pink, 397.

Pip, 132.
Pipe, 387, 389, 469, 507, 538.
Pipe-light, 234.
Pirate, 302, 494.
Pistil, 581.
Pistol, 202, 538.
Pit, 102, 296, 383.
Pitch, 394, 403.
Pitch and toss, 211, 539.
Pitiable, 74.
Pity, 186, 188, 195, 195, 195, 351.
Placard, 160.
Place, a, 76, 100, 101, 103, 106, 249, 297, 458.
Place, to, 103, 135, 201, 215, 228, 237, 242.
Placenta, 428.
Plague, 353.
Pliant, 508.
Plain, 66, 114, 164, 283, 402.
Plait, 120, 220, 409, 473.
Plan, a, 61, 190, 249, 298, 389, 475, 477.
Plan, to, 100, 469, 485.
Plane, 46, 222, 307.
Plane-tree, 278.
Plank, 249, 262, 266, 267, 441.
Plant, 63, 223, 272, 290, 443, 447.
Plantain, 507.
Plaster, 104, 246, 398, 434.
Plat, 107.
Plate, a, 360, 372.
Plate, to, 59, 437.
Platfrom, 280, 438.
Platter, 372.

(767)

PLA-POT.

Play, 3, 79, 199, 202, 205, 421.
Playing cards, 331.
Plead, 478.
Pleasant, 82, 129, 181.
Pleasantness, 575.
Please, 484.
Pleased, 89, 187, 281, 365.
Pleasing, 500.
Pleasure, 21, 281, 301.
Pledge, 204, 347.
Plentiful, 43, 546.
Pliable, 446.
Plinth, 373.
Plot, 163, 427, 485.
Plough, 20, 333, 422, 422.
Plough-share, 539.
Pluck, 205, 231.
Plum, 264, 274.
Plumb, 78.
Plume, 417.
Plump, 299.
Plunder, 54, 221, 229, 230.
Plural, sign of, 10, 23, 117.
Ply, 427.
Poached, 448.
Pocket, 59, 227, 471, 472.
Pod, 378, 476.
Poem, 481.
Poetry, 481.
Point, 149, 214, 374, 592.
Poison, 292, 353, 465.
Poisonous, 353.
Poke, 226, 228, 516, 615.
Pole, 232, 276, 387, 393.
Policeman, 4, 114, 158, 267, 339.
Polish, 373, 494.

Polite, 122.
Politeness, 138.
Pomegranate, 279.
Pommel, 598, 604.
Pond, 296.
Ponder, 81, 270.
Pontoon, 302.
Pool, 138, 299, 300.
Poor, 7, 98, 142, 172, 300, 353, 373, 384, 455, 491, 575.
Poorhouse, 133.
Pop, 224, 328, 609.
Poppy, 415.
Popular, 294.
Population, 200.
Porcelain, 373.
Porcupine, 336.
Pore, 132.
Pork, 425, 450.
Porridge, 418.
Port, 72, 87.
Portcullis, 545.
Porter, 542.
Portion, 599.
Portrait, 363.
Position, 38, 58, 288, 506.
Possess, 260.
Possession, 202.
Possessive, sign of, 356.
Post, 159, 264, 268, 280, 415.
Post-horse, 578.
Posterity, 470.
Post-house, 109, 578.
Posthumous, 523.
Post-office, 161.
Pot, 115, 358, 358, 360, 415, 537.

(768)

Potato, 442, 446.
Pot-luck, 162.
Potsherd, 308, 331.
Pottery, 384.
Pound, 119, 248, 438.
Pour, 4, 24, 40, 248, 315, 318.
Pout, 594, 615.
Poverty, 97, 306, 491.
Powder, 262, 397, 589.
Power, 53, 57, 285.
Practice, 378.
Practise, 236, 419, 439, 466.
Praise, 94, 121, 163, 212, 380, 417, 439, 481, 488, 565.
Prawn, 585.
Pray, 296, 377.
Preach, 138, 486.
Precarious, 197.
Precaution, 186.
Precedence, 166.
Precedent, 20.
Precept, 198, 221, 271.
Precinct, 100.
Precious, 144, 490.
Precipice, 111, 156.
Precipitous, 156, 549.
Precise, 539.
Pre-eminence, 57.
Preface, 166.
Prefect, 166, 367.
Prefecture, 166, 169.
Preference, 191.
Pregnant, 132, 197, 429.
Prejudiced, 25.
Preparation, 41.
Prepare, 490, 511, 547, 595, 616.

Prescription, 6, 91, 249.
Presence, 502.
Present, a, 29, 46, 145, 189, 245, 295, 376, 497.
Present, the, 12, 22, 47, 50, 73, 101, 255, 339, 361, 364.
Present, to, 219, 513.
Present, to be, 50.
Preserve, 132.
Preside, 6, 75.
Press, 28, 58, 113, 120, 169, 278, 499, 513.
Press, a, 278.
Pressing, 21, 182.
Presume, 146, 185, 245.
Presumptuous, 31, 514.
Pretence, 16, 24.
Pretend, 20, 24, 398, 479, 614.
Pretext, 204.
Pretty, 18.
Prevalent, 43.
Prevent, 264.
Price, 22, 29, 160, 268, 518.
Prick, 149, 535.
Prickly-heat, 247, 349.
Priest, 29, 43, 82, 90, 114, 139, 149, 330, 376.
Priesthood, 139.
Prime, 114.
Prime minister, 140.
Princely man, 80.
Principal, 155, 287, 542.
Principle, 407, 579.
Print, 48, 65, 281.
Prison, 97, 332, 336, 339, 359.
Prisoner, 97, 334, 542.

PRI-PRO.

Private, 98, 146, 257, 377.
Privately, 550.
Privates, 3.
Privily; 40.
Privy, 67, 176, 445.
Prize, 233, 496.
Probably, 63, 116.
Proclaim, 172.
Proclamation, 80, 374.
Procrastinate, 223, 237, 522, 523.
Procrastinator, 408.
Procure, 210.
Prodigal, 234, 303.
Prodigally, 317.
Produce, 43, 343.
Prodnction, 343.
Profane, 472.
Profit, 45, 536.
Profligate, 186.
Profound, 297, 305, 308.
Progenitor, 509.
Prognostication, 32.
Progress, 517.
Prohibit, 287, 560.
Project, 384.
Prolapsus, 426.
Prolong, 78, 169.
Promiscuously, 304.
Promise, 196, 479, 485, 493.
Promote, 53.
Prompt, 195, 241, 567, 579.
Promulgate, 569.
Pronunciation, 563.
Proof, 195.
Prop, 231, 232, 232, 235, 241, 265, 269, 331, 610.

Propagate, 27, 517.
Proper, 287, 382, 447, 466.
Properly, 67, 81, 125, 136, 147, 387.
Property, 136, 183, 343.
Proprietor, 400.
Prospect, 33.
Prosper, 253, 439, 445.
Prosperity, 252.
Prosperous, 77, 359, 551.
Prostitute, 125, 128, 129, 454.
Protect, 18, 20, 487, 522.
Protector, 122, 389, 391.
Protracted, 408, 515.
Protruding, 595, 612.
Proud, 28, 313, 578, 580.
Proud-flesh, 428, 431.
Provender, 248.
Proverb, 21, 483.
PROVERBS on :—
　Ability, 385.
　Acquaintances, 487.
　Adaptation, 395.
　Adoption, 518.
　Adultery, 127, 133.
　Adversity, 555.
　Advice, 420.
　Affairs, 198.
　Affinity, 410.
　Age, 293, 420, 575.
　Anger, 180.
　Animals, 441.
　Atonement, 497.
　Beggary, 70.
　Bereavement, 91.
　Blame, 172.
　Boasting, 481.
　Bribery, 467.
　Business, 151, 189, 328, 466.
　Caterpillars, 463.

(770)

PROVERBS

Caution, 207, 597.
Certainty, 381.
Chance, 601.
Changeableness, 69.
Character, 148.
Charity, 51.
Clothes, 36, 470.
Coldness, 40.
Conduct, 614.
Confession, 536.
Control, 441.
Conversation, 483.
Correction, 196.
Courtesy, 38.
Criticism, 80, 530.
Crookedness, 174.
Crops, 252.
Crows, 586.
Daring, 382.
Daughters, 495.
Death, 14, 233, 289, 289, 480.
Debt, 30, 216, 225.
Deception, 286.
Deeds, 9.
Dew, 558.
Difficulties, 104.
Diligence, 51, 56, 57, 203, 251.
Discontent, 500.
Disgrace, 528.
Dishonesty, 494.
Disposition, 241.
Distribution, 59.
Doing, 72.
Doubt, 187.
Drink, 526.
Eagles, 156.
Early rising, 251.
Ease, 544.
Economy, 42, 303.
Endurance, 90.
Enmity, 12.
Envy, 131.
Error, 158.
Etiquette, 211, 376.

Evil, 237, 293, 376.
Evil speaking, 52.
Exhortation, 58, 58.
Expecting, 485.
Experience, 37, 124, 580.
Faithfulness, 180.
Fame, 71.
Farming, 56, 512.
Fate, 83, 83, 83, 210, 345, 410, 452.
Fear, 182.
Feasts, 157.
Feelings, 401.
Filial piety, 54, 86, 133.
Finding, 73.
Fingers, 214.
Fire, 335.
Fishes, 254, 584.
Fitness, 614.
Folly, 276.
Foot-binding, 101, 148.
Foresight, 344.
Forethought, 164, 194, 547.
Forgiveness, 286.
Forgiving, 141, 573.
Fortune, 71.
Friends, 260.
Friendship, 17, 57, 70, 521.
Futurity, 176.
Gain, 7, 125, 253.
Gambling, 497.
Girls, 123.
Giving, 221.
Gods, 75, 151, 439, 556.
Gold, 530.
Good, 293, 376.
Good and evil, 223.
Good men, 469.
Goods, 496.
Gossip, 177, 254, 515.
Graves, 111.
Greed, 230.
Grief, 192, 192.
Grieving, 364.
Guests, 74.

(771)

PROVERBS.

Habit, 322, 419.
Happiness, 257, 376.
Hardship, 68.
Harmony, 82.
Harshness, 336.
Health, 162, 342.
Hearing, 424.
Heaven, 119, 490, 559.
Heaven and earth, 118.
Hell, 119.
Help, 77, 229.
Honour, 173, 379.
Hospitality, 119, 513.
Households, 139.
Hunger, 384.
Hunting, 240.
Husbands, 130.
Hypocrisy, 342.
Idle words, 382.
Idolatry, 164, 320.
Implicating, 85, 515.
Increase, 381.
Indulgence, 126.
Infants, 329.
Ingratitude, 69.
Injury, 139.
Insight, 347.
Insincerity, 361.
Intercourse, 251.
Justice, 164.
Kindred, 475.
Knowledge, 512.
Labour, 53, 157.
Leadership, 274.
Leading, 171.
Learning, 433, 477, 480, 574.
Lending, 111.
Lewdness, 482.
Liberality, 148.
Life, 33, 74, 160, 188, 194.
Litigation, 474, 509.
Longevity, 147.
Loyalty, 180.
Luck, 83, 521.

Lust, 51.
Magistrates, 106, 294.
Magnanimity, 143.
Manner, 82.
Marriage, 129, 130.
Matrimony, 17, 22, 52.
Meanness, 148, 148.
Meddling, 203, 544, 547.
Medicine, 27, 250.
Meeting, 515.
Middlemen, 130.
Mischief makers, 615.
Misfortune, 522.
Misleading, 392.
Mistakes, 537.
Money, 439, 465, 491, 531, 586.
Mortality, 115.
Moths, 234.
Murder, 30.
Nature, 155.
Necessity, 149.
Neighbours, 152, 475.
Niggardliness, 68.
Obedience, 565.
Obstacles, 552.
Occupation, 114.
Offspring, 343.
Old age, 62.
Omniscience, 366.
Opinions, 367.
Origins, 260.
Orphans, 363.
Parents, 119, 305.
Parricide, 170.
Parsimony, 111.
Parting, 513.
Peacemaking, 245.
Plainness, 159.
Pleasures, 91.
Plenty, 324.
Poison, 139.
Policemen, 158.
Possessions, 475.
Poverty, 152, 155, 261, 384, 491.

(772)

PROVERBS.

Prayer, 296.
Precedence, 33.
Presents, 33, 513.
Priests, 127.
Presumption, 232.
Procrastination, 305.
Prodigals, 303.
Profit, 46.
Progress, 303.
Prominence, 209.
Promises, 479.
Propriety, 46, 221.
Prosperity, 439.
Providence, 119.
Prudence, 414, 457, 596.
Purposes, 368.
Quarreling, 552.
Rashness, 65.
Reaping, 148.
Reciprocity, 212.
Recklessness, 610.
Recompense, 124.
Rectitude, 610.
Reform, 439.
Regicide, 170.
Repentance, 37, 186.
Reproof, 181, 492.
Responsibility, 293.
Retaliation, 13.
Retribution, 22, 108, 135, 218, 517, 525.
Rewards, 91, 108.
Riches, 173, 491.
Righteousness, 418, 491.
Rights, 137.
Ruin, 439.
Rulers, 137.
Saving life, 244.
Scandal, 191.
Scheming, 485.
Schooling, 488.
Self-restraint, 74, 547.
Servants, 439.
Shame, 219.
Shepherding, 79.

Sï-ch'uan, 584.
Sickness, 125, 179, 182.
Sincerity, 363.
Slander, 149, 209, 403, 488.
Slighting, 490.
Sons, 116, 126, 305.
Sorrow, 194.
Sowing, 148, 380.
Speaking, 73.
Spirit, 183.
Stealing, 309.
Study, 56, 488.
Stupidity, 34, 373.
Suffering, 223.
Summer, 257.
Sunshine, 60.
Superstitions, 119, 156.
Support, 456.
Suspicion, 348, 348.
Talkativeness, 145.
Teaching, 97.
Teasing, 614.
Thief, 119, 127.
Thieves, 326, 458, 482, 497.
Tigers, 128.
Time, 33, 112, 145.
Trade, 456.
Transgression, 519.
Trials, 324.
Trouble, 91, 234.
Truth, 307.
Uncertainty, 12, 155.
Understanding, 187.
Unfairness, 52.
Union, 78.
Uprightness, 246, 287, 361.
Vegetarianism, 245.
Vexation, 191.
Villains, 473.
Villainy, 18, 24.
Virtue, 495.
Visiting, 566.
Visitors, 346.
Vows, 479.

PRO-QUA.

Want, 324.
Wealth, 80, 142, 152, 155, 187, 261, 521.
Weather, 7, 77, 162, 334, 461, 501, 557.
Wickedness, 189.
Will, 183, 371.
Wine, 238, 442.
Wisdom, 276.
Wives, 126, 130, 495.
Women, 442.
Words, 208, 576.
Work, 54.
World, 188.
Wounds, 336.
Yielding, 152, 514.
Youth, 54.

Provide 511, 547, 572.
Providence, 119.
Province, 362.
Provincial, 526.
Provision, 26, 72, 267, 405, 435, 570.
Provoke, 190, 209.
Public, 36, 36, 137, 244, 363.
Publish, 88, 138, 226, 565.
Pudding, 327.
Puddle, 138.
Puddly, 327.
Puff, 311.
Puffy, 432.
Pug-dog, 335, 460.
Pull, 205, 209, 210, 211.
Pulp, 341.
Pulpit, 438.
Pulse, 428.
Pumelo, 270, 283.
Pump, 507.
Punch and Judy, 26.
Punctuate, 592.

Pungent, 328, 511.
Punish, 51, 298, 416, 492, 511.
Punishment, 45, 416, 416.
Punt, 45.
Pup, 34, 156, 335.
Pupa, 461.
Pupil, 134, 171, 177, 339, 366, 452.
Puppet, 26, 30, 262, 426.
Purchase, 493.
Pure, 40, 62, 276, 307, 403, 500, 612.
Purgative, 318.
Purify, 315, 316.
Purple, 404, 445.
Purpose, 76, 146, 180, 190, 295, 333, 467, 603.
Purposely, 190.
Purse, 408, 448; 472.
Pursue, 500.
Pus, 435.
Push, 212, 218, 219, 222, 237, 239, 241, 265, 541, 592, 613, 615.
Pushing, 58.
Put, 16, 68, 136, 242.
Put away, 68.
Put into, 32, 136, 238.
Put off, 144, 220, 237, 549.
Put out, 17, 221.
Put up, 3, 203.
Pyrus, 277.

Q.

Quail, 587.
Quality, 18, 84, 183, 442.

(774)

Quarrel, 72, 205, 235, 388, 476, 529, 545, 552.
Quarrelsome, 505.
Quarry, 368.
Quash, 172.
Queen, 338.
Question, 88, 360.
Quern, 373.
Queue, 236, 413, 424, 562.
Quick, 57, 149, 195, 210, 240, 311, 602, 611.
Quicken, 28.
Quickly, 31, 148, 181, 394, 408, 516, 602.
Quick-tempered, 148, 319.
Quiet, 104, 141, 187, 307, 308, 428, 554, 559.
Quietly, 187.
Quilt, 466, 535.
Quince, 341.
Quite, 30, 143.
Quiver, 390, 568.
Quote, 171.

R.

Rabbit, 34.
Rack, 173, 233.
Radical, 250, 292.
Raft, 388.
Rafter, 249, 273, 278, 283.
Rag, 331.
Ragged, 328, 369, 472, 473, 606.
Raid, 422.
Railing, 284.
Rain, 119, 311, 451, 556.
Rainbow, 461.
Rain-cloak, 453, 468.
Rainy, 305.
Raise, 106, 171, 212, 220, 299, 306, 426, 439, 498, 549, 569.
Rake, 329, 390, 602, 613.
Ram, 36, 370, 391, 417.
Ramble, 514, 515, 520.
Ramrod, 272.
Rancid, 92.
Range, 156.
Rank, 54, 84, 221, 466, 533.
Rank (adj.), 418, 433.
Ranks, 15, 466, 551.
Rap, 73, 228, 243, 246.
Rape, 127, 450.
Rapid, 181, 318, 523.
Rapier, 539.
Rare, 46, 415, 515.
Rarity; 160.
Rascal, 276.
Rash, 247, 349, 349, 353.
Rat, 382, 422, 593.
Rather, 141.
Rationalist, 519.
Rations; 399, 571.
Rattan, 561.
Rattle, 229, 274, 563.
Rave, 252.
Raw, 343.
Ray, 293.
Razor, 44.
Reach, 69, 227, 238, 311.
Read, 133, 181, 361, 488.
Ready, 1, 26, 124, 152, 221, 339, 490, 616.

(775)

REA-REM.

Ready-made, 198, 339.
Real, 101, 322, 481, 535.
Reality, 143.
Really, 20, 67, 101, 143, 266, 290, 370, 559.
Ream, 44.
Reap, 52, 69.
Rear, 233, 272, 360.
Reason, 49, 189, 201, 242, 270, 312, 329, 339, 519.
Reasonable, 170.
Rebel, a, 293.
Rebel, to, 69, 71, 187, 206.
Rebuild, 529.
Recall, 208, 232.
Recede, 304, 514.
Receipt, 69, 334, 391.
Receive, 19, 69, 69, 121, 177, 205, 209, 222, 298, 384, 452, 512, 566, 597.
Reception-hall, 106.
Recite, 87, 482.
Reckless, 180, 316, 454, 530, 599.
Recklessly, 38, 485.
Reckon, 13, 391, 477, 485, 600.
Recognise, 482, 487.
Recommend, 439, 455, 616.
Recompense, 108, 519.
Reconcile, 58, 82.
Record, 37, 508.
Recorder, 37.
Recover, 350.
Recreate, 517.
Red, 263, 327, 400, 430, 557.
Redeem, 497.
Redouble, 529.

Redress, 17.
Reduce, 42, 205, 304, 362, 451.
Reed, 393, 445, 456.
Reel, 405.
Refine, 28, 62.
Reflect, 180, 514, 591.
Reflector, 429.
Reform, 224, 287, 302, 523, 560.
Refuse, 308, 312.
Refuse, to, 65, 511, 598.
Regard, 362, 391, 474, 476, 496, 568.
Regardless, 509.
Regimentals, 458.
Regicide, 170.
Region, 162.
Register, 38, 330, 487.
Regret, 186, 188.
Regularly, 59.
Regulate, 23.
Rein, 55, 242, 411, 422.
Reiterate, 472, 529.
Reject, 4, 50, 405.
Rejoicing, 492.
Relapse, 420.
Relationship, 23.
Relative, 139, 199, 356, 475, 579.
Relax, 543.
Relent, 195.
Reliable, 125, 137, 381, 503.
Relieve, 494.
Religion, 139, 243, 542.
Relinquish, 66.
Rely, 13, 15, 496, 608.
Remain, 136, 356.
Remedy, 244, 456, 476.

(776)

Remember, 20, 181, 191, 242, 478.
Remind, 225.
Remiss, 459.
Remit, 34.
Remonstrate, 484.
Remorse, 186.
Remount, 224.
Remove, 50, 217, 227, 227, 232, 379, 500, 523.
Render, 13.
Renounce, 275, 428.
Rent, 18, 144, 378, 607.
Repair, 23, 165, 208, 216, 470.
Repay, 110, 495, 523.
Repeat, 428, 472.
Repeatedly, 3, 38.
Repent, 37, 70, 186, 197, 241, 510, 513.
Replace, 224, 283.
Reply, 178, 389.
Report, 80, 108, 122, 569.
Reporter, 75, 122.
Repress, 90, 113.
Reprimand, 27, 41, 90, 207, 345, 567, 592.
Reproof, 231.
Reprove, 214, 488, 492, 603.
Repulsive, 555.
Reputation, 77, 78, 261, 331, 424, 436, 543, 560, 569.
Request, 296.
Require, 474.
Rescue, 215, 229, 244.
Resemble, 29, 175, 362.
Resentful, 183.

Reservoir, 108.
Resetter, 384.
Residence, 166, 388.
Resist, 206, 212.
Re-smoke, 420.
Resolutely, 218.
Resolve, 6, 211, 214.
Resource, 16, 53, 121, 502.
Respect, 211, 245.
Respectful, 245, 447.
Respectfully, 185, 211.
Respond, 56, 196, 485.
Response, 72, 483.
Responsible, 492.
Responsibility, 14, 20, 236.
Responsive, 558, 577.
Rest, 17, 82, 143, 186, 193, 276, 286, 326, 422, 451, 544, 581, 608.
Restive, 578.
Restless, 530.
Restore, 30, 178, 523.
Restrain, 180, 216, 250, 264, 401.
Restraint, 374.
Restrict, 426.
Restriction, 47.
Restaurant, 167.
Result, 151, 404.
Resurrection, 178.
Resuscitate, 583.
Retail, 213, 556.
Retain, 56, 95, 218, 492, 533, 575.
Retainer, 29.
Retard, 506.
Retch, 94.

PRI-PRO.

Private, 98, 146, 257, 377.
Privately, 550.
Privates, 3.
Privily; 40.
Privy, 67, 176, 445.
Prize, 233, 496.
Probably, 63, 116.
Proclaim, 172.
Proclamation, 80, 374.
Procrastinate, 223, 237, 522, 523.
Procrastinator, 408.
Procure, 210.
Prodigal, 234, 303.
Prodigally, 317.
Produce, 43, 343.
Production, 343.
Profane, 472.
Profit, 45, 536.
Profligate, 186.
Profound, 297, 305, 308.
Progenitor, 509.
Prognostication, 32.
Progress, 517.
Prohibit, 287, 560.
Project, 384.
Prolapsus, 426.
Prolong, 78, 169.
Promiscuously, 304.
Promise, 196, 479, 485, 493.
Promote, 53.
Prompt, 195, 241, 567, 579.
Promulgate, 569.
Pronunciation, 563.
Proof, 195.
Prop, 231, 232, 232, 235, 241, 265, 269, 331, 610.

Propagate, 27, 517.
Proper, 287, 382, 447, 466.
Properly, 67, 81, 125, 136, 147, 387.
Property, 136, 183, 343.
Proprietor, 400.
Prospect, 33.
Prosper, 253, 439, 445.
Prosperity, 252.
Prosperous, 77, 359, 551.
Prostitute, 125, 128, 129, 454.
Protect, 18, 20, 487, 522.
Protector, 122, 389, 391.
Protracted, 408, 515.
Protruding, 595, 612.
Proud, 28, 313, 578, 580.
Proud-flesh, 428, 431.
Provender, 248.
Proverb, 21, 483.
PROVERBS on :—
   Ability, 385.
   Acquaintances, 487.
   Adaptation, 395.
   Adoption, 518.
   Adultery, 127, 133.
   Adversity, 555.
   Advice, 420.
   Affairs, 198.
   Affinity, 410.
   Age, 293, 420, 575.
   Anger, 180.
   Animals, 441.
   Atonement, 497.
   Beggary, 70.
   Bereavement, 91.
   Blame, 172.
   Boasting, 481.
   Bribery, 467.
   Business, 151, 189, 328, 466.
   Caterpillars, 463.

(770)

Rocket, 40.
Rockwork, 155.
Rod, 45, 139, 266, 272, 387, 538.
Roe, 132, 460.
Rogue, 602.
Roguery, 170.
Roll, a, 220.
Roll, to, 172, 204, 220, 229, 235, 235, 288, 313, 407, 409, 471, 593, 608.
Roller, 235, 372, 509.
Roof, 359.
Roof of mouth, 595.
Room, 98, 101, 200, 595.
Roost, 99.
Root, a, 270, 280.
Root, to, 137, 463.
Root out, 52.
Rope, 393, 402, 413.
Rosa, 285.
Rose, 338, 340.
Rosin, 267, 574.
Rot, 605.
Rotation, 22, 509.
Rotten, 52, 113, 263, 328.
Rottlera, 273.
Rouge, 226, 429.
Rough, 103, 316, 396, 397, 440.
Roughly, 293, 447.
Round, 59, 81, 98, 99, 99, 100, 260.
Round-about, 522.
Rouse, 123.
Rout, 121.
Roving, 303.
Row, a, 79, 196, 221, 282, 545.
Row, to, 45, 222, 282.

Rowlock, 280.
Royal, 286, 356.
Rub, 87, 209, 224, 226, 238, 370, 373, 485, 501, 611.
Rubbing, a, 226.
Rubbish, 312.
Rubble, 9.
Rude, 120, 172, 265, 398, 449, 530, 546, 575.
Rudely, 183.
Ruffian, 177.
Rug, 293, 294, 472.
Rugged, 103.
Ruin, 23, 65, 91, 112, 114, 244, 328.
Rule, a, 47, 49, 272, 298, 367, 379, 475.
Rule, to, 6.
Ruler, 137, 140, 161, 405.
Rumbling, 510.
Ruminate, 37, 97.
Rumour, 101, 423, 424, 486, 569.
Run, 53, 121, 304, 424, 501, 517, 519.
Runner, 175, 339, 608.
Running, 301, 447.
Rupee, 302.
Rush, 111, 310, 419, 447, 453.
Rust, 535, 537.
Rustic, 188.
Rustling, 384.

S.

Sable, 490.
Sack, 73, 469.
Sackcloth, 159.

PRI-PRO.

Private, 98, 146, 257, 377.
Privately, 550.
Privates, 3.
Privily; 40.
Privy, 67, 176, 445.
Prize, 233, 496.
Probably, 63, 116.
Proclaim, 172.
Proclamation, 80, 374.
Procrastinate, 223, 237, 522, 523.
Procrastinator, 408.
Procure, 210.
Prodigal, 234, 303.
Prodigally, 317.
Produce, 43, 343.
Production, 343.
Profane, 472.
Profit, 45, 536.
Profligate, 186.
Profound, 297, 305, 308.
Progenitor, 509.
Prognostication, 32.
Progress, 517.
Prohibit, 287, 560.
Project, 384.
Prolapsus, 426.
Prolong, 78, 169.
Promiscuously, 304.
Promise, 196, 479, 485, 493.
Promote, 53.
Prompt, 195, 241, 567, 579.
Promulgate, 569.
Pronunciation, 563.
Proof, 195.
Prop, 231, 232, 232, 235, 241, 265, 269, 331, 610.

Propagate, 27, 517.
Proper, 287, 382, 447, 466.
Properly, 67, 81, 125, 136, 147, 387.
Property, 136, 183, 343.
Proprietor, 400.
Prospect, 33.
Prosper, 253, 439, 445.
Prosperity, 252.
Prosperous, 77, 359, 551.
Prostitute, 125, 128, 129, 454.
Protect, 18, 20, 487, 522.
Protector, 122, 389, 391.
Protracted, 408, 515.
Protruding, 595, 612.
Proud, 28, 313, 578, 580.
Proud-flesh, 428, 431.
Provender, 248.
Proverb, 21, 483.

PROVERBS on :—
 Ability, 385.
 Acquaintances, 487.
 Adaptation, 395.
 Adoption, 518.
 Adultery, 127, 133.
 Adversity, 555.
 Advice, 420.
 Affairs, 198.
 Affinity, 410.
 Age, 293, 420, 575.
 Anger, 180.
 Animals, 441.
 Atonement, 497.
 Beggary, 70.
 Bereavement, 91.
 Blame, 172.
 Boasting, 481.
 Bribery, 467.
 Business, 151, 189, 323, 466.
 Caterpillars, 463.

(770)

Scorpion, 464.
Scour, 306.
Scourge, 561.
Scout, 86.
Scowl, 558.
Scramble, 329.
Scrap, 331.
Scrape, 47, 49, 51, 206, 241, 385, 613.
Scraper, 47.
Scratch, 204, 230.
Screen, 109, 113, 154, 228, 239, 323, 394, 488, 522.
Screw, 463.
Scribe, 144, 259.
Scrofula, 8, 352.
Scroll, 91, 147, 154.
Scrutinize, 227.
Scum, 299, 529.
Scurf, 153.
Sea, 302.
Seal, 64, 100, 145, 200, 386, 392.
Seam, 274, 411.
Search, 142, 227, 283.
Sea-sickness, 257.
Season, 13, 133, 255, 575, 608.
Seasonable, 255.
Seasoned, 8, 182.
Seasoning, 72.
Seat, 18, 103, 473.
Seaweed, 162, 450.
Secluded, 559.
Second, 10, 50, 177.
Secondary, 18.
Second-hand, 446.
Secret, 5, 141, 282, 377, 500, 550.

Secretary, 161, 163, 263, 380.
Secretion, 153.
Secretly, 40, 81, 187, 257, 550, 591.
Sect, 542.
Section, 154.
Secure, 161, 347, 535.
Securely, 16, 125, 332, 559.
Security, 204.
Sediment, 399.
Seditious, 61.
Seductive, 442.
See, 261, 361, 362, 366, 367, 474, 475.
Seed, 132, 380, 397, 456.
Seedling, 378, 445.
Seed-pod, 393.
Seek, 147, 204, 402, 478.
Seem, 175.
Seize, 15, 75, 204, 206, 210, 225, 240, 454.
Seldom, 149, 348, 415.
Select, 71, 75, 216, 224, 236, 523.
Self, 158, 437, 475.
Self-esteem, 493.
Selfish, 148.
Selfishly, 377.
Self-reliant, 185.
Self-respect, 245, 338, 530.
Sell, 355, 495, 564.
Seller, 495.
Semen, 398.
Semi-circular, 172.
Semi-conscious, 267.
Send, 27, 141, 158, 242, 355, 418, 521.

Senior, 17, 542.
Sense, 106, 198.
Sentence, 74, 480, 488.
Separate, 44, 46, 52, 544, 545, 552.
Separately, 75.
Separation, 46.
Sequence, 388.
Serge, 272.
Serious, 182, 363.
Serpent, 463.
Serried, 71.
Servant, 2, 19, 20, 129, 161, 161, 164, 542, 560, 598.
Serve, 9, 22, 121, 261, 406.
Serviceable, 406.
Sesame, 443, 574, 590.
Set, a, 51, 117, 396.
Set, to, 137, 156, 234, 238, 246, 272, 451, 548, 565.
Set down, 66, 242, 451.
Set fire to, 326.
Set time, 262.
Set up, 136, 211, 214, 228, 385.
Set upon, 298.
Settle, 9, 14, 124, 125, 135, 137, 152, 153, 154, 161, 163, 239, 249, 289, 304, 347, 385, 404, 493, 545.
Seven, 2.
Seventh, 2.
Several, 3, 165.
Severe, 139, 276, 511, 530, 552.
Sew, 202, 411, 424, 471, 531.
Sexual, 127.
Shabby, 557.

Shade, 322, 416, 522, 550.
Shadow, 175.
Shady, 550.
Shaft, 302, 394.
Shake, 56, 207, 219, 229, 238, 239, 386, 557, 598.
Shallow, 104, 307.
Shame, 168, 184, 189, 418, 615.
Shameless, 66, 168, 184, 436.
Shape, 470.
Share, 45, 164, 427.
Shark, 585.
Sharp, 46, 149, 181, 534.
Sharpen, 49, 373.
Sharp-tongued, 95.
Sharp-witted, 425.
Shave, 23, 49, 49, 240, 533.
Shavings, 46, 262, 443.
Shear, 51.
Shears, 120.
Sheath, 115, 561.
Shed, a, 67, 161.
Shed, to, 112, 303, 305.
Sheep, 417.
Sheep-fold, 98.
Sheet, 172, 357, 469, 472.
Shell, 115, 345.
Shield, 331, 522.
Shift, 339.
Shifty, 510.
Shin, 430, 579.
Shine, 323.
Shirk, 25, 506, 511.
Shirt, 296, 468, 471, 472.
Shiver, 42, 568, 578.
Shoe, 154, 219, 561.

Shoe-horn, 231, 311.
Shoot, 146, 355, 609.
Shop, 100, 102, 167, 200, 440, 440, 467.
Shore, 155.
Short, 21, 149, 167, 184, 307, 329, 367, 368, 368, 508.
Shortcomings 459.
Short-cut, 223.
Shorten, 411.
Short-sighted, 475, 475.
Short-tempered, 295.
Short-winded, 294, 497.
Should, 481.
Shoulder, 427, 431, 579, 580.
Shont, 80, 479.
Shovel, 217, 220, 499, 538.
Show, 200, 214, 256, 302, 472, 553, 568, 612.
Shower, 316, 549, 556, 557.
Shred, 405, 443.
Shrewd, 19.
Shrill, 149.
Shrimp, 397.
Shrine, 169, 585, 596.
Shrink, 411.
Shrivel, 410.
Shuffle, 501.
Shun, 180.
Shut, 3, 109, 223, 230, 432, 543, 547.
Shutter, 542.
Shuttle, 274.
Shuttlecock, 294.
Sick, 349, 527.
Sicken, 435, 529.

Sickle, 540.
Sickness, 257, 349.
Side, 26, 63, 110, 113, 250, 364, 423, 524, 560, 609.
Side by side, 5.
Side-room, 67, 168.
Side-shoot, 263.
Sideways, 26.
Sidle, 12.
Sieve, 393, 417.
Sift, 393.
Sigh, 94, 185.
Sign, 201, 213, 227, 347, 374, 395, 458, 478, 479.
Signal, 458, 478.
Sign-board, 209, 330, 458.
Silenced, 188.
Silent, 141, 220, 424.
Silk, 141, 271, 308, 405, 406, 407, 408, 417.
Silkworm, 465.
Silly, 125, 302.
Silver, 534.
Simple, 44, 263, 283, 309.
Simpleton, 188.
Sin, 135, 334, 416.
Since, 251, 437.
Sincere, 74, 283, 481, 497.
Sincerely, 481.
Sincerity, 21, 595.
Sinew, 388.
Sinewy, 598.
Sing, 74, 87, 90.
Singe, 321, 325.
Single, 91, 337.
Singly, 91.

Sink, 111, 112, 297, 550.
Sip, 222.
Sir, 32, 33, 70, 71, 75, 118, 147, 161, 545, 576.
Sister, 126, 126, 126, 127, 128, 579.
Sit, 102.
Site, 57, 105.
Situation, 106.
Six, 36.
Sixth, 36.
Size, 117, 372.
Skeleton, 269.
Sketch, 100, 144, 225, 347.
Skilful, 91, 157, 202, 580.
Skill, 290, 326.
Skim, 234, 315.
Skin, 50, 51, 266, 356, 434.
Skinny, 426.
Skirt, 470.
Skull, 115, 568.
Sky, 119, 382.
Sky-light, 383.
Sky-rocket, 40.
Slacken, 543, 581.
Slander, 23, 146, 148, 291, 488.
Slanting, 248, 604.
Slap, 159, 212, 231.
Slat, 396.
Slatternly, 473.
Slaughter, 140, 154, 291.
Slave, 5, 29, 123, 129, 465, 582.
Slavers, 307.
Slay, 291.
Sleep, 143, 363, 364, 365, 366, 437, 476.

Sleeve, 218, 275, 469.
Sleight of hand, 165.
Slender, 91, 270.
Slice, 51, 109, 140, 331.
Slight, 29, 180, 314, 491.
Slightly, 124, 178.
Slip, 120, 163, 310, 396, 543.
Slip-knot, 122.
Slippery, 310, 311.
Slope, 104.
Sloping, 604.
Sloppy, 312, 606.
Slops, 380, 611.
Slovenly, 524.
Slow, 125, 172, 307, 357, 365, 522, 532, 566, 604, 612, 614.
Slow-coach, 180, 408.
Slowly, 193, 409.
Sluggard, 180.
Sluggish, 193.
Sly, 187.
Smack, 93, 440.
Small, 67, 101, 141, 148, 174, 254, 383, 404, 414, 455, 471.
Smallest, 293.
Small-pox, 89, 351, 443.
Smart, 19, 57, 58, 338.
Smart, to, 316, 325, 600.
Smartweed, 453.
Smash, 291, 369.
Smear, 209, 226.
Smell, 424, 436, 437, 574.
Smelt, 27, 538.
Smile, 79, 387, 604, 605.
Smirk, 605.
Smoke, 80, 90, 321, 324, 325, 327.

Smoky, 321.
Smooth, 33, 153, 210, 321, 325.
Smoothly, 519.
Smother, 288, 608.
Smuggle, 25, 313, 377.
Snail, 463.
Snake, 460, 462, 499, 586.
Snap, 244.
Snare, 122.
Snatch, 122.
Sneer, 246, 387.
Sneeze, 96, 96.
Snib, 612.
Snore, 185, 594, 610.
Snout, 95, 463.
Snow, 556, 570.
Snow-flake, 331.
So, 124, 201, 322.
Soak, 227, 298, 299, 304, 314.
Soap, 429.
Soap-bean, 356.
Soap-berry, 280.
Society, 62, 259.
Sock, 562.
Socket, 364, 435.
Soda, 588.
Sodomy, 127, 345.
Soft, 82, 131, 268, 294, 299, 408, 436, 446, 508, 606.
Softly, 508.
Soft-tongued, 342.
Soil, 100, 103, 159.
Sold out, 307.
Solder, 532, 536.
Soldier, 36, 55, 274, 330, 399.
Sole, 166, 266.

Solicit, 57, 60.
Solid, 535.
Solitary, 133.
Solitude, 559.
Solution, 385.
Sombre, 592.
Some, 10, 260.
Somersault, 248, 272, 420, 502.
Sometimes, 199, 545.
Son, 2, 34, 80, 132, 135, 330, 340, 490, 525, 576.
Song, 258, 286.
Son-in-law, 63, 130, 131, 576.
Soon, 512.
Soot, 321.
Sophora, 279.
Sorcerer, 158, 387.
Sorceress, 161.
Sorcery, 525.
Sore, 328, 352.
Sorrow, 188, 191, 194.
Sorrowful, 191, 194.
Sorrowfully, 84.
Sort, 138, 230, 389, 441, 568.
Soul, 583, 583.
Sound, 326.
Sound, a, 369, 424, 563, 563.
Sound, to, 93, 222.
Soup, 309.
Sour, 412, 527, 527, 528, 573, 615.
Source, 312.
South, 64.
Southern, 64.
Southern-wood, 452.
Sovereign, 80.

Sow, a, 292, 336.
Sow, to, 234, 234, 380, 592.
Sow-thistle, 454.
Soy, 301, 528.
Space, 47, 101, 271, 288, 458, 466, 600.
Spacious, 143, 407, 546.
Span, 64.
Spare, 132.
Sparing, 189, 362.
Spark, 319, 324.
Sparrow, 587.
Sparse, 379.
Speak, 73, 79, 94, 196, 482, 595.
Speak for, 81, 93, 106.
Spear, 69, 367.
Specialist, 378.
Speciality, 146.
Specially, 146, 333.
Species, 380.
Speck, 592.
Spectacles, 383.
Speech, 483.
Speechless, 384.
Spell, 44, 565.
Spend, 20, 68, 240, 241, 245, 344, 443, 518.
Spermatorrhoea, 523.
Spice, 575.
Spider, 462, 609.
Spike, 531.
Spill, 234, 319.
Spin, 208, 401.
Spinach, 449.
Spindle, 534.
Spinning-wheel, 507.

Spiral, 463, 463, 464.
Spirit, 32, 183, 375, 398, 558, 583, 583, 584.
Spiritless, 134.
Spit, 78, 83.
Spite, 184.
Spittle, 295, 307.
Spittoon, 352.
Splash, 231, 303, 318, 557.
Spleen, 432, 432, 435.
Splendid, 367.
Splendidly, 476.
Splendour, 279.
Splice, 222, 411.
Splinter, 395, 396.
Split, 49, 50, 52, 513.
Spoil, 113, 150, 170, 194, 195, 263.
Sponge, 217, 351, 413, 433, 608.
Spongy, 299.
Spool, 396, 411.
Spoon, 418, 438, 586.
Spot, 247, 353, 592.
Spotted, 247, 443.
Spout, 95, 355, 389.
Sprain, 226, 237, 288, 391, 543.
Sprawl, 202, 500.
Spread, 27, 234, 238, 239, 241, 479, 534.
Spring, 253, 300, 343, 428, 444, 498.
Sprinkle, 301, 315, 316, 600.
Sprite, 13.
Sprout, 387, 444, 609.
Spry, 301, 505, 517.

Spurt, 96, 310, 314, 609.
Spy, 25, 86, 157, 222, 364, 384.
Squabble, 2, 87, 95, 440, 545.
Squander, 422.
Square, 97, 112, 151, 249.
Squash, 341, 354.
Squat, 431, 501.
Squeak, 96.
Squeeze; 120, 207, 237, 273, 600.
Squid, 584.
Squint, 248, 366.
Squire, 87.
Squirt, 93.
Squirrel, 490.
Stab, 48.
Stable, 98, 98, 161.
Stablish, 98.
Staff, 263, 269.
Stage, 109, 200, 280, 386.
Stagger, 25, 616.
Stagnant, 289.
Stain, 298, 315, 350.
Stair, 112, 274.
Stake, 280, 386.
Stalactite, 155.
Stale, 550.
Stalk, 387.
Stall, 107, 239, 269.
Stallion, 577.
Stamen, 581.
Stamina, 32.
Stammer, 77, 120, 486.
Stammerer, 120.
Stamp, 64, 100, 200, 265, 395, 504, 504, 505.
Stamped, 400.

Stand, 70, 103, 385.
Stand aside, 218, 543, 545.
Standing, 57.
Standard, 251, 281, 414, 487.
Staple, 95, 166, 533.
Star, 141, 254, 512.
Starch, 302, 314.
Stare, 510, 572.
Start, 4, 56, 238, 354, 498, 544, 549.
Startle, 96.
State, 99, 108, 345, 376, 480, 511.
Statement, 160, 376.
Statesman; 437.
Station, 18, 103, 136.
Stay, 346, 422, 506.
Steadfast, 184, 252.
Steadfastly, 16.
Steadily, 59, 332.
Steady, 212, 347, 381.
Steal, 25, 70, 359.
Stealthily, 231.
Steam, 252, 294, 321, 322, 327.
Steamer, 342, 396, 441.
Steed, 103.
Steel, 535, 540.
Steelyard, 199, 378.
Steep, 313, 549.
Steer, 577.
Steersman, 274.
Stem, 163, 273, 379, 387.
Stench, 294, 437, 616.
Step, 59, 274, 288, 402, 430, 502, 503, 503.
Step-father, 330, 357.

Step-mother, 176, 256, 413.
Stepping-stone, 112.
Step-son, 357, 413.
Sterculia, 275.
Stern, 152.
Stew, 324, 328.
Stick, a, 272, 276, 320, 536.
Stick, to, 158, 200, 223, 233, 394, 397, 493, 600, 609.
Sticky, 591.
Stiff, 28, 50, 184, 371.
Still, 12, 141, 187, 336, 499, 523.
Sting, 325, 327, 465, 535.
Stingy, 92, 193, 601.
Stink, 434, 436, 528, 612.
Stipend, 169, 434.
Stitch, 237.
Stir, 44, 56, 190, 216, 234, 240, 312, 343, 422, 517, 545.
Stirrup, 540.
Stob, 280.
Stock, 172, 280, 609.
Stocking, 562.
Stocks, 217.
Stolen, 591.
Stomach, 72, 102, 356, 426, 429.
Stone, 112, 270, 272, 351, 368, 372, 397, 579.
Stoop, 18, 105, 152.
Stop, 14, 16, 26, 70, 83, 108, 109, 145, 228, 239, 242, 249, 287, 312, 368, 416.
Stopper, 615.
Store, 8; 154, 455, 470.
Storehouse, 383.

Story, 154, 280.
Stout, 112, 245, 611.
Stove, 321, 328, 541.
Straight, 147, 287, 361, 386, 389.
Straighten, 17, 153, 401.
Straightforward, 203, 295.
Straightway, 394.
Strain, 317, 318, 612.
Strainer, 313.
Strait, 407.
Strange, 121, 125, 160, 182, 346, 480.
Stranger, 116, 138.
Strangle, 55, 405.
Strap, 413, 473, 594.
Straw, 320, 447, 455.
Strawberry, 608.
Straw-cutter, 540.
Stream, 156, 311, 427.
Streamer, 163, 251, 251.
Street, 467, 467, 519.
Street-gate, 268.
Strength, 53, 54, 57, 245, 388, 530.
Strengthen, 106.
Stretch, 17, 121, 172, 172, 239, 278.
Striæ, 433.
Strict, 97.
Stride, 502.
Strife, 163, 198, 375.
Strike, 5, 39, 47, 56, 202, 212, 219, 238, 246.
Strike, a, 47, 614.
String, 5, 78, 162, 218, 220, 382, 403, 413, 598, 612.

Stringy, 598.
Strip, 51, 217, 272, 357, 405, 602, 604.
Strive, 122, 329.
Stroke, 347.
Strong, 24, 50, 58, 98, 114, 143, 168, 173, 385, 426, 529, 553, 607.
Strongly, 332, 412, 537, 540.
Strut, 238.
Stub, 391.
Stubble, 280.
Stubborn, 184, 566.
Stuck, 64.
Student, 386, 492.
Study, 112, 134, 425, 488, 595.
Stuff, 226, 235, 611, 613.
Stump, 265, 280.
Stumpy, 265, 615.
Stunted, 103.
Stupefy, 188.
Stupid, 110, 162, 187, 188, 189, 196, 209, 264, 266, 304, 341, 353, 385, 388, 436, 522, 532, 566, 599.
Stupidity, 187.
Stupidly, 309, 398.
Sturgeon, 585.
Stutter, 486.
Style, 278, 287, 344, 392, 458, 553.
Stylish, 560.
Subdue, 202, 548.
Sub-hire, 242, 314.
Subject, 294, 387, 427.
Sub-let, 510.

Sublime, 62.
Submissive, 185.
Submit, 260, 548.
Subside, 103, 148.
Substance, 174, 433.
Substitute, 219, 259.
Subtract, 549.
Succeed, 93, 205, 413.
Success, 190.
Successful, 11, 134, 519, 565.
Successive, 288.
Succour, 215, 244.
Suck, 83, 83, 159, 605.
Suckle, 86.
Sudden, 319.
Suddenly, 7, 53, 55, 181, 257, 335, 549.
Suet, 300.
Suffer, 70, 90, 223, 517.
Suffering, 277, 326, 445, 555.
Sufficient, 117.
Suffocate, 93.
Sugar, 295, 397, 399.
Sugar-cane, 342, 453.
Suggest, 225.
Suicide, 147, 291, 360.
Suit, 76, 122, 124, 208, 380, 552.
Suitable, 76, 184.
Sullen, 256.
Sulphate of iron, 356, 374.
Sulphur, 370.
Sum, 246, 412.
Summer, 115, 257.
Sun, 118, 251, 551.
Sunburnt, 258.
Sunflower, 450.

(789)

SUN-TAI.

Sunken, 109, 608, 610.
Sunny, 118, 551.
Sun-shade, 27, 416.
Superbly, 38.
Superficial, 307, 314.
Superintend, 360.
Superior, 3, 580.
Superlative, 293.
Supplementary, 548.
Supplicate, 195.
Supply, 493.
Support, 19, 206, 239, 241, 423, 426, 496.
Supporter, 26.
Suppose, 24, 124, 444, 479, 487.
Suppress, 52, 173.
Suppurate, 318.
Supreme, 3, 118.
Sure, 179, 372.
Surety, 6, 111, 212, 370, 431, 435, 568.
Surface, 560.
Surgical, 116.
Surname, 127.
Surpass, 359, 499.
Surplus, 51, 572.
Surprise, 21, 415.
Surround, 99, 113, 412.
Surrounding, 81.
Suspect, 336, 348.
Suspend, 78, 197, 410.
Suspense, 197, 220, 507.
Suspicious, 116, 130, 348.
Sustain, 232, 402.
Swagger, 221, 229.
Swallow, a, 327.

Swallow, to, 81, 85.
Swap, 157, 222.
Sway, 231, 543.
Sweat, 295, 296.
Sweep, 203, 221, 239.
Sweep-net, 239.
Sweet, 342, 342, 462, 605.
Sweetmeats, 570.
Swell, 355, 364, 426, 431, 432, 593.
Swelling, 59, 353.
Swift, 408.
Swiftly, 182, 570.
Swim, 302.
Swindle, 210.
Swindler, 138.
Swing, 150, 561, 562, 592.
Swirl, 314.
Switch, 240, 390.
Swivel-hook, 341.
Swollen, 302, 432.
Sword, 44, 52.
Symbol, 288.
Sympathize, 186.
Syphon, 596.
Syringe, 538.

T.

Tabby, 351.
Table, 42, 271, 275, 284.
Tablet, 331, 371.
Tack, 172, 414.
Tactics, 562.
Tael, 35.
Tail, 152.
Tailor, 469.

(790)

TAK-TEN.

Take, to, 129, 162, 203, 206, 209, 210, 210, 225, 261, 369.
Take back, 71, 81.
Take down, 2.
Take in, 4, 347.
Take off, 224.
Take out, 71, 228, 603.
Take over, 564.
Take up, 15, 223, 534.
Take with, 227.
Tale, 309.
Talented, 564.
Talk, 86, 95, 238, 244, 480, 484, 486, 515, 520, 569.
Talkative, 86.
Talker, 95.
Tall, 247, 424, 506, 506, 580.
Tallow, 300.
Tally, 77, 208, 395, 396.
Talon, 329.
Tame, 47, 140.
Tan, 370.
Tank, 109, 296, 414.
Tanner, 357.
Taoist, 582.
Tap, 246.
Tape, 162, 410.
Tapering, 149.
Tardy, 408.
Tare, 205, 235, 407.
Tares, 380.
Target, 561.
Tarn, 302.
Taro, 442.
Tartar, 428, 595.
Task, 56.

Tassel, 111, 251, 407, 414, 582.
Taste, 93.
Tasteless, 306, 608.
Tattoo, 48.
Tax, 66, 400, 483, 509.
Tea, 446, 452.
Teach, 214, 243, 422, 477, 482.
Teacher, 33, 118, 161.
Team, 576.
Tea-money, 148.
Tea-pot, 115.
Tear, 205, 227, 235.
Tears, 295, 305, 558.
Tease, 190, 614.
Tea-shop, 508.
Teat, 131.
Tedious, 308.
Telegraph, 556.
Telescope, 539.
Tell, 27, 50, 78, 82, 208, 391, 404, 424.
Tell-tale, 122.
Temper, 179, 183, 188, 294, 295, 429, 432, 466.
Temper, to, 24, 306.
Temperament, 376.
Temple, 169, 388, 449, 476, 567, 582.
Temporarily, 416.
Temporary, 257.
Ten, 61, 277.
Ten feet, 2.
Tench, 585.
Tend, 332, 362.
Tender, 131.
Tenant, 18, 138.

(791)

TEN-THU.

Tenon, 279.
Tent, 161, 200, 276.
Tenth, 44, 61, 536.
Termagant, 316.
Terra-cotta, 104, 531.
Terrible, 128.
Test, 49, 104, 151, 373, 421, 481.
Testicle, 65, 432.
Testify, 479.
Testimony, 19.
Thank, 56, 128, 191, 205, 236, 237, 240, 316, 486, 492, 520, 555.
Thankful, 191.
Thank-offering, 192.
Thanksgiving, 528.
That, 201, 262, 484, 525.
Thatch, 445, 447.
Theatre, 107, 200.
Theme, 361, 567.
Then, 21, 150, 414, 525.
There, 525.
There is, 260.
Thereabout, 3.
Therefore, 13, 201, 243.
Thereupon, 322.
Thermometer, 142.
These, 514.
They, 13.
Thick, 66, 309, 398, 529, 591.
Thicken, 380.
Thickening, 444.
Thief, 8, 25, 86, 127, 173, 231, 390, 494.
Thief-catcher, 114.
Thieve, 385.

Thigh, 429, 434.
Thin, 174, 307, 379, 423, 455, 570, 603.
Thing, 267, 332, 474.
Think, 181, 183, 191, 416, 485, 591.
Thinly, 91, 348.
Third, 3.
Thirst, 309.
Thirsty, 309.
This, 12, 262, 287, 484, 514, 590.
Thorn, 48, 275, 447.
Thorough, 382.
Thoroughfare, 516.
Thoroughly, 178, 326, 571.
Those, 525.
Thought, 15, 181, 193.
Thoughtlessly, 91.
Thousand, 62.
Thrash, 166, 203, 216, 236.
Thread, 382, 409, 443.
Three, 3.
Threshing-floor 107.
Threshold, 545.
Throat, 85, 88, 92, 96, 430.
Throne, 105, 144, 168.
Through, 178, 369, 382, 451, 516, 518.
Throughout, 406.
Throw, 4, 150, 203, 211, 212, 237, 344, 531, 611, 613.
Thrum, 173.
Thrush, 347.
Thrust, 17, 597.
Thud, 105.

(792)

Thumb, 214.
Thumb-ring, 565.
Thump, 225, 226.
Thunder, 203, 556, 557, 558.
Thus, 287.
Tibet, 456.
Tibetan, 120, 347.
Tick, 590, 592.
Ticket, 281, 375, 570.
Tickle, 230, 239, 615.
Tidy, 112, 160, 234.
Tie, 205, 218, 218, 230, 402, 599.
Tiff, 72.
Tiger, 457.
Tight, 353, 407.
Tighten, 232.
Tightly, 16, 141.
Tile, 342, 342.
Till, 48.
Till, a, 284.
Till, to, 18.
Tilt, 504.
Timber, 248, 262, 267, 272.
Time, 22, 33, 37, 76, 119, 133, 254, 255, 346, 519, 520, 522, 550, 560.
Timid, 172, 196.
Timorous, 182.
Tin, 540.
Tinder, 319, 324.
Tingle, 232, 557.
Tinsel, 531, 533.
Tip, 149.
Tiptoe, 111.
Tire, 7, 23, 28, 31, 67, 128, 349.
Tiresome, 611.

Title-deed, 121.
Titter, 94.
Tittle-tattle, 254.
To, 3, 18, 48, 76, 147, 175, 347, 404, 438, 518.
Toad, 354, 464, 593.
Toadstool, 448.
Toady, 159, 298, 497, 608.
Tobacco, 295, 450, 452.
Toe, 211, 214.
Together, 1, 36, 76, 78, 502, 502, 515, 594.
Toil, 54, 55, 56.
Toilsome, 56, 492.
Tolerate, 140.
Tomb, 105, 110, 110, 112.
To-morrow, 253.
Tomtom, 563.
Tone, 424.
Tongs, 533, 534.
Tongue, 440.
Tongue-tied, 403.
Tonic, 310, 470.
Too, 118, 525.
Tool, 14, 25, 466.
Tooth, 332, 595.
Toothache, 332.
Toothpick, 395.
Top, 3, 119, 149, 560, 564, 566, 568, 580, 600.
Torch, 206, 319.
Torn, 263.
Tortoise, 596.
Tortoise-shell, 338, 340.
Torture, 215, 216, 273, 275.
Toss, 207.

TOT-TRI.

Total, 36, 405, 412.
Totter, 94.
Touch, 169, 230, 240.
Touch-hole, 543.
Touchstone, 421.
Tough, 357, 408, 421.
Toward, 76, 261, 261.
Towel, 160.
Tower, 280.
Tow-rope, 333, 411.
Town, 467.
Trace, 175, 350, 451, 452, 503, 503, 563.
Traces, 411.
Track, 65.
Tract, 162, 247.
Tractable, 178.
Trade, 11, 87, 166, 190, 308, 326, 456, 466, 492, 511.
Trader, 297.
Trail, 78, 213, 501.
Train, 333.
Traitor, 135.
Traitorous, 124.
Tramp, 297.
Trance, 267.
Tranquillize, 233.
Tranquilly, 30, 164.
Transact, 360, 518.
Transaction, 77.
Transcribe, 205, 486.
Transfer, 234, 379, 477, 484, 486, 564.
Transform, 60, 191, 488.
Transformation 517.
Transgress, 9, 334.

Transgression, 519.
Tranship, 234, 576.
Translate, 412.
Transmigration, 37.
Transmit, 34, 310, 477.
Transparent, 516.
Transport, 227, 227, 521.
Transverse, 281.
Trap, 336, 396, 477, 550, 599, 601.
Trappings, 562.
Travel, 102, 303, 313, 498, 520.
Traveller, 250.
Travelling, 138.
Tray, 204, 212, 279, 358, 360.
Treacherous, 481, 553.
Tread, 501, 503, 503, 504, 504, 505.
Treasury, 167.
Treasurer, 160, 455.
Treat, 245, 362.
Treatise, 487.
Treaty, 401.
Tree, 262, 283.
Trefoil, 444.
Trellis, 269.
Tremble, 207, 568, 604.
Tremblingly, 34.
Trespass, 334, 416.
Trestle, 575.
Triangle, 476.
Tribute, 491.
Trick, 14, 151, 518.
Trident, 69.
Trifling, 178.
Trim, 50, 234, 323, 410, 468, 524.

(794)

Trimming, 524.
Trip, 403.
Tripe, 372.
Tripod, 3, 430, 593.
Triturate, 8, 370.
Triumphantly, 42.
Trivial, 299.
Troop, 241.
Troops, 15, 36.
Trotter, 504.
Trouble, 9, 56, 86, 102, 103, 128, 236, 237, 300, 303, 317, 323, 478, 487, 492, 555, 569.
Troubled, 316.
Troublesome, 306, 309, 411, 492, 611.
Trough, 281.
Troupe, 610.
Trousseau, 122, 398.
Trousers, 148, 468, 472.
Trowel, 46, 219.
Truant, 514.
Truckful, 213.
Truculently, 69, 190.
True, 74, 143, 363, 381, 537.
Truly, 322, 363.
Trump, 164, 225.
Trumpet, 75, 90, 458.
Trumpeter, 202.
Trunk, 272, 279, 392, 506.
Trust, 14, 18, 21, 217, 559.
Trustworthy, 185, 503.
Truth, 119, 143.
Try, 49, 88, 144, 170, 222, 324, 400, 478, 481.
Tub, 211, 358.
Tube, 389, 391.
Tuberose, 13.
Tuck, 204, 403, 405, 409, 473, 600.
Tumble, 111, 272, 284, 608.
Tumbler, 267.
Tumour, 59, 349.
Tune, 484.
Tunnel, 216.
Turban, 122, 160.
Turbid, 272, 309.
Turbulent, 186, 411.
Turmeric, 454.
Turn, 23, 37, 69, 206, 210, 218, 222, 230, 420, 422, 507, 509, 510, 536, 539, 594.
Turner, 507.
Turnip, 453, 457.
Turns, by, 251.
Turquoise, 267.
Turtle, 100, 585.
Turtle-dove, 586.
Tutor, 494.
Twang, 540.
Twig, 274.
Twilight, 238, 249, 252.
Twill, 248.
Twinkle, 363.
Twins, 554.
Twist, 206, 218, 225, 229, 405, 407, 464, 602.
Twitter, 89.
Two, 9, 35.
Typha, 453.
Tyrannize, 457, 509.
Tyrant, 490, 558.

U.

Ugly, 190, 528, 548.
Umbrella, 27, 232, 556.
Unacquainted, 11, 282.
Unalterable, 258, 379.
Unavailing, 69, 560.
Unbearable, 428.
Unbearably, 107.
Unbending, 60, 218.
Unbroken, 99.
Unceremoniously, 225, 228.
Uncertain, 178, 179, 184, 199, 263, 604.
Unchangeable, 258.
Uncle, 17, 70, 330, 438.
Uncommon, 42, 559.
Uncommonly, 431.
Unconventional, 382.
Undecided, 179, 310, 505.
Under, 2, 167.
Undergraduate, 167.
Undergrowth, 446.
Underhand, 178.
Underling, 167, 175, 553.
Undermanned, 415.
Undermine, 458.
Underneath, 167.
Understand, 9, 196, 253, 259, 356, 366, 475.
Understanding, 187.
Undertake, 59, 200, 236, 564.
Undertaking, 151.
Undesirable, 177, 375, 474.
Undeveloped, 381.
Undo, 245.
Undress, 431.
Uneasy, 242.
Unendurable, 70.
Uneven, 164, 443.
Unevenly, 109, 601.
Unexpectedly, 310, 459.
Unfathomable, 310.
Unfinished, 103.
Unfold, 547.
Unfortunate, 520.
Unfriendly, 437, 602.
Ungainly, 388.
Ungovernable, 316.
Ungrateful, 256, 490, 511.
Unicorn, 588.
Uniform, 458.
Unimportant, 158.
Unintelligible, 599.
Uninterrupted, 550.
Unite, 219, 515.
United, 63.
Unjust, 304, 497.
Unjustly, 25.
Unlike, 78.
Unload, 66, 498.
Unloose, 242, 431, 476, 544.
Unlucky, 43, 375.
Unoccupied, 544.
Unpleasant, 500.
Unproductive, 186.
Unprofitable, 186.
Unreasonable, 76, 281, 339.
Unreliable, 137.
Unrip, 213, 407.
Unscattered, 99.

Unscrupulous, 44.
Unskillful, 575.
Unspeakable, 174.
Unstable, 179, 418, 474.
Unstamped, 355.
Unsuccessful, 505.
Unsullied, 253.
Unsympathetic, 184.
Untie, 476.
Untidy, 197, 245, 399.
Until, 438.
Untimely, 119, 289.
Untrustworthy, 418, 559.
Unwavering, 105.
Unwell, 1, 58, 163, 285.
Unwilling, 568.
Unwind, 71.
Unworthy, 181, 347,
Up, 498.
Uphold, 206, 232, 235, 407.
Upper, 561, 562, 566.
Uppish, 576.
Upright, 273, 287, 301, 361, 385, 386, 406.
Uproarious, 563.
Uproariously, 510.
Upset, 420.
Upside down, 568.
Upward, 15.
Urge, 21, 28.
Urgent, 182, 319, 408.
Urgently, 45.
Urinary disease, 351.
Urinate, 151.
Urine, 151, 616.
Us, 199.

Usages, 47.
Use, 20, 56, 107, 146, 170, 240, 344, 458.
Used up, 136.
Useful, 248.
Useless, 163, 168, 391.
Uselessness, 305.
Usual, 162.
Usually, 402.
Usurp, 15, 21, 309, 393, 558.
Utensil, 21, 25, 36, 95, 357.
Utmost, 276.

V.

Vacancy, 415.
Wave, to, 2
Wax, 465.
Way, 192,
516, 56, 86, 94, 116, 318,
Ways a
Wayside
Va, 582, 447, 604.
Vain, 110, 177, 267, 355, 448, 451, 458.
Valiant, 534.
Valuable, 144, 490.
Value, 29.
Vanguard, 534.
Vanish, 250.
Vapour, 294.
Variance, 68, 69, 552, 564.
Variegated, 603.
Various, 555.
Varnish, 315, 603.
Vase, 342.
Vast, 298.

VAU-WAG.

Vault, 382, 458.
Vegetable, 148, 402, 450, 454, 573.
Vegetable-dish, 360.
Vegetarian, 595.
Veil, 160.
Velvet, 404.
Venomous, 292.
Veranda, 78.
Verbal, 72.
Verdigris, 408.
Verify, 243, 577.
Vermicelli, 220, 589.
Vermilion, 263, 370, 400.
Vernal equinox, 253.
Verse, 392.
Vertigo, 257.
Very, 8, 62, 116, 118, 157, 165, 176, 266, 322, 342, 398, 406, 4 , 438, 479, 513, 564, 56 , 597, 602, 604, 607.
Vessel, 95.
Vetch, 446.
Vex, 190, 295.
Vexation, 191.
Viands, 291.
Vice, 50.
Viceroy, 47.
Vicious, 189.
Victorious, 57.
Victory, 12, 223.
View, 190, 256.
Vigna, 489.
Vigorous, 114, 173, 253, 465.
Vile, 234, 265, 381, 528, 548, 580.

Vilify, 486.
Village, 265, 440.
Villager, 526.
Villain, 31.
Villainous, 317.
Vine, 450, 451.
Vinegar, 527.
Violate, 114, 459.
Violence, 16, 288.
Violent, 257, 335.
Violently, 257.
Violet, 445.
Viper, 462.
Virago, 186, 316, 457.
Virgin, 546.
Untrue, 91; 178, 495, 550.
Uniform, 54, 305, 359, 495.
Unimportar
Uninte, 591.
Visit, 48, 68, 200, 211, 261, 422, 498, 503, 559.
Voice, 88, 92, 424, 563.
Voluble, 301.
Volume, 65, 263.
Volunteer, 409.
Vomit, 34, 37, 78, 94.
Vow, 479.
Vulgar, 2, 21, 63, 293, 303, 398, 526, 584.

W.

Wadded, 276.
Waddle, 598.
Wade, 504.
Waft, 234.
Wag, 238.

Wage, 24, 157, 455, 492, 506, 536.
Wail, 459.
Wainscot, 434.
Waist, 433.
Waistband, 472.
Waistcoat, 427, 471, 541, 566.
Wait, 19, 22, 177, 223, 288, 389, 409.
Waiter, 67, 106, 137.
Wake, a, 90.
Wake, to, 528.
Wale, 601.
Walk, 56, 203, 466, 498, 504, 510, 515, 606.
Wall, 103, 104, 104, 112, 113, 201, 397, 590, 601.
Wall-paper, 391.
Walnut, 270, 272.
Wander, 270, 515, 520.
Want, 191, 474.
Wanting, 7, 285.
Wanton, 29.
Wantonly, 119.
Wantonness, 29.
War, 56, 163, 198, 199, 507.
Ward, 100, 540, 547, 592.
Warden, 20.
Warehouse, 466.
Warm, 76, 321, 322, 323, 325, 325, 325, 573.
Warn, 198, 487.
Warp, 282.
Warrant, 375, 396.
War-vessel, 36.
Was, 254.
Wash, 40, 297, 301, 306.

Wasp, 461.
Waste, 109, 258, 279, 446, 511, 522.
Wasteful, 289.
Wasting, 172.
Watch, 364, 367, 468, 512.
Watchman, 136.
Water, 295, 305, 318, 571, 572.
Water-chestnut, 449.
Watercourse, 311.
Watercress, 444.
Waterfall, 318.
Water-wheel, 507.
Waterproof, 301, 556.
Wave, a, 300.
Wave, to, 238, 303, 412.
Wax, 465.
Way, 192, 249, 271, 281, 298, 516, 567.
Ways and means, 286.
Wayside inn, 434.
We, 199.
Weak, 94, 128, 134, 150, 174, 307, 319, 351, 435, 436, 458, 508, 554, 606.
Wealth, 160, 491, 536.
Wealthy, 66, 142, 267, 291, 470, 491, 491.
Wean, 560.
Weapon, 95, 248, 274.
Wear, 113, 200, 223, 382, 499, 501.
Weariness, 31.
Wearisome, 56.
Weary, 31, 98, 183, 349, 576.
Weasel, 152, 490.

(799)

WEA-WIF.

Weather, 22, 119, 295.
Weave, 409, 412.
Weaver, 282.
Web 405, 409.
Web-foot, 219.
Wedge, 149, 226, 235, 277, 342.
Weed, 454, 530.
Weep, 86, 92, 299.
Weigh, 78, 111, 164, 212, 292, 380, 518.
Weight, 35, 111, 370, 372.
Welcome, 177, 512.
Weld, 222, 532.
Welfare, 135.
Well, 10, 102, 123, 135, 392, 437, 456, 518.
Well-formed, 279, 307.
Well-known, 326.
Well-off, 518.
Well-to-do, 66, 251.
Wen, 349, 353.
West, 473.
Wet, 202, 312, 317, 523, 523.
Wether, 417.
Wet-nurse, 130, 131.
Whale, 584, 585.
What, 183, 342, 484, 524, 590, 606, 612.
Wheat, 380, 589.
Wheaten, 589.
Wheedle, 605.
Wheel, 507, 509, 509.
Wheelbarrow, 507.
When, 48, 124, 165, 255, 525.
Where, 524.
Whereby, 16.

Wherever, 552.
Whether, 199.
Which, 134, 165, 524.
While, 6, 47, 107, 286, 549.
Whine, 92, 605, 606.
Whip, 209, 561.
Whirlpool, 37, 301, 305.
Whirlwind, 250.
Whisker, 581.
Whisper, 11, 187.
Whistle, 79, 86, 394.
White, 355, 356, 397, 558.
Whitewash, 48, 397.
Who, 134, 483, 524.
Whole, 1, 35, 59, 62, 76, 164, 206, 246, 273, 309, 313, 360, 403, 515, 516, 517, 547, 599.
Wholesale, 458.
Whorl, 539.
Whose, 524.
Why, 13, 16, 183, 329, 612.
Wick, 179.
Wicked, 32, 288, 401.
Wickedness, 289, 559.
Wide, 143, 168, 244, 379, 407, 546.
Widely, 143.
Widow, 132, 143.
Widower, 143, 585.
Widowhood, 143.
Width, 163.
Wield, 226.
Wife, 35, 81, 128, 128, 129, 129, 130, 135, 138, 139, 153, 447, 496.
Wife's parents, 155.

(800)

WIL-WRA.

Wild, 125, 172, 334, 352, 485, 530.
Wilderness, 258.
Wildly, 9.
Wilful, 184.
Wilfully, 214.
Will, 74, 97, 179, 180, 183, 252, 474, 522.
Willing, 189, 427, 568.
Willow, 270, 278.
Win, 497.
Wind, 151, 464, 569.
Wind up, 404.
Windlass, 507.
Window, 383.
Windpipe, 88.
Wine, 404, 526.
Wing, 419, 432.
Wink, 363.
Winnow, 394, 569.
Winter, 39, 40, 142.
Wipe, 209, 224, 501, 556.
Wire, 405.
Wise, 253.
Wisdom, 192, 256.
Wish, 89, 261, 375, 568.
Witch, 129, 161.
With, 78, 82, 344, 438.
Withdraw, 70, 209, 514.
Withered, 269.
Withhold, 220.
Within, 35, 176, 470.
Without, 322, 549.
Withstand, 209, 212, 229, 240, 246, 269.
Witness, 163, 474, 479.
Wits, 583.

Wizard, 158.
Woe, 135.
Wolf, 335, 335, 490.
Woman, 103, 123, 126, 129, 129, 303, 442, 551.
Womb, 140.
Wonder, 182, 448.
Wonderful, 121.
Won't, 4.
Wood, 262, 266.
Woodcutting, 283.
Woodpecker, 87.
Woof, 396, 410.
Wool, 293.
Woolen, 404.
Word, 133, 477, 480, 483, 485.
Work, 9, 53, 54, 74, 150, 157, 170, 240, 301, 379, 483, 502, 607.
Working, 67.
Workman, 26, 61, 161, 202.
World, 4, 21, 42, 135, 157, 346, 551.
Worm, 461, 461, 463.
Worm-eaten, 203.
Worn, 150, 616.
Worry, 196, 236, 237, 306, 316, 323.
Worship, 93, 193, 211, 245, 377.
Worth, 22, 29, 239.
Worthless, 29, 130, 177, 264, 375, 474.
Worthy, 495.
Would that, 159.
Would, 28, 72, 291, 350, 369.
Wrangle, 79, 89, 96, 329, 388, 505, 582.

(801)

Wrangler, senior, 334.
Wrap, 59, 145, 471.
Wrapper, 59, 357.
Wrest, 481.
Wrestle, 231, 400.
Wretch, 123, 583.
Wretched, 194, 255.
Wriggle, 266, 543.
Wring, 225.
Wrinkle, 357, 357, 410.
Wrist, 510, 566.
Write, 144, 207, 258, 451, 544, 567.
Writer, 258.
Writhe, 266.
Writing-board, 331.
Writing-paper, 259.
Wrong, 158, 210, 258, 559.
Wrong, a, 142, 152, 258, 267, 459, 536.
Wrong, to, 102, 126, 597.
Wry, 25, 288.

Y.

Yak, 250.
Yam, 446.
Yamên, 201.
Yard, 2, 114.
Yawn, 81.
Year, 13, 164, 166, 288, 508, 512.
Yearly, 164.
Yeast, 527.
Yellow, 590, 608.
Yes, 254.
Yesterday, 254.
Yet, 68, 259, 336.
Yew, 267.
Yield, 208, 488, 503, 514.
Yielding, 488.
Yoke, 269.
Yolk, 590.
You, 17.
Young, 73, 131, 142, 148, 149, 156, 164, 165, 509.
Younger, 148.
Youngest, 67.
Your, 17.
Yourself, 77.

Z.

Zealous, 20, 325.

ERRATA.

NOTE:—In order to avoid mistakes, the student is advised to mark the following corrections in their proper places:—

PAGE.	LINE.	ERROR.	CORRECTION.	PAGE.	LINE.	ERROR.	CORRECTION.
9	8	"last"	"fifth"	240	20	"TSO⁵"	"TS'O⁵"
12	30	"we"	"I"	256	20	"LIANG⁵"	"LIANG⁴"
73	32	"rich"	"sick"	276	28	"TS'I"	"TS'I¹"
80	24	"same as 叫"	"same as 叫"	278	8	"TS'IU²"	"TS'IU¹"
120	25	"guage"	"gauge"	288	1	"PU²"	"PU⁴"
148	25	"mind"	"conduct"	294	21	"CH'I"	"CH'I⁴"
149	25	"foot"	"food"	319	27	"LIN⁴"	"LIN²"
154	18	"storeys"	"stories"	321	1	"TIEN¹"	"TIEN³"
212	33	"drop"⁴	"prop"	337	20	"SHUEN²"	"SHÜEN²"
225	12	"trump"	"trump up"	403	30	"SHEN⁴"	"SHEN¹"
264	26	"argument"	"agreement"	444	9	"CH'IN³"	"CH'IN²"
280	6	"rich"	"rice"	448	5	"LI¹"	"LI⁴"
290	21	"have"	"leave"	448	24	"CH ÜIN¹"	"CH ÜIN⁴"
315	20	"skin"	"skim"	452	20	"SHIO¹"	"SHIO⁵"
328	14	"the pop"	"to pop"	499	10	"CH'EN¹"	"CH'EN⁴"
356	25	"tied"	"tidied"	511	24	"PIEN²"	"PIEN⁴"
367	8	"child"	"shield"	523	6	"LIAO⁴"	"LIAO²"
384	17	"inexhaustable"	"inexhaustible"	524	23	"LA⁵"	"LA¹"
				536	17	"TS'IEN⁴"	"TS'IEN²"
454	6	"Pauloowia"	"Paulownia"	573	18	"RAO⁴"	"RAO²"
470	18	"son"	"sentence"	591	4	"LI⁴"	"LI²"
574	28	"making"	"smoking"	597	1	"CHAO³"	"CHAO²"
576	25	"fool"	"foal"	705	10	"Tsüen"	"Ts'üen"
48	1	"TS'I"	"TS'Ï"	69	28	"收"	"收"
75	25	"T'AO"	"T'AO"	71	20	"叠"	"叠"
103	19	"K'UEN²"	"K'UEN¹"	73	29	"叫"	"叫"
110	16	"CH'EN"	"CH'EN²"	124	24	"你"	"他"
134	13	"SHUH⁵"	"SHU⁵"	148	30	"少"	"小"
150	7	"LIAO²"	"LIAO⁴"	231	16	"揎的"	"揎你的"
155	27	"SHIA¹"	"SHIA⁵"	238	9	"了"	"子"
164	28	"NIEN¹"	"NIEN²"	241	16	"子"	"支"
173	18	"K'EO⁴"	"KEO⁴"	278	29	"那在裏"	"在那裏"
178	12	"SÜIN⁴"	"SÜIN²"	391	4	"了"	"丁"
186	24	"KAN¹"	"KAN⁴"	461	5	"晒"	"西"
193	7	"K'I⁴"	"CH'I⁴"	512	3	"奏"	"辰"
207	5	"P'AN⁴"	"PAN⁴"	515	3	"客"	"容"
219	19	"P'O'NG⁴"	"P'ONG¹"	602	13	"了"	"丫"
236	1	"P'IE⁵"	"P'IE²"				

Page 9, line 1, should read, "rubble; unhewn stone; coblestones."
,, 76, ,, 22, should follow line 23.
,, 115, ,, 8, delete brackets.
,, 289, ,, 5, "fall back to" should be "(fall back to)"
,, 330, ,, 4, should read, "a kind of god-father."
,, 405, transfer line 16 to line 14.
,, 653 delete 杠 charcoal, 292.

(803)